American Public Policy

An Introduction

FOURTH EDITION

American Public Policy

An Introduction

FOURTH EDITION

Clarke E. Cochran
Texas Tech University

Lawrence C. Mayer
Texas Tech University

T. R. Carr
Southern Illinois University at Edwardsville

N. Joseph Cayer
Arizona State University

St. Martin's Press　　　*New York*

To
Anne
Etta
Lucy
R.G.C.

Senior editor: Don Reisman
Managing editor: Patricia Mansfield-Phelan
Project editor: Erica Appel
Production supervisor: Katherine Battiste
Cover design: Celine Brandes

Library of Congress Catalog Card Number: 92-50014
76543
fedcba

For information, write:
St. Martin's Press, Inc.
175 Fifth Avenue
New York, NY 10010

ISBN: 0-312-06190-0

Preface

We have made a variety of significant changes for the fourth edition of *American Public Policy.* Having completed this edition during the 1992 election year, we have tried to keep our text current with the issues that have been prominent in the political debate: We have updated coverage of proposals for health care reform, affirmative action, the abortion controversy, free and hateful speech, AIDS, education reform, and foreign policy. Each substantive chapter considers the major policy changes of the early 1990s in detail, and the final chapter provides a comprehensive summary.

American Public Policy is an introductory undergraduate text that focuses on the substantive issues of public policy. Most texts stress methods of policy analysis, models of policy, or the policymaking process. Although these topics are important, their dominance at the introductory level often makes the subject too abstract to engage students' imaginations. In our own teaching, we have found that an interest in more rigorous analysis grows most naturally out of a lively classroom discussion of specific, substantive policy issues—for example, welfare, abortion, tax reform, or nuclear weapons. We believe our book is unique in its emphasis on such issues, combining history and description with debate about alternative solutions.

This text is intended for the first undergraduate course in public policy, either in the form of a one-semester course or as part of a two-semester sequence that includes both political institutions and public policy. We do not assume any prior knowledge of basic policy issues on the student's part, although we do presume an understanding of the basic structure of American government. Therefore, we present the policy material step by step, building a picture of existing policy that the student can use to evaluate alternatives.

Each chapter follows the same outline of four major sections for easy access and comparison. The first section, "Issue Background," provides information the reader needs to know about the background of the particular topic, including descriptions of early policy actions. The second, "Contemporary Policy," outlines the evolution of present-day governmental policy in that area. The section on "Policy Evaluation" presents an in-depth discussion of the principal successes and failures of policy relating to the particular issue under study. Finally, the "Future Alternatives" section evaluates possible alternatives to existing policy. The book compares a wide range of perspectives—from conservative to liberal to radical—but does not take any ideological positions. Instead, students are challenged to develop their own evaluations of the alternatives proposed in contemporary policy controversies.

The book does not neglect the state and local dimensions of policy issues, but the focus is primarily on national policy and national policy debate. Cross-national comparisons of policies and their impacts are presented when relevant. Each chapter ends with a summary of important points and a list of suggested readings for further study.

Chapter 1 introduces the study of substantive issues of public policy. Major policy concepts are defined, and the contexts in which contemporary public policy operates—institutional, economic, demographic, cultural, and ideological—are delineated. Each succeeding chapter examines an individual area.

Chapter 2 gives attention to questions of economic regulation, leaving an entire chapter (Chapter 3) for macroeconomic policy, including the ramifications of the federal budget deficit and international competitiveness. Chapter 4 deals with both environmental and energy policy, which allows us to highlight the important interaction between these two policy areas.

Chapter 5 focuses on the policies that link the different levels of our federal system, policies such as revenue sharing and grants-in-aid. In Chapter 6, the creation of specific policy to respond to the growth of crime is considered. In particular, the chapter evaluates the impacts of policies specifying an individual's constitutional rights: confessions and the right to counsel, the exclusionary rule and search and seizure, and capital punishment.

Chapter 7 looks at the double bind of income support and welfare dependence, beginning with a definition of the term *poverty* and an account of the creation of the welfare system. Expanded attention is given to poverty among children, homelessness, and the underclass. In the chapter that follows, the nation's health care is discussed in terms of a different kind of double bind, one of unlimited needs but limited resources. Medicare and Medicaid are examined, and the issues of bioethics, AIDS, and long-term health care are evaluated. Current proposals for health care reform are summarized.

In Chapter 9, the tradition of free public education in the United States is shown to be in jeopardy. The chapter has been rewritten to consider such problems as poor student achievement, teacher competence, inequities resulting from the system of local control, and inequality in education due to the growth of private schools. The idea of equality, both legal and social, is discussed in Chapter 10. Programs of the 1960s and 1970s—those aimed at achieving equality in the schools and in employment and securing the right of abortion for women—are now questioned seriously. This seeming turnabout in priorities is studied. An entire chapter is then devoted to the issue of first amendment freedoms in an open society, with a special focus on the many safeguards to these freedoms that have been developed over the years and on continued conflicts regarding most of them (for example, the role of religion in American education). Finally, Chapter 12 discusses the primary policy issues facing the United States in the post–Cold War, post–Persian Gulf war world.

American Public Policy can be used in a variety of ways. Instructors may choose to consider all of the policy areas presented or to select a group of them for special emphasis. Chapter 1 should be read first, but the rest of the chapters can be assigned in any sequence the instructor prefers. Supplementary readings focusing on particular issues may be conveniently added.

Many people have read and commented on this fourth edition, and we wish to thank particularly the following persons: John Quincy Adams, Millsaps College; Timothy S. Brady, California State University–Bakersfield; Euel Elliott, University of Texas at Dallas; Don F. McCabe, Southern Illinois University at Edwardsville; and Elena Padilla, New York University. We are grateful for their interest and suggestions. Don Reisman, Frances Jones, and Erica Appel of St. Martin's Press provided invaluable editorial assistance.

Clarke E.Cochran
Lawrence C. Mayer
T. R. Carr
N. Joseph Cayer

Contents in Brief

Contents

Issues and Public Policy

Public policy significantly affects the life of every American, including college students. In public colleges and universities, students benefit directly from the decisions of policymakers, who ultimately dictate whether or not to build and maintain their institutions and to subsidize their tuitions with state or local funds. Such students may also receive federally guaranteed tuition loans or grants. Students attending private schools are also eligible for such assistance. Moreover, public policy provides research grants, building loans, and work-study funds to private as well as public institutions. Even those few schools that resolutely refuse all public money must abide by health and safety laws and equal admissions rules. Though many readers may find it difficult to believe, dormitory cafeteria food must pass local public health inspection!

Public policy in America affects each citizen in not just one way but in hundreds of ways, some of them familiar and some unsuspected. Citizens directly confront public policy when they are arrested for speeding, but they seldom remember that the advertising on the television shows they watch is regulated by the Federal Communications Commission and the Federal Trade Commission. Many citizens who complain loudly at tax time about government bureaucracy and overregulation have forgotten the fire and police protection those revenues provide or the paved streets they drive on to work. Indeed, public policy in America affects a vast range of activities, from nuclear warheads to bathroom plumbing, from arresting lawbreakers to providing medical care for the elderly. This book aims to help students grasp some key dimensions of this ubiquitous influence on American life and to initiate them into the debates swirling around its major controversies. It takes an *issue-oriented approach* to the beginning study of public policy.

STUDYING PUBLIC POLICY

What Constitutes Public Policy?

Even though examples of public policy come readily to mind, defining public policy in clear and unambiguous terms is not easy. Political scientists have devoted considerable attention to the problem without reaching a consensus.[1] Nevertheless, the term *public policy* always refers to the actions of government and the intentions that determine those actions. Making policy requires choos-

1

ing among goals and alternatives, and choice always involves intention. The federal government, for example, chose to establish fifty-five miles per hour as the national speed limit in order to reduce gasoline consumption. Thus public policy is defined in this book as an intentional course of action followed by a government institution or official for resolving an issue of public concern. Such a course of action must be manifested in laws, public statements, official regulations, or widely accepted and publicly visible patterns of behavior. It is rooted in law and in the authority and coercion associated with law. (The terms *public policy* and *policy* will be used interchangeably.)

Two qualifications are necessary, however, for this definition of public policy. First, the idea of an intentional course of action includes decisions made *not* to take a certain action. For example, Congress voted in 1988 not to continue to send weapons to the Nicaraguan contras. It was therefore public policy in the United States not to support them militarily. Second, the requirement that official actions be sanctioned by law or accepted custom is necessary because public officials often take courses of action that step outside public policy—for example, they sometimes take bribes or exceed their legal authority. Such deeds should not be considered public policy—that is, unless they are openly tolerated in a particular political system. Of course, laws or official regulations should not be mistaken for the whole realm of policy. The mere proclamation of a particular course of action is only a first step; the implementation, interpretation, enforcement, and impact of laws and regulations, discussed later, are also part of policy.

Why Study Public Policy?

Students of political science have several reasons for studying public policy. The first is theoretical: Political scientists seek to understand and explain the world of politics—that is, they attempt to develop and test explanatory generalizations about the political behavior of individuals and institutions. Because public policy is a part of politics, political scientists are concerned with how it is related to such things as political party structure, interest groups, interparty competition, electoral systems, and executive-legislative relations.

A second reason for studying public policy is practical. Political scientists and students of policy apply scientific knowledge to solve practical problems. They are interested in how policy-making can be made more rational and effective, how the obstacles to implementing policy decisions can be removed, and how those policies affect the quality of individual and social life.

A third reason for studying public policy, related to the second, is political: Study helps policymakers make intelligent choices. Debate and controversy over public policy in America is not new, but today the range of issues over which serious disagreement occurs is far greater than in the past. So many issues are placed before the public—strategic arms limitation, welfare reform, crime prevention, economic crises, and AIDS prevention at the national level; taxation and spending, teacher competency testing, and public utility regulation at the state level; zoning, mass transportation, and property taxation at the local level—

that mental circuits begin to overload. As citizens, political scientists and college students hope the study of public policy will help them find their way through the tangle of complex issues and sophisticated policy proposals. They seek, in other words, to find policy proposals that they can support as rational and moral means for addressing serious concerns. As political scientists Duncan MacRae and James A. Wilde pointed out, the study of public policy requires "the use of reason and evidence to choose the best policy among a number of alternatives."[2]

The emphasis of this book is on the third reason for studying policy—the political focus—but it draws also on the first two, for intelligent policy selection depends on the analyses and understanding developed by the theoretical and practical findings of political science.

DEFINING MAJOR CONCEPTS

Two Approaches to Policy Study

Generally, the study of public policy may be divided into policy analysis and policy advocacy. *Policy analysis* is principally concerned with describing and investigating how and why particular policies are proposed, adopted, and implemented. It focuses on explanation rather than prescription, on searching scientifically for the causes and consequences of policy, and on general explanatory propositions.[3] *Policy advocacy,* on the other hand, is primarily devoted to examining policies, along with the alternative policy proposals made in the issue areas, with a view toward discovery and recommendation of the best course of action. Policy advocacy draws particularly on ethical principles and ideological perspectives. Thus principles such as freedom, equality, justice, decency, and peace are invoked in policy advocacy, along with ideologies such as liberalism, conservatism, socialism, and Marxism.

Those who would sharply separate policy analysis and policy advocacy make a grave mistake. On one hand, policy advocacy without the findings of analysis is blind. A policy option must be evaluated in the light of what studies have revealed about its chances of being adopted, the probable effectiveness of the option, and the difficulties of implementation. A proposal for increased spending for high school education, for example, would need to be tested against data on the impact of increased spending on student achievement levels. Advocates of a guaranteed annual income would need to take into account the political inertia favoring only incremental welfare reform. On the other hand, policy analysis without awareness of ethical and ideological perspectives is lame. This is particularly true when evaluating the impact of policy. Ethical principles must be brought to bear on the discovery of the good and bad effects of policy. Such principles not only measure success and failure; they also provide insight into consequences that otherwise would not be revealed. Marxist analysis, for example, may expose hitherto hidden functions of welfare policy. Liberalism's emphasis on the subtle link between freedom of choice and personal well-being may provide an otherwise unavailable insight into the negative consequences of censorship.

Stages of Policy Development

The discussion so far has used a number of terms, such as implementation and impact, that refer to important elements of public policy. For example, policies as courses of action have a number of stages, and implementation is one. An impact, on the other hand, is a product of one of these policy stages.

The development of a public policy begins with the public recognition that a problem exists. There are three of these *prepolicy stages:* (1) problem definition or issue formation, (2) policy demands, and (3) agenda formation.

Before a policy is adopted, an issue or problem of public concern must be perceived. Ethical and ideological perspectives play an important role during this first stage, because different perspectives will "see" and define problems differently. For example, imagine how the same social phenomenon might be viewed by people of differing moral values—in this case, the growing pornography industry. Some might view an increase in sexually explicit literature as a manifestation of a socially open and healthy attitude toward sexuality. Others might see it as a symptom of an unhealthy obsession with sex and a turning away from higher values. Depending on what group is doing the defining, different formulations of the issue will result. Thus the issue formation stage leads to the next stage, policy demands: Now opposing demands are made for government action. For example, some people want the smut shops closed down and the owners thrown in jail. Others want the authorities to keep out of what they see as the private business of individual citizens (a demand for government nonaction). Gradually, this social give-and-take coalesces into a perception that policymakers must deal with this problem, and so the agenda formation stage begins. The various demands and perspectives create an agenda of alternative proposals for dealing with the issue. Some proposals and demands never make it to the agenda; others are put on the agenda in altered form.

Following the prepolicy stages, the next major stage in the development of a public policy is deliberation and *policy adoption.* From the policy agenda, decision makers with the input of interest groups, policy experts, and constituents debate and bargain over alternative policy formulations, selecting an alternative or a combination of alternatives to respond to the problem. Decisions are made; policies are formulated; and policy statements are issued. These statements may take the form of orders, regulations, laws, or altered behaviors, but they must be publicly exhibited.

Unfortunately, policy statements are not the whole of policy-making. If they were, policy analysis would be easy. Rather, policy decisions must be implemented—that is, steps must be taken to put the policy statement into practice in order to achieve the policymaker's goals. *Policy implementation* means money spent, laws enforced, employees hired, and plans of action formulated. A policy making stealing illegal would hardly be a policy if no public resources were devoted to preventing thefts and apprehending thieves. In implementation, "there's many a slip twixt cup and lip." Even seemingly simple programs involving little conflict can be difficult to implement if there are numerous participants with differing perspectives and if many particular decisions have to be made before the policy is fully implemented.[4]

Policy implementation includes outputs and impacts. *Policy outputs* are the tangible manifestations of policies, the observable and measurable results of policy adoption and implementation. Stated another way, outputs are what governments in fact do in a particular policy area: The policy outputs of the food stamp program, for example, include money spent, stamps printed, poor persons served, employees hired, and regulations issued. All of these are tangible. Outputs may also be symbolic: Public statements of encouragement and hope are symbolic outputs of the food stamp program. Exercising defense policy includes making threats, posturing, and issuing conciliatory statements. Just as policy analysts can observe and measure money spent and employees hired, they can also record, classify, and count symbolic outputs, though doing so is more difficult.

Policy impacts (sometimes called outcomes) are the effects that policy outputs have on society. They are the policy's consequences in terms of the policy's stated goals as well as of the society's fundamental beliefs. For the food stamp program, major impacts would naturally include changes in recipients' diets. The outcomes of a defense policy would include military strength vis-à-vis other nations and some measure of national security, as well as various economic effects of defense spending.

Policy impact is a major component of an important focus of this text, the evaluation of public policy. *Policy evaluation* focuses principally on the impact of policy, because it is largely from the performance and consequences of policy that we assess its success or failure. Policy can be debated, problems defined, agendas built, and programs adopted and implemented; but what difference does all of this mean for improving the life of society as a whole or of its particular parts? This is the question of impact. Evaluation attempts to assess the outcomes of policies—their effects on society—in order to compare them with the policies' intended goals. It asks whether the goals have or have not been met, with what costs, and with what unintended consequences. It considers whether policy is equitable and efficient and whether it has satisfied the interests demanding action. For example, policy evaluation would ask whether the welfare reforms legislated in 1988 did in fact reduce poverty or improve the lives of the poor. Policy evaluation of antipoverty programs would necessarily also discuss questions of justice, the value of work, and the place of poverty in an affluent society. Thus a policy can be evaluated only after it has been implemented. Attempts to assess the impact of a policy before implementation are more appropriately referred to as estimations or forecasts. For example, students of policy might estimate the educational impact of increasing teachers' salaries in order to support or oppose higher taxes for that purpose.

Aspects of Policy Evaluation

Evaluating policy has both normative and empirical dimensions. The *normative dimension* refers to values, beliefs, and attitudes of society as a whole, of particular groups and individuals in society, and of the policy evaluators themselves. Persons of different values and ideologies use different normative concepts to evaluate policy. Liberals, conservatives, socialists, communists, and anarchists differ fundamentally in their understanding of such concepts and in their ranking of them. Conservatives, for example, believe that free competition and protection of private property are the fundamental values to be pursued by economic policy. Socialists, on the other hand, see a just distribution of the social product as the principal value. Different policy evaluators and different political groups, then, will evaluate public policy differently. Normative perspectives come into play, not only in assessing the goals of policy, but also in analyzing how well policy accomplishes the desired goals.

Normative evaluation, however, is not enough. The *empirical dimension*—that is, understanding the facts—must precede judgment. Before praising or damning the Supreme Court's freedom-of-the-press decisions, one must examine the actual decisions and attempt to assess what difference, if any, they have made or are likely to make in the day-to-day operations of the press. And before criticizing "welfare fraud," one should obtain the most accurate statistics available on money lost through fraudulent claims. Policy evaluation without empirical analysis of policy content, output, and impact is like voting for an all-star team without information on players' batting, earned-run, or fielding averages.

In evaluating a public policy, we distinguish between its intended and unintended consequences. *Intended consequences* are the stated goals of policy—that is, the effects that the policymakers want for the policy. Policy evaluation asks: How well have these goals been met? For example, the Federal Housing Administration mortgage loan guarantee program was intended to increase private home ownership. The intended goal has been substantially accomplished. The percentage of owner-occupied homes in America is the highest in the world. But policies also have *unintended consequences,* those not intended or foreseen by policymakers. FHA loans, more readily available for new homes, also encouraged middle-class movement to the suburbs, contributing to decaying inner cities. Thus the policy of the FHA to encourage the building and buying of newly constructed housing had the unintended consequence of hastening the decline of many urban centers.

Moreover, policy evaluation distinguishes direct policy impact from indirect impact. The consequences of policy, both intended and unintended, on the policy's target population are its *direct impact.* The target population is the group of persons or institutions that the policy is principally designed to affect. For example, in the interstate highway construction program, the target population is the trucking industry and automobile drivers. Public policies, however, often have *indirect impacts* on third parties, which are referred to as spillover effects or externalities. The construction of good roads contributed to the decline of the passenger train and, to a lesser extent, of railroad freight business.

Such spillovers are the indirect impact of the policy. Whether for good or ill, they can be substantial. For example, federal farm programs often have the indirect effect of boosting consumer prices.

In a similar way, policy evaluation also involves what are known as direct and indirect costs. A policy's *direct costs* are the expenditures of time, energy, power, and money in the policy area itself. *Indirect costs* are no different except that they are incurred in areas indirectly affected by the policy—including the lost opportunities to do other things with the resources devoted to the policy in question. Spillover effects involve indirect costs.

Short-term and *long-term effects* must also be distinguished by policy evaluation. Policies cannot be fairly evaluated until their long-term effects can be reasonably assessed. It may take decades, for example, before the full effect of the Persian Gulf war can be known.

Finally, policy evaluation must assess both *symbolic* and *tangible impacts,* just as it must do with outputs. Many policies have as important a symbolic effect as they do a material one. This may be intended or unintended. The Vietnam War, for example, generated cynicism about many time-honored American beliefs, such as respect for the flag, America as a world peacekeeper, and the concept of national honor, all unintended (and negative) symbolic impacts. The Reagan administration's rhetorical output helped to restore in many citizens confidence in American abilities and dedication to symbols such as the flag.

Policy evaluation, then, is clearly a complex matter, requiring diverse skills, insights, and information. This book cannot even begin to make a complete evaluation of each of the policies and issues it covers. It does, however, describe the most important policies in each area, offer data on their most significant outputs and impacts, and suggest the contending perspectives on each of the issues and on the policy alternatives currently under discussion. Each chapter is designed to give readers enough information so that they may begin their own evaluations of these policies and of new ideas and proposals they will encounter in newspapers and magazines, on television, and in their own political activity.

THE CONTEXTS OF CONTEMPORARY PUBLIC POLICY

The debate and shaping of public policy take place, of course, within the general social, political, and economic environment of the American nation. But they take place as well within contexts specific to each policy area. These specialized influences will be outlined in the substantive chapters, but it is important here to discuss some general factors that will influence policy in a variety of issue areas during this last decade of the twentieth century.

The Institutional Context

Obviously, the unique features of the American political system, its basic structures—federalism, the party system, the power of the presidency, and the system of checks and balances—will continue to shape policy as they always have. Policy in the area of civil rights, for example, will continue to be shaped substantially by the federal courts, because of the constitutional system of government and the courts' power of judicial review. The federal system will make national education policy difficult to formulate, because education is primarily a responsibility of state governments. Indeed, the 1980s saw the growth of state and local policy initiative as the federal government contracted its policy innovation. This trend continued in the early 1990s.

In addition to these lasting features of the American political system, however, a serious distrust of institutions, particularly political ones, has surfaced in the last twenty years. President Jimmy Carter made lack of confidence in American political leadership, especially his own, the major theme of the dramatic speech that followed the Camp David "domestic summit" of July, 1979. And President Ronald Reagan made restoration of confidence in American institutions a major symbolic theme of his administration. Yet the statistics illustrate the American public's lackluster response to the political process: The percentage of the eligible population voting in presidential and congressional elections has declined substantially since 1960, with only half of voting-age Americans now voting for president and even fewer voting for other offices (see Figure 1-1). At the same time, opinion polls reveal a growing lack of confidence in the future, with more people expressing the belief that the quality of life will decline in the next ten years rather than improve. Polls on confidence in leadership reveal substantial declines in the trust the public holds for leadership in all areas of life.[5] The popularity of term limitations for elected officials, the candidacy of Ross Perot, and cynicism about politicians testify to growing distrust.

We need not go far to seek the sources for the decline in trust of government. The Vietnam War, the protests and social divisions it spawned, and its tragic impact on many veterans put American foreign policy leadership under a cloud from which it has only partially emerged. Findings of corruption and illegality at the highest levels of government have fed distrust; such revelations have included illegal CIA and FBI surveillance of people and political groups; the Watergate conspiracy; criminal charges against President Carter's Office of Management and Budget director, Bert Lance; criminal investigations of major Reagan administration officials, such as Edwin Meese, Michael Deaver, Lyn Nofziger, Rita Lavelle, and Oliver North; and the resignation of House Speaker Jim Wright in the face of ethics charges. The Iran-Contra affair and the "Keating Five" senators kept the scandal pot at the boiling point. Discovery of corruption and lawlessness in politics is nothing new, but the disclosures of the 1970s, 1980s, and 1990s have been so serious and widespread and have occurred in such rapid sequence that public trust in the ability and willingness of public officials to produce policy in the public interest has been eroded.

At the same time that public distrust has been growing, the presence of the federal government in economic, cultural, and social life has been expanding. Federal regulations, federal spending, and federal deficits increase each year. Suspicion that such growth is inevitable no matter which party is in power, that neither party has an interest in halting it, and that such growth has produced no

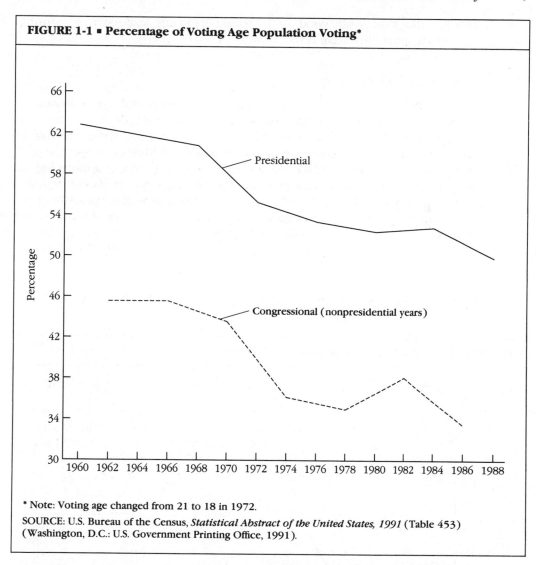

FIGURE 1-1 ■ Percentage of Voting Age Population Voting*

Presidential

Congressional (nonpresidential years)

Percentage

1960 1962 1964 1966 1968 1970 1972 1974 1976 1978 1980 1982 1984 1986 1988

* Note: Voting age changed from 21 to 18 in 1972.

SOURCE: U.S. Bureau of the Census, *Statistical Abstract of the United States, 1991* (Table 453) (Washington, D.C.: U.S. Government Printing Office, 1991).

noticeable and dramatic improvement in the quality of life has contributed to distrust in government and to substantial resistance to new policy initiatives in welfare, health, education, and consumer protection, to cite only a few cases. The Republican victories in 1980, 1984, and 1988 and the "taxpayer revolt" that began in the late 1970s have been the most tangible fruit of this phenomenon. Political scientists Theodore J. Lowi and Alan Stone have argued that the growth of national government, coupled with its failure to "produce" real benefits, jeopardizes the legitimacy of the political system itself.[6]

Suspicion is growing among the public that the national government has been captured by corporate and other interest groups who use it for private benefit rather than public good. In the technocratic age, leadership, responsibility, and accountability seem divorced from ordinary citizens.

The Economic Context

Through the rest of the century, economic instabilities and uncertainties are likely to shape new policy initiatives and cause the reevaluation of old ones. The last half of the 1980s saw a substantial reduction of unemployment and of inflation. Yet the nation entered a period of recession and high unemployment in 1990. Moreover, a new specter was added in the 1980s—an enormous federal budget deficit that grew more rapidly during the Reagan presidency than at any time in history (see Figure 1-2). Reducing the deficit is a major priority of the Bush administration and of Congress, but they disagree over how to do it, and programs in many different policy areas have become hostage to the budget debate. Savings and loan company and bank failures are simply the most dramatic symptoms of a chronically sick economy.

The deficit is not the only economic issue coloring the general policy debate. The United States now runs a deficit in its international trade accounts,

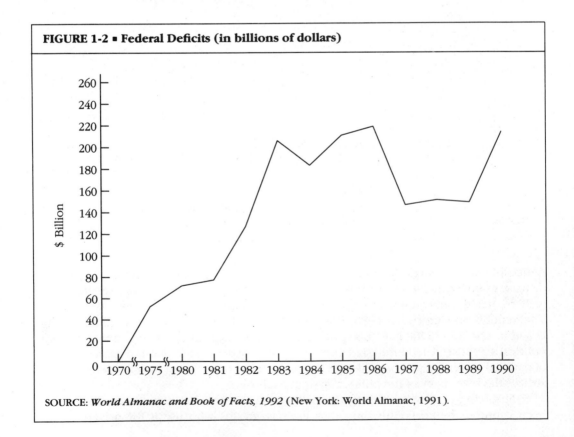

FIGURE 1-2 ▪ Federal Deficits (in billions of dollars)

SOURCE: *World Almanac and Book of Facts, 1992* (New York: World Almanac, 1991).

and the dollar has become weak in relation to other international currencies. Simply put, the United States is no longer the dominant world economy. Europe and the vibrant economies of the Asian Pacific Rim now compete aggressively in American and world markets. Economic, political, and military power have become more fragmented.

American economic thinking increasingly focuses on the scarcity of resources. The economic pie no longer seems indefinitely expanding, and the question of how to manage scarce resources and to distribute them fairly is asked in a variety of policy areas. The changing family income structure in the last fifteen years illustrates this concern. Median family income in inflation-adjusted terms, which increased steadily from the 1950s through the early 1970s, did not grow substantially in the 1980s. The need to absorb millions of new workers, the decline in family size, trends in divorce, and the movement toward two-wage earner families all produced an economic squeeze on the lower and middle classes. Inflation-adjusted income declined for much of the 1980s and 1990s for the poorest 40 percent of families and expanded only modestly for the middle 40 percent, while growing substantially for the richest 20 percent. Young males and single females, young families, and older blue-collar workers face a highly uncertain economic future. The percentage of young families who own their own homes actually dropped in the 1980s.[7]

These matters will be more fully discussed in later chapters, especially those on economic policy (Chapters 2 and 3) and income maintenance (Chapter 7), but it is important to recognize here that these economic trends will have an impact well beyond strictly economic issues. Major spending programs in education, crime control, and health, for example, will have difficulty being enacted. Racial tensions increase during hard economic times. Policy areas closely tied to the economy, such as regulatory policy and spending and tax policy, increased in emphasis during the 1980s and will continue to overshadow other domestic issues in the 1990s.

The Demographic Context

The generational, racial, and residential characteristics of a nation's population change constantly, reflecting new trends in birthrates, life expectancy, job opportunities, and migration patterns. Some of these trends will directly affect future policy-making.

The children born during the "baby boom" after World War II have reached their forties. The proportion of the population under twenty-five, which rose until the mid-1970s, will continue to decline until the mid-1990s when it will level off for a generation. This drop in the number of young people will not only seriously affect education policy but will affect other areas as well. One good impact might be a slowdown in the rate of increase in violent crime, because persons between the ages of fourteen and twenty-five commit a highly disproportionate number of such crimes (see Chapter 6). Economic policy will also be affected, as increasing numbers of men and women in their thirties and forties compete for prestigious positions. Economic performance from 1960 to 1985 was substantially affected by the need to absorb millions of new, young workers.[8]

At the same time, the proportion of the population sixty-five and older, now about 12 percent, is increasing at twice the national population rate and is likely to be 20 percent by 2030 (see Figure 1-3). Those over eighty-five are the fastest-growing segment of the population. Because only a small proportion of persons in this age group work full-time and because their health care requirements exceed those of the rest of the population, pressure on the Social Security system and on health care policy will be intense. Moreover, because life expectancy for women is significantly higher than that for men, in the future most of those over sixty-five will be widowed women, living alone or in some kind of institution, such as a nursing home or apartment complex for the elderly. It is also possible that the working population will come to resent supporting such a large number of retired persons. On the other hand, because the elderly are increasing in number and vote more regularly than the young do, the aged themselves have become a large and powerful political force for the protection of their own interests.

Immigration will continue to change the shape of the American population and present challenges to both federal and local policy. The decade of the 1980s saw legal immigration approach the record of 9 million persons set in the decade from 1901 to 1910. Immigration accounted for one-third of U.S. population growth in the 1980s. These immigrants, primarily of Asian and Hispanic descent,

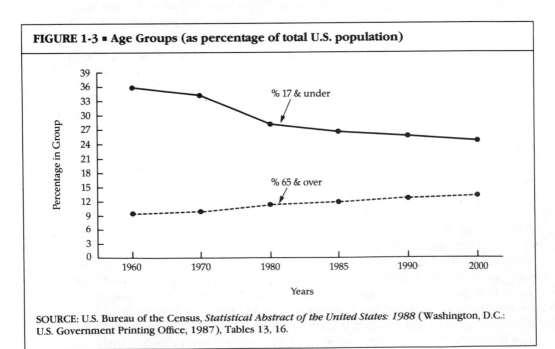

FIGURE 1-3 ▪ Age Groups (as percentage of total U.S. population)

SOURCE: U.S. Bureau of the Census, *Statistical Abstract of the United States: 1988* (Washington, D.C.: U.S. Government Printing Office, 1987), Tables 13, 16.

present both opportunities for dynamic expansion of the economy and challenges for services in housing, schools, jobs, and health care. Moreover, the impact of immigration is not spread evenly across the country. About 70 percent of the new residents settle in Texas, California, Florida, New York, Illinois, and New Jersey, placing a critical assimilative burden on these states.

Public policy in a number of areas will also have to respond to changes in the racial mix of the population. Non-Hispanic whites made up 90 percent of the population in 1955. By 1990 the proportion had declined to 76 percent. Because of illegal immigration and the younger average age of the Spanish-surname population, the Hispanic proportion of the population is rapidly approaching that of the African-American, or black, population. By 2000, Hispanic Americans will number 30 to 35 million or 12 percent of the population; they comprised 6 percent in 1980. Though they share many problems with blacks, poverty and racism being the most important, Hispanics also bring with them a different language and culture. Bilingualism and biculturalism have become more important as issues in education, social services, and employment policy. Historically, such combinations of simultaneous racial change and economic uncertainty have been volatile.

In the next two decades, Hispanics will account for 25 percent of American population growth, and whites will become a minority in California, Texas, and New York as a result of immigration and higher birthrates among Asians and Hispanics. The mix of legal and illegal immigrants may change during the 1990s as over 2 million persons gain legal status through the Immigration Reform and Control Act of 1986. This act allows undocumented aliens who have lived in the United States since before January 1, 1982, to gain legal status and, eventually, citizenship.

Changes in marriage and family life have had a major impact on policy. The increasing percentages of working wives, the high divorce rate, the high rates of illegitimate births, and the increasing numbers of single-parent families have affected labor policy, welfare expenditures, child care, schools, and sexual equality policies (see Figure 1-4). These trends have produced the "feminization of poverty," closely linking women's issues with income maintenance and health care policies. Black families are most strongly affected by these demographic trends. Today over 50 percent of black children are born out of wedlock, and over half live in female-headed, single-parent families. Nearly 50 percent of all children born in the late 1970s experienced family breakup at some time prior to their sixteenth birthday. Poverty, race, and changes in family life create an economic and demographic prison, a situation to be discussed in Chapter 7.

In addition, the "baby boomlet" that is occurring as the baby boom children reach their child-bearing years means that policy in the 1990s will increase its focus on education, child care for working parents, and health care and income support for children in poverty. Also debated will be the effect of family changes on crime, drug addiction, teenage suicide, educational achievement, and other issues.

Finally, the declining population of large urban centers such as New York,

FIGURE 1-4 ▪ Demographic Trends

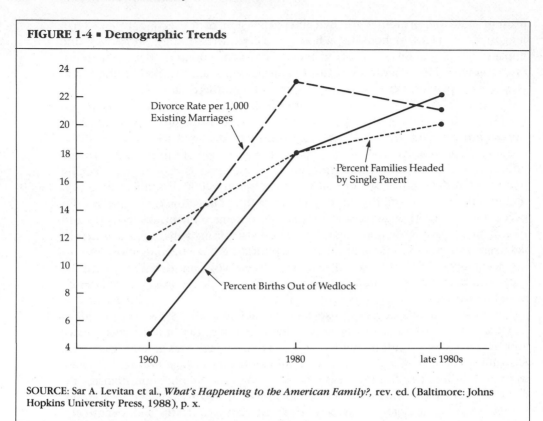

SOURCE: Sar A. Levitan et al., *What's Happening to the American Family?,* rev. ed. (Baltimore: Johns Hopkins University Press, 1988), p. x.

Baltimore, Chicago, and Cleveland and the rising population of rural, suburban, and small urban areas, especially in the South and Southwest, will continue to influence a broad range of policies. Controversies will rage over how the federal government should allocate its grant-in-aid money for urban rehabilitation, jobs, housing, education, unemployment assistance, water and sewer projects, and many other needs. Formulas for allocating these funds, based on such measures as population size, unemployment rate, poverty rate, per-capita income, age of housing, and percentage of delapidated housing, currently favor the frost belt states and cities. But as the sun belt states gain population and political power, they will demand the rewriting of these formulas. The 1980 census produced seventeen new congressional seats for the South and West, while the North and Northeast lost fifteen seats. The 1990 census produced a further reallocation of political power with the West and South gaining another fifteen seats and the Northeast and Midwest losing fifteen.

The Ideological Context

Although perspectives on American public policy have always ranged along a broad spectrum of ideological beliefs—including extreme positions at either end, such as Marxism or militant reactionary viewpoints—historically, conservatism and liberalism have dominated policy-making and evaluation in America. This dominance stems from the common roots of both in nineteenth-century liberalism's commitment to economic, political, social, and religious freedom. The majority of Americans, including policymakers, are some variety of liberal or conservative, despite small and periodically powerful numbers of adherents to other ideologies. Although liberals and conservatives in America share a great many commitments to abstract ideals, such as freedom, democracy, the market system, and individualism, they also disagree on the principles to be used in making and evaluating policy. First, they disagree over the meaning of freedom and its proper limits: Conservatives tend to value civil and personal freedoms less and are more willing to limit them; liberals are more ready to limit economic freedom. Liberals have a deeper commitment to equality than do conservatives. Conservatives are committed to tradition and authority, which is balanced by the liberals' commitment to change and individual choice in moral and social behavior. Liberals tend to have faith in the power of political action to make the world better; conservatives have a more pessimistic attitude toward the potential of politics. These disagreements affect policy debates in all areas, particularly because the role of government itself and the extent to which market forces may be relied on for economic and social health are the main issues in public policy today.

Apart from traditional conservatism and liberalism, in recent years, new ideological viewpoints have surfaced from the two mainstream movements. Neoconservatism has been increasing in influence in the last decade, as has the influence of the New Right. Neoconservatives support a strong national defense, and they advocate resistance to Third World radical or communist movements. In domestic policy, neoconservatives are critical of the government's regulation of business enterprise. The New Right, on the other hand, directs most of its attention to social issues. They oppose abortion, civil rights for homosexuals, feminism, pornography, and what they see as government interference in religious expression. Included in the New Right are the fundamentalist religious groups that became a prominent part of electoral politics in the 1980s.

Leftist radical movements are harder to define and classify. Communists and socialists stress fundamental change in the social and economic system, government control of the basic means of production, and equal distribution of income. Other radicals stress democratic control of the means of production through worker self-management and local, direct democracy. Still others make feminism, environmental protection, or increased individual freedom in personal life the centerpiece of their policy advocacy. Libertarians combine a conservative economic agenda with a liberal social agenda.

The Reagan administration's policy initiatives illustrate well the ideological shift toward conservatism. That administration proposed, and was partially successful in obtaining, substantial parts of the conservative/neoconservative/New Right agenda. These included increased defense spending, tax reduction, deregulation of parts of the economy, abortion restriction, and budget reductions in and elimination of programs of environmental protection, education, and assistance for the poor. At the same time, the fact that President Reagan's victories were only partial illustrates the continued strength of liberal ideology, both in Congress and in the public.

Indeed, we can expect that this decade will witness continued American preference for divided government, in which the Congress remains under Democratic—and therefore relatively liberal—control and the presidency under Republican—and therefore relatively conservative—control. Many citizens certainly *perceive* a failure in domestic policy programs, and this perception supports a conservative politics. Yet, at the same time, Americans are wedded to the benefits that government programs bring them, their cities, and their employers. Voting for the kind of Congress that will continue such benefits fits their plans.[9] During the 1988 campaign President Bush himself promised increased attention to education, child care, and environmental cleanup, all targets of budget cuts in the Reagan administration.

Issue definition is not a neutral, apolitical process. The ideological perspectives just described affect the appearance of issues on the policy agenda. The definition of a policy problem is always a matter for disagreement among people of competing beliefs and principles. Poverty, for example, was not seen as a problem to be solved until the 1930s. Before that, it was held to be an inevitable social condition. Conservatives still tend to view it, at least partially, in this way. Radicals, on the other hand, view poverty as a requirement of capitalist society; from this standpoint, welfare policy becomes simply a device used by capitalism to maintain itself, not a response to a "neutral" problem.[10] Even the statistics used to illustrate the dimensions of an issue will frequently vary depending on the perspective from which the issue is being defined. For example, as we shall see in Chapter 7, liberals and conservatives cite the same poverty statistics, but draw opposite conclusions from them. Care must be exercised in using and interpreting statistics—even those presented in this book!

The Cultural Context

During the 1980s, it became increasingly clear that many policy issues were caught up in a cultural conflict of increasing dimensions. Culture refers to the pattern of fundamental beliefs, principles, traditions, and social assumptions that characterize a society. During the 1980s, political conflict touched on the meaning of these fundamental values in the United States and on whether American culture was undergoing and should undergo key changes.

Demographic changes discussed above, particularly those affecting the family, directly affect this issue. The family is an important carrier of culture. As family life changes, other parts of culture are thrown into question. The family is one of the primary ways of passing on moral understandings, but clearly standards of morality with respect to sexuality, competition, money, material goods, and work, to name just a few, are hotly debated today.

Among many, especially conservatives, there is a perception that something is wrong with the fabric of national life, starting with the family, but also reflected in crime, economic noncompetitiveness, and political and social corruption and greed. According to conservatives, television and movies increasingly portray and advocate ways of life at odds with traditional American values. Abortion, pornography, and sexual promiscuity are openly advocated. Prayer is not permitted in the schools, and the educational system fails hundreds of thousands of young people. The role of women in the workplace and in public life also raises questions about the meaning of traditional cultural values, as does recognition and acceptance of homosexual behavior.

Liberals, no less than conservatives, recognize fundamental changes in gender, sexual, and cultural roles of all kinds. Rather than fearing these changes, liberals tend to accept many of them. They support legislation protecting the right to abortion. They want fundamental political, social, and economic rights available to all persons, regardless of gender or sexual orientation. To the extent that traditional family life oppresses women and children, liberals are prepared to accept necessary change in family structures.[11]

These cultural issues thus run through many of the policy issues that appear in the following chapters. They have also been significant in electoral politics. The effect of these issues has been very dramatic in weakening the Democratic coalition in presidential elections. Indeed, it was cultural issues that were in many respects most significant in the elections of Ronald Reagan and George Bush. The battles on college campuses during 1991 over the question of "political correctness" were simply the tip of an iceberg of cultural politics looming over the whole political system.

APPROACHES TAKEN BY THIS BOOK

This text covers areas that are of permanent major interest and controversy. Though some issues—for example, the legal drinking age—occasionally rise to prominence, the issues we discuss—welfare, constitutional rights, defense, economic regulation—are issues of long-range interest and controversy.

Chapter Plan

The chapters that follow present the major policy issues in American politics. Each chapter follows a similar pattern.

Issue background.   Each chapter discusses the basic issue, problem, or dilemma toward which public policy is directed, that is, the general background. Policies do not arise in a vacuum, as we have already noted, but, rather, grow in response to developments that the public, or some part of it, perceives as requiring government action.

Contemporary policy.   Each chapter describes the evolution of present public policies in their areas of concern. The major features of substantive public policies, as they have been adopted and implemented, are sketched in some detail. The principal goals and target populations intended by the policymakers are also outlined. Although absolute neutrality and objectivity are impossible, we have tried to be as unbiased as possible.

Policy evaluation.   Policy outputs and impacts are evaluated, empirically and normatively, in as full detail as possible. Here our concern centers on the major successes and failures of policy in responding to the dilemmas specified. Our focus is on the ability of existing policies to reach their goals and to have maximum beneficial effect, and we discuss the main differences of opinion on the good and bad effects of the policies.

Future alternatives.   Each chapter lists the major policy alternatives and their supporting arguments as specifically as possible. Here again, different values, different definitions of the issue, and different predictions for policy options will be presented. The authors do not put forth their own proposals but, rather, attempt to help the reader make sense of the welter of policy proposals, statistics, and competing values. The arguments of conservatives, radicals, and liberals, as well as a variety of interested parties, find their way into the following pages in order to illustrate the range of alternatives from which policy selections may be made.

Finally, each chapter ends with a summary of its major points and a list of suggested readings to guide study and reflection.

National Focus

Our text concentrates on public policy at the national level, though the chapters on education and intergovernmental relations discuss state and local government activity. For the most part, however, our attention will be on the national arena, for the issues at stake on the state and local level, given the tremendous variation in their social, political, and economic climates, are less clear and less easily presented than those at the national level. Therefore, although state and local policies are obviously important, here they are discussed as they relate to national policies.

Comparative Information

Many chapters discuss comparable policies in other modern industrial nations. American health care policies, for example, are compared with policies in Great Britain, Germany, and Sweden. Noting international trends is essential if U.S. public policy is to be properly evaluated.[12] To discuss American health care policies as though they were the only kind possible or practiced would be like discussing American wine as though France and Germany grew no grapes. Moreover, issues of crime, employment, economic stagnation, immigration, social welfare spending, and cultural change have begun to affect other advanced nations in ways similar to those occurring in the American context.[13] But the focus of this book is on *American* public policy.

SUMMARY

Public policy is defined as an intentional course of action followed by a government institution or official for resolving an issue of public concern. Policy is manifested in laws, public statements, and official regulations and in widely accepted and visible patterns of behavior. A course of action is understood to include the intentional choice *not* to take an action.

Public policy is studied for theoretical, practical, and political reasons. The emphasis of this book is on the third, helping the reader to understand and respond to contemporary policy issues—that is, to become a better citizen.

There are two approaches to the study of public policy. Policy analysis deals with how and why policy is proposed, adopted, and implemented. Policy advocacy is devoted to examining policy issues and alternatives in order to discover and recommend the best course of action. The methods of analysis and advocacy should be employed in tandem, for using one without the other tends to produce either useless information or biased, unsupported judgments.

Political scientists describe the development of a public policy as having a number of distinct stages. The prepolicy stages are issue formation (some sector of the public recognizes that an issue or problem exists), policy demands (people of differing ideological perspectives make demands for action—or non-action—based on their divergent understanding of the issue), and agenda formation (government assimilates and legitimizes various conflicting demands and creates an agenda of alternative proposals for dealing with the issue). The next stages are deliberation and policy adoption (decision makers select a policy from the agenda and commit themselves publicly to that course) and policy implementation (concrete steps are taken to achieve the policymakers' goals).

Policy evaluation is concerned with assessing the success and failure of policy, especially by examining the policy's impact. We shall evaluate policy from two perspectives: normative dimensions, which comprise subjective or ideological values, beliefs, and attitudes; and empirical dimensions, which comprise the neutral observation of the history and facts surrounding any given policy. In evaluation, further distinctions are drawn based on whether a particular policy effect falls inside or outside its stated policy goals and target population (intended and unintended consequences, direct and indirect impact, direct and indirect cost), based on time (short-term and long-term effect) and the abstract as opposed to the concrete returns of a policy (symbolic and tangible impact).

Each of the policy areas outlined in this book is affected by both specific and general influences. These form the environment or context in which each policy area operates. Many of these influences are subject to constant change, but there are five "policy contexts" that will remain more or less constant during the 1990s:

1. The growing distrust of American political and social institutions as a result of the Vietnam War, political scandals, and doubt about the performance of large national government will dominate the institutional context of public policy.
2. The economic context will be dominated by instability and uncertainty. Economic policy as well as initiatives in other policy areas will be influenced strongly by continuing federal deficits, trade imbalances, and an uncertain world economy.

3. Public policy will be influenced by dramatic changes in the distribution of various age groups in the U.S. population: There will be a lower proportion of young people and an increasing number of persons over sixty-five between now and 2000. The demographic context will also see dramatic growth in the proportion of racial and ethnic minorities and a movement of population from the large urban centers of the North and East to the sun belt of the South and Southwest. Changes in family life also strongly influence policy.

4. Policy-making will be affected by the changing balance of ideological forces in the future. The ideological context of the 1990s seems to favor conservatism, but liberals will continue to exert influence.

5. Cultural conflict, focused on different visions of American society, will strongly influence issues of crime, education, social welfare, equality, and the meaning of fundamental freedoms.

Each issue area is approached in a similar, four-part format: (1) its general background, (2) its existing policies, (3) their successes and failures, and (4) the principal policy alternatives. Although the book focuses on national themes of public policy, most chapters compare American policy with the policies of other developed industrial nations. This is essential to gaining a better perspective on what otherwise might seem to be uniquely American problems.

NOTES

1. James E. Anderson, *Public Policymaking: An Introduction* (Boston: Houghton Mifflin, 1990), pp. 4–8; Thomas R. Dye, *Understanding Public Policy,* 5th ed. (Englewood Cliffs, N.J.: Prentice-Hall, 1984), pp. 1–3.

2. Duncan MacRae, Jr. and James A. Wilde, *Policy Analysis for Public Decisions* (North Scituate, Mass.: Duxbury Press, 1979), p. 4.

3. Dye, *Understanding Public Policy,* pp. 7–8. See also Melvin J. Dubnick and Barbara A. Bardes, *Thinking about Public Policy* (New York: John Wiley, 1983).

4. See the pioneering study by Jeffrey L. Pressman and Aaron Wildavsky, *Implementation,* 3d ed. (Berkeley and Los Angeles: University of California Press, 1984). Note that some political scientists are attempting to move beyond the policy stages framework used in the text; see Paul A. Sabatier, "Toward Better Theories of the Policy Process," *P.S.: Political Science & Politics,* 24 (June 1991), 147–156.

5. Dan Balz and Richard Morin, "An Electorate Ready to Revolt," *The Washington Post National Weekly Edition,* November 11–17, 1991, pp. 6–7.

6. Theodore J. Lowi and Alan Stone, *Nationalizing Government* (Beverly Hills, Calif.: Sage Publications, 1978), p. 12.

7. See Paul Blustein, "Peace for All, Prosperity—for Some," *The Washington Post National Weekly Edition,* October 3–9, 1988, p. 8; "Are You Better Off?" *Time,* October 10, 1988, pp. 28–30; John E. Schwarz, *America's Hidden Success* (New York: Norton, 1988), pp. 14ff, 99ff, 147–185; Joseph J. Minarik, "Family Incomes," in *Challenge to Leadership,* ed. Isabel V. Sawhill (Washington: Urban Institute Press, 1988), pp. 33–66; and Frank Levy, "The Vanishing Middle Class and Related Issues: A Review of Living Standards in the 1970s and 1980s," *PS,* 20 (Summer 1987), 650–655.

8. Schwarz, *America's Hidden Success,* pp. 116ff.

9. Schwarz, *America's Hidden Success,* chap. 6; Sawhill, ed., *Challenge to Leadership;* and B. B. Kymlicka and Jean V. Matthews, eds., *The Reagan Revolution?* (Chicago: Dorsey, 1988).

10. See Edward S. Greenberg, *Serving the Few* (New York: John Wiley, 1974), for such a reference.

11. See Joel Lieske, "Cultural Issues and Images in the 1988 Presidential Campaign: Why the Democrats Lost Again!" *P.S.: Political Science & Politics,* 24 (June 1991), 180–187. For broader discussion of cultural conflict and of the policy issues directly involved, see James Davidson Hunter, *Culture Wars: The Struggle to Define America* (New York: Basic Books, 1991) and Raymond Tatalovich and Byron W. Daynes, eds., *Social Regulatory Policy: Moral Controversies in American Politics* (Boulder, Colo.: Westview Press, 1988).

12. Two fine comparative policy books are Arnold J. Heidenheimer, Hugh Heclo, and Carolyn Teich Adams, *Comparative Public Policy,* 3rd ed. (New York: St. Martin's Press, 1990); and Howard M. Leichter and Harrell R. Rodgers, Jr., *American Public Policy in a Comparative Context* (New York: McGraw-Hill, 1984).

13. See, for example, Joel Kotkin, "Europe's Continental Drift," *Washington Post National Weekly Edition,* September 23–29, 1991, pp. 23–24.

SUGGESTED READINGS

Anderson, Charles W. "The Place of Principles in Policy Analysis." *American Political Science Review,* 73 (September 1979), 711–723.

Anderson, James E. *Public Policymaking: An Introduction.* Boston: Houghton Mifflin, 1990.

Dye, Thomas R. *Understanding Public Policy,* 7th ed. Englewood Cliffs, N.J.: Prentice-Hall, 1991.

Heidenheimer, Arnold J.; Heclo, Hugh; and Adams, Carolyn Teich. *Comparative Public Policy.* 3rd ed. New York: St. Martin's Press, 1990.

Heineman, Robert A., et al. *The World of the Policy Analyst: Rationality, Values, and Politics.* Chatham, N.J.: Chatham House, 1990.

Kymlicka, B. B., and Matthews, Jean V., eds. *The Reagan Revolution?* Chicago: Dorsey Press, 1988.

Leichter, Howard M., and Rodgers, Harrell R., Jr. *American Public Policy in a Comparative Context.* New York: McGraw-Hill, 1984.

Nachmias, David. *Public Policy Evaluation.* New York: St. Martin's Press, 1979.

Portis, Edward Bryan, and Levy, Michael B., eds. *Handbook of Political Theory and Policy Science.* New York: Greenwood Press, 1988.

Pressman, Jeffrey L., and Wildavsky, Aaron. Implementation. 3rd ed. Berkeley and Los Angeles: University of California Press, 1984.

Robertson, David Brian, and Judd, Dennis R. *The Development of American Public Policy: The Structure of Policy Restraint.* Glenview, Ill.: Scott, Foresman, 1989.

Sawhill, Isabel V., ed. *Challenge to Leadership: Economic and Social Issues for the Next Decade.* Lanham, Md.: Urban Institute Press, 1988.

Schwarz, John E. *America's Hidden Success: A Reassessment of Public Policy from Kennedy to Reagan.* Revised ed. New York: Norton, 1988.

CHAPTER 2

The Economy: Changing Government-Business Relationships

American government has always been preoccupied with economic activities. During the first century of America's nationhood, the main concerns of the early administrations were preserving the property of citizens. Although property rights still hold a high place in American values, other economic concerns—such as economic growth, level of employment, international competition, and the scarcity of natural resources—have gradually replaced preservation of property rights as a major focus of government. Yet one factor has remained constant over the years: government and economic activity are inextricably intertwined, and therefore activity in one sector automatically has major consequences for the other. At the same time, quality of life and the relationship of economic development to the environment represent current issues for economic policy.

ISSUE BACKGROUND: KEY CONCEPTS IN ECONOMICS

Economic systems produce and distribute wealth among people in the form of goods and services. Different systems perform these functions in different ways. In theory, a market system operates according to the concept of supply and demand—that is, it responds to peoples' demands by supplying what they want, for a profit. The key to understanding the market system is that both prices and the allocation of goods and services are determined impersonally. That is, they are not set by any actor or institution according to some rational criterion, but rather are produced by the interaction of the impersonal forces of supply and demand. This simplified view of economic systems is predicated on the expectation that there will be a balance between supply and demand and that the economic actors have essentially equal ability to bargain with one another. In reality, however, people vary in the economic power they have, and other factors affect the supply-demand relationship. As economist John Kenneth Galbraith noted, people band together in organizations to acquire power.[1] These organizations often serve their own economic self-interest, not that of society. Because some individuals and organizations have more money, property, or political access than others do, imbalances in the distribution of wealth develop. Governments often intervene to protect the interests of those with power or to rebalance the system, and economic policy deals with these governmental efforts.

The Free-Enterprise System

Industrialized nations are characterized by a variety of economic systems. They can, however, be roughly divided between two extreme alternatives of economic organization: market capitalism, or free enterprise, and socialist, or public, ownership. Although each individual economy more closely approximates one of these two extremes, most combine elements of free-market enterprise and government control. One may actually conceptualize three types of economic system. Free-enterprise capitalism implies both the market system defined earlier and the private ownership of the major means of production, distribution, and exchange, with such means run for the profit of their owner. Socialism involves the public or governmental ownership and control of these major means of production, distribution, and exchange, presumably run for the public interest. In this system, prices and the allocation of goods and services are planned by government agents according to rational considerations. Between these polar opposites is the system practiced in most industrial democracies, a type called welfare-state capitalism. In this system, the allocation of goods and services, and frequently prices, are to a large extent planned, but the major means of production are still in private hands and run for profit.

The major systems champion economic development and industrialization, but they favor different methods for achieving them. Proponents of free-market capitalism justify it on the grounds that the private ownership of firms provides incentives for production. They believe the state should refrain as much as possible from interfering with the conduct of economic activity. In the socialist approach, on the other hand, the political system plays a major role in the conduct of economic activity. Such a system is based on the assumption that economic wealth should be fairly equally distributed among the population and that such distribution improves social welfare. Socialists reject the assumptions that underlie the market system. From the socialist perspective, capitalist societies are dominated by a few wealthy owners and managers of private enterprise, policymakers who are neither chosen by nor responsible to the people as a whole. Proponents of capitalism see the same problems in a socialist economy, namely, that government officials concentrate economic power along with political and social power in their own hands, but capitalists view this as a threat to individual liberty.

In socialist economies such as those in the pre-1989 Soviet Union and the formerly communist countries of Eastern Europe, government ownership predominated. Thus government controlled economic activity through its normal decision-making processes. Even within such societies, however, there were variations, and some had more mixed economies than others. Eastern European nations, in particular, permitted private enterprise, particularly in agriculture, to coexist with the state-owned economic entities. East Germany, Yugoslavia, and

Czechoslovakia diverged from total government ownership, often at the expense of incurring Soviet enmity and sometimes intervention. Relatively independent of Soviet dominance, Yugoslavia, for example, because of the decentralization of its productive mechanisms, had most of its prices determined by market forces. The Solidarity labor movement in Poland also demonstrated that socialist governments cannot always maintain total control over economic activities.

In the 1980s, Soviet leader Mikhail Gorbachev launched *perestroika,* which refers to market-oriented reforms in the economic system. *Perestroika* led to some competition and private enterprise. When communism fell apart in late 1989 and Eastern European countries liberated themselves from Soviet control, the command economies collapsed. As a result, the development of the free-market system accelerated. Currently, the former Soviet Union, its newly independent republics, and Eastern European nations are struggling with the transition to a market economy. Although the future is uncertain, it is very likely that these countries will develop mixed economies reflecting elements of command and free-market systems.

In most industrialized nations—such as the United States, France, Germany, Italy, Sweden, and Japan—a capitalist approach dominates, but it is inevitably a mixture of private ownership and public control that characterizes such systems.[2] Government monopolies invariably run postal services and, in many nonsocialist nations, other economic activities, such as telephone and telegraph services and transportation. These activities are often viewed as being so basic to the maintenance of society that government monopoly is justified.

What differentiates capitalist and socialist economies for purposes of government-economic interaction is that socialist states, as we have seen, have built-in controls through public ownership and operation of economic enterprise. Capitalist economies, on the other hand, utilize other kinds of intervention as a means of guiding or controlling the activities of the private sector. Socialist states do not need the regulation or economic stimulation common in the West, as they exercise direct control, whereas capitalist economies use numerous methods to try to influence economic enterprise.

Among the industrial nations, the United States is one of the most purely capitalist in the way its economic activity is organized. The United States is especially distinguished by the extent to which it still relies on market forces. The majority of economic enterprise is privately operated, and few activities are totally publicly owned. Nonetheless, although economic activity is primarily privately owned, the United States does intervene in economic activity to a great extent. Thus people in the United States, who pride themselves on having a nearly pure form of "free" market capitalism, actually function within a regulated economy.

The economist Milton Friedman, probably the preeminent defender of the free-market system, suggested that a pure free-enterprise economy would be based on

1. A self-adjusting free market independent of any government intervention.

2. Human beings who seek to maximize their own economic self-interest.
3. Competition—stimulated by individual self-interest—that produces maximum benefits for all.
4. Private ownership of the means of production and distribution, which leads to competition, which results in the best quality of product at the lowest price.[3]

Critics of Friedman's position argue that the free-market approach is based on several assumptions that simply are not valid, at least as the so-called free market is known in the United States. Free-market theory rests on the imperfect assumptions that

1. Human beings are essentially motivated by economic wants.
2. People have perfect information on which to make rational economic choices.
3. Demand is elastic (adjusts to changing prices).
4. Production and price are elastic (producers can respond easily to shifts in demand).
5. There is perfect competition.[4]

These assumptions are frequently not representative of real-life economics. The market often fails because human beings act on bases other than economic rationality. Producers, for example, often create demand through advertising—that is, they create artificial "needs" in people purely through the power of persuasive advertising and then fill these new "needs" at a profit to themselves.[5] Furthermore, people often do things because they enjoy doing them, even though there may be negative economic consequences. People do not have perfect information about goods and services and would probably not be able to assimilate and analyze all the information even if it were available. Time is limited, and choices must be made.

Nor is there perfect competition in the market. Instead, the economy is characterized by an unevenness in the resources among producers. Some students of economic systems suggest that our economy actually is made up of two different groups of economic entities.[6] On one side are the large, powerful firms that are few in number but have the resources to persist and to influence other actors in the economy. Then there are many very small firms that find it difficult to compete because they lack the resources to keep up with technological innovations. They often are absorbed by the large firms or are forced out of existence because they are not competitive. Consumers, by the same token, have little ability to influence the powerful producers. The result is that little effective competition takes place in the economy, and therefore prices do not follow the supply-and-demand curve. What happens is that those with resources end up dominating the market, taking advantage of their power to further their own interests.

Finally, consumers' choices within the market may be limited. Even though the cost of gasoline may be very high, some people have no other way to get to work than by automobile and thus are limited in how much they can reduce consumption. Similarly, regardless of cost, a sick or injured person needs medical assistance.

Because of the failure of the free-market system to operate perfectly, many governments intervene to guide and control the economic system. Much government policy is based on the intent to protect citizens and consumers against fraud and abuse, to control monopolies (and thus help make the market truly free), and to protect against inequities and inefficiencies. On the other hand, if those with economic power also have political power, as is often the case, government policy also may be oriented toward protecting their interests. Still other goals of economic planners have been to keep the economy operating on a stable basis and to avoid constant sharp fluctuations between inflation with full employment and recession with unemployment. As the analysis in this chapter will demonstrate, such often-conflicting objectives have been difficult to pursue, and economic policy has been characterized by numerous unintended consequences and indirect impacts.

History of Government's Role

Many critics of government policies seem to believe that the United States began as a nation in which economic enterprise flourished free of intervention by the political system. This view is inaccurate. Policies to influence economic activity have been a part of the American political landscape since the inception of nationhood. The American Revolution resulted, in part, from financial grievances of the colonists, who felt the British monarchy was unfairly impeding colonial development through its taxation policies. After the Revolution, policies affecting economic well-being continued to be a major concern. Witness the controversy surrounding the establishment of a national bank and its relationship to the national debt during the Washington administration.

In its early history, the United States government stimulated the economy through public investment or attempts to create an environment in which the economy could prosper. The national government subsidized development through land grant programs to the railroad industry and to states to establish educational institutions that would, in turn, focus on supporting the agricultural economy. State governments set many precedents during this time in their attempts to spur economic growth. And roads and canals also were built with government subsidy, further illustrating government's efforts to stimulate development.

Although citizens became accustomed to government's playing a supportive role in economic activity, they did not appear willing to accept government interference beyond that role. During the latter part of the nineteenth century, a very strong antigovernment sentiment developed. The national government had begun to develop regulatory policies aimed at curbing some of the abuses of large corporate enterprises. Industry, however, was influential politically and was successful in convincing the political leadership to take a laissez-faire approach to economic activities.[7] It was not until the 1930s that government re-

turned to an interventionist approach. The severe economic depression following the market crash of 1929 led people to accept a greater government role, but
even then there was a great deal of hesitation about permitting government to
become too deeply involved in private enterprise.

When the Depression first hit, the immediate response of President Herbert Hoover's administration was to raise taxes and try to balance the budget.
Unfortunately, these actions exacerbated the problem. The nation, in no mood
for half-measures, sought a new leader in the next election. Franklin D.
Roosevelt, the new president, quickly took another approach. With the strong
support of Congress, he obtained legislation to create a number of agencies and
programs to deal with the extraordinary problems of unemployment and the
slump in production. This whirlwind of legislative action was unprecedented;
within the first one hundred days of Roosevelt's first term, Congress had

1. Passed the Emergency Banking Act, which was intended to put the
   banking industry back on a solid foundation.
2. Created the Civilian Conservation Corps, a public works program to
   hire the unemployed directly by government.
3. Funded state welfare programs through the Federal Emergency Relief Act.
4. Passed the National Industrial Recovery Act to regulate wages, collective bargaining, and work hours and to permit business to organize
   combinations to eliminate waste and some forms of competition.
5. Created the Agricultural Adjustment Administration to support agricultural production and prices.
6. Created the Securities and Exchange Commission to protect investors.

The above represent only a few of the new programs; an era had begun in which
governmental intervention in economic matters would grow immensely. It is
important to note, however, that these programs maintained the tradition of
government support for economic prosperity and that intervention was limited
to rebuilding the economy through aid to particular enterprises. Later came
government efforts to influence the private sector to perform in a particular way,
sometimes against its will. These programs helped in curing the ills of the Depression, but they did not lead to complete prosperity for the economic system.

During the late 1930s, many leaders, including Roosevelt, became convinced that the free-market system could not regulate itself satisfactorily. The
Depression had shown that some of the assumptions of free-market theory, discussed earlier, were not valid. Now it was recognized that for a variety of reasons, sometimes severe fluctuations in the market economy were inevitable without government intervention. Influenced by the ideas of John Maynard
Keynes, whose *General Theory of Employment, Interest, and Money*[8] suggested
new approaches to the relationship between government and the economy,
Roosevelt and his administration began to modify public policy. Not until the
economic impact of World War II became apparent, however, was the immense

power of the political system in influencing the economy recognized. Active government intervention began in virtually every aspect of the economy.

The wartime economy, dictated in large part by the government, had clearly stimulated employment and economic growth. Recognition that government spending could create such dramatic effects created the foundation for sustained government action to influence desirable economic activity and to correct problems in the economy. It was, then, during the 1940s that maintenance of prosperity became a major public issue. Today this recognition remains one of the most, if not *the* most, important concerns of any national administration. The American people now expect the government to take action to resolve problems in the economy, but there are major differences of opinion on just what action will produce the desired results. The contrasts between the philosophies of Friedman and Galbraith outlined at the beginning of this chapter are examples of opposing perspectives on what the role of government should be.

Today, few argue that the government has no appropriate role in the economic sector. Instead, controversy exists over where government should intervene, and for whom. We already have reviewed most of the areas of responsibility. Traditionally, one purpose of government economic policy has been to stimulate economic growth. In the 1970s, however, many economic policies also had to address problems of scarcity, particularly in energy and food. Another purpose of economic programs is protecting and supporting the private-enterprise system through promoting full employment, protecting the well-being of citizens, and controlling the pressures of inflation and/or recession. Ultimately, economic policies also result in redistributing resources among the various groups in society.

Inflation and Recession

Inflation is a rise in price of goods and services, even though the actual value of those goods and services does not increase. Thus, although prices increase, production does not keep pace, resulting in a decline in the purchasing power of money—that is, each dollar purchases less than it did in the past.

Inflation may occur when the demand for goods and services grows at a faster rate than available supplies. Competing consumers drive up the prices for such goods. This type of inflation is known as *demand-pull inflation.* Another type, *cost-push inflation,* refers to an increase in the cost of a product, even though demand remains constant or drops. It occurs when prices are regulated in some way rather than impersonally set by supply and demand. The rise in oil prices, for example, is a form of cost-push inflation, as are rises in labor wage rates without a corresponding rise in productivity. Normally during periods of demand-pull inflation, employment goes up, although this may not be true during times of cost-push inflation. We shall see later why different remedies are appropriate to these different inflation forms. The inflation of the 1970s and early 1980s seemed to result from a combination of demand-pull and cost-push factors. The demand-pull inflation was clearly initiated by the attempt to fight the

Vietnam War without a tax increase. Military spending pumps many additional dollars into the economy without generating a corresponding increase in consumer goods and services those dollars can buy and is therefore the most inflationary kind of spending. Once this inflation is generated, the wage-price spiral of cost-push inflation perpetuates it.

Recessions are periods in which there is a decline in economic activity arising from a slump in effective demand for goods and services. An oversupply of goods and services may cause a drop in production, leading to increased unemployment. Unemployed people are able to purchase less, thus further nourishing the recession. Recessions have hit the United States twice in recent years, from 1981 to 1982, and in 1991. Prolonged recessions are called *depressions.*

Microeconomic Approaches to Managing the Economy

Government concerns about the economy fall into two groups, microeconomic and macroeconomic policy. Generally, microeconomic policy refers to government activities regarding particular firms and businesses, and macroeconomic policy refers to the overall management of the economy. Examples of microeconomic policy are regulation and subsidy programs. Macroeconomic policy includes monetary and fiscal policies. Microeconomic approaches are the subject of the rest of this chapter; macroeconomic approaches are examined in the next chapter.

Government intervention now extends to almost every aspect of our lives in efforts to protect the health, safety, welfare, and environment and to promote economic and social justice. The emphasis in this chapter, however, is on economic intervention. Other chapters address government activities as they relate to other substantive areas such as the environment, health, education, and equality of opportunity.

Economic regulation, in the form of early antitrust laws, began originally as a way of controlling concentrations of wealth and power in large private-sector economic enterprises; the purpose was to ensure that private economic gain did not hurt the public interest. Guarding the public interest has generally meant protection against economic abuse of citizens by prohibiting such practices as charging unreasonable prices, selling products hazardous to the health and safety of the public, and harming resources that belong to all—that is, air, water, and other elements of the natural environment. Basically, the regulators are meant to be watchdogs for the public.

Regulatory agencies normally have a fair degree of independence from other governmental institutions. In establishing regulatory agencies, legislative bodies have delegated certain of their policy-making powers to them and have tried to protect them as much as possible against interference from the executive branch. A regulatory agency such as the Federal Trade Commission (FTC), for example, is created by legislative action. The mandate that Congress gave to the FTC is somewhat vague: to regulate in the interest of ensuring competition and preventing deceptive advertising by industry. Three commissioners serve staggered six-year terms on this agency, with the provision that no more than two may be from the same political party. The president designates one member as chairperson of the commission. Once appointed by the president and confirmed by the Senate, a commissioner may not be removed by the president except under unusual circumstances. Other regulatory agencies are similarly created and members similarly appointed, although the number of commissioners varies from agency to agency. Much regulating also is carried out by units within regular operating departments of the executive branch which are therefore less independent of the president. One example is the Food and Drug Administration in the Department of Health and Human Services.

Congress gave regulatory agencies relative independence from the president because it felt that partisan politics had no place in regulation, and it did not want to surrender its powers to the executive branch. Another reason why Congress delegated its powers was simply that it did not have the time, expertise, or other resources to carry out the specialized activities for which regulatory agencies were created. Ideally the application of expertise and technical judgment is supposed to be free of politics. Though insulated from partisan political forces to the extent that board or commission members have fixed terms and ordinarily cannot be removed by the president, regulatory agencies have not entirely escaped politics. Rather, they are subject to many political pressures from interest groups, legislative committees, and the White House. Because Congress and the president have much to say about the budgets and, indeed, the very existence of regulatory agencies, the agencies pay attention to opinions from those sources.

In applying their expertise to problems, regulatory agencies give meaning to the general policies developed by the legislative bodies. To do so, regulatory agencies pass rules and regulations that have the force of law. Unlike legislative policymakers, however, regulatory agencies also enforce and serve as judges regarding this policy. Thus, once they draw up a rule or regulation, they have the responsibility of seeing that the regulated party abides by the rules. They also decide whether a rule has been violated by an individual party and fashion a punishment appropriate for the violation.

Of course, a commission itself cannot do all the work of a regulatory agency and usually performs only the policy-making and judging functions. Commission policy is executed by its staff, although the staff also creates policy and does the major work in investigating and hearing evidence on cases in which violation of policy is charged.

Once a hearing examiner has heard and evaluated the evidence, the examiner makes a recommendation on how the case should be decided. Normally, the commission accepts the examiner's recommendation, although changes may be made by the commission.

Because certain types of behavior are encouraged, required, or prohibited by the regulator, regulatory policy affects economic activity. Regulation is an attempt to stabilize the economy and protect the interests of the general public. We already have looked at the most common form of regulation in the United

States, agencies that create specific rules and regulations to control the behavior of economic enterprises. Control of activities also is accomplished in several other ways. These include government ownership and the creation of government corporations. Ownership of public lands by the Department of the Interior is an effective way of controlling how the land is used. The U.S. Postal Service and the Federal Deposit Insurance Corporation are government-owned corporations that regulate and control many postal and banking activities. In addition, there are many programs and policies to protect particular economic interests. In agriculture, for example, many of the programs and policies subsidize particular economic entities and interfere with the free market. The case studies examined below include elements of both regulation and other types of intervention to support economic enterprises.

CONTEMPORARY POLICY: FOUR CASE STUDIES IN ECONOMIC INTERVENTION

In the following section we will examine how the many forms of intervention have been applied to four specific areas of the economy—antitrust policy, broadcasting, agriculture, and transportation. Virtually every aspect of the economy is subject to some intervention by government, but to inventory them all here would clearly be impossible. These four case studies will illustrate most of the pertinent approaches to today's economic policy.

Antitrust

Around the close of the last century and the beginning of the twentieth, various energetic business entrepreneurs managed to acquire near monopolies on many American industries, including steel and the railroads. These concentrations of power in a few hands were accompanied by many abuses. Consumers were charged exorbitant prices, small companies were bullied into selling out or were ruined by the large firms, and local governments were pressured into making concessions. Workers in such monopolies, with almost no bargaining power, were exploited at will by ruthless employers. All of these factors led to the reaction, by the public and politicians alike, that concentration of economic power in a small number of enterprises was not in the public interest. A movement grew in the United States to regulate industry through antitrust policy (a *trust* is a combination of several companies, especially one that limits competition). In time a series of laws was enacted that forms the framework of today's government controls over such economic concentration.

Antitrust policy is aimed at preventing one or a small number of firms from directly dominating most or all of a particular market. It also attempts to prevent private firms from agreeing among themselves to restrict competition. Thus antitrust policy prohibits both monopolies and agreements that fix prices, divide markets, or collude on bidding. To control monopolies and to dissolve those that had already come into being, Congress passed the Sherman Antitrust Act in 1890. The Federal Trade Commission Act of 1914 went further by creating the Federal Trade Commission (FTC) to stem the development of monopolies and prevent practices that would lead to unfair competition. Because these laws were only partially successful, the policy was strengthened in 1950 with the Anti-Merger Act, which gave enforcement powers to administrative agencies.

Taken together, the antitrust laws give government a number of enforcement tools. The Sherman Act, and subsequent legislation, make illegal any action in restraint of interstate commerce. Government attorneys, currently the Antitrust Division of the Justice Department, can choose criminal prosecution against companies charged with this violation. The Antitrust Division also has the authority to approve or disapprove mergers. In recent years, the Justice Department took essentially a hands-off approach which led to virtually uncontrolled mergers. Additionally—and with greater effect—the Antitrust Division may initiate civil suits to obtain court orders requiring firms to cease practices that are found to be in restraint of trade. A similar proceeding may require a firm to break up into several units; the Standard Oil Corporation, for example, was divided into a number of companies in this way during the early part of this century. AT&T, which controlled 83 percent of the telephone market, was the object of antitrust litigation. Because the government's case was so strong, the company settled out of court in 1982 and agreed to dissolve, resulting in the current decentralized telephone structure.

Another weapon that can be used is a suit by an individual who has been hurt by an antitrust violation. Current law permits court awards of triple the amount of damages suffered. But relying on such suits is not a very effective method of enforcing regulations: Both lack of interest and the large amount of time required of the litigants and courts in such procedures discourage victims from suing. It is not an efficient method of controlling behavior unless all the parties affected join in a class-action suit.

Class-action suits are those in which an individual or individuals sue on behalf of all people who are in a similar situation. Thus a female employee who has been discriminated against in pay and promotional opportunities may sue her employer for remedy and may include all other female employees who had worked for the employer during the same period of time. Those female employees would be part of the "class" on whose behalf litigation was being initiated. Because of the large number of people who may be affected in such cases, and because courts usually have required litigants to demonstrate personal injury in order to be a party to a court action, class-action suits have been difficult to pursue. Also, courts often require the litigants to identify and notify all members of the class. This requirement can be difficult to meet because the people are hard to locate, and many may be too indifferent to respond. As a result, class-action suits are not a major means of accomplishing regulation, although they are used on occasion.[9]

FTC hearings. Until the late 1930s, antitrust legislation was not very effective because the Supreme Court was unsympathetic to such regulation. In particular, judges were hesitant to rule in favor of restrictions on the use of private property—owners were protected in their right to use their property as they saw fit. In its first decision regarding the Sherman Act, for example, the U.S. Supreme Court held that manufacturing was exempt from the act because it was not commerce.[10] Ironically, the Sherman Act became an ally of business because the court interpreted it to restrict labor unions as restraints of trade.[11] After 1937, however, the Supreme Court's receptivity to antitrust action grew, and the Federal Trade Commission became more active in pursuing antitrust violators. In recent years, cases have involved action against Exxon Oil Corporation, International Telephone and Telegraph, four cereal companies, and Coca Cola and PepsiCo along with five other soft drink companies. The FTC, however, has not been very successful in these cases.

The Federal Trade Commission, like most regulatory agencies, has a small staff and budget compared to the corporations it confronts in its work. The opportunities for violators to delay or buy time are many, some the results of procedural protections required by the courts or the FTC's own rules. These requirements give FTC proceedings the aura of a courtroom process. Complaints are investigated by the staff and a formal hearing may be set up. The hearing requires notice to the parties involved, and each has the opportunity to present its case. In recent years, parties under investigation have inundated the agency with volumes of testimonial material. This considerably lengthens the time it takes for the investigation and hearing to be completed. And afterwards, the hearing examiner, also called an administrative law judge, must still evaluate the record before making a decision. With the record often comprising thousands of pages of very complex material, the examiner has a formidable task and needs time to reflect on the evidence.

Once the process is completed, a party to the case may appeal the decision of the examiner. The full commission then hears the case as if it were a totally new proceeding. The same opportunity for delays exists here. After the commission makes its decision, the defendants in the case may appeal to the courts, and—given the high stakes in many cases—litigation can drag on for years, first through the appellate courts, then on to the Supreme Court. A case involving the makers of the diet supplement Geritol, for example, took thirteen years to resolve, although the FTC was finally successful in getting Geritol's ads—which claimed the product cured "tired blood" and "iron deficiency anemia"— removed from the air.[12] The amount of time and money expended caused many to question whether the whole process was worth it.

The FTC is also subject to political whims. Members of the commission are political appointees of the president and, of course, tend to reflect the president's political philosophy. Additionally, Congress controls the FTC's budget; thus, there is a tendency to be careful not to offend important members of Congress. During the 1960s, for example, Ralph Nader and his Center for the Study of Law in the Public Interest conducted a study of the Federal Trade Commission and castigated it for being timid and unresponsive to the consumer. A similarly critical report was issued by the American Bar Association in 1969.

With the popularity of the consumer protection movement increasing in the 1960s and into the 1970s, members of Congress prodded the FTC to become aggressive in protecting the consumer. The agency responded and became active in pushing consumer rights.

By 1979, the commission had become so aggressive that many industries began to exert pressure on Congress to limit its activities. During 1979 and 1980, for example, the funeral industry, life insurance industry, and many professionals including doctors, dentists, and lawyers all brought pressure on Congress to limit the authority of the FTC to regulate their business practices. Many members of Congress agreed with their complaints, and it appeared that the powers of the FTC might be severely limited. Although Congress ultimately did not follow this policy, the prospect of such restrictions does illustrate the tenuous position of the agency. Created to protect the consuming public, the FTC often finds itself the object of intense political pressures to conform to industry's position on regulation. The election of Ronald Reagan as president in 1980 led to a swing entirely in the opposite direction from the consumer protection focus of the 1970s. During the 1980s, the FTC became a protector of private enterprise, and budgets and staff were severely slashed. Since 1989, with President Bush's appointment of Janet D. Steiger to the chair, the FTC has developed a balanced stance. It is now enforcing laws. It is actually opposing mergers and for the first time in almost eight years is pursuing price-fixing cases. The current position of the FTC appears to be that the free market can work but that consumers have rights as well, and a balance between those interests is the best policy.

The role of the Justice Department's Antitrust Division in the Reagan administration led to an era of almost uncontrolled mergers. The Antitrust Division stopped challenging mergers except in rare cases. As a result, some very large mergers, which probably would not have been approved in any previous administration, were completed. The $20.3 billion Kohlberg Kravis and Roberts Company deal to buy RJR Nabisco attracted a lot of attention in December, 1988. The deal was the most expensive ever. There are many implications, not the least of which is that approval by the Justice Department signaled that mergers are not of much concern to it. The Bush administration appears to favor some regulation of mergers, and 1990 did witness a decline in the number and value of mergers (see Table 2-1). The causes may be economic as much as policy-based.

In addition to the support of the Reagan administration for less stringent rules on mergers, the courts have been less hostile in this respect. In the past, market share was a very important consideration in decisions on mergers. The FTC and the courts were likely to disallow any merger that increased market share of a corporation by even as much as ten percent. In recent years, mergers have been allowed wherein market share was increased as much as 40 percent. The courts have sanctioned such mergers even when the FTC has been opposed.

Weaknesses in U.S. antitrust policy are the result of many factors. One is a lack of clarity about goals. Given the responsibility to restore competition and prevent deceptive advertising, the FTC and the Justice Department would seem to have easily understood objectives. However, these are rather ambiguous goals in

---

TABLE 2-1 ▪ Mergers and Acquisitions—Historical Summary: 1965–1990

Item	Mergers and Acquisitions, net[a]	Dollar Value Paid (billions)	$100 Million-plus Deals
1965	2,125	NA	NA
1970	5,152	16.4	10
1980	1,889	44.3	93
1981	2,395	82.6	113
1982	2,346	53.8	116
1983	2,533	73.1	138
1984	2,543	122.2	200
1985	3,001	179.8	270
1986	3,336	173.1	346
1989[b]	4,763	377.9	NA
1990[b]	4,486	199.9	NA

NA = not available.
[a] Represents announcement.
[b] Data from *Arizona Republic,* December 27, 1990, p. C1.
SOURCE: United States Department of Commerce, Bureau of the Census, *Statistical Abstract of the United States 1988* (Washington, D.C.: U.S. Government Printing Office, 1987), p. 504.

---

terms of the precise actions that might be taken to achieve them. Another factor also explains the sometimes erratic performance: The commission and the Justice Department have discretion as to which of these objectives they emphasize. As different presidents influence these regulators through their appointments, the perspectives of the agencies vary. Thus uneven attention is given to enforcement of rules and regulations. Ambivalence about how strongly antitrust policy should be pursued also provides regulated industries with opportunities to articulate their positions. Industries have the resources and contacts to make their concerns known to regulators, who are often sympathetic in the first place. They are usually effective in mobilizing political forces to reduce the intensity of the enforcement efforts.

International approaches to antitrust. Industrialized nations generally favor some form of control over monopoly and restraint of trade, although some nations such as Italy have virtually no antitrust or antimonopoly laws. While many of the Western European nations use approaches similar to that of the United States, there are variations. Some countries have weaker policies. For example, in Great Britain the approval of Parliament is required before the Monopolies Commission can prevent mergers. This provision opens regulation much more directly to political pressures and thus lessens its effectiveness. So long as mergers are not found to be contrary to the public interest, they are not prohibited. Very seldom does British government find them to be harmful.

Germany represents the opposite end of the spectrum. There, government approval is required before mergers of large corporations can occur. More significantly, the German Cartel Office also has the authority to dissolve a corporation brought about by merger. Most European nations employ an approach somewhere between these two extremes. In Europe, merger activity appeared to be down in 1989 with 8,157 mergers totalling $441.6 billion compared to 8,822 worth $643.6 billion in 1988.

Broadcasting

Regulation of the broadcast industry started from a need to control access to crowded radio channels, brought about by rapid increases in the 1920s in the number of radio stations attempting to operate. At first, the stations themselves tried to work out time-sharing arrangements. Unable to reach an accord, the industry asked for government regulation. In 1927, the Radio Act created the Federal Radio Commission, which was made up of five members appointed by the president with Senate confirmation. Because it was authorized only for one year as an experiment, the commission was in a weak position to accomplish much. Congress also limited its effectiveness by extending its life only one year at a time. The commission was under congressional pressure annually as its existence was debated and renewed.

The Federal Communications Commission.   Finally, in 1934, Congress created the Federal Communications Commission (FCC) through passage of the Federal Communications Act. Established as a seven-member panel, this new body's scope of activities was expanded to include all areas of communications except for the print media. The commission was charged with regulating communication so that "the public interest, convenience, or necessity would be served." The mechanism for regulation was the licensing authority of the FCC.

Whether broadcasting should be regulated at all generates controversy. Some opponents suggest that the First Amendment's protection of freedom of expression means that government should not control broadcasting and, particularly, that it cannot constitutionally control the *content* of programming. They charge that legislation authorizing regulation "in the public interest" has led to the FCC's developing many rules and regulations that amount to censorship of programming. Critics argue that such regulation violates the Constitution.

On the other side of the issue is the view that the public airwaves are a scarce national resource owned by the public as a whole. Therefore, to insure that all citizens' interests are served, it becomes necessary to provide for the orderly use of air channels. The FCC entrusts the licensee with the responsibility to serve the public as a "public trustee." Currently, the authority of the FCC to regulate is relatively well accepted, but controversies over specific regulations still abound— namely, what can or cannot be broadcast.

Another aspect of the FCC that raised complaints was its "equal time" provision, part of the Fairness Doctrine, which required broadcasters to air both sides of controversial issues. Usually, whenever a broadcaster or a program took a stand on an issue, the broadcaster was required to make equal time available for opposing viewpoints. While the doctrine was relatively easy to comprehend, it was not always easy to implement. Do opposing viewpoints concerning advertising have to be aired, for instance? If advertisers take positions—as they often do—some critics believe those who disagree should have the opportunity to explain the other side. The Fairness Doctrine also created problems in election years. If major candidates are given air time to address the public, is the broadcaster required to give the same time to all candidates? Usually Congress resolved the issue by exempting broadcasters from the provision during election years. Of course, members of Congress have no small interest in the matter since they are frequently candidates for reelection themselves.

In 1987 the FCC rescinded its equal-time requirement at the prodding of broadcasters. Public interest groups generated pressure in Congress to reinstate it. While Congress passed the bill reinstating the policy, President Reagan vetoed it. It appears that the policy will not be revived, at least in the near future.

Technological advances also create new demands and problems for the FCC. The development of FM radio broadcasting, television, and the citizens band radio are indicative of the rapid changes that can occur in this field. Regulations that were appropriate to the AM radio broadcasting industry are not adequate for these new technologies. Satellite communication is also within the FCC's jurisdiction and is certain to raise new problems.

Yet another challenge involves the rapid spread of the cable-television industry, which is becoming a very controversial area of broadcast regulation. As it now stands, the national government has handed regulatory responsibility over to local governments. Regulation occurs through the power to issue and revoke charters for service. Each municipality grants charters to cable companies to operate in its jurisdiction. Naturally, the competition for such charters is intense, and many city councils and administrators have experienced great pressure from competing companies. Because of this pressure, some political leaders recently advocated federal control over cable television to bring some uniformity to its regulation. But local government leaders, who have spent much money and time in developing policy for granting franchises to operate, are understandably displeased with such suggestions, and the industry itself prefers to take its chances with local governments, which are more easily approached. Therefore cable television is likely to remain essentially in the regulatory province of local governments, although some intervention also is occurring at the national level.

The FCC had a long history of low visibility and of being viewed as the protector of the industries it regulated. For example, it maintained a close relationship with the telephone monopoly AT&T. It banned competition in telephone equipment by prohibiting non-AT&T equipment from being connected to telephone lines. It also prohibited competing long-distance companies. During the 1980s, dramatic changes took place as competition was permitted in both areas. Beginning in 1968, the FCC permitted some competitive long-distance companies and gradually permitted use of non-AT&T equipment. With the emphasis of the Reagan administration on deregulation, the restrictions were virtually eliminated in the 1980s.

Similarly, in broadcasting, the FCC relaxed its rules on children's programming, allowing more commercialization of such programs. It also eliminated limits on length and frequency of television commercials and relaxed requirements for public-service programming. Congress responded to these actions by passing legislation limiting commercials in children's programs and requiring stations to provide informative programming for children. President Reagan pocket-vetoed the legislation that would have required the FCC to enforce these provisions in its licensing processes. It is also now easier to transfer licenses for radio and television stations, and the same owner can now have up to twelve each of television, AM, and FM stations instead of seven, thus permitting control over a greater share of the market. Currently, the FCC is considering further loosening of rules on ownership.

International regulation approaches.   The major alternative to the U.S. style of broadcast regulation is government ownership and operation of the industry. The British Broadcasting Company and the Canadian Broadcasting Company are examples of this approach. Great Britain also permits a privately owned Independent Broadcasting Authority to operate a commercial broadcasting network. This more direct government influence has led to generally more restrictive rules on what can be broadcast, although the policies have been liberalized greatly in recent years. Sweden, however, with publicly operated broadcasting, places very few limits on what can be broadcast. Of course, in the Soviet Union and most Eastern European countries, broadcasting has been operated and closely controlled by government. Since 1989, however, there has been a freer flow of information.

Agriculture

Agriculture always has had a special place in the sentiments of the American people. Perhaps because Americans tend to trace their roots to the farm and because so much of early American economic development was keyed to agriculture, Americans seem to idealize the family farm. Certainly the vital need of everyone for dependable food production causes people to place agriculture in a special category of respect and concern. Americans also idealize the family farm because of the virtues and values associated with its work ethic and life-style. Politicians capitalize on the special place agriculture holds in American society. This favored status is translated into special governmental protections for agriculture. In particular, rhetoric about preserving the family farm forms the justification for much farm policy, although few policies really do much to accomplish this objective.

Because of this idealization of the farm, probably no activity of economic life is the subject of more legislation than agriculture. Government intervention in agricultural activity ranges from price supports for farm products to tax incentives to regulation of livestock diets and the uses of chemical pesticides. Policy also provides for research and education and gives agriculture preferential treatment in antitrust and unemployment compensation matters. While not all of these policies are regulatory in nature, many do regulate agricultural activities.

The need for government economic intervention in agriculture stems largely from the need to stabilize the farm economy. Farm production is dependent upon many factors, some of which are unpredictable and uncontrollable. A good crop is the result of numerous, very changeable factors: the application of the best technology, good land management, soil quality, water, and the weather. Some factors can be controlled almost completely by the farmer, some only partially, and some—like the weather—not at all. As a result, a farmer may have a good crop one year and lose it all the next because of adverse weather conditions. Even if the crop is a good one, the farmer may suffer because technology has made it possible for farmers to produce bountiful supplies, driving prices below production costs. Thus "oversupply," as in any industry, may lead to a price decline ruinous to the farmer, and frequent price fluctuations—even upward ones—make it difficult for the farm community to plan. Over the years, therefore, farm policy has encouraged stabilization of the agricultural economy.

In 1862, Congress created the Department of Agriculture for the purpose of assisting farmers. Its services have grown over the years to include subsidies, marketing, education, research, stabilization, and development programs, as well as regulation.

That same year, another early statute related to farming, the Morrill Act, granted public lands to states for the purpose of creating "land grant" colleges, institutions that today still have prime responsibility in agricultural research and education. These schools currently operate extensive research programs and educate millions of college students. They also provide support and educational services for farmers through Agricultural Extension Services throughout the country. The Department of Agriculture continues to support these efforts, along with the individual states in which the colleges and universities are located. These programs serve government agricultural policy by improving productivity and the quality of farm goods.

Farm price supports.   The secretary of agriculture is empowered to "regulate" markets and prices by the Agricultural Marketing Act of 1937. Marketing supports and regulations involve assistance in finding markets, regulating methods of marketing, and regulating the quality of goods so as to protect farm-product consumers. Controls over farm commodity transactions and the prices that can be charged for given products support markets for farm goods. The farmer is protected through the establishment of grading systems for various agricultural products and through the development of advanced technology for transportation, storage, and processing.

Although declared unconstitutional by the Supreme Court in 1936, the 1933 Agricultural Adjustment Act provided the foundation on which much subsequent agriculture policy has been based, including artificial protection and stabilization of farm markets. Stabilization programs involve efforts to support the prices of goods and also to insure the ability of farmers to produce goods. Price supports were first provided to encourage farmers to work together and mutually benefit through agreements on restriction of production. They would be rewarded through cash payments made possible by a tax on the processors of agricultural goods. The act also provided for buying up of surpluses and providing incentives to farmers in the form of loans to withhold goods from the market.

The Soil Conservation and Domestic Allotment Act of 1936 and a new Agricultural Adjustment Act, in 1938, again attempted to entice farmers into taking surplus crops out of production and offered price supports for those farmers who agreed to reduce production to specified levels. Price supports are based on a concept known as "parity," which refers to keeping a price equivalent to what it was during an alleged "normal" period. The equivalence is measured in terms of buying power and is intended to adjust for inflation. Thus, if a bushel of wheat sold for a dollar in the target period but inflation made it such that two dollars today buys what one dollar then bought, the price support for wheat would require a two-dollar per bushel price. Another way of looking at parity is to compare the cost of a farm product with another product. For example, if the cost of a bushel of wheat was one dollar and the cost of a shirt was three dollars in the target period, the parity price could be measured in comparison of changes in the costs of the two products. Thus, if the cost of the shirt went up to six dollars in current dollars, wheat would have to go up to two dollars per bushel to maintain parity. The period used for comparison was 1909–1914, a relatively prosperous time for farmers, and this period still provides the baseline for agriculture parity programs. Price supports are used typically with grain crops such as corn, oats, and wheat.

Most post–World War II controversy over price supports has been concerned with whether government should try to keep prices high or let them be set by the market and have government support the farmer through other means. Generally, the price-support mechanism has prevailed, but a staple of policy since 1964 has been increasing reliance on incentives to keep farmers from producing. Through set-aside programs, farmers agree to keep land out of production in return for direct subsidies. Various modifications in the program have produced numerous changes, so that now target prices are established according to the market price for goods. If goods sell below the target prices, farmers are given subsidies. If goods sell at or above the target price, however, government makes no payment. This system is more acceptable to many people, since it both supports farmers and at the same time gives the free-market system an opportunity to work. Set-asides, however, have been limited by the fact that demand for agricultural goods has been high, in part because of world market demands.

Despite this high demand, farmers have not been satisfied. Because they must sell in a relatively free market but buy in a controlled one, their income has not kept pace with their costs. The American Agricultural Movement (AAM), which has been very active since 1977, was born of the frustration farmers face in trying to stay economically solvent. To express its concerns, the movement organized demonstrations and tractor drives to Washington, D.C. On one hand, AAM wanted government to quit regulating farmers, but on the other, it wanted government guarantees of prices. Such a contradiction in desires is not atypical of regulated industries in general.

Price supports also are maintained by loans to farmers. Loans are made using crops as collateral. If the price for the crop exceeds the loan, farmers sell their product and repay the loan. If the price is less than the loan, they can default and the government keeps the crop. Supply is thus controlled and prices maintained.

During the late 1970s and 1980s, the farm economy once again took a downturn. Because there was much speculation in land in the 1970s, farmland became very valuable. Farmers borrowed heavily against their land at high interest rates, partly in response to government encouragement to increase productivity. In the 1980s, however, there was a severe downturn in the economic fortunes of farmers. The value of farmland decreased by as much as fifty percent in many states, and interest rates also decreased. At the same time, costs of production for farmers increased. Many farmers were left with large loans on land they could not sell and interest rates higher than current rates. Their income was insufficient to service their loans.[13] Allied industries in farm communities also have been devastated by the economic problems of farmers.

Farm organizations brought pressure on Congress to take action, and in 1985, it passed the Food Security Act, which put nearly $27 billion into price-support programs and also helped with low-interest loans. In many cases, farmers and others banded together to help those facing foreclosure. Farm Aid concerts were a staple of the late 1980s. Celebrities organized and contributed performances to these concerts, which raised money to help pay off farmers' debts.

Prices also are supported through government-sanctioned marketing agreements among producers. Milk, citrus fruit, and nuts are examples of crops for which the government permits such agreements, called marketing orders. Producers often form cooperatives to regulate production levels. By controlling the amount a farmer can market, price levels are maintained.

Import quotas are another form of regulation that protects the interests of some farmers. Sugar import quotas help maintain artificially high prices for domestically produced sugar.

Stabilization also is achieved through control of the resources for production. Soil-conservation programs help protect one essential resource—good farmland. Programs that train farmers in the optimum use of land are common, as are programs to construct barriers that protect soil from the natural elements of wind and water. Rotation of crops and planting of protective vegetation are other ways soil conservation is supported by agricultural policy. Land protection has not been without its lapses, however. Recently, concern has grown regarding the loss of millions of acres of prime agricultural land to highways and suburban development. Some state and county governments have begun addressing the issue, and the Farmland Protection Act of 1981 directs the Department of Agriculture to provide education and technical assistance to state and local governments in developing programs to protect agricultural land.

Agricultural development policies also involve other specific attempts at stimulating a healthier farming climate. Much of this policy relates to preservation of the family farm, which has been declining (see Table 2-2). Other measures include programs for aiding poor farm families through loan and resettlement programs, which help farmers move from unproductive to productive land. The familiar farm cooperatives across the nation have been supported as a means of

TABLE 2-2 ▪ Farms: The Number of Farms, Land in Farms, and Average Size of Farms in the United States, 1977–1990

Year	No. of Farms[a]	Land in Farms (1,000 Acres)	Average Size of Farms (Acres)
1977	2,455,830	1,047,785	427
1978	2,436,250	1,044,790	429
1979	2,437,300	1,042,015	428
1980	2,439,510	1,038,885	426
1981	2,439,920	1,034,190	424
1982	2,406,550	1,027,795	427
1983	2,378,620	1,023,425	430
1984	2,333,810	1,017,803	436
1985	2,292,530	1,012,073	441
1986	2,249,820	1,005,333	447
1987	2,212,960	998,923	451
1988	2,197,140	994,543	453
1989	2,170,520	991,153	457
1990[b]	2,143,150	987,721	461

[a] A farm is an establishment that as of June 1 sold or would normally have sold $1,000 or more of agricultural products during the year.
[b] Preliminary
SOURCE: United States Department of Agriculture, *Agricultural Statistics 1990* (Washington, D.C.: U.S. Government Printing Office, 1990), p. 356.

stabilizing the farm economy. The Rural Electrification Administration (REA) is another exemplary development program, enabling small farmers to get electricity and much modern technology.

Farm regulations extend beyond efforts to support prices and income. For example, farmers increasingly are subject to environmental regulations, especially concerning pesticides. With urban areas infringing on farmland, farmers must be careful in spraying pesticides so that urban residents are not harmed by the spraying. Because of other environmental concerns, many sprays effective in killing weeds or harmful insects are closely regulated or banned. Alternative sprays are not always effective; therefore costs for repeated spraying increase. Less effective chemicals also subject the farmer to more potential devastation from predators. The income of the farmer is then effectively reduced. The benefits to society at large have economic costs to the farmer.

To sum up, government intervention in agriculture serves both conflicting goals and conflicting needs. The unintended consequences of farm policy are many. In part, it attempts to protect the interests of the small farmer. But it also supports new technology and new approaches to agriculture, which often lead to expensive technology that can be afforded only by the wealthy farmer—normally, the corporate farmer. The improved technology also leads to higher levels of production, which, in turn, lead to lower prices and thus lower income for farmers.

These effects then require new policy initiatives to assist the farmer. Although still attached to the romantic notion of the family farm, the American consumer wants inexpensive food, and the two ideals often seem inconsistent.

Agriculture is one area of the economy in which the consumer has almost always been excluded from decision making. The result is that most agriculture policy falls in the realm of creating supportive climates for economic activity rather than regulating in the interest of the consumer. The full extent of interaction between government and agriculture is huge, and the issues explored here represent only the major aspects of agriculture policy.

International farming experiments.   While the family farm has long been promoted—in words, if not always in practice—as the centerpiece of American agriculture, other nations have viewed it as an inefficient method of agricultural production. For example, collective farms in communist nations were efforts at cooperative approaches to agriculture. The Soviet collectives were not particularly successful, a poor performance many critics blamed on their lack of individual incentive. These critics argued that individual ownership leads to greater effort, and there are movements away from collective farms in the formerly communist world. The Israelis have also experimented with collective ownership in the form of the kibbutz. These experiments appear to have been very successful. The fact that people voluntarily join the kibbutzim, as opposed to the forced participation in the Soviet system, may account for some of the difference.

Transportation

Because systems of transportation are important to the economic development, political integration, and national security of a nation, the transportation industry is the subject of much regulation both in the United States and abroad. Transportation includes railroads, motor carriers, highway systems, and air travel. Although it also can be considered to include pipeline transportation of water, oil, and natural gas, these are more appropriately covered in Chapter 4 on energy policy. The discussion here deals with the first items.

Government regulates the transportation industry through a variety of controls over: (1) entry into and exit from the industry, (2) rates and fares, (3) routes served, (4) finance, and (5) safety. The basic objective of transportation regulation is to ensure that adequate service is available to most of the population at a reasonable cost. Therefore regulation traditionally has centered on economic regulation, although in some instances environmental and safety controls have been important concerns.

The railroads.   The railroad industry was the first element of the transportation sector to be regulated by government. During the late nineteenth century, many abuses were prevalent in railroad transportation. Local governments were bullied by rail companies into donating rights-of-way; if a town refused, the railroad would take an alternate route and the town would die. Public funds were provided for railroad subsidies and, in many cases, the money was pocketed by the railroad magnates. Unreasonable or fixed prices and discrimination in services were common. Because railroads were important to economic development, particularly to movement of agricultural products, government turned to regulation. In 1887, the Interstate Commerce Commission was created, but not until passage of the Mann-Elkins Act of 1910 were teeth put into the enforcement of rail regulations.

This early regulation of the railroad industry resulted much later in adverse conditions for the U.S. rail system. The provisions had created a protected industry with controlled competition. Ticket prices and freight rates were restricted. Railroads also found themselves affected by labor agreements and legislation that limited their ability to modernize and use improved technology. Trucking and air-freight competition took their toll, in part supported by government subsidies, especially in construction of the interstate highway system. As a result, during the late 1950s and 1960s, many railroads suffered serious financial difficulties and equipment began to fall into disrepair. Passenger service, in particular, deteriorated badly. The federal government provided loans and guarantees in an attempt to subsidize the ailing private railroads while they regrouped, but nothing seemed to help.

That impasse led Congress, in 1970, to take an important step. Crossing the boundary between regulation and direct administration, Congress created a new public corporation to bail out the dying system. Known as Amtrak, it in effect put government partially in the business of running the passenger-carrying railroads. Although it did not nationalize the entire industry, as in Great Britain, the United States operates the passenger arm of some railroads, while private industry continues most freight-hauling operations. Thus the United States moved from no regulation to actual operation of part of the system in little over eighty years.

Because of the complex web of regulations under which it operated, the railroad industry strongly supported deregulation. In the mid-1970s, the industry and railroad labor unions pressured the Interstate Commerce Commission (ICC) and Congress to develop deregulation policy. As part of his industry-by-industry approach to deregulation, President Jimmy Carter submitted railroad deregulation legislation in 1979. The Staggers Rail Act was passed in 1980, permitting railroads flexibility in rate setting and route service and abandonment. Nonetheless, railroads continue to be more strictly regulated than any other transportation industry.

Trucking and bus transportation.   Motor-carrier regulation and development of the national highway network have gone hand-in-hand. Over the years, the motor carriers—that is, bus and truck companies—have been ardent supporters of highway construction and improvement efforts. The trend began when the national government stimulated states to act through the Good Roads Act of 1916, which provided federal funds for state construction of better roads with standardized road signs and numbering. In the 1950s, the Interstate Highway System was initiated, and federal funds were poured into development of this nationwide program. Federal funding was justified formally on the basis of national defense (in case of emergency, this network of roads would facilitate movement of military vehicles and supplies), even though economic demands were of greater actual significance.

Motor-carrier transportation service and pricing also are regulated. To cope with excessive competition and to make regulations compatible with railroad regulations, the Interstate Commerce Commission was given authority by the Federal Motor Carrier Act of 1935 to license transportation by bus or truck in interstate commerce through the issuance of a certificate from the ICC. Interestingly enough, trucks carrying agricultural goods were exempted. Certification provided the mechanism whereby specific regulations could be imposed.

In the 1970s, some parts of the trucking industry, particularly independent drivers, complained that they could not operate efficiently under the restrictive controls imposed upon them. An especially sore point was the restrictions on the rates they could charge, since their costs, especially for fuel, had skyrocketed. Demonstrations and strikes by truckers in 1979 resulted in some flexibility by the ICC, such as allowing fuel cost increases to be passed on to the shippers. Ironically, while complaints against restrictions were numerous, suggestions for deregulation from the executive branch resulted in union and industry opposition. While the large trucking companies tended to cite as their objection the potential chaos that might ensue with deregulation, they also benefited greatly from controlled competition. The large trucking companies were protected from competition from smaller companies by ICC regulations. The ICC was perceived by many as being the protector of the trucking industry, rather than its regulator, through policies that limited entry into the market and discouraged competition.

In 1982, legislation deregulating intercity bus lines was passed. The legislation, supported by the industry, permitted easier entry into the industry and greater flexibility in fares. It also preempted state regulation in some activities such as policies that prohibited dropping passengers off at intermediate points on routes.

Despite disagreement regarding deregulation, Congress did pass the Motor Carrier Act of 1980, which deregulated the industry on a limited basis. Designed to conserve energy and provide better service at less cost to the consumer, the legislation eliminates some regulations that have limited competition. Circuitous routes (such as requiring a firm hauling freight from Phoenix to Denver to go through Oklahoma City) and prohibitions on intermediate stops and backhauling (carrying freight on a return trip) were eliminated by the act. Although many of these changes were welcomed, the big trucking companies were also afraid that small carriers would pick up the lucrative routes and make business less predictable.

Air transportation.   The airline industry first became the object of government regulation with the Air Commerce Act of 1926. This legislation imposed safety requirements but contained no economic regulations. Government also supported the industry through awarding of mail contracts from the Department of the Post Office.

In 1938, the Civil Aeronautics Act was passed, bringing the airline industry under economic regulation for the first time. The Civil Aeronautics Board (CAB), created by the act, was assigned responsibility to control interstate airline routes and the fares charged. Until 1958, it also had responsibility for development of safety rules and regulations. Routes were controlled through the issuance by the

CAB of a certificate of "public convenience and necessity," which authorized an airline company to serve a given route. Abandonment of routes was also subject to CAB approval. Rates charged were set by the CAB, and fare changes were subject to its authorization.

By the 1970s, many people in and out of the airline industry began to call for deregulation. Since state regulatory agencies permitted lower fares, the competition from intrastate airlines on some lucrative routes in states like California and Texas made it difficult for CAB-regulated carriers to compete in price. President Carter proposed deregulation as one of his major campaign themes during the 1976 election. With his victory, the impetus for major reform became strong. Deregulation of the airline industry became the first case in his industry-by-industry deregulation strategy.

The Airline Deregulation Act of 1978 created many changes. For example, the CAB relaxed its controls and permitted airlines relatively free entry into or exit from any route, though they were limited to one new route per month. Minimum prices also were deregulated, although maximum price increases still required approval. The immediate effect of the deregulation was a drop in airfares for passengers and a realigning of routes. Major carriers often cancelled unprofitable routes, while commuter airlines were created or expanded to fill the void in these smaller markets. There were complaints about deterioration of service to smaller cities. Sharp fare increases in early 1989 caused critics of deregulation to raise questions about the long-term effects.

The CAB is an example of dramatic turnaround in agency perspective. In the early 1970s, the CAB was viewed as the captive of the industry, intent on protecting existing airlines from competition. By the late 1970s, however, under the leadership of Alfred Kahn, a strong proponent of deregulation, the agency was proposing legislation and taking internal steps to deregulate. Its support of the Airline Deregulation Act of 1978 signaled its shift away from protection of the industry to a laissez-faire perspective. Ultimately, the legislation provided for the gradual decline of CAB functions, culminating in its dissolution in 1985.

Another aspect of airline industry regulation is maintenance of safety. Originally the ICC, and later the CAB, had this responsibility. In 1958, however, the Federal Aviation Agency (FAA) was created as an independent body for all safety-related monitoring and regulation of the industry. Its authority extends to airport facilities as well as airline companies. In 1967, the National Transportation Safety Board was created; part of the Department of Transportation, its job is to investigate accidents. This reform was made in the belief that the FAA, which develops regulations, might have a conflict of interest investigating accidents potentially resulting from its own ineffectiveness or misjudgment.

Deregulation of the airline industry has had dramatic effects. Since deregulation in 1978, passenger boardings have increased from 275 million to nearly 500 million in 1988, and the average cost of fares has declined, although fares have increased sharply on noncompetitive routes. There are many critics of deregulation, however, who note many problems. In particular, concerns about safety and airport congestion are now commonplace. It has been charged that in the drive to boost profits, air carriers are less interested in service and maintenance of the fleet. Uncontrolled entrance of carriers into the best markets and bunching of flights at peak travel hours have created long lines and delays in landing and takeoff.

There was a burst of new entries into the market after deregulation (see Table 2-3). In recent years, however, control of the industry has become concentrated. The four largest carriers now carry about 70 percent of the traffic. Of more concern is the almost complete dominance of some airports and routes by one carrier. In such a situation, price competition does not exist. Airports with competition from smaller regional carriers experience much lower fares than those without the competition. The Transportation Department, consistent with the hands-off approach of the Reagan and Bush administrations, approved every one of the airline mergers it was asked to review. The long-term effects are still uncertain, but continued concentration of the market among smaller numbers of large carriers is likely to lead to higher fares. The closing down of Pan American in 1991 brought the issue clearly to the public spotlight.

International air regulation.   At the international level, there are few similarities to the U.S. airline regulatory pattern. Other nations such as Great Britain, Sweden, Mexico, and the Soviet Union operate their airlines as government industries and therefore regulation is unnecessary. Through outright own-

---

TABLE 2-3 ▪ Airline Deregulation: Status of air carriers that began service after airline deregulation in 1978.

Air Carrier	Start-up	Status	Date
Air Atlanta	1984	Failed	1987
Air One	1983	Failed	1984
American Intl.	1982	Failed	1984
America West	1983	Operating under financial hardship	
Braniff	1984	Failed	1989
Florida Express	1984	Acquired	1988
Hawaii Express	1982	Failed	1983
Jet America	1981	Acquired	1987
McClain	1986	Failed	1987
Midway	1979	Failed	1991
Muse	1981	Acquired	1985
Northeastern	1983	Failed	1985
Pacific East	1982	Failed	1984
People Express	1981	Acquired	1986
Presidential	1985	Failed	1989
Regent Air	1985	Failed	1986
StatesWest	1986	Operating	

SOURCE: Congressional Budget Office.

ership they control the industry directly. However, Canada, Chile, and Australia have followed the United States in deregulating.

Conclusion. The basic goal of regulation of the transportation industry in general has been to encourage creation of as much transportation capacity as possible. At the same time, transportation policy has attempted to insure that adequate and safe service is available and reasonably priced. The next decade will probably see continuing increases in the cost of transportation services.

POLICY EVALUATION: ENCOURAGING COMPETITION OR DISCOURAGING INNOVATION?

Deregulation

A clear trend since the mid-1970s has been the deregulation of industries previously heavily regulated. The Carter administration began the process gradually by examining individual regulatory agencies and the industries they regulated. The Reagan and Bush administrations took a more sweeping approach to deregulation, reflecting strong commitment to a market economy free of governmental constraints. Ideologically, conservatives have been strong supporters of deregulation.

With deregulation came many benefits to consumers and some parts of industry. Some businesses also suffered economic reversals under deregulation. In the airline industry, for example, consumers benefited from increased competition as airfares declined. In the long run, airfares increased again, but competition has sustained many bargain fares. Service to smaller communities has suffered on occasion, and bunching of departure times around peak travel hours has led to complaints of inconvenience. However, the public seems to prefer the bargain fares over matters of scheduling and service.

Large airline companies, which benefited most from regulation, have faced some tough times with deregulation. Financial problems plagued Eastern Airlines and Pan American, which ceased service in 1991. America West and Continental have filed bankruptcy petitions and even USAir, American, and TWA face financial difficulties. Other airlines have disappeared as they merged with or were acquired by yet another carrier. Frontier and Western Airlines no longer exist. At the same time, there have been a number of new airlines since deregulation, competing very aggressively with the established giants of the industry. Southwest is the last surviving example of such assertive companies. Some new entrants into the field did not last long. For example, McClain Airlines, which attempted to appeal to the more affluent traveler who wants first-class amenities, found little market for its product. Similarly, People's Express and Midway foundered after a few years of impressive growth as no-frills airlines.

The trucking industry demonstrates similar effects from deregulation. Consumers benefit from much lower rates on many shipments. Entry of new companies into the market has been extensive, especially in the short-haul routes. At the same time, some long-route national companies (e.g., Time D-C and McLean Trucking Company) have gone out of business because of financial reversals brought on by the competition.

The relaxation of regulation has had broader implications. The Reagan and Bush administrations have been much less rigorous in their implementation of such policies as antitrust, equal employment opportunity, and labor relations. The business sector finds the administrators of these programs willing to interpret policies in ways more sympathetic to business. Thus the National Labor Relations Board and the federal courts have changed the direction of much of labor law. They have permitted the use of bankruptcy laws, for example, to release corporations from contract obligations under collective bargaining agreements, as happened with Continental Airlines and the Manville Corporation. One effect is that labor unions are accepting bargaining agreements that scale back their earnings and benefits. Corporations thus clearly have a stronger hand in controlling their own destiny.

Similarly, antitrust policy under the Reagan administration was much more flexible. The Federal Trade Commission seemed less interested than ever before in prohibiting mergers based on the size of the market controlled. Merger mania began in the late 1970s and accelerated in the 1980s as the Reagan administration relaxed rules. Many of these mergers are "hostile" takeovers in which entrepreneurs take over undervalued corporations. The managers of the take-over targets usually are the most resistant to takeovers, although many stockholders also question the long-term wisdom of such actions.

Yet another aspect of the current business environment is the policy regarding international trade. Although the Reagan and Bush administrations strongly supported free trade as a stated policy, they did exert pressure on foreign competition. Other nations were pushed to agree to voluntary import quotas on such items as steel, textiles, and automobiles. The expectation was that import quotas would improve the prospects of domestic industry to sell its products. After the 1984 election, the administration lessened its efforts in maintaining voluntary quotas. Without the political pressures of an election, it was easier for the administration to act consistently with its free trade stance. However, as the Reagan administration left office, it became involved in a trade war with members of the European Economic Community, who banned U.S. beef that had been fed growth hormones. The administration retaliated with duties equal to 100 percent of the value of food imports from those nations. At the same time, a free trade agreement was made with Canada. The Bush administration has signed a free trade agreement with Mexico but has been less inclined to do so with Western Europe and others.

All of these elements of policy add up to an industrial policy by piecemeal actions. The Bush administration, consistent with its position that government should reduce its activity, shies away from an explicit industrial policy. However, the free-market approach becomes an industrial policy, and the specific elements of policy noted here constitute an industrial policy sympathetic to the business community.

The theoretical effects of government intervention in the economy were examined at the beginning of this chapter, but actual outcomes do not always match the expected results. Critics of regulation note that although much regulation is justified as a means of promoting competition, it often actually tends to stifle that competition. By making entry into a market very difficult, for example, regulation often restricts competition. Competition is also reduced by price controls, as was true in the airline industry until recently. Ironically, for this same reason many industries also defend regulation. Assured of a comfortable environment in which to do business, industry can count on a certain profit margin. Complete competition would make its situation less predictable. The consumer, or consumer advocate, objects to this arrangement because it results in higher prices.

Effects of regulation.   One impact that industry often complains of is that government regulation interferes with its capacity to operate efficiently in a free society. According to this charge, regulatory agencies have become pervasive in all economic areas, and their red tape and complex regulations make compliance almost impossible. Many agencies make conflicting demands on industry, and paperwork has increased to the point that industry must employ people solely to deal with government regulation. Confusion abounds: industries are firmly instructed not to consider race, sex, age, or religion in personnel decisions and, at the same time, are required to submit data on their work force according to the same taboo categories. Moreover, many critics wonder whether regulations are developed to benefit society or simply to keep the wheels spinning so the agency will have something to do.

Regulation may also have unintended consequences in terms of its effects on innovation. Generally, regulated industries appear to be less inclined to adopt new technology and improve their methods of doing business than are nonregulated industries.[14] As a result, regulated industry is likely to be outmoded and less efficient. This is especially true when regulation guarantees a profit—and the losers are consumers.

Regulation also is criticized for contributing to the cost of doing business. In their proposals for deregulation, Reagan's staff members often suggested that the costs of regulation could exceed $100 billion a year. Putting that kind of money into nonproductive efforts diverts it from productive ones. However, critics of the administration—though usually agreeing that regulation had become excessive—are also anxious that deregulation not go too far, that is, to the point of eliminating legitimate controls over economic behavior.

A common complaint of consumer-oriented critics is that regulation is dominated by the regulated industries themselves, which have the money and other resources to keep abreast of policy. Consumers, especially individuals, find access to regulatory agencies difficult because they lack knowledge of procedures and because of the costs associated with input into decision making. Because regulators constantly deal with people from the regulated industries, they develop strong rapport with them. It is only natural that the regulators should consider their interests when making decisions. After all, the regulators would have no one to regulate if they did not help promote their survival! This close relationship often results in strong industry influence and sometimes control over regulators. The interests of consumers may be ignored.

Closely related to the access issue is the complaint that regulatory agencies are outside normal political activities and therefore are not answerable to anyone but themselves and the industries they regulate. It is unreasonable to expect agencies to respond to the major concerns of society if they do not have to answer to the political leadership produced by that society. Of course, regulatory agencies were created to be independent of direct political pressure so that they could consider a wider "public interest." This criticism goes to the heart of the original reason for creating "independent" regulatory agencies in the first place. Independence has both benefits and costs.

It is sometimes argued that government is too involved in too many aspects of everyday life. Government seems to take the position that people need guidance in everything they do, and so virtually no activity is free of government intervention. Duplication of effort, red tape, and examples of bureaucratic bungling, constantly given coverage in the news media, reinforce negative images of regulation. Tax revolts and a rejection of governmental paternalism have led to serious questioning of regulatory efforts. As antigovernment feelings seem to grow, regulatory agencies face major challenges to their activities.

A new twist to these regulatory processes is the effort of the current Federal Trade Commission (FTC) to keep state and local governments from interfering with competition in the marketplace. Most notable have been those cases in which the FTC has successfully sued municipalities to force deregulation of taxicab companies and their fares as a restraint of trade. This emphasis is a new use of antitrust law but is consistent with the administration's pro-business, free trade stance.

Deregulation is promoted as a consumer-oriented policy that will result in more competition and lower prices. In the rush to deregulate in the late 1970s and early 1980s, there was little consideration of the social benefits of regulation. But the recent experience of the airlines is causing some reevaluation. Passenger delays, safety concerns, the loss of service in many cities and regions, and the real cost increases in some fares have caused many to question the benefits of deregulating the airlines. Similarly, the deregulation of the banking industry has been accompanied by record numbers of bank failures and sudden increases in service fees, especially for small depositors. The savings and loan industry collapse after deregulation is the most dramatic case. Also, the increasing costs of telephone service across the country have led many consumers to ask whether divestiture was in their interest. The benefits of regulation in protecting consumers from capricious action, ensuring a reasonable distribution of important services at a fair cost, and protecting the health and safety of the community are now reemerging concerns as the effects of deregulation are assessed. As with any policy, deregulation has resulted in both positive and negative consequences.

Changes in Regulation

Changes in economic regulation have been many, and the effects have varied greatly. For example, the effects of deemphasis of antitrust policy are very difficult to assess. While the business world generally applauds the reduction of control over its activities, consumers are not so sure of the benefits. The rash of mergers and leveraged buyouts create impressive profits for many opportunists, but there are usually losers as well. Many employees, especially white-collar employees, lose their jobs and pensions as a result of the inevitable restructuring of the corporations that are merged. New and reorganized companies often pay lower wages and provide fewer benefits. For the consumer, of course, mergers can lead to less competition and eventually higher prices. Stockholders also are potential losers as total corporate debt increases, exceeding total corporate assets.

Much deregulation in the business sector reduced sensitivity to safety concerns that affect employees. Thus the effect on employees has been negative. Similarly, the elimination of regulations on product safety can benefit producers in the short run and hurt consumers. In the long run, producers may also be hurt as lawsuits over liability for injury create major financial setbacks.

Mergers themselves do not always work out well. Many of them are undone through divestiture or spinning off parts of the acquired companies. For example, Mobil Oil Corporation bought Montgomery Ward and Company. After spending billions of dollars in attempting to shore up its acquisition, Mobil finally gave up and sold it off. There are numerous examples of similar experiences in which neither party to the merger benefited. In recent years, many of those companies that had diversified have begun divesting in order to narrow their focus and concentrate on what they do best. In this scenario, competition increases. Among those splitting up and paring down are RCA Corporation, ITT, Gulf and Western, and Textron. Supporters of deregulation claim that this trend also is a result of the greater flexibility allowed by deregulation.

In broadcasting, deregulation has opened up competition, thus placing the major networks in less dominant positions. The variety of television fare, for example, has increased dramatically across the country. At the same time, critics complain that quality is diluted because of the large number of outlets struggling to put together programming. The effects on profits for the major networks have been significant, leading to restructuring and highly publicized cutbacks in news budgets and programs. At the same time, new networks or cable superstations are emerging, adding to what is available.

Everyone has been affected by the deregulation of telephone service. Long-distance costs are dramatically lower as a result of competition. However, local service is under extreme price pressure because long-distance charges no longer subsidize the local service. Similarly, consumers face confusion in dealing with different companies for different services.

There are many positive results arising from deregulation of the transportation industry. Consumers in major markets certainly have benefited from lower prices for air travel. However, in recent years, mergers of airlines have resulted in diminishing competition and rising prices in many markets. Similarly, those consumers living in small cities and rural areas have experienced deterioration in service and increased costs. At the same time, rail and bus service has all but disappeared from many of those communities. Many critics argue that deregulation has also resulted in less safe transport.

Increased competition in the trucking industry produced very positive results in terms of prices and service delivery. Given the number of bankruptcies among trucking firms, however, it is possible that competition will decrease in the long run.

An area of the economy that did not seem to benefit from the hands-off policies is agriculture. Farmers have had several difficult years in which they have had to borrow heavily in hopes of good crops and prices. Many borrowed to expand their operations because their land values rose during the late 1970s and early 1980s and the market for their crops looked promising. Once land values and incomes dropped, farmers became unable to pay their loans or obtain more credit. Bankruptcy had reached epidemic proportions in the farm belt of the Midwest. In 1987 and 1988, land prices began to rise and the outlook was good. It came too late for many small farmers, however, because they had already gone under. Then the drought of the summer of 1988 brought more economic disaster as crops failed. Hopes were once again dashed. By 1991, farmers had not recovered very well although crops in the Midwest were good that year. The good yields pushed prices on corn and soybeans down. Winter wheat crops were hard hit by disease and profits dropped.

The farm economy continues to swing widely up and down. Farm policies attempt to address particular concerns, but other policies have very strong implications for farmers. Trade policies and agreements, for example, affect the prices farmers receive or how much they can produce. Although the farm economy appears to be emerging from difficult times, with good prospects, it is difficult to know how long the situation will last. Additionally, while overall farm income is improving, there are many small farmers who are still economically on the brink. And the cost of federal farm programs is at a historic high.

Government economic intervention in the form of subsidies and supports for enterprise has raised serious questions as well. The federal government's efforts to stimulate and stabilize financial institutions through loans and loan guarantees, for example, have made them safe places for investors to place their money, but these supports have, at the same time, encouraged risky investments leading to bank and savings and loan failures. Similarly, the federal government provides loans and loan guarantees to home owners, college students, farmers, and others; moreover, it guarantees other financial instruments such as pensions. Currently, the "potential liability" of the federal government for all of these credit programs approaches $6 trillion. Careful regulation and oversight will be necessary to ensure that these potential liabilities do not turn into actual ones, as in the savings and loan collapse.

FUTURE ALTERNATIVES: REFORMING THE RELATIONSHIP OF GOVERNMENT AND THE ECONOMY

There are many suggestions for reform in government's relationship to the economy. As indicated earlier, many of the recommendations deal with eliminating government's intervention in economic activity. Thus creation of a free-market economy independent of government influence is seen as a means to stimulate economic enterprise toward more productivity and to restore the economy to a strong position. However, given the long history of government involvement, it is highly unlikely that such action is possible. As critics of Milton Friedman's ideas (noted earlier) suggest, a true free market is likely to produce a situation in which those groups with power dominate the system. There would not be freedom for all participants to compete equally.

Perhaps the most drastic reform proposal is that regulatory agencies be abolished. Legislative bodies created regulatory agencies because of their own inability to regulate. What happened was that regulatory agencies became little legislatures of their own, enjoying independence from normal political controls. Advocates of reform want a return to citizen control through elected political leaders and believe that redistributing control over economic activities among the three branches of government would permit the public to influence the regulators' activity more effectively. A variation on this theme is that because much regulatory activity ends up in the slow-moving courts, regulatory agencies could be abolished and the courts be assigned the responsibility. Although courts are usually viewed as inappropriate for regulation because of their slowness and lack of expertise, the slowness of regulatory agencies tends to invalidate the argument. Nonetheless, courts may only respond to cases brought to them, and they lack the ability to oversee constantly a particular economic activity.

Abolition of the regulatory agencies may appeal to many, but given the tendency of Congress to create more and more regulatory policies and the agencies to enforce them, it is unlikely that such proposals will enjoy much success. First, there are too many interests that oppose abolition, including the regulatory agencies themselves, their clientele, and the beneficiaries of agency regulation. Consider, for example, the obstacles thrown up against the Reagan administration in its first year as it whittled away at various regulators' powers but failed to dismantle completely all but a few. Second, another factor in opposing abolition is that regulatory policy is likely to have less visibility if placed in a regular administrative department. A particular regulatory policy then may have to compete with other agency priorities and—especially if controversial—may be buried by the agency's politics. Robbed of its independent status, the regulatory unit is likely to be less effective. Hence, for both political and practical reasons, completely abolishing regulatory agencies seems improbable.

Deregulation has become very popular among reformers in recent years and has enjoyed moderate success. We saw, for example, how the airline industry experienced a dramatic deregulation in pricing and, to a great extent, in the geographic areas its various companies could serve. But if some deregulation is good, does that automatically mean that total deregulation would be better? Again, consider the airline situation: although some well-traveled markets prospered, other marginal areas suffered under partial deregulation. The failure of many airlines since deregulation raises fears of concentration of the market in a few companies and of decreasing competition. The question becomes one of weighing costs against social objectives, such as the need to serve communities that cannot support the service on a purely economic basis. Regulation can have several objectives, whereas deregulation proposals often focus on only one factor.

Some of the effects of deregulation have generated suggestions for again regulating some industries, for example, the airline and trucking industries. Representatives of America West Airlines (one of the airlines developed with deregulation) blame chaotic market conditions for the company's current financial troubles and predict disaster for the industry without some controls. They have persuaded Senator John McCain of Arizona to take the lead in proposing new regulations which would be beneficial to America West. Others are concerned that deregulation did not consider social costs and should be reexamined to consider them.

A number of new ideas come from industries that would like to put some controls on what they see as overregulation. One alternative proposed by some is that regulatory policy should focus on results rather than on punishment for violations. If the intent of a policy is to improve safety for employees, for example, the most effective method of accomplishing such an objective might be to reward industries for good safety records.

Another idea is that new rules and regulations should include assessing their economic impact. Congress already considers the economic impacts of its policies. Regulators now are required to make such assessments.

Sunset legislation is yet another favored means of preventing excessive regulation. Sunset legislation requires that agencies and their programs be given specific periods of existence and be reviewed at the end of the time allotted. Thus five years might be a common life span for an agency; at the end of that time it would have to justify its existence. The idea is that the regulatory agency would of necessity eliminate unneeded and nonconstructive activities in order to pass this five-year review. Similar state sunset laws are now in existence. This evaluation can lead to better performance and to a careful consideration by the legislature of whether to continue a regulatory activity.

At the polar opposite of deregulation and regulatory abolition lies nationalization. Nationalization of industry—for example, steel production—would involve government bureaucracy in operating the economic enterprise directly. The criticisms often made of British railroads or the national health service—both nationalized institutions—generate serious opposition to this idea. Neither the American public nor its political leaders appear to feel that nationalization would lead to anything but more red tape and even less efficiency than regulation involves. Therefore nationalization does not appear to be a viable alternative. With the move to get government out of business activities and the privatization of many government activities, the trend is clearly in the opposite direction. The opposition is reinforced by the fact that the current British government is committed to denationalizing some industry.

Another controversial suggestion is to create consumer committees to evaluate economic activities and then make suggestions for change. This is known as direct "consumer oversight." Industry tends to be hostile to this innovation, feeling that consumer groups often focus on one specific issue to the exclusion of the industry's general health. As a result, this proposal has not been accorded serious consideration.

Dramatic new economic proposals are often popular, but the realities of the political process must be faced. The parties with the resources to influence policy usually also have access to the regulatory and economic policy-making system. Thus reform must confront them as well. And the likelihood is that influential interests will prevail, and reform, if any, will continue to be gradual.

SUMMARY

Economic systems perform the function of distributing goods and services among people. Because of differing resources, some people or groups are able to exercise more influence than others can over economic activities. Government policy may work to reinforce the unequal distribution, or it may attempt to redistribute wealth.

Capitalist economies are based on a concept of a free-market system in which competition is open and everyone has an opportunity to participate. A socialist economy is one in which equal distribution of wealth is sought through government ownership and operation of the major means of production, distribution, and exchange. Most economic systems combine these two extremes.

The free-market system does not always operate smoothly because it rests on assumptions that are not completely valid. Thus, as instability in the free-market system develops, governments intervene. Intervention may be through monetary and fiscal policies or through regulation of specific sectors of the economy. Because monetary and fiscal policies are directed at stabilizing activity in the economy as a whole, they are referred to as macroeconomic policies.

Microeconomic policies deal with individual units of private enterprise. Regulation, the primary microeconomic tool, is accomplished in a number of different ways. Antitrust policies attempt to control the overconcentration of economic power in one or a few corporations. Other regulations license firms to perform economic activities, grant licenses to radio or television broadcasters, and award routes to airline, trucking, and bus companies. Microeconomic policies also include interventions to support industries. Thus subsidies for crops and exports provide support for farm industries. Similarly, import quotas shore up domestic industries by shielding them from competition.

Government intervention in economic activities results in a number of major policy outcomes (or impacts), some positive and some negative: (1) an environment supportive of industry through an ensured return on investment and controlled competition; (2) consumer protection against unfair practices and defective goods; (3) increased costs of goods and services; (4) increased red tape and delay; (5) dampening of innovation; and (6) enhanced predictability in provision of services.

The negative outcomes of regulation have resulted in proposals for reform, including suggestions for deregulation, government-industry cooperation, abolition of regulation, and a closer review of agencies through sunset legislation or citizen review committees.

Deregulation has been very popular during the past ten years. Economic policy of the 1980s attempted to soften the effect of regulation. Thus greater flexibility in implementation of policy allowed the market system to operate more freely. Efforts were made to get government off the back of business. The approach of the 1980s had numerous effects, both positive and negative. Industry found itself able to operate with many fewer restrictions and benefited therefrom. Consumers usually benefited as well in the short run from greater competition and lower costs in areas such as shipping and transportation. Nonetheless, the long-term effects have been reduced competition in many markets and increases in prices. Critics of deregulation also point to increasing concentration of economic power in many sectors of the economy as a long-term negative impact and are making proposals for reregulating some industry.

There are inevitably conflicting goals in public policy, and intervention in the economy is no exception. Agencies have to be concerned with protecting the general public, but they also have to be concerned with the health of the economic sectors with which they work. Therefore they often get caught in the middle between advocates of their industries and consumer advocates. It is left to the elected policymakers to mediate these conflicts and to determine what is best for everyone.

NOTES

1. John Kenneth Galbraith, *Economics and the Public Purpose* (New York: Signet, 1973), pp. 3–4.

2. This discussion draws heavily on Richard L. Siegal and Leonard B. Weinberg, *Comparing Public Policies* (Homewood, Ill.: Dorsey Press, 1977), chap. 4.

3. Milton Friedman, in *Capitalism and Freedom* (Chicago: University of Chicago Press, 1962), details this approach.

4. For an excellent critique of Friedman's position, see Rick Tilman, "Ideology and Utopia in the Political Economy of Milton Friedman," *Polity,* 8 (Spring 1976), 422–442.

5. John Kenneth Galbraith explores this and many of the following ideas in three of his books: *The Affluent Society* (Boston: Houghton Mifflin, 1958); *The New Industrial State* (Boston: Houghton Mifflin, 1968); and *Economics and the Public Purpose.*

6. The following position is taken by Robert Averitt in *The Dual Economy* (New York: W.W. Norton, 1968); and by Robert Seidman, "Contract Law, the Free Market, and State Intervention: A Jurisprudential Perspective," *Journal of Economic Issues,* 7 (December 1973), 553–575.

7. Seymour Martin Lipset, in *The First New Nation* (New York: Basic Books, 1963), especially chaps. 1 and 2, traces the changing approaches.

8. John Maynard Keynes, *General Theory of Employment, Interest, and Money* (New York: Harcourt Brace, 1936).

9. G. W. Foster, Jr., *The Status of Class Action Litigation,* American Bar Foundation, Research Contribution No. 4 (Chicago, 1974), examines the development of class-action litigation in the United States.

10. *U.S. v. E.C. Knight,* 156 U.S. 1 (1895).

11. *Loewe v. Lawlor,* 208 U.S. 274 (1908).

12. John A. Jenkins, "How to End the Endless Delay at the FTC," *Washington Monthly* (June 1976), pp. 42–50.

13. F. L. Leistritz and S. H. Murdock, "Financial Characteristics of Farms and of Farm Financial Markets and Policies in the United States," in S. H. Murdock and F. L. Leistritz, eds., *The Farm Financial Crisis: Socioeconomic Dimensions and Implications for Producers and Rural Areas* (Boulder, Colo.: Westview Press, 1988), pp. 13–28.

14. W. M. Capron and R. G. Noll, "Summary and Conclusion," in W. M. Capron, ed., *Technological Change in Regulated Industries* (Washington, D.C.: Brookings Institution, 1971), p. 221.

SUGGESTED READINGS

Cunningham, Donald A., and McManus, B. R. *Preservation of Prime Farmland and Planned Rural Development: A Literature Review.* Knoxville, Tenn.: Tennessee Valley Authority, 1986.

Derthick, Martha, and Quirk, Paul J. *The Politics of Deregulation.* Washington, D.C.: Brookings, 1985.

Felton, John Richard, and Anderson, Dale G. *Regulation and Deregulation of the Motor Carrier Industry.* Ames, Iowa: Iowa State University Press, 1989.

Gerston, Larry N.; Fraleigh, Cynthia; and Schwab, Robert. *The Regulated Society.* Pacific Grove, Calif.: Brooks/Cole, 1988.

Goodman, Marshall R., and Wrightson, Margaret T. *Managing Regulatory Reform: The Reagan Strategy and Its Impact.* New York: Praeger, 1987.

Kornai, Janos. *The Road to a Free Economy.* New York: W.W. Norton & Company, 1991.

McConnell, Grant. *Private Power and American Democracy.* New York: Knopf, 1966.

McKinzie, Lance; Baker, Timothy G.; and Tyner, Wallace E. *A Perspective on U.S. Farm Problems and Agricultural Policy.* Boulder, Colo.: Westview, 1987.

Meier, Kenneth J. *Regulation: Politics, Bureaucracy, and Economics.* New York: St. Martin's Press, 1985.

Murdock, Steve H., and Leistritz, F. Larry. *The Farm Financial Crisis: Socioeconomic Dimensions and Implications for Producers and Rural Areas.* Boulder, Colo.: Westview, 1988.

Reagan, Michael D. *Regulation: The Politics of Policy.* Boston: Little, Brown, 1987.

Stone, Alan. *Regulation and Its Alternatives.* Washington, D.C.: CQ Press, 1982.

Sullivan, E. Thomas. *The Political Economy of the Sherman Act: The First One Hundred Years.* New York: Oxford University Press, 1991.

Tolchin, Susan J., and Tolchin, Martin. *Dismantling America: The Rush to Deregulate.* Boston: Houghton Mifflin, 1983.

Weiss, Leonard W., and Klass, Michael W., eds. *Regulatory Reform: What Actually Happened?* Boston: Little, Brown, 1986.

Wilson, James Q., ed. *The Politics of Regulation.* New York: Basic Books, 1980.

Winston, Clifford; Corsi, Thomas M.; Grimm, Curtis M.; and Evans, Carol A. *The Economic Effects of Surface Freight Deregulation.* Washington, D.C.: Brookings, 1990.

CHAPTER 3

Economic Issues: Taxing, Spending, and Budgeting

The role of the federal government in economic policy has expanded significantly during the twentieth century because of both internal and external pressures. Externalities such as World War I and World War II created an environment in which increased government controls over wages, prices, and private-sector production levels were necessary in order to execute the war effort effectively. Internal pressures arising from the economic upheavals of the Great Depression also contributed to an expanded governmental role in the American economy as a wide range of programs were developed and implemented to promote economic growth. Meeting these pressures required an expanded economic role for the federal government. The economic recovery experienced by the United States after the Depression demonstrated the effectiveness of governmental intervention and provided a foundation for continued economic intervention by the federal government.

These pressures continue to be present as the United States maintains a global diplomatic and military posture and has developed an economy dependent on international trade. Consequently, governmental involvement in economic policy continues to be an item on the policy agenda. Both liberals and conservatives now accept the legitimacy of governmental involvement in economic policy, a marked change from the pre-Depression era when conservatives generally opposed governmental intervention. Liberals and conservatives continue to disagree on the nature of appropriate governmental economic intervention. Liberals tend to favor a managed economy, whereas conservatives tend to favor only governmental utilization of monetary and fiscal policies to promote private-sector initiative.

ISSUE BACKGROUND: CONCEPTS AND ISSUES

The American economic system is best understood as a mixed economy in which the government takes an active role, in a primarily capitalist economy, to promote outcomes that are consistent with social and political values. These values are dynamic rather than static and involve significant levels of conflict. Each value involves questions that must be answered in the context of subjective preferences. Yet it is these values that establish the boundaries of government activity and provide policy direction for public officials.

One value relates to inflation and interest rates. How much inflation is acceptable in order to sustain economic growth? Interest rates tend to mirror inflation and to climb with inflation. What is an acceptable and desirable interest rate that will promote economic growth?

A second value relates to employment and unemployment. What is the desired employment rate? Total employment may not be possible to achieve. What, then, is an acceptable unemployment rate? Economists and the two major political parties now tend to accept 5 percent unemployment as an appropriate definition of full employment.

Employment, inflation, and interest rates are also linked. One effective tool to drive down the inflation rate is to raise interest rates. This acts to cut demand (by increasing the cost of financing consumer goods) and exerts a downward pressure on prices. This strategy was followed in 1981–82 by the Reagan administration and the Federal Reserve with considerable success in reducing inflation. Unfortunately, a reduction in demand for goods also drives up unemployment as producers trim their work force in response to reduced demand. What is an acceptable rate of inflation in order to maintain full employment? Which presents the greater threat to the economic system: inflation or unemployment?

A third value relates to economic growth.[1] The gross national product (GNP) represents the total value of all goods and services produced by the economy. What is the desired rate of growth of the GNP? What should be the role of government in promoting GNP expansion? What level of growth (as measured by GNP expansion) should be actively pursued by the federal government?

A fourth value relates to equality. What should be the role of government in promoting economic equality? Is equality of economic opportunity sufficient, or should government actively pursue policies that seek the redistribution of economic benefits in order to achieve some specified level of economic equality for either social groups or geographic regions of the nation?

A fifth value relates to ideology.[2] What should be the nature and level of government involvement in economic policy? How much governmental involvement is consistent with the free-enterprise economic system? At what level of involvement does governmental action cease to be productive and become a counterproductive restriction on the economic system? This value involves significant social and political conflict over the appropriate role of government in a free-enterprise system.

Economic policy is, then, the total mix of governmental programs and policies that are designed to affect the economy of the nation in a manner consistent with accepted political and social values. In the absence of total agreement concerning economic values, economic policy is the product of political compromises.[3] It is in this environment of political conflict and compromise that economic policy is formulated and executed. The necessity for compromise acts to limit ideological consistency within economic policy. Most economic policies contain both liberal and conservative facets and values. Economic policy in the

United States is neither completely liberal nor conservative but often contains a contradictory combination of values.

Economic Policy Obstacles

Economic policy is the product of compromise in a complex political environment. Consequently, a number of obstacles exist in developing an effective, consistent mix of economic policy options.

One major obstacle is the fragmentation of governmental responsibility for developing economic policy. In the American federal system, state governments share a range of responsibilities with the national government, including economic policy options. Given the diversity of the fifty states, divergent economic policies are often pursued. The economic interests of an agricultural state such as Iowa or Nebraska are not necessarily consistent with those of a heavily industrialized state such as New York or Pennsylvania. The federal system is, then, an environment in which state governments and the federal government often pursue conflicting economic goals.

Fragmentation of responsibility for economic policy also exists at the federal level. The president, representing a national constituency, shares responsibility with Congress for formulating economic policy options. This shared responsibility expands the number of actors who can legitimately participate in establishing economic policy options. This means that every member of the U.S. Senate and the U.S. House of Representatives has a right to exercise a voice in economic policy. Members of Congress tend to represent the economic interests of their state or district with greater zeal than they do the economic interests of the nation as a whole. Conflict between the executive and legislative branches of government over economic policy is a legitimate characteristic of the American political system.

Even the executive branch of government is characterized by a fragmented structure for developing economic policy. A number of cabinet-level departments share in this responsibility, notably the Commerce Department, the Treasury Department, and the Labor Department. This fragmentation of responsibility within the executive branch is extensive. Various agencies below cabinet level also exercise economic policy responsibility. The Office of Management and Budget (OMB), the Council of Economic Advisers, and the independent Federal Reserve Board are three of a larger number of these agencies that exercise an extensive economic policy role.

On the negative side, this extensive structural fragmentation reduces centralized control and coordination over American economic policy. A lack of policy coordination may produce ineffective policy responses to economic problems. On the positive side, fragmentation provides for significant private-sector latitude in economic policy, which is consistent with the values of the free-enterprise system.

A second obstacle involves links between economic policy options. This is a problem because there is often significant conflict between economic goals. For example, the pursuit of full employment will tend to fuel inflation. Policies designed to reduce inflation often produce higher unemployment. This was illustrated in 1982 when federal policies designed to lower inflation acted to increase unemployment across the nation. Similarly, in a system of finite resources, a decision to expand military spending will exert budgetary pressures for a reduction in domestic spending levels. This means that economic policy goals often involve inherent conflicts that can be resolved only through the process of political compromise.

A third obstacle to effective economic policy involves uncertainty over policy outcomes. Economics is a highly quantified discipline characterized by elaborate statistical models. At the same time, it is very imprecise in actual predictive power. This means that even when political consensus is achieved to adopt a specific economic strategy, no guarantee exists that the desired result will be produced. For example, the impact of a tax-rate reduction on economic expansion and tax revenues can be assessed only by implementing the tax-rate change. Economic predictions are therefore subject to debate based on relevant political and financial assumptions used in constructing the model. The conflict generated by this debate in an environment of uncertainty becomes an obstacle to the development of economic policy.

Macroeconomic Approaches

Traditionally, the free-market system was expected to be self-adjusting, ensuring that there would be no sharp swings in the business cycle. But, as we have seen in Chapter 2, because the free-market system has failed in self-regulation, government has intervened to ameliorate the effects of economic dislocations. Congress formally assigned responsibility for maintaining economic stability to the federal government with the passage of the Employment Act of 1946. This act, grounded in Keynesian economic principles, sought to promote full employment through government-stimulated investments and expenditures. This legislation stated that the federal government should "use all practicable means (to achieve) maximum employment, production, and purchasing power." The act did not specify the exact means the federal government should use to achieve full employment. Detailed strategies were left to Congress to formulate. The act did create the Council of Economic Advisers (CEA) within the Executive Office of the President in order to provide the president with advice as economic policy decisions are made.

Two primary instruments, monetary policy and fiscal policy, are used to accomplish macroeconomic goals and achieve stabilization of the economy.

Monetary policy.   *Monetary policy* refers to the efforts of government to control the flow of money in the economy. Money includes not only cash, but also available credit and collateral used for credit or security. The major actor in monetary control is the Federal Reserve Board, commonly known as the Fed, which has several powers that permit it to expand or contract the amount of money in circulation. The Federal Reserve Board oversees the operation of banks participating in the Federal Reserve System and assists them by serving as a clearinghouse for banking transactions and by lending them money. Of particular impact on money supply is the power of the Federal Reserve Board to control the amount of money a bank must keep on reserve, the *reserve requirement.* As the amount required is increased, the banks have less to lend to customers; if the reserve is decreased, banks have more to lend. Banks also borrow from the federal reserve system, and the rate of interest charged by the Fed on such loans, the *discount rate,* affects the ability of banks to lend money to others. Because the interest rates charged by the banks are directly affected by how much the money costs them, the Fed is able to exert control over interest rates charged to consumers. Lower discount rates can be used to stimulate consumer borrowing, whereas higher discount rates discourage such borrowing. The discount rate is a powerful tool available to the Fed for stimulating or cooling off the economy.

The Federal Reserve Board also has the power to buy up government bonds held by people. These are called *open market operations.* Purchasing such bonds places money directly in the hands of potential spenders. Selling bonds, on the other hand, takes money out of circulation.

Another tool exercised by the Fed to regulate the economy involves control over the *money supply.* The currency in circulation does not represent reserves of gold or silver held by the U.S. Treasury Department. The departure from a reliance on these metals is reflected by the words "Federal Reserve Note" on paper currency, a change from "Silver Certificate" of years past. The supply and value of money in circulation is independent of gold and silver.

The value of American currency is determined by the supply in circulation and the level of confidence in the American economy by both citizens and international bankers and investors. The Fed has both the power and the responsibility to control the supply of money in circulation. Increasing the supply of money drives down interest rates and stimulates demand and economic expansion (with the risk of inflation). Decreasing the supply of money drives up interest rates, reduces demand, and cools the economy down (with the risk of higher unemployment rates).

The policies of the Fed are complemented by other government policies. Credit regulations are used as ways of expanding or contracting spending, and numerous government agencies are involved in such activities. Usury laws, stipulating the maximum interest rates that can be charged, are common in state governments. Making loans available to people, such as loans to farmers for seeds and planting or reduced-interest Federal Housing Administration (FHA) loans on housing, also can be used to stimulate economic activity.

Thus, when the economy is in recession, monetary policies are usually directed at encouraging people to spend money. This can be done through lower interest rates and increased availability of money. During inflationary periods, just the opposite is true: Government policy raises interest rates, making it less attractive for people to spend as it becomes more costly to borrow and encouraging savings by making it more profitable for people to save.

Fiscal policy. *Fiscal policy*—which encompasses tax policy, government spending, and debt management—is the other major way in which government attempts to influence economic activity generally. Through tax policy, economic activity can be stimulated or discouraged. Corporations may be encouraged to invest in plant expansion if tax incentives are offered for such activity. Plant expansion ordinarily increases employment and encourages further economic expansion because more people have more money to spend on goods and services. The same is true of a general tax cut: The demand for goods and services is likely to rise if less money is taken from people in the form of taxes. However, depending on the income level of the people involved and the attractiveness of saving, some of the money freed through tax reductions is likely to be saved instead of spent. Thus, when tax rates are changed for reasons of fiscal planning, attention is paid to what the recipients of tax benefits are likely to do with their money. During times of inflation, there is some reason for increasing taxes to reduce the amount of money in circulation. Tax increases may not be appropriate for cost-push inflation, however, because the problem is the result not of increased demand, but of the spiral of controlled prices and wages. The artificially high cost of airline tickets prior to deregulation is an example.

Government spending also affects the amount of money in circulation. If government spends money on contracts and projects, more money will become available to business firms and people employed by them. On the other hand, if government cuts back on spending, less money will be available for spending by others. During the administrations of Lyndon Johnson and Richard Nixon, some delays in awarding contracts for constructing the interstate highway system were justified on the basis that spending that money would be inflationary.

Managing the national debt is another fiscal policy activity that is often the subject of controversy. *Deficit spending* adds to the money supply without adding to production; hence, many critics of the national government suggest that increases in the national debt contribute to inflation.[4] Deficit spending causes inflation when the government artificially expands the supply of money by printing ever-higher quantities of paper currency to pay for government spending. This type of expanded money supply decreases the value of the dollar with a resultant rise in inflation.

It is possible to practice deficit spending without fueling inflation, at least in the short run, by governmental borrowing. This strategy has been employed since 1981 by Presidents Reagan and Bush to finance massive budget deficits with minimal inflationary pressure. The price for this approach is a dramatic increase in the national debt with interest payments consuming an ever-increasing percentage of the federal budget. Currently, about 15 percent of the federal budget is absorbed by interest payments.

These tools of monetary and fiscal policy are complex approaches to stabilizing the economy. There are those who think that government should act directly to increase the money in the hands of consumers in hopes that they will spend it and thus stimulate economic activity. Others argue that government should make more money available to business in the hope that it will expand activities, increasing employment, and putting more money in the hands of employees and therefore of consumers. The first approach, favored by liberals, is referred to as the *percolate-up theory,* and the latter, championed by conservatives, is known as the *trickle-down theory.*

Other measures.   Wage and price levels are affected by direct government action in other ways that are also part of fiscal policy. Some economists advocate *wage and price controls* (as were imposed in 1972–73 during the Nixon administration). Beyond discouraging production, however, wage and price controls are usually difficult to maintain: Everyone has a justification for being exempted, and government agencies become inundated with such requests. Additionally, when controls are lifted, prices and wages surge upward— as happened in the mid-1970s. In another approach, known as *jawboning,* the administration attempts to persuade business and unions to hold the line on increases voluntarily. President Kennedy was successful in such an approach with the steel industry in 1962. Appealing to patriotic feeling and using considerable pressure, such as refusing to make government purchases from those raising prices, he was able to have the price increases rescinded. This kind of approach is not always successful, though, as President Carter found in 1979 when he tried to gain adherence to his voluntary wage and price guidelines.

Wage and price control strategies are microeconomic techniques that are macroeconomic in purpose. These and other microeconomic policies (regulation, for example) have the potential for significant impact on the economy as a whole. Micro- and macroeconomic policies are not necessarily independent economic strategies.

CONTEMPORARY POLICY: APPROACHES TO MANAGING THE ECONOMY

Although there are still controversies concerning exactly how government should approach economic problems, the reality of government intervention has become widely accepted. In the following section, we shall examine approaches to managing the economy, including monetary, fiscal, tax, and deficit policies as part of current macroeconomic policy. Finally, we shall consider industrial policy as an attempt to foster economic development.

Supply-side Economics

The American economy during the 1970s was sluggish. Inflation was high and productivity was below capacity. "Stagflation" was the popular term to describe an economy marked by low levels of productivity and inflation of 10 percent or higher. The sources of this problem appeared to be a combination of factors. The Nixon administration used wage and price controls to limit inflation with only short-term success. When the wage and price freezes were lifted, wages and prices surged upward, thus adding to the inflationary spiral. Dramatic price increases by the petroleum-exporting countries also added to inflation while hindering productivity. Ronald Reagan promised a radical change and was elected in 1980 partly on the basis of the public's expectations that he could turn the economy around.

A major underlying theme of the Reagan administration was supply-side economics.[5] Supply-siders believe that the best method to achieve economic growth is to allow the market system to operate with minimal governmental interference. One basic tenet of the supply-side theory is that the relative price of any good, service, or activity determines how people will act toward it. Consequently, if the market is allowed to operate freely, private demand forces will be sufficient to sustain the economy. Government interference in stimulating demand disrupts the system and has, at best, only a temporary effect on economic growth. Supply-siders believe that government taxes, regulation, and spending only interfere with natural economic activity and that if an emphasis is placed on the stimulation of production, demand will follow naturally as a result of the production process itself.

Supply-side economic theory emphasizes heavy tax cuts in order to stimulate production in the economy. Tax cuts, especially for business and individuals with higher income, leads to consumer saving, which in turn leads to business investment. Investment then leads to economic growth, with the bonus of higher levels of employment, a classic trickle-down argument. Supporters of supply-side economics believe that tax cuts pay for themselves from economic growth, because growth creates more prosperous taxpayers to replace the tax money that was eliminated in the tax cut. A fundamental tenet of supply-side economics is that the propensity to invest is a direct function of the tax rate on such risk-taking economic activity. This idea originated with the economist Arthur Laffer and is represented by the Laffer curve (see Figure 3-1). Therefore most supply-side tax cuts are to be directed at upper-income levels, especially corporate profits and capital gains, which would constitute the most likely sources of significant investment. The theory is that as tax rates rise above a certain level, they so discourage economic activity that total tax revenue is reduced. Hence a tax cut can raise revenue and reduce deficits by stimulating economic expansion.

The tax cuts resulting from the Reagan administration's supply-side proposals were a 5 percent cut in personal income taxes in 1982 and 10 percent cuts in 1983 and 1984. An indexing provision was added to the tax law so that taxpayers would not be hurt if inflation was the primary cause of increases in salaries and wages. Since 1985, the federal income tax tables have been adjusted to account for inflation by indexing the tax rates according to the consumer price index, thus minimizing the effect of "bracket creep."

Corporate taxes were also reduced by enabling corporations to depreciate equipment more easily. This depreciation reduced the overall tax burden on corporations and at the same time was intended to encourage them to invest in new equipment because the write-offs increased corporate profits.

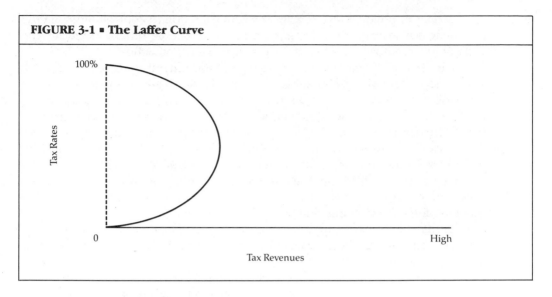

FIGURE 3-1 ▪ The Laffer Curve

Results. Unfortunately, these supply-side expectations were not realized. Not all of the money derived from the lowered tax rates was plowed back into new investment. Significant amounts of the tax windfalls went to horizontal expansion, in which companies bought into other fields (such as Mobil Oil's purchase of Montgomery Ward and the purchase of food-processing companies by tobacco industry giants), expenditures that add nothing to economic growth and did not increase the gross national product.

Though the tax reductions were aimed at increasing the amount of money available for investment and thus for production, other aspects of the new economic policy were viewed as being just as important to economic growth. Regulation was perceived as being burdensome to industry, and so the Reagan administration accelerated the deregulation efforts of the Carter presidency. Conservatives and the business community consider regulations to be costly.[6] Reducing regulation means reducing expenses, thus allowing for investment of those funds. Much of the Reagan administration's deregulation did not occur through changes in law or policy directives as such. Instead, appointments to boards and commissions led to significant shifts in policy interpretation and implementation. The Equal Employment Opportunity Commission, Civil Rights Commission, Federal Trade Commission, and National Labor Relations Board (NLRB) are examples of some of the agencies whose presidential appointees reinterpreted policy to fall in line with the perspectives of the administration. As a result, dramatic shifts in policy have created a climate much more favorable to business. The NLRB, for example, seems to be much more sympathetic to management than to labor. Labor always considered the NLRB to be a protector of its interests and an insurer of fairness. Now it is viewed as an ally of management.

Monetary policy is less easy for the administration to control. Although the president may attempt to move in a particular direction, others, especially the Federal Reserve Board, are free to follow their own approaches.

The Fed was created with the passage of the Federal Reserve Act of 1913. The Federal Reserve System sought to stabilize the banking industry through regulations developed and imposed by the seven-member board. Board members are appointed by the president, with Senate confirmation, to fourteen-year terms. The chairman of the Fed serves a four-year term and is also appointed by the president, with Senate approval. Board members can be removed only by impeachment resulting from the commission of a criminal act. They may *not* be removed over a disagreement about economic policy options with either the president or the Congress. The Fed is therefore a stable, independent, and powerful force in economic policy.

Budget deficits. Supply-side economics did not reduce the budget deficit that President Reagan campaigned against in 1980. In fact, the budget deficits have increased dramatically since 1980 as indicated in Table 3-1. The last president to develop and administer a balanced budget was President Johnson.

As reflected in the table, the $70 billion annual deficit of 1980 had grown to $220 billion by 1986 and was projected to reach a peak of $362 billion in 1992. These deficits are the result of a combination of factors: the large tax cuts

---

TABLE 3-1 ▪ Federal Budget Deficits, 1968–1996 (in billions of dollars)

Year	Surplus (+) or Deficit (−)	President
1968	+3.2	Johnson
1972	−23.4	Nixon
1976	−73.7	Ford
1980	−70.8	Carter
1983	−127.9	Reagan
1984	−207.6	Reagan
1986	−220.7	Reagan
1988	−155.1	Reagan
1990	−220	Bush
1991	−282	Bush
1992	−362*	Bush
1993	−278*	—
1994	−234*	—
1995	−157*	—
1996	−156*	—

* As projected by Congressional Budget Office.

SOURCE: *Statistical Abstract of the United States, 1988* and *1990*; and Congressional Budget Office.

in 1981–83, increased levels of defense spending during the 1980s, the Persian Gulf war of 1991, and the recessions of 1981–82 and 1991–92, which lowered tax receipts and increased federal expenditures for welfare and unemployment.

Interest on the national debt is now the third-largest federal budget item, behind Social Security payments and national defense spending. By 1990 approximately 15 percent of the annual budget was consumed by interest payments servicing a national debt of over $3 trillion. By 1995, interest on the national debt will consume almost 20 percent of the federal budget. This percentage will increase as the cumulative level of debt continues to increase. It is important to understand that the interest payments of $220 billion in 1990 did not pay for any public services in past years or the current year. It was only an interest payment on money borrowed during earlier years.

The impact of increasing deficits on other parts of the economy is manifold. Increasing deficits drive up interest rates because of the increased competition for available money as the federal government competes with private-sector borrowers. The higher interest rates and increasing scarcity of capital may then discourage investment and weaken economic expansion. Higher interest rates mean less spending by consumers, who find loans too expensive, and so domestic purchasing declines. Interest rates for home mortgages and consumer loans were in the 3 to 4 percent range during the 1960s, a period of balanced federal budgets. Significant efforts by the Fed in 1991–92 resulted in home mortgage rates in the 8 percent range in 1992, a reduction from the 10 to 12 percent ranges of the 1980s. Consumer loans remained at the 10 to 12 percent level. The deficit is the major cause of these high interest rates.

Additionally, high interest rates usually cause foreign interests to convert their currencies to U.S. dollars, thus driving the value of the dollar upward relative to that of other currencies. The rise in the value of the dollar makes it difficult for U.S. firms to compete in world markets and therefore leads to a trade imbalance.[7] The strength of the dollar is a measure of the ability of the dollar to purchase (or be purchased by) foreign currency in international money markets. In early 1989, the dollar traded for 189 Japanese yen, considerably fewer than it had a few years earlier. The more yen the dollar trades for, the stronger it is said to be. A strong dollar translates into greater purchasing power for the American dollar in the Japanese market, since a strong dollar will buy more Japanese goods than a weak dollar. At the same time, the strong dollar decreases Japanese purchasing power in the American market, since it requires more yen to buy American goods. As the Fed acted to drive down interest rates in an attempt to stimulate recovery from the recession in early 1992, the dollar traded for 130 yen, 59 less than in 1989. The strength of the dollar is partially determined by interest rates.

A strong American dollar contributes to the trade deficit, which stood at nearly $101 billion in 1990, by driving down the cost of foreign imports to Americans and driving up the cost of American exports to foreign customers. The size of the trade deficit has made the United States the world's largest debtor nation.

Tax Reform

The Tax Reform Act of 1986 was an effort to establish a federal tax system that was fairer, simpler, and more efficient than the previous federal income tax structure.[8] Rhetoric surrounding the tax reform movement indicated that the reform would produce greater efficiency and provide economic incentives for greater national productivity. Accordingly, tax reform does relate to economic policy.

Fairness.   Much of this act was targeted toward creating greater fairness in the federal tax system. The act retained most of the major deductions previously used in itemizing: home mortgage interest, charitable contributions, medical expenses, certain other taxes, and business expense deductions. By lowering the maximum tax rate for individuals from 50 percent to 28 percent, Congress sought to increase taxpayer confidence in the system and to reduce attempts to avoid tax liability. The act also sought to broaden the tax base of the federal government by eliminating certain deductions such as interest on consumer loans and by placing restrictions on the number of home mortgages that could be claimed. Due to the significant tax cuts of 1981–83, Congress did not feel a need to reduce taxes further. In fact, the reform was praised as being "revenue neutral" in its impact. The act did provide some aid to low- and middle-income families by increasing the standard deduction, and it did provide limited tax relief to the elderly.

Simplicity.   The tax reform sought to simplify the tax structure by reducing the paperwork and computations involved in preparing and filing a tax return. There are now only three individual tax brackets (15, 28, and 31 percent).

Efficiency.   Efficiency is probably the most significant component of the tax reform act. The act sought to reduce potential interference with business and investment programs by the tax structure. Under the old tax structure, tax liability could be reduced through unprofitable investments. The reformers argued that such a structure encouraged waste and inefficiency because investment decisions were made not on the economic merits of the investment, but on its impact on tax liability. The tax reform sought to diminish the importance of tax laws in business decision making. Tax reform served as an economic policy instrument to expand the federal tax base and to change investment patterns.

Industrial Policy

As the United States entered the decade of the 1980s, Americans began to question the ability of domestic business to compete successfully in the international market. The country no longer enjoyed a trade surplus and was experiencing a continued annual trade deficit, importing more goods and capital than it exported. The Japanese and other trading partners of the United States were experiencing significant trade surpluses at the expense of American industry. Industrial policy advocates unsuccessfully sought an expanded role for the federal government in managing the economic system in order to make American business more competitive.[9]

Under this approach, the government would have sought to identify industries that could compete successfully in the international arena and provided those firms with legal, technical, financial, and regulatory assistance. Firms that were identified as being noncompetitive would have been given aid to reduce the domestic economic impact of a corporation in decline. The federal government would have provided incentives (tax breaks, financial aid) to encourage industries to increase their competitive abilities in the international market.

Such an industrial policy would have involved an active role for the federal government in industrial planning. Governmental intervention in investment, production, and marketing decisions would have become the cornerstone of an integrated economic policy that sought to increase American success in exporting goods and services.

Critics of this proposed industrial policy argue that the environment in the United States is not conducive to establishing an integrated and rational industrial policy strategy. First, such a policy requires that cooperation and unity characterize the relationship between the public and private sectors as industry surrenders entrepreneurial authority to the federal government. This is not a characteristic of the American free-enterprise system.

Second, such an industrial policy requires that the government actively determine which firms and activities would *not* be targeted for growth and expansion but would be relegated to economic decline. Critics argue that the operation of market forces is more effective in determining "economic losers" than is a government agency.

Third, critics argue that the fragmentation of the American political system would produce a policy in which all industries (competitive and noncompetitive alike) would be targeted for expansion. Such a strategy would not enhance the competitive edge of the United States in a global economy, since significant resources would be channeled to industries that lacked the ability to compete.

Fourth, critics point out that political power tends to gravitate to centers of wealth. This is significant because wealth is concentrated in older industries that are still powerful even in decline. Newer ventures that are high-technology-oriented lack the wealth of older industries and therefore have less political power. Political power is a major factor in determining the allocation of resources in the American system. Consequently, the political system would have a bias against potentially competitive newer industries.

Industrial policy of the type just discussed has not been a central element of American economic policy. The trend over the past hundred years has been for government to enter the marketplace to prevent abuses by those economic actors with the most resources. Government has also attempted to stimulate particular industrial development through favorable tax laws or other incentives. The Reagan administration supported a change in the role of government in industrial development, subscribing to a laissez-faire approach, in which government refrained from interfering in the economy. This laissez-faire approach remained unchanged during the Bush administration.

International Trade

Yet another aspect of the current business environment is the policy regarding international trade. Though the Reagan administration strongly supported free trade as a stated policy, it did exert pressure on foreign competition. Thus it pushed other nations to agree to voluntary import quotas on such items as steel, textiles, and automobiles. The expectation was that import quotas would improve the prospects of domestic industry to sell its products.

The centrality of free trade to American economic policy was clearly illustrated by the agreement signed in 1988 with Canada that allows for almost total free trade between the two countries. Just as some Americans have been alarmed by the prospect of unrestricted free trade from Asian countries, a significant number of Canadians harbor the same fears concerning a potential influx of American-produced goods. Similar open trade negotiations with Mexico are in progress.

Omnibus Trade Act of 1988.   President Reagan signed the Omnibus Trade bill into law in August, 1988, after having vetoed a nearly identical bill just three months earlier. The trade act was a product of rising concern over the nation's growing trade deficit, particularly the trade imbalance with Japan. It was bipartisan in origin and support and was partially stimulated by a hesitancy on the part of the Reagan administration to address actively the issue of unfair practices by America's trading partners.

Both members of Congress and the American public grew increasingly concerned over unfairness in the international trade arena arising from perceived unfair trade practices by other nations. American trade policy has historically been grounded in the provisions of the General Agreement on Tariffs and Trade (GATT) to maintain an environment that stresses minimal trade restrictions. GATT is a multination international trade agreement that is periodically renegotiated among the member nations.

A major problem for the United States vis-à-vis GATT is that the vast majority of international trade is not covered by the GATT convention. Agricultural products, international investments, service operations, and most other trade commodities tend to be covered by specific nation-by-nation trade conventions. These agreements provide a context for restrictive trade practices that are not consistent with the provisions of GATT.

The Omnibus Trade bill was grounded in the belief that the best weapon to use against nations that engaged in unfair trade practices involves access to the American market itself. Accordingly, any trading partner that imposed barriers to American goods and services would find itself faced with significant restrictions to the American market in the form of tariffs or import quotas.

The trade act required the president to identify those nations with unfair trade practices and a large American trade surplus as targets for trade negotiations. If the negotiation process failed, American trade restrictions would follow as retaliation. The act also created a training program for American workers adversely affected by international trade practices. The act also emphasized promotion of American exports and training programs for American industry in order to enhance the likelihood of success in international trade.

All of these elements add up to an industrial policy by piecemeal actions as the federal government continues to avoid developing an explicit industrial policy. Consequently, some economists argue that the United States is at a competitive disadvantage with other nations which have a more clearly defined industrial policy.

POLICY EVALUATION: SUCCESS OR FAILURE?

In any policy evaluation effort, the perspective of the analyst has an impact on the conclusions. Critics of governmental monetary and fiscal policies claim that such policies tend to favor those who have economic resources. Galbraith, for instance, argues that the economic planning system, well developed and representing the people with money, does not help those who need help the most.[10] He sees monetary and fiscal policy as having been captured by business and financial interests, whereas consumers, workers, and the poor are not given sufficient consideration. The opposite stance is taken by Friedman,[11] who suggests that government controls stifle economic activity because they make business too costly to operate profitably. Regardless of perspective, many critics of economic policies agree that these "solutions" tend to distort economic development and lead to the maldistribution of resources in the society. How that maldistribution is explained depends on the critic's point of view.

Social Orders

To explain preferences for governmental activity in economic policy, the concept of "social orders" as discussed by Aaron Wildavsky is useful.[12] Economic and budgetary policies reflect the values of three social orders that have emerged since the founding of the republic. One social order reflects a commitment to the concept of the preservation of a *social hierarchy* as the standard by which to judge government activity. A second emphasizes the operation of *market forces* as the most appropriate standard for evaluating public policy. The third places an emphasis on *egalitarian values* as the prime standard for public policy. This concept of social orders is consistent with the traditional liberal-conservative classification. It also may be more useful in understanding policy preferences than a simple liberal-conservative dichotomy because it provides additional insights into basic economic and political values.

The order favoring the preservation of a social hierarchy supports an active role for the central government in maintaining the status quo in the distribution of wealth. Social hierarchists hold that society is divided into strata based on a natural order. The distribution of wealth reflects this natural ordering. Government should therefore pursue economic policies to preserve this uneven distribution pattern and avoid policies that would artificially erase these natural distinctions. Promoting equality of economic opportunity is not an appropriate sphere of government activity because individuals are primarily responsible for their own economic status. By extension, this order favors low taxation, vigorously opposes redistributive economic policies, favors low levels of domestic spending, and would support higher levels of defense spending to protect the security of the existing economic system.

The market-oriented social order places emphasis on the allocation of social goods through the values of a free-market framework. Individual competition is valued and encouraged. Therefore government ought to avoid excessive entanglement in economic policy. Government should pursue policies that promote equality of economic opportunity only when such policies enhance market operations. Accordingly, this order favors a limited role for government in economic policy, opposes adoption of redistributive economic policies, favors low levels of domestic spending, and also supports higher levels of defense spending.

The egalitarian social order places an emphasis on social and political equality. Government is viewed as an appropriate mechanism to regulate the distribution of economic benefits in such a manner as to promote individual equality. The emphasis on equality directly affects economic policy preferences. Simple equality of economic opportunity, as advocated by the market approach, is an overly limited goal, for it does not entail actual achievement of equality. Egalitarians emphasize redistributive policies to achieve a degree of economic equality. They also favor higher levels of taxes, support higher domestic spending, place reduced emphasis on defense spending, and favor a generally stronger role for government in economic policy.

Historically, American economic policy has been a function of the equilibrium between these three social orders and a shared commitment to a balanced budget with a minimal national debt. Economic choices made since the mid-1970s indicate that the compromises necessary to maintain a balanced budget have ceased to be a priority for these social orders. During the 1980s the federal government pursued conflicting policies favored by each of the three groups. Social hierarchy and market advocates were rewarded with supply-side tax cuts, a reduction in regulation, and significant spending for national defense. Egalitarians were able to achieve increases in entitlement programs.

Federal spending dramatically exceeded federal revenues as the theorized supply-side revenue increases failed to materialize and massive budget deficits were generated. In order simultaneously to satisfy all groups, the commitment to a balanced budget was abandoned and budget deficits embraced. In order to finance the massive budget deficits, the decision was made simply to borrow the money and shift financial burdens of present programs to future generations.

Inflation

The Reagan administration was dominated by individuals drawn from the market and social hierarchy orders. This helps to explain the administration's emphasis on inflation as a greater economic problem than unemployment. Inflation threatened the smooth operation of the market and eroded the wealth of the wealthier strata in society.

The Reagan administration did wage an effective campaign against inflation during the early 1980s and achieved a drop in the inflation rate, from 10.3 percent in 1981 to a low of 1.9 percent during 1986, as reflected in Table 3-2.

During the latter half of the 1980s, economic growth in the United States remained slightly over 3 percent of GNP, as reflected in Figure 3-2. The planned recession of 1982, and its negative GNP growth rate, was followed by an eight-year period of economic expansion. The economic policies of the 1980s are associated with domestic economic growth.

A decline in interest rates of almost eight percentage points between 1981 and 1989 accompanied the economic policies of the 1980s. As Figure 3-3 indicates, interest rates have remained relatively constant since 1986. Interest rates depicted in the figure do not necessarily reflect the rates on consumer loans for that period. Home-mortgage interest rates, on 30-year fixed-rate notes, tended to be four percentage points higher. Between 1986 and 1989, these rates were in the 10 to 11 percent range. In order to counter the recession of 1991–92, the Bush administration encouraged the Fed to lower interest rates in order to stimulate consumer purchasing. By early 1992, mortgage rates were permitted to drop to the 8 percent range in an attempt to invigorate the housing industry.

Fiscal Policy

Critics of the Reagan strategy argued that the inflation of the 1970s was the result of some special circumstances, especially the large increases in the costs of energy and food, which have now leveled off or decreased and are unlikely to recur in the near future. They believed that some reduction in inflation was bound to occur anyway. Egalitarian critics felt that the drop in inflation was obtained at an unacceptable cost in unemployment between 1980 and 1982. Unemployment levels approached 10 percent in that period. Reagan administration officials countered that unemployment eventually decreased to around 6.5 percent, which is near pre-1980 levels.

TABLE 3-2 ▪ Inflation Rates, 1981–1990

Year	Inflation Rate
1981	10.3%
1984	4.3%
1986	1.9%
1988	4.1%
1990	5.4%

SOURCE: *Statistical Abstract of the United States, 1991* (Washington, D.C.: U.S. Government Printing Office, 1991), Table 765.

FIGURE 3-2 ▪ Economic Growth, 1981–1991 (as a percentage of GNP)

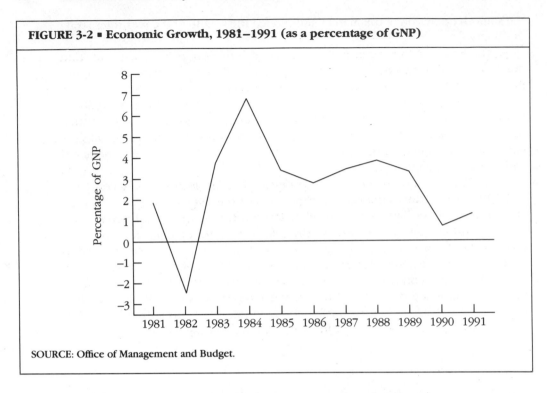

SOURCE: Office of Management and Budget.

The Reagan administration took pride in the fiscal and monetary policies that it claimed fueled the economic recovery of the 1980s, which lasted longer than any other recent period of recovery. The tax reductions allowed more money to be pumped into the economy, aiding in an industrial investment boom.

Critics of these tax and spending policies focused on two issues. The first became known as the fairness issue and relates to the equity of tax and spending reductions. A constant theme of the administration's opponents was that its policies favored the rich and hurt the poor. Studies of the impact of the domestic budget cuts did indicate that those in the highest income categories increased their real income and that the majority experienced no increase or a decline. Of course, unemployment hits low- and moderate-income people almost exclusively and contributes to their lower income.

The second issue raised by critics was that of the deficit. Although the deficit may not have much impact immediately, there is concern that its long-range consequences could be severe. The deficit places the national government in the position of competing with consumers and business to borrow money. The result is higher interest rates, which place American industry at a competitive disadvantage with foreign industry. Foreign investment pours into the United States, with the result that a large portion of the national debt is foreign-owned and the value of the dollar rises relative to that of other currencies. This exacerbates the difficulty American industries face in international trade because they cannot compete in

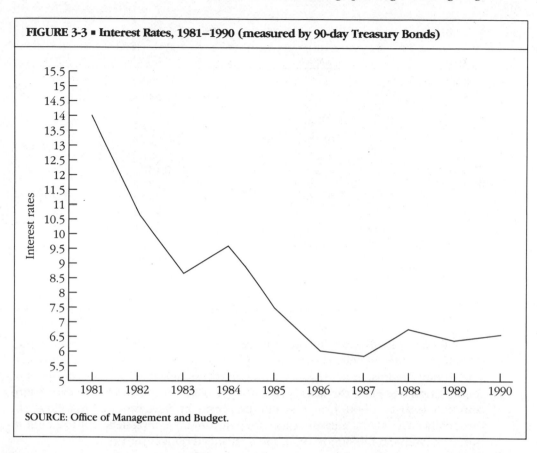

FIGURE 3-3 ▪ Interest Rates, 1981–1990 (measured by 90-day Treasury Bonds)

SOURCE: Office of Management and Budget.

prices. Also, the poor nations that need to borrow money are faced with high interest rates that make it difficult for them to develop their economies. The long-term consequences for international trade and domestic industry could be significant. The growth of the national debt is indicated in Table 3-3. Between 1981 and 1987 the national debt increased by $1.5 trillion. The level of national debt continues to increase, by an additional $800 billion between 1987 and 1991. The United States economy now carries over $3 trillion in debt. This debt can be translated to a $40,000 obligation for every family of four in the United States. The deficit spending of the 1980s has created two policy problems. First, a habit of annual deficit spending has been created. Second, and probably more severe, is the ever-increasing size of the national debt.

The size of the deficit presents long-term costs to the wealth of the nation. Even if the annual deficit were eliminated in 1993 (and this is not a current economic goal) the interest payment on over $3 trillion would consume over 20 percent of the federal budget. Stated another way, interest payments absorb nearly $300 billion of federal spending per year, spending that is diverted from productive uses.

TABLE 3-3 ▪ National Debt, 1960–1992 (in billions of dollars)		
Year	*Deficit*	*Total Debt*
1960	$ 0	$ 290.0
1965	1.4	323.2
1970	2.8	382.6
1975	53.2	544.1
1980	73.6	914.3
1983	207.8	1,381.9
1986	220.7	2,132.9
1987	149.7	2,282.6
1988	155.1	2,437.7
1989	153.4	2,591.1
1990	220.4	2,811.5
1991	282.0	3,093.5
1992	362.0	3,455.5

SOURCE: *Statistical Abstract of the United States, 1989* and Office of Management and Budget.

Gramm-Rudman.   In order to reduce the deficit, Congress passed the Balanced Budget and Emergency Deficit Control Act of 1985, otherwise known as the Gramm-Rudman Act. This act resulted in two significant changes in the federal budget process. First, the act specified target deficit levels for fiscal years 1986 through 1991 that both Congress and the president were required to follow. As originally enacted, the measure called for a maximum federal deficit of $72 billion for 1989 and $36 billion for 1990, and a balanced budget by 1991.

The second provision of the act required that automatic spending cuts be imposed by the comptroller general across the board if the targeted budget deficit levels were exceeded. This process of "sequestration" would be used if the Congress and the president were unable to agree on spending priorities that would reduce the deficit.

The sequestration provision was modified in 1987 to meet constitutional requirements. The comptroller general is the head of the General Accounting Office (GAO), a congressional agency that is not part of the executive branch of government. The Supreme Court ruled that only an officer of the executive branch could order spending cuts and that this provision of Gramm-Rudman was unconstitutional. Under the revised Gramm-Rudman process, the director of the Office of Management and Budget (OMB; an executive branch office) imposes the necessary spending cuts.

The amended Gramm-Rudman process established new budget deficit goals with deficit targets of $100 billion for 1990, $64 billion for 1991, $28 billion for 1992, and a balanced budget for 1993 (Table 3-4). In the event that sequestration is mandated, half of the spending cuts must be imposed on defense spending, with the other half falling on domestic spending.

TABLE 3-4 ▪ Gramm-Rudman (1987) Federal Budget and Deficit Projections, 1990–1993 (in billions of dollars)

	1990	1991	1992	1993
Revenues	$1,059	$1,140	$1,212	$1,281
Spending	1,151	1,207	1,244	1,279
Deficit or surplus	−92	−67	−32	+2

SOURCE: Office of Management and Budget, *Fiscal 1990 Budget.*

Sequestration can be avoided. Even after the director of OMB announces the imposition of sequestration, the president and the Congress have the power to avoid the Gramm-Rudman spending-cut formula by developing an alternative spending reduction plan.

Results. The Office of Management and Budget in the mid-1980s developed projections for revenue and spending patterns that would eliminate the deficit by 1993, as indicated in Table 3-4. These optimistic projections were not achieved. In fact, the 1992 budget will have a record deficit of $362 billion. The OMB projections were unrealistic for several reasons. First, they were based on overly optimistic annual GNP growth rates of 3.5 to 4.0 percent. During the 1991–92 recession, the GNP grew at less than 2 percent per year, and revenues fell while income support payments rose. Second, the Persian Gulf conflict created unexpected budget demands. Third, the cost of the bailout of the savings and loan industry has strained limited federal resources. Finally, the absence of public consensus surrounding spending priorities encouraged the president and Congress to spend federal dollars at ever higher levels.

Gramm-Rudman has proved ineffective in reducing the federal budget deficit. One reason for its ineffectiveness is that Gramm-Rudman required that deficit targets be met at the beginning of a fiscal year based on revenue and spending projections. It was therefore possible to achieve compliance only on paper. The actual deficit at the end of the fiscal year continues to be higher than the target deficit level because of differences between projections and actual revenue receipts.

Congress and President Bush acted to change the rules of the budget process in 1990. These changes will remain in effect until 1995 and shift the focus of the process away from the issue of the size of budget deficits. The new budget rules avoid sequestration if spending is the result of events "beyond the control" of the president and Congress. Spending associated with the Persian Gulf war, the savings and loan bailout, and the 1991–92 recession recovery will not be counted as part of the budget deficit. This allows the deficit to exceed the Gramm-Rudman limits and avoid the draconian cuts associated with sequestration. Gramm-Rudman is effectively suspended until 1995.

A major part of the 1990 budget compromise between Congress and the president was an increase on the national debt ceiling to $4.145 trillion. The increase is intended to last until 1993 and exempts Congress from a traditional annual vote on the debt ceiling.

When the deficit is measured as a percent of GNP, as in Figure 3-4, it tends to remain below the 6 percent level. If the GNP expands, the annual deficit becomes a smaller percentage. But during times of economic recession (1991–92, for instance) it tends to increase. This can be interpreted to mean that the deficit is a minor economic headache. The problem with this kind of analysis is that it ignores the impact of servicing the debt on the federal budget.

Federal revenues and spending.   Figures 3-5 and 3-6 provide a visual display of federal revenues and federal spending. Individual income taxes and Social Security taxes account for 67 percent of federal revenues. Corporate income taxes comprise only 7 percent of federal revenues. A significant point is that federal borrowing provides more revenue than corporate taxes. Borrowing will be the third most important source of federal revenue in 1992. If borrowing is to be eliminated or reduced, and if federal spending is to increase at 9.4 percent, then either new taxes or tax increases are necessary.

Reducing federal spending as a mechanism to reduce the deficit, however, presents significant problems. Social Security, Medicare, national defense, and interest payments consume nearly three quarters of total federal spending. Grant programs to state and local governments absorb 11 percent of the federal budget. If these programs are cut, significant state and local tax increases will be necessary to replace the eliminated federal dollars.

All other federal programs, including education, space, energy, environmental protection, drug programs, and law enforcement, consume only 7 percent of the federal budget. The abolition of these programs would not eliminate the deficit.

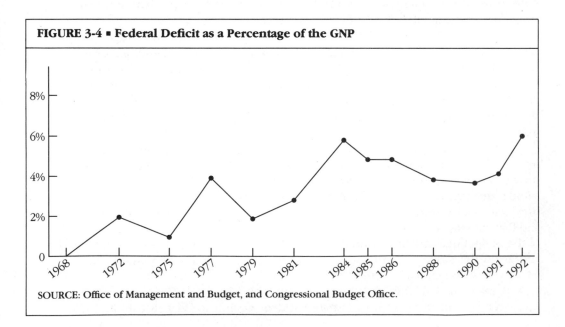

FIGURE 3-4 ▪ Federal Deficit as a Percentage of the GNP

SOURCE: Office of Management and Budget, and Congressional Budget Office.

FIGURE 3-5 ▪ Federal Revenues by Source, 1992

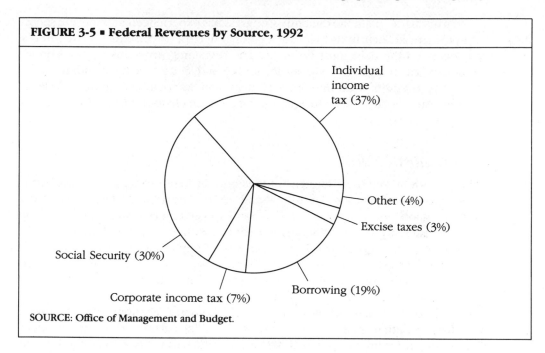

Individual income tax (37%)

Other (4%)

Excise taxes (3%)

Borrowing (19%)

Corporate income tax (7%)

Social Security (30%)

SOURCE: Office of Management and Budget.

FIGURE 3-6 ▪ Federal Spending by Category, 1992

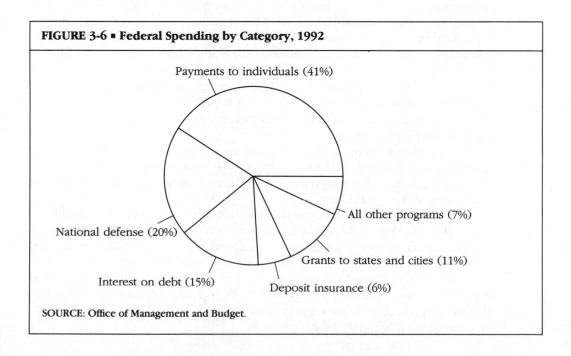

Payments to individuals (41%)

All other programs (7%)

Grants to states and cities (11%)

National defense (20%)

Deposit insurance (6%)

Interest on debt (15%)

SOURCE: Office of Management and Budget.

This may explain the difficulty Congress has experienced in imposing spending cuts. Social Security is "sacred." National defense is "essential." The interest payments on the debt must be made. The remaining programs do not contain sufficient "fat" to provide a significant source of deficit-reducing spending cuts.

The magnitude of the national debt and international trade imbalance present the United States with major economic challenges during the decade of the 1990s.

The Trade Deficit

The pattern of American foreign trade is also an item of increasing concern in economic policy. During the 1960s and 1970s, the United States recorded a surplus of foreign trade. That is, the nation exported more than it imported. This foreign-trade surplus typically ranged between $2 billion and $9 billion annually between 1960 and the early 1970s and was an important element in American economic expansion and prosperity. The last year that a trade surplus was recorded ($9.1 billion) was in 1975. As reflected in Figure 3-7, the U.S. foreign trade balance sheet reflects a pattern of dramatic trade deficits.

The trade deficit has an impact on the domestic economy by fostering a transfer of wealth from the United States to its trading partners as dollars are spent abroad to pay for imported goods. When the trade balance is in near equilibrium between two countries, both economies benefit from stimulated demand. When a trade deficit occurs, economic expansion tends to accrue to the nation with a trade surplus. A trade surplus reflects a demand for goods, which creates a need for production, which leads to creation of jobs. A trade deficit reflects a lessening of demand for goods, reducing the demand for production and, in turn, resulting in job losses and higher unemployment. The trade deficit is a problem for the American economy because the United States has a deficit with many trading partners.

A related issue involves increased levels of foreign investment in the United States. Commerce Department data indicate that foreign investors currently hold roughly $250 billion in American assets. This includes banks, land, buildings, and industrial plants. American foreign investments are around $300 billion, and the gap is quickly narrowing.

Critics of these high levels of foreign investment argue that the American economic system will increasingly be responsive to, and subject to the influence of, foreign nationals. This has led to a call for the imposition of limits on this type of investment by foreign sources.

Supporters of foreign investment argue that there is little to fear from higher levels of foreign ownership. State and local governments actively court foreign investments as a source of jobs and an expanded tax base. Others argue that foreign investment has been a source of funds to finance the national debt and that these funds have allowed the American economy to expand significantly during the 1980s. Some economists also note that the returns on American investments abroad still exceed those of foreign investment in America, which still provides the economy with at least one positive benefit.

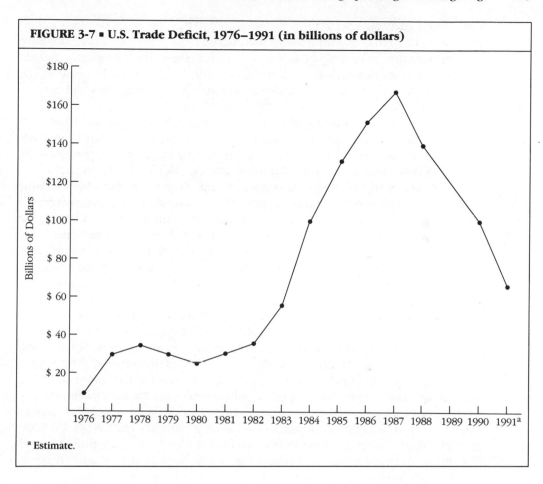

FIGURE 3-7 ▪ U.S. Trade Deficit, 1976–1991 (in billions of dollars)

ᵃ Estimate.

Because these differences of opinion exist, and because the long-term effects of a trade deficit and high levels of foreign investment cannot be accurately predicted, these issues will remain on the economic policy agenda.

FUTURE ALTERNATIVES: SPENDING, TAXES, AND THE DEFICIT

Debate over economic policy is marked by conflict. The issue of governmental involvement in the economy is complex and reflects basic ideological values. During the 1980s, the policy-making departments of the executive branch of government were guided by a desire to reduce the role of government in the economy. Others outside the executive branch argue that more, not less, government intervention is necessary to stabilize the economy. The liberal wing of the

Democratic party appears to be most committed to this approach, with its egalitarian values. Its partisans want policies that increase the power of those who have little opportunity to participate in the economic system. Their proposals include such items as industrial policy, plant closure warnings, and an increase in the national minimum wage. Such policies would intensify coordination and centralization of economic policy.

Taxes.   Tax reforms are also proposed regularly. Tax cuts are often confused with tax reform, though the two are not the same. *Tax reforms* change the basic type and incidence (who pays) of taxation, and *tax cuts* merely reduce the rate of taxation. The tax reform achieved in 1986 has acted to shift tax incidence. Critics of the tax reform claim that deductions and exemptions favor high-income brackets and hurt middle-income people and the poor. Middle-income taxpayers bear the largest burden of national income taxes. Pressure to alter and modify the tax reforms to influence tax incidence continue as economic agenda items.

An item on the economic agenda for President Bush centers on tax policy to lower the deficit and reduce the national debt. President Bush proposed reduction in capital gains taxes, but congressional democrats favor some combination of middle-income tax cuts and tax increases on the wealthy. This means that tax policy questions will remain on the economic agenda in the 1990s. If the deficit is to be reduced significantly, strong new sources of revenue will be necessary.

Alternatives include the flat-tax proposal such as proposed by Jerry Brown during his 1992 bid for the Democratic presidential nomination. The flat-tax approach would eliminate many deductions and reduce the number of tax brackets.[13] Additionally, the proposals call for lowering the maximum rate that everyone would pay. The tax reform of 1986 incorporated some very limited components of a flat tax. Although a true flat tax is unlikely because of the many special interests supporting deductions and other advantages, it is almost certain that there will be additional changes. The major conflict is how and where to generate additional tax revenues.

Another tax reform proposal is a value-added tax to supplement income taxes. The value-added tax is like a national sales tax and taxes goods as they pass through each phase of the economic system. As value is added to each natural resource or good, the tax is imposed on the increase in value. Members of the Brookings Institution have proposed yet another approach, a cash-flow tax that would be based on a household's gross income minus savings. Thus all income would be included in figuring the tax. This proposal would encourage saving, as savings would be subtracted from total income for tax purposes. A similar reform would be made in corporate taxes. Again, this proposal is appealing in that it is simple and arguably fair. Political reality, however, suggests that those with a vested interest in the current complex tax system would work hard to retain their special position.

The value-added tax does have the advantage of being a less visible tax than the income tax, which may be a factor in its consideration in the 1990s.

Industrial policy also occasions differing perspectives. Believers in the free market currently have great influence. There are others, however, who believe that government has a responsibility to try to influence business activity, and therefore research and development efforts are supported as legitimate areas of government action. Free-market advocates believe that imports and exports should not be restricted. Additionally, domestic markets should not be interfered with, and industries should stand on their own ability to compete. On the other side are advocates of government subsidies to assist major industries, such as the steel and automobile industries, when they are in trouble. Protectionist policies such as tariffs and import quotas are often recommended as necessary to support domestic industry and workers. Tax breaks are also suggested as important to the sustained health of the American economy.

Deficit reduction.   Concern with deficit reduction remains a major factor in economic and budgetary policy. The requirements of the Gramm-Rudman deficit reduction act have been effectively neutralized. It is increasingly clear that neither the president nor the Congress has the ability to impose drastic spending cuts to achieve a balanced budget. Tax policy questions remain a major issue for the 1990s.

During the 1988 presidential campaign, George Bush repeatedly said, "Read my lips. No new taxes!" After the election, he sought increased funding for a number of programs that had been targeted for cuts by President Reagan. These included child care, education, the environment, and other social programs. The problem that faced the administration was how to reduce the deficit, expand social programs, and avoid tax increases. The pledge proved impossible to keep.

Rather than ask for new taxes, Richard G. Darman, who was appointed by Bush to head the Office of Management and Budget, raised the issue of imposing "user fees" to pay for government services. Accordingly, user fees could be imposed on broadcasters for use of the airwaves, on savings depositors to pay for federal deposit insurance, on telecommunications systems to pay for regulatory efforts, on airline passengers to pay for air traffic control, and in an unlimited number of other areas as well. Democrats immediately challenged the concept that a user fee is not a tax. Darman acknowledged their protest: "I think [it's] a version of the duck test: If it looks like a duck, it's a duck." Therefore user fees are taxes.

The Bush presidency sought to devise ways to increase federal revenues without using the "T-word" (taxes) as it backed away from the user-fee proposals. "Revenue enhancement" was the description used to justify the relatively small federal tax increases imposed during the first two years of the Bush presidency.

The Bush administration has stressed the importance of maintaining low interest rates in order to stimulate economic growth and increase federal tax revenues. The Federal Reserve Board was in conflict with President Bush in 1989 as it followed a monetary policy of increasing rather than decreasing interest rates in order to reduce inflationary pressures. During late 1991, the Fed began to decrease interest rates in an attempt to stimulate recovery from the recession.

The 1992 budget reflects significant changes in spending priorities for the Bush administration from those of the Reagan administration. Defense spending will be reduced to 20 percent of the budget. Consequently, the size of the

American military is being reduced, and weapons systems once targeted for production (such as the B-2 Stealth Bomber, now costing in excess of $1 billion each) will be purchased in very limited quantities. Defense planning no longer calls for a 600-ship navy. Military units are being withdrawn from Europe and other areas. Defense spending became a target for even sharper budget cuts during the early 1990s.

Other issues.   A number of other major economic issues remain on the policy agenda. One issue involves the move by the European Economic Community (EEC) to develop an integrated economy. In 1985, member nations of the EEC developed a detailed plan to achieve a unified economic system by the end of 1992. Restrictions on trade, services, the flow of capital, and the labor supply would be eliminated. The goal of this plan is to create an environment that stimulates economic growth in member nations. Significant progress has been made toward adopting the necessary agreements to achieve economic unity among EEC nations. Table 3-5 reflects the relative economic size of the EEC, the United States, and Japan.

Successful implementation of the EEC economic system has the potential to provide major economic competition for the United States in a global economy. The EEC represents a potential market of over 300 million consumers with a significant commercial and industrial base. To date, the United States has yet to

TABLE 3-5 ▪ Characteristics of the EEC, the United States, and Japan, 1990

Country	Population	GNP ($ Billions)	GNP (Per Capita)
EEC Countries			
Belgium	9,909,285	153	$15,454
Denmark	5,131,217	101	19,862
France	56,358,331	943	16,749
Germany	78,475,370	1,415	18,051
Greece	10,028,171	43	4,350
Ireland	3,550,352	28	8,171
Italy	57,664,405	825	14,322
Luxembourg	383,813	5	12,894
Netherlands	14,936,032	223	14,966
Portugal	10,354,497	33	3,252
Spain	39,268,715	288	7,346
United Kingdom	57,365,665	758	13,228
EEC Combined	343,425,853	4,817	14,027
Japan	123,642,641	1,800	14,563
United States	248,709,873	5,200	20,908

SOURCE: *The World Almanac, The Universal Almanac.*

develop a comprehensive economic policy to address the potential impact of such a change in Europe.

A second issue involves the impact of energy costs on the economy. The price of oil has fluctuated since 1973 (see Chapter 4) with significant economic consequences. The drop in oil prices has had a direct economic impact by exerting a downward pressure on inflation. As of 1991, oil prices remained low (in the $16 per barrel range). If OPEC member nations are able to achieve tighter control over oil production and increase the market price for oil, inflationary pressures will be exerted on the American economy.

A third issue is the budget deficit and the national debt. As annual budget deficits continue, an ever increasing percentage of federal spending will be consumed by interest payments. At some point in the future, political forces may be tempted to pay for the debt by printing more money and accepting the resultant increased inflation rates. When this strategy has been followed in other countries, annual inflation rates in excess of 100 percent have been observed.

SUMMARY

The role of the federal government in the area of economic policy has expanded significantly during the twentieth century in response to both internal and external pressures. These pressures persist and form the foundation for continued intervention in the economic arena.

The role of the government in regulating the economy is related to a number of values which have differing policy implications and divergent goals. These values include questions surrounding inflation, unemployment, level of economic growth, equality, and ideological orientation.

Obstacles exist in developing economic policy. The separation of powers at the national level, fragmentation of responsibility within the executive branch, and the division of power between state and federal government act to hinder the development of a coordinated national economic policy.

Monetary policy refers to regulating the flow of money in the economy and involves control over interest rates and the reserves that banks must maintain to cover their deposits.

Fiscal policy concerns such things as tax policies, wage and price controls, and government spending. Changes in these policies are made to combat inflation or recession. Inflation occurs when prices are increasing and the output of goods and services is not. In a recession, there is a drop in demand for goods and services, and there is little or no growth in the economy.

Supply-side economics characterized the policy of the Reagan administration. This policy was based on the premise that if taxes were reduced, the economy would be stimulated. The resulting economic expansion would provide increased tax revenues even with significantly lower tax rates. The promise of supply-side economics was never realized. Tax rates were cut but tax revenues did not increase as supply-siders had predicted. The national debt increased dramatically and now consumes 15 percent of the annual federal budget.

Attempts to reduce the federal budget deficit have been largely unsuccessful. The Gramm-Rudman mechanism to reduce the deficit proved ineffective. Budget agreements between President Bush and Congress in 1990 effectively removed the threat of sequestration until fiscal 1995. Economic and budget pressures associated with the budget deficit will drive economic policy through the 1990s.

Western Europe has a stated goal of achieving economic unity by the end of 1992. The impact of an integrated European economic system on the American economy remains an uncertainty.

Tax rates and tax reforms are popular issues for political debate. Reduction in tax revenues without similar reductions in government spending have led to record deficits, thus sparking continuing debate over appropriate government policy.

Because of the dramatic increase in the size of the federal deficit, the issue of tax policy will be on the economic agenda for the 1990s.

Debate over American industrial and trade policy, particularly with Japan, will also continue through the decade.

NOTES

1. Herbert Stein, "Should Growth Be a Priority of National Policy?" *Challenge* (March/April, 1986), 11–17. Late in 1991 the Commerce Department changed its economic measure from Gross *National* Product (GNP) to Gross *Domestic* Product (GDP). Figures in this book are given for GNP.

2. Anthony Solomon, "Economics, Ideology, and Public Policy," *Challenge* (July/August, 1986), 11–17.

3. Edward R. Tufte, *Political Control of the Economy* (Princeton, N.J.: Princeton University Press, 1978).

4. Thomas J. Cunningham, "The Long-Run Outcome of a Permanent Deficit," *Economic Review* (May, 1986), 25–33.

5. Arthur Laffer, "Supply Side Economics," *Financial Analysts Journal* (September/October, 1981).

6. Marc Levinson, "The Verdict on Deregulation," *Dun's Business Month* (November, 1986), 30–34.

7. C. Fred Bergsten, "The Second Debt Crisis Is Coming," *Challenge* (May/June, 1985), 14–21.

8. "Tax Reform—At Last," *Business Week,* September 1, 1986, 54–58.

9. Congressional Budget Office, *The Industrial Policy Debate* (Washington, D.C.: Government Printing Office, 1983).

10. John K. Galbraith, *Economics and the Public Purpose* (Boston: Houghton Mifflin, 1978).

11. Rick Tilman, "Ideology and Utopia in the Political Economy of Milton Friedman," *Polity* 8 (Spring, 1976), 422–442.

12. Aaron Wildavsky, "Budgets As Compromises Among Social Orders," in *The Federal Budget: Economics and Politics* (New Brunswick, N.J.: Transaction Books, 1982).

13. Robert Hall and Alvin Rabushka, *Low Tax, Simple Tax, Flat Tax* (New York: McGraw-Hill, 1984).

SUGGESTED READINGS

Averch, Harvey. *Private Markets and Public Intervention.* Pittsburgh: University of Pittsburgh Press, 1990.

Collender, Stanley E. *The Guide to the Federal Budget.* Washington, D.C.: Urban Institute Press, 1992.

Dolan, Edwin G., and Goodman, John C. *Economics of Public Policy.* St. Paul, Minn.: West Publishing, 1989.

Emmott, Bill. *The Sun Also Sets: The Limits to Japan's Economic Power.* New York: Times Books, 1989.

Galbraith, John K. *The New Industrial State.* 4th ed. New York: Penguin, 1978.

Gianaris, Nicholas V. *The European Community and the United States.* Westport, Conn.: Praeger, 1990.

Friedman, Benjamin. *Day of Reckoning: The Consequences of American Economic Policy.* New York: Vintage Books, 1990.

Friedman, Milton. *Capitalism and Freedom.* Chicago: University of Chicago Press, 1981.

Hartley, Keith. *The Economics of Defense Policy.* London: Brassey's, 1991.

Keynes, John M. *The Collected Writings of John Maynard Keynes.* Edited by David Laibman and Edward Nell. Cambridge: Cambridge University Press, 1973.

Kuttner, Robert. *The End of Laissez-Faire: Economics and the National Interest After the Cold War.* New York: Knopf, 1991.

Nell, Edward. *Prosperity and Public Spending.* Boston: Unwin Hyman, 1988.

Sahu, Kanandi P., and Tracy, Ronald L. *The Economic Legacy of the Reagan Years: Euphoria or Chaos?* Westport, Conn.: Praeger, 1991.

Stabile, Donald R., and Cantor, Jeffrey A. *The Public Debt of the United States: An Historical Perspective, 1775–1990.* Westport, Conn.: Praeger, 1991.

Thurow, Lester. *The Zero-Sum Society: Distribution and the Possibilities for Economic Change.* New York: Penguin, 1981.

Wildavsky, Aaron. *The New Politics of the Budgetary Process.* 2d ed. New York: Harper Collins, 1992.

CHAPTER 4

Energy and Environmental Policies: Conflicting Values and Policy Options

Concern with the development of a national energy policy and with environmental-protection strategies were not major public policy issues in the United States until the latter half of this century. Access to a seemingly unlimited supply of energy facilitated America's emergence as the economic, political, and military leader of the Western world. This abundant supply of cheap energy acted to minimize public concern over energy policy. In large part, the economic prosperity of the United States can be attributed to the availability of an abundance of inexpensive energy combined with the absence of policies designed to prevent environmental despoilation. At least until the end of the nineteenth century, the dominant attitude was that with such vast natural resources available to the nation, regulatory and protective environmental policies were unnecessary.

ENERGY POLICY ISSUE BACKGROUND: COMPLACENCY AND CRISIS

Prior to 1973, most Americans were unconcerned with either energy consumption patterns or energy policy. That year proved to be a watershed in U.S. energy history, however, as the first Arab oil embargo triggered what would become a new era in the nation's public policy on energy resources. As a consequence, energy policy in the United States can be divided into two periods, with the 1973 Arab oil embargo serving as a line of demarcation. The period before 1973 can be called the traditional period, and the years following the embargo, the period of crisis, uncertainty, and complacency.

Traditional Energy Policy

As the United States entered the decade of the 1970s, the prospect of an energy shortage seemed remote. Gasoline regularly sold at less than 35 cents a gallon, natural gas was abundant and, along with fuel oil, was rapidly replacing coal as a source of industrial energy. Nuclear power plants were being licensed and built to provide an unlimited supply of electricity. The energy future of the United States seemed bright.

Energy policy in the United States mirrored this rosy picture in a confident manner. Prior to 1973, energy policy was premised on the conviction that an unlimited supply of inexpensive energy could be produced by the private sector. Indeed, the nation did benefit from an abundance of fossil fuels: coal, oil, and natural gas, all provided by private-sector initiative. To the extent that government regulations did exist, they were designed not to promote conservation but to maintain a stable price to protect the economic security of the energy producers. Therefore U.S. energy policy was unprepared for the 1970s, when world events would threaten the nation's energy supply and thrust the politics of energy into public consciousness. Energy policy prior to 1973 consisted of a patchwork of state and federal actions designed to encourage consumption as opposed to an emphasis on efficiency and national sufficiency in energy production.

Coal. The primary source of energy in the United States until the late 1920s was coal. Most of the regulation of the coal industry involved labor-management relations. The abundant coal supply acted to depress prices, which mandated low wages for miners. Only when supply was controlled could the market price rise to allow wage increases in the coal fields.

A major force shaping policy in the coal industry was the United Mine Workers (UMW). The UMW struggled to achieve government controls on the price and production levels of coal in order to achieve adequate wages. By the early 1920s, a combination of federal and state policies did act to protect the coal industry from oversupply and unlimited competition and to achieve a degree of wage stability as the use of coal hit its high point. But the mid-1920s marked a shift from coal to oil as the fuel of choice for homes and industry. As the demand for coal leveled off and decreased, the industry began a long and gradual slide into depression, taking the union with it. This decline lasted for decades, and most of the activity in energy policy prior to 1973 focused on UMW efforts to limit production and elevate wages in the face of decreasing demand. Only when coal production was limited by government, industry, or union action could the market price rise to provide both profits to the owners and an adequate wage to the miners.

Oil. In the United States, oil has had a long history of government regulation. Basic to oil policy was the element of government protection for the industry. Much of the early regulation involved attempts by the states and the federal government to limit production and create a balance between supply and demand. Production limits were set by state agencies for producers; oil-rich states made mutual agreements concerning production and distribution of their lucrative resource; and federal controls were erected on the interstate transportation of oil.

The protective nature of these policies is best exemplified by the adoption of the oil depletion allowance by the federal government in 1926. The U.S. Geological Survey (USGS) predicted at the end of World War I that the nation's known oil reserves would be depleted within ten years. Proponents of this tax break for the oil industry argued that just as machinery wore out and buildings deteriorated, oil wells also lost their value over time as the underground reservoir emptied. Congress and the president responded favorably, passing a law that allowed an oil company to deduct 27.5 percent of its gross income from its taxable income, provided that the total amount deducted did not exceed 50 percent of the company's net income. The prediction by the USGS proved inaccurate as oil exploration efforts led to the addition of vast reserves in Oklahoma and East Texas by the 1930s. The industry has continued to argue successfully that the oil depletion allowance should be retained because it protects the producer's profit margin, which, they claim, encourages continued exploration across the United States and around the world as the tax savings are plowed back into new oil-drilling expeditions.

Natural gas.   Natural gas has a similar long history of regulation. It was typical for natural gas to be discovered along with a reservoir of oil and for both fuels to be pumped from the same well. As an odorless, invisible, poisonous, and explosive substance, it created problems for the early oil companies and was typically piped a short distance from the well and burned. It was not until the 1920s that welding technology was sufficiently developed to allow the construction of long-distance, high-pressure pipelines to transport the gas to a ready market.

Natural gas production is not labor-intensive, because very little refining is needed to prepare it for commercial use. The bulk of labor is involved in building and maintaining pipelines. Natural gas production involves three major activities: production in the field, distribution through pipelines, and a specialized distribution network to consumers at the end of the pipeline.

Regulation of natural gas was divided between the federal government and the states, with the federal government regulating interstate transportation (pipelines) and state government regulation focusing on production and final consumption. Under the provisions of the 1938 Natural Gas Act, regulatory authority at the federal level was assigned to the Federal Power Commission (FPC). The FPC was charged with regulating the price of natural gas in the interstate market and with approving pipeline construction and deactivation. The intent of these regulatory powers was to maintain a supply of low-cost energy for the consumer.

This regulatory power of the FPC was marked by conflict. The extent of FPC power was not fully defined until 1947, when the Supreme Court ruled that the FPC had regulatory control over both production and interstate distribution of natural gas. This regulatory power was not exercised because a majority of the members of the commission felt that extensive regulation of the industry was inappropriate government policy. Even though later court cases in the 1950s and 1960s mandated an active role for the FPC, regulation was slow and incomplete.

FPC regulation tended to maintain low rates for natural gas consumers. The interstate rates for natural gas were often one-fourth to one-fifth of the unregulated intrastate rates. Gas selling for $2.50 per thousand cubic feet in the intrastate market could be sold for only $1.00 in the interstate market. An unintended consequence was wasted energy; the artificially low price did not encourage consumer efficiency. This low market price also acted to discourage exploration to meet increased demand, as it offered little profit. Therefore production of natural gas could not keep pace with demand.

Nuclear power.   During the 1950s and 1960s, nuclear power was viewed as a potential major source of energy for both the United States and Western Europe. The Atomic Energy Commission (AEC) was established to promote and control the development of this new source of power, with development of nuclear reactors for commercial generation of electricity assigned to the private sector. The dual role of advocate and regulator of nuclear power ultimately produced policy conflicts for the AEC.

Western Vulnerability: OPEC and the Arab Oil Embargo

Not only was America comfortable at home with what it believed to be a nearly inexhaustible supply of energy; it also had access to—and often control over—foreign energy resources. The most important of these were the oil fields of the Middle East and North Africa. Prior to the 1973 Arab oil embargo, the oil-producing countries were not in control of the oil industry within their own borders. Instead, major American and European oil companies were able to exercise nearly complete control over the production of oil, its selling price, and the meager share of profits with which they chose to reward a host nation's compliance.

The power of Western oil companies.   How did Western private enterprise consolidate this near stranglehold on the oil resources of the nations that were to comprise the Organization of Petroleum Exporting Countries (OPEC)? As the oil industry developed in the 1930s, seven major companies dominated oil production and distribution: Standard Oil of California (Chevron), the Texas Company (Texaco), Socony-Vacuum (now Mobil), Gulf Oil, Standard Oil of New Jersey (Exxon), Royal Dutch Shell, and British Petroleum. These industry giants often found cooperative arrangements in their best interests in oil exploration efforts in the Middle East. The result was a reduction in competition in the international oil market. This competition was further reduced when the Arabian American Oil Company (Aramco) was organized by four companies (Standard Oil of New Jersey, Standard Oil of California, Socony-Vacuum, and Texaco) in 1947 to exploit the enormous resources of Saudi Arabia. This and other cooperative efforts were so successful that by 1952, the seven oil giants exercised control over 90 percent of the total crude oil production outside North America and the communist nations.

This control was so effective that the companies were able to resist governmental actions taken by producing nations. When Iran attempted to nationalize the Anglo-Iranian Oil Company from 1951 to 1953, the combined resistance of the major companies eliminated the market for Iranian crude oil. Production was simply increased in the fields of other countries to offset the boycott of Iranian oil. A similar situation occurred when Iraq nationalized its oil fields in 1961.[1]

The origins of OPEC.   It was in this climate of exploitation that the Third World oil-producing states first banded together in one organization with the aim of achieving equitable price and production levels for its members. OPEC was created in 1960 with the membership of seven Arab nations—Algeria, Iraq, Kuwait, Libya, Qatar, Saudi Arabia, and the United Arab Emirates—and six non-Arab nations—Equador, Gabon, Indonesia, Iran, Nigeria, and Venezuela. Several factors acted to undermine the strength of the organization in the 1960s. First, the United States was nearly self-sufficient in the production of oil with relatively little need for imported oil. Second, the cooperative agreements among the major oil companies created an international oil cartel with near-monopolistic powers. Belligerent actions by a producing nation could, as in the case of Iran and Iraq, be met with a boycott of that nation's crude oil. Third, the production of crude oil exceeded international demand, which produced a buyer's market and constrained the power of suppliers. High production levels and the assumption that international oil reserves were infinite acted to keep the price of oil depressed. The low price of oil prevented producing nations from generating sufficient oil tax revenues for economic development and from exercising political and economic power in the international oil market. Only by acting in concert could the producing nations achieve a measure of control over the production and price of their oil reserves.

The 1973 Arab oil embargo.   October 6, 1973, marked the opening date of the Yom Kippur War between Israel and the Arab states. This event provided the catalyst for Arab unity and demonstrated the power of collective action available to OPEC members.[2] On October 17, the Arab oil ministers met in Kuwait and resolved to use oil as a weapon in the struggle with Israel. Accordingly, a 5 percent monthly reduction in exports would be imposed on nations supporting Israel. Consumer nations supporting the Arab cause would not be at risk of an oil embargo. The embargo had limited impact on oil imports by the United States as non-Arab sources, primarily Venezuela and Iran, were readily available. The embargo against the United States was lifted in March, 1974, following the January Egyptian-Israeli cease-fire. Yet the embargo did achieve some of its original political objectives, as support for Israel in Western Europe and Japan was softened. The real value of the 1973 Arab oil embargo was the dramatic example of power through unified policy that it gave to OPEC nations. OPEC ministers realized that if action were taken in concert by all thirteen member states, their demands would be impossible to resist. This period marked the beginning of a rapid escalation in the price for OPEC oil and of systematic controls on production levels. Figure 4-1 shows the price paid for light crude oil between 1965 and 1992.

The swift jump in oil prices depicted in Figure 4-1 coincides with the 1973 embargo. Within its first three months, the price of Arabian oil had increased dramatically from $3.00 per barrel to $11.65 per barrel. This does not mean that the Arab-Israeli conflict directly caused the oil price rise; rather, it was the mechanism that graphically demonstrated the power of collective action. The actual factors that pushed prices up were primarily economic. Oil-exporting nations began to recognize that their oil reserves were finite and that the historic price for oil was artificially low. The industrialized nations were gaining economic benefits from cheap energy at the expense of the oil-producing nations.

The price increase for oil was therefore in part a product of economic pressures in the marketplace. Moreover, as the cost of oil increased, inflationary pressure was exerted on the economies of the oil-consuming West. This inflation led to higher prices for goods consumed by OPEC nations as well as a reduction in

FIGURE 4-1 ▪ Cost of Arabian Light Crude Oil, 1965–1992

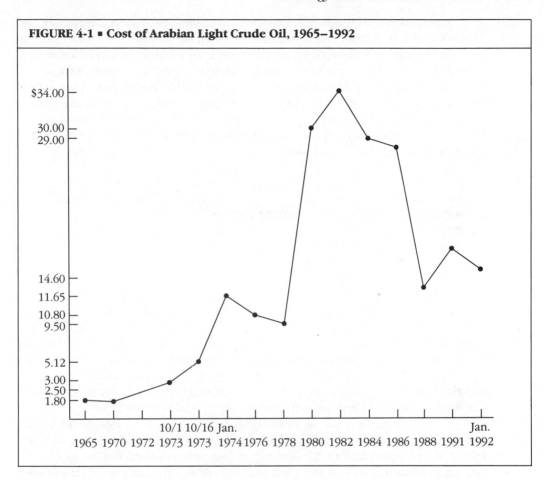

the purchasing power of Western currency, especially the American dollar, paid to OPEC nations. Inflationary pressures and a need by OPEC nations to generate revenues to fund economic development acted to fuel an upward spiral in oil prices. During the late 1970s, OPEC was unable to agree on a fixed price for oil, so a price increase by one nation stimulated similar increases by other producers as well.[3] The reality of oil selling at $50 or even $100 per barrel seemed imminent. It was not until 1982–84 that a combination of forces, including a reduction in demand, discovery of reserves outside OPEC, overproduction, and OPEC disunity, brought about a drop in global crude oil prices through 1988.

The price of oil is vulnerable even to seemingly minor interruptions in supply. During the spring of 1989, two events increased the price of crude oil by several dollars to approximately $21 per barrel. The tanker Exxon Valdez ran aground in Prince William Sound, Alaska, resulting in a temporary closing of the port to oil shipments. In the North Sea a major oil producing platform was severely damaged by fire, which interrupted the flow of oil from that field.

The Persian Gulf war of 1991 also caused a brief upswing in the price of oil. Oil production in Kuwait was reduced to zero during the war and a strict United Nations embargo was placed on Iraqi oil exports. This loss was offset by increased production levels from other oil exporting nations, particularly Saudi Arabia.

These events represented only short-term supply interruptions but had a significant impact on the price of oil-based energy. Gasoline prices in the United States temporarily increased by 10 to 20 cents per gallon. The consequences of a longer-term supply interruption would dramatically increase the price of oil, possibly to the $30 per barrel range.

CONTEMPORARY POLICY: FROM CRISIS TO COMPLACENCY

Energy Problems Emerge

The Arab oil embargo coincided with the end of American energy self-sufficiency. Prior to World War II, the United States was an exporter of oil, but by 1947, the nation was forced to import oil for domestic use. The amount was minimal—less than one-half of 1 percent of total oil consumption—but it would grow. By the mid-1950s, foreign imports accounted for 10 percent of America's oil consumption in part because of the lower cost of imported oil, typically about half that of domestic oil. Thus a refinery on the Eastern seaboard would pay $3.00 for American oil but could obtain imported oil of the same quality for $1.50.[4]

In order to protect the domestic oil industry from cheap foreign oil, President Eisenhower first recommended in 1954, and then imposed, in 1959, an import quota equivalent to 12 percent of domestic production. The quota remained in effect throughout the 1960s. Oil consumption increased at a faster rate than domestic supply. By 1973, American oil consumption reached nearly 17 million barrels per day, while domestic production levels were slightly less than 11 million barrels per day. This gap between supply and demand prompted President Nixon to remove all import quotas on oil in the spring of 1973, which allowed imported oil to rise and reach the current figure of almost 42 percent of total American oil consumption (see Figure 4-2).

Natural gas is the cleanest-burning of the fossil fuels but is not as abundant as domestic oil. Domestic natural gas production reached a peak of 24.7 trillion cubic feet in 1975 and then began a gradual decline. Currently, annual consumption levels are exceeding additions to known reserves. In order to meet demand, it is necessary to import increasing amounts of natural gas. *Nuclear power* appeared to be a potential source of unlimited energy, but this potential has not been achieved because of problems with the safety of the technology. The major accident in 1979 at the Three Mile Island nuclear plant in Pennsylvania and less serious incidents at other nuclear-power facilities acted to shift American policy priorities away from this energy option in the eighties. The abundance of *coal* affords a potential energy option, but serious environmental problems exist with this energy source. Gases

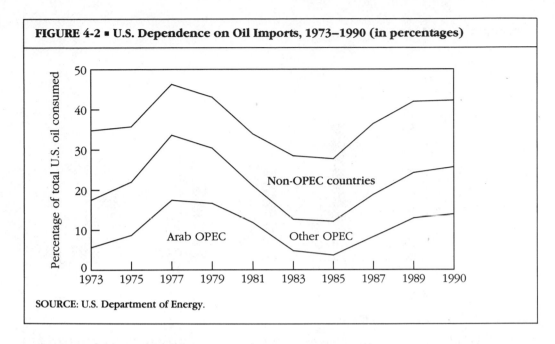

FIGURE 4-2 ▪ U.S. Dependence on Oil Imports, 1973–1990 (in percentages)

SOURCE: U.S. Department of Energy.

produced when coal is burned contribute to the phenomenon of acid rain, and mining activities necessary to produce sufficient quantities of coal have negative impacts on the physical environment. Reliance on coal as a primary energy source acts to degrade environmental quality. *Other sources* of renewable energy such as solar power, wind power, and geothermal technologies have yet to be developed sufficiently to take up the slack left by the depletion of oil and natural gas. The United States continues to depend on fossil fuels as the primary source of energy. This reality has resulted in a continued reliance on oil imports.

Global Dependence on Fossil Fuels

Dependence on oil as the primary energy source continues to be a worldwide trend. Figure 4-3 reflects the shift from coal to oil and the increasing importance of oil and natural gas as energy sources. From 1950 to 1990, the proportion of energy provided by these two sources increased from 36.6 percent to 60.1 percent of total global energy consumption. When energy consumption is examined on a regional basis, the increased importance of oil and natural gas to the industrialized world becomes even more evident. Between 1950 and the mid-1980s, coal had declined as a primary source of fuel in Western Europe from slightly over 85 percent to less than 25 percent of total energy consumption. The same pattern holds true for Japan, as reliance on coal dropped from over 86 percent to less than 20 percent of total energy consumption. Oil and natural gas are now the world's primary energy sources, except in Eastern Europe and Communist Asia, where coal remains the primary energy source even though oil and natural gas are becoming increasingly important as fuels.

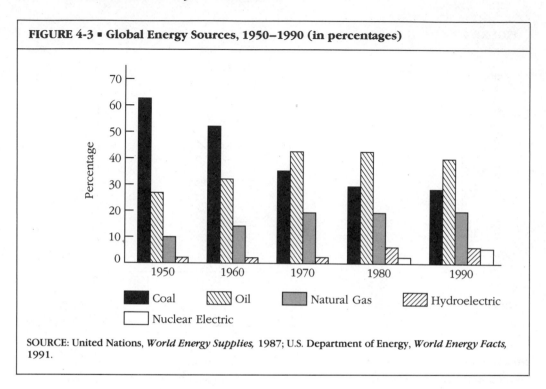

FIGURE 4-3 ▪ Global Energy Sources, 1950–1990 (in percentages)

SOURCE: United Nations, *World Energy Supplies,* 1987; U.S. Department of Energy, *World Energy Facts,* 1991.

Dependence on imported oil is especially significant for the industrialized democracies of the free world.[5] As of 1990, the United States imported 41.9 percent of its oil from foreign sources. The figure is substantially higher for Europe and Japan, with oil imports accounting for 74 percent of European oil consumption and 99 percent of Japanese oil consumption. An important source of oil for Western Europe and Japan is the Middle East and North Africa. Approximately 59 percent of the oil that Japan imports originates in the Islamic world, a drop from the 80 percent range of the late 1970s. The United States has established a pattern since the mid-1970s of obtaining approximately 15 percent of its imports from Islamic nations. This means that the West's economic stability is tied to the uninterrupted flow of oil from the Islamic world and therefore to political stability in the Middle East.

Energy Policy After 1973

The disruption of oil supply and the economic consequences of the rapid increase in the cost of oil created by the imposition of the oil embargo in 1973 created an environment in which the role of the federal government in energy policy expanded.[6] This increased federal role was a foundation of "Project Independence" (billed as the path to American energy self-sufficiency by 1980) as announced by President Nixon on November 7, 1973. The basic elements of the Nixon proposal were (1) imposition of a national speed limit; (2) adoption of daylight-saving time on a year-round basis; (3) increased federal funding for energy research and development; (4) standby authority for gasoline rationing; (5) relaxation of environmental standards to increase the use of coal; (6) deregulation of natural gas; (7) construction of the trans-Alaska pipeline; and (8) the creation of a federal Department of Energy.

Political and technological constraints made self-sufficiency by 1980 an unrealistic goal. By 1974, complete energy independence was replaced by the goal of independence from uncertain foreign oil sources with 1985 as the new target date. With the lifting of the Arab oil embargo in the summer of 1974, the crisis atmosphere surrounding energy began to evaporate. Energy policy floundered as debate over the direction it should take continued and agreement on a unified energy policy proved elusive.

The federal government did take a number of significant actions. Congress acted to authorize construction of the trans-Alaska pipeline over objections of environmental groups. The fifty-five-mile-per-hour speed limit was adopted by Congress in December, 1974. Two new governmental agencies were created in 1974, the Federal Energy Administration (FEA) and the Energy Research and Development Administration (ERDA). These agencies were charged with developing and coordinating new federal energy policies. This increased federal role peaked with the creation of the Department of Energy in 1977 under the Carter administration.

Legislation.   The *National Energy Act of 1978,* enacted five years after the Arab oil embargo in response to President Carter's extensive energy proposals, provided a framework for the future direction of energy policy. The act sought to encourage increased energy efficiency, reduce consumption, and change energy use patterns. First, *natural gas* was deregulated over a three-year period as federal price controls were ended in an effort to encourage increased exploration. Second, the act contained provisions aimed at reducing consumption of oil and natural gas to encourage conversion to *coal* as a major fuel source in generating electricity. Third, the act mandated changes in *utility rate* structures to represent the real cost of supplying electric service to customers. "Declining block rates," in which the unit cost of electricity decreased as the level of consumption increased, could be retained only if the reduced rate actually represented the costs of providing the electricity. These increases in the cost of electricity were designed to reduce oil and natural gas consumption by reducing the demand for electric power produced through the burning of both fuels.

Finally, the act relied on *taxes* and *tax credits* to encourage a reduction in energy consumption and development of "renewable," nonfossil energy sources. Homeowners were given an income tax credit for a percentage of the expenses spent on insulation or other energy-conserving improvements. The tax credit also applied to the installation of solar, wind, or geothermal energy equipment in homes. An important provision of the act included a tax, to be paid by the manufacturer, on "gas-guzzling" cars. The tax initially ranged from $200 to $500 for the 1980 model year and would gradually increase to a range of $500 to $3850 by the 1986 model year. The Corporate Average Fuel Economy (CAFE) standard required that the automobile industry produce a mix of cars with an average fuel efficiency of 27.5 miles per gallon by 1985. The tax and CAFE standard did contribute to a change in the size and fuel efficiency of automobiles, which reduced oil consumption by American drivers. Only Chrysler Corporation was able to achieve total compliance with the new standards. When faced with the prospect of imposing severe tax penalties on General Motors in 1986 (the fleet of GM cars could not meet the new standards), Congress balked and the CAFE standard was reduced to 26.0 mpg for the 1986 model year. The auto manufacturer was given more time to achieve compliance in order to protect the jobs of GM workers. Neither Ford nor General Motors could reach the 27.5-mpg fleet standard for the 1989 model year. In October, 1988, the Department of Transportation adjusted the CAFE standard to 26.5 mpg. Both General Motors and Ford were able to comply with this reduced efficiency standard.

The National Energy Act of 1978 did have an impact on energy consumption patterns, but it clearly did not move the nation toward the long-range goal of U.S. energy self-sufficiency. The act encouraged increased efficiency and conservation but did not contain provisions to develop major alternative energy sources. Therefore American dependence on foreign oil supplies continues.

Decontrol and the windfall profits tax. Federal regulation of domestic oil prices began under the Nixon administration in 1971 as one mechanism to control inflation. As American consumption of oil continued to increase in the 1970s, proponents of decontrol argued that the removal of price controls would reduce oil consumption by up to 100 million barrels of oil per year, because the price rise would stimulate consumer conservation. A second impact would be the stimulation of domestic production as increased profits encouraged additional exploration efforts. Critics of decontrol argued that, although consumption might be reduced and domestic production increased, significant social and economic problems would also emerge because the poor and elderly would face additional financial burdens during winter months and because increased energy costs would add inflationary pressure to the economy.

Under the provisions of the Energy Policy and Conservation Act of 1975, President Carter announced on April 5, 1979, that all price controls on domestic oil would be eliminated by 1981. In order to reduce the opposition to decontrol, the president proposed a "windfall profits" tax that would reduce the increased oil company profits. The Crude Oil Windfall Profit Tax Act, passed on April 2, 1980, stipulated that a tax rate in the 30 percent range (with a host of exemptions) would be levied until $227 billion in revenues were reached, with the tax being phased out between 1990 and 1993. The revenues would go toward (among other things) helping the poor and elderly cope with energy costs.

Energy policy moved in two conflicting directions. Decontrol was designed to provide economic incentives to spur domestic production and exploration. At the same time, taxes were imposed to reduce the magnitude of the economic incentives provided by decontrol. Following decontrol there was a huge increase, followed by a decline, in the level of oil and gas exploration in the United States (see Table 4-1).

Energy Policy after 1980

The basic assumptions guiding energy policy changed dramatically following the 1980 election. President Carter, acting on the assumption that global and domestic energy supplies were dwindling, sought to reduce consumption by emphasizing energy conservation. President Reagan firmly rejected the concept of dwindling energy supplies, arguing that the United States had massive undiscovered oil and gas reserves and that energy policy of the 1970s had discouraged domestic explo- ration and production. Reagan's energy policy sought to emphasize private sector responsibility and to reduce the role of government in energy policy.

Reagan advocated a range of energy policies designed to stimulate market forces and increase energy supplies. His policies emphasized the decontrol of oil, opposition to the windfall profits tax, and increased offshore exploration for oil and gas. His administration favored opening federal lands to oil and gas explora- tion, opposed government mandates designed to achieve a shift from oil to coal in American industry, and opposed strict environmental standards that restricted exploration activities.

Reagan policy values.   The energy policy of President Reagan reflected three values. First, the United States has an abundance of energy supplies.[7] This resulted in the rejection of energy conservation and regulation strategies. Policy efforts were directed toward increasing production and consumption.

Second, the emphasis on clean energy was rejected by the Reagan adminis- tration as a policy value. According to Reagan, the environment should not take precedence over energy policy, and environmental standards for clean air and

TABLE 4-1 ▪ **U.S. Domestic Oil and Gas Exploration**

	Number of Wells Drilled		
	OIL	NATURAL GAS	DRY HOLES
1975	16,276	7,654	10,786
1980	28,553	15,225	18,233
1982	35,865	17,052	23,735
1984	38,976	14,893	23,251
1985	34,570	14,100	20,510
1986	18,290	7,840	12,140
1987	15,820	7,520	10,820
1990	11,340	10,130	7,760

SOURCE: *Statistical Abstract of the United States 1988* (Washington, D.C.: U.S. Department of Commerce, 1987); *Monthly Energy Review* (Washington, D.C.: U.S. Energy Department, 1991).

water should be relaxed. The operation of the market economy would create optimal environmental standards with a balance between energy for growth and a clean environment.

Third, a secure energy supply for the United States could best be achieved by market operations, not by government action. Import quotas, conservation measures, and allocations systems were inappropriate and counterproductive. The private sector could rise to the occasion and provide a secure energy supply for the future needs of the United States.

Energy policy in the 1990s.   These values resulted in a significant change of direction in energy policy. *Solar energy* developmental support was cut by 70 percent by 1982 and continues to be de-emphasized as an area of federal funding for research and development. *Conservation programs* have been reduced due to the conviction of Presidents Reagan and Bush that market forces are the most appropriate means of regulating energy consumption. The one link to the past is a continued emphasis on *nuclear energy* in the form of federal research and development funding. Federal support for research and development of *synthetic fuels* has been curtailed in favor of private investments (which have not been forthcoming). Although efforts by President Reagan to abolish the Energy Department were unsuccessful, the department was assigned a reduced role in *oil and gas* regulation, distribution, and production.

There exists significant conflict over American energy policy directions, and attempts in 1991 to enact energy policy legislation were not successful. Since 1980, energy policy has generally sought to reduce the role of government and rely on incentives to the private sector through the operation of market forces. It should be noted that the United States has never followed a program of unrestricted competition in energy policy. Regulations were imposed by the federal government and the state governments only after industry demanded protection from unlimited competition—that is, from threats to their continuing profits. The cries for deregulation today are not motivated only by an ideological commitment to the free-enterprise system, but also by a desire to shift the costs to consumers as a vehicle for maintaining industry profits.[8]

POLICY EVALUATION: CONTINUED FOSSIL FUEL DEPENDENCE

Because of the higher prices and the emphasis on energy conservation during the late 1970s, there has been a significant change in energy consumption levels and patterns in the United States. Figure 4-4 and Table 4-2 summarize some of these changes.

Evaluating the actual impact of energy policy in the United States from 1973 to 1990 raises a number of questions. It is clear that the level of energy consumption has dropped significantly. Oil and natural gas consumption have decreased, balanced by a rise in the use of coal, nuclear, and hydroelectric power. Some

FIGURE 4-4 ▪ U.S. Energy Consumption by Source, 1973–1990 (as a percentage of consumption)

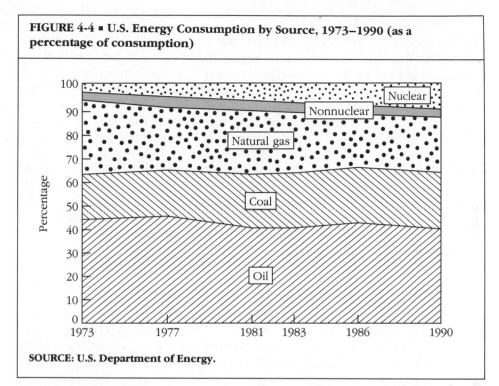

SOURCE: U.S. Department of Energy.

analysts argue that changing consumption patterns have been the result of economic conditions, not energy policy or technological changes in energy. In fact, both economic stagnation and restructuring have indeed occurred in the United States during the past two decades. As the decade of the 1990s unfolds it will be possible to evaluate the long-term impact of the shifts in energy policy decisions.

TABLE 4-2 ▪ U.S. Domestic Energy Production, 1980–1990

	1980	*1990*	*% Change*
Coal[a]	830	1,029	+19.3
Oil[b]	10,214	8,925	−14.4
Natural gas[c]	20,180	17,609	−14.6
Hydroelectric[d]	2,021	2,231	+9.4
Nuclear electric[d]	265	576	+53.9

[a] millions of metric tons
[b] thousands of barrels per day
[c] trillions of cubic feet
[d] billions of kilowatt hours

SOURCE: *Statistical Abstract of the United States, 1988* (Washington, D.C.: U.S. Government Printing Office, 1987); *Energy Review,* 1991 (Dept. of Energy).

Alternatives to Fossil Fuels

The energy crisis of the 1970s increased the political popularity of alternative sources of energy such as solar, wind, and geothermal power. Before the rapid rise in the cost of fossil fuels, these alternatives were too expensive to be utilized as major energy sources, and that fact largely explained why there was little investment in development of the relevant technology. With the drop in the price of oil to less than $17 per barrel by 1992, the economic incentives for continued research and development of alternative energy sources were again minimal.

Solar energy.   An element of President Carter's energy programs was the proposed national goal that by the year 2000, the United States should meet 20 percent of its energy need by solar power. This goal was not adopted, and solar power has experienced relatively little development in the United States. The major piece of legislation so far has been the Solar Heating and Cooling Demonstration Act of 1975. This act created a limited solar demonstration program and clearinghouse. To date, the president, the Congress, and private-sector energy companies have not yet established solar power as a major source of energy in the near future.

Coal liquefaction.   The liquefaction of coal into a crude-oil substitute provides the ability to convert coal into a clean-burning fuel. This technology was developed in Germany before World War I and was the source of 90 percent of the aviation fuel used by the German air force in World War II. Currently, South Africa is the only nation with a commercial coal-liquefaction plant in operation. Authority for federal funding for research and development of this technology was provided by the 1980 Energy Security Act, which created the Synthetic Fuels Corporation. The drop in the market price of crude oil that began in 1986, combined with an abundant global oil supply, has limited the economic viability of coal liquefaction. Owing to the shift in emphasis to private-sector responsibility, this energy source remains undeveloped.

Geothermal energy.   Tapping the heat deep within the earth to convert water to steam produces electricity and geothermal energy. The Reagan administration was reluctant to fund research and development for geothermal energy, and this source remains undeveloped.

Nuclear Power

The growth of the nuclear energy industry and the emphasis on nuclear technology as a source of energy were the products of the government's desire to use nuclear energy for peacetime purposes. There are two different nuclear processes, fission and fusion. Fission is splitting atoms; fusion produces energy by fusing atoms. To date, fusion technology is still in the early stages of development.

Nuclear-fission technologies grew out of the nuclear submarine program of the U.S. Navy, in which light-water reactors (LWR) use uranium 235, a relatively scarce substance, to produce heat for steam generation of electricity. Fusion technologies use the more abundant uranium 238, converting it into plutonium 239. A prototype liquid-metal, fast-breeder reactor (LMFBR) of this type was under development at Clinch River, Tennessee, but the project, mired in conflict over questions of cost and safety, was terminated.

The nuclear energy option remains questionable because it has yet to overcome three problems: safety, waste disposal, and decommissioning strategies. Initial research indicated that *nuclear safety* would not be a problem. The 1975 Rasmussen Report issued by the Nuclear Regulatory Commission (NRC) concluded that nuclear accidents would probably never occur and provided a foundation for continued nuclear expansion. But the March, 1979, accident at Three Mile Island in Pennsylvania dramatically demonstrated the inaccuracy of the Rasmussen Report. This was followed by the 1981 discovery that the earthquake protection system at the Diablo Canyon, California, nuclear power plant was installed backwards. Nuclear safety has not been guaranteed and remains a major technological problem.

Safety.   The issue of nuclear safety continues to have significant impact on energy policy in the United States. Flaws in construction have plagued the nuclear industry. Adequate training and supervision of plant personnel remains a major issue for the industry. Adequate planning in the event of a major accident has also been difficult to achieve, as indicated by the difficulties of operators of the Seabrook nuclear plant in New England to gain approval for emergency evacuation plans.

A major indication of the potential problem with nuclear safety is illustrated by the experience of the Department of Energy (DOE) with nuclear reactors utilized by the Department of Defense to produce material for the nation's atomic arsenal. Most of these facilities were constructed in the late 1940s and the 1950s and are approaching the end of their useful life. Construction standards in place at the time were less stringent than those of today. In late 1988, it was revealed that these nuclear facilities were responsible for significant environmental contamination and had major safety defects. Cracks were found in reactor vessels, deficiencies were identified in emergency cooling systems, fire-protection systems were found to be defective, obsolete and deteriorated equipment was often used, and routine maintenance had not been performed. In response to these and other difficulties, the Energy Department acted in the late 1980s temporarily to close the facilities at Savannah River, South Carolina; Hanford, Washington; Mound, Ohio; and Rocky Flats, Colorado.

Waste.   *Nuclear waste* disposal has also proved to be a problem without a solution. Initially, it was assumed that the spent fuel could be reprocessed into new fuel. This technology did not develop. Given the failure of the reprocessing option, the problem of long-term disposal of nuclear wastes remains unsolved.

Nuclear waste production is not expected to reach the levels projected during the 1970s. This is primarily because utility companies have not ordered any new reactors for over ten years. While the volume of waste generated has not reached projected levels, the costs associated with nuclear waste management have skyrocketed dramatically. In 1983, DOE estimates for nuclear waste management were $23 billion. By 1988, this had been revised to almost $40 billion. It is safe to assume that these costs will continue to escalate given the technological difficulties of managing nuclear waste.

Another difficulty with nuclear waste management involves the identification of old, inactive sites that pose a threat to health and the environment. As of 1987, some 982 inactive waste sites had been identified, and DOE officials expect to identify over 800 more abandoned sites as the process continues. The majority of these sites do not provide adequate containment of the radioactive waste, and the costs associated with providing adequate storage cannot be accurately estimated until each site is thoroughly and systematically evaluated.

Nuclear plant age and decommissioning.   The nation's nuclear generating plants operate under forty-year licenses issued by the NRC. These licenses will begin to expire in the year 2000 for the oldest plants, and by 2020 the licenses of over half of the current 111 nuclear power plants will expire. The potential loss of these plants represents a serious energy problem since they generate 20 percent of the nation's electricity. One potential solution is to extend their operating license by an additional ten to twenty years. Current estimates indicate that operating license extensions may be sought for eighty nuclear power plants during the 1990s.

License extensions are a source of intense controversy. Opponents argue that it is unwise to extend the operating life of nuclear plants to fifty to sixty years when they were designed and manufactured for a forty-year life cycle. Neither the NRC nor the nuclear industry has data on the structural integrity of materials in a reactor that have been continuously exposed to radiation. Supporters argue that with proper maintenance and repairs the life cycle can easily be extended. As of 1991, the NRC was considering extending the operating license for two plants, one in Minnesota and one in Massachusetts.

Decommissioning a nuclear power plant means shutting down and deactivating the plant to the extent that the site poses no environmental threat. To date, the NRC has not specified the guidelines and standards that will apply to future decommissioning activity. There are three options: dismantlement, mothballing, and entombment. Dismantlement presents problems of storage, because the fuel rods, containment buildings, and the reactor vessel will be radioactive for several thousand years. Some estimates indicate that up to eight hundred tons of radioactive material will require permanent storage from each nuclear unit dismantled.

Mothballing simply means locking the facility behind a security perimeter and waiting several thousand years until the radioactive material decays on its own. This approach has been entitled SAFSTOR, or safe storage, by the NRC. Entombment takes mothballing a step further by constructing a large concrete structure around the facility. Both options present problems of protecting people and the environment from dangerous material for up to eighty thousand years.

The actual costs for decommissioning a nuclear power plant are subject to debate. In 1978, the NRC estimated that costs would range between $43 million and $58 million, but the Rand Corporation published information that these costs might be in the $500 million range. The actual costs to achieve a partial decommission at Three Mile Island have exceeded $1 billion.

By 1987, the NRC had increased its estimates to between $100 and $135 million to decommission a 1,100-megawatt reactor. Costs to decommission the small 72-megawatt Shippingport, Pennsylvania, reactor have approached $100 million and will not be fully known until the process is completed. Most experts agree that the NRC estimates are excessively low.

The uncertainty is high because no major nuclear power plant of commercial size has been decommissioned in the United States, so the technology and the actual methods to be used have yet to be tested. Decommissioning nuclear reactors in submarines remains a problem for the U.S. Navy, as well. The Navy was unsuccessful in its proposal to tow obsolete nuclear submarines to isolated areas and sink them in the ocean.

A policy to apportion the costs of decommissioning a nuclear power plant has yet to be developed. Some early plans call for the states to be involved and the federal government to assume all costs. The financial liability of the utility company that constructed and operated the plant has yet to be determined, and the impact on consumers served by utility companies operating nuclear power plants also is not known.

An unresolved policy issue is how to keep future generations informed (for 10 to 80 thousand years) concerning the location and lethal nature of radioactive wastes. If such a mechanism had been in place since 1940, policymakers would know the location, nature, and the threat posed by nuclear wastes to the public and the environment today. No mechanism has been developed for either short-term (50–100 years) or long-term (thousands of years) transmittal of knowledge. Policy adopted by the Department of Energy in 1980 states, "Although this generation bears the responsibility for protecting future societies from the waste it creates, future societies must assume the responsibility for any risks which arise from deliberate and informed acts which they choose to perform."

The future.   The United States is moving away from nuclear technology as an energy option. Power plant construction has slowed, projects have been canceled, and the licensing procedure has been stiffened. Since 1978, no new orders for nuclear power plant construction have been placed by the utility industry. Nuclear power will not expand as a major source of energy in the near future in the United States. Plant construction was virtually complete by 1990 (see Table 4-3). This pattern does not hold true for other nations. Currently there are 312 nuclear power plants in operation outside the United States, with over 200 more facilities under construction and still more in the planning phase. The current status of global nuclear power plants is reflected in Table 4-4. On a global scale, nuclear power continues to be a major source of energy. Only two European countries are reducing their dependence on nuclear power. Austria has deactivated its only nuclear power plant, and Sweden has announced plans to eliminate nuclear power plants by the year 2010.

Global emphasis on nuclear power can be traced to two factors. First, construction of nuclear power plants represents an investment of billions of dollars. The size of this investment exerts economic pressure to maintain the nuclear power plants in order to obtain a return on the massive construction expenditures. Second, many countries simply have no other currently available viable source of electricity. As of 1988, approximately 15 percent of global elec-

---

TABLE 4-3 ▪ Operating Nuclear Power Plants in the United States

Year	Number of Operating Plants
1975	54
1978	70
1980	70
1982	77
1987	95
1988	108
1990	111
1991	111

SOURCE: *Statistical Abstract of the United States, 1988* (Washington, D.C.: U.S. Government Printing Office, 1987); *Energy Review,* 1991.

---

tricity is the product of nuclear power. Within two years, by 1990, this figure had increased to over 20 percent. Even a major nuclear accident such as that at Chernobyl in the Soviet Union has not deterred emphasis on nuclear power plants on the international scene.

Political Impact of Continued Oil Dependence

There are two central political consequences of the free world's dependence on oil imports. The first is *the uncertainty of supply*. The West's economic, political, and military power can be severely weakened if the supply of oil is interrupted or

---

TABLE 4-4 ▪ Operating Nuclear Power Plants, by Country, 1990

Country	Reactors	Country	Reactors
Argentina	2	Japan	39
Belgium	8	South Korea	9
Brazil	1	Netherlands	2
Bulgaria	5	Pakistan	1
Canada	18	South Africa	2
Czechoslovakia	8	Spain	10
Finland	4	Sweden	12
France	55	Switzerland	5
Germany	28	Taiwan (China)	6
Hungary	4	United Kingdom	39
India	7	United States	111
Italy	3	Soviet Union (former)	43
		Yugoslavia	1

threatened. In a very real sense, the West's Achilles' heel is its dependence on imported oil. Interrupt the oil flow, and the West is threatened with economic collapse. Yet the foreign reserves the West must have to survive are mainly situated in the highly volatile Middle East. Conflict is rife both within the Islamic camp itself and between that camp and Israel.

As a consequence, the Western world has been drawn into increased military and political involvement in the Persian Gulf region, with a primary goal of promoting internal stability in order to maintain an adequate oil supply.[9] Western involvement ranges from military sales and assistance to air and naval bases in the Middle East. Currently, the United States has either an established presence or arrangements for military bases in Oman, Egypt, and Saudi Arabia, which helped offset the loss of Iran in 1979 as a major American ally in the region. In response to the war between Iran and Iraq, Western navies assigned warships to patrol the Persian Gulf.

The United States military presence expanded dramatically in 1990–91 in response to the Iraqi invasion of Kuwait. Under operations Desert Shield and Desert Storm the United States led and coordinated a major military campaign to remove Iraqi forces from Kuwait and protect Saudi oil fields (see Chapter 12).

The dissolution of the Soviet Union is a source of concern for stability in the Middle East. Some of the newly independent republics have a predominantly Islamic population and the known oil reserves in what was the Soviet Union are unevenly distributed among the new republics. Two factors, religion and the need for oil, have the potential to attract these new nations into Persian Gulf politics. The foreign policy values and orientations of these new nations are not at this point clear, and the political, military, and economic consequences for stability in the Middle East remain uncertain.

International trade.   A second consequence is *the impact on the annual trade deficit.* By early 1992, imported petroleum products accounted for almost 50 percent of the trade deficit (see Figure 4-5). While much attention has been directed toward a trade deficit with Japan, particularly with regard to automobiles, there has been little attention given to the economic cost of imported oil.

American reliance on imported oil has the potential to contribute a structural element to the trade deficit. This means that the United States must achieve ever-higher trade surpluses with trading partners who do not export oil to offset a continuing energy trade deficit. The cost of imported oil saddles the American economy with an additional international trade burden.

OPEC.   An additional consequence of Western dependence on imported oil has been *the inability to control the price of oil.* When OPEC acted from a position of strength, the oil-consuming West demonstrated a marked inability to limit price increases. This was a major problem in the late 1970s, when an upward spiral in oil prices placed increased inflationary pressure on Western economies. The erosion of OPEC unity has been a major factor in the dramatic drop in global oil prices.

OPEC disunity is a function of disagreement over oil prices, production levels, and political conflicts. In 1981, Western oil consumption was still high, and

FIGURE 4-5 ▪ Impact of Oil Imports on the U.S. Trade Deficit, 1985–1990

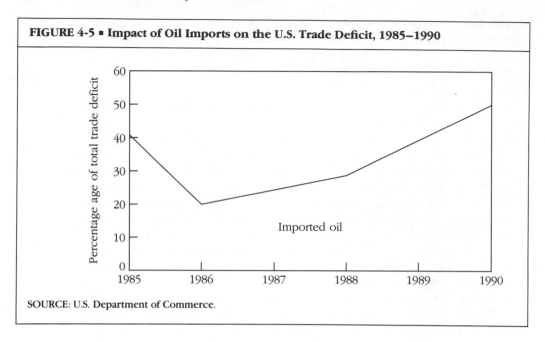

SOURCE: U.S. Department of Commerce.

OPEC oil was selling for $32 per barrel. Some members were calling for an increase in price to $41 per barrel. But Saudi Arabia, the largest oil exporter, opposed the increase and refused to raise the price of its oil, effectively thwarting the proposed price increase.

The Saudis advocated a policy of gradual, moderate price increases. In the Saudi view, oil selling in the $40 to $60 per barrel range would lead to more conservation measures and escalate the rate of development of alternative energy sources in the consuming nations. As these alternatives became available, they would reduce the demand for oil, causing a loss of revenue for the oil exporters and a loss of global political power for OPEC. The Saudi viewpoint was not shared by all OPEC members, several of whom have embarked on major economic development programs and need increased oil revenues to achieve their goals of modernization. In the 1980s, OPEC was unable to hold all its members to agreed price and production levels for its oil.

Disagreement over production levels has also reduced OPEC unity. As the West began to become more energy efficient, demand for oil also began to decrease slightly. The most appropriate strategy to maintain price when demand drops is to reduce supply. OPEC has not been able to establish an allocation formula for reducing production levels. Member states, in need of revenues, have continued to produce at levels higher than global demand, which has acted to drive oil prices down dramatically.

Political disunity also is a factor. The prolonged war between Iraq and Iran contributed to higher production levels as each nation sought revenues to fund the war effort. In the aftermath of the Persian Gulf war of 1991, Iraqi production was at minimal levels and the oil fields in Kuwait were inoperable until the fires were extinguished in late 1991. By early 1992, production from the Kuwaiti fields was being restored. The potential for military and political conflict in the Persian Gulf contributes to uncertainty over oil production levels.

OPEC was unsuccessful in its attempt to establish and apportion production quotas among member countries, and as of early 1992 oil sold for $16 per barrel. There is little doubt that OPEC will continue to seek to limit production and increase the price of oil and is therefore an unknown element in the energy supply equation.

Although OPEC is in disarray, it would be a mistake to assume that the organization will have little impact in the future. Internal events in the member nations can disrupt production and external events can provide OPEC unity, as demonstrated during the mid- to late 1970s.

FUTURE ALTERNATIVES: ENERGY POLICY COMPLACENCY

The "energy crisis" of the early 1970s appears to have evaporated, and the public concern that stimulated energy policy activity has diminished. The close of the 1980s was marked by both lower energy prices and an adequate supply, and these factors have contributed to an attitude of complacency toward energy policy. Is the current attitude of complacency justified? Was the extent of the energy crisis overestimated, or did energy policy responses act to solve the problem of energy scarcity?

One factor that contributed to the energy shortfall of the early 1970s was a product of faulty demand projections by the energy companies and governments. During the 1950s and 1960s, demand for oil was always underestimated. Ten-year projections were off by as much as 25 or 30 percent.[10] A gap of five to ten years exists between the time a decision is made to seek additional oil and gas reserves and actual production from those new sources. Prior to the 1970s, the routine underestimation of demand failed to stimulate sufficient exploratory efforts to maintain a balance between supply and demand. By the early 1970s, energy consumption patterns, which were the cornerstone of forecasting, produced projections of dramatic increases in energy demand for the decade of the 1980s and beyond. The OPEC unity achieved in 1973, which provided a framework for price increases and limited production quotas, added credibility to the projections of a continuing future gap between supply and demand. Between 1973 and 1978, the growth in the demand for oil did exceed the growth in the oil supply, with several consequences. First, decisions were made to increase the oil supply by exploring the North Slope in Alaska, to increase exploration in the North Sea, and to intensify exploration efforts in other regions of the world as well as across the United States.

Second, the increase in the cost of energy produced slow but continuous changes in consumption patterns. A gradual change was made to more energy-efficient automobiles. Homes were insulated. The efficiency of residential and commercial heating units was increased. Fuel efficiency became an important value in the transportation industry as new trucks and aircraft were designed and manufactured. Changes in manufacturing techniques also provided increased energy efficiency. These changes acted to decrease the rate at which energy demand grew.

Third, OPEC economies were becoming increasingly dependent on the oil consumption patterns of the West. Modernization and development programs created an ever-increasing demand for oil revenues within OPEC nations. The need to market oil and maintain production became a driving force within OPEC nations.

Gradually, demand was reduced to levels lower than global supply. Between 1974 and 1988, non-OPEC oil production increased by over 80 percent, from 17 million barrels per day to over 31 million barrels per day. This increase in production, combined with the improvement in energy efficiency and other conservation measures, acted to create an imbalance in which supply exceeded demand by 1988.

The condition of adequate energy supply and lowered prices has had a major impact on the United States. Public concern has been replaced by complacency as oil remains a primary energy source. This complacency may not be justified. Contrary to public perceptions, the energy system is considerably more volatile and dynamic now than in the past. Prior to 1973, the supply and price of energy were controlled largely by the actions of the international oil companies. During the 1970s, the OPEC oil cartel acted to control oil supply and prices. The power of these two systems of control has evaporated as oil supply, production, and cost respond to international market forces and competing international interests.

This has at least two policy implications for the United States. First, continued dependence ties American economic strength to access to foreign energy sources. Any disruption in oil supply will have potentially profound economic consequences. Second, low international prices will act to reduce domestic oil production in the United States. Forecasts for the early 1990s indicate that the cost of oil will not escalate drastically and that global supply will continue to exceed demand. In order for OPEC eventually to achieve higher prices for its oil it must (1) maintain high production and low prices to discourage the development of alternative energy sources, (2) minimize expansion of non-OPEC oil sources, and (3) increase dependence on OPEC as a primary source of energy.

Thus complacency may create a future in which the United States will find itself vulnerable to a situation similar to what it experienced in 1973.

ENVIRONMENTAL POLICY

Public concern over environmental policy was minimal until the end of the nineteenth century. As the United States expanded westward, the horizon seemed to present an unlimited supply of land, water, mineral deposits, and timber. Farming techniques reflected little concern for minimizing soil depletion. Forests were cleared without concern for reforestation or the devastation of soil erosion. Minerals were mined and metals smelted without concern for their effects on fresh-water supplies; when contamination did result, it seemed a minor problem, because alternative sources of water seemed endless.

Once the nation began to reach the limit of its geographic expansion, to industrialize, and to experience rapid population growth, however, the problem of environmental preservation and protection could no longer be so easily avoided. From the 1870s through the 1930s, conservation was the dominant theme of environmental policy. Examples include the establishment of Yellowstone Park as the first national park in 1872 and 1897 legislation that created an extensive national forest system. Although the conservation standard provided a general policy focus, there was significant disagreement over what specific strategies should be employed. To some, conservation meant resource management for effective utilization, such as scientific forestry; others viewed conservation primarily as wilderness preservation. This conflict over strategy is still present today and remains a major policy issue.

Despite a history of conservation policies, fundamental concerns over environmental protection were still absent from the policy agenda as late as the 1950s. The publication of *Silent Spring* in 1962 drew attention to the dangers of pesticides, such as DDT, in the food chain.[11] This book acted as a catalyst to mobilize a heightened environmental consciousness. The sense of social responsibility that emerged in the 1960s also moved environmental policy from the background to the forefront of the policy agenda.

ISSUE BACKGROUND: A LEGACY OF ENVIRONMENTAL ABUSE

The long period of indifference and neglect has left its mark on the physical environment of the United States. The environmental problems the nation now faces are the product of the historic lack of public concern with the unintended but harmful consequences of the economic growth and development of an industrialized society. Air pollution, water pollution, solid-waste pollution, toxic- and hazardous-waste pollution, acid rain, and changing land-use patterns all pose important problems.

Air Pollution

Air pollutants can be categorized in two groups: particles and gases. Particulate matter includes such material as ashes, soot, and lead (a noncombustible gasoline additive). Though particulate pollution is a problem, the dangers presented by the release of gases into the air are just as real but probably less well understood by the general public. The major air pollutants can be grouped into the following five categories:

Carbon Monoxide (CO). Carbon monoxide is a colorless by-product of the incomplete combustion of carbon fuels. Gasoline engines are its primary source.

Sulfur Dioxide (SO_2).   Sulfur dioxide is produced by the combustion of fuels containing sulfur. When combined with water vapor, it can form sulfuric acid and fall as "acid rain."

Hydrocarbons (HC).   Hydrocarbons, consisting of various combinations of hydrogen and carbon, are the unburned fuel resulting from incomplete combustion. The compounds have a major impact in the production of photochemical smog in urban areas.

Nitrogen Oxide (NO).   Nitrogen oxide is a by-product of fossil fuel combustion at high temperature levels. It combines with hydrocarbons to produce smog.

Particulate matter.   Particulates include liquids or solids released into the atmosphere.

From trends projected in 1980 through the year 2000 by the Environmental Protection Agency (EPA), it is safe to assume that air pollution will continue to be an environmental problem.[12] Total emissions of particulate matter were projected to double by that year. Generation of sulfur dioxide was projected to increase at a rate of 4 to 6 percent annually. Emissions of nitrogen oxides should grow dramatically as coal continues to be an important fuel source: By the year 2000, they could be 90 percent higher than in the late 1970s. Hydrocarbon emissions were projected to remain at a constant level or to increase slightly by the year 2000. Emissions of carbon monoxide also were projected to rise. That these projections have not stimulated significant policy responses may be attributed, in part, to the fact that in the short run the level of most air pollution emissions has remained somewhat stable as indicated in Figure 4-6.

Figure 4-6 should be interpreted with care. That the level of emissions has remained constant or decreased slightly should not be interpreted to mean that the problem of air pollution has been reduced. The atmosphere continues to be polluted with over 100 million tons of emissions each year.

The focus on measuring the raw amount of individual pollutants produced can be a deceptive approach to the problem, because studies have shown that serious health problems can result from either short-term exposure to high levels of these compounds or long-term exposure to relatively low levels. There is also evidence that these pollutants act synergistically on animal and plant life. This means that exposure to the compounds together produces more harmful impacts than would result from exposure to them separately.

Not all emissions can be easily categorized as either harmless or polluting. Such is the case with carbon dioxide (CO_2). So far, CO_2 has not been clearly identified as a major pollutant, and there are no regulations governing its emission in the United States. But scientists are increasingly concerned that high levels of CO_2 in the atmosphere may warm the earth and result in major climatic changes (see Figure 4-7). This is known as the "greenhouse effect." Increased atmospheric levels of CO_2 trap the earth's heat by reducing the escape of infrared radiation from the surface into space. There is debate within the scientific community over the

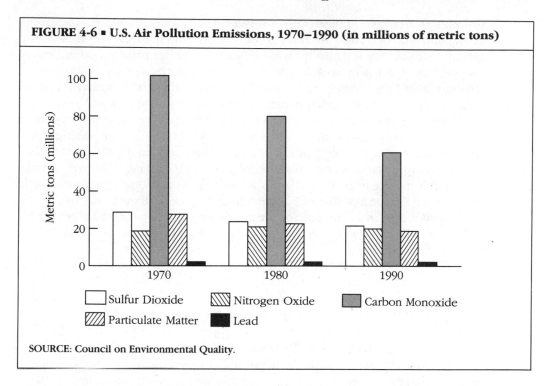

FIGURE 4-6 ▪ U.S. Air Pollution Emissions, 1970–1990 (in millions of metric tons)

SOURCE: Council on Environmental Quality.

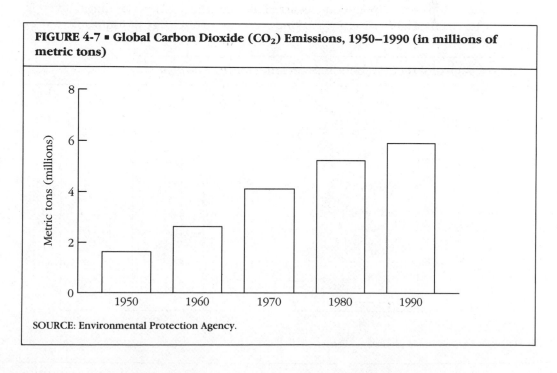

FIGURE 4-7 ▪ Global Carbon Dioxide (CO_2) Emissions, 1950–1990 (in millions of metric tons)

SOURCE: Environmental Protection Agency.

seriousness of the greenhouse effect. One aspect of the debate concerns the causes of the drought of 1988—whether it can be attributed to early stages of the greenhouse effect or is a manifestation of normal weather-pattern cycles. Debate also focuses on the origins of the rising levels of atmospheric CO_2. Some experts attribute high CO_2 levels to the use of fossil fuels; others believe that the rapid deforestation in Africa, South America, and Asia is the primary cause.[13]

Ozone layer.   The earth is protected from excessive ultraviolet rays by a thin layer of ozone some thirty miles above the surface. The production and continued use of chlorofluorocarbons (CFCs) now threaten the integrity of that protective layer. Scientists have discovered a hole in the ozone layer over Antarctica roughly the size of the United States. A thinning of the ozone layer above North America and Europe has also been documented. Depletion of the protective ozone layer would result in a higher incidence of skin cancer, cataracts, and other health problems. This is primarily due to the harmful nature of ultraviolet-B radiation from the sun.

Chlorofluorocarbons are the primary cause of ozone depletion. When CFC molecules reach the ozone layer, they split and recombine with ozone molecules to form chlorine monoxide and oxygen, gases which do not block ultraviolet radiation. Figure 4-8 indicates the continuing increase in global CFC emissions.

Water and Solid-Waste Pollution

Water pollution.   Neglect of the nation's waterways has been a major environmental problem. Perhaps the most dramatic incident illustrating the seriousness of water pollution occurred in the 1960s: The Cuyahoga River in Cleveland caught fire as a result of the extensive discharge of flammable wastes

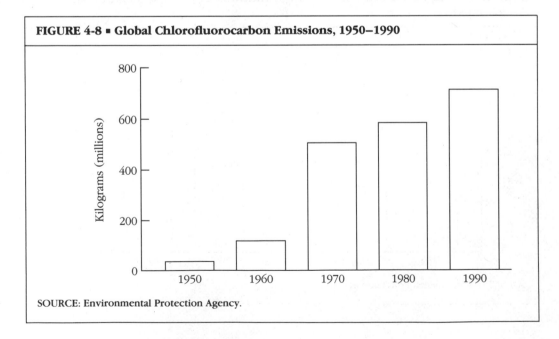

FIGURE 4-8 ▪ Global Chlorofluorocarbon Emissions, 1950–1990

SOURCE: Environmental Protection Agency.

into the river. Although this is not a typical event, virtually all surface waterways have experienced some type of pollution.

Even though water pollution is a well-documented nationwide problem, its severity varies considerably among the different regions of the country. Waterways of the industrialized Northeast and Midwest have been especially abused. Even though sources of water pollution vary greatly, it is possible to classify most pollutants into four categories.[14]

Industrial wastes contain a wide range of organic and inorganic compounds, including heavy metals such as mercury and zinc. A relatively new water-pollution phenomenon is thermal pollution; the cause is the discharge of heated water into rivers and lakes after it has been used to cool equipment used primarily in electric power plants. Thermal pollution heightens the toxicity of some other pollutants and, by accelerating the decomposition of organic matter, lowers the oxygen level in surface waters.

Domestic and municipal wastes include human wastes and other compounds disposed of by people in their day-to-day lives.

Agricultural wastes include animal waste and other compounds that may pose health risks, such as fertilizers and pesticides that run off into waterways and enter the food chain.

Miscellaneous pollutants may be "natural" and include silt and sedimentation entering surface waters following rains. Also included are more serious pollutants such as those from accidental oil spills. While offshore oil spills from supertankers and drilling accidents receive publicity due to their magnitude, the hundreds of other smaller spills that occur each year receive relatively little attention. Mining activity also adds to water pollution: Where strip mining is practiced, sulfur compounds in the exposed soil react with rain to form sulfuric acid, which then runs off into surface waters. Already a major pollutant in Appalachian mining regions, this is becoming a problem in Western states where coal mining has been on the increase.

One approach to reducing water pollution involves aggressive waste-water treatment by cities and industry to eliminate most of the contaminants before they enter surface waters. There are three levels of waste treatment. Primary treatment is the basic form and uses settling chambers to remove solid contaminants before the water is released. Secondary treatment filters the remaining wastes through beds of rock and sand to remove organic contaminants, with the addition of chlorinates to kill bacteria. Tertiary systems use additional filtration (such as activated charcoal) to remove inorganic compounds and heavy metals.

There is no lack of waste-treatment technologies available to municipalities and industry to minimize the discharge of contaminants. The major obstacle has been cost. Construction and operation of a tri-level treatment system has been beyond the financial means of many cities and industries because such a system can cost three to four times as much as a bi-level treatment system. The reality of immediate economic costs has historically acted to shift policy options away from a completely aggressive waste-treatment strategy.

Solid-waste pollution.   Solid-waste pollution is linked directly to the level of economic activity. The United States produces over six billion tons of solid

wastes each year. This includes *agricultural* solid wastes (2.5 billion tons annually), *residential and commercial* solid wastes (250 million tons), *industrial* solid
wastes (1.5 billion tons), and *mineral* solid wastes (1.8 billion tons of slag and mill
tailings).

The traditional approach has been simply to bury the waste in landfills, an
option that is less than satisfactory given the projections that solid-waste production may double by the year 2000. Despite this veritable landslide of solid waste,
recycling is not a major priority in the United States.

As indicated in Figure 4-9, solid waste from municipal areas has more than
doubled since 1960. Recycling has not yet reached the level to have an impact on
the solid-waste disposal problem. It is economically expedient, in the short run, to
discard processed materials and utilize new raw materials in the production
process. For example, it is cheaper to use pulp timber than to recycle paper.
Government action, which would itself be costly, could institute mandatory recycling, as already done in some localities, but that does not seem likely at the
national level within the next decade. Perhaps only when the supply of raw
materials is depleted will the economic basis of the "throwaway" society change.

Toxic and Hazardous Waste

Hazardous wastes are those wastes that pose a significant threat to either health or
the environment due to their "quantity, concentration, physical, chemical, or

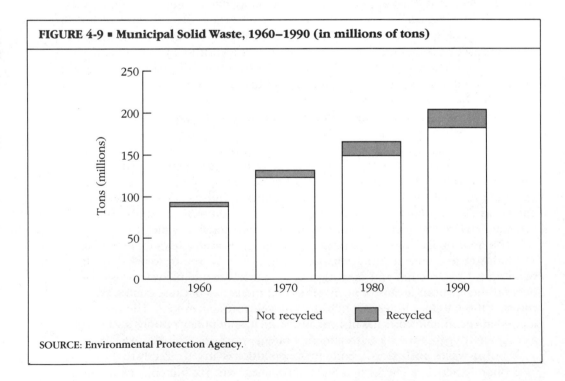

FIGURE 4-9 ▪ **Municipal Solid Waste, 1960–1990 (in millions of tons)**

SOURCE: Environmental Protection Agency.

infectious characteristics."[15] The EPA estimates that between 38 million and 60 million tons of hazardous wastes are produced each year in the United States and that 65 percent of these toxic substances are produced in ten states: California, Illinois, Indiana, Louisiana, Michigan, Ohio, Pennsylvania, Tennessee, Texas, and West Virginia.[16]

Seldom are hazardous wastes disposed of in a safe manner. In fact, some estimates indicate that less than 10 percent of toxic wastes are disposed of safely. Of the remaining 90 percent, half is relegated to nonlined surface lagoons, 30 percent is buried in nonlined landfills, and the remaining 20 percent is spread on roads, burned, or dumped into sewers or directly into surface waters, or injected into deep wells where subsurface waters can be contaminated.[17] The amount of this waste will continue to increase to the point that by the year 2000, approximately 75 million tons will be produced annually.

The impact of improper toxic-waste disposal may emerge only decades later, as illustrated by the events at Love Canal in Niagara Falls, New York. The Hooker Chemical Company buried more than twenty thousand tons of chemical wastes containing over three hundred different chemicals at Love Canal in the 1950s. Two decades later, in the 1970s, residents in the Love Canal area were experiencing mounting incidences of health problems that were directly attributed to the buried toxic wastes. Over $30 million was needed to clean up the site and relocate residents.

Toxic wastes can threaten communities far removed from toxic-waste sites and the chemical industry. The case of Times Beach, Missouri, illustrates this point. Times Beach was located on Interstate 44, about twenty-five miles southwest of St. Louis. This small rural community appeared safe from the threat of toxic wastes; yet events were to prove otherwise. Oil contaminated with dioxin was spread over the gravel and dirt streets of the town at levels high enough to make the whole city a health risk. Eventually, the entire city was purchased by the federal government, and residents were relocated to surrounding communities. Today, Times Beach remains a ghost town as the EPA and the state of Missouri seek a long-term disposition for the contaminated city. The difficulty of assessing toxic-waste threats was brought home in late 1991, when some members of the scientific community argued that the threat from dioxins has been overstated. They contend that Times Beach need not have been evacuated.

One type of increasingly important—and controversial—hazardous waste is *radioactive* waste. The two main sources of radioactive waste are the nuclear-weapons program and nuclear power plants used to generate electricity. Some of these high-level wastes are so toxic that they must be stored for *500,000* years. Low-level wastes also pose a major problem. The United States produces over 3 million cubic feet of this waste, which requires safe storage for hundreds of years. Nuclear waste-management policy is an area marked by controversy and uncertainty.

Safe disposal of radioactive wastes has continued to prove an elusive goal. As the United States began to develop nuclear technology during World War II, minimal concern was shown for finding safe disposal techniques. Radioactive wastes were typically burned, buried in shallow pits, or simply dumped into the existing sewage system. The governing philosophy was that safe disposal involved simply the dilution of radioactive wastes, which facilitated dispersal of the wastes in the environment. During the late 1940s and the 1950s, ever-higher quantities of radioactive wastes were produced. The high volume of waste required that a new disposal system be developed: ocean dumping. This technology involved using containers (primarily 55-gallon drums) to hold radioactive wastes. These containers were then filled with concrete and dumped off the coast of the United States.

Between 1945 and 1967, the United States dumped almost one hundred thousand of these containers into the waters off the Atlantic and Pacific coasts. This practice was terminated by 1970 because of the long-term threats posed to the environment. Gradually, the containers corrode and the wastes are exposed to the ocean currents and enter the food chain. Currently, ocean dumping of radioactive waste is not a policy of any nation.

With the elimination of ocean dumping, land disposal is now the method of choice. The only problem is that a viable technology for long-term disposal has not yet been developed. Current surface facilities are rapidly reaching or exceeding capacity. A safe, technologically feasible storage system has not yet been found, and the level of radioactive waste continues to accumulate, as indicated in Figure 4-10.

One policy obstacle to solving the problem of toxic-waste dumps is that

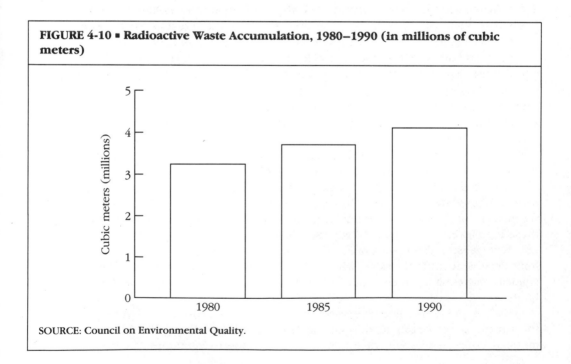

FIGURE 4-10 ▪ **Radioactive Waste Accumulation, 1980–1990 (in millions of cubic meters)**

SOURCE: Council on Environmental Quality.

many sites have yet to be identified. The EPA has located over seventeen thousand potentially dangerous sites, but possibly many thousands more still wait to be discovered. Virtually every state in the union contains at least one hazardous toxic dump. The EPA has not been provided with the budget and the personnel to complete this critical first step.

Acid Rain

An environmental problem of growing concern is the phenomenon of acid rain. This is produced when air pollutants, primarily sulfur dioxide, nitrogen oxides, and hydrocarbons, are chemically converted by sunlight into sulfates, nitrates, and other acidic compounds, which are returned to earth by rain and snow and gradually change the acidic balance in both water and soil.

Acidity is measured in pH units on a scale ranging from 0 to 14, with the pH value of 7 representing neutrality. Values greater than 7 represent alkalinity, and values less than 7 represent acidity. The logarithmic nature of the scale means that a pH level of 5 is ten times more acidic than pH 6 and that pH 4 is one hundred times more acidic than pH 6. For example, a lake that increases in acidity from pH 4.5 to pH 4.2 has *doubled* its level of acidity. A lack of understanding of pH levels has minimized public concern with the potential threat posed by acid rain.

When acidity in a body of water exceeds the level of pH 5, the ability to support fish and plant life is diminished. Given that over 20 million tons of sulfur dioxides and 20 million tons of nitrogen oxides are released into the atmosphere each year, the United States faces a potential problem of enormous magnitude. Data from the EPA indicate that the acidic level for rain and snow is below the level of pH 5 for the entire eastern half of the nation. This means that virtually all rivers and lakes in the affected region are threatened by increased levels of acidity. There are geologic differences, however, that can reduce the impact on bodies of water in this region. For example, the limestone floors of some lakes in New England neutralize some of the acidity. The problem of acid rain is that more acidity can be deposited in a lake or stream than can be neutralized naturally.

Acid rain also harms agriculture and forestry. The U.S. Office of Technology Assessment (OTA) has estimated that agricultural production in the United States has been reduced by 6 to 7 percent because of acid rain and that up to 20 percent of the land in the eastern United States is seriously threatened by it.[18]

The Environmental Legacy

The absence of an aggressive environmental-protection strategy has left the nation with potentially severe air, water, and toxic-waste problems. A range of other environmental issues also pose problems for the nation. Both conventional and strip *mining* activities continue to have significant impacts. Without extensive reclamation efforts after strip mining, the land is permanently unusable for productive or recreational purposes. The tailings from conventional mining activity also present problems as wind and rain transport contaminants into the ecosystem.

This is a significant problem for uranium mining, because radioactive debris is left in the open in mammoth sand piles. *Land-use patterns* are also an issue of concern. Topsoil erosion, the loss of wetlands, and forestry practices remain areas of policy conflict. An area of increasing concern is *indoor air pollution.* The traditional view presumed that pollution was only an "outdoor" problem: People could escape the problem by remaining indoors. But such is not the case, as serious indoor health hazards such as formaldehyde foam (used in building insulation), asbestos, and other toxic substances have been documented.

As with energy, the environmental policy legacy has been one of historical neglect in terms of environmental protection, which allowed environmental abuse to develop into a significant public policy problem.

CONTEMPORARY ENVIRONMENTAL POLICY

Although there unquestionably are severe environmental problems facing the United States in the 1990s, efforts have been undertaken to ameliorate them. This section will look at these major policy responses, including the historical background of some environmental legislation, and will outline the most important features and goals of the evolving public policies.

Water-Pollution Policy

Leadership in this policy area has been gradually and partially assumed by the federal government. The origins of the federal role can be traced to the Refuse Act of 1899, which sought to limit the blockage of navigable rivers by municipal and industrial debris. Although the act was largely ignored, it did indicate the necessity for action by the federal government to respond to a problem that extends beyond state borders.

Congressional action would gradually expand this federal role. The Water Pollution Act of 1948 provided federal funds for sewage-plant construction, leaving standards and enforcement largely to the states. In 1956, this act was amended to authorize federal funds to sponsor conferences on water pollution. The Public Health Service (PHS) was also assigned a permanent role in monitoring water-quality standards in municipalities across the nation. The 1961 Water Pollution Control Act and the 1965 Water Quality Act continued to provide federal funds for sewage-plant construction and to assign primary responsibility for water standards and enforcement to the states.

The underlying assumption of the emphasis on state responsibility held that states would be vigilant in protecting their own water resources, but this was not typically the case. State governments proved unwilling to enact strict standards for fear of driving industry into other states with less stringent standards. The result? Most adopted very weak water-quality standards.

The Clean Waters Restoration Act of 1966 signaled the beginning of the transfer of water-quality enforcement responsibility from the states to the federal government as it assumed the power to initiate court action to force municipal and industrial compliance with water-quality standards.

The Water Pollution Control Act Amendments of 1972 continued this trend of increased federal responsibility. The unrealized goal of this act was to end the discharge of pollutants into waterways by 1985 by mandating that industry and municipalities adopt the "best available" sewage-treatment technology. The 1974 Safe Drinking Water Act continued the emphasis on federal action by assigning to the EPA responsibility for establishing minimum standards for drinking water.

Air-Pollution Policy

Attempts to control and improve air quality in the United States have followed a similar pattern of a gradually expanding federal role. The first action taken by Congress, the Air Pollution Control Act of 1955, did little more than fund research on air quality. The federal role was gradually increased as the Clean Air Act of 1963 provided funds for state air-quality programs and the Motor Vehicle Air Pollution Control Act of 1965 empowered the Department of Health, Education and Welfare (HEW) to set automobile-emission standards. This was the first federal program to regulate emissions directly. The program was expanded by the National Emissions Standards Act of 1967.

The 1970 Clean Air Act Amendments signaled a major change in air-pollution policy in the United States. These amendments sought to reduce, by 1975, all air pollutants that constituted a health threat. Primary responsibility for establishing standards and enforcement of those standards was delegated to the EPA. Initially, these standards were expected to reflect a primary emphasis on protection of public health and welfare, with a secondary emphasis on economic issues. These high standards were modified by the 1977 Clean Air Act Amendments, in which the federal government responded to the energy crisis and to protests from industry. Emission standards were relaxed, and lax compliance deadlines were established.

Congress enacted another series of amendments to the Clean Air Act in November, 1990. These amendments are designed to move air quality toward the standards that were originally to be achieved by 1975. One specific provision includes reducing SO_2 emissions in order to reduce the threat of acid rain by the year 2000. The amendments also allow some air-quality standards to be tailored to the degree of pollution in individual communities as opposed to setting uniform nationwide standards for all emissions. Critics of these amendments argue that they do not contain sufficiently stringent nationwide air-quality standards. Supporters hold that these amendments do embody a move in the direction of the standards in the original Clean Air Act.

The National Environmental Policy Act (NEPA)

The National Environmental Policy Act, which was signed into law on January 1, 1970, by President Nixon, reflected a major change in environmental policy by the federal government.[19] The act placed greater emphasis on federal leadership in formulating national environmental policy through the creation of the Council on Environmental Quality (CEQ), within the Executive Office of the President, to provide advice on environmental policy issues. Although the CEQ was largely an advisory body with no direct power to stop pollution violations, its existence within the Executive Office provided the framework for a strengthened federal role under the leadership of the president. The legislation also mandated that the president submit an annual "environmental quality report" to Congress and that federal agencies submit "environmental impact statements" on any action that would affect the environment.

The impact statements are filed with the CEQ and are open for public inspection. The act sought to force public agencies to undertake a deliberate and thorough analysis of the potential environmental consequences of any projects under their control, and to investigate the feasibility of using alternatives to achieve the same goals if the proposed activity would have a significantly adverse effect on the environment.

The *Environmental Protection Agency (EPA)* was created by President Nixon in 1970 as part of a reorganization of the federal bureaucracy. The EPA combined some fifteen offices and agencies into a single agency assigned responsibility for (1) water pollution, (2) air pollution, (3) solid-waste management, (4) radiation control, and (5) pesticide and toxic-substance control. The new agency was intended to centralize federal power in environmental policy by eliminating the previous pattern of fragmentation and decentralization.

Unlike the advisory Council on Environmental Quality, the EPA is a regulatory agency with power to establish and enforce policy. The actual impact of the EPA on environmental issues is a function of the values and assumptions of the president and of the administrator he selects to guide the agency in interpreting and enforcing environmental rules and statutes. The agency is influenced by political values and arrangements. Under the direction of Anne Gorsuch Burford between 1981 and 1983, the EPA was criticized for making "sweetheart deals" with major industrial polluters and for scheduling EPA cleanup projects based on political considerations instead of environmental concerns.

The Hazardous Waste Superfund.   One program that continues to be long on controversy and short on actual delivery is the Superfund, created during the Carter administration by the 1980 Comprehensive Environmental Response Act. The Superfund provided the EPA with the authority and the funds to assist in cleanup operations at toxic- and hazardous-waste sites across the country. The creation of the fund was intended to allow an active role for the EPA in dealing with emergency situations and with abandoned toxic-waste sites. By 1984, over seventeen thousand disposal sites had been identified, with estimates that an additional five thousand sites will be documented. EPA estimates indicate that the cleanup operations at the two thousand most dangerous sites would cost between $8 billion and $16 billion, roughly five to ten times the size of the original level of the Superfund.

Relatively few sites have actually been cleaned up under the provisions of the Superfund act. In fact, a number of the sites have been cleaned not by disposal but by simply transferring the wastes to another toxic-waste site. This transfer of wastes from one location to another does not indicate progress in a cleanup program. The program failed to have a significant impact during the 1980s, owing to the lack of financial support by the Reagan administration.

POLICY EVALUATION: SEARCHING FOR DIRECTION

Current Policy Direction and Values

The 1960s and 1970s were decades in which extensive environmental legislation was enacted and regulatory policies and agencies created. The trend toward increased regulation and federal leadership changed as new values became the source of environmental policy during the Reagan administration. Its position was to relax standards and to reduce federal regulatory activity.[20] Reagan opposed the provisions of the Clean Air Act and sought to reduce the enforcement role of the EPA. He was successful in securing funding to research possible sites for dumping wastes into the ocean, with the EPA charged with the identification of appropriate dump sites. Yet illegal ocean dumping by private businesses and inadequate municipal sewer systems resulted in the closing of large sections of the nation's beaches during the summer of 1988, as trash and dangerous medical wastes were washed ashore.

The "bubble concept" that applies clean-air standards to a plant as a whole, rather than focusing on specific points of emission, means that increased levels of pollution at one source within a plant will be accepted if the overall levels of contaminants for the particular plant remain within EPA guidelines. President Reagan did not make specific environmental promises in either his 1980 or 1984 campaigns and expressed a desire to utilize cost-benefit analysis and market forces as the most appropriate mechanisms for guiding environmental policy. He stressed that environmental protection issues should not be allowed to impose unrealistic and burdensome restrictions on economic growth. The negative environmental impacts are the result of a value system that emphasized economic activity and reduced environmental standards.

The Bush administration established a continuity with the environmental values of the Reagan administration. Accordingly, market values were viewed as an appropriate mechanism for determining environmental policy. President Bush also held to the view that environmental policy should be evaluated in the context of costs and benefits to society. Environmental protection policies were to be avoided if the associated costs to society were higher than the monetary benefits.

President Bush also favors a stronger role for state governments, as opposed to the federal government, in enacting environmental legislation.

The Politics of Regulation

The regulatory process itself is subject to political pressures from competing interests within society, which can influence the formulation of an effective environmental policy. One political factor that affects regulation is the pressure on administrators and elected officials to emphasize short-term economic benefits as opposed to long-term consequences of environmental damage. A second factor involves emphasis on the primacy of economic growth as a basic value in the political system. Economic growth carries an environmental cost almost universally, and the American system has historically concentrated on the desirability of growth. A third factor that directly affects the regulatory process is the value placed on compromise in our political system. The Constitution itself is a product of compromise, and the American system places a great deal of importance on seeking the middle ground. Although compromise is a politically expedient technique for making policy, it is not necessarily the best approach in establishing an effective environmental policy. Compromise becomes a factor in the delay and weakening of environmental-protection policies.

Given the nature of the political system, regulatory policy tends to be a product of political pressures, a fact that hinders development of effective policy choices. And even if policy could be formulated without these factors, problems with enforcement would remain.

Enforcement Problems

Effective enforcement of environmental policy is difficult to achieve for a variety of reasons. A major obstacle is the climate in which the EPA must operate. The EPA was charged with providing the scientific evidence to support the environmental standards established by Congress. The procedure of establishing a solid scientific base for its regulations required more financial and personnel resources than the EPA had available. Increasingly, the courts placed the burden of proof on the EPA to defend the standards it was expected to enforce. Gathering and documenting this evidence is a time- and resource-consuming activity.

From the late 1980s onward, the EPA received less political and budgetary support. This decline in support eroded the ability of the agency to pursue aggressively a policy of strict enforcement.

FUTURE ALTERNATIVES: UNRESOLVED POLICY ISSUES

The preceding discussions have dwelt primarily on the nature and extent of environmental pollution and the evolution of public policy designed to address those environmental concerns. There remain several unresolved issues in the policy area, questions concerning the role that government ought to take and the strategies that ought to be followed.

Self-regulation of the Market

Should government take an active role in planning and regulating activities that affect the environment? Or can this issue best be solved by a minimal governmental role, with the primary responsibility shifted to the operation of the free-market system?[21]

Conservatives who advocate reduced environmental regulation and increased reliance on the market point to the negative consequences of environmental regulations. Regulations mean higher costs to business and so contribute to inflationary pressures on the economy. These critics also contend that regulations interfere with national business planning, are difficult to comply with, are often arbitrary, and lack a scientific consensus. They point to the once-stringent clean-air standards, which they contend are a good example of arbitrary and unrealistic standards forced to bend to more practical needs.

Market-oriented individuals argue that the market economy would not produce rampant environmental spoilage. Rather, the free market would produce conditions that make it profitable for the private sector to recycle waste products and to develop technologies to reduce pollution at the source. The level of pollution that did exist would be a product of the relationship between the costs and benefits to society.

Liberals, however, strenuously disagree.[22] They point out that consumers tend to purchase the least expensive item when quality is similar. Industry would never voluntarily install pollution-control equipment that would drive up the prices of its goods and put them at a competitive disadvantage. Thus the market could not provide a basis for making intelligent environmental policy choices. Therefore liberals argue that without governmental regulation, the environment will continue to deteriorate. Pollution is an externality, an indirect impact of market activity, that will continue to have costly social and economic effects without the policy hand of government to minimize them.

Taxes and Legal Action

There are several alternatives to the current administrative enforcement mechanisms for achieving environmental goals and compliance with environmental regulation.[23] First, the system of rules, regulations, guidelines, and air- and water-quality standards might be replaced by taxes or fees for the discharge of pollutants. Such a system represents a modified market approach popular with many neoconservatives. It would, they argue, reduce the administrative costs associated with regulation and allow industries to calculate the costs and benefits of environmental damage themselves. Critics of this alternative point out that some level of government would have to monitor discharges precisely in order to compute the tax; taxes would have to be set and adjusted continuously for particular pollutants;

and companies in noncompetitive sectors of the economy could simply continue to pollute and pass the cost of the tax to consumers.

A second alternative, which is employed in some situations today, is the use of injunctions to halt pollution. This means obtaining a court order requiring that pollution be eliminated or reduced by a specified time or the polluter will be forced to cease operation. This strategy has the advantages of clarity and finality, but it can be used only on a case-by-case basis.

A third alternative rewards enterprises that reduce pollution by awarding them tax subsidies or underwriting the cost of pollution-control equipment. This approach provides economic incentives to cease pollution activities and has a parallel in the tax credits already given industries that install energy-conservation equipment. Yet tax subsidies ultimately transfer the cost of environmental protection from the polluter to the general public.

Stiff fines and jail sentences are a fourth approach to the problem. They would impose a strong negative incentive to cease polluting. But enforcement problems remain. Even when a conviction is obtained, jail terms are almost never imposed in these types of white-collar crimes, and fines—considering the resources of big industry—may be absorbed as routine business expenses.

Other alternatives to enforcing environmental compliance have been debated and sometimes used, but, like those discussed here, they have met with limited success, and no consensus has been reached. An effective strategy to achieve compliance with pollution standards remains elusive.

The Role of State Governments

The issue of state responsibility for environmental enforcement remains unresolved. Early regulatory efforts concentrated authority in the hands of state government, with limited success. There is evidence that a reduction of the role of the federal government and transfer of responsibility for environmental policy to the states will result in a general weakening of standards.

One reason is that the governing coalitions within state governments have a relatively narrow political base. In other words, compared with the national level, the proportion of the population concerned with political events at the state level is relatively small. Public-opinion polls indicate that less than 30 percent of the electorate regularly follows state government actively. Consequently, it is relatively easy for a special-interest group to gain considerable power in state government.

State governments also face severe staffing problems. Job vacancies reach levels as high as 20 percent in the regulatory agencies of some states, and the turnover of trained, qualified personnel is also a problem. Limited fiscal resources are a primary source of this problem.

A third problem emerges when federal agencies, primarily the EPA, fail to issue regulations in a timely manner. The result is a negative impact on state enforcement procedures. Inconsistency, confusion, and delay follow as states operate without federal leadership.

A fourth problem grows from a perception that federal regulations fail to appreciate the states' unique needs, producing inflexible program requirements. The inflexibility is viewed by the states as a barrier to state initiative, as states are faced with implementing rigid programs that may not meet their needs.

A fifth problem stems from the perception that federal EPA officials may not be interested in establishing meaningful communication with the states. A lack of responsiveness by the EPA builds perceptions at the state level that the "feds" do not understand and do not care about the problems and issues faced by state officials.

A sixth problem is conflicting interests among the states themselves. Not all states are threatened to the same degree by the same environmental pollutants. Acid rain is unevenly distributed across the nation and is not an issue in certain areas of the country. States vary with respect to their economic base. Strict environmental policies have differing levels of economic impact across the nation. Given the differences among the states, dissatisfaction with environmental policies adopted at the federal level will be manifested at the state level, and interstate conflict may lead to policy deadlocks in Congress and the EPA.

These six problems relate to the issue of dividing leadership responsibility between the federal government and the fifty states. Leadership requires the expenditure of financial resources. It was the policy of the Reagan administration to reduce the degree of leadership and financial responsibility of the federal government, but the states have not been overly eager to assume the leadership role in enforcement policy.

Energy and the Environment

Regulatory policies designed to protect the environment often conflict with policies intended to increase the supply of energy available to the nation. The onset of the energy crisis and emphasis on economic growth created pressures to postpone compliance deadlines and to relax environmental standards and rules. This linkage between energy policy, economic expansion, and environmental policy is a source of conflict, as was graphically demonstrated on March 23, 1989, when the Exxon Valdez ran aground in Prince William Sound and spilled between 10 and 12.5 million barrels of oil in the coastal waters of Alaska. The long-term environmental consequences are not yet clear, but the impact on fish and wildlife is extensive. Effects on the $2 billion fishing industry can be fully assessed only over several years.

This spill, the largest in American history, illustrates a basic public policy conflict: the desire for a pristine environment and a commitment to produce energy to maintain economic stability. Efforts to expand oil exploration in Alaska's Arctic National Wildlife Refuge will be slowed as the impact of the Exxon Valdez accident is assessed.

Continued economic growth seems to necessitate energy production and consumption patterns that threaten the environment. Continued reliance on fossil fuels results in massive emissions of carbon dioxide, which may generate a greenhouse effect in which the earth's atmosphere warms excessively. At the very least, continued reliance on fossil fuels will increase the incidence of acid rain.

Emphasis on development of coal as a major fuel source intensifies several environmental problems. Increased utilization of coal will generate higher levels of CO_2, because coal contains higher levels of carbon than either oil or natural gas. This strategy would also result in higher emissions of sulfur dioxides, a major factor in the acid-rain phenomenon.

The process of energy resource development also poses significant environmental threats. Strip mining for coal denigrates the environment as the ground surface is removed to reach the coal beds. Shaft-mining techniques for coal and uranium present problems, because an effective policy for handling the tailings from the mines has yet to be developed and implemented. Offshore oil drilling efforts present significant environmental threats as well. Oil spills, leaks, and seepage threaten both water quality and wildlife.

The process of developing synthetic fuels from nontraditional fossil fuel sources (obtaining crude oil from oil shale or from the process of coal liquefaction) also presents significant environmental risks. These include surface and subsurface water contamination, air pollution, and disposal of the tailings and other solid waste from the associated mining activities.

Nuclear energy exploitation also presents significant environmental threats. Miners are exposed to carcinogenic radon gas, and the mine tailings contain low-level radioactive materials that are scattered beyond the immediate mining area by the process of wind and water erosion. The wastes from nuclear plants present an environmental risk apart from the potential damage from a nuclear accident, such as the disaster at the Chernobyl facility in the Soviet Union.

Given the close relationship between energy-use patterns and the environment, basic values within society come into conflict. The American public has a long history of valuing nature, and the history of environmental legislation reflects this. One example is the creation and expansion of the national park system. At the same time, the American public has come to expect continued economic growth and personal prosperity. The result is a willingness to accept potential risks to the environment to guarantee a ready supply of energy. The guiding assumption is that any environmental damage that is produced will have little impact on environmental quality. Given its traditional confidence in science and technology, the American public finds it plausible to believe that an optimal "scientific" mix for energy and environmental issues can be established.

The integral bonds between energy and environmental policies are the political, social, and economic issues and the conflicts they produce. The task for political institutions and actors is to resolve or minimize the conflicts and develop policies that promote growth in the energy supply and the economy while protecting the environment.

SUMMARY

The United States has grown accustomed to an abundant supply of cheap energy, and the consumption patterns that have developed place primacy on economic growth. Today, despite the addition of new domestic fossil-fuel reserves, domestic supply has failed to outdistance demand. The result is an increased dependence on imported oil supplies.

International events in 1973 combined temporarily to provide the Organization of Petroleum Exporting Countries (OPEC) with the power to control global oil prices, which resulted in dramatic price increases during the 1970s. Disunity within OPEC combined with increased exploration and conservation measures by Western consuming nations contributed to the significant drop in oil prices between 1986 and 1988.

Attempts to establish a policy leading to energy independence in the United States have been unsuccessful. The comprehensive proposals of Presidents Nixon and Carter were not enacted by Congress. The goal of American energy independence seems an elusive, if not impossible, goal.

The development of alternative energy sources has moved at a slow pace because the technology is both complex and expensive. The lack of profit potential for business has caused corporate policymakers to withhold their support, thus retarding development. Current federal policy has reduced financial assistance for research and development in this area.

The political values that mold energy and environmental policies have changed significantly during this decade. The expanded role of the federal government in formulating energy policy has gradually been replaced with an emphasis on market forces. In a major policy reversal, the leadership role of the federal government has been reduced in favor of uncoordinated efforts by the private sector in response to market forces.

During the twentieth century, the federal government's role in environmental policy has grown tremendously. This is true for air pollution, water pollution, and most other areas of concern. The 1960s and 1970s saw the passage of such pivotal legislation as the Water Pollution Control Act, the Clean Air Act, and the National Environmental Policy Act, among others.

Given the nature of the American political system and the necessity for compromise, even environmental policy strong on intent may be weakened in the area of enforcing regulations. For a variety of reasons—the climate of legal challenge in which the EPA must operate, fuzzy lines of responsibility with state governments, the difficulty in gathering scientifically based information on which to base regulations—regulation as it does exist is not always enforced to its fullest.

The role of government itself has become a major policy issue. There is opposition to government regulation and the financial burden that this regulation imposes. The administration of President Reagan advocated increased reliance on the operation of market forces as the most appropriate mechanism for determining policy options.

Environmental policy and energy policy are inextricably linked. With the onset of the energy crisis, efforts to increase coal production and use and to develop synthetic fuels became aggressive. Yet the production of these energy sources has a substantial negative impact on the quality of the environment. At the same time, environmental regulations add to the already high cost of energy production and consumption. The energy crisis and an emphasis on economic expansion have tipped the energy-environment balance toward relaxation of some environmental standards and regulations.

NOTES

1. Raymond Vernon, ed., *The Oil Crisis* (New York: W.W. Norton, 1976).
2. Melvin A. Conant and Fern R. Gold, *The Geopolitics of Energy* (Boulder, Colo.: Westview, 1978).
3. David Davis, *Energy Politics,* 2nd ed. (New York: St. Martin's Press, 1978).
4. See Seymour Warkov, *Energy Policy in the United States* (New York: Macmillan, 1978).
5. Douglas Evans, *Western Energy Policy* (New York: Macmillan, 1978).
6. Marc H. Ross and Robert Williams, *Our Energy: Regaining Control* (New York: McGraw-Hill, 1981).
7. Don Kash and Robert Rycroft, *U.S. Energy Policy* (Norman: University of Oklahoma Press, 1984).
8. For a complete discussion of cost allocation, see Lester Thurow, *The Zero-Sum Society* (New York: Penguin, 1980).
9. Hanns Maull, *Europe and World Energy* (London: Butterworth, 1980).
10. Peter Schwartz, "What Happened to the Energy Crisis? The Dilemma of an Energy Decision Maker in a Dynamic World," in Jack M. Hollander, Harvey Brooks, and David Sternlight, eds., *Annual Review of Energy* (Palo Alto, Calif.: Annual Reviews, 1987).
11. Rachel Carson, *Silent Spring* (Boston: Houghton Mifflin, 1962).
12. *Environmental Outlook, 1980* (Washington, D.C.: U.S. Environmental Protection Agency, 1980) provides a detailed projection of pollution trends to the year 2000 for geographic regions in the United States.
13. See C. E. Boes, Jr.; H. E. Goeller; J. S. Olson; and R. M. Rotty, "Carbon Dioxide and the Climate: The Uncontrolled Experiment," *American Scientist,* 65 (1975).
14. For example, see Environmental Protection Agency, *Quality Criteria for Water* (Washington, D.C.: Government Printing Office, 1976) and "Water Pollutants," *Environmental Outlook, 1980,* chap. 6.
15. The Resource Conservation and Recovery Act, PL 94–580, Section 4001 (1976).
16. Environmental Protection Agency, "Hazardous Waste Fact Sheet," in *EPA Journal: Waste Alert,* 5 (February, 1979).
17. See T. H. Maugh, "Toxic Waste Disposal: A Growing Problem," *Science,* May 25, 1979.
18. Office of Technology Assessment, *Acid Rain and Transported Air Pollutants: Implications for Public Policy* (Washington, D.C.: Office of Technology Assessment, 1985).
19. National Environmental Policy Act, PL 91-190, January 1, 1970.
20. George C. Eads and Michael Fix, eds., *The Reagan Regulatory Strategy: An Assessment* (Washington, D.C.: Urban Institute Press, 1984).
21. See Guy Benveniste, *Regulation and Planning* (San Francisco: Boyd and Fraser, 1981) and Thurow, *Zero-Sum Society.*
22. See Benveniste, *Regulation and Planning,* chap. 9.
23. Stuart S. Nagel, "Incentives for Compliance with Environmental Law," in Lester W. Milbrath and Frederick R. Inscho, eds., *The Politics of Environmental Policy* (Beverly Hills, Calif.: Sage Publications, 1975).

SUGGESTED READINGS

Barbour, Ian; Brooks, Harvey; Laboff, Sanford; and Opie, J. *Energy and American Values.* New York: Praeger, 1982.

Burch, William R., and DeLuca, Donald R. *Measuring the Social Impact of Natural Resource Policies.* Albuquerque: University of New Mexico Press, 1984.

Burns, Michael E. *Low-Level Radioactive Waste Regulation: Science, Politics, and Fear.* Chelsea, Mich.: Lewis Publishers, 1988.

Carroll, John E. *Environmental Diplomacy.* Ann Arbor: University of Michigan Press, 1984.

Conservation Foundation. *State of the Environment: A View Toward the Nineties.* Washington, D.C.: Conservation Foundation, 1987.

Edmonds, Jae, and Reilly, John M. *Global Energy: Assessing the Future.* New York: Oxford University Press, 1985.

Gilleland, Diane S., and Swisher, James H., eds. *Acid Rain Control: The Costs of Compliance.* Carbondale, Ill.: Southern Illinois University Press, 1984.

Hollander, Jack M., ed. *Annual Review of Energy.* Palo Alto, Calif.: Annual Reviews, 1987.

Kash, Don, and Rycroft, Robert. *U.S. Energy Policy.* Norman: University of Oklahoma Press, 1984.

Knoepfel, Heinz. *Energy 2000: An Overview of the World's Energy Resources in the Decades to Come.* New York: Gordon & Breach Science Publishers, 1986.

Jan Krann, Dick, and Veld, Roeland J. *Environmental Protection: Public or Private Choice.* San Diego, Calif.: Academic Press, 1991.

Office of Technology Assessment. *Acid Rain and Transported Air Pollutants.* Washington, D.C.: U.S. Government Printing Office, 1984.

Rosenbaum, Walter A. *Environmental Politics and Policy.* Washington, D.C.: Congressional Quarterly Press, 1991.

Stewart, Hugh. *Transitional Energy Policy, 1980–2030.* New York: Pergamon, 1982.

Thurow, Lester C. *The Zero-Sum Society.* New York: Penguin, 1980.

Vig, Norman J., and Kraft, Michael E. *Environmental Policy in the 1990s.* Washington, D.C.: Congressional Quarterly Press, 1991.

CHAPTER 5

Intergovernmental Policies: A New Federalism?

The United States' political system is based in part on a separation of responsibilities among different units of government. Those problems that must be addressed by government, however, do not respect jurisdictional boundaries, and therefore intergovernmental actions have become common in dealing with modern problems. Intergovernmental relations refers to the relationships among governmental jurisdictions. For our purposes, the term *intergovernmental relations* will mean the relationships between the national government, on one hand, and the states and local governments, on the other. Interactions between and among states and local governments are also part of the concept.

ISSUE BACKGROUND: THE FEDERAL SYSTEM

The federal system established by the U.S. Constitution ensured that there would be much flexibility in the way that governmental units interacted with one another, and the fact that a federal system was created ensured the need for interactions. As most American government textbooks point out, federalism is a middle ground between a unitary system of government and a confederation. In a unitary system, the central governmental unit controls the system's operation and the distribution of powers. Although the central government may delegate certain powers to local governments, the national level may change those powers or take them away without the consent of the local units. Great Britain is an example of a unitary system.

In a confederation, the local, or constituent, units control the fate of the government. Specifically, the constituent units control the final power to make and enforce laws over their own subjects, a concept called *sovereignty.* In such a system, the central government is created by the other governmental units. The powers of the central government are determined by the local units. The United Nations is a confederation made up of nations. Our government under the Articles of Confederation was such a system, and the weaknesses of that experiment led to the creation of our federal system. With the dissolution of the Soviet Union, eleven former republics have formed a confederation called the Commonwealth of Independent States.

In federalism, the relationships between central and constituent units can be changed only with the consent of both levels. The system of government estab-

134

lished by the Philadelphia Convention of 1787 was a federal system the responsibilities of which were divided between the national government and the states.

Issues in a Federal System

In a federal system, numerous issues arise concerning the proper role of the federation's respective units. Because the U.S. Constitution is not always clear on what exactly the division of responsibility should be, the issues become matters of public debate. Because no one office, division, agency, or branch of government has exclusive responsibility for intergovernmental relations, more confusion arises.

The principal issue in intergovernmental policies is what role each level of government should assume. The authors of the Constitution were wary of too strong a central government and cognizant of the problems of one too weak. They felt that it was necessary to have a national government that could reasonably coordinate the actions of the states, but they also wanted to give the states the autonomy to deal with their own concerns. In the evolution of relations among the states and the national government, there have been periods when the states were relatively stronger and periods in which the national government appeared to dominate. Generally, the states were relatively strong from the beginning of the Republic until the 1930s. After the 1930s, the national government assumed greater and greater responsibility until 1980. In 1980 the election of Ronald Reagan as president presaged an effort to reduce the influence of the national government.

The form of these interactions is also an issue. Should governmental units work together on common problems? Should the national government deal through the states to work with local units of government? Questions also arise as to whether the national government should only help other levels of government deal with their problems or whether it should also implement programs at the state and local levels.

Yet another concern is who should control program implementation. If the national government's money is used in programs, it is not surprising that the national government will want some control over how the money is spent. Without such control, the national government would take the blame for raising tax revenue but would have no say in how it was spent. Those responsible for raising money are not usually willing to give up that say. On the other hand, state and local officials wish to retain as much discretion as possible and do not want to be told by federal bureaucrats how to conduct their business, because they believe they can better address their own differing needs and situations.

Red tape is always an issue when intergovernmental relations are discussed. The controls and duplication of effort that often accompany programs developed at the national level but administered at state and local levels occasion much debate. Efficiency is thus an issue. Opponents of national government effort usually argue that state and local governments can more efficiently deliver needed programs on their own. On the other hand, many programs may be developed on the national level that would not get off the ground on the lower levels, programs that require the tremendous capital and other resources available only to the national government or that require consistent application throughout the nation.

Many national government programs are created to stimulate states or local units to take action in areas in which they have been reluctant to do so or in which there are great inequities among the states or localities. For example, intergovernmental programs may be created to eliminate inequity in education, health, or welfare programs. Other programs may stimulate states to improve transportation, the environment, or work safety when they would not be so inclined without federal government prodding. Of course, critics argue that federal programs reduce the initiative and creativity of local or state units. If left to themselves, without the carrot of federal monies, they might experiment more and develop innovative approaches to solving problems. Innovative approaches often have difficulty getting by the federal bureaucracy.

The form of funding also occasions differences of opinion. Most federal funding has been in the form of categorical grants in which money is provided for a specific project with stipulations on exactly how the money can be used. A grant to develop a program for gifted children is an example.

Advocates of fewer restrictions support block grants, which give money to state or local units for general purposes instead of a specific project. For example, instead of grants for a program for gifted students, a state may receive an education block grant. The state then determines how best to use the education funds.

General revenue sharing, which refers to the transfer of money from the national government to state and local units with little or no restriction on its use, was another popular form of fiscal intergovernmental relations. A formula is used to determine how much money each jurisdiction is entitled to receive.

Participants in Intergovernmental Relations

Numerous groups or special interests also affect intergovernmental policies. Congress and the executive branch interact in the politics of developing intergovernmental policies at the national level. The national government's actions are affected by the concerns of state and local governmental officials. The mayors and governors, through their conferences and organizations, make pronouncements on those national government policies that affect them. Within their own parties, they also attempt to influence the direction of national leaders on relevant issues. Governmental agency officials, especially national government administrators of intergovernmental programs, also have considerable influence on policies. They give legislators their recommendations, and in the policy's implementation, their interpretation or action gives real meaning to the policy. Many of the complaints of state and local officials are directed at federal government administrators. State and local administrators also make their concerns known to policymakers at all levels of government.

The recipients of services under intergovernmental programs often voice their feelings. For example, when aid to education is slated for change or reduction, teachers and school administrators are likely to make entreaties to Congress and the president. Similarly, changes in welfare programs bring reactions from welfare recipients. Other groups that might not directly benefit from a program may also participate in intergovernmental policy development; a program to develop a recreational lake is likely to stimulate environmental groups to take a stand on the issue. Of course, the taxpayer is another interested party, one the Reagan administration appealed to often in its efforts to reduce federal government spending. The main contention is that federal government involvement creates unnecessary administrative expenses that taxpayers have to absorb.

A special interest is taken by the Advisory Commission on Intergovernmental Relations (ACIR), which advises the president and Congress. It was created in 1959 to review the federal system and recommend improvements in the relations among the units. The commission conducts studies and publishes them with recommendations.

With all the participants in the process, it is little wonder that there are conflicts over the direction that intergovernmental relations should take. The courts can resolve the legal and constitutional issues, but differences of opinion within the limits of the law are resolved through the political process, if at all.

CONTEMPORARY POLICY: INTERGOVERNMENTAL REALITIES

During the first century and a half of United States history, the federal system changed gradually. Because the nation was essentially rural and society relatively uncomplicated, the responsibilities of the national government and the states could be relatively easily defined. Although there were major controversies, as illustrated by states' rights conflicts, essentially the powers of the national government were interpreted to be rather narrowly defined. Citizens dealt primarily with state and local jurisdictions. Overriding the separation-of-powers concept was the general philosophy that government at all levels should be restricted in scope. With such an approach, the early history of the United States did not have a great deal of intergovernmental interaction.

During the late nineteenth century, intergovernmental relationships began to develop more formally. In 1862, for example, the Morrill Act provided land grants for agricultural education programs, and the land grant universities are the result of this program. Hatch Act grants beginning in 1887 were the first actual cash transfers from the national government to the states for specific program development. These grants were for establishing agricultural experiment stations. Still, the growth in intergovernmental activities was gradual, and this trend continued through the first three decades of the twentieth century. From the 1930s onward, however, changes occurred much more rapidly. And it is now a settled issue that the powers of the national government are not limited by any specific state powers by virtue of the supremacy clause in Article VI of the Constitution.

Modern Intergovernmental Relations

The term *intergovernmental relations* is sometimes used interchangeably with federalism, but the two really do not mean the same thing. Federalism refers to the formal, legal structure of the political system, whereas intergovernmental relations refers to all the interactions of governmental units within the political system. Therefore, although not provided for specifically in the formal document establishing the political system, some intergovernmental activities occur anyway. The origin of the term intergovernmental relations is somewhat unclear, but political scientist Deil Wright believes that it originated in the New Deal of the 1930s.[1] Given that the New Deal really spawned a large part of what we now know as intergovernmental relations, it is appropriate that the term should have originated from those programs.

If the New Deal symbolizes the development of modern intergovernmental relations, then the Social Security Act of 1935 is the New Deal foundation of many intergovernmental relations activities.[2] This act, and the various amendments to it such as Medicare and Medicaid in 1965, created programs in social welfare that continue to underpin much of the nation's welfare policy today, although the programs' form and organization have changed. These programs began a trend toward federal financing of the programs' activities. They had shared funding with the states and were administered through the state governments. Contacts with the local governments were minimal. But during the mid-1930s, some programs began to bypass the states and deal directly with the municipalities. The public housing program begun in 1937 is an example of such a program.[3] The New Deal programs introduced a new element into the relations between the national government and state and local units. Rules and regulations were developed to implement the federally funded programs. State and local governments permitted the national government to restrict their independence in order to acquire money for programs they had not yet developed, even though they had the authority to do so. Another important legacy was the categorical grant-in-aid, in which funds were provided for specific purposes such as urban renewal, airport construction, and highways.

World War II preoccupied policymakers at all levels, and the development of intergovernmental programs diminished during that time. The immediate postwar activities included a gradual expansion of programs involving state, local, and national governments. Categorical grant-in-aid programs continued to dominate the system. The Kennedy and Johnson administrations of the 1960s brought a dramatic growth in federal programs attempting to solve the problems of American society. During the Johnson administration, in particular, the War on Poverty and Great Society programs spent federal funds in an effort to eliminate poverty and solve other problems of society. During these years, society became highly urbanized, and much of the response to urban problems was to extend programs directly to the cities rather than channel them through the state governments, which were often unsympathetic to urban concerns. By the beginning of the Reagan administration in 1981, there were approximately six hundred separate funding programs for state and local governments.[4] To the dismay of many state and local government administrators, these programs carried with them many detailed administrative regulations.

A major legacy of the 1960s and 1970s was the development of project grants, such as Community Development Block Grants, which required application for funds by the state and/or local government. The national government funding agency would then have to approve the grant. In doing so, the agency could pressure the jurisdiction receiving the money to structure the project or program as the agency wanted. Thus the discretion of state and local units was further lessened. Of course, many entitlement grants continued to exist and expand. In those grants, the jurisdiction would be automatically eligible for funds according to some formula or criterion. Nonetheless, the emergence of the project grants requiring application increased the influence of the national government in programs at the state and local levels. Complicating the matter was that each program had its own application procedures and requirements.

Changes in the 1970s

Not surprisingly, state and local governments and many aspirants to national office criticized the federal grant-in-aid program. As a result of mounting pressures, the programs began to be consolidated in the late 1960s and early 1970s. President Nixon highlighted this consolidation as part of his domestic policy. General and special revenue sharing were created as means of lessening the detailed national control of state and local programs using federal funds. Only general revenue sharing actually was funded by the Congress, but some programs, such as the Law Enforcement Assistance Act, consolidated monies for a particular type of program and gave more discretion to state and local authorities on exactly how the money would be spent. Under general revenue sharing, state and local governments would receive an amount of federal tax dollars according to a formula. With minor exceptions, the money could be used for virtually any purpose that the receiving jurisdiction chose. Instead of specific conditions and limitations on use of the money, new general requirements had to be met by all programs. Equal employment opportunity would be required, and common accounting procedures would have to be used in all governments receiving funds.

The concerns of those who were critical of federal intervention in all aspects of society were adopted by presidential candidate Ronald Reagan, who promised to reverse the trend toward more federal government involvement. Although many preceding presidents had promised to return power to the state and local governments, none had attempted to accomplish that objective quite so dramatically as did President Reagan.

The Reagan Administration

The Reagan administration came to office with a public commitment to reduce federal spending and limit the role of the federal government in what it perceived to be the affairs of state and local governments. Spending cuts and other changes were directed at altering that intergovernmental relationship. Although other administrations had attempted to reverse some of the increases in federal government activity, they accepted the idea that the national government has responsibility for the social welfare system and worked basically to curtail federal control while retaining funding responsibilities. But the Reagan administration perceived things quite differently and worked from a commitment to eliminate the national government's involvement in funding or managing such programs.[5] The Carter administration had in fact begun many of these reductions but progressed slowly; the significance of the Reagan approach was largely in its pace and the extent of restricting federal government influence.

There is a strong political consideration in the approaches of differing administrations to reducing the influence of the national government. Both the Nixon and Reagan administrations focused on giving responsibility to elected officials for local programs. Democratic party administrations, on the contrary, emphasized giving responsibility to various interest groups and organizations. The Republican rationale for moving to a block grant concept was prompted by practical political and economic concerns. Elected officials wanted more of the action, and the federal government did not have the money to expand federal grants. Shifting the power over programs from bureaucratic agencies to elected officials strengthened Nixon's political base. Reagan adopted a similar strategy. The Model Cities program of the 1960s, an experiment in broad funding to localities for comprehensive purposes, provided the model for the block grant concept.

The principal instrument for reducing federal government involvement was the Omnibus Reconciliation Act of 1981, which brought about spending cuts and other policy changes intended to scale back the role of the federal government in domestic affairs. For the first time in twenty-five years, the absolute dollar level of funds to state and local governments actually declined.[6] Policy shifts included reorienting welfare policy and channeling the administration of the programs through the state governments. Instead of following the lead of the Nixon, Ford, and Carter administrations in offering incentives to welfare recipients by allowing them to keep portions of their benefits if they found jobs—so that they could improve their situation by working—the Reagan administration sought to eliminate assistance to working poor. Additionally, reductions were achieved by requiring able-bodied recipients to participate in work programs.

The administration of many programs was centered in the states through the consolidation of more than fifty categorical programs and $7.2 billion into nine block grants.[7] With the block grants, many of the grants that had gone directly to local units of government now were administered by the states. Each state had to draw up guidelines and distribution criteria for using the monies. One aim of the administration was to reduce the contact between the national government and the local units. The states were expected to assume a more aggressive role in programs. Of course, less funding for programs also meant that state and local governments would have to decide whether or not a program was worthwhile. Thus power would be returned to state and local governments, and the national government's role would be diminished. Another argument for the reductions was that the states would save money by not being subject to so many overlapping regulations. Yet, because administrative costs never equaled the cuts, case loads and services were reduced in many programs. Cuts were also demanded by the Reagan administration during 1981 to provide for increases in defense spending and for tax cuts.

Federal aid to state and local governments now totals about $170 billion (see Figure 5-1), representing 18 percent of all state and local government expenditures (see Figure 5-2). In 1979, federal aid reached a peak of 23 percent of all state and local expenditures and has been on a downward trend since then. The Reagan administration successfully halted the growth in the proportion aid represents of both federal and state and local funds. Nonetheless, the absolute dollars continued to climb (see Table 5-1).

Revenue sharing, along with many social programs, was a target of the Reagan administration. Revenue sharing was scheduled to expire on September 30, 1986, but the Reagan administration in 1985 proposed ending it a year earlier. Because of opposition from congressional and local government officials, the program continued until its original expiration date. Although local officials and others supported the $4.6 billion-a-year program because it allowed almost complete control over funds by the receiving governments, there were opponents as well. Some members of Congress opposed it because they wanted Congress to be able to control the spending of the money it raised. Perhaps most controversial, however, was that there was no criterion of need associated with general revenue sharing. Wealthy and poor communities alike received funds. Palm Springs, Cali-

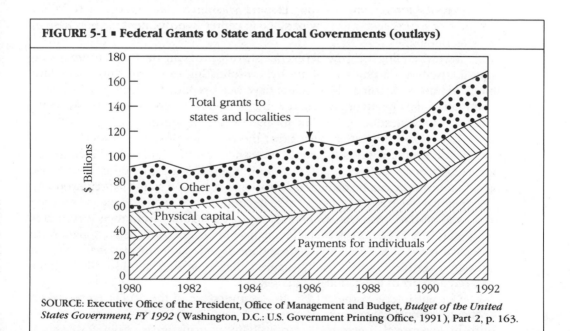

FIGURE 5-1 ▪ Federal Grants to State and Local Governments (outlays)

SOURCE: Executive Office of the President, Office of Management and Budget, *Budget of the United States Government, FY 1992* (Washington, D.C.: U.S. Government Printing Office, 1991), Part 2, p. 163.

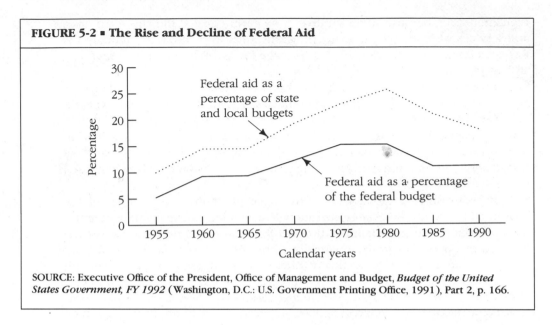

FIGURE 5-2 ■ The Rise and Decline of Federal Aid

SOURCE: Executive Office of the President, Office of Management and Budget, *Budget of the United States Government, FY 1992* (Washington, D.C.: U.S. Government Printing Office, 1991), Part 2, p. 166.

fornia; Scottsdale, Arizona; and Grosse Pointe, Michigan, received funds along with Youngstown, Ohio; Newark, New Jersey; and Brownsville, Texas.

Some communities became dependent on general revenue sharing, whereas others used it for extras. Poor communities were likely to use it along with normal tax revenues for operating expenses, and wealthier communities used it for projects or extras such as a new park, civic center improvement, or purchase of new technology.

Besides ending the general revenue sharing program, the Reagan administration focused on cutting federal aid by consolidating categorical programs into block grants. Now some block grants have been reduced as well. For example, community development and energy grants declined between 1980 and 1992 and seem to be destined to decline for the foreseeable future.

Tax reform suggestions also affect the revenues of state and local governments. Allowing taxpayers to deduct state and local taxes on federal income tax forms creates an indirect transfer of funds. State and local taxes are also more acceptable if they can be deducted on national taxes, and so the flat-tax proposal, as explained in Chapter 3, affects these deductions and is often opposed by state and local officials, who fear they will face greater hostility from their electorates without it. The 1986 tax reform included the elimination of the deduction for state and local sales taxes. Reaction of state and local government officials was swift and strongly negative. Political reality suggests that some state and local deductions will remain part of the national tax code.

Current intergovernmental policy is a mixture of the recent emphasis on reducing national government prominence in public affairs and the historic development of national government responsibility in many areas of public concern.

TABLE 5-1 ▪ Federal Grant Outlays By Function (in billions of dollars)

Function	Actual 1990	Estimate					
		1991	1992	1993	1994	1995	1996
National defense	0.2	0.3	0.1	0.1	0.1	0.1	0.1
Energy	0.5	0.5	0.4	0.3	0.3	0.3	0.3
Natural resources and environment	3.7	4.0	3.8	3.9	3.7	3.3	2.9
Agriculture	1.3	1.4	1.4	1.5	1.6	1.6	1.7
Transportation	19.2	19.8	20.2	21.5	21.9	21.8	23.3
Community and regional development	5.0	4.8	4.3	4.0	3.7	3.6	3.6
Education, training, employment and social services	23.1	26.8	27.6	27.8	28.1	28.5	28.9
Health	43.9	54.9	63.4	72.3	82.2	92.6	103.7
Income security	37.0	42.7	46.3	49.2	52.3	54.7	55.6
Veterans benefits and services	0.1	0.2	0.2	0.2	0.2	0.2	0.2
Administration of justice	0.6	0.9	0.8	1.0	0.7	0.7	0.7
General government	2.3	2.3	2.2	2.2	2.2	2.2	2.3
Total outlays	136.9	158.6	171.0	184.0	197.0	209.9	223.2

SOURCE: Executive Office of the President, Office of Management and Budget, *Budget of the United States Government, FY 1992* (Washington, D.C.: U.S. Government Printing Office, 1991), Part 2, p. 164.

Since the New Deal, the emphasis has been on creating programs and policies to cope with society's problems, and it was unlikely that one administration could totally undo what had taken forty-five years to develop. Thus it is not surprising that the current situation reflects elements of many perspectives.

During the Bush administration, the trend toward reducing federal government expenditures continued with little action regarding funding of increased responsibilities for state and local governments which had to pick up programs. The end of the cold war led many to hope that the peace dividend would allow for relieving state and local governments of their financial pressures. However, the Persian Gulf war and persistent public debt have made it difficult for financial relief to come from the national government. State and local officials worry that they are presented with increasing numbers of federal mandates and shifting of more responsibilities while the national government provides no funding for them. Although the administration seems interested in increasing federal financing of some parts of programs, it also shifts larger parts to state and local levels, further undermining the ability of state and local governments to finance programs and services.[8]

Other Forms of Intergovernmental Interaction

Because money provided by the national government is a major source of funding for intergovernmental activity, the emphasis in intergovernmental relations is often on fiscal relationships, but there are other forms of interaction as well. Intergovernmental relations include cross-cutting regulations such as nondiscrimination requirements in the state and local units' personnel actions, cooperative efforts in law enforcement, and cooperation in tax enforcement.

Although critics usually portray the national government as growing at the expense of the state and local governments, all levels of government have expanded through intergovernmental programs. Thus, in regard to budgets, number of personnel, taxes, number of services, number of people served, and the like, state and local governments have kept pace with the national government in growth. For example, federal government expenditures increased from about $300 billion in 1974 to nearly $1.5 trillion in 1992. From 1974 to 1988, the state and local governments' expenditure of their own revenues grew from a little over $160 billion to over $765 billion.[9] Many of the activities creating this growth are cooperative programs among the national, state, and local governments. The fact that our federal system creates some confusion over responsibilities leads to the cooperative efforts.

The cornerstone of President Reagan's New Federalism was the reversal of the national government's involvement in state and local affairs. In order to achieve that goal, the president tried to curtail the amount of money transferred from the national government to state and local units. Though 25 percent of state and local expenditures were federal funds when Reagan took office, his intention was to cut that portion to approximately 4 percent by 1991. To do so, he proposed swapping responsibility for some programs, such as leaving welfare to the states and accepting Medicaid as a federal responsibility. But Congress did not go along with those suggestions, in the face of widespread state and local opposition.

Specific elements of the administration's program were consolidation of many grants under block grants, elimination of some grant programs, reductions in others, and elimination of rules and regulations imposed on the receiving jurisdictions.[10] In 1981, the administration was successful in cutting real dollar federal aid by about 12 percent. Although real dollar expenditures increased again by 5 percent between 1985 and 1987, they had dipped 18 percent by 1990.[11] Even during the difficult economic times of 1982 and 1983, the administration did not reverse its stance that federal government efforts should be reduced. Instead of drawing up plans to provide emergency aid to state and local units hard hit by the sluggish economy, the administration continued its push for reducing the federal governmental role. As a result, the long-standing view that the national government should come to the rescue in times of trouble appears to have been reversed. The Bush administration exhibited a similar attitude during the 1990–91 recession.

The Reagan administration eliminated some federal rules and regulations as well as some grants. For example, in the Community Development Block Grant programs, the grant recipients no longer have to target their programs to low- and moderate-income persons. Additionally, many programs such as legal services to the poor were simply terminated by the administration's decision not to spend the funds.

Of course, the administration was not able to accomplish all that it set out to do. Because Congress had to act on most of the proposals, there was a lot of political pressure to kill many of the administration's proposals. Efforts to reduce funding for environmental programs, for example, met with strong opposition. Similarly, the administration's attempts to scale back or eliminate cabinet departments such as Education and Energy were unsuccessful. Suggestions that general revenue sharing be eliminated, however, were successful despite opposition by state and local political leaders.

In addition to the financial relationships between the national government and other units of government, there are many national programs and requirements that affect state and local activities. National government legislation on health and safety, environmental protection, consumer protection, civil rights, and other issues requires or encourages state and local entities to take or refrain from particular action. For example, federal law permits the states to have a sixty-five-mile-per-hour maximum speed limit on some interstate highways in order to receive federal highway funds. Water-quality and air-quality standards are imposed on state and local governments as well. These are areas in which the national government has not had the major responsibility because they are considered reserved powers of the states. In recent history the national government has established requirements that state and local governments must follow in order to receive grants. In some cases, the requirements are viewed as usurping state and local government responsibilities.

The U.S. Supreme Court decided in *Garcia* v. *San Antonio Metropolitan Transit Authority* (1985) that state and local governments are subject to the Federal Fair Labor Standards Act. As such, state and local units have to pay minimum wage and overtime rates and comply with other reporting and employment requirements. The decision overturns the Court's 1976 ruling that exempted these jurisdictions from coverage by the act. The ruling imposes requirements upon the state and local governments and gives the U.S. Department of Labor authority over them. It represents a reversal of the efforts of the Reagan administration to lessen restrictions.

Despite the Reagan administration's efforts to alter significantly the shape of American federalism, the national, state, and local governments continue to work interdependently.

State governments also provide grants-in-aid to local governments. School districts receive the largest share of state aid by far. Municipalities and counties receive most of the rest, although there are some funds that go to special districts and townships. The same issues that exist between the national government and state and local governments arise in state grants to local jurisdictions. Because of the closeness of the actors involved, the conflicts can become even more intense. During the 1980s, it was expected that states would increase their levels of support to local governments in response to federal cutbacks. The evidence suggests that there has been little real change.[12]

POLICY EVALUATION: CHANGING
INTERGOVERNMENTAL RELATIONS

Complaints about the intergovernmental system usually have focused on the growth of the national government at the expense of state and local autonomy. The criticisms are there today just as they were before the advent of President Reagan's New Federalism. However, some analysts have found that the general criticism is often not present in the comments of state program managers when they discuss particular programs.[13] Nonetheless, David Walker characterized the federal system as one of system overload, with the national government imposing heavy burdens on the state and local governments.[14] Regardless of one's perspective, it is clear that state and local governments have grown as the national government has expanded its involvement in domestic policy issues. The result has been more and more intergovernmental activities and a more complex web of relations. Of course, the intention of the Reagan administration was to reverse that complexity and lighten the hand of the national government in the affairs of state and local governments.

Administrative Problems

Perhaps the most common complaint about the federal government is that it imposes too much red tape on the state and local recipients of aid. The national government also is criticized for attempting to regulate too many areas of activity outside grant programs. State and local administrators complain about the amount of paperwork in applying for and administering grants. The paperwork increases the costs to the recipients and delays the project's completion. Much of the difficulty arises because the regional administrators of federal agencies cannot make the final decisions on most grants. Instead, they advise the central agency office, which in turn makes the final decision. Disputes in interpreting program criteria and rules and regulations take a long time to resolve, and conflicting rules and regulations and duplication of effort only compound the problem. Even more difficult for the state and local agencies is the need for clearance from numerous agencies for local officials on up to federal agency managers.

All of these requirements lead to inflexibility in the categorical programs. Local officials feel that their needs cannot be met; rather, the program requirements appear to be oriented more to the needs of the federal agency. Additionally, many of the categorical programs are so narrowly defined that it becomes difficult to fit them to the particular needs of the state and local governments.

Block grants and general revenue sharing were supposed to eliminate some of the administrative problems noted above. Giving state and local officials more discretion in the structure of their programs would subject the money to fewer restrictions. Although block grants generally begin with such aspirations, state program administrators seem to recategorize them as part of their actual implementation. Conflicts develop within the state block-grant administrative agencies. Program specialists fight for funds for their programs, and the funds end up being allocated on a program basis. The result is that after they reach the state level, the block grants often begin to look again like categorical grants. Additionally, national government policy seems to reimpose conditions. For example, general revenue sharing was found to contain the compliance requirements of fifteen different federal agencies just four years after its adoption as federal aid without strings.[15]

Another effort to reduce the overlap in administrative rules was the Joint Funding and Simplification Act of 1974, which authorized one set of administrative rules for programs funded jointly by federal government agencies. The idea behind the act was to allow state and local governments to develop coordinated programs with funds from various grant programs to address local problems. But there has been little success because there have been few joint funding programs. The program-specific detail of the federal agencies tends to ignore the more general problems faced by the state and local communities. As a result, the centralization inherent in most categorical grant programs often is another source of friction for state and local program administrators.

Monitoring

Related to administrative problems is monitoring by federal agencies. In granting money to other units of government, the national government tries to see that the money is used properly and for beneficial programs and to that end has devised elaborate monitoring arrangements. Among the most important is the A-95 review process, which refers to Circular A-95 of the Office of Management and Budget. This review procedure requires that proposals be commented on by some unit other than the local government requesting funds. Typically, a regional council of governments or regional planning commission is made responsible for reviewing and commenting on grant applications. Additionally, the request usually must be commented on by some statewide agency or office before going to the federal agency. The reason for these requirements is to reduce overlapping projects and to ensure that one project does not work at cross-purposes with other projects in the area. It also permits the coordination of projects that would benefit an area. The end result should be cost savings to the taxpayer and more efficient use of grant monies, but there is no hard evidence that such objectives have been met.

There is no question that the review process has had many beneficial effects in generating greater cooperation among units in a region. Nonetheless, the instrument has not been entirely successful. Because the regional councils of governments and the like are made up of representatives of the area's jurisdictions, they pursue their own interests in making decisions. Coalitions of jurisdictions often work to the advantage of some and to the disadvantage of others. Typically, many small units of government may coalesce around issues and hamper the efforts of the one largest city in the region. It therefore is common for the largest city to withdraw from the regional association, thus closing the door on coopera-tive efforts. In instances in which representation on the regional association depends on the population of the constituent units, this may have the opposite effect. The larger jurisdictions may control and ignore the legitimate needs of the smaller units. But the A-95 review has been important to the intergovernmental grant system, despite these problems.

Monitoring occurs within agencies as well. The recipient of a grant normally has to be reviewed by the granting agency. Most federal agencies have so many programs and grants to monitor that it is impossible to do a complete job of monitoring, so recipient governments may find ways to get around or ignore compliance with impunity. And when an agency decides to take action against a unit, the affected government has many options at its command to lessen the agency's ability to do so. Because the agencies rely on congressional support to continue their activities, the affected government can turn to members of Congress to put pressure on the granting agency. The agency also depends on its clientele, the recipient units of government, to ensure support for its programs. Thus agency administrators usually see the advantage of working things out with the state or local units rather than fighting with them.

Finances

Another feature of the intergovernmental system is the financial relationships between and among units. Because the national government increased the numbers of funded programs during the mid-twentieth century, intergovernmental transfers of funds became significant. The problem with providing federal funds lies in who controls the use of those funds. With categorical grants, the national government clearly established criteria for using the money. With block grants and general revenue sharing, the expectation was that the national government would loosen its control. Of course, the main purpose of Reagan's domestic policy was the loosening of restrictions coupled with major cuts in domestic spending.

With grants, the state and local levels are never certain what amount of money is going to be available from year to year. This uncertainty in the level of funding makes it more difficult for them to plan their own activities and budgets. Another irritating aspect of most federal grants for the recipient units is the maintenance of effort requirement, which means that state and local governments cannot use federal money to replace their own spending on the affected program. The receiving governments are locked into spending patterns if they wish to receive the grants with such requirements. For example, Community Development Block Grants could not be used to reduce the amount of money that the local government spent on redevelopment. Instead, a government would be required to continue to spend at the level at which it had spent in the past, or it could not continue to receive Community Development funds.

Block grants and general revenue sharing combined with the Reagan administration's cuts in domestic spending have had several effects on state and local governments. State and local units were faced with absorbing the costs of many programs if they were to continue to provide services, especially social and human services programs. Studies of the effects of block grants so far have indicated that the state replacement of lost federal funds has been relatively low.[16] The principal question is whether the state and local governments wish to continue programs and whether they have the resources to do so. The shift to block grants increased the internal competition for funds in state governments. Another feature of the funding shift has been to show the states how they can influence local units to a greater degree. And the states are themselves now using the block grant approach to fund many programs.

Structural Effects

The federal patchwork of grants affects the way state and local governments operate. One of the many criticisms of federal funding in the past has been that it distorts the priorities of state and local governments. The argument is that governments go after money where it is available. They are unlikely to spend money on programs or projects that are needed but pursue less-needed projects because they can get federal help with them. Because there are categorical grants for almost anything imaginable, it is less likely now than it was in the 1950s and 1960s that this criticism is accurate. However, federal priorities may become state and local priorities if the incentive is great enough.

Probably the greatest effect of Reagan's domestic program was that it sustained the emergence of the states as strong partners in the federal relationship. The evidence is clear that the states were beginning to gain influence during the Nixon administration and through the Carter presidency. Reagan's emphasis on returning power to the states and eliminating many federal activities accelerated that trend and probably ensured that it would not be reversed. The fact that block grants go through the states for distribution places state government in a strong position to determine how the money will be used and what units of government will use it. Thus the states won more independence from the national government at the same time that they increased their ability to control the distribution of money to the local units.[17]

Another structural legacy of Reagan's program is that the issue of intergovernmental relations has been raised as a prominent item on the national policy debate agenda. The relationship between the state and local governments and the national government became a major component of political discussion during the 1980s, and a serious consideration of altering that relationship resulted.

FUTURE ALTERNATIVES: CONTINUING ADAPTATION OF THE INTERGOVERNMENTAL SYSTEM

Intergovernmental policies continue to evolve as differing demands are made on the political system. Glendening and Reeves characterized the federal system as a pragmatic one,[18] adapting to changing conditions and assuming new forms to accommodate political, economic, and social realities. Thus it is safe to say that there will be changes in intergovernmental policies, but it is the directions of those changes that are at issue, and the proponents of alternative intergovernmental arrangements will attempt to shape the new intergovernmental policies.

The Reagan administration was the proponent of one type of inter-governmental redistribution of power. As already noted in this chapter, proponents of this type would like to see the system change so that the national government can reduce its influence in domestic affairs and leave most government activities to state and local governments. The programs of the Reagan administration have increased the status and influence of state governments and diminished national government involvement in many activities. The block grant programs were viewed by the Reagan administration as only a step to further withdrawal by the national government, with the hope that federal involvement in many of the block grant programs would eventually be eliminated.

The National Governors Conference, the Conference of State Legislatures, and the Advisory Commission on Intergovernmental Relations believe that the roles of the national government and states can be better defined. The problem is determining exactly which functions should be the responsibility of the national government and what should be the responsibility of state and local units. Commonly, suggestions are made that the national government assume all responsibility for health and income support programs and shift the responsibility for all other social programs to the states. Governors occasionally call upon the national government to assume all responsibility for funding welfare programs, in return for the states' picking up other programs such as education and transportation. Again, the primary emphasis is on turning over many functions to the state and local governments while reducing federal involvement, but there is little agreement on exactly how the division should be made.

The process of dividing responsibility suggests a view of intergovernmental relations in which functions can be neatly separated. But history has suggested that such neat divisions are unrealistic. Since most policy activities affect more states than one, it is unrealistic to leave such activities exclusively under the control of one or more states. That would leave the citizens of some states affected by policy-making activity by a governmental body in which they were not represented. This consideration was a primary factor in replacing the Articles of Confederation with the present Constitution, which provides for a national sovereignty. Therefore it is improbable that any system could be devised that abolished sharing and cooperation. Nonetheless, proponents of this view expect that progress will be made toward their objectives. The success of the Reagan administration in redirecting the relationship suggests that some shift is possible.

Opponents of the shift of responsibility to the states argue that states are not able to assume that responsibility. States are not likely to have the resources to fund the programs adequately, and, as we noted above, states may not always be inclined to continue such programs. The administrative complexity of fifty states administering programs, as under the block grants, is seen as burdensome and inefficient by the opponents of these proposals. There are also concerns that some states will be less sensitive to issues such as equity, fairness, and civil rights in developing and implementing programs.

Those favoring the centralization of programs also are concerned about the complexity of the problems facing American society. They see problems as being so complex that only the national government can possibly marshal the resources to address them and provide a coordinated effort.

Some people advocate a radical change in the structure of the federal system that would greatly change intergovernmental policy.[19] They suggest that the states be eliminated and replaced by regional governments. The number of units would be reduced from fifty to about twelve; this smaller number would mean more efficiency, and interactions between the national and constituent governmental units would be less complex. Under the regional system, the national government would exercise more control over regional units than it currently does over the states.

The advocates of change are not likely to see their proposals realized completely, but some shifts are certain. It appears certain that fiscal changes will continue: The trend toward fewer real dollars in grants is not likely to be reversed, especially with the federal deficit pressures. As a result, there will be fewer dollars for state and local units to share. Competition for those dollars is bound to increase, and some analysts suggest that changes in political coalitions of public interest groups would result, as they now oppose one another, rather than work together, on grant requests.[20] With fewer dollars available, fiscal relationships are likely to give way to cooperative efforts in other ways and to the national government's attempts to regulate activities of states and local governments through general policy. Such general policy is likely to increase the costs of state and local government without providing federal monies to cover those costs.

It is hard to predict what will happen with the block grants. These programs appear to be popular with the general public and with state officials because they imply few strings. However, the general public is ineffective in pressuring Congress to sustain these programs. Because the Reagan administration viewed block grants as one step toward federal withdrawal from such programs, they might not have a secure future. Categorical grants most likely will continue to be the most significant element of the fiscal relationship, because the interests affected by them often are strong and can influence Congress when cuts are contemplated. Even with the consolidation of programs into block grants, there has been little effect on the number of categorical grant programs. There were approximately five hundred federal grant programs in 1978 and still over four hundred in 1987. More significantly, categorical grants still account for more than 80 percent of grant funds.

SUMMARY

Intergovernmental policy is a natural outgrowth of the federal system, in which government responsibilities are loosely distributed between the national government and the states. The nation started with the states being relatively strong while the national government sought its proper role. Later intergovernmental interactions occurred through land grant programs and cooperative efforts to develop the economy. But until the twentieth century, the national government was not closely involved in domestic policy, which was seen as the realm of state and local governments.

The twentieth century marked the era of escalating intergovernmental programs. During the 1930s, many national government programs were created to help the nation out of the Great Depression, and those programs signaled a strong national involvement in social and economic policy. Until the 1970s, the national government increased its involvement through many grant programs and took responsibility for the nation's general welfare. During the 1970s, however, national leaders began to question the propriety of the massive federal programs and began to return many of these responsibilities to the states.

Reagan's election in 1980 accelerated the trend toward reducing the influence of the national government and increasing the state governments' power. To do this, categorical grants were deemphasized, and block grant funding was favored. Categorical grants fund a specific project subject to federal government rules and regulations. Block grants fund general program areas such as education and permit the states to determine how the money will be spent within this area. General revenue sharing was an even broader-based transfer of funds in which a state or local government received money with no strings from the federal government. The money was then spent as the state or local government decided.

The issues in intergovernmental relations concern which level of government has the authority, inclination, and resources to engage in a particular activity. The national government entered many domestic program areas such as social and educational programs because states either did not have the resources or were not interested in providing some services. To ensure equity of services, the national government offered grants to the states to encourage them to draw up particular programs. But with the grants came numerous restrictions and controls as well, which have prompted many state and local government officials to press for a different arrangement whereby they would have maximum flexibility in using federal funding. The 1980s brought those concerns to the forefront of the political debate. The 1990s began with a similar approach, although the major complaint now is that programs and mandates are passed on to state and local governments without money to fund them.

NOTES

1. Deil S. Wright, *Understanding Intergovernmental Relations* (North Scituate, Mass.: Duxbury Press, 1978), pp. 6–7.

2. Arnold M. Howitt, *Managing Federalism: Studies in Intergovernmental Relations* (Washington, D.C.: Congressional Quarterly Press, 1984). Much of this historical discussion draws on Howitt's account, pp. 1–35.

3. Ibid., pp. 5–6.

4. Parris N. Glendening and Mavis Mann Reeves, *Pragmatic Federalism,* 2d ed. (Pacific Palisades, Calif.: Palisades Publishers, 1984), p. 72.

5. See Samuel Beer, "Foreword," in John William Ellwood, ed., *Reductions in U.S. Domestic Spending* (New Brunswick, N.J.: Transaction Books, 1982).

6. Richard P. Nathan, Fred C. Doolittle, and Associates, *The Consequences of Cuts* (Princeton, N.J.: Princeton University Urban and Regional Research Center, 1983).

7. Ibid., p. 4.

8. Michael A. Pagano, Ann O'M. Bowman, and John Kincaid, "The State of American Federalism, 1990–1991," *Publius,* 21 (Summer 1991), 1–26.

9. Advisory Commission on Intergovernmental Relations, *Significant Features of Fiscal Federalism, Revenues and Expenditures,* vol. 2 (Washington, D.C.: U.S. Government Printing Office, August 1990), pp. 2–7.

10. For an excellent discussion of these issues, see George E. Peterson, "The State and Local Sector," in John L. Palmer and Isabel V. Sawhill, eds., *The Reagan Experiment* (Washington, D.C.: Urban Institute Press, 1982), pp. 157–217; and Michael J. Ross, *State and Local Politics and Policy* (Englewood Cliffs, N.J.: Prentice-Hall, 1987), chap. 2.

11. Executive Office of the President, Office of Management and Budget, *Budget of the United States Government, Fiscal Year 1992* (Washington, D.C.: Government Printing Office, 1991), Part 2, p. 166.

12. Pagano, Bowman, and Kincaid, "The State of American Federalism."

13. See Daniel J. Elazar, *American Federalism: A View from the States,* 3d ed. (New York: Harper & Row, 1984).

14. David B. Walker, *Toward a Functioning Federalism* (Cambridge, Mass.: Winthrop, 1981).

15. Lawrence D. Brown and Bernard Frieden, "Guidelines and Goals in the Model Cities Program," *Policy Sciences,* 7 (December 1976), 488.

16. Palmer and Sawhill, *The Reagan Experiment,* chap. 6; and Nathan and Doolittle, *The Consequences of Cuts.*

17. Nathan Glazer, "The Social Policy of the Reagan Administration: A Review," *Public Interest,* 75 (Spring 1984), 76–98; Donald Axelrod, *A Budget Quartet: Critical Policy and Management Issues* (New York: St. Martin's Press, 1989), pp. 135–152; and Ross, *State and Local Politics,* chap. 2.

18. Glendening and Reeves, *Pragmatic Federalism.*

19. For example, Rexford G. Tugwell, *Model for a New Constitution* (Palo Alto, Calif.: James E. Freel and Associates, 1970).

20. George E. Hale and Marian Lief Palley, *The Politics of Federal Grants* (Washington, D.C.: Congressional Quarterly Press, 1981), pp. 169–170.

SUGGESTED READINGS

Axelrod, Donald. *A Budget Quartet: Critical Policy & Management Issues.* New York: St. Martin's Press, 1989.

Barfield, Claude E. *Rethinking Federalism: Block Grants and Responsibilities.* Washington, D.C.: American Enterprise Institute, 1981.

Elazar, Daniel J. *American Federalism: A View from the States.* 3d ed. New York: Harper & Row, 1984.

Ellwood, John William, ed. *Reductions in U.S. Domestic Spending.* New Brunswick, N.J.: Transaction Books, 1982.

Fix, Michael, and Kenyon, Daphne A., eds. *Coping with Mandates.* Washington, D.C.: Urban Institute Press, 1990.

Glendening, Parris N., and Reeves, Mavis Mann. *Pragmatic Federalism: An Intergovernmental View of American Government.* 2d ed. Pacific Palisades, Calif.: Palisades Publishers, 1984.

Gosling, James J. *Budgetary Politics in American State Governments.* New York: Longman, 1922.

Hale, George E., and Palley, Marian Lief. *The Politics of Federal Grants.* Washington, D.C.: Congressional Quarterly Press, 1981.

Keller, Morton. "State Power Needn't Be Resurrected Because It Never Died." *Governing,* 2 (October 1988), 53–57.

Nathan, Richard P.; Doolittle, Fred C.; and Associates. *The Consequences of Cuts: The Effects of the Reagan Domestic Program on State and Local Governments.* Princeton, N.J.: Princeton University Urban and Regional Research Center, 1983.

Pagano, Michael A.; Bowman, Ann O'M.; and Kincaid, John. "The State of American Federalism, 1990–1991." *Publius,* 21 (Summer 1991): 1–26.

Palmer, John L., and Sawhill, Isabel V., eds. *The Reagan Experiment.* Washington, D.C.: Urban Institute Press, 1982.

Palmer, Kenneth T., and Moen, Matthew C. "Intergovernmental Fiscal Relations in the 1980s." *Public Budgeting and Financial Management,* forthcoming 1992.

Ross, Michael J. *State and Local Politics and Policy.* Englewood Cliffs, N.J.: Prentice-Hall, 1987.

Swartz, Thomas R., and Peck, John E. *The Changing Face of Fiscal Federalism.* Armonk, N.Y.: Sharpe, 1990.

Wright, Deil S. *Understanding Intergovernmental Relations.* 3d ed. Pacific Grove, Calif.: Brooks/Cole, 1988.

CHAPTER 6

Crime and Criminal Justice: Dilemmas of Social Control

The public today perceives crime as having reached intolerable levels, especially in America's major cities. This perception has created a widespread demand that government do something to attack the problem. This demand was manifested in the 1988 presidential campaign, when one of the most effective campaign techniques of the winner, George Bush, was to imply that his opponent, Michael Dukakis, was more concerned with the rights of criminals than with those of their victims.

This chapter will describe policies developed to deal with crime, analyze the impact of these policies, and suggest alternatives presently available. The chapter will focus on one widely assumed strategy for the prevention of crime, *deterrence*. Deterrence refers to the discouraging of criminal acts by imposing prohibitive costs on criminals. In general, this means severe punishment. Research shows, however, that a high probability of punishment and the swiftness of suffering the punishment after committing a crime are more conducive to deterrence than is increasing the severity of the punishment. The chapter will examine the factors that may impede such punishment and those that keep the perpetrators of crime out of jail or allow them to escape with punishments less severe than those allowed by law or demanded by a widespread sense of justice.

Evaluating the impact of public policy on crime depends on knowing the nature and extent of crime. It is therefore necessary to assess the extent to which the incidence of crime has actually increased in recent years. It is important to note that crime is not an undifferentiated phenomenon. There are different types of crime with different rates of occurrence and different causes, and they require different policies to reduce their incidence. Policies designed to reduce one kind of crime may have no effect on, or may even increase, other types of crime. The unintended consequences, or *spillover effects,* of public policy are crucial to the evaluation of crime policies.

Too often, politicians generalize about one type of crime, for example, "crime in the streets," as if that type of crime encompassed the universe of the crime problem. Actually, crime is any behavior that some duly constituted legislative body has chosen to make illegal. These behaviors include crimes against property (robbery and auto theft), crimes against persons (assault, murder, and rape), white-collar crimes (stock fraud and price fixing), "victimless" crimes against a dominant moral code (sodomy, fornication, adultery, and the sale of pornography), and political crimes (illegal campaign contributions and bribery). **155**

These are distinct types of activities, the causes and prevention of which differ. Even within these categories, many distinctions may be discerned. Carefully planned murders, spontaneous killing in anger or in a fight, and violent rape born out of a general hatred of women—all crimes against persons—will not respond to the same remedies. Because the concept of crime covers too diverse a category of actions to be analytically useful, this chapter will distinguish various types of illegal activities with respect to their causes and means of prevention.

ISSUE BACKGROUND: THE GROWTH OF CRIME

The Extent of Crime

It is not difficult to find factual support for the perception that crime in general has increased at an alarming rate in recent decades. The crime rate, as defined by the Federal Bureau of Investigation's *Uniform Crime Report,* rose dramatically for the two decades after the current method of tabulating the FBI index went into effect, until 1981. This crime index refers to the number of crimes per 100,000 population for seven categories of crime: (1) murder and manslaughter, (2) forcible rape, (3) robbery, (4) aggravated assault, (5) burglary, (6) larceny and theft, and (7) auto theft. The rise in index crimes of violence from 1967 to 1978 was 192 percent, and the rise in index crimes against property was 168 percent.[1] Clearly, these statistics represent significant increases, whatever the definitional problems. The crime index from 1981 to 1990 is shown in Table 6-1.

Except for a leveling off and brief dip from 1981 to 1984, the crime rate has grown steadily over the past three decades (see Figure 6-1). From 1960 to 1990, the rate of violent crimes per capita, the kind of crimes that generate the most fear and have a consequently severe impact on urban life, increased *355 percent!* In particular, a rise in violent crime against random victims, crime unrelated to the identity or behavior of the victim, has exacerbated the widespread fear of crime. This fear and the perception of victimization are illustrated by the fact that, according to the February 9, 1992, edition of the *New York Times,* sales of home alarm systems increased from 1986 to 1992 by 80 percent.

White-collar crime. Problems of the definition and interpretation of crime statistics abound, however. The crime index does not exhaust the universe of illegal activities. For example, the index does not include most white-collar crimes, which cost the American public more in lost dollar value than does the total of all the index crimes.[2] The U.S. Chamber of Commerce has estimated that embezzlement, fraud, commercial theft, and "business-related arson" cost the public over $40 billion per year in the late 1970s, ten times the value of the property lost through street crime. FBI figures estimate that for 1988 the total loss to victims of street crime was $16.6 billion, if one adds in less direct costs such as pain, suffering, and the risk of death. Antitrust violations may cost another $160 billion per year.[3] Edwin Sutherland found that a number of large corporations have

TABLE 6-1 ▪ Index of Crime, 1990

	Total Crime	Violent	Property	Murder and Manslaughter	Forcible Rape	Robbery
Rate per 100,000	5820.3	731.8	5088.5	9.4	41.2	257.0
Percent Change since 1989		10.4	.2	8.0	8.1	10.3
Percent Change since 1981		23.1	−3.3	−4.1	14.4	−7.0

	Aggravated Assault	Burglary	Larceny	Motor Vehicle Theft
Rate per 100,000	424.1	1235.9	3194.8	657.8
Percent Change since 1989	10.8	−3.2	.7	4.3
Percent Change since 1981	46.4	−25.1	1.8	38.6

SOURCE: U.S. Department of Justice, Federal Bureau of Investigation, Uniform Crime Reports, *Crime in the United States,* released August, 1991 (Washington, D.C.: U.S. Government Printing Office), p. 50.

been convicted of numerous violations of law over the years, a record that would cause an individual to be penalized as a "habitual offender."[4] A price-fixing scheme that sent some lower-level General Electric and Westinghouse executives to jail in the 1960s was estimated to have cost the American public some $800 million.[5] Clearly, it would require many muggings to equal that sum. General Electric was at it again in the 1980s, pleading guilty in 1985 to defrauding the Air Force of $800,000 in 1980 on a Minuteman missile project. Other major corporations convicted or charged with substantial, recent violations are General Dynamics, E. F. Hutton, and the Bank of Boston. In late 1988, the securities firm of Drexel Burnham Lambert pleaded guilty to felony counts involving mail, wire, and securities fraud, and paid a fine of $650 million.

The late 1980s witnessed new levels of money lost to the public through white-collar crime. Stockbrokers such as Ivan Boesky and Michael Milken were convicted of having illegally made tens of millions of dollars by dealing in stocks on the basis of inside information not available to the general public, thus deriving an unfair advantage over others who invest in the market. Boesky was convicted of fraud and paid a fine and penalty of $100 million. An even bigger scandal involved the financial collapse of a large number of savings and loan institutions, forcing the government to cover billions of dollars in insured deposits. The total sum that will eventually have to be made up by taxpayers is not yet precisely fixed but the estimates are continuing to expand and now range in the neighborhood of $500 billion. It became apparent that these institutions had been engaged in making

FIGURE 6-1 ▪ Crime Rates 1960–1990

Number of incidents per 100,000 Americans.

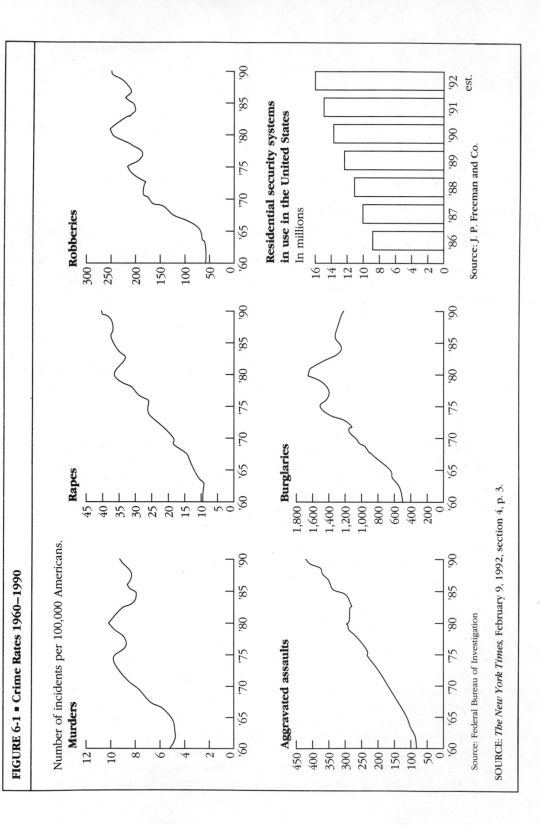

Source: Federal Bureau of Investigation

SOURCE: *The New York Times*, February 9, 1992, section 4, p. 3.

large risky loans to speculators, especially in real estate, and substantial investments in a junk-bond market. They were able to escape the scrutiny of government oversight and regulation with the assistance of several United States senators to whom the savings and loan executives had made large campaign contributions. The appearance of malfeasance in high places at the public's expense was exacerbated by the revelation that President Bush's son Neil was among the savings and loan executives involved in the scandal.

The public officials elected to uphold and implement the law can prove to be among the more flagrant white-collar criminals and add to the atmosphere of disrespect for the law. Public officials may betray their trust in various other ways. Revelations in October of 1991 showed that members of Congress had written over eight thousand bad checks against the House Bank. The bank had long made a practice of forgiving such overdrafts. At the same time, it became apparent that members of Congress regularly were having their traffic tickets forgiven. Such casual disregard for the rules on the part of people who may act as role models for many young Americans may make others regard with respect those who successfully break the law.

Street crime. Although white-collar crime may cost American society in the aggregate more money than street crime does, James Q. Wilson persuasively argued that what is called crime in the streets has a more negative impact on America's sense of community.[6] Even for those who are not actually victims of crime, the fear of street crime alters one's life-style and patterns of interaction. People may no longer feel free to walk the streets and in effect become prisoners in their own homes. In many cities, downtown businesses have failed to prosper because people no longer feel safe in those areas, and such failures can be considered to be an indirect cost or spillover effect of street crime, a cost that does not enter into the crime statistics themselves. Moreover, the perception that there is a relationship between street crime and violence adds to fear and makes even the prospect of such crime more traumatic than that of white-collar crime, regardless of the dollar value lost. Furthermore, the perception that there is a relationship between potentially violent street crime and race or ethnicity exacerbates the problem of prejudice against and distrust of America's minorities.

Reported crime. The FBI index includes only reported crimes. Sample surveys, on the other hand, report that two to three times more crimes are committed than are reported. This rate of underreporting, such "victimization surveys" indicate, varies according to geographical area. The crime rate as indicated by the index therefore depends on what proportion of actual crimes is reported and becomes a statistic. A greater proportion of crimes being reported would lead to an increase in the crime rate in the index even if the actual crime rate did not increase. Such a reporting increase has occurred.

There are two reasons why the proportion of crime that is reported and recorded in the crime index has increased in recent years. The first reason is that the development of computers and other data-processing equipment has facilitated the accuracy and completeness of collecting and tabulating crime data. The second reason is that more stolen property is now insured, and in order for the benefits of such a policy to be claimed, a police report must normally be filed. In past years, the likelihood that the perpetrator of a crime would be apprehended or that stolen property would be recovered was always low; therefore there was little incentive outside insurance considerations to report crimes. Now, because more property is insured, it is likely that a greater percentage of crime is being reported. As noted, this would generate a rise in the crime index even if the number of actual crimes committed were to remain constant. Some types of crime (for example, murder) are more likely to be reported than others (robbery). Rape has been seriously underreported, in part because of the kind of treatment rape victims once received in court. With court reforms easing the potential embarrassment of victims in pressing charges, the rate of reporting rape may be going up significantly, in turn affecting the statistics for that crime.

Reasons for the Crime Increase

It is important to keep in mind that a "crime" is an activity that some legislative body has chosen to make illegal. This activity may be one that harms persons or property; it may be an activity that offends some ethical principle adhered to by the segment of society that dominates the lawmaking process; or it may be some silly or innocent activity the illegal status of which is inexplicable. For example, in Idaho it is illegal to fish from the back of a giraffe, and in Massachusetts it is illegal to eat peanuts in church. Old laws are seldom repealed, whereas new ones are continually being passed as each generation seeks to ban something that it finds odious. The number of proscribed activities has expanded over time. Clearly, the more things that are declared illegal, the greater the crime rate will be, even if behavior patterns remain constant. A statistical increase in crime does not necessarily reflect changes in behavior patterns.

"Victimless" crimes.   Acts among willing adults that violate some moral principle supported by the dominant forces in society constitute a substantial fraction of crimes. Although some such acts may in fact inflict genuine harm—for example, drug use that leads to crimes to pay for the habit, or prostitution that spreads disease—they are called "victimless crimes" because participation in such activity is presumed to be voluntary. Estimates vary with the definition of the term and the range of activities proscribed, but in many estimates arrests for victimless crimes account for over half the total number of arrests. Such laws often attempt to ban conduct that is widely practiced. Consequently, they are often ineffective in altering the actual behavior of people strongly disposed to engage in the proscribed conduct. Thus the impact of these laws is not to prevent the conduct in question but rather to criminalize large segments of the American population. If the Kinsey Report is correct, some 95 percent of Americans at some time in their lives violate some of the laws regulating sexual behavior. These laws include bans on sodomy, fornication, and adultery. Sodomy refers to unnatural or abnormal sex. Because what is natural or normal in sexual behavior is a subjective judgment over which reasonable people disagree, many respectable citizens violate vaguely drawn sodomy statutes. Such statutes often prohibit any form of oral-genital sex, even among married partners, with prison penalties of up to thirty years. Georgia, for instance, forbids "carnal knowledge and connection against the law of nature." Yet not only has the existence of morals legislation failed to prevent the conduct being banned; there are indications that with the growing secularization of our society and with the "sexual revolution," the rate of such conduct is actually increasing. Despite all efforts to punish prostitution, it continues unabated. Whatever the causes of homosexuality, it is apparently a deep-seated predilection undeterred by the threat of legal punishment, although the threat of death from AIDS has apparently reduced the incidence of certain high-risk behaviors among homosexuals. Because the behaviors or services proscribed by such legislation are strongly demanded by certain segments of the population, an illegal network has been created to take the risks of supplying them. Thus the development and maintenance of organized crime is a spillover effect of banning strongly desired behaviors for moral purposes.

Drugs.   Drug abuse may constitute a special category among victimless crimes. When a nonaddicted youth is seduced into drug use by a "pusher," the concept of voluntary behavior is stretched quite thin. Because many mind-altering drugs are physically or psychologically addicting—or both—the demand for them by the addicted is largely unaffected by costs, including potential punishments for their use. Consequently, the disposition to use such drugs is unlikely to be deterred by the threat of punishment. The legislative control of drug use in the United States is far from a recent phenomenon; however, this legislation has failed to stem a sharp rise in the use of mind-altering drugs in recent decades.

Drug users in search of money to finance their expensive habits have brought higher rates of property crime along with the drug epidemic. In the mid-1970s, the Drug Enforcement Administration estimated that an average heroin habit cost $57.50 per day, or $21,000 annually to support.[7] This cost is beyond the financial capability of typical upper-middle-class people, not to mention addicts who have a diminished capacity to pursue middle-class careers. Consequently, addicts have little choice but to turn to crime to support their habit. Given the rigid demand, the successful interception of the drug supply would only make the drugs more scarce and more expensive. This would produce the spillover effect of increasing the crime rate even further.

Heroin was the drug of choice in the post–Vietnam War period. Cocaine, even more expensive, was primarily used by middle- and upper-class addicts. However, in recent years, a cheaper version of cocaine called "crack" has made that drug easier to obtain on the streets and less expensive than heroin. Hence crack has become the drug of choice on the streets. The extent of the steady and substantial rise in drug addiction is indicated by the data in Table 6-2, which reports the rate of arrests for drug violations.

The enormous increases in both total sales and possession of drugs between 1980 and 1988 (2.14 times as many sales and a 61 percent increase in total possession) are found despite the fact that marijuana use decreased significantly in that period. The arrests for the sale of the two most addictive drugs went up over seven times in that period while arrests for possession increased slightly less than

TABLE 6-2 ■ Drug Arrests per 100,000 Population				
	1980	*1985*	*1987*	*1988*
Total for Drug Sales	57.9	82.0	103.6	123.9
Heroin and Coke Sales	10.8	27.8	56.7	74.8
Marijuana Sales	28.4	36.4	28.1	25.4
Total for Possession	198.1	264.1	297.2	326.0
Heroin and Coke Possession	22.2	74.4	126.2	153.7
Marijuana Possession	146.2	156.1	138.8	130.1

SOURCE: *Statistical Abstract of the United States, 1990* (Washington, D.C.: U.S. Government Printing Office, 1989), p. 78.

that. Clearly, increases of this magnitude must necessarily lead to significant increases in the rate of crime committed to sustain such addictions. Moreover, the spread of crack cocaine in America's inner cities has been accompanied in recent years by the formation of rival youth gangs seeking to control the inner city for the sale of crack. These gangs have been engaged in an armed struggle of unprecedented violence among themselves for control of that turf. This violence has claimed the lives not only of rival gang members but of innocent bystanders as well, frequently children, who are caught in crossfire.

Demographic change.   Other categories in the crime statistics increase with the influence of demographic trends, such as the urbanization of America. Cities offer a greater crime potential than do smaller towns and rural areas. The high concentrations of people in America's urban population centers mean more interaction among people, more opportunities for crime, and less chance of being apprehended. There is normally a greater selection of valuable, concealable, and transportable goods in cities than in rural areas. Furthermore, the anonymity of a city makes it easier for the perpetrator of a crime to escape detection or capture. Until recently, crime has been a distinctly urban phenomenon, and the fact that a greater proportion of the population lived in urban areas has meant more crime. In recent years, however, crime in small-town and suburban settings has been increasing faster than has crime in urban areas, and the gap between the two types of settings is narrowing (see Table 6-3). The reasons for this trend are not yet clear.

Another demographic trend contributing to the increased incidence of crime is that those categories of people statistically more likely to commit crimes have been growing as a proportion of the total population. Lower-class people in general and lower-class blacks and Hispanics in particular tend to have higher birthrates and higher crime rates than do middle-class whites. Youth is also an important crime indicator. Until recently, there was a growing proportion of the population under 25, due in part to the postwar baby boom, and crime has statistically been a young man's phenomenon. However, this trend has apparently ended, and with increasing longevity, the proportion of the older population is

TABLE 6-3 ▪ **Urban-Rural Distribution of Crime Rates per 100,000 Population for 1986 (percentage change over 1978 in parentheses)**

	1986			1978		
	STANDARD METROPOLITAN STATISTICAL AREAS	OTHER CITIES	RURAL	STANDARD METROPOLITAN STATISTICAL AREAS	OTHER CITIES	RURAL
Violent crime	732 (25.3%)	350 (23.2%)	175 (0%)	584	284	175
Property crime	5,504 (4.1%)	4,443 (8.9%)	1,770 (−2.9%)	5,286	4,079	1,823

SOURCE: U.S. Bureau of the Census, *Statistical Abstract of the United States, 1988* (Washington, D.C.: U.S. Government Printing Office, 1987).

beginning to rise. This fact could account for the aforementioned downturn in crime rate statistics from 1982 through 1984.

The fact that crime is very much a young man's activity—especially with respect to "street crimes"—further weakens the deterrent impact of the criminal justice system. Much of the most vicious crime is committed by juveniles, and the most active part of a career criminal's life is over by around the age of twenty-five or thirty. By one set of data, slightly over 35 percent of those arrested in one year for index crimes were juveniles. Marvin Wolfgang and his associates, however, find that a small number of delinquents—juveniles who have had five or more recorded contacts with police—are responsible for a majority of all crimes and two-thirds of all violent crimes.[8]

Yet the criminal justice system does not fully accept the responsibility of minors for their actions. Sentences usually are lighter; alternatives to actual incarceration are preferred; and the police records of minors are erased when they reach their majority. Long-term imprisonment is generally not a likely possibility until an adult record is well established, and, as we have seen, this is usually after the most active part of the criminal career is over. Hence the prison system functions more as a source of room and board for semiretired criminals than as a means of removing from our midst those who present the greatest current and future danger to society.

For many juveniles in lower-class neighborhoods, a brush with the law is not the mark of shame among one's peers that it would be to middle-class youths. Rather, it is often a source of pride and status for having stood up to the system. The kinds of light punishments at stake in the juvenile justice system do not present credible deterrents to the growing army of teenage recidivist criminals who grow to understand that they can continue to flout the law with impunity as long as they are minors.

Ethnicity.　A cultural factor that may be contributing to the crime increase is the growing awareness by different ethnic or racial groups of their distinct identities and interests, that is, a growing sense of identification with particular interests that may not be compatible with the interests of the community as a whole. This phenomenon has created a sense of particularistic rights and entitlements that seems to be rising faster than the capacity of the political system to satisfy these new demands. In other words, the cumulative total of what these groups have perceived as their just desserts exceeds the finite resources that society has to distribute. This inability to satisfy demands leads to a widespread perception of justice impeded, which in turn generates frustration. And a well-developed literature in social psychology and political science links frustration with violence.[9]

The major identity-conscious ethnic group with a rising sense of having experienced egregious injustice is the black population. In 1990, with blacks making up less than 13 percent of the national population, 28.9 percent of the persons arrested for serious crime were black, a figure that is down from its level of 33.8 percent in 1978. The figure for blacks under 18 years of age is 26.2 percent. These data are summarized in Table 6-4.

It is true that the problem of a high black crime rate is not a recent one. Blacks have long been statistically more likely than whites to possess the various attributes associated with criminality: living in urban areas, having a large youth population under twenty-five, coming from broken homes, and living in poverty. But according to Harvard political scientist and urban specialist Edward Banfield, during the early 1960s black crime rates began to exceed those of whites even when these foregoing crime-inducing attributes were statistically controlled.[10] In other words, Banfield suggested that blacks have become statistically more likely than whites to engage in criminal behavior even if they do not differ from whites in social class, level of urbanization, average age, and so forth. There are some data and literature to support this claim; however, others hold that in comparable

---

TABLE 6-4 ▪ Arrest Rates by Race, 1990

	White	Black	Native American	Asian or Pacific Islander
Under 18	1,239,241	455,164	18,416	25,859
Percentage under 18	71.3	26.2	1.1	1.5
Total	7,712,339	3,224,060	122,586	92,383
Percentage of Total	69.2	28.9	1.1	.8

SOURCE: U.S. Department of Justice, Federal Bureau of Investigation, *Uniform Crime Report,* released August, 1991, p. 193.

circumstances black and white crime rates would not significantly differ. Therefore, with regard to the question of whether blacks are more crime-prone than whites even when all other attributes are controlled, the evidence is inconclusive. Although blacks are more likely to commit crime than whites are, it should be noted that most black crime is directed at black victims.

If blacks are found to remain more crime-prone than whites are when individual attributes are controlled, the difference may be due to a heightened sense of injustice. This rising perception by blacks of justice denied may in turn be partially attributed to the very success of the early phases of the civil rights movement, a success that many feel generated premature expectations of basic social change. The perception of justice denied is periodically renewed and exacerbated when the violent treatment of blacks is apparently not prosecuted and punished with the same vigor as would be the comparable treatment of whites. In late 1980, the acquittal of three Miami policemen after they had beaten a black suspect to death and the acquittal of several Nazi party members and Ku Klux Klansmen of killing some North Carolina radicals pressing for black advancement, as well as the 1991 videotaped beating by Los Angeles policemen of a black man, Rodney King, illustrate the kinds of events that generate a perception of injustice.

This perception may have lent some legitimacy to black crime and violence. Many of those committing arson, looting, and assault during the 1992 Los Angeles riots certainly saw their action as somehow justified by the acquittal of the four police officers charged with Rodney King's beating. Perceptions of a racist criminal justice system may increase the propensity to crime. Looters would rather see themselves as "urban guerillas" attacking white racism than as scavengers of kitchen appliances. The aura of political legitimacy surrounding otherwise criminal behavior is further encouraged by those whites who attribute looting in predominantly black neighborhoods to political motivations rather than greed. This view of black crime as a reaction to racism would attribute part of the increase in crime to a growing awareness of social and economic disabilities faced by those most likely to commit crime.

Ideology.   Certain types of crime are clearly related to poverty and unemployment, a fact that accounts for much of the apparent correlation between crime and race or ethnicity. The philosophical question is to what extent persons, regardless of their individual circumstances, remain free to choose between criminal and law-abiding behavior and hence are responsible for their actions. To the extent that criminality is a choice made under conditions of free will, one cannot posit socioeconomic conditions as a cause of certain types of criminality. Conservatives tend to emphasize free will and individual responsibility for criminal behavior, whereas liberals are more likely to attribute such behavior to sociological circumstances such as poverty and racism, which they claim "cause" the individual to act in aberrant ways. Of course, sociological conditions are more amenable to public policy solutions than are defects in individual character, and liberals tend to be more optimistic than conservatives are about the prospect of reducing crime by improving the environment in which people live.

Whatever conclusions one wishes to draw about this essentially unresolvable philosophical question, the fact remains that people in certain socioeconomic circumstances are statistically more likely to engage in criminal behavior. Accordingly, whether such circumstances are a cause of crime or a rationalization for it, a reduction in such circumstances may subsequently reduce the rate of certain types of crime.

CONTEMPORARY POLICY: CONSTITUTIONAL RIGHTS AND THE DETERRENCE OF CRIME

Common sense tells us that criminal behavior can be prevented by confronting the prospective perpetrator with the threat of punishment. Accordingly, the conventional idea is that severe treatment of criminals will deter subsequent criminality and that lenient treatment will encourage it.

This conventional outlook has attributed the problem of rising crime in large part to a significant expansion in the rights of persons accused of crime, an expansion that was associated with the Supreme Court under the chief justiceship of Earl Warren (1953–1969). This expansion has, however, been largely halted with the appointment of several Supreme Court justices under the Reagan and Bush administrations who are thought to be politically conservative and less sympathetic to an expansive view of individual rights implicitly protected by the Constitution. This Court, headed by Chief Justice Rehnquist and buttressed by the addition of Justices O'Connor, Scalia, Kennedy, Souter, and Thomas, now has a solid conservative majority. It is unclear at this writing to what extent the Court will try to reverse the aforementioned revolution in procedural rights. We will see below that some modifications and qualifications have already occurred. Clearly, further expansion of the rights of the accused is unlikely for the foreseeable future. However, the respect that legal scholars in the Anglo-American common law system have for the force of precedent will probably limit the extent to which the Court can undo that revolution.

Because in our system the accused is presumed innocent until proven otherwise, the rights of the accused are the rights of the innocent. These rights require the judicial system to proceed according to the rules of evidence, rules that prevent people from being punished on the basis of hearsay, rumor, emotional prejudice, or other factors that do not objectively establish guilt. Given the choice of punishing all of the guilty, even if some innocent are also caught in the net, or taking care not to punish the innocent, even if some guilty people thereby escape punishment, Western society has opted for the latter alternative. It must be remembered that each of these procedural rights or "legal technicalities" came into being in response to a particular abuse of government power. As Justice Felix Frankfurter once said, "The history of liberty has largely been the history of procedural safeguards."

This expansion of rights has come about in two ways. First, it has involved an expanded meaning of the U.S. Constitution's Fourteenth Amendment to incorporate progressively more of the guarantees in the federal Bill of Rights. The Bill of

Rights limits the national government's criminal law and trial procedures only in federal courts. Most crimes, however, are violations of state law, and most criminal trials are resolved at that level. It is only through that ambiguous phrase of the Fourteenth Amendment that "no State shall deny any person life, liberty or property without due process of law . . ." that the U.S. Constitution imposes any restriction on state criminal procedure. Reasonable people on the Supreme Court and elsewhere can and do disagree on which of the specific provisions of the Bill of Rights applicable to criminal justice are or should be implied by that "due process" clause. Although the Court has always formally subscribed to the standard that only those rights that are "fundamental" or part of "the essence of ordered liberty" should be incorporated, the Court in practice has now incorporated most of the listed rights of the Second through Eighth Amendments in addition to several inferred or unlisted ones, called "penumbra rights," such as the right to privacy.

The second mode of expansion of the rights of the accused has been through a broadened interpretation of existing rights. With each of these rights, the question was not whether it existed but rather what it meant or implied. The expansion of the rights of the accused has generated the most controversy in three areas:

1. The right to counsel and the admissibility of confessions.
2. The exclusionary rule and the admissibility of illegally obtained evidence.
3. Constraints on the use of capital punishment.

Confessions and the Right to Counsel

It was decided quite early that the right to counsel applied to state criminal proceedings. What this right entails, however, has changed over the years. To the Founding Fathers, it was understood by its common-law meaning: the right to hire an attorney. The concept that the state had any obligation to pay for one's attorney is a modern extrapolation from this earlier concept. The practice of providing defense counsel in federal criminal trials had long been standard procedure but not a constitutional requirement. Although the first expansion of the right to counsel occurred in 1932 when the Supreme Court held in the infamous Scottsboro case that the accused had in capital cases (cases in which the death penalty is a legal possibility) the right to be provided with effective counsel, the Court resisted the logic of its argument in refusing to extend that right to all felony trials. The Scottsboro opinion noted that even intelligent laypersons lack "skill in the science of the law." Clearly, the prosecution is legally trained and, in an adversary proceeding, has a distinct advantage in knowing how to manipulate the rules of evidence and procedure. However, the Court did not extend the right to counsel at state expense to all felony trials until the *Gideon* v. *Wainwright* case of 1963.[11]

Even this expansion of the meaning of the due process clause did not satisfy all the needs of defendants for counsel in state criminal processes. Most convictions in fact have been obtained from confessions, often through plea bargaining, before the cases ever come to trial.

Plea bargaining is a frequently used process involving an agreement be-tween the prosecution and the defendant by which the latter is allowed to plead guilty to a lesser crime than he or she is charged with. In return, the prosecution drops the more serious charge. The prosecution in this way avoids the necessity of satisfying the burden of proof for the more serious charge; the crowded court docket is relieved of another time-consuming case; and the defendant is freed from the threat of the more serious punishment.[12] This "bargain" is generally offered to a defendant with either the implicit or explicit threat that if the deal is rejected, successful prosecution under a more serious charge will be the outcome. Even innocent people may in such circumstances be persuaded to "cop a plea" in order to escape the threat of dire punishment. Furthermore, prosecutors sometimes overcharge in order to allow themselves room to bargain. At the same time, plea bargainers who have committed serious crimes may get by with more lenient punishment and early release from detention. The pressure from overcrowded court dockets on harried, overworked prosecutors to dispose of cases in this short-cut fashion can thus frustrate the goal of physically removing dangerous criminals from society for long periods of time and detract from whatever deterrent effect serious punishment may exercise on subsequent crime. Potential criminals thus have good reason to assume that they can obtain leniency by plea bargaining.

Escobedo **and** *Miranda*.   Thus, for a period of time, many cases were being settled in the pretrial stage, when defendants did not have a guaranteed recourse to counsel. This problem was addressed by the Court in the *Escobedo* v. *Illinois* (1964) case, when it extended the right to counsel to that point in the pretrial process when "the investigation is no longer a general inquiry into an unsolved crime but has begun to focus on a particular suspect"—in other words, at the point of arrest.[13] This decision further held that the accused must be informed that he or she has a right to remain silent. The rights of the accused were further extended in the famous *Miranda* v. *Arizona* (1966) decision, a case involving an Arizona rapist who, when faced with damaging evidence of his guilt and not informed of his rights, confessed "with full knowledge of my legal rights."[14] The Court vacated the conviction in holding that Miranda should have been informed of the following rights at the point of arrest: (1) his right to remain silent, (2) his right to know that anything he said could and would be used against him in court, and (3) his right to be represented at that time by counsel, at state expense if necessary. Before any confession or damaging statement can be entered as evi-dence, all of the above rights must be consciously waived. Of course, the first thing that an attorney is likely to do is advise his or her client to say nothing, thereby placing the burden of proof on the police or prosecution to prove their case. This would seem on the surface likely to reduce the rate of convictions, because so many are obtained by confession. Furthermore, the decision seemed to mean freeing, on a legal technicality, a person who had voluntarily confessed to a heinous crime. For many, it epitomized a dangerous precedent for freeing other criminals on similar technicalities. This decision was widely perceived as symbolic of a trend toward an obsessive concern for the rights of the accused at the expense of the swift and severe punishment of criminals, and it was therefore roundly criticized by many as an excellent example of misguided liberalism interfering with the maintenance of law and order.

The Exclusionary Rule and Search and Seizure

The exclusionary rule is the principle that evidence obtained in an illegal search and/or seizure may not be admitted in a court of law. The Fourth Amendment merely proscribes "unreasonable searches and seizures"; the Constitution is altogether silent on the admissibility of any evidence gathered. The core of the argument that the Fourth Amendment ought not to be construed as excluding illegally obtained evidence is that such a principle would protect only the guilty, whereas constitutional rights are designed to protect the innocent. Furthermore, if one is not guilty of a crime, an unreasonable search and seizure will not yield any incriminating evidence. The secondary argument against the exclusionary rule is that other remedies are available to deter police from illegal searches; namely, police can be sued or arrested for such behavior.

    Mapp v. *Ohio.*   Despite these arguments, the Supreme Court held in the famous *Mapp* decision that the due process clause of the Fourteenth Amendment requires the exclusion from court of illegally obtained evidence.[15] In *Mapp* v. *Ohio* (1961), the Court rejected the argument that the exclusionary rule protects only the guilty. The Court found that other remedies were ineffective; hence the exclusionary rule was a necessary means to enforce the admittedly fundamental right to be free from such illegal searches. The rule protects more than the guilty, only because if illegally obtained evidence is inadmissible, there is no motive for police to make illegal searches of the guilty or the innocent. Police are less likely to undertake illegal searches if they know that they cannot use any incriminating evidence they find through such searches. The Court in *Mapp* cited evidence that alternative procedures to deter illegal searches have been ineffective; therefore, the exclusionary rule is a necessary deterrent to illegal searches. Moreover, the Court noted that an increasing number of states have voluntarily adopted the exclusionary rule, a fact that weakens the argument that the exclusionary rule goes against custom and practice in the United States.

    Despite these data and arguments, the Court in 1984, driven by then Chief Justice Burger's avowed hostility to the exclusionary rule, continued to chip away at the rule without specifically overturning it. The Court announced a decision in the case of *Nix* v. *Williams* (1984) that held that illegally obtained evidence would now be admissible if the Court found that the police would have discovered the evidence sooner or later by legal means. This pleased conservatives, who argued that it would render clearly guilty people less likely to be released on a mere "technicality." But liberals fear that this dampening effect on the disposition of the police to engage in illegal searches may be seriously weakened by this case. Subsequently, the Court made another inroad on the exclusionary rule in the case of *U.S.* v. *Leon* (1984), in which it held that if the police acted in "good faith" that the search was legal, the fact that the search turned out to be technically illegal would not be grounds for suppressing any evidence found.[16]

Capital Punishment

The third area in which the expansion of the rights of the accused has provoked the most controversy is that of capital punishment. The relevant constitutional provision is the Eighth Amendment protection against "cruel and unusual punishment," which opponents of the death penalty have variously held either prohibits the imposition of capital punishment itself or, failing that, at least limits the mode and circumstances of its imposition. Given the ambiguity of the words "cruel and unusual punishment," their implications for the practice of capital punishment are something on which reasonable and informed legal scholars can and do disagree. The controversy is exacerbated by serious disagreement over the importance of capital punishment as a deterrent to capital crime.

The Supreme Court has affirmed that there are two legitimate social purposes that may be served by the death penalty: deterrence and retribution. Most of the published arguments supporting the retention and use of capital punishment have focused on its putative value as a deterrent to future crime; the essentially normative, retributive argument is apparently distasteful to many scholars. Yet for the person in the street, retribution is also a real consideration. Clearly, there are some crimes for which mere imprisonment seems an inadequate punishment. Many people's intuitive sense of justice is deeply offended when a brutal mass murderer, such as Charles Manson, the instigator of the Sharon Tate murders, James Gacy, the sex murderer of over twenty young boys, or Jeffry Dahmer, convicted in 1992 not only of killing and sodomizing but also of cannibalizing his victims, is allowed to live on in prison. As an ethical argument, the issue of retributive justice cannot be resolved; yet it may more easily withstand scrutiny than the more frequently relied-upon deterrence argument.[17]

Although the retributive argument regards capital punishment as an end in itself, the deterrent argument regards capital punishment as a means to the end of preventing serious crimes. Accordingly, the question of whether capital punishment is in fact an efficient means is in principle an empirical question, a question resolvable by observable data.

Deterrence?   If, on the basis of common sense, it seems clear that punishment deters proscribed acts, it follows that death should deter such acts more effectively than less severe punishment will. As the British Royal Commission on capital punishment stated in 1953, *"Prima facie,* the penalty of death is likely to have a stronger effect as a deterrent to normal human beings than any other form of punishment. . . ." There is in fact evidence that punishment in general does deter crime. However, another body of research indicates that it is the swiftness and certainty of punishment rather than its severity that most effectively operates as a crime deterrent. Yet, the death penalty, in the American context, can neither be swift nor certain. It is hedged by automatic appeals and the right of almost any judge personally to stay an execution based on any question about the manner of arrest or conviction. It is limited also by the reluctance of judges and juries to impose the death sentence and the even greater reluctance of states to carry it out. Sociologist Thorsten Sellin has reported that historically, the risk of suffering the death penalty in the United States if caught and convicted of capital murder *during a period of widespread executions* (1933–1950), was only 3.67 percent. When one considers the arrest rate for felonies, the risk factor diminishes even further. For instance, between 1961 and 1968 in Chicago, only 0.7 percent of the persons charged with capital murder and 1.5 percent of persons convicted of that crime were even sentenced to death, let alone actually executed.[18] A person sentenced to die can usually find a judge to stay the execution on some grounds, delaying the implementation of the death penalty for lengthy periods. There is less than a one percent probability that a convicted murderer will be executed; but, more important in terms of the deterrent effect of "swift and certain" punishment, there is virtually no chance that a murderer will be executed within two years of conviction.

There is very little doubt that if every person convicted of murder were to be immediately dispatched, other murders would be deterred. However, the foregoing data suggest that there is very little likelihood of such a policy being implemented. First, the system seeks through appeals and rehearings to resolve all uncertainty before carrying out an execution. Second, America's more secularized society is uncertain about judging who deserves to live and die. Finally, there appears to be a cultural strengthening of the sanctity of life itself under way in the nation. Consequently, to execute promptly all or even most people convicted of murder is politically unthinkable. And failing that extreme approach, it is hard to see how capital punishment can have a greater deterrent effect than do other forms of punishment.

There are some data on the actual deterrent effect of the death penalty, but they are inconclusive.[19] For example, studies have compared homicide rates between states that administer the death penalty and states that have abolished it. If the administration of executions were in fact a deterrent to capital crime, the murder rates in death penalty states should be significantly lower than those in the abolitionist states. Table 6-5 presents such a comparison among three states from the same geographic region (ensuring that variations between the states in homicide rates cannot be attributed to regional cultural differences). Contrary to expectations, the two death penalty states in fact had slightly higher mean homicide rates than did the abolitionist state. The mean rates for the years shown are Massachusetts (death penalty), 1.95; Connecticut (death penalty), 2.28; Rhode Island (abolitionist), only 1.8. These differences are not, however, statistically significant; they could easily have occurred by chance if we assume that the categories (abolitionist and death penalty states) do not explain any of the variation in homicide rates.

This failure to find a significant impact of the death penalty on capital crime may be attributable in part to the fact that murder, the major capital offense, is, relative to property crimes, one of intense passion. Whether much rational calculation goes on in the mind of a murderer about the probable costs (punishment) of

TABLE 6-5 ▪ Crude Homicide Death Rates per 100,000 Population Comparing an Abolitionist State, Rhode Island, with Two Death Penalty States, Massachusetts and Connecticut

Years	Rhode Island	Massachusetts	Connecticut
1920–1924	2.5	2.6	3.3
1925–1929	2.5	2.1	2.8
1930–1934	1.9	2.1	2.6
1935–1939	1.6	1.6	2.0
1940–1944	1.1	1.3	2.0
1945–1949	1.5	1.4	1.7
1950–1954	1.2	1.1	1.6
1955–1959	1.2	1.0	1.5
1960–1964	1.2	1.6	1.7
1965–1969	2.4	2.7	2.5
1970–1974	3.3	4.0	3.4

$F = 1.098$ (for one-way analysis of variance with no interaction effects). Critical level of F at .05 with 30 and Z degrees of freedom = 3.32.
SOURCE: Adapted from National Office of Vital Statistics, *Vital Statistics in the United States* (Washington, D.C.: U.S. Government Printing Office, 1974).

the act is a doubtful question to many. It seems fair to conclude, then, that the death penalty as it may conceivably be practiced in the United States would not have a significant deterrent effect on the crime of murder. Therefore, the *justification* of capital punishment would have to rely on the retributive argument (an issue that will be discussed shortly).

Capital punishment and the law.   The legal status of capital punishment itself has always been accepted by a majority of the Supreme Court. The Eighth Amendment prohibition of cruel and unusual punishment, however, does constrain the *manner of execution.* Reasonable people differ on what forms constitute cruelty. It is safe to presume that practices of medieval torture, such as the use of the rack or the screw, burning victims alive at the stake, drawing and quartering, or crucifixion, would violate the amendment, but beyond such obvious cases, states have been given wide latitude. Although once all were believed to be humane methods, it is now thought that hanging, electrocution, and execution by firing squad are neither quick nor painless; yet all are still legal (though increasingly out of vogue).

Although practice and precedent in our common-law system support the legality of the death penalty itself, such common-law principles should also reflect evolving community standards. Public opposition to the imposition of the death penalty was strong in the decades before 1970, but opinion has now moved in the opposite direction. Conversely a number of states have voluntarily abolished the death penalty. Legal principles responsive to community standards have become more restrictive on the manner and circumstances of imposing the death penalty, and it is in this area that constitutional challenges to the death penalty have been based.

First, death has not been regularly assigned to those convicted of murder. As noted, only a minority of those prosecuted for murder are even charged with capital murder. Capital murder is homicide for which the death penalty may be assessed. It is limited to premeditated murder and, since *Gregg* v. *Georgia* (1976), limited to certain types of premeditated murder such as multiple killings, homicide committed in the course of another felony, or killing a police officer in the line of duty. Moreover, even conviction for capital murder in a death penalty jurisdiction far from guarantees that the death penalty will actually be assigned. In California in the period from 1950 to 1975, only 104 of the 2,111 persons convicted of capital murder were sentenced to die.[20] This raises the question of whether there are consistent criteria for determining why one murderer is sentenced to die and another is not, criteria based on the nature of the act itself.

Research shows that rather than the nature of the act, factors such as the defendant's race, socioeconomic status, or gender have proved to be better predictors of whether the death penalty will be assigned. Blacks have been executed in disproportionate numbers in American history, especially in southern states. For instance, a study of executions in North Carolina from 1933 to 1937 showed eighty-one blacks but only forty-five whites being executed. A study of capital cases in Texas from 1924 to 1968 produced a higher percentage of convicted blacks being executed than convicted whites, and the difference was statistically significant.[21] Furthermore, socioeconomic status has been an important determinant of suffering or avoiding the death penalty, because such status is related to the ability of one's lawyer.

Such data on the impact of race constituted the bases of several challenges to the constitutionality of the death penalty. The Supreme Court under Chief Justice Rehnquist, however, does not appear to be receptive to such challenges. Most notably, in 1987 in *McCleskey* v. *Kemp,* the Court rejected the argument that the Georgia death penalty statute should be invalidated because the death penalty was more likely to be assigned when the victims of capital murder were white than when the victims were black, as well as more likely when the perpetrators were black than when they were white. Julian Epstein, an aide to Michigan Representative John Conyers, reported a study of thirty-two states that revealed that killers of whites have an 11.1 percent chance of reaching death row, whereas the killers of blacks have only a 4.5 percent chance. In some states, the discrepancy is even greater. For example, in Maryland, the killer of a white person is eight times more likely to receive the death penalty than the killer of a black.[22] The Court appears to be backing away from inferring racial bias from the fact that race is a good predictor of who actually is sentenced to death.

Gender, though not widely discussed in this context, is perhaps an even better predictor than race is. Women are far less likely to be assigned the death penalty than men are. From 1930 to 1967, of the 3,334 persons executed for murder in the United States, only 30, or 0.8 percent, were women.[23] Of course, such data should be seen in relation to a comparison of capital crime convictions of men with those of women. Unfortunately, such convictions are not broken down by sex in the available data. However, statistics do provide clues: in 1978, there were 12,736 arrests of men for murder and nonnegligent manslaughter (the index category that includes capital murder) and 2,234 such arrests of women. Because women, who accounted for about 17.5 percent of capital murder arrests, also accounted for less than one percent of the executions in earlier years, the conclusion that women are significantly less likely than men to be assigned the death penalty appears to be reasonable.

Furman v. *Georgia.*   It was the importance of such determinants on who receives the death penalty—rather than the nature of the criminal act—that the Court found objectionable in the landmark case of *Furman* v. *Georgia* (1972), in which the Court laid down the first major explicit constitutional restraints on the practice of capital punishment in the United States.[24] Although a majority clearly rejected the notion that capital punishment is inherently cruel and unusual, five justices agreed that it was cruel and unusual as it was then practiced in this country. There is no single pattern of reasoning to be discerned in these five diverse opinions, but one concept is that the imposition of capital punishment shall not be arbitrary. That is, its imposition must be on consistent criteria grounded in the nature of the criminal act.

POLICY EVALUATION: FLAWS IN THE CRIMINAL JUSTICE SYSTEM

In the preceding section, the evolution of contemporary policy in the area of constitutional rights and the deterrence of crime was studied with an emphasis on the two reasons for the expansion of such rights: (1) the expanded meaning of the U.S. Constitution's Fourteenth Amendment to incorporate more of the *federal* Bill of Rights guarantees, and (2) the broadened interpretation of *existing* rights. It is this second category that has generated the most controversy in three areas:

1. The right to counsel and the admissibility of confession, as interpreted in the case of *Miranda* v. *Arizona.*
2. The exclusionary rule and the admissibility of illegally obtained evidence, as interpreted in the case of *Mapp* v. *Ohio.*
3. Constraints on the use of capital punishment, as interpreted in the case of *Furman* v. *Georgia.*

Confessions and the Right to Counsel

As already seen, *Miranda* v. *Arizona* pointed up the legal ramifications of not informing a suspect of his or her rights before entering any confession or damaging statement as evidence. Many feared that the rights of the accused would be excessively protected at the expense of obtaining otherwise valid confessions and swift punishment. But the available evidence does not support this fear.[25]

However, *Miranda* may have lowered the rate at which confessions are obtained in the first place. One study found that in Pittsburgh, in 1964, the police obtained confessions in 54.5 percent of the cases before *Miranda* procedures were implemented and in only 37.5 percent of the cases after the procedure was implemented.[26] Moreover, studies of the frequency of suppressing confessions on *Miranda* grounds do not take into account cases dismissed in preliminary stages or arrests not made because of the requirement of the *Miranda* rule.[27]

The impact of *Miranda* on reducing the number of confessions may be ameliorated by the fact that a large number of arrestees, having been informed of their *Miranda* rights, still decline to exercise them. In one study, a third of eighty-five defendants processed did not choose even to avail themselves of the services of a lawyer on hand in the police station for that purpose; 75 percent of the defendants did not exercise their option for counsel other than the station house counsel; and 40 percent chose to make incriminating statements after having waived their *Miranda* rights.[28] These somewhat startling data become explicable in the light of the findings in the same study that 15 percent of the eighty-five defendants failed to understand their right to remain silent, 18 percent did not understand their right to the presence of counsel at that time, and 24 percent failed to understand that the state would appoint counsel at its expense. In order to exercise a right, one must not only be informed that he or she has the right, but one must also understand what that right means. These considerations cast doubt upon the expectation that *Miranda* should significantly reduce the rate at which convictions are obtained.

A related question is the extent to which confessions are necessary to dispose of cases. The *Miranda* case illustrates this point. The victim's bloodstained effects were found in Miranda's car; Miranda could not account for his whereabouts at the time the crime occurred; and he was identified by the victim. Hence Miranda confessed when confronted with an overwhelming case against him. When the Supreme Court quashed the conviction on the admissibility of the confession, it did not acquit Miranda. Rather, when the Court nullifies a conviction on constitutional grounds, it is saying that there is a problem with the manner in which the conviction was obtained, but the Court is not determining guilt or innocence. The case is remanded back to the prosecution, which may then choose to retry the accused in a manner consistent with the Supreme Court ruling. Miranda was in fact convicted on other evidence.

The point is that if the only ground for conviction is a confession obtained from an uninformed suspect under the psychological stress of an intense interrogation, the possibility exists that the suspect may in fact be innocent. If the accused is guilty, there should be a good chance that physical evidence or witnesses can be found to implicate him or her in the crime without a pressured confession. Moreover, when it is easy to pressure a confession from any plausible suspect, police may be tempted to use that technique to avoid the difficulty of seeking evidence to find out who really committed the crime. Convictions *per se* do not aid the cause of law and order if society erroneously convicts the innocent while actual perpetrators of crime remain free.

The Burger Court and *Miranda*.   The Burger Court made some decisions that have had the effect of narrowing the impact of *Miranda* without actually overruling it. Chief among such decisions is *Harris* v. *New York* (1971), which held that statements made by a defendant without *Miranda* warnings could be used to impeach his or her credibility. *Oregon* v. *Haas* (1975) extended the *Harris* principle to a defendant whose request for an attorney had been ignored. However, that same year, in *Brown* v. *Illinois,* the Court held that a confession is inadmissible, even though voluntarily made, if the arrest that preceded the confession was invalid (that is, made without warrant or probable cause).[29]

A 1981 Court ruling extended the *Miranda* principle to hold that the testimony of psychiatrists who have examined a defendant cannot be used to justify the imposition of capital punishment if the defendant was not accorded *Miranda* warnings before the psychiatric examination. The Court that year also extended the *Escobedo* and *Miranda* principles on the right to counsel, holding that once an accused requests counsel, interrogation of the accused alone must cease even if the accused is willing to continue talking. These unanimous decisions suggest that even the conservative Burger Court did not abandon the controversial *Miranda* principle. The even more conservative Rehnquist Court is unlikely to be more sympathetic to *Mapp* and *Miranda.* However, the Reagan-appointed justices on the Rehnquist Court are known to respect precedent and the importance of continuity in the law.

The Exclusionary Rule and Search and Seizure

We have already discussed the immediate importance of *Mapp* v. *Ohio,* that is, that the Court had reversed its earlier position and declared that the due process clause of the Fourteenth Amendment requires the exclusion from court of *illegally obtained evidence.* In effect, the Court rejected the argument that the exclusionary rule only protects the guilty; instead, it felt that if illegally obtained evidence is inadmissible, there is no motive for police to make illegal searches of the guilty or the innocent.

However, Chief Justice Burger disagreed. In his attack on the exclusionary rule, he made two claims: that it has a negative effect on successful prosecutions and that there is no evidence that it has a countervailing effect of deterring illegal police behavior. But according to data cited by Stephen Wasby, Burger was wrong on both counts. With regard to Burger's fears that *Mapp* will allow guilty people to "get away with it," Wasby did note a substantial decrease of some 41 percent in the number of suspects actually reaching trial in New York in 1961, immediately following *Mapp*. However, he found that the rate of successful prosecutions rose again the following year, suggesting that police were becoming adjusted to the new constraints on their behavior. With regard to Burger's claim that *Mapp* produced no benefits, Wasby quoted former New York City Police Commissioner Michael Murphy and former Philadelphia District Attorney (now Senator) Arlen Specter to the effect that police behavior was "revolutionized in many states." Political scientist Stuart Nagel also found increased police adherence to the rules on legal searches and seizures.[30]

The states, however, have varied in the strictness with which they have applied the *Mapp* ruling. The dictates of the Supreme Court are not self-enforcing; the mere handing down of a ruling does not automatically alter behavior. That is why there is a growing body of research on the compliance with and the impact of such rulings.

Beyond the exclusionary rule, the other major question on illegally obtained evidence that the courts have had to deal with is what constitutes an unreasonable search and seizure. The issue here is under what conditions it is permissible to search for and seize evidence without first obtaining a search warrant. Issued by a judge, a search warrant authorizes a public official to search private property without the consent of the property owner and specifies what is being sought.

The rules on what constitutes a legal warrantless search emerge from a complex array of cases and appear to be formulated with the goal of protecting police from the danger of hidden weapons. At the same time, these rules must protect the expanding concept of privacy immune from government intrusion. In a lawful arrest in which a warrant has not first been obtained, the following forms of search may be made: (1) the person and pockets of the arrestee and (2) the arrestee's car or the room in which he or she was arrested ("the area under his possession"), but not the entire house.[31] A person merely stopped for questioning may be subjected to a pat down or frisk for weapons, but pockets may not be searched.[32] The very complexity of these rules illustrates the difficulty that the courts have in trying to balance two important conflicting values: the right of individuals to be free from governmental oppression or harassment and the control of crime and punishment of criminals. The expansion of limits on search and seizure to include electronic surveillance illustrates this growing concept of the right of privacy and at the same time illustrates the problem of constraining police use of an important law enforcement tool.[33]

Capital Punishment

The *Furman* v. *Georgia* case was the first in which the Supreme Court laid down the law about the major constitutional restraints on the practice of capital punishment in America. One major decision was that the imposition of capital punishment should not be arbitrary. But it is important to keep in mind that *Furman* did not outlaw capital punishment as such; it outlawed capital punishment only as it was practiced circa 1971. Therefore numerous states accepted the implicit invitation of the Court to bring their death penalty statutes in line with the decision. One group of such laws viewed the arbitrariness referred to in *Furman* as being rooted in the "untrammeled discretion" of judges and/or juries in deciding whether a convicted murderer should be put to death. These laws tried to meet the objections of *Furman* by making the death penalty mandatory for certain types of crime; the decision to execute or spare the defendant theoretically would then be a consistent one, independent of such attributes of the defendant as race and social status. However, these laws robbed judges and juries of the ability to take account of the individual circumstances of the criminal act, rendering the imposition of capital punishment still somewhat arbitrary; and so mandatory death penalty statutes were also struck down by the Court.[34] The Court approved new death penalty statutes, however, as written for Florida, Georgia, and Texas (and presumably any other states enacting laws along the same lines). These approved statutes listed specific mitigating and aggravating circumstances as guides to be considered in deciding whether to assign the death penalty in a particular case, rather than making the imposition of the penalty mandatory for an entire category of crimes.[35] The legality of capital punishment has in this way been explicitly reaffirmed by the Court. Liberals have expressed the fear that this would bring about a flood of executions as states acted on the backlog of inmates now occupying death row. At first, the rate of executions began slowly, with three of the first four post-*Furman* executions being "voluntary," the condemned man himself eschewing further appeals. However, the rate has increased, especially in the southern states, and by 1985 over forty post-*Furman* executions had been carried out, including that of a North Carolina grandmother, the first woman to be executed in twenty-two years. By 1989, over 2,200 persons were under sentence of death.

Debating capital punishment.   The capital punishment issue epitomizes the widespread confusion with regard to the purposes of punishment. Although capital punishment is usually defended in terms of its deterrent effect, it is clear from the foregoing that capital punishment, as it can conceivably be practiced in the United States, is unlikely to have any significant deterrent effect on crime. It is possible, however, that many of those who defend capital punishment on deterrence grounds are really concerned about maintaining its role in retribution. The Court has explicitly said that retribution is a constitutionally valid purpose of punishment, stating in *Gregg* v. *Georgia* (1976) that

> . . . capital punishment is an expression of the society's moral outrage at particularly offensive conduct. This function may be unappealing to many, but it is essential in an ordered society that asks its citizens to rely on legal processes rather than self-help to vindicate their wrongs. . . . Retribution is no longer the dominant objective of the criminal law . . . but neither is it a forbidden objective.[36]

Many claim that the Eighth Amendment ought to be interpreted as banning capital punishment *per se,* but much of this argument is framed in ethical terms. Justices Brennan and Marshall, in making this argument, repeatedly evoked "the evolving standards of decency that mark the progress of a maturing society" to argue that a penalty that was permissible at one point in our history is no longer permissible today.[37] The precise content, however, of such "evolving standards of decency" is a subjective judgment on which reasonable people may disagree; the issue of whether the Eighth Amendment does or should prohibit capital punishment becomes instead the refining issue of how morally abhorrent capital punishment has become.

Execution of minors.   The constitutionality of applying the death penalty to capital crimes committed while the perpetrator was a minor has been a hotly debated issue in the 1980s. Opponents characterize the practice as "killing our children" and point out that the United States is virtually the only remaining Western nation that executes teenagers. The presumption of such opponents is that minors are not fully aware of the nature and consequences of their actions; therefore, they should not be held as fully responsible for their actions as are adults.

Those who support the application of the death penalty in these cases argue that violent and even vicious crimes increasingly are committed by teenagers. The growing problem of gang warfare in our large urban centers, a phenomenon discussed elsewhere in this chapter, only highlights the violence and mayhem that can be committed by teens. As noted earlier in this chapter, crime is to a large extent a young person's phenomenon; therefore the policy of protecting the very sector of the population most likely to commit serious crimes from serious punishment weakens whatever deterrent effect that punishment might have.

Opponents argue that evolving standards of decency in the Western world are violated by the execution of "children." They say that the rarity of such executions supports the claim of an evolving consensus that they violate the Eighth Amendment ban on cruel and unusual punishment. (In the twentieth century, there have been twenty executions for crimes committed by persons under 16 years old; none of these has taken place since the death penalty was revived by *Gregg* v. *Georgia.*)

The Court addressed the question of teenagers on death row in the 1988 case of *Thompson* v. *Oklahoma.*[38] In 1987, William Thompson, a fifteen-year-old with a record of three convictions for violent assaults with deadly weapons, murdered his brother-in-law by savagely beating him, shooting him, and then cutting his carcass up with a knife, a crime for which he received the death sentence. It is reported that Thompson had expressed the opinion that his age would protect him from severe punishment; nevertheless, it is not likely that many prospective teenage perpetrators engage in such calculations. The Court overturned the death sentence on a five-to-four vote; however, only four justices held that the death sentence for crimes committed by people under sixteen years old is necessarily cruel and unusual. The fifth justice, Sandra Day O'Connor, voted with the majority on narrower grounds. This leaves the possibility of executing teenagers open; however, the case indicates that a growing segment of the population is very uncomfortable with the idea of putting minors to death, and it is likely that states will remain reluctant to do so.

Limits on the death penalty.   Although there remains significant public support for the retention of the death penalty, the Court continues the general trend of increasingly circumscribing its application without invalidating the penalty itself. In *Sumner* v. *Shuman* (1987)[39] the Court struck down the Nevada statute that made the death sentence mandatory for murder perpetrated by a prisoner who was serving a life sentence without the possibility of parole at the time of the crime. Justice Blackmun, writing for the Court, argued that the mandatory nature of the sentence did not allow consideration of mitigating circumstances or factors and therefore did not allow the punishment to be clearly related to the individual or unique nature of the crime. This is consistent with the concern over arbitrariness expressed in *Furman* and the mandatory penalty cases that followed, such as *Woodson* v. *North Carolina* (1976) and *Roberts* v. *Louisiana*

(1976). Proponents of the law argued that the death penalty was the only thing that would deter such prisoners already serving life sentences from committing homicide. Blackmun addressed such claims, however, with the judgment that the *possibility* of a death sentence would be a sufficient deterrent.

This case, together with the aforementioned *Thompson* case and the case of *Maynard* v. *Cartwright* (1980),[40] appear to indicate that even this putatively conservative Court will continue to insist upon circumscribing the imposition of the death penalty with a set of carefully drawn and precise mitigating and aggravating factors as a guide to tie the penalty to the nature of the individual act. In the *Maynard* case, the Court struck down an Oklahoma death-penalty statute on the grounds that the state's phrasing of aggravating circumstances as crimes that are "especially heinous, atrocious or cruel" was unconstitutionally vague. The dire predictions of many civil libertarians that the "Reagan Court" would open the floodgates to a wave of executions do not appear to be supported by this Court's death-penalty decisions so far.

The disposition of the Court to circumscribe the means and conditions under which the death penalty could be assigned and to insist further that the decision to assign the death penalty be a function of the particular circumstances of the crime had earlier been manifested in the victim impact cases *Booth* v. *Maryland* (1987) and *South Carolina* v. *Gathers* (1989), which ruled that evidence about the impact of the crime on the victim or the victim's family must be excluded from consideration in assigning punishment.[41] A new disposition of the more conservative Court of the 1990s to pull back from its previous defendant's rights emphasis, perhaps informed by the public's demand for a greater stress on victim's rights, was manifested in a series of decisions in 1991, beginning with *McCleskey* v. *Zant* (1991), which overruled *Booth* and allowed victim's impact statements to be read with regard to sentencing decisions.[42] The *McCleskey* decision permitted statements read by the families of a murder victim testifying as to the devastating impact of their loss on their lives, statements that were followed by a death sentence to McCleskey. The liberal defense position continued to be that such statements constitute an emotional appeal that is extraneous to the hard facts of the case and therefore ought not to be salient in the assignment of appropriate punishment. However, information about difficulties and deprivations in the background of the convicted perpetrator have long been admissible in sentencing decisions.

Conclusion: Crime and Criminal Procedure

These issues surrounding capital punishment apply in large part to the broader question of the impact of expanded rights of defendants on the crime rate. Any rights that affect only the severity of punishment are unlikely to have an adverse impact. Rather, it is the rights that actually diminish the likelihood or swiftness of punishment that could lessen the deterrent effect and thus "encourage" more crime. The principal question in deterrence, therefore, is the perceived probability that the person who commits a crime will in the foreseeable future have to face some serious punishment.

Have expanded defendants' rights indeed served to hobble the deterrent effects of punishment? Before answering such a question, it is important to keep in mind that the theoretical route from criminal act to punishment is marked by numerous exit points, only one of which is an overturned conviction due to the expansion of defendants' rights (see Figure 6-2).

First, the rights of the accused can only come into play *after* a suspect is arrested. In fact, however, it is unlikely that any given criminal act will ever lead to an arrest. One scholar estimates about twelve arrests for every one hundred crimes in the United States.[43] James Q. Wilson claims that the odds are fourteen to one that the perpetrator of any given felony will not be caught.[44] In any event, the chances that a given criminal act will never lead to an encounter with the criminal justice process are extremely high, probably over 80 percent; therefore the nature and content of that process remain largely irrelevant to crime deterrence (see Figure 6-3).

A second factor detracting from the deterrent effect of punishment is the bail system together with the delay of trial. In those cases coming to trial, everyone except those accused of the most heinous capital crimes is accorded the option of posting bail and remaining free until the trial. For a large percentage of the accused who can afford the cost of bail, punishment is postponed until after the trial—and sometimes until after a series of appeals. Given the slowness with which our overburdened judicial system operates, punishment could and often does take years. Yet it is the swiftness and certainty of punishment that most deter crime. Studies show that from 30 percent to 70 percent of robbery suspects out on bail are rearrested for the commission of other crimes.[45]

Finally, because of the overcrowded nature of the judicial system, over three-quarters of convictions are obtained through plea bargaining, as noted before. This fact also gives potential criminals reason to believe that they can escape serious punishment even if they are caught.

Thus the expansion of defendants' rights has played a very small role in impeding or postponing the punishment of those who commit serious crimes. On the other hand, these rights do help protect the innocent and enhance the perception of the system as a just one, thereby contributing to the legitimacy of the system. It can be concluded that the restriction of defendants' rights does not offer a cost-efficient method for controlling crime. However, alternative policy options do exist, and these will be explored in the following section.

FUTURE ALTERNATIVES: POLICY OPTIONS FOR REDUCING CRIME

One obvious goal of public policy aimed at reducing crime is to increase the cost of illegal activity to the criminal, a result that a classic economic model predicts should reduce the quantity of crime.[46] These costs include material costs, time costs, and psychic costs as well as the familiar costs of expected punishment.

For example, encouraging or even requiring increased security devices in homes and businesses can add both to the time and the materials needed to

FIGURE 6-2 ▪ Exit Points in the Criminal Justice System

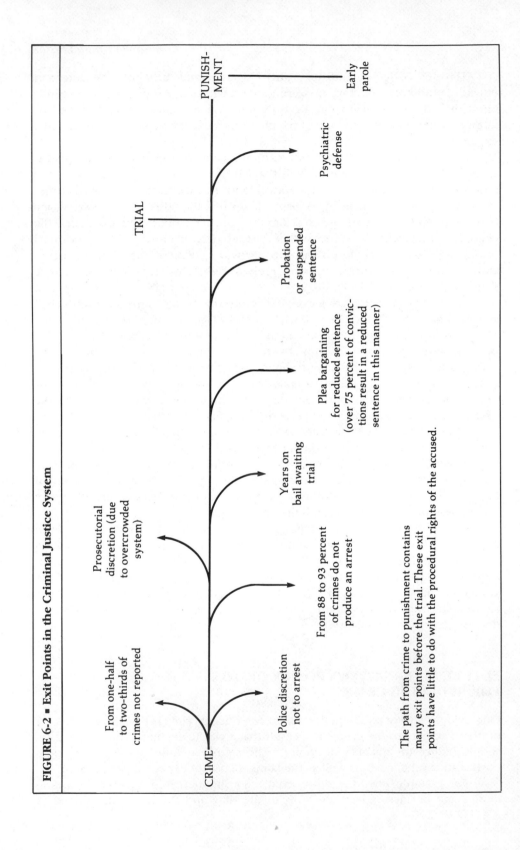

CRIME

PUNISH-MENT

TRIAL

From one-half to two-thirds of crimes not reported

Prosecutorial discretion (due to overcrowded system)

Police discretion not to arrest

From 88 to 93 percent of crimes do not produce an arrest

Years on bail awaiting trial

Plea bargaining for reduced sentence (over 75 percent of convictions result in a reduced sentence in this manner)

Probation or suspended sentence

Psychiatric defense

Early parole

The path from crime to punishment contains many exit points before the trial. These exit points have little to do with the procedural rights of the accused.

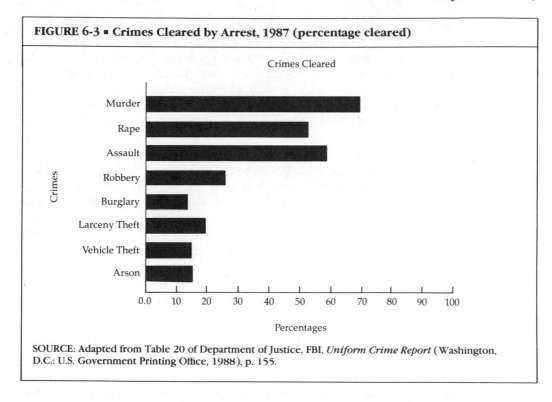

FIGURE 6-3 ▪ Crimes Cleared by Arrest, 1987 (percentage cleared)

Crimes Cleared

SOURCE: Adapted from Table 20 of Department of Justice, FBI, *Uniform Crime Report* (Washington, D.C.: U.S. Government Printing Office, 1988), p. 155.

commit a crime. Logically, it may be surmised that if the perceived opportunities for earning a better return by noncriminal means exceed the opportunities for the return from crime (breaking into the now electronically secure business has become too much trouble), assuming an equal expenditure of time and effort, the potential criminal would find it rational to opt for noncriminal pursuits and crime would be reduced. (This kind of analysis points to an oft-cited conclusion: that programs to reduce unemployment and to provide jobs for the most crime-prone segments of the population would cut crime.)

The logic of this argument presumes that criminals are rational, economically motivated beings. This assumption is only imperfectly valid. It would most likely apply to property crimes, but crimes against persons are frequently acts of passion or anger that have nothing to do with the rational pursuit of economic rewards. Even in the case of some property crimes the economic assumption remains imperfectly valid, most notably in crimes to support drug addiction.

Drug-Related Crimes

Estimates vary on what proportion of street crime (for example, mugging, robbery, and auto theft) is committed to support an addiction to illegal drugs;

however, such estimates uniformly place the figure at over half and sometimes as high as three-quarters. As explained earlier, the high cost of addictive drugs on the illegal market combined with an inflexible and economically inelastic demand for such drugs almost requires the addict to commit crime to support the addiction. Clearly, a reduction in the extent of drug addiction should lead to a reduction in crimes against property. Moreover, since intravenous drug users now constitute the primary source of new AIDS cases, reducing drug addiction would affect the spread of that disease.

Attacking supply.   The first strategy to reduce drug addiction—and perhaps the most popular to the public—is to try to intercept the supply. President Nixon, for example, initiated the much-heralded "Project Intercept." This strategy was reemphasized in the Reagan and Bush administrations. Though the heroic efforts of federal agents to catch drug smugglers, punish them, and confiscate their wares make sensational newspaper headlines, such efforts do not have a positive impact on the extent of drug addiction. The supply may be temporarily diminished, which raises the price of the remaining available drugs. The demand for drugs, however, is not sensitive to price. Therefore the higher price probably has the effect of driving addicts to commit more crime in order to afford the higher prices.

Efforts to intercept the drug supply can never be completely successful. The nation's borders are too extensive, and the many ways of concealing smuggled illegal drugs make thorough searches impractical. For example, smugglers now swallow balloons full of pure cocaine and retrieve them when they have passed through their alimentary canal after clearing customs. Because most drugs, such as cocaine and heroin, are highly diluted for street sale, a valuable quantity of pure, uncut white powder occupies very little space. Furthermore, the stakes are so high and the potential profits so great that there will always be someone willing to take virtually any risk or go to any lengths to supply the drugs.

Attacking demand.   A second strategy in dealing with the drug problem is to attempt to rehabilitate the addict. This means assigning criminal addicts to a hospital-type facility rather than a prison. Here the addict could receive psychological counseling in conjunction with medically supervised withdrawal. Yet records indicate the failure rate of such programs to be well over 90 percent.[47] Smaller community rehabilitation efforts have had a somewhat better record, but they process too few addicts to resolve the drug problem. Moreover, addicts frequently return to heroin use even years after withdrawal. Apparently, the anxieties that produce the heroin hungers still exist for such people, even though the physical addiction may be over.

A third strategy is maintaining the addict on a heroin substitute, usually methadone (a synthetic narcotic developed by the Germans in World War II). Methadone maintenance programs have achieved some success in stabilizing known addicts and removing them from the drug subculture, which leads to a life of crime and other antisocial behavior. One study of one thousand patients in such a program reported a 92 percent reduction in arrest records over a four-year period. This study also reported a substantial increase in the rate of employment, from 26 to 61 percent at the end of one year.[48] Methadone is, however, an addictive drug itself, and a black market has grown up around the legal dispensing of methadone. Moreover, methadone has proved to be less than a totally satisfactory substitute for heroin from the addict's point of view, in that methadone can only relieve the agonies of heroin withdrawal—it cannot duplicate the euphoric "highs" that heroin offers to new addicts. Therefore a market for expensive heroin continues to exist, and pushers still have the economic incentive to find new addicts.

A fourth strategy is the British policy of legally dispensing maintenance doses of heroin itself to confirmed addicts. The Dangerous Drug Act of 1920 allowed physicians to prescribe such drugs to addicted patients. Until about 1950, the number of known addicts in Britain slowly declined to around 400. In the next two decades the number of addicts in Britain began to increase, reaching a level of around 3,000 by 1970. This contrasts with estimates of the total number of heroin addicts in the United States in 1972 at around 300,000. Thus the United States had about one hundred times as many addicts with only four times as many people, a clear failure of the punitive and intercept strategies that have dominated our policies regarding the drug problem. The causes of the rise in the British rate of addiction were twofold: abuses by physicians in the dispensing of such drugs and the growing legitimacy of the counterculture movement throughout the Western world, in which drug use for emotional satisfaction was characteristic. The British policy changed in the face of this rise in addiction. Today drugs are dispensed through clinics run by the National Health Service, a practice that affords the opportunity for greater control over drug distribution. Since the advent of this newer procedure, the number of addicts in Britain has stabilized, whereas the number of addicts in the United States has increased fivefold over the same time period.[49] This manifestly advantageous result raises the question of why the British plan of controlled maintenance has been able to stem the rise in heroin use in that country but the American policy of punishment or supply interception has had no detectable ameliorative impact.

The British system appears to succeed because it removes the economic incentive to take the risks of smuggling drugs and creating new addicts. It is virtually impossible to stop completely the influx of addictive drugs by force. One can, therefore, either raise the risks and the economic costs of doing that kind of business or reduce the potential benefits. As we have pointed out, someone will always be willing to bear the costs and take the risks as long as the prospect of fabulous profits remains. This prospect disappears under the British program of the free dispensation of addictive drugs; hence, the potential benefits of being a drug dealer no longer outweigh the risks. The British system rejects the long odds against successfully and permanently reforming existing addicts (and accepts a small government-dependent population) in order to reduce the creation of new addicts. The data suggest that they are succeeding.

The drug epidemic in the United States has been exacerbated in the late 1980s with the introduction of crack, which is apparently more highly addictive than ordinary cocaine and even more so than heroin. Moreover, its misuse can easily result in death. The spectacular death of basketball star Len Bias in 1987 from cocaine highlighted the less publicized but equally tragic deaths of thousands of young people from the misuse of this highly lethal substance every year. Crack is fast replacing heroin as the drug of choice in the inner-city slums.

We have already alluded to the growth of gang warfare associated with the crack epidemic. Gangs frequently possess sophisticated weapons, especially semi-automatic assault rifles such as the Israeli-made Uzi and the Chinese-made AK-47. Eruptions of gang violence often involve drive-by shootings in which innocent bystanders are killed. This has caused geometric increases in the murder rates in some areas. Washington, D.C., for example, has become the murder capital of the world largely because of such shootings.

A public outcry to control the widespread ownership of these weapons, stimulated by the random shootings of schoolchildren, motivated the previously anti–gun control President Bush to impose a ban on the importation of assault rifles. The decisions of whether to make the ban permanent and of how to address the domestic production of these kinds of weapons have not been made at this writing. Other proposals to address this phenomenon include committing federal resources to the task of policing Washington, D.C. In 1991, with its counterintelligence functions rendered largely moot by the end of the Cold War, the FBI announced that it was diverting many of its resources to a program of cooperation with the Washington, D.C., police department to curb the soaring crime rate and in particular to combat the growing problem of gang violence in that city.

Violence against Women

The crime of rape and other forms of violence against women have come into increasing focus in recent years, due in part to the rising prominence of the feminist movement. Technically, rape consists of using force or the threat of force to obtain sexual interaction with a woman against her will. Rape has come to be widely perceived not merely as a means of obtaining sexual gratification but rather as an extreme manner of expressing hostility to women. This broader definition of the term is related to the heightened awareness that far more often than not sexual aggression occurs within the context of courtship or friendship relationships (called "acquaintance rape" or "date rape") or even that of marriage. Although serious discussion of acquaintance rape has arisen only recently, Laurie Bechofer and Andrea Parrot trace it back to the biblical book of Samuel.[50] Susan Brownmiller, in *Against Our Will,* calls rape "nothing more than a conscious process of intimidation by which all men keep all women in a state of fear";[51] and Andrea Dworkin goes further, arguing that heterosexual coupling is a form of dominance in a context of unequal roles and that what appears as consent on the woman's part is simply a form of collaboration obtained by the man in the inevitable war between the sexes.[52]

The problem of male power over women also arises in the matter of sexual harassment, here defined as the behavior (including speech) of a man who, holding some form of dominance over a woman, attempts to initiate a sexual relationship (broadly defined) with her. This relationship may take the form of conversation or subtle pressure that makes the woman in question feel uncomfortable, offended, or embarrassed. The essential elements are expressed or implied male power in an asymmetrical relationship and some form of sexual content. If a man were to require his secretary to pick up his laundry, it would be harassment, but not sexual harassment. This form of sexual intimidation came most acutely to public attention in October, 1991, when Supreme Court nominee Clarence Thomas was accused of such harassment by law professor Anita Hill, a former employee. The Senate Judiciary Committee conducted a highly publicized hearing of the allegations. The truth behind the charges was never conclusively established, but the perceived hostility and skepticism with which Hill was treated by the committee enraged many people.

Despite their vicious and exploitive nature, the crime of rape and the related civil wrong of sexual harassment present unique problems for the criminal justice system, which is, after all, dedicated to providing due process for those accused of even the most heinous acts. With this expanded definition of rape, rape and sexual harassment confound a *sine qua non* of criminal law: that the behavior being proscribed be precisely defined. For sexual activity to be rape, it must occur against the will of the victim. Prosecutions for rape have always been weakened by problems of evidence and especially by the ages-old myth of implied consent, that is, the assumption or the assertion that although the woman said no, she must really have meant yes. The 1992 rape conviction of former heavyweight boxing champion Michael Tyson may have been a major step in establishing the credibility of rape victims in denying such implied consent, although even in this case the defense argued that if the young woman was in the man's room at two o'clock in the morning, she must have expected sexual advances. Moreover, even expressed consent is frequently held by some to be implicitly coerced by the asymmetrical power relationship between men and women, a position reported by law professor Susan Estrich, who indicates, "many feminists would argue that so long as women are powerless relative to men, viewing yes as a sign of true consent is misguided."[53]

The recognition that the forms of coercion used by men over women can go beyond direct and overt use of force brings legal theory closer to reality. However, some scholars fear that the expanding conceptualization of rape and the imprecise definition of sexual harassment serves to blur the distinction between this kind of vicious behavior and other widespread forms of interaction between the sexes. These problems in defining behavior can exacerbate the difficulty in obtaining rape convictions from male jurors who may perceive an uncomfortable similarity between some of their own past actions and those of a defendant in such cases.

Clearly, there is heightened sensitivity to the problems of rape and sexual harassment that will lead to accelerated efforts in legal and legislative policy formation. The challenge is to fight rape and harassment in all their forms while protecting the rights of women and men.

Crimes of Violence and Gun Control

Drug-related crimes are primarily crimes against property, that is, theft in order to support expensive addictions. Of course, violence is frequently involved in such crimes as a means of obtaining the economic benefit. When the violence becomes the end in itself, the causes and the means of combating such crime are quite different from those in the case of crimes against property.

When the goal of the crime is material gain, a certain amount of rational calculation—cost-benefit analysis—may indeed go into the decision to commit the crime. Even drug-related crimes, with the addict's inelastic demand, can be curbed by removing the pusher's economic incentive and the addict's economic need. When the goal of the criminal act is violence to another person, however, the element of rational calculation diminishes. Although there may be certain psychic benefits that accrue to the perpetrator of a crime of violence, it is doubtful whether much rational calculation is involved. Rape, for instance, is now thought by most psychologists to be an act of violence (an act of woman hating) rather than an act motivated by sexual passion or need. For example, rapists have been known to commit their crime within hours of experiencing consensual sexual relations.

The point is that in such crimes the traditional theory of deterrence breaks down. Because the benefits are emotional, the decision to commit the crime is, by definition, nonrational. This is why the data fail to show that the death penalty deters capital crimes of rape or murder. One policy option on crimes against persons is to contain the proliferation of the instruments of violence. In practical terms, this means gun control.

Guns and violence.   In the United States, the proliferation of firearms far exceeds that in any other civilized nation. Estimates of the number of privately owned firearms in the United States range from 50 to 200 million guns in the possession of some 40 million individuals. Firearms have been used to shoot over 200,000 people per year, some 20,000 of whom die. In 1976, the United States had a homicide rate of 9.1 per 100,000 population, a rate among twenty-five industrial nations exceeded only by Northern Ireland (a nation beset by widespread internal terrorism). This rate rose to 10.2 per 100,000 by 1980. The American rate was 355 percent higher than the next nearest nation, another frontier country, Australia, which had a rate of 2.0. Although this American rate declined to 8.3 by 1985, it was still substantially higher than other nations (see Figure 6-4). In 1987, there were 17,859 murders known to police, of which 10,556, or 59 percent, were committed by firearms. In 1986, 8,572 people were killed by handguns. Indeed, more people in America were killed by handguns during the years of the Vietnam War than American soldiers were killed in Vietnam.

Estimates for 1987 indicate that some 20,000 to 22,000 people are killed by handguns each year, if approximately 12,000 annual suicides using these weapons are included. Experts estimate that only one person in ten who attempts suicide really intends to die. Many stage the attempt to draw sympathy or get attention. However, the presence of a gun renders many of these suicides successful, whereas someone swallowing pills or standing on a window ledge may be saved.

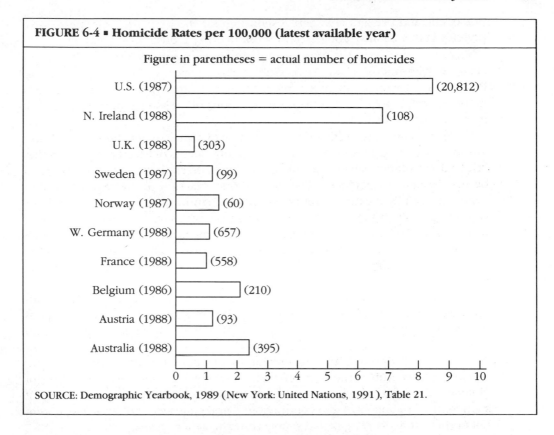

FIGURE 6-4 ▪ Homicide Rates per 100,000 (latest available year)

Figure in parentheses = actual number of homicides

SOURCE: Demographic Yearbook, 1989 (New York: United Nations, 1991), Table 21.

Moreover, the proliferation of guns has meant that many of them inevitably fall into the hands of children, who are less likely to use them responsibly. In 1987, an average of one child under the age of fifteen died in the United States each day from a handgun accident and ten others were injured, according to the Center to Prevent Handgun Violence. Moreover, from 1987 to 1989 there was a 34 percent increase in the number of children under fifteen killed by guns, according to the Coalition to Stop Gun Violence. Many of these tragedies occur because gun owners leave their weapons where children can find them. Accordingly, by late 1991 a number of state and local governments had either adopted or were considering legislation holding gun owners responsible under both civil and criminal laws for any harm caused by their leaving weapons accessible to children. Not surprisingly, the powerful National Rifle Association (NRA) opposes such legislation insofar as it covers young people fourteen years of age or older, claiming that fourteen-year-olds are capable of making their own decisions about guns. The NRA legislative counsel further opposes legislation that mandates criteria for storing weapons. As we shall see again below, this powerful lobbying group for gun owners has consistently opposed any effort to regulate firearm possession and use and is in part responsible for the extraordinarily permissive policies in this country compared to those in other industrialized nations.

As we have seen, the growing phenomenon of gang violence in the underclass neighborhoods of our large cities thrives on easily obtainable weapons. Police forces are increasingly seeking to counter the firepower of street gangs with more powerful and more sophisticated weapons of their own, creating a kind of domestic arms race.

There is no question that the proliferation of firearms contributes to their use in shooting people. Despite the cliché of the opponents of firearm regulation that "Guns don't kill people; people kill people," the correlations are far too strong to be dismissed as coincidental. The international reaction to the murder of John Lennon forcefully illustrated this phenomenon. Nations that restrict firearms have far fewer people shot. Japan, with half as many people as we have, had 46 handgun deaths in 1985; Great Britain had only 8 handgun murders that year among its 54.5 million people; whereas Houston, Texas, had approximately 150 such murders among only 1.5 million people in 1986 (based on a reported rate of 22.9 murders per 100,000).

Opposition to gun control.   Despite these data, there are two rationales for the opposition to gun control. The first is the belief that gun control would not correct the crime problem. The second is that it would violate rights of gun owners.

A key assumption of the first rationale is that guns are not the only available deadly weapon. Knives and blunt instruments can and do serve as instruments of violence; yet no one seriously advocates the restriction of the private ownership of such items. Opponents of gun control hold that if guns were not available, potential perpetrators of crime would simply resort to other means.

It is further argued that persons determined to commit crimes would find illegal ways of acquiring firearms even if laws banned them. Prohibition did not prevent the use of alcoholic beverages, nor do laws eliminate prostitution, pornography, or illegal drugs. Therefore gun control would by definition take guns away from law-abiding citizens only and leave them in the hands of criminals.

Neither of these arguments invalidates the utility of gun control legislation in reducing the number of people who are shot each year. First, it is both physically and psychologically easier to kill someone with a gun than with a blunt instrument or with a knife. It takes a greater degree of strength, passion, commitment, and insensitivity to bash in a head with an andiron or to plunge a knife between someone's ribs than it does to stand across a room and pull a trigger. Furthermore, the possibilities of resistance are much greater in a knife or club attack, means requiring physical proximity, than when one is shot from a distance. The proliferation of firearms, the data show, not only correlates with the number of people who are shot but also with the total number of people who are murdered. Guns in general and handguns in particular account for a preponderant proportion of homicides in this country. Nationwide, 60 percent of all murders are committed with firearms, and 45 percent with handguns. This far outstrips other methods of committing homicide, as shown in Table 6-6. In a recent year, Rhode Island, with

TABLE 6-6 ▪ Murders in the United States in 1988 (percentage by weapon)

Weapon	Percentage
all guns	60.7
handguns	45.3
cutting and stabbing	19.1
blunt object	6.3
hands, feet, etc.	6.2
strangulation	2.2
fire	1.4
other	4.1

SOURCE: The Department of Justice, FBI, *Uniform Crime Report* (Washington, D.C.: U.S. Government Printing Office, 1990), p. 13.

strict gun control laws, had 1.4 total murders per 100,000 population, whereas Texas, with a high incidence of gun ownership, had 9.7 murders per 100,000 population.

The ease of taking lives with firearms as opposed to alternative methods is clearly shown in the figures for suicides by firearms in Table 6-7. It should be noted that despite the availability of numerous other means to commit suicide, firearms were used in over half the cases and came through the 1970s to account for almost two-thirds of all suicides. Taking one's own life is frequently an essentially irrational or impulsive act, and one that might not have taken place had the victim been forced to cool off in the light of day or to use some other, possibly unsuccessful, means.

The third corollary, that banned firearms would still be available by illegal means, presumes a determined criminal who plans his or her use of the gun in advance. In fact, the majority of homicides are not premeditated but are crimes of

TABLE 6-7 ▪ Suicides in the United States

Year	Total Number	Number by Firearms	Percentage by Firearms
1970	16,629	9,707	58.4
1975	16,622	12,185	62.1
1980	20,505	12,937	63.1
1983	21,786	13,959	64.1
1985	23,145	14,809	64.0
1986	24,226	15,518	64.1

SOURCE: *Statistical Abstract of the United States, 1991* (Washington, D.C.: U.S. Government Printing Office, 1991), table 125.

passion committed on the spur of the moment. The argument that would end with a punch when a gun is not available may end with someone dead if a gun *is* available. Many shootings occur in domestic quarrels or in drunken arguments in bars. If the combatants had to go out the following day and seek a firearm from illegal sources, surely some of their passion would have cooled off in the sober light of day.

Unquestionably, some determined criminals would still seek out firearms by illegal means and use them. But, equally undeniable, other potential killers would cool off and not pursue a weapon. The claim is not that gun control would totally prevent murder, but rather that gun control would save many lives. The issue is, then, how much a human life is worth against the convenience of a law-abiding gun enthusiast's unrestricted access to firearms.

The second rationale against gun control is its alleged infringement on the right of law-abiding citizens to keep and own firearms, supposedly a constitutional right based on the Second Amendment, which reads:

> A well regulated militia, being necessary to the security of a free State, the right of the people to keep and bear arms, shall not be infringed.

It is important to note that there are two parts to this sentence. Presumably the opening gerund phrase, if it is not redundant, modifies the main clause. Therefore it is reasonable to conclude that the purpose of the amendment was to prevent the national government from disarming the state militias. The Constitution therefore does not unambiguously prevent Congress from choosing to regulate private ownership of firearms. It is essentially a political rather than a constitutional question.

Regulation of guns.   Even on the assumption that Congress could regulate firearms if it chose to do so, it is argued that Congress ought not to do so because such regulation would interfere with the rights of two groups of people who require firearms. The first group consists of those who hunt game for recreation. A large part of this difficulty could be dealt with by distinguishing among kinds of firearms. Most hunting is done with rifles, whereas most crime is committed with concealable handguns; thus the fairest solution would be to prohibit the handguns that kill people and not ban rifles. Allowing hunting rifles would not eliminate the occasional crime committed with one, and handgun control might inconvenience the adventurous soul who chooses to hunt wild boar with a snub-nosed .38; but the overall impact would be unimpeded hunting recreation for the sportsperson and a significant reduction in homicides. Or guns could be distinguished by barrel length and/or melting point, criteria that would distinguish the cheap, small handguns used in much crime from rifles and longer-range handguns occasionally used in hunting.

The second group consists of people who genuinely need a gun for protection. This would include those who work in high-crime neighborhoods, those who must travel late at night, and those whose safety has been threatened.

The needs of this second group constitute another important argument against gun control legislation. The argument is that law enforcement institutions and the justice process are unable to protect citizens from being victims of serious crime; therefore such people have the right and the obligation to seek protection for themselves and their families. The argument states that if potential criminals believed that most people kept guns in their homes and knew how to use them, the number of break-ins would decrease dramatically.

FBI statistics do not support this argument, however. Their data show that a handgun used for "self-defense" is *one hundred times* more likely to kill or injure its owner than it is to stop a potential criminal. The owner will tend to be less ruthless than the criminal in shooting another human being or may be less adept than the criminal in handling the gun. Permits can be issued on an individual basis to anyone who makes a case for a genuine need for a gun and who does not appear to present a high risk of using that gun for undesirable purposes.

Therefore gun control does not have to ban guns from the entire population. It may be confined to the requirement that prospective purchasers of weapons be identified and the records checked to see whether they fall into one of the high-risk categories before they are allowed actually to possess the weapon. Such regulation might even be confined to small handguns. It is perhaps not too much to ask that a gun seller not be permitted to sell an arsenal to someone recently released from prison or from an institution for the criminally psychotic.

The requirement that prospective purchasers of handguns undergo background checks is the essence of the Brady Bill. The bill was named after presidential aide James Brady, who was critically wounded in John Hinckley's attempt to kill President Reagan in 1981, and after Sarah Brady, his wife, who has become one of the leading activists for handgun control. The proposed background checks would take a day or two and purchasers would have to wait seven days before taking possession of guns, a period of time that could also serve as a "cooling-off period." In 1991, Congress came close to passing the Brady Bill, lending some hope to proponents of gun control.

Semi-automatic weapons. The debate on the control of semi-automatic weapons, which hold many rounds of ammunition and allow many more rounds to be fired in less time, was activated by several mass killings, one having been the murder of five children and the wounding of some thirty others in a Stockton, California, elementary school in 1989 by a deranged man named Patrick Purdy with a Chinese-made AK-47. In the wake of that killing, the Bush administration banned the import of assault rifles such as the AK-47 and the Israeli-made Uzi but refused to extend the ban to the domestic manufacture of such weapons, even though three-fourths of the country's weapons are produced domestically. This debate continued when a Glock 17 was used by another deranged gunman, George Hennard, to kill twenty-two people and wound many others in a Killeen, Texas, cafeteria in October, 1991. The Glock, in addition to being able to escape detection by some airport metal detectors, has the advantage of being semi-automatic with a large seventeen-round clip like an assault rifle, which renders it efficient in killing large numbers of people. It is a 7.4-inch-long, 21.8-ounce pistol that, unlike an assault rifle, is concealable.

A provision in the omnibus crime bill of 1991 provided for the ban on the domestic manufacture and sale of thirteen types of these semi-automatic weapons and would have limited the size of ammunition clips. Although this provision would not have outlawed the Glock, it would have prevented the legal sale of the 17-round clip able to kill so many so quickly. Just one day after the Killeen massacre, however, the House voted by the substantial margin of 247 to 177 to pass Representative Harold Volkmer's (Democrat, Missouri) amendment to the crime bill to delete the ban on automatic weapons and large ammunition clips.

The polls have shown for some time that a substantial majority of Americans support some form of gun regulation. For example, a 1977 poll asked a national sample the following question: "Would you favor or oppose a law which would require a person to obtain a police permit before he or she could buy a gun?" Seventy-two percent of the respondents favored such a law; 26 percent opposed it; and 2 percent answered that they did not know. Furthermore, 70 percent of that sample agreed that "the only way to control handguns is by federal law."[54] Why, then, has this policy not been adopted on a national level?

The answer lies in the efforts of one of the wealthiest and most powerful interest groups in the nation, the National Rifle Association, whose zealous and intense efforts to oppose almost any form of firearm regulation epitomize the ability of a passionate minority to overcome a passive majority. The NRA supports or opposes politicians on the single-issue "litmus test" of their position on gun control, and the group's vociferous opposition to politicians who support gun control has been a major factor in defeating some candidates.

Decriminalization and Deterrence

Recall that the swiftness and certainty of punishment are thought to be the major ingredients in deterring crime. There are two factors at work in the criminal justice system that greatly slow down the meting out of that punishment. One is the long wait that criminals spend free between arraignment and trial, and the other is the enormous case load of "victimless crime" defendants.

A substantial portion of the total justice system case load is processing the so-called victimless crimes. The people who are arrested for such things as prostitution, public intoxication, or drug abuse take up a very large portion of the court time in any large city, time that might otherwise be used to prosecute more swiftly the perpetrators of crimes against persons or property. To the court time spent on victimless crime must be added the use of such resources as prosecutorial forces, court-appointed defense attorneys, and police time. Such laws often demean law enforcement officers, who must consort with prostitutes, homosexuals, and gamblers in order to catch them. Police are pressured to apprehend such people, not because of any threat they pose to public safety, but solely because they offend the dominant morality. Having to assume undercover roles that themselves violate accepted morality detracts from the public image and self-image of the police. These laws are also selectively enforced against social undesirables. Police arrest streetwalkers but rarely arrest expensive call girls. Lower-class people are arrested for public intoxication on the street, but middle-class people are rarely bothered for intoxication except when driving. These laws also encourage organized crime, which provides criminalized services. Finally, these laws fail to prevent the conduct they proscribe; they may not even substantially reduce such conduct. *Decriminalization,* the legalization of such conduct, is a policy option that would permit a reallocation of criminal justice resources to crimes against persons and property.

It is protested, however, that the legalization of such "immoral" conduct would in effect constitute a legitimization of it, an official stamp of approval that would result in its expansion. Laws against murder do not prevent the crime from occurring, but they reduce its incidence and place society squarely in the position of saying that murder is not tolerable. It is argued that there are principles of ethical conduct that define the essence of society as a community and that society's officially sanctioned code of conduct must embody these principles.[55] The Reagan administration strongly favored moving toward greater use of the state's powers to protect its view of public morality.

Others argue that there is a basic difference between laws proscribing crimes against persons and property and laws proscribing conduct that a dominant group finds immoral. With the former case, there is a widespread consensus on the wrongful nature of acts such as murder, robbery, and rape. With the latter, there is no such consensus on the immorality of such conduct as getting intoxicated, sexual "swinging," or homosexuality. The legislation of morality is thus an attempt to impose a moral unity in a society in which ethical pluralism is a fact of life. In fact, the toleration of such pluralism has long been held a hallmark of an open society. Moral and philosophical homogeneity can be imposed only at the cost of considerable resources of coercion and legitimacy. If such resources are scarce and finite, the criminalization of what dominant groups consider to be immoral may have the effect of reducing society's ability to control crimes against persons and property. Therefore one effective method to reverse the situation—to free up the criminal justice system's resources to deal with priority crimes—is to decriminalize the kinds of victimless offenses discussed in this section.

Strengthening the Police

Providing for more police or enhancing their technical law enforcement capabilities would seem to be an effective means of deterring crime. It is not clear, however, what effective actions specifically can be taken to secure this end. Some of the most obvious innovations have been tried and shown not to be effective.

For instance, an experiment has been conducted on the effect of increasing the numbers of police in a given geographical area. Political scientist Robert Lineberry reported on an experiment in Kansas City that reduced the police presence in one section of the city, greatly increased the police presence in a second section, and left a third section unchanged with respect to police presence. The experiment failed to reveal significant differences in crime rates among the three neighborhoods.[56] The report did not deal with arrest rates, however, and the experiment was in place only a short period of time. Obviously, one study is inconclusive, and increasing the police in one area may simply displace crime to other areas.

Increased physical paraphernalia, such as riot control vehicles, or higher police salaries and sophisticated recruitment practices, have also not been shown to have a significant impact on police effectiveness. Although increasing the resources allocated to police may give the psychological satisfaction of supporting the forces of law and order, it does not hold out much promise of contributing to the goal of deterring crime.

Penal Reform, Sentencing, and Recidivism

Criticisms of the disposition of our criminal justice system to impose insufficiently harsh penalties are frequently directed at the discretion available to judges to impose sentences. The issue over whether the maximization of jail time served will in fact reduce the crime rate involves assumptions about the impact prison time served has on the criminal. It is widely assumed that discretionary sentencing has resulted in excessive leniency for serious criminals, as well as resulting in unjustly harsh sentences that depended on which judge was presiding in a given case. It is assumed, in other words, that society cannot trust judges to mete out punishments that are suitable to the circumstances and nature of each particular crime. These assumptions have led to a demand for a standardization in sentencing.

Mandatory sentencing proposals at the state level may mean limiting the alternatives to jail time served, or it may mean imposing a minimum of time served before parole eligibility. However, the impact of such laws would be undercut by plea bargaining and the greater disposition to enter such bargains in the face of a mandatory sentencing law. At the federal level, an elaborate and comprehensive set of guidelines for the standardization of sentencing was enacted into law in 1987 and subsequently upheld by the courts. Of course, such federal laws have no impact on the vast preponderance of crime that involves state law, except insofar as the federal policy serves as a model for the criminal justice systems of several states.

The fact that most career criminals will serve prison time at some point in their lives renders the recidivism rate one of the more important facts about criminality. *Recidivism* is the rate at which crime is committed by people who have been convicted of previous crimes. A high recidivism rate indicates that people who have been punished for committing at least one crime have a higher probability of committing subsequent crimes than do people who have never been so punished.

One authority has estimated that as many as 80 percent of all felonies are committed by people previously convicted of other felonies; others place the rate as low as one-third.[57] Widely accepted estimates suggest that recidivists account for around 60 percent of all felonies. One study of 18,000 people arrested in 1963 found that within three years, 55 percent had been arrested again, and another study of persons arrested for robbery found that only 38 percent went back to jail within two years.[58] Problems of definition and data gathering account for the wide variation among these statistics.

The serious implication of the high recidivism rate is that rather than deterring individuals from committing additional crimes, punishment and incarceration appear to make it more likely that they will engage in criminal behavior again. The recidivism rate attests to the failure of our prison system. Its importance becomes even more obvious in light of the more than 600,000 people incarcerated in American prisons, and the desire to curb this relentless relapse into criminality has inspired an increasing concern for the reform of the prison system. Putting more people in jail has not lowered the crime rate (see Figure 6-5).

Many charge that the prison system increases the inmates' tendency toward criminality. First, the system is seriously overcrowded. This fact in turn results in the bitterness and dehumanization that occur when people must spend years in substandard conditions. President Bush's $1.2 billion major crime proposal in 1989 focused on allocating nearly $1 billion for new federal prison construction. The new space, however, would immediately be filled by new inmates, as will similar spaces built in state prisons. Second, prisons are understaffed with respect

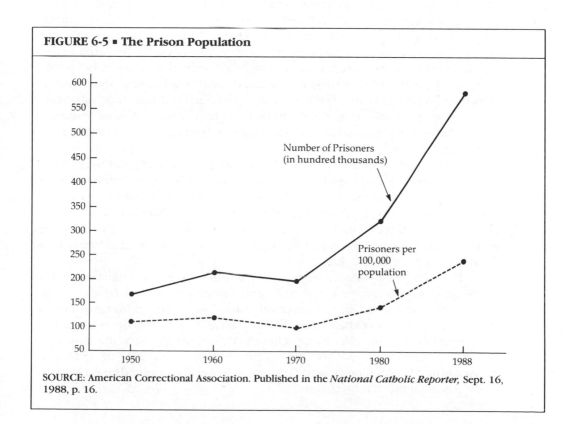

FIGURE 6-5 ▪ The Prison Population

SOURCE: American Correctional Association. Published in the *National Catholic Reporter,* Sept. 16, 1988, p. 16.

to trained personnel who could help rehabilitate inmates. Third, improper supervision by staff and a lack of standards for choosing them results in such brutalizing experiences as beatings by guards, homosexual rape, and interracial violence.

Yet it is dangerous to characterize the prison system as if it were an undifferentiated whole. Although clearly some prisons have been notoriously brutalizing places—city jails such as the Cook County Jail in Chicago and the Tombs in New York City are frequently cited in this regard—other places are well-staffed, modern facilities that resemble college campuses as much as institutions for punishment.

Another characteristic of the prison system alluded to by its critics is a failure to prepare inmates to lead productive lives upon their release. Little is done to impart the skills needed to make the inmates more employable than when they turned to crime. There is little call in today's economy for laundry workers or license plate manufacturers.

Drugs are easily available within many prisons, and under the pressures of prison life, addicts are sometimes created. This addiction, of course, almost guarantees the subsequent criminal activity of such inmates.

Among the suggested strategies in prison reform are better vocational training and improved psychological counseling, rehabilitative services aimed at changing the circumstances in which the individual became a criminal in the first place. (This argument assumes, however, that "environment" breeds criminality, an assumption not universally accepted.) Overcrowded conditions can be addressed by building more facilities, by shorter sentences, by probated or suspended sentences, by work release programs, and by early paroles. Work release programs offer the added benefit of additional vocational training. More rigorous standards and better training for supervisory personnel and even "conjugal visits" from the mates of prisoners, which permit them to maintain a normal heterosexual life, have been suggested as means of mitigating the dehumanizing nature of the prison experience.

The controversial nature of these proposals is due in large part to confusion and ambivalence over the goals of the prison system. Liberals and social scientists assume that the main purpose of the prison system is rehabilitative and correctional. Prisons are in fact frequently called "correctional facilities." Others stress the deterrent effect of punishment. Still others see prisons as places to house and isolate crime-prone individuals from society, thus physically preventing them from inflicting any further harm.

The kind of malevolent conditions that would seem best to fulfill the function of punishment are different from the more benevolent prison conditions frequently held to encourage rehabilitation. Therefore those who seek to use the prisons for punishment charge that they are "schools of crime" because convicts are treated too kindly.[59] Yet many believe that by making prisons more brutal in order to punish criminals effectively, we make prisons less able to rehabilitate criminals into law-abiding citizens. The recidivism estimates cited above are used as evidence for this interpretation.

The main impediment to serious prison reform is financial. As it stands, the nation already spends over $10 billion per year on its prison system, and taxpayers are reluctant to spend a great deal more. Prison reform would almost certainly require substantial tax increases. More and more such increases are mandated by federal court decisions requiring states to end overcrowding.

Limiting the Alternatives to Punishment

The deterrent effect of prospective punishment is further reduced by the various mechanisms for circumventing the full weight of the law even when a person is convicted. The widespread availability of such mechanisms gives criminals reason to believe that the chances are remote that they will ever suffer the maximum punishment provided by law. These mechanisms include the defense of insanity, indeterminate sentencing with the widespread use of parole, probated or suspended sentences, and the separation of juvenile offenders from the regular criminal justice system. All of these mechanisms except the insanity defense reflect the problem of our overcrowded criminal justice system. They promote the release of inmates short of the maximum penalty provided by law, thereby freeing prison facilities for the continued influx of new inmates. *Indeterminate sentencing* means that the judge specifies a range of time for incarceration, say, two to ten years. The inmate then becomes eligible for parole any time after the minimum period is served. There is a movement to specify mandatory sentences of determinate length for certain types of crimes. Indeterminate sentencing is still the norm, however, because penologists feel that it offers the needed flexibility to fit the punishment to the unique circumstances of each case.

Parole is a process by which a convicted inmate is released from prison before serving the full extent of the sentence; a parole board decides whether an inmate can and probably will lead a socially constructive existence. Such a parolee must report for the duration of his or her sentence to a supervisory official known as a parole or probation officer. A judge may, at his or her discretion, *suspend* the sentence, in effect waiving all incarceration for the convicted criminal. The only thing the convicted criminal suffers is the onus of having the conviction on his or her record. A *probated sentence* means that incarceration is not imposed, but the judge imposes a requirement that the convicted criminal must report to a probation officer at specified intervals. Judges have the discretion to hand down suspended or probated sentences for a wide range of crimes. Although this discretion clearly lowers the deterrent impact of legally possible punishment, the mandatory incarceration of all convicted felons, especially for the length of their maximum sentences, would necessitate a substantial increase in available jail space. Many people want all criminals locked up, but few people are willing to have a prison built near them or to pay for such prisons. Neoconservatives tend to favor reducing these alternatives in favor of more determinate but shorter sentences. Their motive is both for the deterrent effect (every conviction means jail) and for the retributive effect (determinate sentencing as punishment).

Earlier we alluded to the fact that juveniles commit much of the violent crime in this country. Yet because we do not hold juveniles fully responsible for their actions, they are immune from the regular punishments of the criminal justice system. Moreover, their juvenile record does not carry over beyond their minority; they begin adulthood with a clean slate, regardless of the number or nature of their criminal acts as minors. Whatever deterrent effect the punishments of the criminal justice system may provide, it does not apply to teenagers, the age group most likely to commit crimes against persons and property.

The idea that children cannot be held responsible for their actions in the same ways as adults can appeals to our sense of fairness. After all, little children cannot be expected to possess the powers of judgment to discern right from wrong. But it is not clear that this inability to discern right from wrong also applies to people in their middle to late teens, the time of greatest criminality. Therefore there are those who suggest that for violent and serious crimes, the laws of the regular criminal process ought to apply at a younger age. Obviously, we would not want to imprison a five-year-old, regardless of what act was perpetrated. But few would have problems with incarcerating a seventeen-year-old murderer, rapist, or mugger. It is this gray area in between where the lack of consensus exists. At what age do we draw the line? Alternatively, it has been suggested that juvenile records be carried into adulthood to establish recidivist patterns immediately upon coming of age.

Psychiatric defenses came into being because American society chooses not to punish illness or its consequences. Insanity defenses are based on the belief that some actions are the consequence of pathological conditions beyond the control of the person committing them. The guiding law holds that if the court, on advice of the psychiatric profession, officially pronounces that a person, due to mental illness, was incapable of discerning right from wrong at the time the crime was committed, that person is innocent by reason of insanity. Of course, persons who are declared innocent of a serious crime by reason of insanity are not turned loose on the street; they are "sentenced" to an institution for the insane. However, it is much easier to be pronounced "cured" by the staff of such institutions and freed than it would be to obtain parole or release if one were imprisoned for the same crime. The perpetrators of the most heinous of murders, if declared insane, may be eligible for release from the mental institution in a very few years. The successful use of the psychiatric defense by John Hinckley, the man who shot President Reagan, renewed interest in and controversy over this issue.

The difficulty with the psychiatric defense resides in the imprecise state of psychoanalytic theory. The profession is unable to state whether a person was legally insane at the time of a crime with the same objectivity that a physician can claim in stating that a person has cancer or appendicitis. The concepts of the various kinds of psychosis do not have precise observable equivalents, and so a conclusion about the condition of a defendant in this situation is an educated judgment over which reasonable and trained persons can disagree. One psychiatrist at a given trial may testify to a person's legal insanity, and another psychiatrist may testify for the prosecution that the person was legally sane. Thus, often the appropriateness of relying on a psychiatric defense rests more on whether one has the funds to hire the most impressive psychiatric testimony than it does on any objective test of sanity. Thomas Szasz, a noted psychiatrist himself, has written extensively about what he sees as the fraudulent nature of psychiatric defenses.[60] But two noted scholars from Harvard have argued (with a considerable body of supporting data) that there are constitutional (genetic) and personality factors in explaining criminal behavior.[61]

It is likely that psychiatric defenses may become somewhat more numerous, owing to a 1985 Supreme Court decision holding that the states are obligated to pay for psychiatrists for those who claim such defenses but cannot afford the costs of psychiatric consultation. A number of states had already provided such state aid, but this decision extends the protection to all fifty states. If the availability of such defenses makes it easier to avoid serious punishment for serious crimes, it will weaken the deterrent impact of such punishments. Yet it appears clear that mental illness, however imprecise its conceptualization, is real and that persons so afflicted ought not to be punished for their affliction. The conservative position on such issues is to emphasize the need for personal accountability for one's actions. This position's adherents tend to be skeptical of the precision and objectivity with which legal insanity can be determined. After all, they might argue, the commission of heinous or vicious crimes almost by definition involves some loss of reason. The distinction among the measures of madness that permeate such crimes and legal insanity is the judgment of a psychiatrist, a judgment made without precise criteria. Such conservatives would generally prefer to circumscribe the availability of psychiatric defenses.

The furor in the 1988 presidential campaign over the furlough granted to a convicted rapist and murderer, Willie Horton, during the Dukakis administration in Massachusetts illustrates a widespread perception, especially among conservatives, that the preferred strategy toward the crime problem is to lock up those individuals who are a threat to society and to keep them locked up. Specifically, this would involve *preventive detention* and *selective incapacitation.* The former strategy would authorize judges to deny bail to accused persons that they consider likely to commit additional crimes. The latter would target chronic offenders for long-term incarceration. Samuel Walker, in his recent book analyzing policy alternatives to deal with the crime problem, argues that both strategies would fail significantly to reduce crime because of two factors: the prediction problem and the costs of incarceration.[62] The prediction problem means that we cannot really identify who is dangerous and likely to commit more crimes, and we cannot predict which criminals would likely commit violent crimes. Therefore we would not incarcerate those who would actually commit the crimes we are trying to prevent, while we would incarcerate many people who are not really dangerous. The cost problem is that these policies would significantly increase the population of our already overcrowded prison facilities. The estimated cost for new facilities is between $45,000 and $70,000 per inmate. Costs of keeping an inmate in prison vary from $8,000 to $50,000 per inmate. Using the lower estimates, Walker calculates that the cost of implementing preventive detention and selective incapacitation over the next five years would be around $120 billion, an astronomical sum in an era of budget deficits.[63]

Crime Reform at the Federal Level

The Comprehensive Crime Control Act of 1984 was signed into law by President Reagan, implementing a number of the strategies to control crime discussed in this chapter. However, the act applies only to the federal criminal process, whereas 95 percent of crimes violate state laws, and it is unlikely that the law will have a significant impact on the nation's overall crime problem.

Specifically, the law replaces indeterminate sentencing with strict sentencing guidelines for judges. Any departure from these guidelines must be explained in writing by the judge. In addition, the law provides for preventive detention (the denial of bail) to accused criminals whom the judge deems dangerous. Civil libertarians argue that such a provision amounts to a denial of liberty without due process of law, in violation of the Fifth Amendment. They further contend that it amounts to reversing the historic burden of proof in the American judicial system to being held guilty until proved innocent. The burden of proof is clearly shifted in insanity pleas from the prosecutor, who formerly had to prove that the defendant was not insane, to the defendant, who now must prove that he or she is.

Given the small fraction of criminal cases that are prosecuted at the federal level, the chief significance of this law is the extent to which it will stimulate similar legislation at the state level. The states often regard federal law and policy as a model to emulate. The bill seems to represent the direction of public opinion toward less sympathy for the rights of the accused, an opinion shift that may facilitate state legislation along these lines.

SUMMARY

Rather than being a single undifferentiated phenomenon, crime comprises a variety of manifestations, each with its distinct "causes," and its own possible "cures." The causes discussed in this chapter include the following:

1. The increasing number of acts designated as crime, including the vast category of crimes against a dominant moral standard rather than against persons or property.
2. The increasing abuse of addictive drugs that in turn leads to more property crime and violent crime to support the habit.
3. The urbanization of America, the increasing percentage of the population included in the most crime-prone groups, and poverty and a pervasive sense of injustice among subordinate groups.

The most commonly prescribed cure for the problem of crime is the deterrent effect of severely punishing criminals. In this regard, many conservatives feel that the expansion of the rights of the accused by the U.S. Supreme Court has prevented the punishment of many guilty people, thereby encouraging more crime.

These rights have been expanded by the increasing incorporation of the Bill of Rights into the meaning of the Fourteenth Amendment—thereby applying them to state criminal processes—and by the broadened interpretation of the rights themselves. The most controversial expansion of the rights of the accused occurred in three areas: the right to counsel, the exclusionary rule, and capital punishment.

The expanded *right to counsel* makes it mandatory that one be informed at the point of arrest of the rights to remain silent and to be provided with a lawyer by the state. The *exclusionary rule* is an interpretation of the Fourth Amendment right to be secure against unreasonable searches and seizures; it holds that illegally obtained evidence cannot be admitted in a court of law. *Capital punishment* must now be imposed according to consistent standards related to the nature of the act being punished and not in an arbitrary or capricious manner.

Most scholars believe that the swiftness and certainty of punishment, more than its severity, deter crime. Factors other than the rights of the accused have most often impeded this swiftness and certainty of punishment. These factors include the low probability that the perpetrator of any given crime will be arrested; the overcrowded criminal justice system that requires plea bargaining, light sentences, early parole, and probated and suspended sentences; diversion of the police and prosecutors to the enforcement of "victimless crimes"; and the principle fundamental to the criminal justice system, the granting of the benefit of the doubt to the accused. There is little evidence to support the proposition that crime has been encouraged by the expansion of the rights of the accused.

Yet crime remains a serious problem calling for some effective remedies from the makers of public policy. Several policy options and their potential effectiveness have been presented. Among those with the most promise are the British policy of the controlled dispensation of addictive drugs; the expansion of both our judicial and prison systems, combined with the decriminalization of truly consensual behavior among adults to cope with the impact of overcrowded court and jail systems; and some constraints on who may own certain types of firearms. Unfortunately, these are, for political and cultural reasons, among the options most difficult to implement. Other choices, such as buying more hardware for law enforcement or employing more police officers, have been shown to have little impact on the crime problem. These choices, being simpler and less costly, have great appeal, although they are less effective. Reforming the juvenile justice system, the psychiatric defense, and federal criminal laws was the centerpiece of crime control debates in the 1980s. The public itself will have to face these choices and decide whether it wants to pay the ideological and economic costs of confronting the crime problem in the 1990s.

NOTES

1. From U.S. Bureau of the Census, *Statistical Abstract of the United States,* 100th ed. (Washington, D.C.: U.S. Government Printing Office, 1978), p. 177.

2. For a detailed description, see Mark Green, Beverly Moore, and Bruce Wasserstein, "Criminal Law and Corporate Disorder," in Jerome Skolnick and Elliot Currie, eds., *Crisis in American Institutions,* 4th ed. (Boston: Little, Brown, 1979), pp. 527–547.

3. Cited in Michael Parenti, *Democracy for the Few,* 2nd ed. (New York: St. Martin's Press, 1980), p. 122. Compare with David Hellman, *The Economics of Crime* (New York: St. Martin's Press, 1980), Table 2–1, p. 23.

4. Edwin Sutherland, *White Collar Crime* (New York: Holt, Rinehart & Winston, 1949), pp. 210–222. The seventy corporations studied had been found guilty 980 times for illegal activities.

5. See Richard Smith, "The Incredible Electric Conspiracy," *Fortune* (April 1961), 161–224.

6. James Q. Wilson, *Thinking About Crime,* rev. ed. (New York: Basic Books, 1983), esp. chap. 2.

7. Hellman, *The Economics of Crime,* p. 147.

8. Cited in Samuel Walker, *Sense and Nonsense about Crime,* 2d ed. (Pacific Grove, Calif.: Brooks-Cole, 1989), pp. 38, 55.

9. For example, see John Dollard et al., *Frustration and Aggression* (New Haven, Conn.: Yale University Press, 1939); and Ivo K. and Rosalind Feierabend, "Systematic Conditions of Political Aggression: An Application of the Frustration Aggression Theory," in Ivo K. Feierabend, Rosalind Feierabend, and Ted Gurr, eds., *Anger, Violence and Politics* (Englewood Cliffs, N.J.: Prentice-Hall, 1972), pp. 136–183.

10. Edward Banfield, *The Unheavenly City* (Boston: Little, Brown, 1970), p. 172. Earl Moses, "Differentials in Crime Rates Between Negroes and Whites Based on Comparisons of Four Socio-Economically Equated Areas," *American Sociological Review,* 12 (August 1974), 411–420; Edward Green, "Race, Social Status and Criminal Arrest," in Charles Reasons and Jack Kuykendall, eds., *Race, Crime, and Justice* (Pacific Palisades, Calif.: Goodyear, 1972), pp. 103–123.

11. *Powell* v. *Alabama,* 287 U.S. 45 (1932); *Betts* v. *Brady,* 316 U.S. 455 (1942); *Gideon* v. *Wainwright,* 372 U.S. 335 (1963).

12. The Supreme Court has ruled that once a guilty plea has been entered under such a plea bargain, the prosecution's side of the bargain must be kept. Failure by the prosecution to keep its bargain will cause the court's judgment to be vacated. *Santobello* v. *New York,* 404 U.S. 257 (1971).

13. *Escobedo* v. *Illinois,* 378 U.S. 478 (1964).

14. *Miranda* v. *Arizona,* 384 U.S. 436 (1966). See the excellent discussion in Richard Cortner and Clifford Lytle, *Modern Constitutional Law* (New York: Free Press, 1971), especially pp. 159–160.

15. *Mapp* v. *Ohio,* 367 U.S. 643 (1961).

16. *Nix* v. *Williams,* 104 S.Ct. 2501 (1984); *U.S.* v. *Leon,* 104 S.Ct. 3430 (1984).

17. See the argument that the criminal justice system must be perceived as "just" in James Q. Wilson and Richard J. Herrnstein, *Crime and Human Nature* (New York: Simon and Schuster, 1985), pp. 506–507.

18. Thorsten Sellin, *The Penalty of Death* (Beverly Hills, Calif.: Sage Publications, 1980), pp. 70, 71.

19. Isaac Ehrlich, "The Deterrent Effect of Capital Punishment: A Question of Life and Death," *American Economic Review,* 65 (June 1975), 398. Peter Passell and John Taylor, "The Deterrence Controversy: A Reconsideration of the Time Series Evidence," in Chester Pierce and Hugo Bedau, eds., *Capital Punishment in the United States* (New York: AMS Press, 1976), p. 359. Sellin, *Penalty,* chap. 10.

20. These figures are extrapolated from Sellin, *Penalty,* p. 52.

21. Guy Johnson, "The Negro and Crime," *The Annals of the American Academy of Political and Social Science,* 217 (1941), 100; cited in *Furman* v. *Georgia,* 408 U.S. 238 (1972).

22. Cited in *Dallas Times Herald,* November 17, 1985. *McCleskey* v. *Kemp,* 107 S. Ct. 1756 (1987).

23. Sellin, *Penalty,* p. 66.

24. *Furman* v. *Georgia.*

25. James Ridella, "Miranda: One Year Later—The Effects," *Public Management,* 49 (July 1967), 183–190; this author found in a St. Louis survey that less than one percent of those arrested have been freed on *Miranda* grounds.

26. Richard Seeburger and Stanley Wetlick, "*Miranda* in Pittsburgh: A Statistical Study," in Theodore

Becker and Malcolm Freely, eds., *The Impact of Supreme Court Decisions,* 2nd ed. (New York: Oxford University Press, 1973), p. 154.

27. Stephen Wasby, *The Impact of the United States Supreme Court: Some Perspectives* (Homewood, Ill.: Dorsey Press, 1970), p. 156.

28. Richard Medalie, Leonard Zeitz, and Paul Alexander, "Custodial Police Interrogation in Our Nation's Capital: The Attempt to Implement Miranda," *Michigan Law Review,* 66 (May 1968), 1347–1422.

29. *Harris* v. *New York,* 401 U.S. 222 (1971); *Oregon* v. *Haas,* 420 U.S. 714 (1975); *Brown* v. *Illinois,* 422 U.S. 590 (1975).

30. Wasby, *Impact,* p. 162; Stuart Nagel, *The Legal Process from a Behavioral Perspective* (Homewood, Ill.: Dorsey Press, 1969), p. 314.

31. *Chimel* v. *California,* 394 U.S. 752 (1969).

32. *Terry* v. *Ohio,* 392 U.S. 1 (1968); *Sibron* v. *New York,* 392 U.S. 40 (1968).

33. *Katz* v. *United States,* 389 U.S. 347 (1967). Wiretaps can be used under a warrant requested by the Justice Department or when the president makes a demonstrable finding that national security is at stake. Such a finding is, however, subject to judicial scrutiny.

34. *Woodson* v. *North Carolina,* 428 U.S. 280 (1976). *Roberts* v. *Louisiana,* 428 U.S. 35 (1976).

35. *Proffit* v. *Florida,* 49 L. Ed. 2d 913 (1976); *Gregg* v. *Georgia,* 428 U.S. 153 (1976); *Jurek* v. *Texas,* 49 L. Ed. 2d 929 (1976).

36. *Gregg* v. *Georgia.*

37. Marshall in *Furman,* 408 U.S. 238, p. 329; Brennan, p. 269.

38. *Thompson* v. *Oklahoma,* 108 S.Ct. 2687 (1988).

39. *Sumner* v. *Shuman,* 107 S.Ct. 2716 (1987).

40. *Maynard* v. *Cartwright,* 108 S.Ct. 1853 (1988).

41. *Booth* v. *Maryland,* 107 S.Ct. 2529 (1987); *Payne* v. *Tennessee,* 59 LW 4814 (1991).

42. *McCleskey* v. *Zant,* 59 LW 4288; *Coleman* v. *Thompson,* 59 LW 4789; and *Yost* v. *Nunnemaker,* 59 LW 4809 (1991).

43. Attributed to Norval Morris, as reported in Norton E. Long, "The City as Reservation," *Public Interest,* 25 (Fall 1971), 31.

44. Wilson, *Thinking About Crime,* p. 118.

45. Wayne H. Thomas, *Bail Reform in America* (Berkeley: University of California Press, 1976).

46. Hellman, *The Economics of Crime,* p. 49.

47. Alexander Smith and Harriet Pollach, *Some Sins Are Not Crimes* (New York: New Viewpoints, 1975), p. 100.

48. Cited in ibid., p. 104.

49. Ibid., pp. 98–99.

50. Andrea Parrot and Laurie Bechofer, *Acquaintance Rape: The Hidden Crime* (New York: John Wiley, 1991), p. 15.

51. Susan Brownmiller, *Against Our Will: Men, Women and Rape* (New York: Simon & Schuster, 1975), p. 15.

52. Andrea Dworkin, *Intercourse* (New York: The Free Press, 1988), pp. 125–126.

53. Susan Estrich, *Real Rape: How the Legal System Victimizes Women Who Say No* (Cambridge, Mass.: Harvard University Press, 1987), p. 102.

54. U.S. Department of Justice, *Sourcebook of Criminal Justice Statistics* (Washington, D.C.: U.S. Government Printing Office, 1980), pp. 205, 208.

55. For this kind of argument, see, for example, Clarke Cochran, "Authority and Community," *American Political Science Review,* 71 (June 1977), 546–558.

56. Robert Lineberry, *American Public Policy* (New York: Harper & Row, 1977), p. 189.

57. Daniel Glaser, "The Effectiveness of a Prison Parole System," cited in Vergil Williams, *Dictionary of American Penology* (Westport, Conn.: Greenwood Press, 1979), pp. 217–219.

58. Cited in Duane Lockard, *The Perverted Priorities of American Politics,* 2nd ed. (New York: Macmillan, 1976), p. 206.

59. For example, Clark, *Crime,* chap. 13; Lockard, *Perverted Priorities,* p. 206.

60. Thomas Szasz, *The Manufacture of Madness* (New York: Harper & Row, 1970); and *Psychiatric Justice* (New York: Macmillan, 1965).

61. Wilson and Herrnstein, *Crime and Human Nature,* esp. chap. 20.

62. Walker, *Sense and Nonsense,* pp. 63–75.

63. Ibid., p. 79.

SUGGESTED READINGS

Berns, Walter. *For Capital Punishment: Crime and Morality of the Death Penalty.* New York: Basic Books, 1979.

Cole, George. *Criminal Justice: Law and Politics.* 4th ed. Monterey, Calif.: Brooks-Cole, 1984.

Hellman, David. *The Economics of Crime.* New York: St. Martin's Press, 1980.

Jenkins, Phillip. *Crime and Justice, Issues and Ideas.* Pacific Grove, Calif.: Brooks-Cole, 1984.

Jacob, Herbert. *The Frustration of Policy: Responses to Crime by American Cities.* Boston: Little, Brown, 1984.

Menninger, Karl. *The Crime of Punishment.* New York: Viking, 1968.

Morris, Norval, and Hawkins, Gordon. *The Honest Politician's Guide to Crime Control.* Chicago: University of Chicago Press, 1969.

Schur, Edwin. *Crime Without Victims.* Englewood Cliffs, N.J.: Prentice-Hall, 1965.

Sellin, Thorsten. *The Penalty of Death.* Beverly Hills, Calif.: Sage Publications, 1980.

Smith, Alexander, and Polloch, Harriet. *Some Sins Are Not Crimes.* New York: New Viewpoints, 1975.

Sutherland, Edward. *White Collar Crime.* New York: Holt, Rinehart & Winston, 1949.

Tullock, Gordon. "Does Punishment Deter Crime?" *Public Interest,* 36 (Summer 1974), 103–111.

Van Den Haag, Ernest, and Conrad, John B. *The Death Penalty: A Debate.* New York: Plenum, 1984.

Walker, Samuel. *Sense and Nonsense about Crime.* 2nd ed. Pacific Grove, Calif.: Brooks-Cole, 1989.

Wilson, James Q. *Thinking about Crime.* 2nd ed. New York: Basic Books, 1984.

CHAPTER 7

The Double Bind: Income Support or Welfare Dependence?

American citizens display positive attitudes toward the poor, especially the aged and disabled, and support public programs to assist them. Yet these same citizens exhibit highly negative attitudes toward the programs, generally known as "welfare," developed to furnish assistance to the poor. The term *welfare* conjures up images of dependency, irresponsibility, laziness, and illegitimacy, of people who have no reason to be poor, except their own lack of initiative.[1] These antiwelfare attitudes have serious implications, because public spending on the general category of income support, which includes welfare, is the largest and, until the Reagan administration, the most rapidly increasing budget item at the federal level. When this fact is combined with budgetary pressures as government copes with economic uncertainty and massive deficits, these programs easily become a battleground of contending interest groups and ideologies.

Social programs cover a broad range of activities, including Social Security, public assistance, job training, public health, unemployment compensation, education, and many other programs. Obviously, not all of these programs are aimed at relieving poverty. This chapter is concerned only with the following: *social insurance programs,* which provide for the aged, disabled, widowed and orphaned, and unemployed; *public assistance programs,* which provide for the alleviation of poverty for those not covered by social insurance; and *antipoverty programs,* which are designed to provide jobs, job training, or other assistance to those needing help to lift themselves out of poverty. Collectively, these programs are referred to as *income maintenance* or *income support programs.* Other social programs will be covered in later chapters. The policies to be discussed here and the health policies discussed in the next chapter, however, do constitute about half of all federal spending!

ISSUE BACKGROUND: DISAGREEING ON THE MEANING OF POVERTY

There are many measures employed in the United States to prevent, alleviate, or cure poverty and to maintain adequate incomes for certain sectors of the population. But before we can examine these efforts in detail, we must know more about poverty itself, what people think it is, how widespread the problem is, and to what causes it is attributed.

Defining Poverty

Poverty may be defined in absolute or relative terms. An absolute definition defines a minimal level of well-being in nutrition, shelter, clothing, health, and so on and then determines what income is sufficient to maintain this level, taking into account family size and perhaps other factors such as ages of family members and location of residence. This minimum level changes with fluctuations in the general standard of living and in the value of money. Though always tied to the cost of certain kinds of material goods, this minimum income level also implies psychic consequences for those living below its standards:

> Poverty should be defined psychologically in terms of those whose place in the society is such that they are internal exiles who, almost inevitably, develop attitudes of defeat and pessimism and who are therefore excluded from taking advantage of new opportunities.[2]

Feelings of helplessness and powerlessness in the face of overwhelming political, economic, and social forces help keep such persons mired in poverty.

Relative definitions of poverty do not relate it to a particular level of material well-being but to the well-being of other members of society. In this definition a family is poor if its resources place it well below a normal standard of living, no matter how moderate or extravagant that standard might be. Thus most relative definitions define poverty as any family income below one-half the nation's median family income.

The type of definition chosen makes a big difference in evaluating policy. Under most absolute definitions, poverty has varied in the last thirty years, but under relative definitions, the proportion of poor Americans has remained constant during these years.

Absolute definitions.   There are a number of possible absolute measures of poverty. Conservatives normally accept the most parsimonious measure, liberals the most generous. The most widely used measure of poverty is the Social Security Administration (SSA) figure. This figure is calculated each year by determining the cost of the Department of Agriculture's Economy Food Plan and multiplying it by three (the "multiplier"), on the assumption that a poor family of four spends approximately one-third of its income for food. Slightly different multipliers are used for other family sizes. This figure is calculated anew each year as food costs change and is calculated for different family sizes. Thus the poverty standard for a family of four in 1991 was $13,400. (The poverty standard in 1991 ranged from $6,620 for a one-person family to $22,440 for an eight-person family.) The SSA figure is compared with the income levels of the population as reported by the Bureau of the Census, and the number and percentage of persons below the poverty level are calculated (see Table 7-1).

TABLE 7-1 ▪ Number and Percentage of Persons below SSA Poverty Standard

	White Persons (in millions)	Black Persons (in millions)	Spanish Origin (in millions)	Total (in millions)	Percentage of Population
1960	28.3	9.9	N/A	39.8	22.2
1965	22.5	8.9	N/A	33.2	17.3
1970	17.5	7.5	N/A	25.4	12.6
1975	17.8	7.5	3.0	25.9	12.3
1980	19.7	8.6	3.5	29.3	13.0
1985	22.9	8.9	5.2	33.1	14.0
1990	22.3	9.8	6.0	33.6	13.5

SOURCE: U.S. Bureau of the Census, *Current Populations Reports,* Series P-60, No. 175: *Poverty in the United States, 1990* (Washington, D.C.: U.S. Government Printing Office, 1991), Table 2.

Although the SSA standard is the most widely cited and is the official definition for all government statistics on poverty, its value has been severely criticized by liberal and radical students of poverty.[3] Their basic argument can be condensed into five points. First, the food budget central to the calculation is too low, allowing (in 1991) about $3.00 per person per day for food. This food budget, they argue, is barely adequate for survival and is inadequate for long-term good nutrition and health. Thus the budget may have been chosen not because it was adequate but to keep the poverty standard low. Second, the SSA standard does not take account of regional variations in cost of living. Third, the SSA standard is adjusted annually according to the Consumer Price Index rather than to the actual cost of food. Fourth, the SSA standard counts before-tax income, not actual cash on hand. Finally, the multiplier is artificially low; research in the late 1970s showed that poor people actually spend about 28 percent of their income on food, sometimes needing to spend up to 50 percent on shelter. For all these reasons, liberals argue, the official poverty figure is too low, substantially underestimating the number of poor in America and the government effort needed to eliminate poverty.

There are other ways of computing the poverty line, although few studies of poverty are based on them. For example, the same multipliers as the SSA standards applied to a more generous "low-cost food plan" designed by the Department of Agriculture would set the poverty line approximately 25 percent higher than the SSA, meaning that the poverty line for a nonfarm family of four in 1991 would have been $16,750. Because SSA estimates are very low, a sound case can be made for this approach. Use of this standard reveals that 43.5 million persons, or 18.1 percent of the population, were poor in 1987.[4]

Relative definitions. Relative definitions of poverty are favored by many because they emphasize the continuing inequality of income and wealth in the United States. Even though incomes and the standard of living have been rising since World War II, a family is poor, many argue, if its income is insufficient to bring it close to the current median standard of living in society. In the last forty years, income distribution has not changed significantly. Compared with the median standard, a constant one-fifth of the population has been in poverty during that time; that is, 20 percent of families earned less than half the median income. In 1990, median family income was $35,353, and about 21 percent of families earned less than $17,700. As Table 7-2 indicates, the lowest fifth of the population consistently receives under 5 percent of before-tax income. The distribution of wealth is even more unequal, with the wealthiest 20 percent consistently controlling over 90 percent of corporate stock and 70 percent of total wealth. Moreover, after a long period of decline, wealth inequality began to rise in the 1980s. The richest one percent now hold 25 percent of wealth.[5] The measure of income concentration has shown no significant change. Indeed, the most recent years have shown a growing inequality of income distribution. (See Figure 7-1.) In real (inflation-adjusted) terms, the median family income in 1987 returned to 1973 levels, and the income is now concentrated in fewer hands. In 1973, the typical 30-year-old man could make payments on a median-priced home with 21 percent of his salary. By 1984, these payments would have taken 44 percent of his salary.

The United States now seems to be in a situation of rising economic inequality, complicated by its changing demography. For example, if two wage earners making $35,000 each per year marry, they create one very well-to-do family out of two middle-income families. If divorce occurs in a family earning the median income, it creates two families—one likely to be poor—out of one.

Use of a relative measure of poverty, conservatives and neoconservatives point out, has certain disadvantages.[6] First, family composition and age have a great deal to do with income. The growing number of retired persons and students living independently—traditionally, two groups with low incomes—distorts the income distribution figures by substantially reducing the income going to the

TABLE 7-2 ▪ Share of Aggregate Family Income (Unrelated Individuals Excluded)

	Poorest 20%	*Second 20%*	*Third 20%*	*Fourth 20%*	*Richest 20%*	*Richest 5%*	*Index* of concentration*
1967	5.4	12.2	17.5	23.5	41.4	16.4	.358
1972	5.5	11.9	17.5	23.9	41.4	15.9	.355
1977	5.3	11.6	17.5	24.2	41.4	15.7	.363
1982	4.8	11.2	17.1	24.2	42.7	15.9	.380
1987	4.6	10.8	16.8	24.0	43.8	17.2	.393
1990	4.6	10.8	16.6	23.8	44.3	17.4	.396

* Note: The higher the index, the more unequal the distribution of income.
SOURCE: U.S. Bureau of the Census, *Current Populations Reports,* Series P-60, No. 174: *Money Income of Households, Families, and Persons in the United States: 1990* (Washington, D.C.: U.S. Government Printing Office, 1991), Table B-3.

FIGURE 7-1 ▪ Income Distribution (Family)

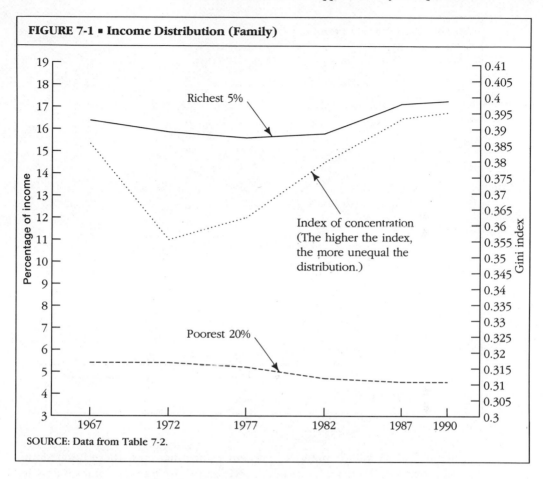

SOURCE: Data from Table 7-2.

bottom fifth. The data above, however, exclude such persons. Second, more generous welfare benefits, only partly counted as income, encourage more single-parent families to set up independent households, again biasing the figures toward the low end. Third, the income picture is falsified by concentrating on percentages and on the low end of the scale. Many families in the top 20 percent actually have incomes in the $65,000 to $80,000 range. (In 1990 the income range for that group began at $61,490, and the top 5 percent began at $102,358.) Thus opponents of the relative approach to poverty argue that the facts cited are misleading and that poverty should not be confused with inequality.

How Many Poor?

Determining the size of the poverty population once again depends on the definition of poverty selected. As can be seen from Figure 7-2, SSA-defined poverty declined sharply between 1959 and 1970, from 40 million poor (22 percent of the

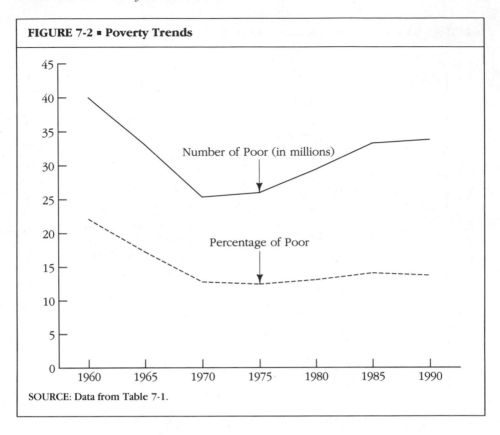

FIGURE 7-2 ▪ **Poverty Trends**

SOURCE: Data from Table 7-1.

population) to 25 million poor (13 percent); since that time, there has been no lasting reduction. We must be careful, however, not to draw too quick a conclusion from these figures. Often they are cited by both conservatives and liberals to show that America has made substantial progress in reducing poverty—conservatives because they oppose substantial expansion of public assistance and the SSA figures show that enough progress has been made, and liberals because they propose even greater efforts along the same successful lines to reduce the current number. On the other hand, radicals and spokespersons for minority groups point to the failure to reduce poverty in the last decade as evidence of failure, not success, and of the need for fundamental reform.

The Census Bureau data used in Figure 7-2, however, disguise a basic reality generally accepted by both conservative and liberal economists. These data are based on pretax cash income, including government transfer payments. That is, social insurance and public assistance cash benefits are counted as family income. Thus, if by "poverty" one refers to income earned without government help, removing cash payments from the measure reveals that nearly 25 percent of the population is poor, even at the very low SSA definition of poverty. Thus one-quarter of the entire American population is unable to avoid poverty without government help. Radicals use this figure to indict the American economic system. Moreover, the share of *aftertax* income going to the wealthiest increased more rapidly in the 1980s than their share of *pretax* income. On the other hand, the official poverty figures do not take account of the income value of in-kind benefits, such as medical care and food stamps, or employer-provided health care or other benefits, nor are they adjusted for the tendency of people to underreport income. Adjusting for these factors leaves about 10 percent poor, a figure cited in support of the enormous success of income maintenance and job programs.[7] Thus, although official statistics disguise the number of persons highly dependent on government aid, they also hide the success of federal programs in reducing poverty. Although European poverty rates are generally substantially lower than American rates, the trends over time are very similar.[8]

Who Are the Poor?

The incidence of poverty does not fall evenly across the nation; particular areas, groups, and classes bear a far higher incidence of poverty than others. Although a majority of the poor are white, the incidence of poverty is higher among racial minorities, reflecting racial prejudice, low job skills, and poor education. Whereas 11 percent of whites are poor, 28 percent of Hispanics and 32 percent of blacks are poor. Poverty among Native Americans is even higher.

Age is also associated with poverty. Although government cash and in-kind benefits have reduced poverty substantially among the elderly, youth poverty is alarming. Almost 40 percent of the poor are under eighteen, and their number is increasing. One of every five children lives in poverty. Benefits to the elderly, principally Social Security, are generally indexed to keep pace with inflation. Benefits for others are not indexed and therefore decline over time in terms of real purchasing power.

There is increasing reason to refer to the "feminization of poverty." The majority of the poor now live in female-headed families, and the number of such families is growing, with 34 percent of such families (versus 6 percent of two-parent families) classified as poor (including half of black and Hispanic female-headed families). Half of poor families are now headed by women, compared with 26 percent in 1960.

The feminization of poverty reflects the demographic changes discussed in Chapter 1. Increasing rates of divorce and illegitimacy have placed more women with small children in poverty. Lacking adequate child care facilities and so unable to work full-time and care for their children, they fall below the poverty line. Sometimes these women do work full-time, but at jobs that do not pay enough to support their families. For most of these female-headed households, poverty is a painful but temporary phenomenon that lasts until marriage or remarriage places them in a two-earner situation. Yet for many it is a more or less permanent condition. Evidence is growing that single parenthood has dire consequences for future generations with respect to education, illegitimacy, and welfare dependency.[9] Figures 7-3 and 7-4 present some of the disturbing statistics on families

FIGURE 7-3 ▪ Single-headed Families

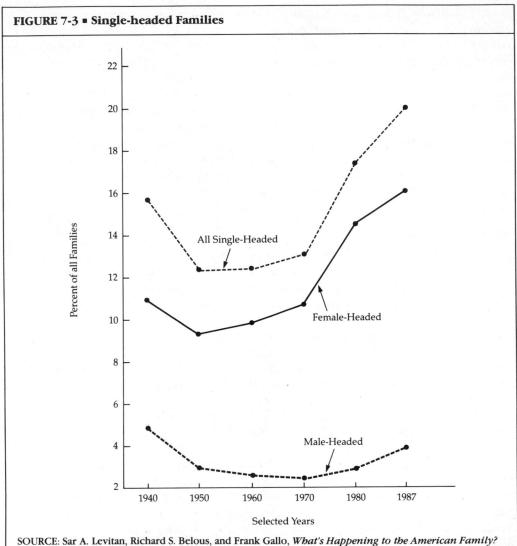

SOURCE: Sar A. Levitan, Richard S. Belous, and Frank Gallo, *What's Happening to the American Family?* Rev. ed. (Baltimore: Johns Hopkins University Press, 1988) p. 111.

and poverty. The poverty statistics also include a substantial number of elderly widows attempting to live on meager Social Security, pension, or public assistance checks.

Education and residence are also correlated with poverty. Persons lacking a high school diploma are disproportionately poor, as are those who live in the core of large metropolitan cities and in rural areas.

Despite the stereotypes, very few of the poor are lazy, work-avoiding, welfare dependents. Except for mothers staying at home to care for small children, most of

FIGURE 7-4 ▪ Families in Poverty

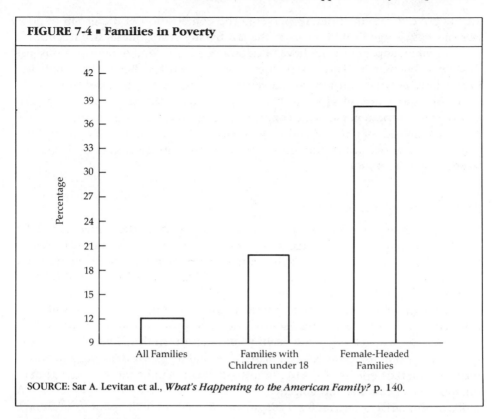

SOURCE: Sar A. Levitan et al., *What's Happening to the American Family?* p. 140.

the poor work either full- or part-time or have become unemployed because of technological changes. Many workers in low-skill jobs are in or near poverty because of low wages, seasonal work, inflation, and high taxes. For example, a person working full-time for fifty-two weeks at the 1991 federal minimum wage of $4.25 an hour would have an income of $8,840. This is $4,560 less than the poverty level income for a family of four persons. Such people lack opportunities for advancement, and if older workers (forty and over) lose their jobs through recession or technological change, they are unlikely to find new employment at the same level or pay. Accompanying this dismal employment picture are feelings of rejection, defeat, and powerlessness. Indeed, mental illness has a higher incidence among the poor than in other strata of society.

The persistence of poverty reflects a complex conjunction of factors. First, demographic trends swelled the ranks of the elderly, of female-headed households, and of job seekers. Because these groups tend to be at the low end of employability, poverty rates went up. Similarly, a weak economy with static wage rates and growing income inequality contributed to poverty. On the other hand, an expanding number of two-income families helped to offset these trends. Finally, government programs of income support, especially programs targeted at the elderly, helped to push poverty rates down. The result of these countervailing forces was a steady poverty rate of about 13 percent. The composition of the group of poor persons has changed substantially in the last twenty years, but its size has not.[10]

Income support policies have been targeted at the kind of poor persons just described, but there is also a "hard-core" poverty barely touched by these policies. Particularly in large cities there is a small but growing "underclass" among the poor. Members of this class are unskilled, uneducated residents of the most dismal slums. For most poor persons the condition is temporary; the population fluctuates as some climb out of poverty, and some briefly fall into it. But the underclass lives year in and year out in a culture of poverty, thus presenting the greatest challenge to social welfare policy.

The Causes of Poverty

Conservative views.   As much as they disagree about the definition and the incidence of poverty, ideological groups disagree even more about its causes.[11] Conservatives argue that there is little involuntary poverty in the United States. Those who wish to work and to achieve a decent standard of living are able to do so by taking advantage of the free enterprise system's opportunities. For those who are unable to work, because of age, physical handicap, or other disability, sufficient resources are available through social insurance programs and private philanthropy. Those who are adult and healthy but poor are, in this view, poor because they lack the self-discipline to work hard, save, and invest by delaying immediate pleasures for the benefits of a better future—that is, the poor simply choose not to pursue the educational and employment opportunities available to everyone. A more recent variation attributes these supposed qualities of the poor to a "culture of poverty." Individual poor persons learn these attitudes from the culture around them, which teaches satisfaction with a life of casual social relationships, irresponsibility, immediate gratification, and sexual license.

Thus conservatives and neoconservatives also argue that government welfare programs cannot prevent or cure poverty because they do nothing to change the basic attitudinal causes of poverty. In fact, these persons contend, government programs have the unintended consequence of encouraging persons to remain in poverty by guaranteeing a rather generous standard of living to the poor. These programs encourage families to break up, reward sexual license by increasing benefits for additional, often illegitimate, children, and make only very weak work demands on recipients. Cheating and fraud are rampant in public assistance programs in the view of many conservatives.

Conservatives also find government responsible for poverty in another way. The growth of the public sector, with its increasing regulation of and interference in private enterprise, has weakened the productive capacity of business. The resulting economic stagnation means that those at the bottom are unable to advance. Minimum wage laws, for example, have the indirect impact, according to conservatives, of a high rate of teenage unemployment because employers no longer find it economically feasible to hire them.

Liberal views.   Liberals dispute the notion that the attitudes of the poor make them responsible for their poverty. They argue, instead, that the poor are no different from the nonpoor; they simply lack the opportunities for education, employment, job training, and decent housing. If they had such opportunities, they would take advantage of them. There is no firm evidence, they argue, that government programs decrease work effort, increase illegitimacy, or promote family breakup.[12]

Liberal policy focuses on providing opportunity and curing the social and economic causes of poverty. Liberals emphasize that the opportunities offered to the poor must be real. The poor rightly refuse or exploit job-training programs that do not provide salable skills or that provide employment only in temporary, menial work with no future. Thus the basic liberal premise is that lack of genuine opportunity for advancement is the root cause of poverty. Sometimes liberals do accept a variation of the conservative "culture of poverty" argument. They insist, however, that the source of this culture lies in a realistic assessment by the poor of their chances for success in a society and economy structured against them. Changing that structure will weaken and ultimately break the cycle of poverty.

According to liberal theory, racial discrimination against blacks, Hispanics, and other minority groups and sexual discrimination against women, particularly women heads of household, are important causes of poverty among these groups. Discrimination affects progress in school, employment choices, job advancement, wages, and housing conditions. Racial minorities and women have high poverty rates because of the pervasive discrimination they have suffered, discrimination that continues in subtle ways and the effects of which still are felt.

Liberals also see poverty as a result of the harmful side effects, the indirect costs, of a capitalist, free-enterprise economy. Economic progress makes certain job skills obsolete, swelling the ranks of the unemployed. Other jobs are no longer considered skilled, and the pay for them falls so low that even some full-time workers do not make a wage high enough to keep them and their families out of poverty. The doubling of the unemployment rate in the early 1980s also was a major cause of poverty. Economic recession plus public assistance budget cuts produced the sharp increase in poverty in the 1980s.

Radical views.   Marxists and socialists agree with much of the liberal analysis of the causes of poverty, but they see the roots of its family strife, unemployment, and discrimination lying deep within the American socioeconomic system itself. Capitalism, such radicals argue, necessarily requires a large proportion of poor persons, because it exists to create wealth for a small group of controllers of property. Poverty is necessary in a capitalist society because it provides a large pool of surplus labor to do menial and dirty tasks and to keep general wages low. Poverty also acts as a goad to the middle class. Fear of the hardship and shame of poverty keeps it hardworking and subservient to the attitudes and desires of the upper class. The culture of poverty is also useful to the middle and upper classes, as it offers them such outlets as gambling, prostitution, and charity work. Moreover, the violence, crime, and immorality of the poor provide a convenient focus for moral indignation, neatly deflecting attention from the corruption, injustice, and crass materialism of capitalist culture.

Radicals scoff at the potential poverty-relieving effects of programs to create jobs and economic expansion. Such tactics will not work because poverty is built into the structure of the economy itself; only radical economic change will have a positive effect on poverty. Welfare is publicly distributed in ways that keep it demeaning and despised, whereas handouts for the rich are dignified in hidden tax loopholes, investment credits, loans and loan guarantees, and government grants and contracts, especially for military purposes.

Recent changes in the causes of poverty.   Whatever the differences of opinion among ideological groups concerning the fundamental causes of poverty, it is clear that certain changes in the late 1980s and early 1990s have contributed to the current stagnation of poverty at relatively high levels.

First, the real earnings of high school graduates and high school dropouts declined significantly beginning in the late 1970s. At the same time, the real wages of college graduates rose rapidly. This fact contributed to the growing gap between the wealthy and the poor in the most recent years. It also means that jobs with low educational qualifications are less able to keep families above the poverty or near-poverty level.

Second, government programs (as discussed below) became less effective in moving families out of poverty. Third, the economy grew only slowly during the late 1980s and went into recession at the beginning of the 1990s. Families went into poverty when the primary breadwinner lost employment or when one working parent in a two-worker family lost a job.

Finally, handicapping conditions discussed in other chapters, such as violent crime, drug addiction, poor schools, teen pregnancy, and poor health, placed obstacles in the way of thousands of young persons. It is difficult even in booming economic times to escape the drag of such conditions.[13]

CONTEMPORARY POLICY: THE NATIONAL INCOME SUPPORT SYSTEM

As noted in the introduction to this chapter, not all national social programs are aimed at alleviating poverty or helping people stay above the poverty level. In this chapter, income support programs (broadly distinguished as social insurance, public assistance, and antipoverty programs) are the major focus.

Depending on how one counts, there are anywhere from sixty to ninety separate federal programs providing social insurance, public assistance, and antipoverty aid to Americans. These range from huge programs, such as Old Age, Survivors, Disability, and Health Insurance, to relatively small programs, such as the Women, Infants and Children nutrition program. Expenditures for all these programs total over $600 billion per year, and their administration is complex and confusing. Many programs are joint federal-state ventures, requiring fifty different sets of regulations and bureaucracies. At the federal level alone, jurisdiction is divided among numerous committees in the House of Representatives and the Senate, and various executive departments and agencies. The majority of federal aid recipients benefit from two or more of these programs, with most receiving aid from three.

Social Insurance Programs

Substantial American involvement in social insurance began late compared with the world's other industrial democracies. The first federal programs were stimulated during the 1930s by the widespread poverty, hardship, and unemployment of the Great Depression. In this situation of economic disaster, with nearly 25 percent unemployment at its worst point, it became obvious that few of the aged, the poor, the widowed and orphaned, or the unemployed had resources to carry them through the hard times. Therefore President Franklin D. Roosevelt proposed, and Congress enacted, the Social Security Act of 1935 as the centerpiece of federal efforts to provide for these situations. The act's social insurance provisions are the parents of today's unemployment insurance and Old Age, Survivors, Disability, and Health Insurance (OASDHI), the latter popularly known as "Social Security."

Social insurance programs are based on contributions (by both employees and employers) to a trust fund. The only persons eligible to receive benefits are those persons, or their dependents, who have contributed to the program. Benefits are paid out of contributions and are related to contribution amount and to need. Social insurance programs are not, strictly speaking, antipoverty programs, because benefits go to contributors who in many cases are quite well-to-do. They are, however, antipoverty programs in one sense, as their primary goal is to prevent individuals and families from falling into poverty in the event of old age, disability, temporary unemployment, or the death of a family's breadwinner. Workers are required to purchase insurance against these possibilities. The premiums and benefits involved were originally designed to be quite modest, because they were meant to be only a foundation for the worker's own private, voluntary preparations for these contingencies (for example, through pensions or savings). Social insurance, however, has expanded beyond its original goals. Quite unintentionally, it has come to be seen as the primary source of retirement income for many workers.

Social Security today. Originally conceived as an old-age retirement fund, since 1935 OASDHI has been continually expanded with new programs: survivors' benefits were added in 1939, disability insurance in 1956, and health insurance (Medicare) in 1965. Today OASDHI constitutes the largest single item of federal spending. Over 90 percent of the working population, including the self-employed, are covered. Fifteen percent of the population currently receive benefits, expenditures are nearly 30 percent of federal spending, and Social Security taxes account for 30 percent of federal revenues. In addition to the Social Security program covering most workers, the federal government also administers other retirement programs for some federal workers, railroad employees, and veterans. They are not described in this chapter, but they are included in the data for social insurance programs.

OASDHI is financed by a payroll tax, in theory paid in equal shares by employer and employee. Most economists, however, believe that the burden of the employer's share is nearly always passed on to the employee in the form of lower wages. The bulk of the tax goes to two trust funds, Old Age and Survivors' Insurance, and Disability Insurance, which finance the benefits paid out of these programs. The remainder goes to a health insurance trust fund to finance Medicare, the system of health insurance for the elderly, which will be discussed in Chapter 8. Originally set quite low, both the payroll tax rate and the wage base on which it is applied have steadily risen, from the original one percent each for employer and employee on the first $3,000 of wages to 7.65 percent each on a wage base of $53,400 ($125,000 for the Medicare component) in 1991. The most rapid increases have come in the last 20 years because of inflation and the financial difficulties of OASDI described in a later section.

Benefits under OASDI (note that the Medicare health insurance component is not included here) are based on a complicated formula using the worker's previous average monthly earnings and a benefit schedule that pays higher percentages of average earnings for lower income brackets. Thus the highest-paid workers receive higher benefit amounts up to the maximum amount, but lower-paid workers receive higher percentages of their average wages in monthly benefits. Disability benefits are calculated in a similar way.

Benefits and expenditures have risen rapidly with the rise in the number of aged recipients, their longer life span, and liberalized definitions of disability (see Table 7-3 and Figure 7-5). Inflation is also an important factor, because benefit levels have been indexed since 1972 to increases in wage levels and the cost of living through Cost of Living Adjustments (COLAs). It is important to note that Social Security benefits are seldom the only source of income for retired workers and their dependents, particularly those who have earned high wages. Individual

---

TABLE 7-3 ▪ Monthly Benefits under OASDI, Selected Years

	OAS Recipients	OAS Benefits (in $ thousands)	Average Benefit	Disability Recipients	Disability Benefits (in $ thousands)	Average Benefit
1940	222,488	$ 4,070	$18.29	—	—	—
1950	3,477,243	126,856	36.48	—	—	—
1960	14,157,138	888,320	62.75	687,451	$ 48,000	$ 69.87
1970	23,563,634	2,385,926	101.25	2,664,995	242,400	90.96
1980	30,936,668	9,432,229	304.89	4,682,172	1,261,723	269.47
1985	33,151,148	14,441,737	435.63	3,907,169	1,459,906	373.64
1990	35,566,144	19,716,655	554.36	4,256,981	1,970,108	462.90

SOURCE: *Social Security Bulletin,* 54 (Washington, D.C.: U.S. Government Printing Office, October 1991), Table M-8.

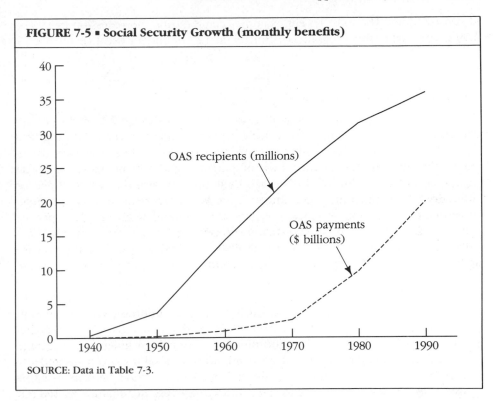

FIGURE 7-5 ▪ Social Security Growth (monthly benefits)

SOURCE: Data in Table 7-3.

private retirement plans have proliferated in recent decades, and Congress acted in 1974 to insure retirees' rights to benefits and the financial integrity of such plans. Total OASDI expenditures are estimated at about $300 billion for fiscal year 1993.

Unemployment insurance.   Unemployment compensation is the other principal form of social insurance. Its purpose is to maintain the income of normally employed workers in periods of involuntary unemployment. About 90 percent of all employed persons are covered. The program provides a federal tax incentive for each state to establish and administer its own program. Thus, unlike OASDI, unemployment insurance is financed and administered at the state level, under general federal guidelines. Taxes are paid by employers based on their payrolls and prior experience with unemployment. Thus tax rates and benefit levels vary from state to state, as does the duration of eligibility for benefits. Persons receiving aid are required to accept a "suitable" job if one is offered, and states must have job counseling and job placement programs. An estimated 3.5 million persons received benefits in March, 1991. State-administered Workers' Compensation programs also help insure against loss of income.

Congress has frequently extended the duration of unemployment insurance benefits and added special supplements to meet emergency needs during recessionary periods. The most recent examples came during the recession in 1991–1992. The cost of this program is estimated at $27 billion for fiscal year 1992.

Public Assistance Programs

Public assistance, generally thought of as welfare, is designed to help certain categories of persons whose circumstances place them in poverty. Its programs are intended to aid either families who are temporarily unable to support themselves through no fault of their own or persons who are ineligible for social insurance but deserving of aid because their poverty was the result of age or disability. Much thinking about the poor in Anglo-American history has been governed by the assumption that public assistance should be given only to people who deserve it, that is, those who are not responsible for their own poverty. Thus public assistance has traditionally been available to children and to adults who are aged, blind, disabled, or guardians of small children. Adults who are none of these are assumed to be undeserving and are seldom eligible for assistance.

Though persons needing help are many and though federal programs to assist them, such as Aid to Families with Dependent Children (AFDC) and Supplemental Security Income (SSI), have their origins as far back as the Social Security Act of 1935, there is little coordination among them and gaps in coverage are substantial. These programs are financed out of general tax revenues, and any person who is a member of an eligibility category may receive benefits. For this reason they are often referred to as *categorical programs.* Benefits are related not to previous earnings but to present need. In the jargon, they are "means tested." Examples of public assistance programs are SSI, food stamps, and AFDC.

Public assistance programs come in two forms, cash assistance and in-kind assistance. Cash assistance is simply a transfer of income from a government agency to an individual—an AFDC check, for example. In-kind assistance refers to programs in which a tangible benefit, but not cash, is given to the recipient. Food stamps, for example, are convertible into food but not into money income, and Medicaid provides direct health care. In-kind benefits, however, have a cost to the government and a value to the recipient that can be computed as part of the recipient's income.

Assistance to the poor also comes in the form of services. Here the benefits are not tangible in the way that cash and food are, but they do have a value. They are often the "glue" holding together a variety of federal, state, and local programs, helping reduce institutionalization, and providing an advocacy for the poor.[14] Examples are marital counseling, literacy training, family planning, and foster care. Although the services provided are valuable to the recipient, because they are so intangible their cash value is more difficult to compute than is the value of other in-kind benefits.

There are three main means-tested cash assistance programs available to the general public: Aid to Families with Dependent Children, Supplemental Security Income, and General Assistance.

Aid to Families with Dependent Children. AFDC began as part of the original Social Security Act on the premise that the children of the poor, who are not responsible for their own poverty, deserve aid. Intended at first as a temporary measure until social insurance took over the full burden, the program was later expanded to include the single mothers of such children. Later still, states were permitted the option of extending benefits to such families with an unemployed father present (AFDC-UP), and approximately half of the states have exercised this option. Under the welfare reform measures passed in 1988 (discussed in the Future Alternatives section below) all states must adopt AFDC-UP provisions. Aid to Families with Dependent Children, the program most persons have in mind when they speak of welfare, is jointly funded by the states and the federal government and administered by state or local welfare departments under federal regulations and state law. Federal funding for AFDC is now approximately 55 percent of the total.[15] Because of the joint federal-state structure and provisions of the funding formula, benefit levels and eligibility vary widely from state to state, the proportion of federal funding being highest in states with low per-capita incomes and low benefit levels.

Each state agency sets its own standard of need for food, clothing, and shelter, and AFDC payments are calculated on this formula. Families with countable incomes below that standard are eligible for aid, but states are not required to pay benefits at 100 percent of need, and few do. Thus benefits are set by subtracting countable income and resources from the maximum benefit level for each family size and circumstance. Actual benefits paid vary enormously from state to state. For example, the median state's *standard of need* in 1987 was $428 per month, which was only 55 percent of the poverty line for a family of three. The median state's *maximum AFDC payment* was only $354 per month for such a family. Benefits for a three-person family ranged in 1990 from $114 per month in Alabama to $647 per month in Alaska. During the 1980s, benefit increases lagged far behind increases in the cost of living. By 1988, only sixteen states paid AFDC benefits above 80 percent of the poverty level for a family of three. Eight states paid less than 60 percent.

The costs of AFDC benefits and the number of persons receiving them expanded rapidly in the 1960s and early 1970s, but leveled off thereafter (see Figure 7-6).

Supplemental Security Income. The SSI program began in 1974, replacing the federal-state programs of old-age assistance and aid to the blind and disabled established by the Social Security Act of 1935. Benefit levels are set by the Social Security Administration and adjusted annually for cost-of-living increases. In 1991, a couple with no other income received $610 per month. SSI was designed to replace the jumble of state and federal programs for the aged, blind, and disabled with a single, centrally administered program. It is also the first guaranteed minimum-income program in the United States funded from general revenues.

Despite the expectation of one simplified, consolidated program, SSI has turned out to be quite complicated. First, the benefits have been insufficient, with

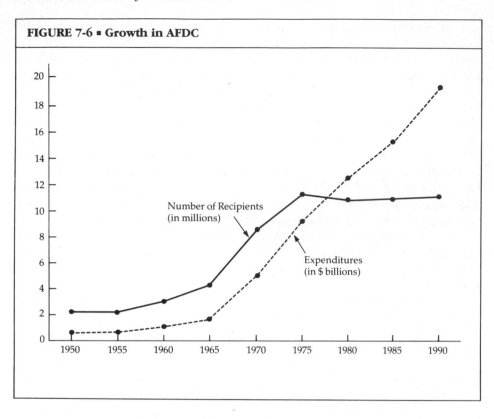

FIGURE 7-6 ▪ Growth in AFDC

Number of Recipients
(in millions)

Expenditures
(in $ billions)

benefit levels low enough so that forty-eight states supplement SSI with their own funds (Texas and West Virginia are the exceptions). Second, the federal government is not the only administrator; twenty-nine states administer their supplemental programs directly. Finally, the use of SSI has crossed over into other federal efforts. SSI can be used to supplement OASDI when its benefits are below SSI standards. In fact, over 70 percent of all aged recipients and nearly 30 percent of all blind and disabled recipients use SSI to supplement Social Security. Federal and state SSI expenditures were $15.2 billion in 1990 for 5 million recipients.

Earned Income Tax Credit. The final major form of federal cash assistance is the Earned Income Tax Credit (EITC), which is of importance to working families near the poverty line. Under the EITC the taxpayer receives a tax credit from the government for each dollar earned up to a certain point; the credits are gradually phased out as income rises. In 1989, for example, the credit disappeared at an earned income of $19,340. This credit is refunded to the taxpayer, providing a benefit of anywhere from a few hundred dollars to close to $1,000 dollars for some working families. In 1988, the EITC benefited approximately 28 million taxpayers at a cost of $5 billion.

General Assistance. General Assistance refers to wholly state funded and administered programs that help individuals, usually on an emergency basis, who are not eligible for other types of cash aid. Virtually all states have such programs, but expenditures are quite modest, amounting to approximately $2.7 billion in 1988.

Despite the modest expenditures associated with General Assistance programs, they were hard hit by state budget cuts during 1991 in response to recession-induced state fiscal crises. Of the 30 states providing general assistance, 14 cut funding levels and 13 froze them. AFDC benefit levels were also cut in many states, the sharpest cuts since 1981.

In-kind benefits. Public assistance in the form of in-kind benefits has grown rapidly since the mid-1960s and now constitutes a higher proportion of public assistance than cash benefits. Yet millions of persons below poverty income receive no in-kind assistance. Medicaid was enacted in 1965 (along with Medicare) as Title XIX of the Social Security Act. With federal money matched by state funds, it offers medical care to low-income individuals. In addition, both the states and the federal government fund numerous other health services that benefit the poor, programs that will be discussed in the next chapter. Here it is enough to say that the poor generally have more serious health problems than other income groups and that medical bills are more financially devastating to them. Medicaid and other health programs, then, have provided important in-kind benefits.

After Medicaid, food stamps are the most significant form of in-kind benefit available to the poor. Indeed, on a day-to-day basis they are more important. In this program, coupons redeemable in grocery stores (for food items only) are given to families below certain income levels. Note that cash is not given directly to recipients for this purpose. The food stamp program well reveals some basic assumptions about welfare and poverty in America, for it is rooted in the desire to see the poor adequately fed but also in a distrust of their spending habits.

The program is administered by the Department of Agriculture, which pays the entire cost of the coupons and almost two-thirds of the state's administrative costs. Benefits are keyed to the price of food, the cost of a decent diet, family size, and income. Because eligibility guidelines are established on a different basis and at different income levels from the cash assistance programs, many persons ineligible for the latter are eligible for food stamps. Still, fewer than half of those potentially eligible for food stamps receive them. Moreover, because AFDC and SSI income are counted in determining eligibility, persons in states with high AFDC and SSI benefits receive fewer food coupons, and vice versa. This feature of the program tends to narrow the interstate disparities of the AFDC program. Finally, the food stamp program is very sensitive to changes in the economy; in times of recession and unemployment the program expands rapidly.

The year 1991 provided a particularly good example of how food stamps respond to the economy. The number of recipients rose to nearly 24 million, or 10 percent of the population. The increase in the number of recipients from 1990 was 15 percent, or 3 million persons. Federal expenditures for food stamps totaled approximately $18 billion in 1991 (see Figure 7-7).

Millions of Americans live in substandard, dilapidated, and overcrowded dwellings. Various programs of housing assistance stretch as far back as 1937,

FIGURE 7-7 ▪ **Increase in the Use of Food Stamps, 1970–1991**

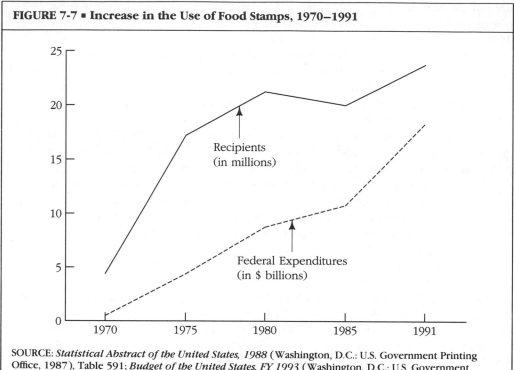

SOURCE: *Statistical Abstract of the United States, 1988* (Washington, D.C.: U.S. Government Printing Office, 1987), Table 591; *Budget of the United States, FY 1993* (Washington, D.C.: U.S. Government Printing Office, 1992), p. A-352.

attesting to government's desire to address this problem. Examples of such programs are public housing, rural farm labor housing, rent and mortgage subsidies, the Community Development Program, and neighborhood rehabilitation. All attempt, in one way or another, to restore urban and rural housing and to provide decent housing for the poor. Yet federal housing aid makes only a small contribution toward relieving this situation, despite a variety of programs providing loans or rent subsidies to low-income families.

Spending grew slowly from $7.8 billion in 1981 to $12.4 billion in 1986 and was $15 billion by 1990. By 1989, only one-fourth of those eligible for federal housing assistance were receiving it, and 40 percent of the nation's 16 million renter households with incomes below $15,000 were paying more than half of their income for rent. Such families live close to the edge of homelessness. Homelessness, as we shall see in the Future Alternatives section below, has begun to receive national prominence as a policy issue.

Other in-kind programs represent far smaller dollar figures than Medicaid, food stamps, and housing assistance. Examples are the school lunch program, nutrition programs for infants and the elderly, social services, and assistance with home weatherization and other energy costs.

Changes in Income Support

The causes of change in the costs of social insurance and public assistance are complex and subject to debate. One factor is obviously the general inflation of the last twenty years. Some programs, such as OASDI and SSI, have a built-in compensator (the COLA) for the effects of inflation. Others are adjusted periodically by legislative action to keep pace with the rise in prices. Much of the growth, then, in income support costs is inflationary, not real growth. Programs not indexed, such as AFDC, tend over time to decline in purchasing power. A second factor is change in the size of population groups, which particularly affects OASDI, federal civil service retirement, and other pension programs. As the proportion of the population over retirement age has increased and as life expectancies for this part of the population have been lengthened, program expenditures have increased. Demographic patterns also affect AFDC. Its benefits are targeted toward one-parent families, especially those headed by women. As divorce and illegitimacy rates climb, so do AFDC expenditures. A third reason why these programs have grown is the high unemployment generally characteristic of the 1970s and mid-1980s, and particularly the sharp recessions from 1974 to 1975, 1979 to 1980, 1981 to 1982, and 1991 to 1992. Programs designed for the working poor and those out of work grow rapidly in such periods. These causes of expenditure growth reflect social and economic patterns external to the income support programs themselves. Other causes, however, stem from policy changes.

During the 1960s and 1970s, legislation created new programs and broadened the coverage and raised the benefit levels of old programs. A larger proportion of the population became eligible for benefits; benefits became easier to receive; and benefit levels were raised toward the poverty line. OASDI coverage, for example, was extended to new categories of workers; the definition of disability was liberalized; and benefit levels were indexed to inflation rates. Medicare and Medicaid were created in 1965. The food stamp program was created during the 1960s and continually expanded. These changes represented both enlarged populations to be served and real growth in terms of costs.

The growth of public assistance programs peaked during the mid-1970s and then began a decline, reinforced during the Reagan and Bush administrations. Democratic support in Congress saved these programs from draconian reductions, but the poor have suffered a steady slippage for fifteen years in programs designed for alleviating poverty. The working poor were the most severely affected by these trends, as education, job training, and social service programs were scaled back. Cash income assistance, for example, declined as a proportion of GNP from 0.37 percent in 1966 to 0.22 percent in 1985. Maximum AFDC and food stamp benefits in the median state declined in constant (1984) dollars from $737 in 1971 to $542 in 1984 (from 87 percent of the poverty level to 64 percent). By 1991 AFDC payments were at 58 percent of 1971 purchasing power.[16] These declines were partially offset by tax reductions for the poor in the 1986 tax-reform package.

The supposed enormous size of public assistance has drawn outraged criticisms; yet mistaken impressions about such means-tested spending must be avoided. Public assistance expenditures are certainly sizable. But in terms of their impact on the total budget, they are dwarfed by the social insurance programs, which account for 80 percent of expenditures in income support programs. Moreover, expenditures for public assistance programs amount to only 5 percent of the federal budget. Widespread dislike of and dissatisfaction with these programs may focus on their cost, but their inequities and inefficiencies are a far more appropriate target for controversy.

Antipoverty Programs

One of the most important causes of early growth in public assistance was the group of 1960s programs known as the War on Poverty. Created by President Johnson and Congress in 1964 as the Economic Opportunity Act and administered by the Office of Economic Opportunity (OEO), these programs were intended to eliminate the causes of poverty. The War on Poverty included a great variety of programs, many that no longer exist and others that have been redefined and absorbed by the traditional administrative departments.[17] Employment programs are now the most significant antipoverty policies.

In 1974, job programs were combined under the general umbrella of the Comprehensive Employment and Training Act (CETA). CETA plus other job-related programs accounted for $11 billion in federal expenditures in 1981. Because these programs provided not only job training but also salaries for participants, they were both antipoverty and income support programs. Training and employment programs provided funds for training welfare recipients in job skills. They offered grants to state and local governments for skills training, counseling, remedial education, subsidized employment, and job creation in areas with high unemployment. They also funded the Job Corps, summer youth employment, and the Young Adult Conservation Corps. But in 1982, CETA was allowed to expire, and job training was redirected toward the private sector. The Job Training Partnership Act promoted by President Reagan and Senator Dan Quayle places most job-training programs in the hands of local Private Industry Councils. These are made up of businesspersons, educators, labor officials, and other community representatives. This program began with $3.9 billion in 1982. Employment and job-training programs suffered severe declines in the 1980s. By the end of the decade, expenditures were about $4 billion.

The primary purpose of job-training programs is to give the poor marketable skills. They must, however, go hand in hand with job creation programs, or the skills will mean nothing. The Work Incentive Program for AFDC recipients, for example, has had little success because of the lack of child care facilities, the low educational level of the trainees, and the lack of jobs once skills are acquired. Other training and unemployment programs have been more successful, although the temporary nature of CETA and public service jobs meant that many of those trained and employed had little prospect for permanent employment.

The Welfare State

The United States is not a welfare state in the way that term is normally understood, despite the extensive welfare programs just described. It is important to stress this point if we are to understand the difference in approach to social welfare between the United States and Western Europe. With the exception of public education, government social services in the United States, including public assistance, social insurance, nutrition, health care, and housing, all are tied to the concept of the deserving poor and therefore to minimum-income criteria (means tests) or to the recipient's previous self-contributions (as in Social Security). Although the means test does exist in Great Britain, Sweden, France, the Netherlands, and other welfare states, it plays a far smaller role than in the United States. The essential feature of the welfare state is that it aims to guarantee minimum standards of life close to society's average through social services, education, public assistance, social insurance, and employment programs to all citizens as a political right, not as charity.[18] In Western Europe, subsidized housing, health services, child care, employment, and other benefits are available not only to the poor, as in the United States, but to all or most citizens.

As in the United States, spending for income support is the largest budget item in all the industrial democracies.[19] The basic programs of social insurance—retirement, disability, and unemployment compensation—are very similar across nations, and the provision of public assistance to the aged, blind, disabled, and children is universal. All, moreover, participate extensively in job training and retraining and job creation. In all of these countries there is also, as we saw in the United States, a tendency to expand the programs once established and to raise benefit levels. There is also the same pressure to moderate growth in spending during the 1990s.

There are, however, significant divergences between American policy and policy in other countries. Nations such as Sweden and Germany, among others, have more extensive programs of sick leave and maternity benefit, and all have programs of family or childrens' allowances, which, in effect, provide assistance to the poor in large families without the stigma of public assistance or the requirement of many American states that no able-bodied male be present in the family. Subsidized housing and child care for extensive segments of the population are also available in Europe, providing decent low-cost housing for the poor and freeing mothers to work. Pressures in the European welfare system are building, however. Housing shortages, for example, are becoming increasingly common and are critical in parts of Britain and the Netherlands, and there is a constant demand for expansion of child care facilities as more women enter the labor force.

The United States has been consistently last in establishing welfare and income support programs, and its funding of them remains at a level well below that of most other developed nations, in which social insurance and public assistance benefits come close to ensuring current average living standards. Because of negative attitudes toward the poor, American benefit levels in most states fall well below the poverty line. Moreover, rates of participation among those eligible for public assistance are higher in Europe than in the United States. Case workers actively seek to enroll eligible people, but in the United States there is still a widespread attitude that public assistance should be difficult to obtain, even for those who qualify.

Note finally that just as a welfare state is a more extensive concept than welfare is, so income support in both the United States and Europe extends far beyond the "needy poor" definition of programs discussed in this chapter. The modern state supports the income and the standard of living of the wealthy and the middle class to an even greater extent than it does the poor. Socialists and Marxists make this fact a central indictment of American policy.[20] Tax deductions for mortgage payments and for medical care and insurance aid millions of middle-class Americans to maintain a high standard of living. Government grants, loans, loan guarantees, and subsidies to farmers, transportation companies, small businesses, large corporations, trade associations, and thousands of other interests help to prop up the incomes of workers, managers, and owners. Income support is a way of life throughout modern nations. The policies considered in this chapter are only a part of these endeavors.

POLICY EVALUATION: ECONOMIC REALITIES AND CRITICAL IDEOLOGICAL VIEWPOINTS

Because of the radical differences in their perspectives on poverty and its causes, critics of various ideological stripes have different evaluations of income support programs.

Conservatives, given their belief that poverty is the fault of the poor and of misguided welfare spending, generally evaluate public programs negatively. Their reforms stress work requirements, tightening benefit eligibility, policing the programs to eliminate fraud and mismanagement, keeping families intact where possible and requiring absent fathers to pay child support when families have broken up. They also believe in keeping benefit levels low to encourage employment among the poor. Finally, they encourage job creation through the private sector.

Liberals, believing that poverty is involuntary and related to lack of opportunity, have a generally favorable evaluation of welfare and income support programs, although they favor reform in the direction of more equal benefit levels and program expansion to cover all eligible persons.

Radicals see poverty programs only as bandages on a wound, neither intended to nor able to accomplish prevention or cure. In their view, tightening program eligibility would only punish the poor more severely. However, they are cynical about the benefits of expanding those programs, which they support only as a step toward their collapse from overgrowth. Collapse would make obvious the need for change from liberal capitalism to the welfare state or socialism.

Social Insurance Policy

Successes.   Although social insurance spending greatly exceeds spending for antipoverty programs and public assistance combined, as noted before, until the late 1970s it generated comparatively little controversy. First, these programs, particularly OASDI, have a good record of accomplishing their goals. Moreover, because benefits are related to the self-contribution mechanism under the insurance aspect of OASDI and unemployment compensation, they are compatible with American value systems. Benefits are seen as returns on an investment, albeit a mandatory one, rather than a handout.

OASDI and unemployment insurance have done a good job of keeping recipients out of poverty, particularly when combined with tax breaks and other benefits, such as SSI, Medicare, Medicaid, and food stamps, for which beneficiaries may also be eligible. Social Security is largely responsible for a poverty rate among the elderly lower than the national average. Retired workers and their spouses generally have from 35 to 100 percent of their preretirement wages replaced by OASDI. The lower replacement rates are generally for higher-income workers who are more likely to have private pension resources as well as Social Security. Moreover, at least until the mid-1970s, Social Security gave retirees, survivors, and the disabled a more than fair return on their investment, as they could expect to receive more in benefits than their taxes had paid for. Current retirees, especially those with lower incomes, will likely recoup their payroll tax contributions.[21] Unemployment insurance benefits and wage replacement rates vary from state to state but are generally sufficient to support the temporary unemployment they were designed for, particularly when combined with the benefits available from some unions and from public assistance. Long-term unemployment is a more serious problem, but the unemployment insurance system was never intended to handle it.

The Social Security dilemma.   Despite the generally acknowledged success of social insurance programs in meeting the goals intended, there are serious issues and controversies surrounding the programs, particularly with respect to long-term financing.[22] Social Security has become a major public issue. For many years, OASDI has been financed, unlike private insurance programs, on a pay-as-you-go basis. Taxes paid into the system go into trust funds, but these funds do not have large enough reserves to cover benefits. As a result, taxes collected each year are expended for benefits in that same year. The taxes of those currently working pay the benefits of the retired. This situation caused no problem so long as benefits were low and the ratio of active workers to beneficiaries was high. The crisis developed when benefits began to expand rapidly because of inflation and a high wage-replacement rate, and it has deepened as the number of retirees has grown and their life spans increased. The financial crisis has been exacerbated by a rapid rise in disability claims as definitions of disability have been expanded, for example, by allowing substantial claims for psychological incapacity to work. The periodic recessions between 1973 and 1992 also contributed to the crisis by reducing tax receipts just as benefits were skyrocketing.

The pay-as-you-go-nature of Social Security means that it is a compact between generations. The present generation in effect agrees to pay for its predecessors' retirement if the following generation will agree to pay for the present generation's retirement. The problem is that economic fluctuations within a particular time period can affect the relative economic well-being of the generations and the ability of the present generation to tax itself to pay the benefits of the retired. Moreover, in the long run, the fact that the generations are of different sizes has enormous implications. As birthrates remain low and life spans lengthen, the number of workers will shrink relative to the number of retirees, straining their ability to pay the taxes necessary to support the system. Those over eighty are the fastest-growing population group in the United States. Although there are three workers today for every beneficiary, in thirty years there will be only two, or possibly even fewer.

Moreover, the indexation of benefits to the cost of living and the high wage-replacement rates encourage early retirement and less work after retirement. This reduces economic output in the economy as a whole. Finally, the large sums absorbed by Social Security may reduce private savings and thus the level of capital available for economic investment. The political clout of an increasing elderly population will work to maintain the costly benefits. It is important to note at this point that these problems, as well as those described below, are endemic to the social security systems of all developed nations.[23]

The crisis in Social Security, then, is as much political as it is economic. It is a crisis of confidence and trust in the system's ability to continue paying benefits through the economic and demographic changes of the coming decades. It is also a challenge of the ability of Congress and the president to fashion policy changes in the midst of strong and conflicting political pressures. They must choose between a reduction in the growth of benefits or continued increases in Social Security taxes. This situation places politicians in a nightmarish double bind: either the beneficiaries—who will become an increasingly potent political force—will be unhappy with reduced benefits, or current workers—on whom revenues and productivity will depend—will react negatively to higher taxes. In 1977, Congress timidly responded by partially eliminating overindexing, which had caused benefits to rise faster than the cost of living, and by enacting a steep rise in the tax rate and wage base.

Social Security reforms of 1983.   In 1983, Congress enacted important changes in the Social Security system in an attempt to resolve these problems and guarantee the system's long-term health. In order to pump more money into the system, Congress required that after January 1, 1984, new federal employees must pay into the system, as well as members of the Congress, the office of the president, the judiciary, and employees of nonprofit organizations. Moreover, Social Security benefits were made subject to taxation for the first time, if half of one's benefits plus outside income exceeds $25,000 ($32,000 for married couples).

In order to hold down costs, the regular Social Security retirement age will be gradually increased from sixty-five to sixty-seven, starting in 2003. Additionally, future COLAs (Cost of Living Adjustments) will be based on the lower of the increase in the Consumer Price Index or the average increase in wages, if the OASDI trust fund falls below a certain level. Other changes were made to encourage workers to continue working full- or part-time beyond the regular retirement age. Whether these changes will bring costs and benefits into long-run balance depends on the population changes and economic performance over the next fifty years.

These financial problems may be alleviated to some extent by two developments. First, the same fertility and mortality patterns that will increase the percentage of future retirees dependent on working people will also mean a decrease in the percentage of children dependent on those workers. Thus the total dependency ratio will not change. This will, however, help the financial burden only if educational and other child-related expenditures decline as the number of children declines. But the power and entrenched position of educational interest groups may very well be able to prevent such relief. Indeed, as Chapter 9 shows, the pressure for more spending for education is now intense. Second, a trend toward later retirement may grow, spurred by the aged who wish to work and by the congressional desire to keep Social Security expenditures low. Later retirement will help, though, only if current restrictions are retained on the amount of income that can be earned without reduction in benefits. These provisions, however, seriously damage the equity of the system, because they make it more unlikely that individuals, particularly those enjoying relatively high incomes as workers, will receive a fair return in benefits for the payroll taxes they have contributed. Moreover, later retirement for older workers may result in fewer job opportunities for younger workers. Thus the solution of one problem can create new problems through its unintended consequences.

Is Social Security fair? The fairness issue stems from a basic disagreement over the goals of OASDI: whether policy should be aimed at the equity of taxes and benefits or at the adequacy of benefits to cover retirement needs. To a large extent, this disagreement divides along conservative versus liberal-radical lines. Equity means that benefits should be proportioned to taxes paid into OASDI: the more a person pays, the more he or she should receive on retirement. Conservatives, who stress equity as the most important element of OASDI, argue that the program should be placed on an insurance basis, that is, funded out of trust funds, not general revenues. The employer-employee tax ratio should remain at one to one, and benefits paid out should reflect taxes paid in. Liberals and radicals stress adequacy of benefits. Adequacy means that benefits should be adequate to keep recipients out of poverty; that is, they should be linked to current need rather than past contributions. Thus lower-income workers would receive proportionately higher benefits upon their death, disability, or retirement—in other words, more than they had contributed. From this viewpoint, the trust fund is an accountant's myth, and contributions from general revenues should be added when necessary to keep benefit levels high. These contradictory goals have always been embodied in the OASDI program, but there was little friction until recently because, as long as financing was no problem, both goals could be met.

In addition to the recent financial problems, the growing gap between financially secure and poor elderly persons exacerbates the equity-adequacy problem. The income of most of the elderly has improved substantially in recent years, especially for those with pensions and savings in addition to Social Security benefits. But those whose retirement depends entirely or largely on Social Security exist at or below the poverty line. A two-class system among the elderly is increasingly a reality.

Moreover, recent increases in the wage base have made for serious equity problems. Higher-income persons, who are paying considerably more in taxes, may not receive in benefits as much as they contribute. Thus Social Security is no longer a bargain for high-income workers. They may begin to demand more equitable benefits or an option out of the system, either of which would deal a damaging financial blow to OASDI. Liberal supporters of adequacy are, however, not satisfied with benefits either, because OASDI for the poorest workers must often be supplemented by public assistance programs and because 60 percent of all OASDI benefits go to those already above the poverty line.

Retaining the restrictions on earnings for those receiving OASDI and taxing benefits pleases liberals because it emphasizes the wage replacement, need-based character of OASDI. But it angers those who see OASDI benefits as an earned right based on contributions made. Benefits should be paid, conservatives argue, irrespective of current income.

The spouse's benefit, a payment added to support the spouse of a retired or deceased worker, also presents important equity controversies. The trends toward two-worker families and toward divorce cloud the purpose of this benefit, which was originally designed to recognize the need of one worker's benefits to support two persons in retirement. Currently, however, it makes a one-worker family proportionately better off in benefits than a family in which two workers pay payroll taxes. Yet eliminating the benefit would be a hardship for women who choose to be homemakers rather than wage earners. And although pegging benefits to the contributions of two earners in a family would please those who stress equity, it would mean more than adequate benefits for many such families. A divorced spouse (male or female) can receive benefits on a former husband's or wife's Social Security record if the marriage lasted at least 10 years. The divorced spouse must be at least 62 and unmarried and must wait until two years after the divorce to receive benefits for the first time.

Unemployment compensation. As we noted in the previous section, fewer than half of the unemployed receive unemployment compensation because of eligibility restrictions and limited benefit periods. Unemployment insurance is of most help to those with stable work histories and good prospects for finding a new position. The poor, who often have weak job skills and erratic work experience, frequently find themselves ineligible for benefits.

These problems of unemployment compensation have become increasingly evident as the American economy goes through fundamental restructuring. Many unemployed persons are not readily qualified for jobs that require new skills or higher education. Moreover, part-time and temporary workers are not eligible for unemployment benefits, and the numbers of these persons losing their jobs has jumped. Large numbers of workers exhausted their basic 26-week benefit period early in the most recent recession. During this period, extended unemployment benefits were created to assist qualified persons for 13 to 20 weeks beyond the normal benefit period.

Longer-term proposals for reform in unemployment compensation call for increasing the wage base for the unemployment tax in order to build up sufficient funds to cover more persons for longer periods of economic stagnation.

Antipoverty Employment Programs

Employment programs are subject to widely divergent evaluations depending on ideological stance. Conservatives have generally evaluated these negatively, with the exception of a few programs for special groups, such as vocational rehabilitation. They believe strongly, however, in mandatory work or work training for those receiving welfare benefits. Conservatives take the view that private industry can best train and employ jobless, able-bodied, adult welfare recipients. Programs such as government job training and public employment, they argue, divert resources from truly productive private-sector employment, fail to train for the actual job market, tend to be simply "make-work" projects, and are basically a hidden form of welfare. Conservatives favor deregulation of industry as a means of encouraging production and increasing employment at all levels. A general tax cut would also stimulate production and employment according to supply-side economics, a theory reviewed in Chapter 3. If direct government stimulation of jobs and job training is necessary, conservatives favor tax credits to businesses that hire or train the jobless.

Liberals, on the other hand, believe that work requirements for welfare recipients, in the absence of other measures such as education and child care facilities, generally fail. They point to the dismal record of work requirements in training and placing welfare mothers and note that few public assistance recipients have the skills, health, or family environment necessary for work programs to succeed in removing them from welfare rolls. Liberals contend that youth and adults whose job skills have become unneeded in a changing economy are better targets for job-training and employment programs. They contend, however, that such programs must be more consistently and generously funded and must be supported by remedial education and child care. Moreover, they support a national full-employment policy, including substantial public employment if necessary. Public service jobs are not "make work" but, rather, contribute to needed construction, rehabilitation, conservation, and beautification projects.

Empirical evidence points to a mixed record for employment and job-training programs.[24] Workers needing job retraining receive few benefits, although women and the young with no previous experience often succeed in finding employment after training. Some Job Corps centers have shown impressive results. Training programs have been more successful than work-experience programs. The modest size of employment and training programs and their substantial funding reductions in the 1980s have meant that they have little impact on poverty or unemployment rates.

As the United States undertakes fundamental economic restructuring, with many old firms permanently reducing their labor forces and new firms emphasizing high technology skills, the entire employment and job-training system must be rethought. Job retraining becomes even more important than training for the first job. No new policy initiatives, however, appear on the horizon. Discussion wallows in the old rhetoric of public versus private employment training responsibilities.

Public Assistance Policy

Because there are so many public assistance policies and because all are aimed at the general problem of poverty and its manifestations in poor health, nutrition, housing, and the like, each program will not be evaluated separately. Rather, the overall success of public assistance, its principal failures and problems, and the major proposals for reform will be considered as a whole.

Accomplishments of public assistance.   Despite highly critical public attitudes toward the American welfare system, its students generally agree that it has been quite successful in accomplishing many of its intended goals. First, public assistance, through its combination of cash and in-kind aid, has moved a large number of Americans out of poverty, and for many of those unfortunate enough to suffer from poverty, it will be a transitory experience ending again in economic health. Admittedly, the definition of poverty operating here is the most stingy; yet, although this success must not be exaggerated, it should still be acknowledged. Moreover, the same programs that, by conservative definition, have nearly eliminated poverty have certainly reduced it substantially if other definitions are used.

Each public assistance program, examined in isolation, has important shortcomings and inequities, but taken together, they balance out to some extent and provide for many of the poor a basic minimum standard of living. This combination effect is why many liberals oppose cutting what appears to be excessive spending in particular programs.

Certainly the food stamp program has contributed to improved nutrition among the poor. Moreover, given the rather broad eligibility standards for food stamps, the near-poor are able to maintain decent living standards when economic hard times place severe restrictions on income. Food stamps have become more than an antihunger program, for they are now an essential part of the network of benefits supporting a minimum income for the poor. Medicaid, housing assistance, and other in-kind programs have also been very important in filling basic needs of the poor for medical care, housing, counseling, and other services. America's great wealth makes its residual poverty shocking; even more shocking would be the extent of poverty if no public assistance programs were available. Public assistance has been more successful than is usually acknowledged in alleviating poverty, hunger, ill health, and inadequate housing.[25]

European programs of income support are even more successful. A similar mixture of cash and in-kind programs plus the rapid expansion of benefits and eligibility has been successful in lifting the low-income population out of poverty. The difficulties of cross-cultural comparison of poverty make precise figures impossible to attain, but generally, European programs support the low-income population at a higher standard of living than do American programs.

The use of public assistance by most American families conforms to the policy's intention, to provide a temporary alleviative measure until jobs are found, health is regained, or the divorced or widowed are remarried. Although the members of the underclass stay on assistance for considerable periods, the average AFDC stay is about three years. Going on welfare is primarily an economic decision influenced by the unavailability of jobs and by prevailing wage rates. Despite widely held opinion, fraud and corruption are no more or less of a problem than in most other government programs or in private business, for that matter.

Liberal critics have obscured the successes by implicitly shifting the issue from poverty to income inequality. During the 1960s, the focus of liberal action was on remedying absolute poverty. During the 1970s, that focus implicitly changed to an attack on relative inequality; the standard of evaluation has been redefined. Although public assistance has made great strides in minimizing the former, it has done little about the latter.[26] However, public assistance's primary goal is not reduction of inequality, but reduction of economic insecurity. Moreover, liberal support has begun to retreat from current welfare programs because liberals have recognized the accuracy of many conservative critiques. Public assistance does contain waste and inefficiency, and it has not come close to curing poverty. Yet liberal loyalty to the welfare idea is still strong. Indeed, liberals still tend to confuse their strong sense of justice and compassion for the poor with the ability to solve the poverty problem. Perhaps a liberal society is to be judged not by whether it ends poverty but by how sympathetic it is to its poor.[27]

Conservatives often fail to see the successes of welfare because they are ideologically predisposed to oppose it. Concentrating criticism, then, on bureaucratic expansion, the explosion of welfare expenditures, and a few spectacular cases of fraud, they indict the entire system of programs. Yet public assistance has helped protect American private enterprise from its own shortcomings. The very successes of welfare in reducing poverty have smothered demands for a more radical reform of the American political and economic system, as liberals and radicals lament.

Failings of public assistance. Public assistance does have numerous serious shortcomings. The six main problems are (1) cost, (2) inadequate benefits, (3) unfairness, (4) work disincentives, (5) excessive complexity, and (6) punitive features in some programs. Conservatives tend to stress the first and fifth; liberals and radicals the second, third, and sixth. All recognize the fourth.

1. Cost. The problem of program cost is a serious one, although it can be exaggerated. Public assistance costs grew rapidly in the 1960s and early 1970s but since then have leveled off. Yet the total cost of all federal public assistance is one-fourth the cost of OASDI and only 5 percent of the budget. Cost increases would be smaller if corrected to reflect inflation, and growth in the number of beneficiaries has slowed in the past decade. Nevertheless, the total cost is quite high, and the proportion of expenditures for administration is very large. Such a large percentage is evidence of inefficiency in getting funds to the target populations. Moreover, because most public assistance programs are jointly funded and administered by federal and state governments and because many states supplement federal funds at a high rate, program growth can put a severe financial strain on some state and local governments, particularly in times of economic recession when tax income falls. Similar financial pressures are present in public assistance in other nations; program expansion has slowed, and political conflict over welfare-state kinds of programs has escalated. (See Figure 7-8.)

2. Adequacy. Another major problem is inadequate benefits. With at least 10 percent of the population, over twenty million persons, still living in poverty (based on the least-generous SSA standard), the failure of public assistance to cope with this shocking deprivation among such plenty has come under sharp criticism. These benefits are barely adequate for most recipients to maintain any kind of decent living standard, particularly as inflation increases the cost of basic goods.

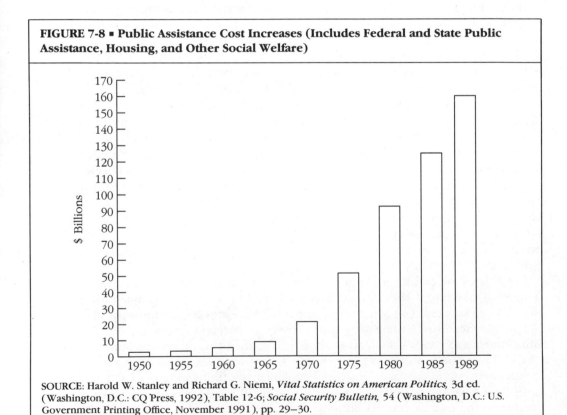

FIGURE 7-8 ▪ **Public Assistance Cost Increases (Includes Federal and State Public Assistance, Housing, and Other Social Welfare)**

SOURCE: Harold W. Stanley and Richard G. Niemi, *Vital Statistics on American Politics,* 3d ed. (Washington, D.C.: CQ Press, 1992), Table 12-6; *Social Security Bulletin,* 54 (Washington, D.C.: U.S. Government Printing Office, November 1991), pp. 29–30.

Recently, the average benefit has been declining as a percentage of median income and of the poverty level. By 1990, the average monthly AFDC stipend had fallen (in constant 1990 dollars) from 1980's level of $148 to $131. This represents less purchasing power than the average stipend had in 1965. The combined AFDC and food stamp benefit dropped 26 percent from 1970 to 1991 in inflation-adjusted dollars. Moreover, there are substantial gaps in public assistance coverage, particularly for single individuals and childless couples under sixty-five. Pegged as they are to the "deserving" poor, public assistance programs contribute little to relieving the poverty of these persons. Few of the programs provide assistance solely on the basis of need; most exclude certain categories of persons from assistance. (See Figure 7-9.)

3. *Unfairness.* Inequity, in two senses, is a problem in public assistance. *Horizontal inequity* refers to the fact that poor persons with the same degree of need frequently do not receive the same degree of aid. *Vertical inequity* refers to a twofold imbalance: the most needy often are not the first to receive aid, and the system sometimes offers very high benefits to some of the poor while providing none for the near poor.

These inequities have two main sources: the variations in benefit levels from state to state, and the categorical nature of the programs. Because eligibility and

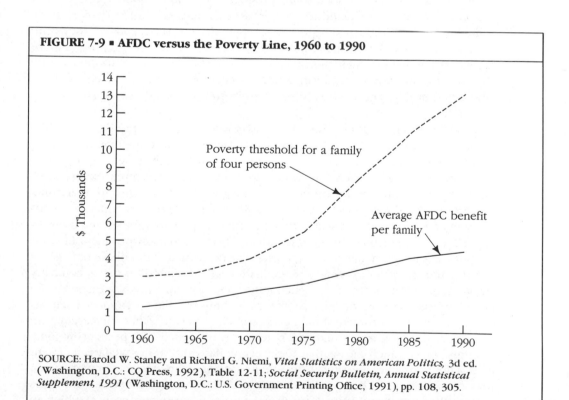

FIGURE 7-9 ▪ AFDC versus the Poverty Line, 1960 to 1990

Poverty threshold for a family of four persons

Average AFDC benefit per family

$ Thousands

SOURCE: Harold W. Stanley and Richard G. Niemi, *Vital Statistics on American Politics,* 3d ed. (Washington, D.C.: CQ Press, 1992), Table 12-11; *Social Security Bulletin, Annual Statistical Supplement, 1991* (Washington, D.C.: U.S. Government Printing Office, 1991), pp. 108, 305.

benefit levels for programs such as AFDC and Medicaid are set by each state, a poor family is eligible for different benefits depending on where it lives. A family with an income of $4,000 in California is eligible for higher benefits (even adjusting for differences in cost of living) than is a family in similar circumstances with the same income in Alabama. It seems inequitable and unfair that families with identical needs are treated differently simply because of where they live. The most generous state provides about six times the AFDC benefit as the least generous state. Similar variations occur because certain categories of people are eligible for benefits but others are not. In some states a poor family with an unemployed father present is eligible; in others it is not. A childless couple under sixty-five may have the same or a greater degree of need as one with one or two children, but they are generally not eligible for benefits. Moreover, families that have an earned income slightly above guidelines are not entitled to support, whereas others without such income may be eligible for a variety of programs, the combined benefit of which makes them better off than the working family. For example, in the average state in 1987, a single mother with three children and no other income was eligible for AFDC and food stamp benefits of $7,656 per year plus Medicaid. The same person who worked all year at a minimum wage job would have an income of $6,968. This kind of vertical inequity contributes to the work disincentive to be considered shortly.

The expansion of the food stamp program and of other in-kind programs has reduced some of these inequities, but substantial ones remain. Moreover, since some kinds of in-kind benefits are tied to eligibility for AFDC and SSI, they reinforce horizontal and vertical inequities. Also, because many in-kind programs are funded at a low level, their benefits are not available to all who are technically eligible. Housing assistance, for example, is received by only a fraction of those who could qualify. Those who receive it are better off than those, equally needy, who do not.

4. Work disincentives. The most universally recognized problem of public assistance is that, despite work requirements, there are discouragements to work built into the very structure of the programs, particularly when the effect of multiple programs is taken into account. Disincentives are often exaggerated, because there is little empirical evidence of large effects, but they are real nonetheless. Work disincentives keep public assistance recipients dependent on assistance even when work is available to them, obviously an unintended and undesirable effect. These disincentives come into play because in many programs benefits are phased out as earned income increases. The rate at which this phase-out occurs is called the *marginal tax rate.* The graduated benefit reductions that accompany rising income were instituted to encourage welfare recipients to work and to be fair to workers not receiving benefits; as a family is able to support itself, its dependence on government should decrease. The problem is that the marginal tax rate of all the programs combined reached or exceeded 100 percent in some circumstances, which means that for every dollar earned, the welfare recipient loses a dollar or more in benefits. Recipients are not inclined to accept work when they can do as well or better without it. In addition to marginal tax rate problems are so-called notch problems. A notch is the point in the benefit scale at which an additional dollar of earnings does not simply reduce benefits but rather makes the person totally ineligible for benefits. The loss of such assistance, particularly of Medicaid for families with health problems, is a strong work disincentive. These work disincentives mean that costs are higher than they could be, that more remain dependent on assistance than is necessary, and that those who work are treated unfairly when compared with those who could but do not.

There are ways of reducing the disincentive, but they have their own problems. Lowering the marginal tax rates and eliminating notches would mean substantial cost increases. Sharply reducing the benefit level would make hunger the spur to work, which is politically and morally unacceptable to most.

5. *Administration.* The problem of administrative complexity is a serious dilemma for public assistance programs of all modern nations and an important reason for their high administrative cost. As Joseph Heffernan pointed out:

> Each program is tailored to a specific problem created by income security (or lack of it), a specific approximate cause of income insecurity, or a specific subpopulation group in need. The result is not an income security system with rationally intersecting and reinforcing elements, but a crazy-quilt pattern of programs, with gaps and over-laps. To the scholar, the public official, the taxpayer, and the recipient alike, the set of programs appears to be a confused tangle because in fact it *is* a confused tangle.[28]

The confusion and complexity are inherent in categorical and means-tested programs because hundreds of questions, forms, and regulations are needed to define categories and levels of need and to establish whether particular persons are needy and fit the defined categories. Multiply this by the determination process for other programs, add periodic rechecking of eligibility to reduce fraud and waste, and the administrative burden of these programs becomes staggering. On top of all this is the complexity of having separate rules and regulations at each level of administration: federal, state, and local. The system is so confusing that substantial sums are often mistakenly overpaid, for the caseworkers are sometimes as bewildered as the clients.

Paradoxically, antifraud regulations contribute to a higher rate of erroneous payments. As more and more regulations are added to close loopholes and as more and more forms are devised to ensure accurate checks of income, the complexity of the program increases. As this happens, program employees are more prone to mistakes; caseworker turnover also increases, and new workers—having had less time on the job—are even more prone to mistake. A double bind operates once more. Public assistance can be either lower in administrative costs and higher in fraud, or higher in administrative costs and lower in fraud. Low overhead and low fraud rates cannot be achieved simultaneously.

6. *Punitive features.* Finally, means-tested public assistance carries with it a degree of degradation for the recipient. Determination of eligibility requires many embarrassing personal questions, long waits in impersonal offices, and possibly home inspections. Often denials of benefits are made for trivial reasons in order to keep the rolls low. The recipient is stigmatized as being poor and unable, or

unwilling, to work. Given American attitudes toward welfare recipients, the use of food stamps brands one as lazy and probably immoral. Although recent court decisions have reduced many of the punitive and degrading aspects of public assistance, others remain.

In sum, the public assistance programs established in the 1930s and modified in the 1960s have worked relatively well for the kinds of poverty they anticipated. They have not worked well for the new poverty found among the underclass, female-headed households, and persons with obsolete job skills. Current reform measures, described in the following section, aim to address the shortcomings of current programs and to attack the new roots of poverty.

FUTURE ALTERNATIVES: SOCIAL SECURITY, WELFARE, THE UNDERCLASS, AND THE HOMELESS

Social Security

There are four different directions in which changes in Social Security can go.[29] The first two do not require fundamental changes; the second two would alter the basic structure of the system. The first direction is to expand the system, particularly by increasing tax revenues to keep the system solvent. The second direction is to preserve the system's solvency by reducing benefits and/or increasing the retirement age. The 1983 reforms combined modest parts of both of these directions, pleasing conservatives with the elements of the second, and liberals with the first. The third direction would change the program's structure by changing the form of the tax or building up a genuine reserve fund from which to pay benefits. The substantial economic consequences of these ideas make them highly improbable. Finally, some propose introducing elements of choice, voluntarism, and competition by wholly or partially replacing the present system with a combination of private pensions and increased public assistance. However, both the entrenched nature of Social Security and the unpopularity of public assistance rule out such a change in the next couple of decades.

Despite its financial troubles, a fundamental reform of Social Security is unlikely. The very size of the program in revenues, expenditures, and number of participants means that any basic change would be a major disruption of the political, economic, and social systems. Moreover, the program changes described in the preceding section have put off the financial crisis for some time and have at least partially satisfied powerful interests. Social Security is a dangerous political issue, one on which to avoid controversy.

Yet pressing issues in Social Security remain. Perhaps the most important is the relationship between the Social Security Trust Fund and the federal budget deficit. Because of the 1983 Social Security reforms, the trust fund builds up surpluses each year. In 1988, the surplus was $40 billion; by the middle 1990s, the surplus will approach $100 billion per year. These surpluses will occur until approximately 2030, reaching an estimated $12 trillion in that year. That enormous sum of money will help pay the Social Security benefits of the baby-boom generation, and these payments are expected to exhaust the surplus by the year 2050.

All of this seems a long way off. What is the immediate problem? Simply this: The Social Security surplus (and smaller surpluses in the Medicare, federal-employee retirement, and unemployment trust funds) is counted against the deficit generated by current spending and taxing. Thus, if the various trust fund surpluses had not been counted, the 1988 deficit would have been $255 billion instead of $155 billion. Moreover, the trust funds are invested in the government securities that fund the deficit. That is, we are borrowing from the trust funds, especially Social Security, to support current deficit spending. The borrowed funds, however, will eventually have to be paid back (ultimately to the tune of $12 trillion) when the trust funds have to be used for paying retirees. That would require an enormous tax hike or other borrowing from the general public.

The alternatives are, first, to continue the present course, which is the most likely because the illusions it depends upon remain politically palatable. This alternative postpones the dilemma for a couple of decades. The second choice is to cut the Social Security payroll tax so that the surpluses do not accumulate. Reduction of Social Security taxes is attractive for another reason. These taxes have accounted for a major part of the heavy tax burden on young middle-class families. Although the income tax burden for such families has increased modestly, their total burden has been greatly increased by the higher rate of Social Security taxes paid on an ever-higher wage base. This choice, however, means that the retirement of the baby-boom generation would have to be supported entirely by payroll taxes of the next generation, an enormous burden at that time. The final alternative is to raise income and other taxes and to cut spending in order to make a substantial dent in the real deficit. This is the most realistic, but also the most politically and economically painful (in the short run) alternative.

Pensions.   As noted in the Evaluation section, private pensions have become a major part of the resources of the elderly, supplementing and in many cases outweighing the benefits of Social Security. In 1974, Congress passed the Employment Retirement Income Security Act (ERISA) in order to provide a federal guarantee for many private pension funds. ERISA was designed to make sure that pension funds would indeed be available at retirement time for those counting on them. This legislation, however, insures only about one of every eight pension plans covering about half of all workers. Other workers have little or no insurance for their pension funds.

Two problems loom on the horizon. First, the twenty-year trend toward growing numbers of workers being covered by pensions reversed itself in the late 1980s. Currently, only about 44 percent of the work force is covered by a pension plan. This means that in the future more workers will be more dependent on Social Security. Second, the pension industry shows signs of going the way of the savings and loan industry. The United States has almost 900,000 private pension plans, with assets of $2 trillion, covering 76 million persons. In 1989, the Department of

Labor's Inspector General's Office issued a warning that over 25 percent of the plans audited were in violation of regulations protecting their funds. In some cases, adequate funds were not being put into the pensions, or funds were being siphoned off by administrators to cover business losses or to pay other business expenses. When a guaranteed pension plan fails, it becomes the responsibility of the federal Pension Benefit Guaranty Corporation to bail it out. The corporation is currently running a deficit of $1.5 billion and may be out of funds by the end of the decade. The federal government will have to act soon to make sure that private pension funds continue to be available to those counting on them.

Public Assistance

Both liberals and conservatives tacitly acknowledge progress in eliminating poverty and focus on the problems in public assistance programs themselves: inequities, cost, disincentives, and administrative complexity. Yet, despite numerous proposals by presidents, legislators, and scholars, welfare reform until recently remained bogged down. First, although most agree on the main issues, they disagree on the priority assigned them. Liberals stress inadequate benefits, horizontal inequities, and indignities to which recipients are subjected. Conservatives stress program cost, vertical inequities, and work disincentives. Radicals argue that the principal need is not welfare reform but income redistribution and basic economic change. Second, the various solutions to the problems in welfare contradict one another. Making benefit levels more adequate would increase program costs, increase work disincentives, and possibly widen vertical inequities. Eliminating notches and lowering the marginal tax rate would boost costs tremendously and make the programs less efficient in reaching those who need the most help. Reducing costs would likely result in inadequate benefits, greater horizontal inequities, greater program complexity, and greater indignity for recipients. The main problems in public assistance are normative, not technical. Any version of welfare reform will require difficult choices among competing values of poverty reduction, benefit adequacy, low cost, equity, incentives, target efficiency, administrative efficiency, and decent treatment of recipients.

Conservative welfare reform.   The conservative program of welfare reform aims at preventing and alleviating poverty but places equal stress on making sure that only the truly needy receive benefits and that the benefits do not create widespread welfare dependency.[30] Conservative proposals are rooted in the concept of the deserving poor as discussed in the Background section on the causes of poverty. Thus they would continue the categorical nature of current programs and increase efforts to eliminate fraud. An enforceable, fair, and clear work requirement would be a condition of receiving aid. Intact families are the best guarantee that women and children will not fall into poverty; therefore conservatives call for policies encouraging families to stay together. Failing that, they believe that child support requirements should be rigorously enforced. Conservative reformists also argue that administrative responsibility should be shifted as much as possible to state and local governments. Because the free market is the best antipoverty mechanism, private institutions to help the poor and to provide job training should be encouraged by continuing tax credits for charitable contributions. If such reforms could be implemented, conservatives argue, unnecessary programs could be eliminated, fraud and waste reduced, the welfare rolls trimmed, and benefits to the truly needy increased.

Critics of this approach point to a number of problems. Emphasizing only the truly needy, tightening work requirements, and attacking fraud and waste all would require additional regulations that would add to administrative costs and confusion. Moreover, critics contend, work requirements have not worked in the past and are unlikely to work in the future unless the kinds of job training and child care facilities opposed by conservatives are available. And shifting administration to the state and local levels may save some money, but only at the cost of increasing inequities. Finally, critics point out, the idea of the deserving poor is obsolete in a modern, affluent, industrial economy. Conservative reforms would leave many of the poor unprotected by public assistance.

Liberal welfare reform.   Liberal proposals for incremental expansion as the mode of welfare reform involve a great many particular measures.[31] The most important would be the establishment of a national minimum benefit by standardizing AFDC and food stamp eligibility and, in many versions, the federal takeover of all funding and administration of these programs. States could supplement the national minimum and receive federal help to do so. The Earned Income Tax Credit should be more generous, and public service jobs should be expanded. Various in-kind benefits such as housing, nutrition, medical care, and job training, should be expanded to cover all eligible. Special emphasis would be on in-kind programs, including food stamps, because public attitudes favor providing services and in-kind benefits more than providing money. Therefore a more adequate standard of living is likely to be supported if in-kind benefits are a significant part of the program. National Health Insurance, discussed in the following chapter, would eliminate an important work disincentive notch.

Opponents of incremental growth see a number of flaws in this set of proposals. First, they make no attempt to reduce the complexity and inefficiency of the present jumble of programs. In fact, by expanding benefits, these proposals would increase administrative costs, fraud, and error. Opponents also argue that the cost of these changes would be enormous. A national minimum benefit would reduce inequities only if it were set so high that the cost would be prohibitive. Expanded benefits and increased adequacy of payments would also not improve work incentives. They might, in fact, increase the disincentive effect. These proposals, critics charge, simply mean more of the same problems, costs, and inefficiencies that now plague public assistance.

Guaranteed minimum income reform.   Those who favor more thorough structural reform of welfare are a mixed group, including liberals, conservatives, neoconservatives, and some radicals, who favor some form of guaranteed minimum cash income to replace the existing structure of cash and in-kind programs.

Proposals for a comprehensive cash assistance program come in a variety of versions, but the basic structure is the same whether they feature a system of income tax credits, a system of grants, or a combination of grants and tax credits. All Guaranteed Annual Income (GAI) or Negative Income Tax (NIT) proposals would reduce the present number of categorical programs and provide a basic cash minimum income (variable according to family size) below which a family cannot fall. Also essential is a break-even point (also variable by family size), which is the maximum income above which assistance would not be given. Between the income floor and ceiling a marginal tax rate of less than 100 percent (usually 50 percent) would be applied to earnings as a work incentive. Suppose, for example, the minimum for a family of four were to be $10,000 and the maximum $18,000. Families with no earnings or earnings below the floor would receive $10,000 per year. Families with earnings between $10,000 and $18,000 would receive 50 percent of the deficit between their earnings and the maximum. Thus a family of four earning $11,000 would receive $11,000 plus $3,500 for a total of $14,500. Families earning $18,000 or above would receive no aid. The idea is that the family always would have more by working than by not working.

Guaranteed Annual Income proposals were made by President Nixon in 1969 (Family Assistance Plan) and by President Carter in 1977 (Program for Better Jobs and Income). Neither plan passed Congress, as the combination of conservative and liberal objections overwhelmed any chance of success. By the late 1980s, public assistance reform issues had moved in a new direction.

Family Support Act.   A consensus among different ideological groups allowed the passage of a welfare reform measure in 1988.[32] Liberals came to understand that the relative unpopularity of public assistance programs allowed President Reagan to succeed in cutting them back. Moreover, the reality of the budget deficit limited new spending initiatives. Finally, states and local governments showed some promise of creative efforts. Thus liberals came to realize that large increases in spending were not possible; that there must be a role for state and local experimentation; that different poverty populations require different solutions; and that new programs must be fiscally sound; that is, savings have to be found to offset new spending.

Conservatives had to concede that their all-out attack on public assistance programs during the Reagan administration had failed to eliminate the basic system of public assistance. Therefore conservatives had to acknowledge that there is a poverty problem and that the federal government will remain the major player in attacking it. Moreover, they admitted that employment and child care programs must be strengthened and that doing so costs money.

These realizations on both sides produced the following rough consensus: First, both public assistance recipients and government have obligations to make welfare a temporary aid to self-sufficiency, as originally intended. In exchange for education, employment training, and benefits for living expenses, the recipient must follow through with seeking and keeping employment. If not, benefits should be reduced. The idea is to break the cycle of poverty by focusing on education, job training, strong family life, and a strong work history. Second, because of the feminization of poverty, child care for recipients must be available and subsidized by government. Along these lines, major federal child care legislation was passed in 1990. It provided federal grants to state governments and to parents to set up and to pay for expanded child care facilities. Third, education is a primary route out of poverty. Parents and children need improved education programs to acquire the skills necessary for self-support. Fourth, fathers must play a more central role in family support. Families should stay together whenever possible; therefore, the AFDC-UP (Unemployed Parent) program should be mandatory in all states. Absent fathers should be required to pay child support; therefore, a federal-state network should be set up to enforce such payments. Fifth, jobs and job training have to be strengthened and recipients required to work whenever possible. Finally, federal, state, and local taxes on the poor and near-poor should be reduced.

There is a recognition primarily that the poor are not an undifferentiated group. There are, first of all, the elderly and disabled, for whom direct income assistance is probably the most appropriate form of aid. Indeed, it is this group that has been most assisted out of poverty in the last two decades, particularly by Social Security increases. But additional public assistance is still needed to help the poorest of the elderly and disabled. A second group of the poor is single mothers with young children. If they are to be moved out of poverty, they need child care, child support from absent fathers, health insurance, and assistance in finding jobs. Another group is the working poor, who are underemployed or employed only part-time or at minimum wage. Their primary need is job training for higher-wage skills, remedial education, health insurance, and unemployment compensation when jobs run out. Finally, there is the urban "underclass," to be discussed below. What is clear is that no single, simple program can address all the needs of these diverse groups.

The Family Support Act of 1988 embodied many of these ideas. The act makes marginal improvements in AFDC benefit levels by making eligibility slightly more generous. It makes the AFDC-UP program mandatory in all states and requires at least one parent in a two-parent AFDC-UP family to work, even if this means community service or other unpaid work. The Family Support Act also requires the states to establish an education, training, and employment program for public assistance recipients. The program is called Job Opportunities and Basic Skills (JOBS), and each state must enroll at least 20 percent of its cases in this program by 1995. Public assistance recipients will be required to participate in the JOBS program as long as adequate child care and other necessary services are available. Recipients who refuse to participate will lose a portion of benefits. The states must also guarantee child care, transportation, and other services needed to allow recipients to participate. The act also mandates stricter enforcement of child support orders, including automatic wage-withholding of court-ordered support payments. In addition, states are required to provide a year of child care and Medicaid benefits to those leaving public assistance for work.

Future issues in public assistance lie in monitoring the success of these measures, for the act leaves much to be done in some of the most important areas. First, it does not appropriate a great deal of money for job-training programs, which are very expensive. In an economy with a rapidly changing technological base, adequate public and private job-training initiatives will be very important in keeping people out of poverty.

The second issue is creating jobs for public assistance recipients. Little in the bill addresses job creation for those required to work as a condition of receiving assistance. If jobs are to be guaranteed to recipients, what effects will this have on local labor markets? Although state experiments with job requirements have had some success, the picture is very mixed and substantial questions remain, including the shape of the economy, the relative effectiveness of services versus sanctions in achieving employment, and the effectiveness of comprehensive remedial programs versus simple job location programs.[33]

Third, the Family Support Act does not go far enough toward managing health care issues, which create the most severe "notch" problems and disincentives to leave public assistance. Families without job-related or other health insurance simply cannot afford to leave public assistance that provides Medicaid benefits. This is especially true of families with children or families with severe health problems, and the poor have generally greater health needs than the rest of the population.

Fourth, child care provisions in the bill do not go far enough toward providing child care assistance for working parents or for setting up additional day-care facilities. More vigorous child support enforcement will remove at most 200,000 families from the welfare rolls.

On all of these issues there are disagreements among liberals, conservatives, and radicals on program emphasis and implementation. Moreover, none of the reforms attacks the problems of inadequacy of benefits or of horizontal inequities in the current system. Even if the Family Support Act is very successful, millions of persons will remain in poverty and on public assistance.

State experiments.   Some states have begun to take a more aggressive stance regarding public assistance. They are experimenting with a variety of incentives and punishments that make benefit levels depend upon the behavior of recipients. Wisconsin has had the most visible profile. Going beyond the work and job-training requirements called for in the Family Support Act, in 1988 it instituted a "Learnfare" program. Learnfare requires children 13 to 19 from welfare families to attend school regularly. Benefits may be cut up to $100 per month if children are truant. States such as California and Maryland have proposed or adopted requirements that would require teenage mothers on public assistance to live with a parent or guardian and to attend school, on penalty of benefit reduction. Other proposals would increase benefits when public assistance parents marry or when women accept long-term birth control implants, as an incentive to break the cycle of single-parent families. New Jersey in 1991 adopted regulations that deny benefits of $64 per month to additional children born while the family is receiving public assistance.

Although the incentives and punishments embodied in these measures seem commonsensical, there has been little research to substantiate any cost savings or effectiveness in moving persons off public assistance. Moreover, critics charge that they are costly to administer, punish children unfairly for the behavior of their parents, and may encourage punished parents to turn to illicit sources of income, such as prostitution and drugs.

Children, the Underclass, and the Homeless

The three most intractable income support issues are those related to the large number of children spending all or part of their childhood in poverty, to the "underclass," and to the growing numbers of homeless persons in our country.

Children and poverty.   As reported in the first section of this chapter, children are disproportionately poor. One out of every five are below the official poverty line at any given time, and many more live in poverty for at least part of their childhood. Moreover, children are increasingly living in single-parent families. Many go for years without seeing their fathers, even for short visits. Twenty-five percent of all children under eighteen live in single-parent households, and about half of all children will live in such a household at some time while growing up.

The problems of children related to poverty and family breakup include poor education, teenage pregnancy, child abuse, suicide, drug addiction, and high crime rates. Moreover, poorly educated, addicted, abused, or imprisoned children will hardly grow up to be productive citizens in a competitive world economy.

Despite these problems, government spending on children has declined in recent years, particularly when compared with spending on the elderly. In 1965, government spending on the elderly was 21 percent of all income maintenance and other social welfare spending while 37 percent went to children. By the late 1980s, spending on children was 24 percent and spending for the elderly reached 33 percent. Such spending lifted out of poverty 82 percent of the elderly who would have been poor without government programs. Only 32 percent of children escaped poverty through such spending.[34]

Other nations have far more generous programs for children, without slighting the elderly. Most, for example, have a universal children's allowance, amounting to from 5 to 10 percent of the median wage. They also provide cash benefits to parents at the time of childbirth, as well as allowances that support a parent for taking time away from work in the first months of the child's life. Preschool and child care programs are also generously supported in other nations.

Many proposals are being advanced at the federal and state level to attack the problem of child poverty and its associated social problems. At the federal level, the equivalent of a children's allowance has been proposed by some members of Congress. This allowance could be in the form of a grant of $1,000 per year for each child in a family. It would cost approximately $65 billion, but some of the cost could be regained if the grant were taxable income to higher-income families. Variations of this proposal involve raising the income tax exemption for dependents, the value of which has dramatically declined as a result of inflation. Some propose doubling the exemption to $4,300 per child or converting it into an $800 tax credit.

Other proposals at the federal and state levels include increased funding for

Head Start and other preschool programs, extending Medicaid coverage to larger numbers of poor children, and expansion of the food stamp and WIC programs to ensure adequate early childhood nutrition. It should be noted, however, that many of these proposals for increased state funding have been accompanied by reductions in the basic AFDC payment, as discussed above. It is often a matter of giving with one hand, while taking away with the other!

One measure that has been widely adopted and has been in place for some time is strengthened enforcement of court-ordered child support payments by absent fathers. Thousands of absent parents are in arrears on these payments, which is one of the reasons why single-parent families have such a high poverty rate. States, in cooperation with the federal government, have developed extensive networks for locating absent fathers and for enforcing child support payments with garnishment of paychecks and threats of imprisonment. If all such awards were collected, it would be possible to reduce AFDC rolls by 20 percent and AFDC costs by one-third. The complexity of the problem, however, is indicated by the fact that the size of awards and rates of payment have actually declined during the 1980s, at a time of increased enforcement efforts.[35]

The underclass.   Definitions and estimates of the underclass vary, and some policy analysts reject the term itself. But, however defined, the problem is serious. *Underclass* certainly does not refer to all or most of the poor, but primarily to the long-term poor. Yet people are poor for years at a time for a variety of reasons; lack of income is only part of the problem. The underclass are those persistent poor, who also have serious educational, family, attitudinal, job-skills, and emotional-psychological problems. They also tend to live in areas in which such problems are endemic to a large proportion of the population.

As Sheldon Danziger points out,

> All agree that the underclass comprises only a small percentage of the poverty population. . . . [It includes] poverty over relatively long periods; poverty that is geographically concentrated; poverty that is associated with dysfunctional behavior; and poverty that is transmitted through its effects on the attitudes and behavior of the next generation.[36]

The underclass, then, refers not simply to the persistently poor, but to the long-term poor also living in desperately run-down neighborhoods, deeply involved in teen pregnancy, drugs, crime, and poor education and job skills. Most estimates of the urban underclass population are about two to three million persons, or about seven to ten percent of the poverty population.[37]

Disagreement about the causes of underclass poverty and its growth during the last two decades are rooted in two different explanations, associated with the liberal and conservative explanations of poverty discussed in the first section of this chapter. Liberal structural explanations focus on racial discrimination and the disappearance of entry-level manual labor jobs in the urban marketplace, combined with the flight of the black and white middle classes to the suburbs. This leaves a sizable population of unemployed and unemployable persons behind, concentrated in the inner cities of major metropolitan areas. The conservative explanation focuses on a culture of poverty, dependency, and antisocial behavior passed from generation to generation in ghetto areas. Many researchers are now coming to accept that both explanations may contain part of the truth.

The underclass presents a special challenge to income support policy. It is particularly hard to reach with traditional programs to alleviate or cure poverty. This class seems immune to periods of economic improvement and to traditional compensatory social programs. Because there are multiple dimensions to underclass poverty, multiple approaches are needed to attack it. Simply increasing public assistance spending will not work. Job skills must be cultivated and transportation to job sites provided so that underclass persons can compete for skilled labor positions.

But job skills depend also on qualities of law-abidingness, marriage before childbirth, going to work every day, literacy, and many other factors that the middle class takes for granted. Programs to change attitudes, provide rehabilitation from drug and alcohol addiction, and improve education and the health of children must all be brought to bear over a long period, not just on a hit-or-miss basis. Many of the child support programs described above are also called for by students of the underclass. What is needed is an intensive effort to enable children to arrive at adulthood properly educated, healthy, and prepared for jobs. To do so takes commitment to the underclass and the money and creativity to support that commitment.

Homelessness. Also important is decent housing. Newspaper and television stories have brought before the American public the plight of one portion of America's underclass, the homeless. For example, a December, 1991, Associated Press story described some of the one hundred or so shantytowns that now exist in New York City. These groupings of "dwellings" made from garbage bags, cardboard, sheets, and wood scraps are located throughout the city, housing some two to three thousand persons, a fraction of the estimated 70,000 homeless in New York.[38]

Homelessness cannot be understood apart from American housing generally. Despite substantial cuts in housing programs for the poor during the 1980s, there were no cuts in housing subsidies for the well-to-do, chiefly mortgage interest deductions but also including FHA and VA insurance. The property tax and mortgage interest deductions were worth $38.8 billion in foregone federal taxes in fiscal year 1988, and 52 percent of those benefits went to the 17 percent of the population making $50,000 a year or more. In contrast, the 58 percent of the population making $30,000 or less received only 30 percent of the benefits.[39] Home ownership is increasingly difficult for the lower-middle class, and housing for the poor becomes scarcer and more expensive.

The problem is not due simply to lack of housing stock. In many cities there are significant vacancy rates. Rather, the problem is lack of affordable low-cost housing. Much of this housing was demolished in recent decades to make room for office buildings and upper-income condominiums. Public housing units have not been built to replace them, nor have housing allowances or subsidies been sufficient to stimulate building or rehabilitation of low-cost units.[40]

At the same time, poverty is increasing, jobs are becoming more scarce for the unskilled, and greater numbers of mental patients have been released from hospitals and residential programs. All of these factors have contributed to the increasing numbers of homeless in the United States. Estimates of the number of homeless persons in this country range from 250,000 to 3 million, but the best estimates seem to be about 350,000 persons in 1988, with the number growing quite rapidly.[41] The long-term homeless are predominantly male, single, living alone, disproportionately nonwhite, and have little attachment to the labor force. They are also mainly young persons with below-average education, low prior incomes, and few job skills. A considerable number, though not a majority, have spent time in mental hospitals, and a fairly large number are alcoholics or drug addicts. The new homeless tend to be women, parents, and married persons with little history of mental illness or alcoholism. Rather, lack of stable family connections and low incomes have forced them from their last housing. For many of the new and old homeless, living on the streets or in shelters is a recurring rather than a permanent phenomenon, but for a substantial number it is a permanent condition.

Although the news media have brought the plight of the homeless directly and poignantly to the attention of ordinary citizens and policymakers, there has been little response at the federal level. Much of what has been done has been accomplished by local governments and private agencies with local funds. These efforts have been addressed almost solely to alleviating immediate needs for food, shelter, and medical care. Local governments and private agencies lack the resources to provide permanent solutions or permanent housing.

The major policy initiatives at the federal level are the 1987 McKinney Homeless Assistance Act and the Cranston-Gonzalez National Affordable Housing Act of 1990. The former provided Emergency Shelter grants to state, city, and county governments from the Department of Housing and Urban Development (HUD) and appropriated $73.2 million for such grants for 1990. HUD also is authorized to develop a Supportive Housing Demonstration Program to provide funds ($126.8 million in 1990) to local governments for projects helping the homeless toward independent living. The act also made available $73.2 million for assistance in renting single-room occupancy dwellings in 1987. Finally, the McKinney Act requires the federal government to identify all surplus federal property that could be used to shelter the homeless.

Funding for the National Affordable Housing Act did not begin until 1992. It provides rental housing assistance in connection with services for homeless people with disabilities, particularly persons seriously mentally ill, having chronic alcohol or drug problems, or having AIDS and related diseases.

The problem of homelessness is really three problems, and each requires a different set of actions to be of real efficacy.[42] The first group is down-on-their-luck individuals and families, especially children. Recession, loss of affordable housing, and marginal job skills affect this group. Many low-income persons are just one paycheck away from homelessness. Loss of the job or serious medical problems push them over the brink. Attacking their lack of housing requires not just housing vouchers or other assistance with shelter, but also remedial education, vocational training, and other employment counseling.

Another large group of the homeless is the seriously mentally ill, especially those suffering from schizophrenia. Their homelessness is at least in part a result of the breakdown of the system of mental health care in the United States. Since 1960, various policies at the federal and state levels have produced deinstitutionalization of many of the mentally ill. However, inadequate community mental health services and lack of a comprehensive system of tracking and supporting the noninstitutionalized mentally ill result in many being left alone on their own meager resources. Attacking the problem of their homelessness means also providing a coherent system of treatment, housing, and rehabilitation.

Finally, alcoholism and drug addiction are the cause for many persons' homelessness. As with the mentally ill, rehabilitation and vocational programs are needed for them as much as provision of food and shelter.

Homelessness is simply the most visible of the serious future issues in the area of income support. Just as important are the intersecting issues of the underclass and the poverty of children. Reform of the present systems of social insurance and public assistance will not be sufficient without a concentrated effort to address these issues as well.

SUMMARY

Poverty may be defined in absolute or relative terms. Absolute definitions vary, but the most widely used are the Social Security Administration's definition and a measure based on the Department of Agriculture's "economy food plan." Relative poverty is usually defined as half the median family income.

The extent of poverty in the United States depends on the definition used. The SSA standard estimates poverty at 13.5 percent of the population, whereas other definitions produce a higher proportion of 20 percent. Counting in-kind benefits, making other adjustments, and using the SSA standard indicate approximately 10 percent of the population in poverty.

Although poverty was reduced during the 1960s and 1970s, the incidence of poverty is still high among racial minorities, children, female-headed families, rural dwellers, central-city residents, and persons with minimal education. The semipermanent poverty "underclass" is a growing problem in many cities.

The causes of poverty are subject to heated ideological debate. Conservatives and neoconservatives largely blame the poor themselves and government programs that encourage dependency. Liberals see lack of opportunity, discrimination, and technological change as the principal causes of poverty. Radicals point to the structural flaws of the capitalist economic and political system.

In this chapter we have examined the national income support system, which may be divided into three categories: social insurance (requiring contributions as a condition of benefits), public assistance (financed categorically from general revenues), and antipoverty programs (various employment and job-training efforts). Aid may be provided in cash or as in-kind benefits.

Social insurance programs began with the Social Security Act of 1935. Old Age, Survivors, Disability, and Health Insurance (OASDHI) is financed by payroll taxes on employers and employees; expenditures have increased rapidly in the last decade. Unemployment insurance is financed by taxes on an employer's payroll, and payments are made to workers who are involuntarily jobless for temporary periods.

Public assistance programs, which provide assistance to certain categories of persons whose circumstances place them in poverty, also trace their ancestry to the Social Security Act. Principal cash assistance programs are AFDC, SSI, and General Assistance. Food stamps, Medicaid, housing assistance, nutrition, and education programs constitute the bulk of in-kind aid. All of these programs grew rapidly until 1975 but then slowed down.

European income support programs are similar to U.S. efforts but are available to a wider spectrum of the population and are less stigmatizing. America lags in expenditures, benefit levels, and family allowances. Despite the claims of some, the United States is not a welfare state.

OASDHI and unemployment insurance have been highly successful, with relatively high public approval. Serious questions, especially with the inflation of the 1970s, have emerged, however, concerning the long-term financial soundness of these programs. Debate focuses on how the program should be financed, how long-term population trends will affect payroll taxes and benefits, the appropriate retirement age, whether equity or adequacy of benefits should be more strongly emphasized, and, in the case of unemployment insurance, the declining percentage of the unemployed who are supported. Important Social Security reforms were enacted in 1983 but are unlikely to solve its long-term problems.

Evaluations of employment policies vary according to ideological perspectives. Conservatives find little value in job training and employment programs unless they are carried out by private enterprise. Liberals find such programs generally successful. Socialists and Marxists argue that such programs are not fully successful unless accompanied by radical change in the economic structure.

Public assistance has had substantial success in alleviating the worst effects of poverty, ill health, poor nutrition, and inadequate housing. Despite stereotypes of "welfare cheaters," most recipients of AFDC, food stamps, and Medicaid use them as they were intended: for temporary emergency relief. The primary failings of public assistance are high total program cost, inadequacy of benefits, horizontal and vertical inequities, work disincentives, excessive complexity and inefficiency in administration, and punitive features in some programs.

Three main types of welfare reform are commonly advocated. Conservatives tend to favor minor restructuring to tighten eligibility, require recipients to work, and reduce fraud and overall cost. Liberals and some radicals favor expanding existing programs in incremental fashion by increasing benefits, broadening eligibility, and raising funding levels. On the other hand, scrapping much of the present system in favor of a Guaranteed Annual Income or Negative Income Tax has found some support across the ideological spectrum.

The most important future issue in Social Security, aside from traditional debates over payroll taxes and benefit levels, is the impact of the current trust fund surplus on the federal budget deficit. With respect to public assistance programs, the most significant future issues are those initially addressed in the Family Support Act of 1988: job creation and job training, work requirements, child care, child support by absent fathers, family stability, education, and adequate benefit levels. The enormous problems of children in poverty, the urban underclass, and the homeless are other issues that will challenge income-support policy in the future.

NOTES

1. Joe R. Feagin, "America's Welfare Stereotypes," *Social Science Quarterly*, 52 (March 1972), 921–933; Lester M. Salamon, *Welfare: The Elusive Consensus* (New York: Praeger, 1978), appendix B. See Hugh Heclo, "The Political Foundations of Antipoverty Policy," in Sheldon H. Danziger and Daniel H. Weinberg, eds., *Fighting Poverty: What Works and What Doesn't* (Cambridge: Harvard University Press, 1986), pp. 312–340. The situation is not very different in other nations. See Richard Coughlin, *Ideology, Public Opinion, and Welfare Policy* (Berkeley, Calif.: Institute of International Studies, 1980).

2. Michael Harrington, *The Other America: Poverty in the United States* (Baltimore: Penguin, 1963), p. 175.

3. Harrell R. Rodgers, Jr., *Poverty amid Plenty: A Political and Economic Analysis* (Reading, Mass.: Addison-Wesley, 1979), pp. 18–30; and Leonard Beeghley, *Living Poorly in America* (New York: Praeger, 1983), pp. 17–38.

4. Rodgers, *Poverty amid Plenty*, pp. 24–25. Data on the number of persons below 125 percent of the SSA poverty figure are from U.S. Bureau of the Census, *Current Population Reports*, series P-60, No. 161 (Washington, D.C.: U.S. Government Printing Office, August 1988), Table 17.

5. Edward N. Wolff, "The Distribution of Household Wealth," in Lars Osberg, ed., *Economic Inequality and Poverty: International Perspectives* (Armonk, N.Y.: Sharpe, 1991), pp. 92–133.

6. See Irving Kristol, *Two Cheers for Capitalism* (New York: NAL, 1978), pp. 203–204 and chap. 23.

7. See Institute for Research on Poverty, *Focus*, 13 (Fall and Winter, 1991), 17–18; also Christopher Jencks, "Is the American Underclass Growing?" in Christopher Jencks and Paul E. Peterson, eds., *The Urban Underclass* (Washington, D.C.: Brookings Institution, 1991), pp. 32–35.

8. See Timothy J. Smeeding, "Cross-National Comparisons of Inequality and Poverty Position," in Lars Osberg, ed., *Economic Inequality and Poverty: International Perspectives* (Armonk, N.Y.: Sharpe, 1991), pp. 39–59; and Arnold J. Heidenheimer et al., *Comparative Public Policy*, 3rd ed. (New York: St. Martin's Press, 1990), chap. 7. Note that all developed countries now find that poverty is increasingly concentrated in female-headed families. See discussion below and Gertrude Schaffner Goldberg and Eleanor Kremen, eds., *The Feminization of Poverty: Only in America?* (Westport, Conn.: Praeger, 1990).

9. Sara McLanahan, "The Consequences of Single Parenthood for Subsequent Generations," *Focus*, 11 (Fall 1988), 16–21.

10. For helpful surveys of these trends, see Isabel V. Sawhill, "Poverty and the Underclass," in Isabel V. Sawhill, ed., *Challenge to Leadership* (Washington, D.C.: Urban Institute, 1988), 215–252; John E. Schwarz, *America's Hidden Success*, rev. ed. (New York: Norton, 1988), chap. 6; and Danziger and Weinberg, eds., *Fighting Poverty*.

11. For a discussion of various theories, see Chaim I. Waxman, *The Stigma of Poverty*, 2d ed. (Elmsford, N.Y.: Pergamon, 1983).

12. For review of the evidence, see Danziger and Weinberg, eds., *Fighting Poverty*, chaps. 3, 9, 10.

13. For summaries of all these causes, see James Tobin, "The Poverty Problem: 1964 and 1989," *Focus*, 12 (Spring 1990), 6–7; and "1991 Green Book," *Focus*, 13 (Fall and Winter, 1991), 14–18.

14. See Michael F. Gutowski and Jeffrey J. Koshel, "Social Services," in John L. Palmer and Isabel V. Sawhill, eds., *The Reagan Experiment* (Washington, D.C.: Urban Institute, 1982), pp. 307–328.

15. For an excellent summary of the development of public assistance programs, see Paul E. Peterson and Mark C. Rom, *Welfare Magnets: The Case for a New National Standard* (Washington, D.C.: Brookings Institution, 1990), esp. chap. 4.

16. Peter T. Gottschalk, "Retrenchment in Antipoverty Programs in the United States: Lessons for the Future," in B. B. Kymlicka and Jean V. Matthews, eds., *The Reagan Revolution?* (Chicago: Dorsey Press, 1988), pp. 131–145; Spencer Rich, "Falling through the Reagan Safety Net," *The Washington Post National Weekly Edition,* December 26, 1988–January 1, 1989, 6–7.

17. For evaluation of the War on Poverty, see Marshall Kaplan and Peggy L. Cuciti, eds., *The Great Society and Its Legacy* (Durham, N.C.: Duke University Press, 1986).

18. See Norman Furniss and Timothy Tilton, *The Case for the Welfare State* (Bloomington: Indiana University Press, 1977); and Alfred J. Kahn and Sheila B. Kamerman, *Not for the Poor Alone: European Social Services* (New York: Harper Colophon Books, 1977). See also Robert Haveman, Barbara Wolfe, and Victor Halberstadt, "The European Welfare State in Transition," in John L. Palmer, ed., *Perspectives on the Reagan Years* (Washington, D.C.: Urban Institute, 1986), pp. 147–173.

19. This section draws heavily on Heidenheimer et al., *Comparative Public Policy,* chap. 7; Richard L. Siegel and Leonard B. Weinberg, *Comparing Public Policies* (Homewood, Ill.: Dorsey Press, 1977), chap. 6; and Kahn and Kamerman, *Not for the Poor Alone.* See also Hugh Heclo, *Modern Social Politics in Britain and Sweden* (New Haven, Conn.: Yale University Press, 1974); and Howard M. Leichter and Harrell R. Rodgers, Jr., *American Public Policy in a Comparative Context* (New York: McGraw-Hill, 1984), chap. 2.

20. Edward S. Greenberg, *Serving the Few* (New York: John Wiley, 1974); Beeghley, *Living Poorly,* pp. 45–48.

21. Martha Derthick, *Policymaking for Social Security* (Washington, D.C.: Brookings Institution, 1979), esp. p. 215. See also Charles W. Meyer and Nancy L. Wolff, "Intercohort and Intracohort Redistribution under Social Security," in Charles W. Meyer, ed., *Social Security* (Lexington, Mass.: Heath, 1987), pp. 49–68.

22. Peter J. Ferrara, *Social Security* (Washington, D.C.: Cato Institute, 1982); Carolyn L. Weaver, *The Crisis in Social Security* (Durham, N.C.: Duke University Press, 1982); Meyer, *Social Security;* and Susan M. Wachter, ed., *Social Security and Private Pensions* (Lexington, Mass.: Heath, 1988).

23. Jean-Jacques Rosa, ed., *World Crisis in Social Security* (San Francisco: Institute for Contemporary Studies, 1982); Heidenheimer et al., *Comparative Public Policy,* pp. 248–265.

24. See Danziger and Weinberg, eds., *Fighting Poverty,* chaps. 6 & 10; also Schwarz, *America's Hidden Success,* pp. 42–48.

25. Schwarz, *America's Hidden Success,* chap. 2.

26. Government tax and transfer payments have little effect on redistributing income among groups and in reducing inequality. See Patricia Ruggles, "The Impact of Government Tax and Expenditure Programs on the Distribution of Income in the United States," in Osberg, ed., *Economic Inequality and Poverty,* pp. 220–245.

27. Glenn Tinder, "Defending the Welfare State," *New Republic,* March 10, 1979, pp. 21–23.

28. W. Joseph Heffernan, *Introduction to Social Policy* (Itasca, Ill.: Peacock, 1979), pp. 161–162. Emphasis in original.

29. For a discussion of these directions, see Ferrara, *Social Security,* and Weaver, *Crisis in Social Security,* pp. 190–193.

30. See Stuart M. Butler and Anna Kondratas, *Out of the Poverty Trap: A Conservative Strategy of Welfare Reform* (New York: Free Press, 1987). For an excellent review of the debate on welfare reform, see Michael Mumper, "Poverty, Work, and Social Policy: Review Article," *Polity,* 19 (Summer 1987), 678–692.

31. See, for example, Harrell R. Rodgers, Jr., *Poor Women, Poor Families: The Economic Plight of America's Female-Headed Families,* rev. ed. (Armonk, N.Y.: Sharpe, 1990). See also Peterson and Rom, *Welfare Magnets,* esp. chap. 5.

32. For elements of the consensus, see Mumper, "Poverty, Work, and Social Policy"; Danziger and Weinberg, eds., *Fighting Poverty,* pp. 15–17, 341–347; Isabel V. Sawhill, "Poverty and the Underclass," in Sawhill, ed., *Challenge to Leadership,* pp. 215–252.

33. For a review of these issues and of state experiments, see the articles by Judith M. Gueron, Robert I. Lerman, and Joel F. Handler in *Focus,* 11 (Spring 1988), 17–24, 24–28, 29–34.

34. Paul Taylor, "Like Taking Money from a Baby," *The Washington Post National Weekly Edition,* March 4–10, 1991, p. 31.

35. "Why Are Child Support Collections Declining?" *Focus,* 12 (Fall and Winter 1989), 23–29.

36. "Overview," *Focus,* 12 (Spring and Summer 1989), 2. For an excellent introduction to the problem, see this entire issue of *Focus;* also see Jencks and Peterson, eds., *The Urban Underclass.*

37. In addition to the sources cited in note 36, see Ruggles, "The Impact of Government Tax and Expenditure Programs," pp. 185ff.

38. *Lubbock Avalanche-Journal,* December 21, 1991.

39. Ann Mariano, "Is It a Mortgage Deduction, or a Housing Subsidy for the Wealthy?" *The Washington Post National Weekly Edition,* October 24–30, 1988, p. 20.

40. See Heidenheimer et al., *Comparative Public Policy,* chap. 4, esp. pp. 124–125.

41. See "Tracking the Homeless," *Focus,* 10 (Winter 1987–1988), 20–25.

42. E. Fuller Torrey, M.D., "Who Goes Homeless?" *National Review,* August 26, 1991, pp. 34–36.

SUGGESTED READINGS

Achenbaum, W. Andrew. *Social Security: Visions and Revisions.* Cambridge: Cambridge University Press, 1986.

Barak, Gregg. *Gimme Shelter: A Social History of Homelessness in Contemporary America.* New York: Praeger, 1991.

Block, Fred; Cloward, Richard A.; Ehrenreich, Barbara; and Piven, Frances Fox. *The Mean Season: The Attack on the Welfare State.* New York: Pantheon Books, 1987.

Cottingham, Phoebe H., and Ellwood, David T., eds. *Welfare Policy for the 1990s.* Cambridge: Harvard University Press, 1989.

Danziger, Sheldon H., and Weinberg, Daniel H., eds. *Fighting Poverty: What Works and What Doesn't.* Cambridge: Harvard University Press, 1986.

Heidenheimer, Arnold J.; Heclo, Hugh; and Adams, Carolyn Teich. *Comparative Public Policy,* 3rd ed. New York: St. Martin's Press, 1990.

Jencks, Christopher, and Peterson, Paul E., eds. *The Urban Underclass.* Washington, D.C.: Brookings Institution, 1991.

Kahn, Alfred J., and Kamerman, Sheila B. *Not for the Poor Alone: European Social Services.* New York: Harper Colophon Books, 1977.

Levitan, Sar A. *Programs in Aid of the Poor,* 6th ed. Baltimore: Johns Hopkins University Press, 1990.

Light, Paul. *Artful Work: The Politics of Social Security Reform.* New York: Random House, 1985.

Mead, Lawrence M. *Beyond Entitlement: The Social Obligations of Citizenship.* New York: Free Press, 1986.

Meyer, Charles W., ed. *Social Security: A Critique of Radical Reform Proposals.* Lexington, Mass.: Heath, 1987.

Murray, Charles. *Losing Ground: American Social Policy, 1950–1980.* New York: Basic Books, 1984.

Osberg, Lars, ed. *Economic Inequality and Poverty: International Perspectives.* Armonk, N.Y.: Sharpe, 1991.

Peterson, Paul E., and Rom, Mark C. *Welfare Magnets: A New Case for a National Standard.* Washington, D.C.: Brookings Institution, 1990.

Rodgers, Harrell R., Jr. *Poor Women, Poor Families: The Economic Plight of America's Female-Headed Families.* Rev. ed. Armonk, N.Y.: Sharpe, 1990.

Wilson, William Julius. *The Truly Disadvantaged: The Inner City, the Underclass, and Public Policy.* Chicago: University of Chicago Press, 1987.

CHAPTER 8

Health Care: Unlimited Needs, Limited Resources

The same perplexing logic and inherent goal conflicts that characterized the policies of public income support studied in the last chapter also plague health care policy. Indeed, an intimate connection between the two areas makes it essential that they be considered together. Health care policy and income support policy are closely linked for two reasons. First, the high costs of health care (for both illness treatment and health maintenance) are primary contributors to poverty or low income for many Americans. Second, the poor and the aged are more likely than the rest of the population is to be afflicted with illness and high medical bills. Therefore many proposals for reform of income support policy include reform of health care policy. Yet, just as with the former, a double bind operates in health care: goals and priorities are in conflict; pursuit of one goal precludes pursuit of others that are equally desirable. The potential need for health care is unlimited; yet individual and social resources for health care are always limited. As political scientist Aaron Wildavsky described this dilemma:

> If money is a barrier to medicine, the system is discriminatory. If money is no barrier, the system gets overcrowded. If everyone is insured, costs rise to the level of their insurance. If many remain underinsured, their income drops to the level of whatever medical disaster befalls them. Inability to break out of this bind has made the politics of health policy pathological.[1]

Health policy is important to American politics because it is closely tied to the issues of poverty, welfare, and social insurance.

Health policy, however, is also important in its own right. Health and medicine are basic concerns of American citizens. Annual expenditures from public and private sources for health care amount to more than one of every ten dollars of the Gross National Product. Americans each year spend more on health care than on national defense, more per capita for health care than for automobiles and gasoline combined. Malpractice cases and medical-ethical questions, such as euthanasia, abortion, and experimentation with new forms of life, claim an increasing share of judicial attention. The power of physicians to affect lives grows because of new medical technologies and the public's great fear of serious disease. Conditions once handled by the moral, religious, or criminal systems, such as alcoholism, sexual deviations, gambling, anxiety, overwork, child abuse, and family violence, now tend to be classified as sicknesses to be treated by mental- or physical-health

258

professionals. The jogging, health food, body building, and other physical fitness movements signal a growing concern for health. And criticism of doctors and hospitals has grown prominent enough to produce its own social backlash in the form of patients' rights movements, midwifery, and self-treatment advocates.

How a society deals with pain, the meaning and value assigned to it, reveals much about its fundamental beliefs and commitments. Pain and death are basic concerns of medicine, but they are also experiences that address the meaning of life, the value of the body, and the significance of the human spirit. Health care policy is fundamental because the resources and attention given to health care, the institutions that deliver it, and the way it is received affect the shape of social relations.

ISSUE BACKGROUND: THE HEALTH CARE SYSTEM AND ITS PROBLEMS

The U.S. System versus Other Approaches

The American health care system is a mix of public and private institutions with little central planning or coordination. At the highest level of the health care profession—among physicians, dentists, psychiatrists, and psychologists—solo, *fee-for-service* practice is the rule. That is, the professional provider of health services in America sets up his or her own office, with perhaps one or two others sharing the same specialty, sees only his or her own patients, and charges a separate fee for each individual service performed. If a patient sees more than one provider, the patient will be billed separately for each service by each provider; for example, a bill might have charges for injections, blood work, urinalysis, an office visit, anesthesia, and so forth. Institutions such as hospitals, nursing homes, clinics, and laboratories also operate primarily on the same fee-for-service basis.

Bills are paid through complicated arrangements among government agencies, individuals, and private insurers. Federal, state, and local governments provide a number of health-related services directly, for example, inoculations, health inspections, vector control, veterans' care, and epidemic control. They also reimburse private providers and individuals through grants and direct payments for services. Individuals pay for a variety of services directly, but they also pay indirectly by purchasing health insurance from private insurance companies and Blue Cross–Blue Shield plans. These companies then reimburse providers for covered services, which vary widely according to the terms of particular policies. Most private insurance is purchased through or provided by employers, with the employers passing their costs on to employees in the form of lower wages.

The U.S. health care system absorbs a tremendous amount of national resources. Total spending from all sources was $666 billion in 1990, a sum that amounted to 12.2 percent of the GNP for that year or an average of nearly $2,600 spent for every man, woman, and child in the nation. That share of the GNP has been growing larger: In 1965, medical expenditures were only 6.2 percent of the

GNP; from 1965 to 1988, they grew between 5 and 16 percent a year. The rate of growth in 1990 was 10.5 percent. Public sources paid 42 percent of the total bill, individuals paid 25 percent directly, and private insurance picked up 33 percent of the tab. These percentages, however, vary greatly with the type of service. For example, direct out-of-pocket payment by individuals for hospitalization represents about 5 percent of the total, whereas direct payment for dental care represents about 75 percent.

Other nations.   The United States is unique among industrial nations in its mix of private insurance, public financing, and direct patient spending. In other nations, health care systems tend to be more tightly organized, with less private, fee-for-service practice.[2] Compensation by salary or by *capitation* (a fixed payment for each patient on a physician's register) is more common. Where fee-for-service practices do exist, private fees are restrained by the fee schedules determined by the government and charged by government physicians. Recent changes in health policy have begun to introduce such elements into the American system.

These foreign systems can be grouped into two main approaches to health care: The central government either (1) operates a national health service, as in Great Britain and the former Soviet Union, or (2) mandates universal insurance coverage through employer or other private policies plus government insurance for the population unable to obtain private insurance, as in Germany, Sweden, France, and Italy. The systems with national health services may properly be called *socialized medicine,* for in them health care institutions are government owned and operated. Physicians and other providers work for the government, and private practice is minimal. *Universal health insurance* systems, on the other hand, vary widely in the amount of government control and are not socialized medicine. For example, in Sweden the central and local governments do not actually operate all health care programs, but they do exercise considerable influence over them; compare this with Germany, where government influence is minimal.

Again excluding the United States, the health care systems of the industrial world have other important features in common (notwithstanding wide differences in organization). In these nations virtually the entire population is covered for all or the major part of its health needs. The only exceptions in some nations are the wealthy, who may seek private health care. In the United States, however, government-supplied care is provided only for the poor and elderly, although tax subsidies encourage it for others. Thus gaps in U.S. health care coverage are more substantial than elsewhere.

Coverage under foreign health care is generally broader than coverage by public or private insurance in America. Coverage for nursing home care, medicines, eyeglasses, and dental services is the norm rather than the exception. Home health care is frequently provided, as in England where health workers regularly visit new mothers and children. In Sweden and the Netherlands, social service agencies visit the elderly regularly to care for their health and other needs. In the case of children, these visits provide low-cost preventive services; in the case of the aged, they limit the need for expensive nursing home care.

Although some systems, such as those in France, New Zealand, and Sweden, employ relatively high deductible and coinsurance requirements, generally third-party payments cover a higher percentage of medical bills than in the United States. Patients have fewer out-of-pocket expenses than Americans do, and in none of these countries are medical bills allowed to place a catastrophic burden on families.

Medical care costs have risen rapidly in the industrialized nations. Although many have more extensive coverage than the United States, none has higher costs (see Table 8-1). Moreover, costs in other nations have stabilized recently while American costs continue to increase. There seems to be no correlation between the type of health care system and the amount of money, public and private, spent on health care. Nor is there any correlation with general levels of citizen health. All nations are seeking ways to hold down costs; yet only the British National Health Service has been very successful in doing so (though with the unintended consequences of physician dissatisfaction and long waits for many kinds of health care).

How Healthy is America?

Health care is not health. Expenditures for care cannot be translated directly into better health or longer life. Money spent on medical technology, however, has certainly kept many persons alive and in good physical condition. Intensive care units, coronary bypass surgery, and hemodialysis, as well as immunizations, fillings of dental cavities, and penicillin, have lessened pain and prolonged life for millions.

The most widely used statistics on health are encouraging. By 1990 life expectancy in the United States was 75.6 years, and the death rate for infants

---

TABLE 8-1 ▪ Total Health Expenditure as a Percentage of Gross Domestic Product

	1963	*1983*	*1988*
Australia	5.0	7.5	7.0
Belgium	3.5	6.5	7.3
Britain	3.9	6.1	5.9
Canada	5.5	8.5	8.5
Denmark	3.6	6.7	6.2
France	4.2	9.2	8.7
West Germany	4.8	8.1	8.6
Japan	3.0	6.8	6.7
Netherlands	3.9	8.8	8.4
Sweden	4.7	9.6	9.0
United States	5.2	10.9	11.2

SOURCE: Edward Cody, "Lessons from Abroad: Is the U.S. Ready for National Health Insurance?" *Washington Post,* July 7, 1987, Health Section, p. 14; *Washington Post National Weekly Edition,* May 1–7, 1989, p. 38; U.S. Bureau of the Census, *Statistical Abstract of the United States, 1991* (Washington, D.C.: U.S. Government Printing Office, 1991), Table 1443.

during the first year of life was only 10.4 per 1,000 live births. These figures represent considerable improvements over previous decades, but they are more than matched by other nations. Even though American medical technology is the most advanced in the world, the United States ranks equal to or behind such countries as Sweden, Japan, the Netherlands, Denmark, Canada, France, England, and others in life expectancy and infant mortality. (See Figure 8-1.)

Obviously, many factors other than medical care influence infant mortality and life expectancy—nutrition, genetics, environment, and risk taking, for example. Yet these figures indicate that there is substantial room for improvement in American health. Other phenomena point to major problems in the U.S. health care system.

The perception is widespread among professionals and public alike that despite improvements in health statistics and advances in medical knowledge and technology, Americans are only marginally healthier now than in previous decades. Despite massive increases in health care expenditures and numbers of medical professionals, the additional benefits have not outweighed the additional costs. Most Americans, although perhaps satisfied with their individual care, are convinced that there is a crisis in the system as a whole.

If all the basic ills of the American health care system are looked at generally, an overall pattern can be discerned: The health care system emphasizes some kinds of care at the expense of others. In particular, cure of acute medical conditions, those lasting less than three months and requiring medical attention or restricted activity, is emphasized over care for chronic conditions, those debilitating illnesses lasting over three months. Expensive, high-technology, curative hospital care, especially for those over sixty-five, is stressed to the neglect of disease detection and prevention, health education, rehabilitation services, low-cost chronic care, and neighborhood health centers. And the structure of health insurance payments reinforces the doctor's natural fascination with acute conditions by paying for most hospital and surgical bills but for few routine office procedures.

The main problems of U.S. health care can be grouped into three categories: access, cost, and quality. The politics of health care is so perplexing because solutions to these three problems are widely regarded as being in conflict. Guaranteeing access to health care for all Americans will very likely increase costs and could reduce quality. Reducing health care costs may require rationing care, thus impairing access and possibly quality. Improving quality of care demands more spending and has unintended access effects. The paragraphs below describe the three problems. The Contemporary Policy and Evaluation sections describe and evaluate federal policies designed to affect them. The Future Alternatives section discusses reform proposals that try to find a way out of the seemingly contradictory goals of broadened access, cost reduction, and high quality of care.

Inequities in Access to Health Care

Medical care is maldistributed; that is, the areas and persons with the greatest needs for health care are not the areas and persons with the greatest access to care. Hospitals, nursing homes, clinics, doctors, dentists, and other health care profes-

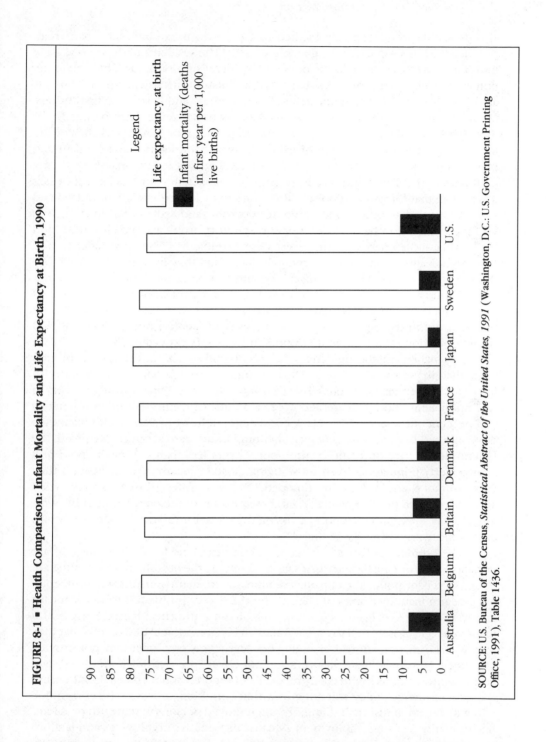

FIGURE 8-1 ▪ Health Comparison: Infant Mortality and Life Expectancy at Birth, 1990

Legend

☐ Life expectancy at birth

■ Infant mortality (deaths in first year per 1,000 live births)

SOURCE: U.S. Bureau of the Census, *Statistical Abstract of the United States, 1991* (Washington, D.C.: U.S. Government Printing Office, 1991), Table 1436.

sionals are disproportionately located in well-to-do urban and suburban areas, because the highest fees can be generated there. The residents of these areas have better access to care than do the poor and residents of rural areas. This phenomenon is particularly true for access to specialized institutions and personnel, but it is also true, to a lesser extent, for general practitioners and basic care institutions. Medical care is distributed on the basis of ability to pay rather than on need.

This limited-access pattern contributes to the poor health and shorter life expectancy of those who are poor or live in rural communities. Black infant and maternal mortality rates are nearly twice those of whites and comparable to many countries in the Third World. The average life expectancy for blacks is six years lower than that for whites. Poor children tend to be inadequately immunized and to suffer more than other children do from chronic and acute conditions, such as vision problems, low hemoglobin, upper respiratory problems, and elevated blood lead levels; and 25 percent have severe dental problems.[3] The poor suffer as well from significantly higher rates of mental illness, and they have significantly more days of restricted activity, bed disability, and lost work than those who are not poor. Thousands of communities have no health care professionals at all. Half of all hospital closures since 1983 have been in rural areas, and one quarter of all rural hospitals are in danger of closing. The number of medical doctors per 100,000 rural population is half that in metropolitan areas. Life expectancy is lower, infant mortality higher, and the incidence of accidents and chronic illness greater in rural areas than in metropolitan areas. The percentage of the population having health insurance coverage has declined since 1980 under the impact of high levels of unemployment and Medicare and Medicaid cuts. Currently, 37 million persons (15 percent of the population) lack consistent public or private health insurance coverage and have serious difficulty obtaining health care services. Medicaid, the federal health care program for the poor, covers less than half of the poor and near-poverty population. Even those living close to health care facilities, if they lack insurance, are likely to be "dumped," that is, transferred to an overcrowded and understaffed public hospital. A large percentage of the population of Brownsville, Texas, for example, reports crossing the border into Mexico because health care is more readily available there![4]

The problem of lack of access has a number of hidden dimensions that are not apparent from the bare statistics given above. As the prominence of health care issues in recent political campaigns demonstrated, many persons who currently have health insurance are still affected by the access problem. Insurance means access to care; loss of insurance means difficulty in getting health care. Since health insurance is so closely tied to employment, many persons feel tied to jobs that they may wish to change but fear changing because a new employer may not provide insurance. Moreover, many insurers will not cover "pre-existing conditions"; as a consequence, workers with costly medical conditions cannot change jobs because the new insurance policy will not cover their condition, or loss of the current job will make them uninsurable. Similarly, unemployed persons with health problems find difficulty securing employment, because prospective employers cannot afford to carry them on their health insurance policies. These problems are now beginning substantially to affect the middle class.

Many contend that where medical institutions and professionals decide to locate is a matter of individual choice, influenced by opportunities for income and leisure, by place of training, by quality of facilities for medical care, and by opportunity to associate with members of a like social class. Similarly, whom they wish to treat is a matter of free choice. Thus, according to this argument, access problems would occur under any system of health care. Others, particularly liberals, argue that public policy affecting such factors as training requirements and financial incentives could help overcome the unevenness. Radicals, on the other hand, believe that "the maldistribution of health benefits is inherent in the private enterprise, fee-for-service character of the medical system and of the class-stratified nature of American society."[5] Only wholesale change in the social, economic, and medical systems would redistribute medical benefits to where they are most needed.

High Cost

The gaps in public and private health insurance are wide enough to let millions fall into financial disaster. Nearly 15 percent of the population has no health insurance, public or private. Fifty million to 60 million persons have no major medical coverage. The result is that nearly 20 percent of all families every year have out-of-pocket medical expenses exceeding 5 percent of their gross income. Most of these families are poor and even $1,000 out-of-pocket is a catastrophic expense. Three million families have medical bills exceeding 20 percent of income.

Cost escalation in the medical field has been constant, and one expert warns that "there are virtually no economic constraints left to prevent decision makers in medical care from doing everything they can think of, no matter how small the benefits nor to whom they accrue; in economic jargon, they are free to head straight for the saturation point. In a complex area like medical care, that point is a distant and moving target."[6] Demand is self-created, and supply does not work to reduce price. Table 8-2 and Figure 8-2 illustrate this trend.

There is no end in sight for skyrocketing costs, nor is there universal agreement among students of the problem on all the reasons for these cost increases or on their order of priority. Some factors, however, are commonly accepted as important.[7]

Certainly general inflationary trends have contributed to the rise in medical costs. But because the cost increases in medicine have been higher than the general inflation rate and because medicine's share of the GNP has been increasing, reasons more particular to health care must be sought to explain the growth in costs.

Third-party payments.   The most important contributor to rising cost has been the growth in third-party payments for medical care. Third-party payers are not health care providers (hospitals, doctors, and the like) or patients but are those who pay the charges to providers on behalf of the patients. The primary third-party payers are governments (particularly through Medicare and Medicaid), the Blue Cross-Blue Shield plans, and private health insurance companies. Formerly, patients paid most health costs directly from their own resources. Now most are paid

TABLE 8-2 ▪ **Aggregate and per Capita National Health Expenditures,**
Selected Years

	Total (in billions)	Per Capita	Percent of GNP
1940	$ 4.0	$ 30	4.0
1950	12.7	82	4.4
1960	26.9	146	5.3
1965	41.7	211	6.0
1970	74.7	358	7.5
1975	132.7	604	8.6
1980	249.0	1075	9.5
1985	422.6	1710	10.6
1990	670.9	2585	12.3
1995[a]	1072.7	3944	14.7
2000[a]	1615.9	5712	16.2

[a] Estimates.
SOURCE: "National Health Expenditures, 1986–2000," *Health Care Financing Review,* 8
(Summer 1987), Table 12; Sally T. Sonnenfeld et al., "Projections of National Health
Expenditures through the Year 2000," *Health Care Financing Review,* 13 (Fall, 1991), Table 6.

indirectly, through privately purchased or employer-provided health insurance or
through public programs. For example, from 1950 to 1977 the proportion of
direct expenditures for hospital care fell from 50 percent to 8 percent, and
third-party payers now reimburse about two-thirds of physicians' services. Third-
party payments contribute to cost increases by hiding the financial burden from
both patient and provider. Providers feel no compulsion to keep fees low, because
they know patients are covered by insurance or public programs. And patients, not
seeing the direct cost, ask for the best in service. The true, total cost of the
procedures is spread throughout society. Moreover, because most insurance plans
pay a greater proportion of hospital costs than physicians' office costs, there is an
incentive to hospitalize patients unnecessarily in order to collect benefits. Additionally, third-party payers have typically reimbursed providers at the "usual,
customary, and reasonable" (UCR) rate prevailing in a particular location. Because
the UCR rate is determined by providers' practices, providers have an incentive to
raise their fees, thus raising the UCR rate. Until the mid-1980s, public and private
insurers did little to hold down costs, preferring the easier route of passing them
on to consumers in the form of higher insurance premiums and taxes.

Third-party payments, particularly Medicare and Medicaid, also contribute
to greater use of old services and growing demand for new ones. People, particularly the elderly and the poor, are now able to avail themselves of health care, thus
placing rising demand on existing resources. Moreover, because these programs
pay for new services, the medical market attracts new providers and new services.
Services sometimes provided to the poor in the past free or at reduced cost now

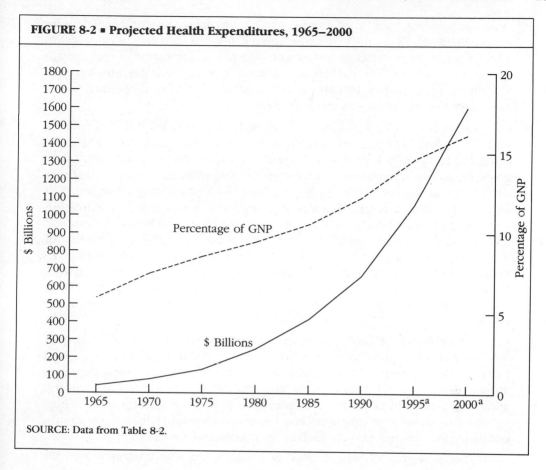

FIGURE 8-2 ▪ **Projected Health Expenditures, 1965–2000**

SOURCE: Data from Table 8-2.

are reimbursed at the going rate. Moreover, the lack of effective competition in the medical market means that the expanded supply of health care providers simply generates higher expenditures. During the 1960s and 1970s, the time of greatest cost increases, the number of physicians per 100,000 population was growing from 150 to 200; yet median physician incomes, far from declining or leveling off, were growing rapidly. Hundreds of thousands of other professionals—nurses, aides, therapists, and administrators—were also being added. The health delivery industry is now the second largest in the nation in terms of workers (7.6 million).

   Fee for service.   There are other reasons as well for the high costs of medical care, and each of them is intensified by the system of third-party reimbursement without effective cost control. The fee-for-service system of payment is inherently inflationary in today's medical "sellers' market." Because each service carries a separate fee and because the knowledge of services lies predominantly with the provider, there is an incentive to offer as many services as possible for each patient, who lacks the knowledge and the financial incentive to call a halt to them. Patient and provider do not bargain over prices. For example, even though nearly one-third of all hospital beds are vacant on any particular day, hospital costs do not decrease. Rather, fees are raised on all services to generate the income necessary to cover the losses on vacant beds.

Labor costs.   Medical care remains a highly labor-intensive field, despite its high technology. The fact that medicine is the only major industry that is both labor and technology intensive is a primary contributor to its high costs. Labor costs, for example, are 60 percent of hospital expenditures. During the last two decades the salaries of hospital workers, which had been abysmally low, began to increase partly as a result of unionization and partly as a result of increasing demand. The rapid jump in labor costs made a major contribution to medical inflation. Interestingly enough, although there was a dramatic rise in the number of workers per patient during this period, there was also a sharp increase in complaints from patients about lack of attention and care. Job responsibilities became fragmented among various levels of nurses, aides, therapists, and orderlies, so that effective supervision was difficult to achieve and productivity per worker decreased.[8]

Malpractice.   A small proportion of health cost increases have resulted from the rising number of medical malpractice suits filed by injured or disgruntled patients. This has resulted in malpractice insurance companies' raising their premiums to providers, who in turn have raised their fees to consumers to cover the additional costs. Moreover, doctors have begun to practice "defensive medicine" by ordering more extensive tests and more of other procedures than strictly necessary in order to guard themselves against possible lawsuits.

Technology.   Modern medical technology has also contributed to increased health care spending. New diagnostic and treatment procedures—such as the computerized axial tomography (CAT) scanner for whole-body X-rays, renal dialysis, neonatal units, chemotherapy, coronary bypass surgery, artificial hearts, and fiberoptics surgery—are tremendously expensive, because of both the equipment and materials themselves and the specialized personnel needed to operate them. Yet there is serious debate about the effectiveness of these measures in saving or extending life.[9] Some argue that they have not contributed to an increased life expectancy and that they carry their own dangers of harm to the patient from risky diagnostic procedures, unnecessary surgery, and drug side effects. Iatrogenic (physician-caused) illness, for example, is a major subject in medical literature. Others contend that such criticisms are exaggerated and that many persons have benefited from the new procedures through longer life and freedom from pain and disability. Moreover, some new technologies do reduce costs. New drugs can treat conditions formerly requiring surgery. Magnetic resonance imaging (MRI) can look inside the body to aid diagnoses that used to need exploratory surgery. Yet most technologies, despite acknowledged benefits, have increased the national health bill. And although many of these technologies service a very small proportion of the population, their costs are shared by ordinary patients.

Technological change also produces increased "service intensity." New procedures do not necessarily replace old ones. Therefore patients tend to receive more procedures today than they did before. Of course, the fee-for-service payment system is also an incentive to service intensity. Service intensity may, indeed, be the most important cause of higher health care costs, because it interacts with all of the other cost increase factors.[10]

Conflicting claims on the relative effectiveness of the new procedures aside, however, there are serious cost problems associated with medical technology that derive from status competition among hospitals and doctors. Helicopter ambulances, open-heart surgery units, and chemotherapy units have become items of high prestige, and often hospitals in the same area will have duplicate versions of the same technology, irrespective of the actual need for them. Doctors, moreover, resist combining or allocating these units among different hospitals; they demand that the best and latest equipment in each field be available from each hospital, threatening to pull out from any one that does not provide such equipment. The result is high acquisition costs, underutilization of equipment and staff, and the danger that skills will become rusty. Each patient entering the hospital helps subsidize the equipment, which lies idle much of the time.

Tax policy. Federal tax policy is another cause of society's high health costs. Tax regulations on medical expenses and health insurance premiums encourage the purchase of health insurance, particularly that including coverage of routine care, thus promoting growth in third-party payments. Contributions from employers to employee health insurance are nontaxable. Moreover, individuals may deduct all medical expenses over 7.5 percent of income. In this manner employees are encouraged to take additional income in the form of insurance benefits and to use deductible medical services. These tax policies are estimated to have cost the treasury approximately $33 billion in 1990, about the same as federal expenditures for health care for the poor under Medicaid. Most of these tax benefits aid the middle and upper classes. When health insurance and treatment were made tax deductible in the early 1950s, it was to make sure that Americans obtained health insurance, but it now has the unintended consequence of driving up health care costs.

Age. The aging of the population plays an increasing role in health cost increases. Life expectancies at ages 60 and 85 began to increase significantly in 1950 (see Figure 8-3). The aged have more severe health care problems. This fact, combined with the aging of the baby boom population, means that, especially after the year 2000, health costs will rise very rapidly.

Finally, health costs are going up rapidly because of the public's exaggerated expectations of medical science, coupled with its unprecedented fear of illness, old age, and death. Americans treat these as abnormal conditions, rather than as

FIGURE 8-3 ▪ Male Life Expectancy at Ages 60 and 85

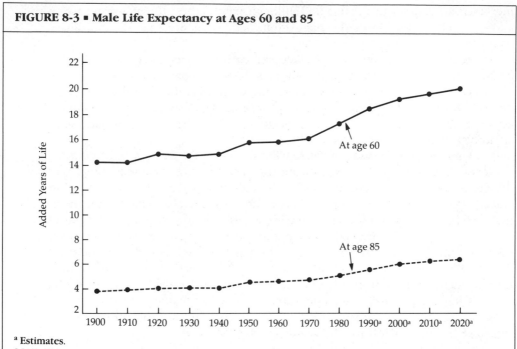

^a Estimates.

SOURCE: S. Jay Olshansky and A. Brian Ault, "The Fourth Stage of the Epidemiologic Transition: The Age of Delayed Degenerative Diseases," in Timothy M. Smeeding, ed., *Should Medical Care Be Rationed by Age?* (Totowa, N.J.: Rowman & Littlefield, 1987), Table 2-1.

part of human life. Thus the sick and aged are increasingly relegated to medical specialists, hospitals, and nursing homes. As the population continues to age, the demand for these kinds of services will increase dramatically. Cures are demanded of medicine, and if they are not forthcoming, a lawsuit may be. Billions of dollars are spent each year on visits to the doctor for colds, flus, and other self-limiting illnesses and for undifferentiated pains and anxieties. As a result, most of a primary care physician's time and a good deal of the specialist's is spent in providing psychological reassurance, rather than in physical "curing."

Quality of Health Care

As suggested earlier, Americans are "doing better, but feeling worse." Health statistics are improving, and most Americans are satisfied with their own health care. Moreover, American medical technology and health care innovation are the best in the world. Yet, fear of high health costs, impersonality, and increased size in the health care field have left Americans feeling uneasy about their health care. In addition, there are significant concerns that efforts to hold down costs and to increase access to health care may adversely affect the quality of care that most Americans receive. Some aspects of the current system do raise serious quality issues.

Contributing to the quality problem is overspecialization. Primary care physicians, that is, family doctors and general practitioners, now constitute a small proportion of American physicians. Cardiologists, neurosurgeons, urologists, and other specialists are the dominant figures in the medical profession. Despite one of the highest ratios of physicians to population in the world, the ratio of primary care physicians is quite low. In 1950, two-thirds of all physicians were general practitioners; today, about one-fourth are. In other nations, the percentages are significantly higher, for example, 35 percent in Sweden and 50 percent in England.

Serious consequences in quality flow from the predominance of specialists. It may help account for the rather poor performance on measures of infant mortality and life expectancy relative to those of other developed nations, because these measures are more sensitive to high-quality routine care than to sophisticated, exceptional procedures. Overspecialization also contributes to the high cost of medical care because specialists charge more and use hospitals more than do general practitioners. Most American physicians are affiliated with hospitals, whereas the typical European doctor is not; hence the American incentive is to use hospitals, where care is expensive. Supply-and-demand economics do not work to reduce prices when the specialized fields become overcrowded. Each doctor sees fewer patients but raises fees in order to keep income high. Between 1975 and 1985, average physician income doubled, going from $57,000 to $113,000. The growing oversupply of physicians, changing from 148 per 100,000 population in 1960 to an expected 250 per 100,000 in 1995, will magnify this problem. (See Figure 8-4.) Overspecialization tends also to mean higher rates of unnecessary surgery and other specialized procedures. Surgeons are trained to do surgery and so recommend it; internists are trained to interpret medical test results and so prescribe extensive tests. Estimates of surgery performed but not actually needed vary, with some running as high as 60 percent.[11] The number of unneeded gall bladder removals, tonsillectomies, and hysterectomies is undoubtedly very high.

Ideological perspectives.   Different ideological camps tend to assess blame in different ways for the health care problems just outlined. Socialists and other radicals blame the corporate structure of health care and the associations of hospitals, doctors, dentists, and other professionals. More and more, they argue, large corporations are expanding their control of hospitals, nursing homes, and drugs. Physicians and other professionals are organized to control prices, types of health care delivery, and entry into professional ranks. Such monopolistic control creates inequitable distribution, high costs and profits, and low-quality care.

Liberals contend that the primary cause of these problems is market mechanisms that do not operate effectively in the sellers' market of medical care. Consumers lack the information to "shop" wisely for medical services, and competition among professionals is absent. Thus, because ordinary controls on prices, location of services, and entry of providers do not work, liberals hold that stricter

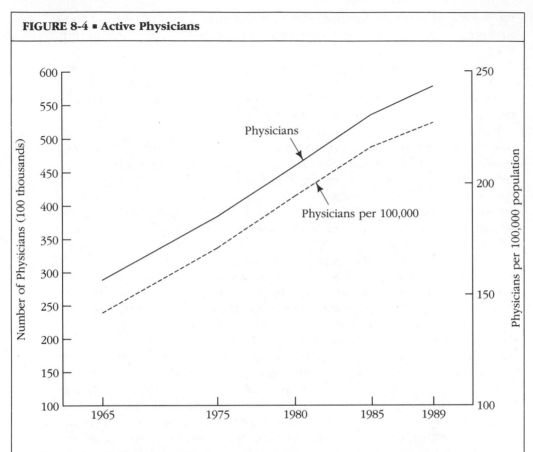

FIGURE 8-4 ▪ Active Physicians

SOURCE: S. T. Sonnenfeld, D. R. Waldo, J. A. Lemieux, and D. R. McKusick, "Projections of national health expenditures through the year 2000," *Health Care Financing Review* 13 (1):1–28. HCFA Pub. No. 03321, Office of Research and Demonstrations, Health Care Financing Administration (Washington, D.C.: U.S. Government Printing Office, October, 1991).

government regulation is needed to offset the failures of the market. Conservatives, on the other hand, argue that there is no inherent reason why market forces could not operate if reduced government regulation and changes in the monopolistic practices by health care providers were allowed to stimulate competition.

Health Policy before 1965

Government involvement in actual public health care until three decades ago was a relatively small part of the overall public health picture. As late as 1965, public health care expenditures represented only 21 percent of the total spent nationally on health care, a percentage that had not changed since the Second World War. Typically at that time, state and local governments provided garbage and sewer services, furnished safe drinking water, and kept rabies, disease-bearing insects, and epidemic diseases under control. The importance of these measures should not be overlooked, as they contributed the principal element to increased life expectancy in the twentieth century. State and local governments did support some health care services, sometimes providing free clinics and immunizations for the poor and supporting charity wards in county hospitals.

In addition to its assistance of state and local public health programs, the federal government has a fairly long history of monitoring the quality and safety of consumer goods that could represent adverse health risks, and this responsibility has been expanded over the years. The Department of Agriculture inspects and grades meat and poultry products. The Food and Drug Administration reviews, tests, and licenses drugs, inspects food processing, and assesses cosmetic safety. The importance of the FDA in this respect was highlighted in the 1992 controversy about banning silicone gel breast implants. It also is responsible for regulating hazardous substances and for radiological safety. The federal government's programs for monitoring air and water purity were described in Chapter 4.

The first building blocks of what was to become today's public health care edifice were mainly in areas of scientific research, mental health, and medical attention for selected groups of the poor. Beginning with the establishment of the National Institutes of Health (NIH) in 1937, the federal government has been active in biomedical research. In addition to NIH, the National Science Foundation, the Department of Health and Human Services, and the Department of Agriculture also support some research. Generally, between 1950 and 1990 federal expenditures for health research and development increased dramatically from $160 million to $10.2 billion, accounting for over two-thirds of the nation's health research spending.

The federal effort before 1965 having the most comprehensive effect on the health care system was the Hill-Burton program, which was implemented by the Hospital Survey and Construction Act of 1946. During the 1950s and 1960s, the Hill-Burton program provided as much as 15 percent of construction funds in some years and exerted leverage on considerably more through its requirement for matching funds. By the 1960s the goal of 4.5 beds per 1,000 population was seen to be too high; large numbers of vacant beds became a problem, and Hill-Burton was phased out.

CONTEMPORARY POLICY: HEALTH CARE FOR THE POOR AND THE AGED

It was not until the mid-1960s that widespread public involvement in health care—at least for certain sectors of the American population—became a reality.

With the Johnson administration's War on Poverty came increasing recognition of the maldistribution of health care, the financial burden of care on the elderly and the poor, and the weak performance of the United States on a number of comparative measures of health. The volume and complexity of federal health legislation increased dramatically, and expenditures exploded. The organization of these programs, with the important exception of Medicaid, bypassed state governments and interlocked directly with local governments and especially with local, private, nonprofit corporations.[12] The federal approach, however, was hardly well coordinated, being instead a "shotgun" attack on American health care problems.

Medicare and Medicaid, the most important programs, were enacted in 1965 after years of debate in Congress over the federal role in providing medical care. Many legislators had long disputed any federal responsibility in this area, and others had advocated a program of national health care along European lines. Under the War on Poverty legislation, a compromise was reached in which social insurance would be extended to cover the serious health needs of the aged; this was the birth of Medicare. Almost as an afterthought, Medicaid was added to help the states pay the medical expenses of welfare recipients. Neither program was designed to change the organization or delivery of health care in America, but only to pay some of the bills and supply care to many not adequately served.[13]

Medicare

Medicare, as noted, was designed not as a program for the poor specifically but as a supplement to Social Security for elderly recipients, who have more extensive medical needs and expenses than the general population. Medicare is designed to protect this aged population against the risks of medical disaster. It consists of two parts: hospital insurance, known as Part A, and voluntary supplementary medical insurance, or Part B. Hospital insurance covers a broad range of hospital and posthospital services, subject to some deductibles and coinsurance. (A deductible is a set dollar amount that a patient must pay directly before insurance benefits begin. Coinsurance is a percentage of the bill that a patient must pay directly after meeting the deductible.) For a given benefit period, beneficiaries must pay a deductible for hospital care set at the approximate cost of one day of hospital care, $652 in 1992. To encourage early discharge from expensive hospital care, Medicare covers certain types of posthospital care, such as skilled nursing facilities and home health service. Beneficiaries must pay one-eighth of the daily cost of from 21 to 100 days in a skilled nursing facility. Thereafter benefits cease. Medicare does not pay for ordinary nursing home or routine home care, but it does pay the reasonable cost of hospice care for terminally ill patients.

Part A of Medicare is financed through the Social Security payroll tax. Both employer and employee pay a tax of 1.45 percent of the employee's wage base ($130,200 in 1992). In addition to the aged, hospital insurance since 1974 also covers two other categories: persons who have become disabled, if they have been entitled to Social Security disability payments for at least two consecutive years, and those with end-stage renal (kidney) disease.

Supplementary medical insurance (Part B) is a voluntary insurance program for all persons age sixty-five and older. Monthly premiums were $31.80 in 1992, and general tax revenues finance expenses not covered by premiums (75 percent). The cost of the insurance is so low that 98 percent of the elderly elect to buy coverage. Part B covers physicians' services, outpatient hospital services, and other medical services. After the yearly deductible of $100 is met, Medicare pays 80 percent of allowed charges (the maximum fees that the government specifies) for covered services. The patient must pay the remainder and any other charges in excess of the allowable amount if the physician will not accept the allowable charge as payment in full. Unfortunately, physicians are increasingly reluctant to accept Medicare benefit assignments, as their fees are rising faster than are Medicare allowables; as a result, patients are paying a larger part of their bills directly or purchasing costly private insurance ("medigap") to supplement Part B. Elderly persons eligible for Mcdicaid are automatically covered by Medicare in most states, which have elected to "buy in" to the program by paying the recipient's premiums, deductibles, and coinsurance.

The costs of Medicare have far exceeded original estimates and have been prime contributors to health cost inflation. Medicare costs were $109 billion in 1990 and were expected to hit $182 billion by 1995. Figure 8-5 shows the increases in costs and numbers of recipients since the program's beginning.

The reasons for this growth are clear. Inflation in hospital costs and physician's fees, paid by Medicare, have already been discussed. Other increases came when the disabled and chronic renal disease patients were added in 1974. Moreover, because the proportion of the elderly is growing and they are living longer, the increase in beneficiaries and the years they are covered contribute substantially to cost increases.

Catastrophic care.   In 1988, Congress and the Reagan administration addressed the enormous impact of medical bills on many of the elderly in compromise catastrophic costs legislation, the largest expansion of Medicare since its beginning in 1965. However, the catastrophic care law was repealed the following year. Beginning January 1, 1989, Medicare Hospital Insurance would have covered all hospitalization costs of Medicare beneficiaries after the patient paid a single annual deductible, about $575 in 1989 and increasing thereafter with inflation. Supplemental Medical Insurance–covered costs were to be capped at $1,370 annually, after which Medicare would have paid 100 percent instead of the current 80 percent of covered physician charges. The cap was to increase each year. The legislation also covered for the first time the cost of outpatient prescription drugs, phasing in coverage in 1991. By 1993, Medicare would have paid 80 percent of the cost of such drugs after an annual deductible of $600. The legislation also made slight expansions in hospice, in-home health care, respite care, and at-home intravenous drug therapy.

The reasons why this legislation was repealed are instructive about the politics of health care.[14] The cost of the new program would have been paid for by a special tax on Medicare recipients themselves, particularly a tax on elderly individuals with incomes over $45,000 per year and elderly couples with incomes over $85,000. Only 40 percent of Medicare enrollees would have had to pay the

FIGURE 8-5 ▪ Medicare Benefits and Beneficiaries

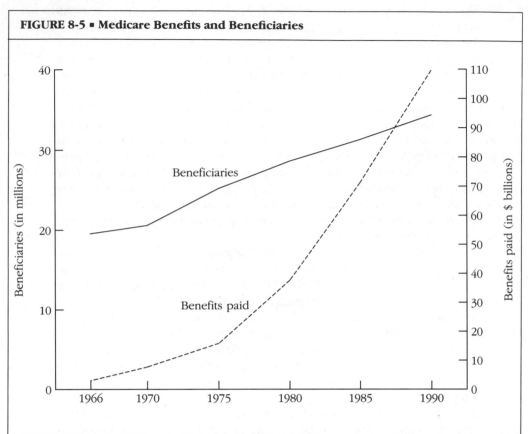

SOURCE: K. R. Levit, H. C. Lazenby, C. A. Cowan, and S. W. Letsch, "National health expenditures, 1990," *Health Care Financing Review* 13(1):29–54. HCFA Pub. No. 03321, Office of Research and Demonstrations, Health Care Financing Administration (Washington, D.C.: U.S. Government Printing Office, October 1991).

supplemental premium financing the catastrophic care legislation. Nevertheless, strong lobbying by interest groups representing the elderly caused Congress in 1989 to retract the law. These groups objected to the precedent that the legislation set: that is, that for the first time in Medicare history a substantial part of the program would have been financed by recipients themselves.

The future of legislation covering catastrophic costs not now covered by Medicare is clouded. The budget deficit and the need to provide access to those citizens with no coverage at all make it unlikely that Medicare will be extended without some financing mechanism that requires higher-income participants to carry some of the load. Moreover, even the repealed legislation did not address the pressing issue of long-term nursing home care for the aged. This topic will be considered in the Future Alternatives section.

Medicaid

Medicaid is a public assistance program funded out of general revenues. Like AFDC (reviewed in Chapter 7), it is a federal-state program with benefits varying among the states. States must cover SSI and AFDC beneficiaries and certain other poor persons, particularly pregnant women and children under nine. To receive Medicaid funds, states must offer certain basic medical services without cost to the patient. Depending on the state's per capita income, the federal government reimburses 50 to 80 percent of the costs for these services. They include inpatient and outpatient hospital services; physician's services; prenatal care; laboratory and X-ray services; home health services; skilled nursing; early screening, diagnosis, and treatment of physical and mental defects in those under twenty-one; and family-planning services and supplies.

Additionally, states may expand the number of those eligible and include other services for which the federal government will reimburse a proportion of costs. Optional services include clinical services, dental care, physical therapy, drugs, dentures, eyeglasses, and nursing home care. All states offer some optional services: some provide all, others as few as three. Because of state variations in definitions of eligibility and in the services offered, the proportion of the poor covered varies. Only 45 percent of the poor receive Medicaid coverage; the percentage varies among the states from 20 to 90 percent.[15]

As noted, almost all states "buy in" to Medicare for elderly Medicaid recipients. The reverse is also true, as many Medicare recipients also are eligible for Medicaid, particularly for nursing home care not covered by the Social Security health program. About one-fourth of all Medicaid recipients are actually supplementing their Medicare, and Medicaid costs reflect this, over 40 percent going for nursing home and intermediate care. Medicaid supplies 85 percent of all third-party payments to nursing homes and nearly half of all nursing home revenues.

States are required to pay the premiums, deductibles, and coinsurance charges for Medicare beneficiaries who have incomes below the poverty line but who are otherwise not poor enough to qualify for Medicaid coverage. States also must provide Medicaid coverage of prenatal care and pediatric care for infants up to age one for families with incomes below the poverty line. By 2000, all states must cover all children in families with incomes below the poverty line.

Just as with Medicare, the costs of Medicaid have exploded far beyond original estimates. Federal and state expenditures were $71.3 billion in 1990 for 25.3 million recipients. Figure 8-6 shows the program's growth in federal and state costs. The reasons for cost increases here are more difficult to pinpoint than for Medicare. Certainly, the number of recipients has increased steadily, a factor controlled by legislation on eligibility. Fraud and inefficiency, although present, have not contributed significantly to cost increases. Most increases are accounted for by medical inflation generally and the high costs of nursing home care for the impoverished elderly and disabled. In recent years, the large number of persons without medical insurance has strained local public hospital budgets, for state law

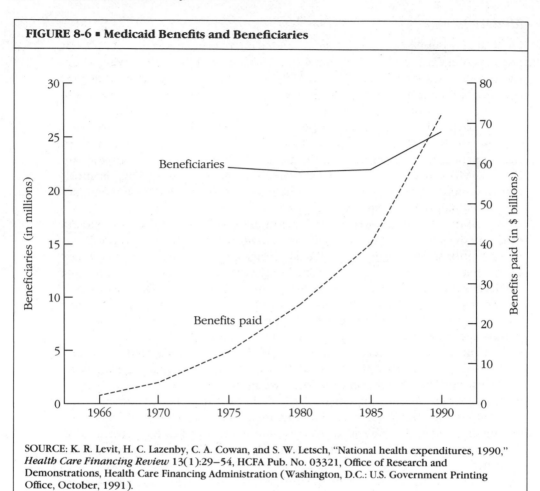

FIGURE 8-6 ▪ Medicaid Benefits and Beneficiaries

SOURCE: K. R. Levit, H. C. Lazenby, C. A. Cowan, and S. W. Letsch, "National health expenditures, 1990," *Health Care Financing Review* 13(1):29–54, HCFA Pub. No. 03321, Office of Research and Demonstrations, Health Care Financing Administration (Washington, D.C.: U.S. Government Printing Office, October, 1991).

often mandates that they provide indigent health care on an emergency basis. Local governments faced with these bills have pressured state governments to make more persons eligible for Medicaid, thus passing part of the costs on to the federal government. Although two-thirds of all Medicaid recipients were eligible through ▪ AFDC, they consumed only one-fourth of expenditures. The aged, blind, and disabled account for three-fourths of all Medicaid spending.

Other Federal Programs

Though Medicare and Medicaid account for 75 percent of all public health expenditures, there are other important federal health programs. Many were developed in the late 1960s and early 1970s to attack the problems of access and escalating health care costs.

Maldistribution of health care providers was the concern of the Neighborhood Health Centers (NHC) program begun in 1966 by the Office of Economic Opportunity (OEO). The creation of these centers was inspired by radical theory. The idea of NHCs was to challenge the health establishment, as Medicare and Medicaid had not done, by organizing comprehensive health care in poverty areas along with counseling, social services, and employment training in health careers. The NHCs were to take an advocacy stance for the poor on health-related issues, not just cure their ailments. The impact of this program has been highly significant for particular underserved areas. By 1982, there were over eight hundred community health centers serving 4.2 million persons, but these were being pushed to abandon their social welfare aspects in favor of more narrowly defined medical practice.[16] During the remainder of the 1980s, growth of NHCs stagnated as their funding was changed to a Primary Care Block Grant and cut substantially. The federal government also funds three other health-related block grants to the states: Maternal and Child Health Services; Alcohol, Drug Abuse, and Mental Health; and Preventive Health Services. Funding for these was cut substantially in the early 1980s.

By the early 1970s the rapidly increasing cost of health care had become a major national concern, and Congress instituted a series of measures in the hope of somehow holding down costs.[17] Congress's first tactic was to create Professional Standards Review Organizations (PSROs). Established in 1972, these groups of physicians and other health professionals were mandated to review and determine the quality and necessity of care given Medicare and Medicaid patients in their areas of specialty. There is no evidence, however, that PSROs affected medical costs. But Congress refused to let them die completely, transforming them in 1982 into Peer Review Organizations (PROs). These are somewhat more independent of the doctors and hospitals they are supposed to police. The PROs (one for each state) must approve each Medicare hospital admission and set targets for reducing unnecessary admissions, surgeries, and deaths.

The federal government began in 1973 to promote Health Maintenance Organizations (HMOs) as an alternative means of health care delivery and a device for holding down costs. The HMO is a form of prepaid group practice. A sponsoring organization—a public, private, professional, business, or consumer group—employs doctors and other health professionals on salary to provide comprehensive health services. Subscribers pay a set fee each month, and all medical needs are covered without additional costs. Incentives to control costs are built into HMOs. Because the premiums are prepaid and providers are salaried, unnecessary or questionable services produce no additional income, only additional costs. Hospital care is not used unless clearly necessary. Physicians, who may be given bonuses if costs are kept low, have an incentive to offer preventive care and early diagnosis and treatment. The 1973 HMO statute provides start-up costs for approved groups and overrides restrictive state laws for the HMOs it supports.

Once considered the wave of the future, the HMO movement has slowed considerably. Today about 650 exist nationwide, enrolling about 34 million persons or 14 percent of the population. There are several reasons for this reduced growth. Professionals resist the group practice and salary features of HMOs. Patients in some plans miss the personal relationship with their private physicians. Estimates of financial savings have not been completely met. Enrollment of the poor and aged, lavish federally mandated benefit packages, and occasional poor administration have driven up costs in federally supported HMOs. Yet some HMOs have demonstrated an ability to reduce costs, treatments, and hospitalization with no decline in quality of health. There is no consensus among experts regarding the causes of success and failure. Nevertheless, the federal government has established strong incentives for Medicare recipients to enroll in HMOs as a way of cutting costs.

POLICY EVALUATION: HEALTH CARE AT THE CROSSROADS

When health care policy is evaluated in terms of its intended goals, a mixed picture emerges. Public policy, particularly Medicare and Medicaid, has been successful in reducing the financial burden of health care for the poor and elderly and in overcoming inequitable distribution of care by lowering financial barriers to medical care. Yet burdens remain for much of the population, and serious problems of access persist. Moreover, unintended consequences are a major concern, as health education policy contributes to the overspecialization of physicians, and recent changes in that policy have not yet shown an effect. Public policy, again particularly Medicare and Medicaid, contributes substantially to the cost escalation in health care. As health care policy reduces the financial burden on specific individuals, it increases it on society as a whole.

Health statistics have improved during the last twenty years, and government support of medical research, federal training programs for health workers, and public financing of medical care for the aged and poor have had an impact on this advance. Infant mortality, for example, has declined 50 percent in the last twenty years. Deaths from heart attack, high blood pressure, and stroke are down substantially, and deaths from most major diseases are decreasing in the forty-five–to–sixty-four age group, meaning longer life expectancies. Medical research has developed chemotherapies for cancer treatment, artificial joints and internal organs, CAT scanners, and electronic fetal monitoring. And medical professionals and the public know far more today than a decade ago about the hazards of drugs, smoking, environmental pollution, and poor diet.

Medicare and Medicaid

Successes.   Some of the most dramatic gains in health are directly attributable to Medicare and Medicaid.[18] Surveys show that people are seeing physicians regularly as a result of their enactment. The poor in fact now visit physicians more frequently, though gaps between poor and nonpoor still persist. Approximately 25 million persons each year benefit from Medicaid and 34 million from Medicare.

The elderly also utilize health care facilities now to a greater extent than before. In 1964, they averaged 190 hospital discharges and 2,300 days of hospital care for every thousand people. By 1973, these figures were 350 discharges and 4,200 days respectively for every thousand.

Measures of health also show improvement for the poor and aged. Data are not available on death rates by social class, but data by race show that age-adjusted rates fell 10 percent for whites and 13 percent for blacks and others between 1965 and 1974. Infant mortality declined in this period by 38 percent for nonwhites and 31 percent for whites. Yet death rates and infant mortality rates are still higher for minorities. Health statistics for the aged since 1965 also show declines in death rates from diseases particularly afflicting the elderly, in days of restricted activity, in the mortality rate of aged males, and in the incidence of acute conditions.

Problems.   Medicare and Medicaid, however, have failed to do all their sponsors had hoped for and have led to increasingly high costs. Both programs have, moreover, some structural flaws that inhibit their ability to deal most effectively with the major problems in health care. Access to health care remains a problem along geographical, racial, and income lines. Large differences in death rates, life expectancy, and infant mortality still exist. Because of state variations in eligibility definitions, over half of the poor are not covered by Medicaid. In fact, the percentage of the poor and near-poor covered has declined from a high of 65 percent in 1975 to about 45 percent today. In many states, qualifying income for Medicaid is well below poverty level. Even so, more applicants are rejected for failure to complete detailed and complex applications properly than for having too high an income. In other words, burdensome procedures on poor, elderly, sick, and often illiterate applicants keep millions of persons from receiving benefits for which they are otherwise qualified. In seventeen southern states, the length of the Medicaid application ranged from three to fifty-two pages.[19] Rural residents still find it difficult to see doctors, dentists, and other providers. There is also some evidence of high rates of unnecessary surgery under Medicare and Medicaid. Moreover, because of state variations in coverage, the amount spent per recipient varies widely. In fact, five states alone account for half of all Medicaid spending. Other states, because of cost increases in the program, have placed limits on levels of coverage that amount to very high coinsurance requirements.

Gaps in coverage exist also within the Medicare program. It is very restrictive on nursing home care; those aged who need this care must "spend down" their financial resources until they are poor enough to qualify for Medicaid. Many of the aged, especially those near poverty, continue to have high out-of-pocket expenditures because of deductibles and coinsurance, averaging 13 percent of income for those near poverty. Medicare pays only about 42 percent of the health costs of the aged. The rest must come from Medicaid, out-of-pocket spending, or privately purchased insurance.

Other problems.   Federal government spending for health care is concentrated on the elderly, to the neglect of children and others. To some extent this concentration is necessary. The elderly need more health care. Yet the consequences of poor prenatal and postnatal care for mothers and their children are serious and long-term. They result in weakened general health, decreased learning ability and poor performance in school, and decreased motor skills, resulting in poorer employability. The cost of basic prenatal care is less than $1,000, while the cost of a neonatal intensive care bed can run beyond $2,500 per day!

Structural problems also inhibit the effectiveness of Medicare and Medicaid, preventing them from accomplishing all their goals. Because they were not designed to alter the health care delivery system but merely to pay a portion of its bills, they have, as mentioned earlier, contributed to cost escalation in health care by underwriting the most expensive forms of care. Medicare regulations allow its most generous payments for acute hospitalization; Medicaid pays nearly half of all nursing home costs and has largely financed the tremendous expansion of that industry during the 1970s. Until recently, neither program had the aim of challenging costly, unsafe, and unnecessary hospital care or the shocking conditions in many nursing homes. PSROs proved ineffective in this respect, and Medicare and Medicaid administrators were largely occupied with check drafting. They have been as big a boon to the health care industry as to patients.

An additional structural problem in Medicaid is that many physicians and dentists refuse to accept Medicaid patients because they must then legally accept the Medicaid fee schedule as full payment. The Medicaid fee structure is about two-thirds less than Medicare for the same procedures. Others accept patients but then illegally charge them the difference between their fees and the Medicaid schedule. A similar problem in Medicare noted earlier is the growing number of physicians refusing to accept Medicare benefit assignments. The result is a barrier to care or a financial burden on the poor. Fraud and corruption on the part of providers is a serious problem, though difficult to document precisely. Some estimates cite fraud at as high as 10 percent in Medicaid; others, much lower. Some dramatic instances of Medicare and Medicaid "mills" have been revealed; here, patients are treated for nonexistent conditions or overtreated for illnesses, with the "clinics" making a tidy profit.

Slowly and grudgingly the federal government has begun to address the cost problems in Medicare and Medicaid and to make changes restricting care and costs.[20] Because Medicare was expected to take in 30 percent less than it expends by the end of the century and to bankrupt the trust fund by 1990, action was clearly needed. In 1981 and 1982, there were reductions in both programs. Medicaid funding to the states by the federal government was cut, and states were given broader discretion in controlling their spending. Medicare replaced its system of reimbursements to hospitals with a system of prospective payments. In 1984, Congress further curtailed Medicare costs by imposing a fifteen-month freeze on Medicare fees charged by doctors and by increasing the monthly premiums for Part B, the voluntary medical insurance part of the program.

Prospective payment.   The most significant of these changes is the prospective payment system. Instead of reimbursing hospitals for their claimed "reasonable costs" for patient care, as in the past, the new system is based on a fixed scale (varying by region and urban-rural locality) for treating 468 different ailments (Diagnosis Related Groups, or DRGs). The hospitals have incentives for cutting costs and making sure that only necessary services are given to patients, for if their costs are higher than the set fee for their treatments, they must still accept the DRG-established fee as payment in full and may not charge the patient the difference. On the other hand, if their costs are below the established fee, they are allowed to keep the difference.

Early results from the Medicare changes show expenditure reductions. Part A expenses, which had risen 10 percent annually from 1973–1982, rose only 5.5 percent in 1985. The Medicare hospital insurance trust fund, which had been expected to be bankrupt by the late 1980s or early 1990s, is now running a surplus. Medicare hospital admissions declined 1.7 percent from 1983 to 1984, and the average patient's length of stay dropped from 9.5 days to 7.5 days. These results will certainly hold down rising costs. Whether they will adversely affect patient care and health, as critics charge, cannot yet be determined.

Prospective payment is now being tried in some Medicaid systems and by some private insurers. The DRG idea is spreading. Yet it has important limits. Hospitals faced with declining revenues may place subtle and not-so-subtle pressures on physicians to discharge patients early, the so-called quicker and sicker alternative. Additionally, the expansion of DRGs may force some hospitals to close unprofitable departments or to "dump" patients to other hospitals when costs cannot be shifted to non-DRG patients. Private insurers are now working increasingly hard to cut their costs and have clamped down on hospitals' ability to "cost shift" Medicare losses to private patients. In turn, this has forced hospitals into rapid restructuring and, in some cases, into severe financial difficulty.

Physician payment reform. Congress acted in 1989 and 1990 to reform the way in which Medicare reimburses physicians. An annual cap is now placed on Medicare physician payments, and a new scale of reimbursement called the "Resource-based relative value scale" (RBRVS) was implemented. Under the RBRVS system, Medicare rates are set not by the prevailing rates in the different medical specialties, but by an evaluation of the relative resources needed to deliver different services. This scale favors cognitive procedures such as office visits and diagnostic services, and devalues procedures such as surgery.[21] Thus, over time, the primary care specialties, such as family practice and internal medicine, will see reimbursement rates increase substantially, while surgeons, anesthesiologists, and ophthalmologists will see their rates decrease. The intended effect is not to save money on reimbursements directly but to encourage more use of lower-cost primary care and less of high-cost specializations, as well as to provide incentives for physicians to enter the primary care fields.

Medicare costs remain very high and are projected to increase to nearly $200 billion in 1995. While the Hospital Insurance Trust Fund should cover these costs during the 1990s, it will begin to disappear by the year 2000. Medicaid costs also continue to grow, and the problem of Medicaid eligibility creates important "notch" problems in the public assistance programs described in the last chapter.

Other Policies

Increases in the cost of medical care, recognized as a serious problem since the late 1960s, have not yet begun to slow down. Many supporters of a more competitive medical market argue that regulation only drives prices up by adding to the administrative costs of providers and by stifling innovation. The HMO program has taken a more direct approach by actually encouraging the rise of new competition in health care service, but the HMO experience has not fully supported hopes of a competitive medical market's ability to hold down increases.

The new PROs have not had enough time for full testing, but there is no early evidence of a substantial impact on either costs or quality of care. There is also an important question whether negative sanctions, such as PROs, are the most effective way to manage a highly fragmented health care system. Legislation in 1986 tried to attack the problem of millions of persons' lacking health insurance. That legislation requires employers with over twenty employees to make group health insurance available for up to three years for widows, divorced spouses, or dependents of employees and for up to 18 months for employees who have quit or have been laid off. Beneficiaries must pay all premiums plus a 2 percent administrative fee. Nevertheless, the number of persons without insurance, now 37 million, continues to grow.

Divergent Political Goals on Health Care

The perceived failure of Medicare, Medicaid, and other programs to attack the serious structural problems of health care may reflect inflated expectations of the effectiveness of public policy, but it certainly also reveals the different perspectives from which individuals and groups approach health policy.[22]

From the political left come charges that the health care system is biased against rural residents, the poor, and racial minorities. According to the leftist view, persons in these groups are less healthy than others because they are powerless, unable to control or to gain equal access to quality health care. Medicare, Medicaid, NHCs, and other programs have alleviated conditions marginally, but only at the cost of leaving control in the hands of hospitals, nursing homes, doctors, and the professional associations that represent them. They point out that one of the most important trends of the last decade has been the entry of for-profit corporations into the health care industry, especially for-profit hospitals and nursing homes. The growth of for-profit hospitals, the decline of public hospitals, and the new emphasis on cost cutting have the potential to reverse the gains made in health care for the poor. Hospitals are beginning to compete for paying patients through advertising and special services, such as valet parking, weight reduction and nutrition programs, and executive suites for business people. The medically indigent patient, whether covered by Medicaid or not, is not a source of profit for the hospital, and such patients may be turned away to overcrowded, declining public hospitals, or to no hospital at all, if a public one is not locally available. Quality care for the poor will be more difficult to obtain. For these reasons adherents of the political left believe that the primary impact of public programs has been to aid the wealthy providers of health care.

Liberals and radicals tend to recommend divergent approaches to overcoming this contradiction. Liberals stress greater federal regulation of the health care system and removal of financial barriers to access by enacting a form of comprehensive national health insurance. Radicals, on the other hand, reject both free-market and bureaucratic control of health delivery in favor of patient rights, affirmative action, equal access to health care, and community control of health care delivery to the poor. As an example, they cite the original intent of NHCs, which were begun as a radical strategy for health care but have gradually become bureaucratized.

Conservatives and neoconservatives find no hope in regulation or community control. The medical market, they argue, although not truly competitive now, could be made much more so. The political right charges that the regulated system penalizes both professionals and the productive public. Excessive government intervention leads to lower medical standards and higher costs. Therefore medical decisions should be left in the hands of the professionals qualified to make them. If government were to cease regulating the medical market and subsidizing third-party payments, they believe, consumers' freedom of choice coupled with the availability of alternative types of health insurance would make the market more competitive, more efficient, and less costly.

Another group of critics contends that the principal problems of health are the fault of an overemphasis on medical care. Greater attention, they argue, should be given to the environmental causes of ill health. The great advances in health and life expectancy made early in this century came through immunizations, inoculations, and public health measures creating a more sanitary environment. Comparable gains will probably not be realized through cancer and heart research and treatment, through preventive medicine, or through increased spending on doctor, hospital, and nursing home care. Rather, progress will come from attending to the cancer- and other disease-causing agents in the workplace, air, and water. Society knows what many of these are and should devote its resources to removing them and preventing their entry into the environment. Those who take this position argue that these environmentally induced cancers, lung diseases, kidney diseases, and other ailments are already costing billions of dollars for health care and lost work time. Expenditures to reduce their causes would be prudent investments in health and economic productivity.

Personal health practices. Accompanying environmental concerns is the notion of preventive self-measures for personal health. The greatest potential for improving health and extending life may lie within the control of the individual. Studies have shown that individuals can add eleven years to their life expectancy by following some basic health habits, such as the following:[23]

1. A balanced diet with regular meals.
2. Breakfast every day.
3. Moderate exercise two or three times a week.
4. Adequate sleep (seven or eight hours a night).
5. No smoking.
6. Moderate weight.
7. No alcohol or only in moderation.

These practices would cost government and society nothing. Government and private industry programs to encourage fitness and to discourage smoking and drug and alcohol abuse may extend life and moderate health care costs as much as any other measures can, and some unions, corporations, and health insurance companies are already offering special benefit packages to nonsmokers and others who practice good health habits.

Liberals who emphasize these ideas are also strong supporters of government programs of occupational safety and health, of strict controls on disease-causing chemicals, of efforts to clean up the environment, and of antismoking campaigns. Conservatives point to individual responsibility, arguing that the choice of whether to practice good health habits is essentially outside government influence and that personal risk taking is not an appropriate area for strong government action. But society even now ends up paying for individual decisions adversely affecting health through Medicare, Medicaid, public hospitals, and increased health insurance premiums. Hospitals and companies are installing health and wellness centers. These can have important positive effects on employee morale, productivity, and health, but there is not much evidence of health care cost savings. Surprisingly, preventive medicine itself does not seem clearly to lead to reduced medical costs, and preventive measures can have serious externalities. Vaccinations may cause serious injuries; life-style factors may be used to deny or raise insurance premiums; health screening may be used to deny or terminate employment or promotions.[24]

Other nations.   We have said that other advanced industrial nations have health care systems rather different from those in America. Because they stress physicians in general practice, strict controls on hospital affiliation, and comprehensive coverage, they have avoided most of America's major problems. The numbers of specialists and primary care physicians are in rough balance, financial burdens from medical care are absent, and, because programs are comprehensive, access is universal.

Yet there are disadvantages and problems in these systems as well. Virtually all are facing cost escalation similar to America's. Even in systems that serve all, regardless of financial status, there are still inequities in access to care and in the health of different classes. In England, for example, there is still a strong correlation between mortality and morbidity rates and social class. The National Health Service has not been able to persuade doctors to practice in sufficient numbers in underserved areas or to overcome the social and economic causes of poor health.[25] Because many of the determinants of health and disease are less medical than individual, social, economic, and environmental, many of the same ideological controversies over environmental health and personal health responsibility rage in Europe.

FUTURE ALTERNATIVES: ETHICS, COST CONTROL, AND ACCESS

The principal current issues in health policy may be grouped into three categories: ethical controversies, questions about reliance on market mechanisms for cost control, and ensuring access to care. In discussing alternatives to the present system of health care, the first two categories have much to do with the third. Each of the three is strongly affected by the problem of spiraling health care costs.

Ethical Issues

Previous chapters demonstrated that evaluations of such moral questions as compassion for the poor, crime and sin, and the value of an unspoiled environment are a fundamental part of public policy debate. Normally, however, these questions are combined with questions of efficiency, cost, and feasibility. Similarly, in health policy this mix of questions prevails for most issues. The issues considered in this section, however, are almost purely ethical. Because pain and death affect perceptions of the meaning of life and the value of the body, medical issues are essentially tied to philosophical, religious, and moral beliefs.

Right to care.   The most comprehensive ethical issue is whether there is or should be a right to health care in America. This issue parallels the question of the right to a basic minimum income discussed in Chapter 7. Closely tied to the issue of a right to health care is the question of whether the right, if it exists, is an equal right. The positions taken on these ethical questions strongly influence where one will stand on the issues of reliance on competition, Medicare and Medicaid spending, and national health insurance, which in its most complete form would provide universal health care for all U.S. citizens. Those who argue that there is a right to health care and that it is an equal right support the most extensive proposals for expansion of health policies to cover all citizens fully.

Advocates of a right to health care contend that health is a requirement for a decent life, just as food, clothing, shelter, and political and civil freedom are. Because law and policy guard these aspects of life, they should guard health by recognizing a right to health care. Therefore government has the responsibility to see that all persons, insofar as humanly possible, have access to the care needed to preserve health. Those who oppose this position contend that the Anglo-American constitutional tradition recognizes political and civil rights such as freedom of speech and the right to a trial by jury, but it has never recognized rights to the public distribution of economic goods, such as food, health care, and shelter. Government may, indeed, help provide these for citizens, but not as rights to which all have a claim. They are given as charity or as services.

Among those who recognize a right to health care there is considerable disagreement over whether it is a right to a basic minimum of care or a right to equal care.[26] Proponents of an equal right point out that health is one of the fundamental goods a person can possess. It affects job, income, education, social status, and sense of worth. Therefore to distribute health care unequally on the basis of income or residence or age is to commit a grave injustice. All must have an equal right to the most extensive health services available. It would be wrong to allow the wealthy to extend their lives by buying access to chemotherapy while consigning the poor to early deaths from cancer.

On the other hand, many believe that providing equal access to the most expensive services available would drive up the demand for them, imposing an enormous burden on society. Also, they argue, visits for minor and imagined illnesses would impose heavy demands on doctors' time. (There is, however, no evidence of such a phenomenon in nations recognizing an equal right to health care.) Those who take this position contend that all have a right to a basic minimum of care necessary for good health, but beyond that minimum, individuals' ability to buy services may be used to allocate resources. Would it be just, they may ask, to demand country club memberships for all because the rich can afford the health-enhancing benefits of golf, tennis, and sauna?

Other ethical issues concern how health policy should allocate limited resources to different kinds of need. The health needs of the young and old differ substantially. Is it more just to invest enormous sums under Medicare and Medicaid in high-cost acute care technologies for seriously ill old persons or in expensive long-term nursing home care, or should these sums go to support the basic medical, dental, and psychological care needed by the young whose lives are just beginning? Similarly, policy advocates debate whether research and treatment should focus on the major fatal diseases such as heart disease and cancer, as they do now, or on the long-term chronic, crippling diseases such as mental disorders, arthritis, and senility. These are moral, rather than medical or scientific, questions, because they involve the values that determine how society should allocate scarce resources among its different segments. Recent debates about how much research funds should be allocated to research into AIDS (acquired immunodeficiency syndrome) illustrates well the moral and political dimensions of health questions.

AIDS.   AIDS, first recognized as a disease in 1981, had become one of the nation's highest public health priorities by the end of the 1980s. The retrovirus, now called human immunodeficiency virus (HIV), responsible for AIDS was identified only in 1983, and the first drug effective in treating AIDS, AZT, was licensed in 1987. AZT was the product of federal biomedical research, with AIDS research funded at $1.2 billion in 1993.

Persons with AIDS and persons at high risk for AIDS (primarily homosexual and bisexual males, intravenous drug users, and the sexual partners of such persons) suffer high potential for employment and other discrimination. Chapter 10 covers the issue of protecting them from discrimination. Other questions concern the allocation of dollars for research. Although AIDS is a terrible and rapidly spreading disease (see Figure 8-7), almost invariably fatal, its current incidence and the number of deaths is very low compared to cancer, heart disease, and the disabling effects of dementias such as Alzheimer's disease. Does AIDS research have too high or too low a federal priority in light of other areas of research?

Other ethical questions involve whether stopping the spread of AIDS justifies distributing clean needles to IV drug users, explicit sex education programs in elementary schools, and condom advertisements on television. Another question is how to distribute the cost of medical care for AIDS victims. This cost can be quite high, as much as $150,000 per case, and could cost the nation as much as $40 billion in 1993. Although this is only about 5 percent of total projected health costs, it will be heavily concentrated in certain cities and states. How can the system of private and public health insurance cope with these costs? Who should pay them?[27]

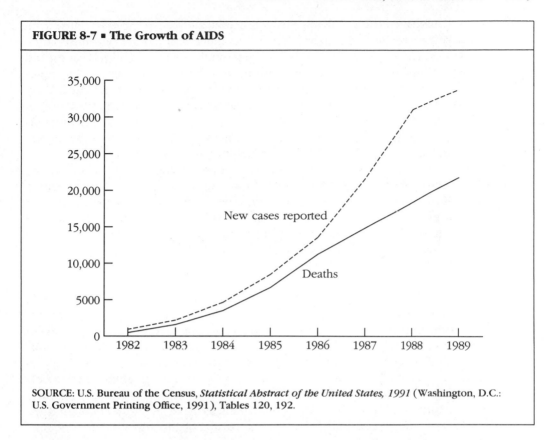

FIGURE 8-7 ▪ The Growth of AIDS

SOURCE: U.S. Bureau of the Census, *Statistical Abstract of the United States, 1991* (Washington, D.C.: U.S. Government Printing Office, 1991), Tables 120, 192.

Funding health care.   The subjects of birth and death raise major policy questions.[28] Abortion, discussed in Chapter 10 in a different context, is such a question. In the realm of health care, debate centers on the Hyde amendment, upheld by the Supreme Court in 1980, which bans Federal Medicaid funding for most abortions. Some argue that this denial discriminates against the poor; others, that it saves the lives of thousands of unborn infants. At the other end of life, debate focuses on whether society should fund or encourage the use of sophisticated medical technology to keep alive those, particularly the aged, with terminal illnesses. Should government discontinue funding such treatments in order to use the resources elsewhere? Similar issues were raised by the "Baby Jane Doe" case and others, which asked whether physicians and parents may withhold life-saving care from severely handicapped newborns. Recent controversies concern the ethics of removing feeding tubes from patients in a "persistent vegetative state." Many support legislation at the state and national levels that would allow a person the right to die in dignity; these measures would remove extraordinary means of life support in terminal cases. Such legislation would also allow physicians and family members to make such decisions without fear of criminal prosecution.

Some states have enacted "living will" legislation, allowing persons to refuse such extraordinary technologies in advance of becoming ill. Still other reformists argue in favor of active euthanasia, that is, allowing terminally ill persons to request and receive an injection or other artificial means to end their lives. Dramatic examples of physician-assisted suicide raised the issue to national prominence in 1991. Many oppose these measures on the ground that they cheapen life, making it a matter of economic calculation. They also believe that such policies diminish the religious value of suffering for the human spirit and that they "play God" by allowing the state, physicians, or individuals to determine the time and manner of death.

By the late 1980s, a debate had opened up regarding the ethics of rationing health care access by age. The principal question is whether certain expensive procedures should be available to all persons or whether they should be denied to persons beyond a certain age, since at that point they are unlikely to prolong the quality or length of life significantly. Examples of such procedures are kidney dialysis, heart transplants, and chemotherapy.[29]

Finally, government support for biomedical research raises serious ethical questions. Particularly troublesome are attempts to create new forms of life through recombinant DNA research and in vitro fertilization ("test-tube babies"), although other research areas raise similar questions. Proponents of government support for scientific research argue that it is essential to advance the frontiers of knowledge and that just as previous research has, it will lead to cures for serious illness and procedures to relieve suffering. Opponents contend that unlike previous scientific breakthroughs, recombinant DNA research involves creating new forms of life, an enterprise not appropriate to human endeavor and one that may likely result in new diseases for which humans have no protection. In vitro fertilization, they argue, interferes with the natural beginning of life and requires immoral experimentation on embryonic human life.

Health Care Cost Control

Market mechanisms.   Most discussions of health care assume, as previous sections of this chapter indicated, that the medical marketplace exhibits only very imperfect competition. Normal economic mechanisms of supply and demand, competition, and informed consumer choice do not operate effectively in it. A vociferous attack on this assumption, however, has been mounted in recent years by conservative and neoconservative policy analysts.[30] These critics argue that if medical consumers were encouraged to "shop around" for the best use of their health care dollars, especially in the purchase of insurance, the medical market would function more competitively. Consumers, in this view, do not need more regulatory protection; they often have enough information from friends and relatives to make intelligent choices among health care providers. Moreover, professional peer pressure, fear of malpractice suits, and competition from alternative care-delivery mechanisms can weaken physicians' ability to control demand for services. These analysts recognize the imperfect nature of present medical markets but attribute much of that imperfection to the monopolistic, anticompetitive practices of professional groups such as the American Medical Association, to excessive government regulation, and to tax policies that subsidize high-cost medical insurance and health care.

One of the most important changes in the modern American health care system is nearly universal recognition of its fundamental economic incentives at all levels. As a result, although general free-market forces are only minimally effectual, selective market mechanisms can be used effectively.

Earlier we noted that market proponents originally placed a great deal of confidence in HMOs as a method of generating competition. Market advocates now suggest four types of action to restore the market's ability to control medical costs and provide necessary services.

1. Greater reliance on deductibles and coinsurance would reduce the percentage of third-party payments and force the consumer to consider medical expenditures more carefully and to shop for less costly alternatives. Replacing current comprehensive health insurance policies with major risk insurance would promote this goal.
2. Tax laws should be modified to reduce deductions for buying expensive insurance or medical treatments, formulas that amount to medical subsidies. Tax law could be rewritten to eliminate deductions or provide fixed ones, instead of the present practice of increasing deductions as an individual or employer spends more on health care.
3. The strong link between employment and insurance should be severed. Instead of having to accept a single employer-provided plan, employees should be encouraged to "shop around" among a variety of plans with various coverages and costs.
4. Insurance providers should be encouraged to control costs by limiting their reimbursements for services to those who hold prices down. They may even form closed-panels, or preferred provider organizations (PPOs) willing to keep costs in line. Coverage might not be provided for non-essential services, such as cosmetic surgery.

These suggestions have grown in popularity in recent years, and government and private institutions have taken some steps in this direction. Income tax deductions for health insurance and health care have been reduced. The 1986 tax-reform bill increased to 7.5 the percentage of taxable income beyond which medical expenses become deductible. Competitive, private-enterprise elements are being introduced as private, profit-making corporations increasingly enter the hospital, nursing home, and health delivery systems formerly dominated by public and private, not-for-profit institutions. Blue Cross and other insurance companies, as well as labor and management in their employee health insurance plans, have begun to experiment with closed panels, voluntary fee restraint, and options for lower-cost, less extensive coverage policies. There is some evidence to indicate that patients' cost sharing does reduce health care usage, and thus costs, without adversely affecting health, and that such cost sharing is being increasingly promoted.[31]

Criticism of medical markets.   Critics of the market advocates' approach point to the unique nature of the health care market. Consumers possess little information about illnesses or the effectiveness of treatments. When they are sick and in pain, patients are too ready to abdicate responsibility to professionals. Some illnesses literally leave persons physically unable to "shop around." Physicians have great leeway in achieving their "target incomes," by determining types of treatments and tests, length of hospital stay, and number of office visits. Critics are also skeptical of the possibility that unorganized consumers will be able to exert substantial influence on the physicians, government bureaucrats, large insurance companies, and hospitals that control medical resources. The following observation spells out the argument against "free-market" medicine. According to H.J. Geiger, "There is no 'effective demand' among American consumers for a barium enema or a heart-valve repair, and there is no 'free market' for hospital rooms as there is for hotel rooms. You don't get them at all without a physician's order: but when a physician orders them, you almost always get them. The suppliers control, even create, the demand."[32]

Those who scoff at a competitive medical market believe that there are only two alternatives for holding down prices and guaranteeing services: (1) government regulation of prices, fees, services, and delivery systems or (2) total government financing of health care. In the former, costs and services are controlled administratively; in the latter, they are controlled by annual appropriations, which cannot be exceeded by providers. Most European nations employ a combination of these strategies. Changes in the 1980s in federal health programs toward prospective payments, RBRVS, and limiting physicians' fees illustrate the administrative approach, although prospective payments are intended to encourage some market efficiencies by hospitals. National systems of health care do not invariably hold down costs, but they give government the opportunity to regulate the salaries of health care workers, especially physicians, and to ration expensive technologies. DRGs are one method of such regulation already employed in the United States. They combine directives and market-oriented savings incentives for hospitals. The Canadian system of universal health insurance and the British system of socialized medicine demonstrate that it is possible to control health costs.[33] The United States, without a system of universal health coverage, has the most costly medical system in the developed world.

Changes already under way in American health care delivery will produce effects on health costs that are not yet well understood. As advances in medicine limit hospital admissions and length of stay, hospitals are closing or redirecting their missions. Those that survive compete for patients and doctors by offering amenities and new preventive medicine services. Outpatient surgeries and free-standing surgical units, as well as minor care clinics ("Doc in a Box"), have directed care away from traditional hospital in-patient care. In 1976, hospital employment accounted for two-thirds of all health care employment; now it is 55 percent. More doctors involved in these practices or in HMOs are on salary, instead of fee-for-service. Their incentive, therefore, is to reduce the number of procedures performed, thereby reducing costs, but leaving the potential for reduced quality of care. A leaner, more competitive medical system may mean less rapidly growing costs. But it also raises questions about how best to care for patients and how much patient freedom of choice will be available.

The question of freedom of choice is raised also by the efforts of the federal government, employers, and private insurers to hold down their costs by requiring patients to see only certain providers, either through an HMO, a preferred provider organization (PPO), or an independent practice association (IPA). The PPO and the IPA are associations of independent physicians who agree to combine their services and to contract with employers or insurers to serve their customers at reduced rates. These new forms of health care delivery are changing the face of American medicine, but it is not clear whether this change will be enough to control costs or whether the new recognition of economic incentives will have an adverse effect on quality of care.

Ensuring Access to Care

Since the passage of Medicare and Medicaid in 1965, major legislative debate has considered the issue of whether the United States should follow the European lead and develop a comprehensive federal insurance scheme covering the major health needs of the entire population. Should the principles of Medicare and Medicaid be extended from the aged and the poor to all citizens? It is possible that within the current political climate the question is a moot one. By the early 1970s, there seemed to be sufficient momentum to support passage of some form of national health insurance. But during that decade liberal sentiments appear to have been replaced by more conservative ones.

A variety of factors stalled the movement. Organized opposition to national health insurance (NHI) continued from professional groups such as the American Medical Association and the American Hospital Association, who drew support away from comprehensive NHI by sponsoring their own proposals for very weak bills. Liberals refused significant compromise on their support for the most extensive forms of NHI; so the opportunity for enacting more limited legislation was lost. By the late 1970s, rampant inflation and large federal budget deficits had halted progress toward NHI, although legislative proposals continued to be introduced. Yet the basic issues and problems in health care, to which NHI is proposed as a solution, continue.[34]

By the early 1990s, the issue of national health care was important once again. The unexpected 1991 Senate election victory of Harris Wofford in Pennsylvania catapulted the issue into the political arena in the 1992 elections. The primary issue is providing access to care for the poor, the uninsured, and the aged needing long-term care. Cost-cutting measures tend to make this care less readily available. Moreover, introducing more competition into medicine makes it difficult for the poor and the uninsured to get care, since they are unlikely to increase the profits of health care providers.

The American health care system is founded on employment-linked health insurance plus Medicare for the aged and Medicaid for the unemployed poor. But, as discussions earlier in this chapter indicated, there has been a decline in the number of poor covered by Medicaid and in the ability of increasingly hard-pressed hospitals and clinics to offer uncompensated care for the poor. Already mentioned in the previous section is 1986 federal legislation mandating employer-provided insurance coverage of former employees and dependents. This measure is particularly important since loss of employment is a major reason for having no insurance coverage. Along the same line are various proposals at the state and federal levels to mandate particular coverages in employer-provided benefits; that is, to make sure that they do reasonably cover serious illness, parental leave after the birth of a child, preventive care for children, psychiatric care, and alcohol and drug abuse treatment.

New proposals.   Proposals for widening access to all Americans, or at least to many more of the poor and the uninsured, fall into three basic types.[35] Each has strong supporters in the political and the health care communities. Whatever fundamental health care reform emerges in the 1990s will be derived from one of these approaches.

Health insurance vouchers.   In his 1992 State of the Union address, President Bush proposed this reform, which is supported by many conservatives. Leaving the basic structure of public and private health care and health insurance untouched, he proposed that the tax system be used to provide health insurance vouchers in the form of refundable tax credits or tax deductions to low-income persons who purchase health insurance policies. Those without insurance would receive up to $3,750 per family per year for this purpose. This approach would require minimal changes in the current system, although Medicare and Medicaid would be cut in order to release funds to pay for the program. The system of private health insurance companies would remain in place. The proposal also claims some of the advantages of competitive approaches described above. Consumers would make choices of insurance among the most cost-effective plans.

The disadvantages of this proposal, however, are very substantial. It does nothing significant to reduce costs, because it leaves virtually unchanged all of the incentives that have made the American health care system the most expensive in the world. Second, it assumes that low-income and other uninsured persons will in fact be intelligent, cost-conscious health insurance consumers and that cost-effective individual or group policies will be made available to them. Finally, and most significantly, this proposal would encourage many small employers to drop their insurance coverage, forcing their employees to resort to the tax-credit–financed individual policies. This would shift more of the cost of health insurance from the private to the public sector.

Other proposals that involve only modest changes in the present system include incremental Medicare and Medicaid expansion to cover adequately the most at-risk groups and government-supported or -mandated risk pools that would enable small employers to obtain lower-cost policies for their workers. These proposals would make only a small dent in the large number of persons uncovered or inadequately covered by insurance.

Mandatory employment-based insurance.   A variety of proposals under this heading build upon the existing system of employment-based health insurance. This approach has the advantage of leaving in place a system of insurance that employers, employees, and health insurance providers are familiar with. But it would extend that system to cover more persons. There are two basic variations of this strategy. The first variation is *compulsory private insurance* through employers, with government insuring the unemployed through an expanded Medicaid. This approach requires every employer to provide a standard health insurance package covering basic health care to every employee. Government would insure the rest. Theoretically, then, every person would have access to health care. Hawaii instituted such a plan in 1974, and it appears to work well.

The second variation goes under the name, *"play or pay."* In this approach, every employer would either have to provide basic insurance to every employee (play) or contribute funds to a public insurance program (pay) that would cover all the uninsured. This approach avoids the problem of requiring employers with few workers to deal with the intricacies of insurance provision and to shop around among programs. They could simply elect to pay a tax (similar to the unemployment insurance tax) for each worker. All such workers would then be under a single government-operated insurance plan.

Compulsory employment-based insurance, particularly the "play or pay" variant, is widely supported in Congress and in sectors of the health care industry. Democratic presidential candidates Bob Kerrey and Paul Tsongas proposed such plans in 1992. This method has the advantage described above of keeping the basic system in place but extending it to all persons. There are, however, major disadvantages to this plan. Again, there is little cost control. The system of private insurance, which produces very high administrative costs in health care and serious inefficiencies, remains in place. Moreover, compulsory insurance under either variant adds a substantial business cost to employers not currently providing health insurance. (Of course, these employers are now at a competitive advantage over employers who do provide insurance.) Not only will such a policy increase business costs, it will also add another layer of government regulation to business. Finally, many employers that now provide health insurance to their workers might decide to cancel that coverage and elect to "pay" the tax, letting their workers be covered under the public program.

All-government insurance.   In light of the complexities and disadvantages of the proposals described above, a comprehensive restructuring of the health care system may be in order. This, at least, is the argument of many liberals inside and outside the health care system. This restructuring would provide public health insurance to every person as a right of citizenship. Health providers would still be private; government would not take over private hospitals or physicians' practices. But such a program would eliminate all private insurance, as well as Medicaid, in favor of a nationally or regionally administered single health insurance program.

This proposal, in the view of its advocates, such as 1992 Democratic presidential candidate Tom Harkin, would have the advantage of eliminating the waste and inefficiency of thousands of private insurance programs, all with large numbers of administrators, different claim forms, and different coverages, in favor of a single payer, with uniform coverage and a single claim form. The administrative savings under such a system might well pay for most of the expanded coverage. Moreover, employers would be free of the burden of health care costs and administration, and all citizens would have access to health care based on their need for it. Such a system would also be in a strong position to negotiate health care cost reductions from doctors, hospitals, and other providers. The Canadian system provides the model for many who favor this approach.

The disadvantages of the proposal are also significant. First, it would require a massive restructuring of health care and health administration, upsetting very powerful and well-established components of the system, particularly the health insurance companies. It would also reduce other kinds of private control over health care, and it would worry physicians and other providers that their freedom of action and their freedom of income would be affected adversely. Second, the all-government system would shift billions of dollars of expenditures from private to public budgets, requiring a massive increase in taxes. Even if taxpayers as a whole saw an off-setting reduction in their private insurance fees and out-of-pocket health expenses, there is substantial resistance to any tax increases in the contemporary political climate.

Managed care.   Managed care is often proposed as a component of the second and third options above, or as an independent set of proposals to obtain cost control. Managed care is already part of HMOs and of many private insurance policies, which may require some combination of second opinions before surgery or hospitalization, prior approval before a major procedure, and patient use of a designated provider or set of providers (PPOs or IPAs). Lower fees are negotiated between insurers and the approved providers.

Some health care reformers see greater use of managed care as a means of getting control of runaway costs. Government regulations could be used to induce or require many public and private insurance providers to use HMOs, PPOs, and other managed care devices. These regulations could also require that all plans and providers offer a similar basic benefit package to all consumers without cancellations and without exclusions on the basis of preexisting conditions, thus increasing access.

Opponents of managed care proposals argue that such limitations on consumer choice and provider judgment of needed treatments will interfere with health care quality. Physicians will not be able to exercise their own professional expertise in treating patients but will be subject to approval or second-guessing by nonphysician administrators of insurance plans.

Conclusion.   Inability to marshall sufficient political strength behind one of the approaches just described has left the issue of health care reform in stalemate. The public increasingly perceives that the health care system has serious problems, but it is difficult to build coalitions for fundamental change when so many groups with different interests have to be brought together. The current political and electoral controversies over health care are part of the process of negotiating reform. There is one issue, however, that requires a different approach from any of those just discussed.

FIGURE 8-8 ▪ Projected Nursing Home Expenditures, 1965–2000

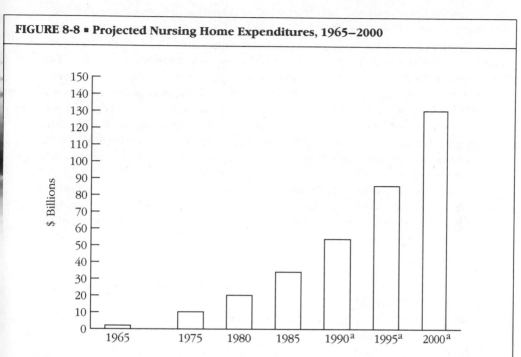

ª Estimates.

SOURCE: S. T. Sonnenfeld, D. R. Waldo, J. A. Lemieux, and D. R. McKusick, "Projections of national health expenditures through the year 2000," *Health Care Financing Review* 13 (1): 1–28, HCFA Pub. No. 03321, Office of Research and Demonstrations, Health Care Financing Administration (Washington, D.C.: U.S. Government Printing Office, October, 1991).

Long-term care.   A second major issue for the future is how to finance long-term care for the elderly. Expenditures on long-term nursing home care have risen dramatically in recent decades, along with the increase in the number of aged persons (see Figure 8-8). When the baby boom generation begins to retire after 2010, the problem will be greatly intensified. Medicare, as previously mentioned, does not pay for ordinary nursing home care, although Medicaid does. Therefore Medicare recipients who need such care must first exhaust all of their resources so that they become poor enough to be eligible for Medicaid.

On any given day about 5 percent of those over 65 and 20 percent of those over 85 are in nursing homes. Moreover, 20 percent of the elderly have some chronic or disabling condition, and nearly one-third of all American health care expenditures benefit the aged. Astonishingly, one-third of all Medicare expenditures are concentrated on caring for the dying in their last year of life.

Most proposals for dealing with long-term care focus on amending Medicare to provide nursing home coverage.[36] But attention must also be given to finding ways to pay for less expensive care that could be provided at home. Nevertheless, any solution will be costly, and little alternative exists to Medicare and Medicaid. Private insurance for long-term care is unlikely. First, it would be prohibitively expensive if purchased after 65; yet the young are unlikely to invest scarce dollars in policies designed to cover their possible nursing home care in old age. We can continue inadequately to finance long-term care through the means-tested welfare solution of Medicaid, or we can reform Medicare. If the latter option is selected, then the question of financing will prove a major political battleground, as it did with the 1988 catastrophic care legislation. Should Medicare recipients finance long-term care themselves, or should it be provided by the working population through payroll or income taxes?

For all of these reasons health care politics will continue to be contentious, and policy will be difficult to form. None of the policy proposals, whether competitive, regulatory, or NHI, can control costs effectively, because control would require substantial structural changes in the health care system, changes affecting everyone as a consumer of health care. Building a coalition for such change would be extraordinarily difficult politically. The costs of health care are distributed widely among the population, whereas the financial benefits are concentrated. Change, therefore, is strongly resisted. Finally, the growing numbers of the elderly and constantly new technology place demands on the system that no reform can change.[37] Health is a basic value in all cultures, and the resources Americans devote to health care indicate its high priority in this culture. Whether these resources can truly be said to advance the goal of good health is the central issue in health care policy.

SUMMARY

The American health care system is a mixture of private individual behavior, private corporate endeavors, and government policy. Lack of coordination characterizes the provision of and payment for services. This system is increasingly dominated by third-party payments, and it absorbs over 12 percent of the GNP. Other nations have more comprehensive systems of health care, but severe cost inflation is a major problem in most countries. American health care lags behind the rest of the world on basic measures of health, and it suffers serious problems of access, cost, and quality.

The most important problem in health care, shared by many nations, is its soaring cost to society. The chief causes of cost escalation in the United States are growing numbers of elderly, overspecialization, maldistribution, third-party payments, modern medical technology, federal tax policy, and the public's exaggerated expectations of medical science.

U.S. public policy in the health field prior to 1965 was largely concerned with public health in regard to regulating and licensing drugs and food, supporting health research, funding hospital construction, and minor efforts aimed at improving the health of the poor. U.S. health care policy was still in its infancy.

This situation was revolutionized in 1965 when the War on Poverty stimulated passage of Medicare and Medicaid. Medicare provides hospital insurance and voluntary medical insurance under Social Security for those sixty-five and older. Medicaid is a cooperative state-federal program offering health care services to the poor. Funded from general revenues, it supports a variety of such services, varying from state to state.

Other federal health care programs include support for professional training, Neighborhood Health Centers, Peer Review Organizations, health-related block grants, and support for Health Maintenance Organizations.

Federal health care policy, particularly Medicare and Medicaid, has been successful in reducing the financial burden of medical care on the aged and the poor, and it has improved both their access to care and their general health. Some of the health gaps between black and white and aged and nonaged have been narrowed.

There still are substantial problems with federal health care policy, however. Many differences in quality and access to care still remain among various groups. Medicare and Medicaid have contributed to health care's inflated costs and have not challenged structural problems in its delivery. And neither regulatory policies nor PROs, PPOs, and HMOs have had the success hoped for in introducing rational coordination and cost control into the system.

Ideological disagreement pervades the evaluation of health care policy. The political left charges that the health care system is biased against the aged, the poor, rural residents, and minorities. The political right stresses the failures of market regulation and advocates less government intervention and more competition in the health insurance sector. Liberals stress the failure of the medical marketplace and the need for government regulation. Other groups see individual responsibility for good health habits as the direction for substantial improvement in health. Similar controversies plague other nations.

Ethical issues are important to health care policy today. Whether there is a right to health care and, if there is, whether it is a right to basic minimum care or to full care for all are central questions.

Another major issue in health care policy centers on the recent conservative attacks on government regulation of markets. They argue that medical markets can function effectively and control costs if consumers can be encouraged to shop for insurance policies, if monopolistic insurance practices can be broken, and if government regulation is weakened. Critics of this approach contend that regulation is necessary because consumers lack adequate information to make intelligent choices, because medicine is a sellers' market, and because of the entrenched power of health care providers.

Access to health care remains a fundamental problem, and policy initiatives in the 1990s will have to address three of its most difficult dimensions: finding ways to provide coverage for the 55 percent of persons below the poverty line not now covered by Medicaid, providing health insurance for millions of workers without employer-provided insurance, and financing long-term health care for the elderly.

NOTES

1. Aaron Wildavsky, "Doing Better and Feeling Worse: The Political Pathology of Health Policy," in John H. Knowles, ed., "Doing Better and Feeling Worse: Health in the United States," *Daedalus,* 106 (Winter 1977) p. 111.

2. The comparative material in this section is based upon Arnold J. Heidenheimer, Hugh Heclo, and Carolyn Teich Adams, *Comparative Public Policy,* 3rd ed. (New York: St. Martin's Press, 1990); Lawrence D. Brown, ed., *Health Policy in Transition* (Durham, N.C.: Duke University Press, 1987), pp. 17–64; Henry J. Aaron, *Serious and Unstable Condition: Financing America's Health Care* (Washington, D.C.: Brookings Institution, 1991), chap.4; and Victor G. Rodwin, "Comparative Health Systems," in Anthony R. Kovner, ed., *Health Care Delivery in the United States,* 4th ed. (New York: Springer, 1990), pp. 435–465. See also Jean de Kervasdoue et al., eds., *The End of an Illusion: The Future of Health Policy in Western Industrialized Nations* (Berkeley: University of California Press, 1984).

3. Harrell R. Rodgers, Jr., *Poverty amid Plenty* (Reading, Mass.: Addison-Wesley, 1979), chap. 6.

4. George Rust, "Sick and Poor, Close the Door," *Health and Development,* 8 (Summer 1988), 3–7; for data on access to health care, see President's Commission for the Study of Ethical Problems in Medicine and Biomedical and Behavioral Research, *Securing Access to Health Care, Vol. I: Report* (Washington, D.C.: U.S. Government Printing Office, 1983), chap. 2.

5. Edward S. Greenberg, *Serving the Few* (New York: John Wiley, 1974), p. 158.

6. Louise B. Russell, "Medical Care Costs," in Pechman, ed., *Setting National Priorities: The 1978 Budget* (Washington, D.C.: Brookings Institution, 1977), p. 182.

7. Carl J. Schramm, ed., *Health Care and Its Costs* (New York: Norton, 1987).

8. Eli Ginzberg, "Health Services, Power Centers, and Decision-Making Mechanisms," in Knowles, *Doing Better,* pp. 209–211.

9. For some of the debate, see Ivan Illich, *Medical Nemesis* (New York: Bantam, 1977); Ivan L. Bennett, Jr., "Technology As a Shaping Force," in Knowles, *Doing Better,* pp. 125–133; and Karen Davis and Cathy Schoen, *Health and the War on Poverty: A Ten-Year Appraisal* (Washington, D.C.: Brookings Institution, 1978), pp. 23–25, 219–224.

10. See Kenneth E. Thorpe, "Health Care Cost Containment," in Kovner, ed., *Health Care Delivery,* chap. 11, and Aaron, *Serious and Unstable Condition,* chap. 3.

11. Kenneth M. Dolbeare, *American Public Policy* (New York: McGraw-Hill, 1982), pp. 201–204; Howard H. Hiatt, *America's Health in the Balance* (New York: Harper & Row, 1987), pp. 4, 27–29, 39–40, 47, 81–84.

12. See William P. Brandon and Carol McPhee, "The Federal Assumption of Responsibility for Health Policy, 1953–1966," paper delivered at the 1979 Annual Meeting of the American Political Science Association, Washington, D.C. For a list of the most important pieces of legislation, see Brown, ed., *Health Policy in Transition,* pp. 1–3.

13. A good summary of the provisions, costs, and impact of Medicare and Medicaid may be found in Davis and Schoen, *Health and the War on Poverty,* chaps. 3 and 4. See also Paul Starr, *The Social Transformation of American Medicine* (New York: Basic Books, 1982), chap. 3; and Rashi Fein, *Medical Care, Medical Costs* (Cambridge: Harvard University Press, 1986), chaps. 5–6.

14. On the politics of the legislation, see Beth C. Fuchs and John F. Hoadley, "Reflections from Inside the Beltway: How Congress and the President Grapple with Health Policy," *PS,* 20 (Spring 1987), 212–220.

15. John F. Holahan and Joel W. Cohen, *Medicaid: The Trade-off between Cost Containment and Access to Care* (Washington, D.C.: Urban Institute Press, 1986).

16. See Davis and Schoen, *Health and the War on Poverty,* chap. 6; also William P. Brandon, "Politics, Administration, and Conflict in Neighborhood Health Centers," *Journal of Health Politics, Policy and Law,* 2 (Spring 1977), 79–99; and H. Jack Geiger, "Community Health Centers," in Victor W. Sidel and Ruth Sidel, eds., *Reforming Medicine* (New York: Pantheon, 1984), pp. 11–32.

17. Paul Starr, "Health for the Poor: The Past Twenty Years," in Sheldon H. Danziger and Daniel H. Weinberg, eds., *Fighting Poverty* (Cambridge: Harvard University Press, 1986), pp. 116–121, and note 10 above.

18. Information on these gains comes primarily from Davis and Schoen, *Health and the War on Poverty,* chaps. 2–4, and Stephen M. Davidson and Theodore R. Marmor, *The Cost of Living Longer: National Health Insurance and the Elderly* (Lexington, Mass: Heath, 1980).

19. Don Colburn, "Medicaid: It's Not What They Make That Counts," *Washington Post National Weekly Edition,* July 4–10, 1988, p. 33.

20. See Schramm, ed., *Health Care and Its Costs.*

21. For a description of RBRVS, see William C. Hsiao et al., "Resource-Based Values: An Overview," *JAMA: Journal of the American Medical Association,* October 28, 1988, 2347–2353.

22. See Victor G. Rodwin, "Perspectives on the State: Implications for the Future," in Kervasdoue et al., eds., *The End of an Illusion,* pp. 35–55.

23. See particularly John H. Knowles, "The Responsibility of the Individual," in Knowles, "Doing Better," pp. 57–80, esp. pp. 61–62.

24. Louise B. Russell, *Is Prevention Better than Cure?* (Washington, D.C.: Brookings Institution, 1986); Jack A. Meyer and Marion Ein Lewin, eds., *Charting the Future of Health Care* (Washington, D.C.: American Enterprise Institute, 1987), Part III; Deborah A. Stone, "The Resistible Rise of Preventive Medicine," in Brown, ed., *Health Policy in Transition,* pp. 103–128.

25. Gillian Pascall, "Health," in David C. Marsh, ed., *Introducing Social Policy* (London: Routledge & Kegan Paul, 1979), pp. 141–164.

26. See, for example, Ronald M. Green, "Health Care and Justice in Contract Theory Perspective," in Robert M. Veatch and Roy Branson, eds., *Ethics and Health Policy* (Cambridge, Mass.: Ballinger, 1976), pp. 111–126; Norman Daniels, *Just Health Care* (New York: Cambridge University Press, 1985); for a comprehensive review of this issue and of a variety of ethical issues in health care, see President's Commission, *Securing Access to Health Care,* and Thomas M. Garrett, Harold W. Baillie, and Rosellen M. Garrett, *Health Care Ethics: Principles and Problems* (Englewood Cliffs, N.J.: Prentice-Hall, 1989).

27. For a review of these issues, see Thomas C. Schelling, "Life, Liberty, or the Pursuit of Happiness," in Isabel V. Sawhill, ed., *Challenge to Leadership* (Washington, D.C.: Urban Institute Press, 1988), pp. 253–277. There is great difficulty in predicting accurately the future course of the disease. See Mitchell H. Gail and Ron Brookmeyer, "Methods for Projecting Course of Acquired Immunodeficiency Syndrome Epidemic," *Journal of the National Cancer Institute,* 80 (August 17, 1988), 900–911.

28. For a convenient summary of some issues discussed in the rest of this section, see Daniels, *Just Health Care;* Carol Levine, ed., *Cases in Bioethics,* 2d ed. (New York: St. Martin's Press, 1989); and Nancy F. McKenzie, ed., *The Crisis in Health Care: Ethical Issues* (New York: Meridian Books, 1990).

29. For introduction to the debate, see Daniel Callahan, *Setting Limits: Medical Goals in an Aging Society* (New York: Simon & Schuster, 1987), and Timothy M. Smeeding, ed., *Should Medical Care Be Rationed by Age?* (Totowa, N.J.: Rowman & Littlefield, 1987).

30. See Clark C. Havighurst and Glenn M. Hackbarth, "Private Cost Containment," *New England Journal of Medicine,* November 23, 1979, pp. 1298–1305; *Health Policy: The Legislative Agenda* (Washington, D.C.: Congressional Quarterly Press, 1980), pp. 35–40; Theodore R. Marmor, *Political Analysis and American Medical Care* (Cambridge, England: Cambridge University Press, 1983), chap. 12, and H. E. Frech III, ed., *Health Care in America: The Political Economy of Hospitals and Health Insurance* (San Francisco: Pacific Research Institute, 1988).

31. See Steven C. Renn, "The Structure and Financing of the Health Care Delivery System of the 1980s," in Schramm, ed., *Health Care and Its Costs,* pp. 8–48, and Malcolm Gladwell, "HMOs: Destined to Succeed in Spite of Themselves," *Washington Post National Weekly Edition,* August 29–September 4, 1988, 22–23.

32. H. J. Geiger, quoted in Ivan L. Bennett, Jr., "Technology As a Shaping Force," in Knowles, *Doing Better,* p. 127.

33. See Henry J. Aaron and William B. Schwartz, *The Painful Prescription: Rationing Hospital Care* (Washington, D.C.: Brookings Institution, 1984) and Robert G. Evans, "Finding the Levers, Finding the Courage: Lessons from Cost Containment in North America," in Brown, ed., *Health Policy in Transition,* pp. 17–47.

34. The arguments of both supporters and opponents of NHI may be found in Karen Davis, *National Health Insurance: Benefits, Costs, and Consequences* (Washington, D.C.: Brookings Institution, 1975), esp. chaps. 1 and 2; Mark V. Pauly, ed., *National Health Insurance: Now, Later, Never?* (Washington, D.C.: American Enterprise Institute, 1980); and Judith Feder et al., eds., *National Health Insurance: Conflicting Goals and Policy Choices* (Washington, D.C.: Urban Institute Press, 1980).

35. For excellent and comprehensive surveys of the proposals, see Aaron, *Serious and Unstable,* chap. 5, and "Caring for the Uninsured and Underinsured," *JAMA: Journal of the American Medical Association,* May 15, 1991, 2491–2567.

36. See Karen Davis and Diane Rowland, *Medicare Policy: New Directions for Health and Long-Term Care* (Baltimore: Johns Hopkins University Press, 1986); Diane Rowland, "Issues of Long-Term Care," in Schramm, ed., *Health Care and Its Costs,* pp. 222–251; William P. Brandon, "Politics, Health and the Elderly: Inventing the Next Century—The Age of Aging," in Theodor J. Litman and Leonard S. Robins, eds., *Health Politics and Policy,* 2d ed. (Albany, N.Y.: Delmar, 1991), pp. 335–355; and

Catherine Hawes, "Nursing Home Reform and the Politics of Long-Term Care," *PS,* 20 (Spring 1987), 232–241.
    37. Marmor, *Political Analysis,* Chap. 3.

SUGGESTED READINGS

Aaron, Henry J. *Serious and Unstable Condition: Financing America's Health Care.* Washington, D.C.: Brookings Institution, 1991.

Aaron, Henry J., and Schwartz, William B. *The Painful Prescription: Rationing Hospital Care.* Washington, D.C.: Brookings Institution, 1984.

Brown, Lawrence D. *Health Policy in Transition.* Durham, N.C.: Duke University Press, 1987.

"The Changing Politics of Health Care." *PS,* 20 (Spring 1987): 197–241.

Davis, Karen, and Schoen, Cathy. *Health and the War on Poverty: A Ten Year Appraisal.* Washington, D.C.: Brookings Institution, 1978.

Davis, Karen, and Rowland, Diane. *Medicare Policy: New Directions for Health and Long-Term Care.* Baltimore: Johns Hopkins University Press, 1986.

Garrett, Thomas M.; Baillie, Harold W.; and Garrett, Rosellen M. *Health Care Ethics: Principles and Problems.* Englewood Cliffs, N.J.: Prentice-Hall, 1989.

Kovner, Anthony R. *Health Care Delivery in the United States,* 4th ed. New York: Springer, 1990.

Litman, Theodor J. and Robins, Leonard S., eds. *Health Politics and Policy,* 2d ed. Albany, N.Y.: Delmar, 1991.

Marmor, Theodore R., *Political Analysis and American Medical Care.* Cambridge, England: Cambridge University Press, 1983.

Payer, Lynn. *Medicine and Culture: Varieties of Treatment in the United States, England, West Germany, and France.* New York: Penguin Books, 1988.

Sardell, Alice, and Catchen, Harvey. "Health Politics in the 1980s: A Review Essay." *Journal of Politics,* 48 (February 1986): 168–181.

Schramm, Carl J., ed. *Health Care and Its Costs.* New York: Norton, 1987.

Starr, Paul. *The Social Transformation of American Medicine: The Rise of a Sovereign Profession and the Making of a Vast Industry.* New York: Basic Books, 1982.

CHAPTER 9

Education: Conflict in Policy Direction

Education policy encompasses the basic interests and values of society. But in a pluralistic society such as the United States, there is often deep disagreement over those values. Such is the case with education. Because policy decisions that affect schools reach so deeply into the life of the American family and affect so many people to such an extensive degree, conflict becomes an integral part of policy-making. Inevitably, therefore, many divergent groups and individuals are drawn into the struggles over formulation and direction of education policy.

Education policy has been marked by changes, and these changes have often created high levels of conflict and public controversy. Much of this conflict can be traced to two opposing traditions within education theory, conservative and liberal thought.

Conservative thought ties personal development to social discipline with an emphasis on individual initiative and responsibility. Conservatives see the degree of initiative and ability as varying greatly among different people. Accordingly, it is the individual who must assume the greater burden for educational achievement and for whatever economic and social opportunities result. The rewards of society are garnered through competition. This emphasis on the individual places traditional conservative thought in general opposition to federal involvement in education policy. Conservatives emphasize the responsibility of the family, state government, local school boards, and private institutions such as the church as the appropriate structures for molding education policy.

The New Right, a conservative movement, also stresses family and local responsibility for education policy. But this group demonstrates a willingness to turn to government structures at the state and federal levels to advance their own beliefs and values. Some prominent examples include attempts to reintroduce prayer and Bible reading, promote "creation science," and prohibit the teaching of "secular humanism" in the public schools.

Liberal thought reflects a concern for societal action to ameliorate individual deprivation resulting from social inequities. Emphasis is placed on the rights of the individual and on efforts to eliminate the effects of privilege and discrimination in the educational system. The concern of liberalism is to achieve educational choices that promote equality of opportunity. Ability, not privilege, should determine access to the educational system and its rewards. This concern with equality leads liberals to advocate an expanded role for the federal government in education policy. Liberal thought underscores the federal government's positive contri-

303

butions in promoting equality in other policy areas, such as civil rights. These contributions have established a framework for advocating an expansion of the federal role in education policy as a means to remedy past policies by local school boards and state governments, which have, as in the case of segregation, supported unequal educational opportunity. It should be noted that both the liberal and conservative schools of thought tie wealth, power, and prestige to educational achievement.

These two traditions have generated cross-pressures and conflicting goals in American education policy. Schools have been assigned the multiple tasks of teaching students the basic skills necessary for a productive life, establishing a positive self-image, offering a system of values by which they may direct their lives, laying the groundwork for an integrated society through contacts with individuals from different racial and ethnic backgrounds, providing the nation with an adequate supply of highly trained citizens for scientific and technical enterprise, and enculturating students politically by creating a sense of loyalty to American values.

ISSUE BACKGROUND: HISTORICAL PERSPECTIVES AND THE ONSET OF FEDERAL INVOLVEMENT IN EDUCATION

Education policy in the United States is based on two principles: first, education should be free and universal, and second, control over education should be centered on the local level.

The Tradition of Free Public Education

After the Revolutionary War, the concept that the newly independent nation should allow or encourage the development of a special privileged class or official aristocracy was firmly rejected. The U.S. Constitution affirmed that government would be bound by the consent of the governed through regular elections, and the founders of the republic turned to education as one mechanism for ensuring that the republic would survive.

The thinking of Thomas Jefferson exemplifies the position that state-supported education for all citizens is a basic requirement for democracy. He wrote in 1816, "If a nation expects to be ignorant and free, in a state of civilization, it expects what never was and never will be."[1]

Jeffersonian thought reflected three educational goals: first, to provide mass literacy training; second, to expand access to higher education to all children without regard to social background and to open positions of leadership to those with high levels of educational achievement; and third, to provide for an educational system in which leaders could be trained in the United States rather than in Europe. It was these values on which the gradual emergence of a free public education system in the United States was based.

The stimulus for a free educational system grew during the early decades of the new nation's life. Education was seen as the means to enable the public to make "right choices" (those consistent with democratic values) and maintain stability within the republic. Thus free education was seen as a strong force for maintaining the existing social order.[2]

A variety of factors encouraged the shift from a private, largely church-based education system to a free public education system. Education became an effective tool for political socialization and was a key element in the "melting pot" approach to nation building. Immigrants to the new nation were heterogeneous with a variety of religions, languages, and customs. Immigrants arriving from countries without democratic institutions needed to develop an understanding of democracy and a new identification as Americans. This integration into the American social and political system was best achieved by means of a free public education system. Education became the instrument for increasing a sense of nationalism and the promotion of national unity. Even though the United States was settled by diverse groups, the educational system promoted a pride in being American over ethnic pride.

The maturing industrial revolution brought a great increase in national wealth, which promoted the concept of free education, and as the national wealth increased, the nation could afford to educate ever-higher proportions of its residents. By the time of the Civil War, slaves were the only Americans denied access to the education system.

The early period of the United States reflects the emerging concern for free public education available to all children. The following decades were marked by conflicts and reforms, but the tradition of free public education had become entrenched in American thought.

The Tradition of Local Control

Although education could have been declared an appropriate national function along with the power to make war and coin money, the U.S. Constitution does not provide for federal control of the educational system. The American system grew out of an English heritage in which the church and home took responsibility for education. Therefore there was little impetus for granting power to the national government to control education in the new nation.

In America, that English heritage evolved into the early district school, which represented a system of complete local control over free education. Each district was an independent political entity that ran all aspects of education as it saw fit. The residents of the district decided all policy issues relating to education: the tax rate, appointment and removal of teachers, school calendar, selection of classroom materials, and resolution of conflicts among teachers, parents, and children. Community control became a basic tenet of American education as manifested in the local school district of today.

An Emerging Role for State Governments

State governments have assumed an increasingly important role in education policy. Local school districts are created by state government and are able to exercise only those powers specifically granted to them by the state. As state funding for local schools has increased in importance, states have exercised greater influence over education policy. State education departments act to formulate education policy guidelines for local districts. It is state government that specifies curriculum models and teacher certification standards and establishes guidelines for "gifted" education programs and the provision of special education services.

State governments also establish the framework for financing education programs. Local districts are free to tax and spend only within guidelines established by the state. State governments have primary responsibility for establishing minimum expenditure levels for local districts. The increased power and influence exercised by state governments conflicts with the tradition of local control.

Federal Involvement in Education

In the last half of the twentieth century, the proper role of the federal government in education policy began to emerge as a major issue. The Constitution does not specifically assign educational responsibility to the national government, and the fear of a strong central government drove the states to guard their authority from intrusions by the national government. Yet the federal government had a minor role in education from the earliest years of the republic. A partial history of major federal education programs appears in Box 9-1.

It should be stressed, however, that even as late as 1958 the various programs described here did not represent a major federal role in education. Federal aid to education was still limited in scope and usually was indirect in nature. Its programs were justified on the grounds that they represented limited solutions to specific problems. Given this orientation, a limited federal role in education was accepted. Efforts to expand substantially the role of the federal government were unsuccessful until 1965.

The Struggle to Enact Comprehensive Federal Aid-to-Education Legislation

The "baby boom" at the end of World War II resulted in a dramatic increase in school enrollment beginning in the 1950s. The problem of meeting this burgeoning student population was exacerbated by policy decisions made in the preceding decade. During the Depression, capital expenditures for education had been reduced, and during the war, they had been almost completely suspended. Thus, after the war, the nation's schools found it difficult to accommodate the demands created by dramatically increased enrollments.

BOX 9-1.
Major Federal Education Programs

1787   *Northwest Ordinance:* required one section of land in each township of the Northwest Territory to be reserved for support of education.

1862   *Morrill Land Grant Act:* provided public land for colleges that would specialize in agricultural and mechanical arts.

1867   *Office of Education Act:* created the U.S. Office of Education.

1917   *Smith-Hughes Act:* provided limited federal funds for vocational education.

1920   *Smith-Bankhead Act:* provided for vocational rehabilitation grants to the states.

1935   *Social Security Act:* provided for vocational rehabilitation of the handicapped.

1944   *Servicemen's Readjustment Act (GI Bill):* provided financial assistance to veterans in education programs; these benefits were extended to Korean conflict–era veterans in 1952 and to Vietnam-era veterans in 1966.

1946   *National School Lunch Act:* provided student nutrition subsidies through school lunch programs.

1950   *Federal Impacted Areas Aid Program:* authorized federal funds for aid to school districts in which large numbers of federal employees and tax-exempt federal property contributed to high school enrollment and a reduced local tax base. School districts serving military installations are typical examples of "federally impacted" areas.

1950   *National Science Foundation (NSF):* was created with the goal of promoting scientific research and improving the quality of teaching in the areas of science, mathematics, and engineering.

1958   *National Defense Education Act:* provided federal financial support to strengthen the areas of science, mathematics, and foreign language instruction; and to establish a system of direct loans to college students. This act was in response to the successful launch of Sputnik by the Russian space program. Dramatic early failures by the United States space program produced a sense of urgency to upgrade American scientific education.

1965   *Elementary and Secondary Education Act (ESEA):* provided financial assistance to local schools for textbooks, libraries, and other instructional materials.

1968   *Elementary and Secondary Education Act Amendments:* provided financial assistance for educating handicapped children.

1974   *Educational Amendments:* consolidated some federal programs and established the National Center for Education Statistics.

1978   *Career Education Incentive Act:* provided for the creation of career education programs in elementary and secondary schools.

1979   *Department of Education Organization Act:* created the cabinet-level Department of Education by consolidating education programs from other federal departments.

Even though public opinion polls indicated strong support for expanded federal aid to education, bill after bill went down to defeat in Congress during the 1950s. Federal aid legislation failed to pass in part because it had become entangled in two broad areas of social conflict: public education versus private sectarian education (the problem of separation of church and state) and integrated versus segregated schools (the problem of racial prejudice). During this period, federal aid bills were of three types:

1. Federal aid with no restrictions concerning race and religion.
2. Federal aid restricted to public schools with no restrictions on segregated systems.
3. Federal aid with no restrictions on religion but with restrictions on segregated systems.[3]

Interest groups already divided along national- versus local-control lines also began to take positions favoring or opposing federal aid. Supporters of increased federal aid viewed the infusion of federal dollars as a means of improving the quality of education available to the nation's children and as a solution to the problem of equity in educational spending. Districts would no longer be tied to unequal local financial resources, and the infusion of federal dollars would equalize per-pupil spending across geographical regions.

Groups opposing federal aid tended to be conservative. These groups included the National Association of Manufacturers, national and local chambers of commerce, and the Daughters of the American Revolution, among others. Much of this opposition was based on the fear that increased federal aid would be translated into greater federal dominance of education. Given the tradition of local control, many conservatives felt that such potential federal encroachment should be resisted at all costs. Other groups opposed aid bills on the grounds of "states' rights." Both local and states' rights groups saw federal aid as the first step whereby parents would gradually lose control of their children's education. A transfer of responsibility for education policy to the federal level was in basic conflict with their commitment to limited government.

Even more controversial than the issue of federal control were the still unresolved issues of race and religion. Minority groups such as the National Association for the Advancement of Colored People (NAACP) and many liberal groups opposed federal aid to segregated schools on moral grounds. The South's educational system was still racially segregated and dominated by the white power structure, and there was little doubt that the proposed federal dollars would be funnelled into the segregated white schools at the expense of the financially strapped black schools. For this reason many liberals wished to prevent the enactment of such legislation until all segregation had been abolished, as mandated by the Supreme Court in its landmark decision in *Brown* v. *Board of Education* (1954), which found unconstitutional the practice of "separate but equal" education (see Chapter 10 for a discussion of *Brown*).

Abandonment of general federal aid and adoption of the Elementary and Secondary Education Act.   In 1964, President Johnson abandoned the strategy of enacting a general program of federal aid and instead focused efforts on passing legislation that would utilize a broad range of categorical assistance programs designed to remedy specific problems, especially the educational needs of disadvantaged children. This new strategy also involved considerably lower levels of federal monies than would have been provided by a program of general federal aid. It also offered a mechanism for resolving the issue of public aid to parochial schools, since children, not the religious schools, would now be the primary beneficiaries. The ESEA was passed in April, 1965.

Under the concept that ESEA gave aid to children but not to schools, funds were authorized to parochial schools for the purchase of nonreligious textbooks and library materials, but teachers' salaries were excluded. These provisions removed the issues of religion and excessive federal control from the federal aid program.

Intergovernmental conflict on ESEA.   Despite the significance of the change in the federal government's relationship to education, an examination of the sources of revenue for education reveals that the role of the federal government in providing financial aid has remained relatively minor. Figure 9-1 indicates that after the passage of ESEA in 1965, the contribution of the federal government increased from 4.4 to 7.9 percent. Since 1965, the federal contribution increased to 9.8 percent in 1980 but dropped substantially through the 1980s. By 1989, it had dropped to 6.3 percent with over 93 percent of education revenue derived from state and local sources. Federal education spending has remained relatively stable since 1980. As indicated in Figure 9-2, the one area of significantly increased federal spending involves university research projects. The level of federal spending for higher education programs has remained stable with a slight dollar increase reflected in funding for elementary and secondary education programs.

State government revenues have continued to increase in importance as a source of revenue for local districts. State governments now supply slightly over 50 percent of the revenues to local districts. This increase in state funding has translated into increased power over education policy for state governments. For example, curriculum content and structure as well as minimum competency standards for students and teachers are now in the domain of state governments. The tradition of local control may be weakened as the role of state government expands.

Problems have also surfaced with the federal government's commitment to remain a "junior partner" in education. Federal officials charge state and local authorities with failure to comply with federal guidelines. On the other hand, state

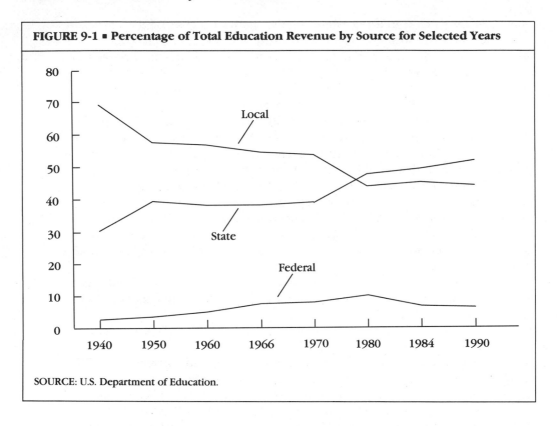

FIGURE 9-1 ▪ Percentage of Total Education Revenue by Source for Selected Years

SOURCE: U.S. Department of Education.

and local officials lament federal mandates, which often fail to include federal funding dollars.

One dimension of the conflict between local and federal officials can be traced to conservative and liberal assumptions held at the two levels of government. During the 1960s and 1970s, federal education programs and guidelines tended to reflect a liberal bias, demonstrated in the concern for equality of opportunity. During this period, federal programs manifested a concern for equalizing resources and achieving a racially balanced educational system. This orientation began to change in 1981 during the Reagan administration and continued under President Bush as a more conservative view guided federal education policies.

Local officials often support policies with a more conservative orientation. The emphasis on local control accepts fiscal inequality among districts and stresses the central importance within districts of the "neighborhood school." Moreover, the conservative viewpoint held fast to the neighborhood school even in the 1960s and 1970s, when it usually prolonged segregation.

These conflicting philosophical positions add to the conflict over education policy. Many local officials fear that the federal government will be able to direct policy as a result of withholding financial aid without adequately considering the values of local residents.

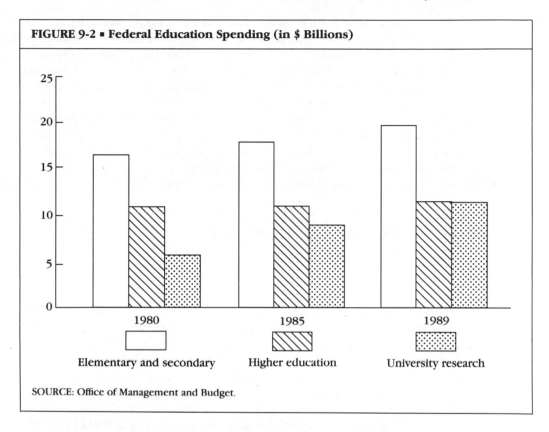

FIGURE 9-2 ▪ Federal Education Spending (in $ Billions)

Elementary and secondary   Higher education   University research

SOURCE: Office of Management and Budget.

The Federal Role in Higher Education

The system of higher education in the United States is dominated today by tax-supported public institutions. During the postcolonial period, private colleges and universities were dominant. This was especially true in the Northeast. The southern states began the tradition of establishing public colleges. Yet it was not until the enactment of the Morrill Act in 1862 that public higher education began rapid and extensive development. The agricultural and mechanical colleges had a practical orientation that attracted students and increased public support. By 1900, there were 977 institutions of higher learning in the United States; by the 1980s that figure had increased to over 3,300. Over 1,300 (or 40 percent) of these institutions are private. Nonetheless, almost 80 percent of the nation's college students attend public institutions of higher education.

Increasing numbers of people have decided to attend college. In the words of a former Office of Education official, "In a democratic society there is really no choice but to accommodate the educational demands of the people."[4] This demand for access to higher education presents the problem of maintaining a quality education while allowing almost unrestrained public access.

State institutions of higher learning rely primarily on state funds for operation, but a variety of federal funding programs exist. The GI Bill provides aid in the form of tuition assistance to veterans. This federal program acted to increase access to college education. Federal aid in the form of grants for research also subsidizes higher education. Universities have utilized this additional money to support research activities and create faculty positions. These federal research dollars have increased the ability of the federal government to exercise influence over the educational policies of recipient institutions. Universities find it necessary to comply with federally mandated policies in order to receive research grants and contracts. The creation of the "basic educational opportunity grant" program in 1972 assisted students with financial needs. Various loan and work-study programs also provide funds. Just as federal involvement has increased at the elementary and secondary levels, it has also increased in the area of higher education.

CONTEMPORARY POLICY: REMEDYING
SOCIAL INEQUALITY THROUGH EDUCATION

Disagreement on the objectives of education has long been a source of policy conflict. Education can serve as an equalizing or leveling institution, or it can be a selection mechanism that perpetuates an existing stratification system. The concept that education is to function as an equalizer was not widely accepted at the time of Washington and Jefferson. Attempts to use education for such purposes only served, in the opinion of many, to "pull down what is above, never raise what is below." This conservative orientation toward protecting established elites was challenged by a more liberal concern for the creation of an egalitarian education and a classless society as the nation continued to grow.

Leveling has been basic to achieving the socioeconomic goals of education. As the children of immigrants were absorbed by American culture, opportunities for economic and social advancement were created. Thus education was perceived by the immigrants as a leveling institution. Leveling is directly related to educational equality. Equalization of educational opportunity provides students with the potential for social and economic advancement. Yet under the provisions of *Plessy* v. *Ferguson* (1896), inequality was legitimized for much of American education. In this ruling, the Supreme Court established the doctrine of "separate but equal" in American life. The Court held that separation of the races did not violate the Constitution if the races were treated equally. One result was the establishment of a dual education system in the South based on race. But this segregated system was unequal, both in physical facilities and in the quality of education provided. This inequality was not effectively challenged because of the support it received from the white power structure and the relative powerlessness of black Americans.

In the South, therefore, the educational opportunities available to blacks were minimal to nonexistent. Poor whites also suffered from a system of education deprivation. Thus education served as an institution for restricting opportunity. As noted earlier, it was not until 1954 that the Supreme Court recognized the effects of separate educational systems and rejected the "separate but equal" doctrine.

But *Brown* v. *Board of Education* only provided a legal basis for eliminating segregation. It was not until the administration of President Johnson that schools were assigned the task of equalizing educational opportunities for all Americans.

The Problem of Unequal Financial Resources

Because of the uniquely American tradition of local control, nearly 44 percent of elementary and secondary school revenues are generated by local property taxes. This practice is rooted in the American tax system itself, as the largest proportion of local tax revenues is generated by the property tax. The result is a system in which local school district funds are limited by the amount of value of taxable property, which varies widely from district to district.

This unequal distribution of resources works to the disadvantage of residents of poor districts. Revenue is a product of the tax rate multiplied by the value of taxable property (the tax base). In a district with extensive property wealth, a large amount of revenue can be generated by a relatively low tax rate. In a less wealthy district, the tax rate would have to be much higher to generate the same amount of revenue. The result is a disparity in per-pupil expenditures.

This situation exists at the state and regional levels as well. For example, with their average lower tax base, the southern states have considerably less to spend per pupil than have the industrialized states of the Northeast and Midwest. The national average for 1989 was $4,509, but Virginia, with $4,744 per-pupil spending, was the only southern state to meet that level of expenditure. All of the remaining southern states spent less than the national per-pupil average.[5] Arkansas spent $2,698 per student in 1989, the lowest of the fifty states. (See Figure 9-3.) The only mechanism to equalize per-pupil spending across the nation involves the infusion of massive federal dollars for education. Such an approach has been rejected as state governments and local districts retain primary responsibility for education policy. Today, more emphasis is placed on state assistance at the same time that surplus state revenues are shrinking. The federal government has not played a role in encouraging financial reform, nor has it attempted to provide assistance to states that are wrestling with the problem.

There are often high levels of financial inequality among districts within a given state. In Illinois, the wealthiest districts spend almost three times as much on each pupil as do the poorest districts in the state ($6,260 as compared to roughly $2,100, a difference of over $4,000). In the case of Arkansas, the local per-pupil revenues for poor districts are only 62 percent of the state average, whereas the wealthiest districts are capable of collecting 145 percent of the state average, almost two and a half times that of the low-wealth districts.[6] Education Department statistics indicate that financial inequality is a problem in most states, with a ratio of unequal spending of 2 : 1 or even 3 : 1 common in states as diverse as Texas, Ohio, New Jersey, and New York.

A number of states have tried to equalize property tax assessment rates in order to increase the equality of educational funding. Findings from the U.S. Census Bureau indicated that these efforts have met with mixed levels of success.

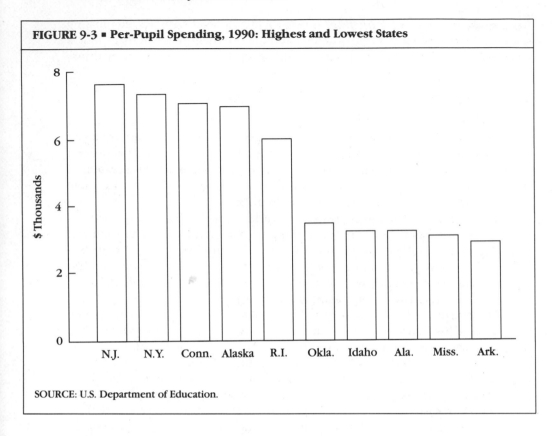

FIGURE 9-3 ▪ Per-Pupil Spending, 1990: Highest and Lowest States

SOURCE: U.S. Department of Education.

Over 58 percent of the local jurisdictions sampled were deemed to have a nonuniform assessment of property. This is one of the reasons why local funding for education continues to be a potential source for the lack of equal opportunity in education.

Low spending levels should not be automatically interpreted as evidence of a low tax effort. In many cases the districts with low levels of spending are taxing at a relatively high rate. They lack the financial base to spend at higher levels.

Increasing numbers of school districts are finding it difficult to generate adequate revenue to support a diversified program of instruction. The demands for increased teacher salaries and expanded educational services conflict directly with taxpayer resistance and economy drives at the state level. In this age of fiscal conservatism, many school boards have been forced to cut programs and increase class size, thus promoting greater inequality in educational opportunity. The large cities of the nation tend to be faced with the problem of low fiscal resources to a greater extent than are suburban and rural districts.

Several factors have combined to increase the pressure on these urban districts. First, most large central cities are faced with a declining tax base as the middle class moves to the suburbs. This declining tax base has eroded the revenue-raising power of the urban school districts. Second, urban districts face higher costs than other districts do. Maintenance, security, and special programs act as a drain on budgets. Teachers have organized and bargained effectively for higher salaries, further adding to costs. Finally, state aid programs tend to favor rural and suburban districts at the expense of urban schools.

The bias of state governments against urban districts can be traced to two factors. First, urban areas were the historically wealthy areas of states. It was the rural areas that then required the greatest proportion of state assistance. Consequently, state aid programs were oriented toward rural needs. As wealth shifted from city to suburb, state aid programs were not restructured to provide increased aid to the urban school districts. Prior to the decisions of the Supreme Court in 1962 and 1964 mandating reapportionment, state legislatures were dominated by rural interests. Attempts to shift state aid patterns met with stiff resistance in the legislatures, which effectively thwarted such efforts. The second factor was the development of a coalition between rural and suburban legislators following the reapportionment mandate. Suburban areas usually gained more strength in state legislatures than did the major urban areas. The suburban legislators tended to reflect a bias against urban areas similar to that of the rural legislator. The result was the formation of a rural-suburban coalition that has continued to reflect an antiurban bias.

Federal aid has not been effective in eliminating fiscal inequities. Although it is true that federal aid programs give more money to urban districts and less to rural and suburban districts, the amount of aid is too little to eliminate differences in per-pupil expenditure. Moreover, the suburban districts have an advantage over urban districts in both state aid and taxable wealth.

Efforts to reform financial disparities.   Attempts have been made at the state level to force school finance reform in the direction of greater equality. The California Supreme Court ruled in *Serrano* v. *Priest* (1971) that under the provisions of the California constitution, education is a fundamental right that cannot be a condition of the wealth of a child's parents or neighbors.[7] This doctrine of "fiscal neutrality" found that reliance on the property tax resulted in excessive financial disparities among school districts. Following the *Serrano* decision, fifty-two lawsuits were filed in thirty-some states in an attempt to spread the California reform. The *Serrano* decision stimulated some states to reform their system of school finance.

The issue of school finance reform was then declared off limits to the federal courts by a crucial U.S. Supreme Court decision. In the case of *San Antonio Independent School District* v. *Rodriguez,* the Court in 1973 refused to equate inequities in property values and the resultant differences in educational expenditures with violation of the equal protection clause of the Fourteenth Amendment.[8] The Court reasoned that the "right" to an education was not explicitly or implicitly guaranteed in the Constitution. Furthermore, differences in spending levels could not be equated with "interference with fundamental rights." The Court supported the continued use of the property tax in Texas by stating that there was no evidence that Texans were deprived of "an adequate minimum educational offering." The state courts and state legislatures provide avenues for challenges and changes to school finance, however, because many state constitutions do guarantee the right to an education.

In the post-*Serrano* period, the implications for school finance reform have become clearer. The reform movement would achieve success only at the state level with a focus on state court systems and state legislatures. The *Serrano* and *Rodriguez* decisions prompted reform efforts to be concentrated at the state level.

During 1990, state supreme court decisions in Texas and New Jersey provided two such victories for the finance reform movement. The Texas Supreme Court ruled that the state must provide funding to overcome unequal per-pupil spending in school districts handicapped by a tax base lower than the state average. Under this requirement, the state government provides revenue to local districts to ensure school districts that tax property at a specified minimum rate will receive equal state dollars. The Texas approach does not impose a ceiling on per-pupil spending by districts across the state. Wealthier districts may still choose to tax and spend at rates higher than the state average. However, state education monies will be first targeted toward poorer districts, a practice that may penalize wealthier areas of the state. Even more dramatically, new legislation passed to comply with the court ruling forces wealthy and poor Texas school districts to share local property tax revenues.

In 1990, the New Jersey Supreme Court ruled that the existing school finance system violated the state constitution. The New Jersey remedy was significantly different from that in Texas. Per-pupil spending must be equal across all school districts in New Jersey in order to comply with the requirements of the state constitution. Wealthier districts initially remained free to tax and spend at a higher level of their own choosing. The state had assumed an obligation to provide funding to allow poor districts to spend at the same level as the wealthiest districts. In order to cap this state financial obligation, the state legislature effectively established a ceiling level above which local districts could not spend. Wealthy districts lost much of their discretionary taxing and spending power.

What factors account for the recent limited successes of the school finance reform movement? While a definitive answer remains elusive, some explanations do exist. First, these reforms occur at a time when the business community is concerned about the need for an educated work force in order to compete in a global economy. Concerns about the link between education and national competitiveness have motivated political and business leaders to call for structural changes in the education system. The nation can ill afford to rely on individuals with a disadvantaged education and remain economically competitive. Second, state governments have taken a greater leadership role in education policy. The focus on accountability, minimum competency testing, and other measures of educational performance are just some manifestations of state government initiative in education policy. Third, the importance of state monies to local districts has continued to increase (see Figure 9-1). Increased levels of state funding have led the public and political leaders to expect financial solutions to education problems from state governments.

Conflict over school finance reform.   Policy conflict is embodied in the reform movement. Conservatives often see finance reform as one more attempt to solve a problem by simply spending more money. Accordingly, they argue that reform efforts should be targeted toward education philosophy, not education finance. Education finance has been traditionally distributive in nature, with little emphasis placed on a redistribution of financial resources. The redistributive nature of school finance reform is in conflict with much conservative thought. Redistributive policies are often viewed as the embodiment of liberal principles.

Proponents of local control are concerned by the increased power and control over education exercised by state governments. Financial reform is therefore viewed as a threat to a basic tradition in the American educational system.

Financial reform is a potential two-edged sword concerning education quality. One goal is clearly to improve quality by making more funds available to poorer districts in a state. Yet New Jersey and California have acted to place ceilings on education spending by local districts because of the potential cost to state government of higher spending to bring all districts up to the wealthiest level. Spending caps effectively limit the scope and nature of programs that wealthier districts could choose to provide to their students. Opponents see this as an undesirable downward leveling outcome.

The controversy over financial equalization reflects the conviction that expenditures are tied to quality of education. The relationship between expenditures and educational achievement, however, is less than clear. Studies in this area have not solved the question because of conflicting results and differing interpretations. There is little doubt, however, that expenditures do affect the educational environment. Wealthy districts are able to pay teachers higher salaries, construct and maintain high-quality physical facilities, maintain a lower teacher-student ratio, and offer a wide range of educational programs, including the option of technical training or college preparatory classes. This is one reason why residents of wealthy districts often oppose school finance reform.

Because the research is ambiguous, it cannot be said unequivocally that students attending districts with high expenditure levels will have higher levels of achievement than will those attending districts with lower expenditure levels. On the other hand, it is clear that the educational options available to students in poor districts are not as extensive as those attending wealthier schools. For example, a difference of $2,000 per child (typical within most states) becomes $60,000 for a class of 30 students. This represents the ability to hire two additional teachers, equip a computer lab, or provide other education programs.

Conventional wisdom holds that the "life chances," or future opportunities, of students attending poor districts are restricted when compared with the life chances of others. Consequently it is assumed that such deprived students will achieve less in life, that is, have lower incomes, find it more difficult to advance socially, and contribute less to making America more economically competitive than will students from wealthier schools.

Part of the problem with building a strong case for school finance reform is the lack of unambiguous evidence that dollars make a difference in educational achievement. If such data existed, the reform movement would be strengthened.

Equality in Education

> All, regardless of race or class or economic status, are entitled to a fair chance and to the tools for developing their individual powers of mind and spirit to the utmost. This promise means that all children by virtue of their own efforts, competently guided, can hope to attain the mature and informed judgment needed to secure gainful employment, and to manage their own lives, thereby serving not only their own interests, but also the progress of society itself.[9]

The concept of equality is a central tenet of the American ideological system. Yet, when asked to define equality, most Americans find it difficult to arrive at an adequate explanation free of contradictions. We have discussed the role of education in supplying the individual with the tools necessary for a productive life. The various Supreme Court decisions that eliminated the segregated education system in the United States—the "badge of inferiority" that marked members of racial minority groups—will receive a thorough discussion in Chapter 10 on legal and social equality.

In the 1950s, the public clamored for a strengthened educational system that would give the nation the ability to withstand the challenge of international communism. During the 1960s, this concern faded and was superseded by the demand that education focus on the elimination of poverty and social injustice. The earlier concerns were not eliminated, however; rather, new ones were elevated to positions of primary importance.

As the decade of the 1960s unfolded, the nation began to realize that in the midst of unequaled prosperity large numbers of Americans were living in poverty and deprivation. The level and extent of poverty were revealed both in the electronic media and in print. Michael Harrington's *The Other America* (1962)[10] had a great impact on President Kennedy. The CBS television documentary "Harvest of Shame" (1960) by Edward R. Murrow was typical of network programs that began to investigate the degree of poverty in the United States. Concepts such as the "culture of poverty" became part of the wisdom of the era. According to this concept, poverty passes from generation to generation. The cycle leads from parents to children to grandchildren in a cycle of poor education, poor jobs, poor housing, poor food, and poor health. The poor seemed locked into this cycle.

The notion of equality of opportunity implies that the rules for success and failure are fair. Although there is disagreement on the definition of what is "fair," the basic principle of fair competition is endorsed by most Americans. As the nation recognized that equality and fair competition did not exist for all groups, public leaders turned to the education system as a technique for eliminating inequality of opportunity and for achieving a degree of social justice for the poor.

The concept of educational equality varies along a liberal–conservative continuum. As we have noted, the conservative orientation holds that individuals are endowed with differing levels of ability. Accordingly, efforts to guarantee an equal education are an exercise in futility. Intelligence rather than equal opportunity determines the individual's life chances. The orientation of classic liberalism emphasized equality of opportunity. All external barriers should be removed to allow complete development of individual potential. Social and background characteristics should not determine individual opportunity.

The definition of equality in education has slowly changed over time.[11] Initially, conflict centered on the appropriate role of government in guaranteeing equal opportunity. Gradually the more liberal position prevailed, and education as a means of achieving equal life chances became public policy. This approach was embodied in the War on Poverty of the Johnson administration. Government would use its power to assure each child an equal education. The emphasis was placed on the inputs of education, that is, on the expansion of special programs designed to give graduates equal standing for competition in a free-enterprise system.

This concern for equality of opportunity is gradually giving way to a concern for representative equality. The focus has shifted from the inputs to the outputs of education policy, that is, with the occupational outcomes of education. Increasingly, education policy is being judged by the degree to which population demographics are reflected in employment patterns. (In the perfect model, for example, the same percentage of blacks as in the total U.S. population would be found employed in, say, engineering careers.) Effectiveness then would depend on the advancement experienced by previously disadvantaged groups. Affirmative action programs are one manifestation of this concern for representative equality. But this shift of concern from the inputs to the outputs of education policy has widened the gaps between conservatism and liberalism.

Equality and busing. In *Inequality: A Reassessment of the Effect of Family and Schooling in America* (1972), Christopher Jencks, then director of the Harvard Center for Educational Policy Research, and a group of seven other scholars identified three assumptions that have supported the move toward equalization of educational opportunity.[12] These assumptions characterize the conventional wisdom on education and the "culturally deprived" that was current in the mid- to late 1960s. First, poverty can be eliminated by helping the children born into it to rise above it. Once an individual has escaped the bonds of poverty, he or she will not fall back into poverty. Second, the main reason that children cannot escape the hold of poverty is a lack of cognitive skills: the ability to read, write, and function effectively in a complex society. Third, the best method for breaking the cycle is through a change in the educational system. Children can be taught the needed cognitive skills by attending schools with middle-class children and through the extension of special programs designed to compensate for past inequities.

This thinking was, in part, an outgrowth of James Coleman's *Equality of Educational Opportunity* (1966),[13] in which he analyzed the relationship between student achievement and education policy. According to Coleman's research, the primary factor that affected student learning was family background, both the individual student's and that of his or her classmates. Family background molded the student's attitude toward education, and this attitude was linked with the student's performance.

Although the Coleman report did not make specific policy recommendations, it was utilized by the federal government as a basis for educational change. The data of the report were reanalyzed by Thomas F. Pettigrew and others for the U.S. Civil Rights Commission.[14] This new analysis indicated that educational achievement scores were higher for black students attending predominantly white schools than for black students attending predominantly black schools. This difference in achievement approached two grade levels. Pettigrew noted that achievement levels of white students were not affected by the presence or absence of small proportions of black students. Also, the analysis showed that special programs designed to aid students in predominantly black schools had only short-range effects.

The commission utilized Pettigrew's analysis to support its advocacy of an end to segregation and racial imbalance in the schools. The findings indicated that the only effective method for improving the achievement levels of black students was to allow them to attend predominantly white schools. The commission attacked the institution of the neighborhood school, which often had led to segregated schools, and advocated busing as an alternative to improve the quality of education available to minority Americans.

Pettigrew drew a distinction between integration and desegregation. Integration was defined as an atmosphere of complete acceptance across racial lines. Desegregation did not imply acceptance, but rather an environment of stress and hostility. Pettigrew believed that achievement could be improved only in the positive environment of an integrated school.

The Supreme Court was influenced, in part, by the work of Coleman, Jencks, Pettigrew, and others when it mandated busing in 1973 as a viable method to achieve racial balance in the nation's schools. Chapter 10 considers the social research on the impact of busing, which has challenged some of the initial findings of the Coleman report.

Educational Inequality outside the United States

Equality as an issue in education is not limited to the United States. There has been concern in Western Europe with the relationship between educational opportunity and life chances available to citizens. Various surveys and studies indicate the existence of a general lack of equality of educational opportunity. Following World War II, although the GI Bill greatly expanded education opportunities in America, only 2 to 5 percent of the same age group in Western Europe were enrolled in higher education.

In Europe, education tends to select individuals on the basis of class, not merit. In postwar Sweden, over 60 percent of university students were drawn from the upper and upper-middle classes. Only 6 to 7 percent were drawn from the lower socioeconomic strata (which made up about 55 percent of the population).

The same was true for all of Western Europe. Studies in Germany, England, and France revealed similar patterns: only a small percentage of university students were drawn from the lower and lower-middle classes. European reform efforts in recent decades have moved to change these patterns.

Equality of educational opportunity is also restricted in the former communist countries. Although the data are not so readily available, some pertinent observations have been made. The vast majority of students attending universities are drawn from the upper socioeconomic levels. The impact of the fall of communism in Eastern Europe and the Soviet Union on educational equality remains to be seen.

Even though the United States is not alone in the struggle to increase educational equality, it has made greater efforts than has Western Europe to achieve equality of opportunity.

POLICY EVALUATION: EDUCATIONAL QUALITY IN THE UNITED STATES

Concern over Poor Student Achievement

During the 1960s and 1970s, many school districts adopted "innovative" programs that reduced the emphasis on the traditional three Rs and instead encouraged the student's emotional growth, self-direction, and individualism. But because of a decline in student achievement, the public came to believe that these curriculum reforms were not academically adequate. The performance levels of students on standardized tests such as the Scholastic Aptitude Test (SAT) have declined since 1967. As indicated in Table 9-1, this downward trend leveled off from 1982 to 1984 and had reversed slightly by 1986, only to continue the downward trend again in 1991. Average verbal scores have fallen by 44 points to a record low of 422 points and average math scores have declined by 18 points since 1967.

Although there is little debate on the fact that the mean level of performance

TABLE 9-1 ▪ Standardized Test Scores (Average), SAT and ACT, 1967–1991

		1967	1970	1975	1980	1982	1984	1986	1988	1991
SAT	Verbal	466	460	434	424	426	426	431	428	422
	Math	492	488	472	466	467	471	475	476	474
ACT	Composite Average		19.9	18.5	18.5	18.4	18.5	18.8	18.8	20.6

SOURCE: College Board, *National Report,* 1991, and Department of Education.

on standardized tests has declined over an extended number of years, there are considerable differences in identifying the causes of the decline. Parental attitudes and societal changes were cited as the major factors contributing to low levels of performance. On the other hand, many parents and tax-payer groups believe that the departure from the basics such as reading, writing, and arithmetic fostered the decline in student achievement.

In 1977, a national panel investigated the decline in the SAT mean scores and attributed it to several factors. More students are taking the test now than in any previous time period. Specifically, there has been a marked increase in the number of students from families that have not traditionally attended college. Low scores by this group tend to lower the mean score on the test as a whole. Accordingly, the SAT average scores should not be used as an accurate barometer of student achievement in the society as a whole. The panel also indicated that television viewing and family instability have lowered the motivation of students to excel. The findings of this and other early studies were not conclusive, and later research into factors that might explain the decline has remained problematic.[15]

As indicated in Table 9-1, student scores on the American College Test (ACT) have remained stable over time. The ACT is a different type of standardized test than the SAT. ACT scores range from 1 to 36, and questions on the test are designed to reflect the high school curriculum in place in participating states. The SAT is constructed in such a manner as to be "blind" to high school curriculum. Consequently, as curriculum declines in rigor, a pattern of consistent ACT scores and declining SAT scores could result. One pattern of student performance on the ACT does raise serious concern. In 1970 14 percent of the students taking the ACT scored more than 25 points and 21 percent of the students scored less than 15 points. The percentage of students with scores over 25 has remained constant since 1970, but the percentage of students scoring less than 15 increased dramatically to 33 percent by 1975 and has remained at that level. This is one indication of a gap between well-prepared and less well prepared students. (See Figure 9-4.)

The College Board, which administers the SAT, has indicated that the decline in SAT scores indicates a "disturbing pattern of educational disparity" in the nation's schools. Students planning to enter the most rigorous colleges and universities (about 20 percent of the total) had much higher average scores (515 verbal and 584 math) than other less well prepared college-bound seniors. The College Board has expressed concern that the nation's schools are producing two categories of students: a small group of well-educated students and a larger group of ill-educated students.

Student SAT performance is clearly related to family background characteristics, as indicated in Figure 9-5. The higher the level of parental education, the higher the average SAT score of the child. Children of parents with a graduate degree had average verbal and math scores of 476 and 528 respectively. Children of parents without a high school diploma had average verbal and math scores of 339 and 409, a difference of 137 points on the verbal scale and 119 points on the math scale! Since level of education is one indicator of socioeconomic status, a positive relationship between socioeconomic status and student performance

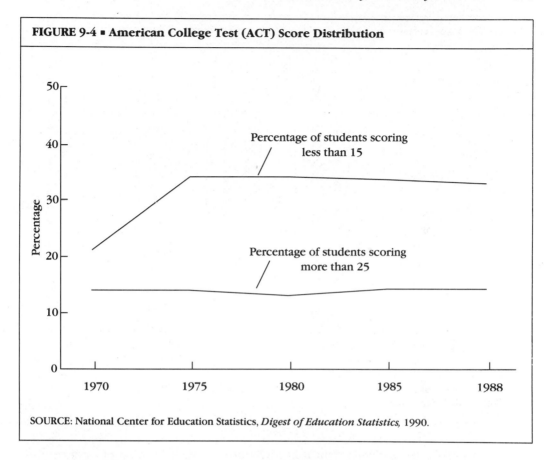

FIGURE 9-4 ▪ American College Test (ACT) Score Distribution

Percentage of students scoring less than 15

Percentage of students scoring more than 25

SOURCE: National Center for Education Statistics, *Digest of Education Statistics,* 1990.

appears to exist. This provides support for concern that American schools may not be providing an equal education to all groups of students.

Minimum Competency Tests. Whatever the cause of the drop in student performance, parents and legislators have become more concerned over students' achievement levels. The result has been the adoption of minimum competency tests (MCTs) in some forty states. The tests are used for a variety of purposes, for instance, as criteria for student promotion, and as diagnostic tools to determine the need for remedial training. Twenty-one states now require that students earn a passing grade on an MCT as a requirement for receiving a high school diploma. Most of the MCT exams require performance on an eighth- or ninth-grade level.[16]

The proliferation of MCT examinations can be traced to the public's concern about the academic content of courses. Gallup polls conducted in the 1970s revealed that two-thirds of the public favored some type of national achievement test. Minimum competency testing has been advocated as a way to force schools to stress the basics of education. Many believe that imposing such tests on students as a requirement for a high school diploma will combat what they perceive as a trend

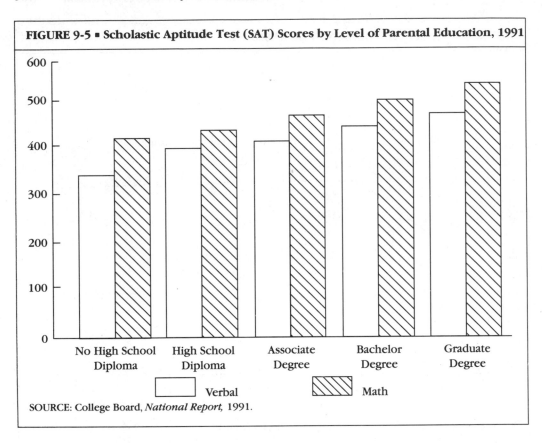

FIGURE 9-5 ▪ Scholastic Aptitude Test (SAT) Scores by Level of Parental Education, 1991

SOURCE: College Board, *National Report,* 1991.

toward lower academic standards. MCTs are one manifestation of a concern for quality education.

Educators tend to be skeptical of the tests as a prerequisite for graduation. The examinations are charged with being biased, statistically unreliable, and a simplistic solution to a complex problem. Such was the case with the Florida MCT.[17] Blacks constituted 19 percent of the 1979 graduating class in Florida. Of the 4,200 students who failed the test three times, 64 percent were black. The pattern of low performance on the Florida MCT persists. In 1990, 83 percent of whites passed the test on the first administration whereas only 65 percent of hispanics and 53 percent of blacks achieved passing scores. A student in Florida may take the test an unlimited number of times to earn a passing grade and the high school diploma.

Representatives of the black community charge that cultural differences and vestiges of segregation are the primary cause of black problems with the exam. Given their disproportionate impact on minority students, it is more likely that MCTs measure the results of racial discrimination in education, not student achievement.[18] History may justify minority groups' fear of testing, for their basic right to vote was denied for many years by means of biased "literacy" tests.

There also may be a danger that the acceptance of MCT programs can lead to a false sense of confidence and accomplishment. Critics argue that MCTs do not measure essential skills or even skills that can be generalized to life outside the classroom.[19] The MCT program tends to emphasize a narrow range of academic abilities rather than providing a framework for establishing a sound education system. Other critics charge that even if the MCT is valid, educators will devote efforts toward teaching students to pass the exam and other advanced academic material will be neglected. One conclusion is certain: The validity of minimum competency tests will always be questioned because there is no universal agreement on what schools should accomplish. MCTs are a fixture on the educational landscape, however, and will continue to be a source of conflict.

Questioning Teacher Competency

Accompanying the concern for student performance has been a concern for the level of teacher competency in the nation's schools. By 1989, Alabama was the only state not using some form of competency testing for initial certification of classroom teachers. Most of the states rely on one of three test forms: The National Teacher Examination or NTE (27 states), the Pre-professional Skills Test (6 states), or a test developed and approved by a specific state (16 states). The NTE was developed by the Educational Testing Service, a major developer of standardized tests. This test requires three hours to complete and is intended to measure general knowledge and the basic skills of reading, writing, and arithmetic.

The validity of the competency tests, however, remains under serious question. There is an absence of data to support the assertion that the tests actually measure competency. In fact, these tests may be biased toward middle-class white Americans just as MCTs are biased toward middle-class white high school students. There are two components to effective teaching: mastery of knowledge and mastery of teaching strategies. Even if competency tests do validly measure mastery of academic material, their power to assess mastery of teaching skills remains unconfirmed. Despite the problems with determining teacher competency, both the use of and debate over such testing will continue into the next century.

Concern over the issue of teacher competency extends to teacher education programs at the university level. When the SAT scores of freshmen education majors are compared with those of students with other majors, a disturbing pattern emerges. As a group, education majors have lower combined math and verbal SAT scores (812 average) than do students majoring in math (1,050 average), English (1,010 average), or engineering (1,050 average). In fact, the average combined SAT score for all entering freshmen is higher (893 average) than for education majors. If SAT scores do measure achievement and ability (this assumption is open to challenge), then why do education programs fail to attract brighter students (as defined by their SAT scores)?

One plausible, partial explanation for the recruitment disparity centers on the starting salaries of program graduates as indicated in Table 9-2. This gap in

TABLE 9-2 ■ Average Starting Salaries of Selected College Graduates, 1989

Profession	Average Starting Salary
Teaching	$ 20,100
Engineering	$ 30,600
Accounting	$ 26,568
Sales-Marketing	$ 25,572
Business Administration	$ 24,372
Liberal Arts	$ 24,348
Chemistry	$ 28,488
Economics	$ 25,332
Computer Science	$ 27,756
Mathematics	$ 26,340

SOURCE: U.S. Bureau of the Census, *Statistical Abstract of the United States, 1991* (Washington, D.C.: U.S. Government Printing Office, 1991).

salaries does not disappear as teachers gain experience and earn master's degrees. Many experts argue that, given the lack of financial rewards after graduation, teacher education programs will continue to have difficulty in recruiting students of the highest academic caliber.

The rise of the women's movement in the United States has also affected the career options of some of the brightest women, for they now have career choices in business, law, and medicine that were traditionally denied to them. This means that especially bright women can seek training in other academic disciplines besides teaching.

The policy implications arising from this situation present genuine difficulties in any attempt to improve the quality of education. First, in order to enhance the appeal of teaching as a career, salary levels may have to be raised. Second, projections indicate that the demand for teachers will exceed the supply in a number of disciplines. This is currently a problem in the areas of math and science. The challenge is to produce an adequate supply of high-quality teachers in an environment that has failed to recruit and retain the best and the brightest. The issue of teacher competency is bound up in the policy of teacher compensation as reflected in the issues of merit pay and master teachers.

Merit Pay and Master Teachers

Merit pay. The current emphasis on quality education has led to a widespread advocacy of merit pay as an appropriate way to attract and retain quality teachers. Polls indicate that over 61 percent of the public and over 62 percent of teachers endorse the concept of merit pay.[20] The Report of the National Commission on Excellence in Education (*A Nation at Risk*) recommended that merit pay plans be adopted across the nation. President Reagan voiced his support of merit pay by stating that "teachers should be paid and promoted on the basis of their merit and competence. Hard-earned tax dollars should encourage the best. They have no business rewarding incompetence and mediocrity."[21]

State governments are in the early stages of experimenting with various types of merit pay provisions for teachers. As of 1990, fifteen states had developed some variant of teacher incentive pay plans: Arizona, Connecticut, Idaho, Indiana, Iowa, Massachusetts, Missouri, New Jersey, New York, North Carolina, Pennsylvania, South Carolina, Tennessee, Texas, and Utah. There is little doubt that the issue of merit pay for teachers will be on the policy agenda during the foreseeable future.

Although merit pay does appeal to the public and the teaching profession, there are problems in implementing the concept. First, because the merit pay concept is intended to attract and retain exceptional teachers, it is best implemented after teachers' salaries are elevated to levels competitive with those of the private sector. Merit pay is not a substitute for an adequate salary scale.

A second problem with the concept is the validity of merit pay as a motivating force in teacher behavior. Because many of the nation's quality teachers continue in the profession despite low salary scales, salary may not be the main factor in recruiting and retaining the highest-caliber teaching force.

A third problem is establishing an unbiased operational definition of merit as applied to teachers. No group, whether it be teacher organizations, school boards, state education commissions, or federal agencies, has been able to determine exactly what constitutes merit or effective teaching. For example, student performance is not an acceptable measure, because intelligence is widely viewed as an innate quality; therefore teachers are very much captives of the students assigned to their classrooms. Merit reflects the values of the school system and is linked to the goals of the education system. Without agreement on values and goals, the concept of merit will remain elusive.

A fourth problem with merit pay will arise if it can be defined in specific, unambiguous terms and standards. In order to qualify for merit pay, teachers may abandon their own creativity in order to comply with a rigid set of standards. Merit pay may become a threat to teachers' experimentation and creativity if teachers follow established guidelines to meet merit standards.

A fifth problem with merit pay is cost. The total cost of a merit pay plan has yet to be established. It is clear that a genuine merit plan would increase costs to local districts. The federal government, under Presidents Reagan and Bush, opposed expanding its role in financing teacher salaries. Given the climate of opposition to local property taxes, school boards will find it more difficult to pass "revenue-enhancing measures." This means that state governments are the only viable source of revenues to pay for a merit plan. At the same time, because of fiscal limitations, state legislatures are resisting demands from a range of sources to assume greater responsibilities in financing programs.

A sixth problem is indirectly related to merit pay and concerns the appropriate role that market forces ought to play in establishing salary scales. Merit pay proposals assume that market forces would apply only in general terms and that all teachers, regardless of academic discipline, would qualify for the same level of merit increase. A true market approach would differentiate among academic disciplines and offer significantly greater merit increases to those teachers in high demand in the private sector, currently the science and math teachers. Such an approach would have adverse effects on teacher morale, as teachers in "low demand" areas, such as English, realize their lower value to the district. The concept of merit pay is not necessarily consistent with market forces in establishing teacher salary scales.

Merit pay has been supported as a major innovation and remedy for the nation's education system. But during the 1920s the concept of merit pay was widely supported in the United States,[22] and the rhetoric of that period closely resembled that of today. But merit pay plans failed to be adopted then because of the problems of defining merit and evaluating teachers. Only when these problems are solved can a truly effective merit pay plan be implemented.

Master teachers.   The concept of classifying master teachers is closely related to the concept of merit pay. This system includes merit pay components as well as career ladders for teachers as they progress. Master teachers could provide a variety of services and fill a range of roles, depending on the educational climate and needs of each school district. Typically, a master teacher plan would include the identification of exceptional teachers, a system of merit-based financial rewards, and the use of master teachers as resource personnel in a supervisory capacity over other teachers to encourage higher levels of teaching effectiveness.

Several issues must be resolved before a master teacher classification system can be implemented. The selection criteria have yet to be established, and the responsibility for setting these criteria has not yet been assigned. The role of teacher organizations in the process has also not yet been defined. Master teacher programs will also cost money, and assigning financial responsibility for such programs will prove difficult. Despite these problems, the concept has much support.

Parent groups support the concept but have not yet acquired extensive information on implementation issues and lack the necessary political alliances to push for a major shift to a system of master teachers. Teacher groups support the provisions for extra pay but have serious reservations about the selection criteria to be used and about the role of their professional organizations in the selection process. State education commissions and departments support the concept as a method to recruit and retain high-quality teachers but have reservations about the role of state government in financing the concept. The federal government supports the idea but has stated that all financial costs must be shouldered by the local districts and the state.

Even though major issues remain unresolved, the concept of master teachers will remain on the policy agenda. Enrollment patterns and increased demand for quality teachers make it attractive to all groups active in the area of education policy.

Bilingual Education

Bilingual education programs grew out of Title VI of the Civil Rights Act of 1964 and the Equal Educational Opportunities Act (EEOA) of 1974. These acts mandated that the states and local school districts set up programs to rectify language deficiencies of students from non-English-speaking families. These acts did not specify a particular program but left it in the hands of state and local education officials. The Bilingual Education Act of 1974 provided federal funds to meet the language needs of non-English-speaking students. Throughout the 1970s, bilingual education was favored as the appropriate method to remediate language difficulties.

By the early 1980s, over 830,000 students were enrolled in some type of bilingual education program. These programs were developed in areas with high concentrations of minority students, over 70 percent being in the Southwest and Pacific coast area.

Bilingual programs were devised to remedy language difficulties and enhance the equality of educational opportunity for non-English-language students. When bilingual programs were evaluated, their effectiveness in improving educational achievement was challenged. Even though several studies found that bilingual programs were not effective, the issue has not yet been resolved. The methods employed in the critical studies weakened the validity of the conclusions; problems included extremely small sample sizes, inconsistent research designs, and the inability to control critical learning variables.[23] Advocates of bilingual programs have thus been able to reduce the impact of the negative evaluations. On the positive side, there is evidence that bilingual programs may reduce dropout rates and facilitate the political socialization of non-English-speaking students into American culture.

Bilingual education is gradually coming to be viewed as simply one among a variety of suitable programs to remedy language deficiencies. Bilingual programs are increasingly defined not as a right or entitlement but simply as an available policy option. These views stem, in part, from efforts to reduce the role of the federal government in establishing education policy. The Reagan administration proposed that states assume greater financial responsibility for bilingual programs, and this remains the view of the Bush administration. In the absence of federal mandates to provide bilingual programs, any reduction in federal funds for these programs would place their future entirely in the hands of the state governments. Given the costs of the programs, the lack of positive evaluations, and the current financial stress of state governments, the future of bilingual education programs remains in doubt.

Multiculturalism

In order to establish a greater appreciation for the contributions of all the various ethnic groups in the United States, a movement describing itself as "multiculturalism" has emerged and is having a direct impact on education policy as it seeks to change public perceptions by reexamining traditional views of the Western European impact on the Americas. The resulting emphasis on redefining the diverse and disparate ethnic elements in American society and revising the history books accordingly will have significant consequences for curricula.

Redefinition of the African-American contribution, for instance, requires that African culture and values be identified and taught. Accordingly, a Portland, Oregon, syllabus states that "Africa is the cradle of civilization," and an Atlanta, Georgia, syllabus says, "Nothing in the twentieth century has touched humanity so totally as those things which were first accomplished by Africans." These curriculum revisions have the effect of expanding students' knowledge of cultures too often ignored in the educational system. The emphasis on Afrocentrism arises from a conviction that black students' educational performance improves with a heightened sense of cultural pride.

The multicultural movement appeals to many groups, the long-settled as well as recent arrivals. Hispanic Americans, Asian Americans, and Native Americans all see an opportunity to erase traditional stereotypes and create a more positive view of their own cultural heritage.

The curriculum changes that accompany the multicultural movement generate considerable conflict. The emphasis on self-definition by various ethnic groups requires that their contributions and the Western heritage both be revised. The result can be a significant alteration of traditional views. Some critics of the new trend argue that basic American values brought from Europe—democratic principles, the Anglo-Saxon legal system, the importance accorded the individual, science and technology—will not receive sufficient attention in a revised curriculum.

A case in point is the controversy that surrounded the so-called correct interpretation of the discovery of the Americas in 1492 by Christopher Columbus. As the five-hundredth anniversary was celebrated, many multiculturalists argued that more emphasis should have been placed on the destructive effects of conquest, economic exploitation, and disease that did in fact accompany European colonization in the Americas. At the same time, Americans of European ancestry discovered that these aspects of colonization contradicted what formerly had been treated in their history books.

Multiculturalism is also at odds with the view of America as a "melting pot," wherein an undeniable measure of political and social integration was synthesized from innumerable ethnic elements. The multicultural curriculum may be better characterized as a "salad bowl" view of America, stressing diversity rather than homogeneity.

Opponents of the multiculturalist current note the ethnic conflicts accompanying the dissolution of the Soviet Union and the civil wars following the disintegration of Yugoslavia. They fear that too great an insistence on cultural diversity could lead to serious conflict, fragmentation, and weakness.

Discussion of the appropriate role of multiculturalism will be an integral part of education policy debate over the next decade.

FUTURE ALTERNATIVES: COMMUNITY CONTROL, PRIVATE SCHOOLS, A CHANGING FEDERAL ROLE, AND CONFLICTING PRIORITIES

The questions regarding equality and education, the ability of white-dominated schools to educate minority students, and the competence of both students and teachers have produced calls for alternatives to the public school system as it has been traditionally organized. Two courses dominate current discussion of educational reform. One is to reemphasize local governance through community control of schools. The other is to deemphasize public schools through measures to strengthen private and church schools.

Community Control and Decentralization

Members of minority groups have begun to advocate effective local participation in school decision making in order to exercise power over the institutions that directly affect their lives. This same demand has been made by other groups resisting federal and state intervention in local schools. The busing controversy is a case in point. Other examples include controversies over textbooks, school prayer, and student drug abuse. Today, citizens expect education to be both technically advanced and responsive to the public, and conflict often permeates the relationship between professional educators and citizen groups over such expectations. Often communities, angered by what they perceive as the failure of their schools to educate well, will balk at paying any more in taxes for a system that is outside their control.

The role of professional educators. Professional educators have opposed the movement toward decentralization and community control. One reason they present is the public's alleged lack of expertise, which prevents the effective evaluation of alternatives. The evidence does support this position. In surveys that have asked the public to name those officials responsible for education policy, the majority have been unable to supply even one name. But people in a community often have strong opinions about education and do usually agree on the general criteria for judging a school: qualified teachers, classroom discipline, and physical equipment, although they may find it difficult to supply adequate definitions of such terms.

Historically, education policy has been molded by professional educators who tended to dominate state and local education bureaucracies. The professional education establishment would be inclined to resist giving power to groups it perceived as less well informed and unqualified. But minority groups have a vested interest in education policy, and in order to guarantee educational equality, many blacks, Hispanic Americans, and others are convinced that they should have a large measure of control. Community participation in education also serves to move minority Americans into wider-ranging positions of power and responsibility.

District consolidation and decreased local power. The issue of community control is linked to the evolution of the education power structure. The structures adopted during this century have progressively reduced the role of parents and the public while expanding that of professional educators and various governmental institutions at the state and federal level. The move to consolidate school districts weakened the power of the community. Nationally, the number of school districts fell from over 100,000 at the turn of the century to fewer than 16,000 today.

The emphasis of the consolidation movement was on operating efficiency, which could be achieved by an economy of scale. Larger districts, averred the proponents, offer more and better services at a lower cost than smaller districts. But consolidation also has curtailed interaction between the public and school boards. Prior to consolidation, each elected board member represented a small constituency of a few hundred people. Consolidation reduced the number of school boards, thereby dramatically increasing constituency size. These constituencies now number in the thousands and in large urban areas can include several hundred thousand. Consolidation also acted to diminish the ability of parents to influence education policy. The resultant sense of powerlessness has led some parents to turn to private schools, which they feel may be more responsive to their needs.

A central question is the assignment of governmental responsibility for education. As creations of the state, school districts possess limited power in setting revenue, spending, and curriculum policy and are subject to the policy dictates of state government. The federal government has also dictated policy to local districts, primarily in the areas of integration and educational quality. Yet it has been hesitant to provide funds to assure compliance with the federal guidelines. Consolidation and the shift of power to state governments have been driven by economics, and there has been little public debate about local control and accountability. Only as the impact of these changes has become evident have segments of the public become involved.

The Department of Education.   Another source of conflict over decentralization and community control is the role of the U.S. Department of Education (DOE). The department was created by Congress in 1980 during the term of President Carter. As originally proposed, the department would have consolidated virtually all programs relating to education then scattered among the various federal departments and agencies. As approved by Congress, however, the new department consisted only of programs housed primarily in what had been the Department of Health, Education and Welfare (HEW). Although some 152 education-related programs were transferred, a significant number of education programs remain outside the present department's control. Federal education programs are also administered by, among others, the Department of Energy, the Department of Defense, and the Department of Health and Human Services. The Department of Education remains a relatively weak federal department.

The Department of Education does have the potential to expand its role and become a major force in policy formulation. This potential power is an issue of concern, especially from the conservative perspective, for the department can expand its power only at the expense of state and local community control. Conservatives argue, quite forcefully, that the creation of the department extends the power of the federal government into an area in which it has no right to be involved.

Generally speaking, this point is much less important to liberals. They defend the department as primarily a coordinator for education programs and policies. It also gives the federal government the necessary organizational structure to address effectively the problems in this critical policy area.

The Issue of Private Schools

Since the 1970s, there has been some shifting of students from urban and suburban public schools to private schools. Busing and a fear of minority students have been contributing factors, but most parents justify the shift to private schools as a concern for quality education. Parents also often object to "mainstreaming," whereby students with disabilities (mental or physical) are integrated into regular classrooms to the fullest extent possible. This practice has led to charges that teachers had to spend excessive time with the special students and neglected the needs of others. Parents claim that their children are simply "warehoused through" the twelve grades. Evidence for these views came in the form of a study in 1981 by James S. Coleman, cited earlier for his theories on educating minorities, which showed educational achievement scores by private school students of all races and classes to be higher than those of public school students.[24]

Parental concern over religious beliefs and values has added to the growth of private schools affiliated with fundamentalist churches. Enrollment in these schools has increased from 140,000 to nearly a half-million today. Although the Supreme Court prohibited prayer and Bible reading in public schools during the early 1960s, this action did not provoke a rapid expansion of private Christian schools. Only after the Supreme Court mandated busing to achieve racial balance did these schools begin to grow in size and number. Although there is little doubt that busing and integration were early forces stimulating the growth of these schools, to attribute their continued enrollment stability to racism would be a mistake. A major factor now appears to be a desire for an educational system that follows traditional values and is committed to teaching moral absolutes.

As reflected in Figure 9-6, the percentage of students attending private schools of all types increased until 1980 and has remained stable since then. This indicates that public schools will continue to face competition from private schools during the decade of the 1990s. This competition will involve not only enrollment numbers, but also curriculum content, student achievement levels, social values, and financial support.

Education vouchers and tax credits.   One proposed reform of education financing is a system of vouchers or tax credits that would allow parents to select the school best suited to the needs of their children. This reform has strong conservative support as well as support from private schools and the Bush administration, which proposed a voucher plan in 1992. Vouchers represent public tax

FIGURE 9-6 ▪ Private School Enrollment, 1970–1995 (as a percentage of total enrollment)

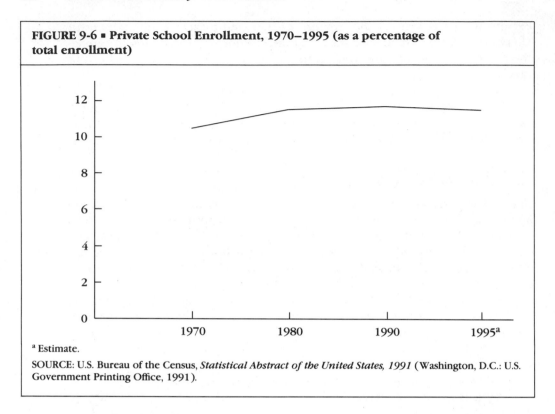

[a] Estimate.

SOURCE: U.S. Bureau of the Census, *Statistical Abstract of the United States, 1991* (Washington, D.C.: U.S. Government Printing Office, 1991).

dollars redeemable for education services. The voucher system would allow parents to use them as tuition payment at either public or private schools.

Proponents of the voucher plan argue that it is necessary to overcome the inflexibility of the existing local public school districts. This view holds that public schools, dominated by rigid bureaucracies, are incapable of developing the programs and incentives necessary for an effective teaching and learning environment. Supporters claim that such a system is compatible with the competitive spirit of free enterprise: public and private schools would either develop quality programs or cease to exist as their enrollments evaporated.

School choice plans have emerged in several states. Milwaukee, Wisconsin, is experimenting with a pilot program that allows some students to attend private nonreligious schools through the provision of a $2,500 state financial grant. The plan is under court challenge but has the support of both Republicans and Democrats in the state legislature. Minnesota has also experimented with a form of limited school choice, and the voters of Michigan considered a plan in 1992.

School choice plans vary significantly. Some concern public schools only and allow parents to send their children to any public school regardless of district of residence. Other plans encourage the option of attending private schools (including religious schools) through grants, tax credits, or tax deductions. Tax credits would allow parents to deduct educational expenses from their actual federal or state income tax bill. In effect, parents would be allowed to use money for private education expenses instead of paying it as income tax and would therefore be free from the burden of paying both tuition costs for a private education and contributing to the upkeep of public schools that their children do not attend.

The adoption of a system of vouchers or tax credits might spur the movement toward private schools, which is opposed by liberals and public educators on egalitarian grounds. Prior to desegregation, a duality existed in the education system based on race. If middle-class students are removed from the public system, a new duality would arise based on socioeconomic status, and a two-tiered educational system would be the end product. Private schools, funded with public tax monies, would constitute the upper tier, with public schools relegated to the bottom. Supporters of vouchers and credits counter that the financial aids would be used by students from all economic classes.

The use of a voucher system might create nationwide social problems, according to opponents. The educational system acts as a major vehicle for political socialization through which the young achieve a common set of values and level of knowledge concerning the political and social system. This is combined with a common curriculum and the opportunity to interact with students from diverse backgrounds. A voucher system would segregate students in accordance with parental preferences, and the diversity of experiences available to public school students would disappear.

Private religious schools provide students with an educational environment in which religion is an integral part of the curriculum. Modern jurisprudence has no argument with such mixed secular and religious training. Rather, it is the question of financial aid from government for religious education that instantly evokes the doctrine of separation of church and state. Several Supreme Court decisions have defined the rights of parents and the proper role of the state (see Chapter 11). Here it is sufficient to say that the Court has struck down as unconstitutional state programs of general aid to religious schools. The changing composition of the Supreme Court (resulting from appointments by Presidents Reagan and Bush) may provide a different policy direction. Proposals for assisting private and religious schools face a serious constitutional challenge, the outcome of which is in doubt.

Crisis in Education

> If an unfriendly foreign power had attempted to impose on America the mediocre educational performance that exists today, we might have viewed it as an act of war. As it stands we have allowed this to happen to ourselves.[25]

So states the 1983 report of the National Commission on Excellence in Education. The report was critical of the current state of the nation's education system and concerned about the implications for the future. The ability of the United States to maintain a preeminent position in commerce, industry, science, and technology is, in the words of the commission, "at risk." Competition from Japan, South Korea, and Western Europe places a burden on our education system to produce skilled, creative individuals in order to ensure economic strength.

The commission's concerns extended beyond economic matters to the role of education in strengthening the foundations of a free and open democratic society. The commission shared Jefferson's conviction that an educated public is necessary to supply intellectual and moral strength to the Union. Education also offers an appreciation for a pluralistic society and fosters a common political culture. According to the commission, the problems in education quality are the functional illiteracy of 23 million Americans, American students' lower performance than students from other industrialized nations on nineteen academic tests, the continued decline in achievement test scores, and the proliferation of remedial courses at the college level. In addition, for the first time in American history, the educational skills of the current student generation will be lower than those of their parents.

The commission's report is significant because it reflects the concern of elected officials, education professionals, and the general public about the perceived decline in the quality of education. The commission's recommendations focus on curriculum reform, with a renewed emphasis on the basics of education (English, science, math, and social studies) and on a longer school day and year (seven-hour day, 220-day academic year). The commission also endorsed the concepts of merit pay, competency testing for students and teachers, and the implementation of a master teacher program. It is significant that the commission gave the primary responsibility for financing education to the local school districts and the states, therefore limiting the federal government's role.

The failure of the United States to make significant progress toward overall educational excellence was documented in October, 1991, with the release of the report of the National Assessment of Educational Progress, prepared by the National Education Goals Panel, a group of governors and federal officials. The report depicts a bleak overall picture of nationwide academic achievement. Some specifics of the report:

- Advanced math: Fewer than 1 percent of fourth-graders and eighth-graders and 2.6 percent of high school seniors could perform at the advanced level.
- Basic Math: Only 60 percent of students in grades four, eight, and twelve could solve simple math problems.
- Fewer than 20 percent of the students could perform math skills on their grade level.

Student performance in the areas of science, social studies, and language arts was no better.

The high school dropout rate is another continuing problem, the magnitude of which is presented in Figure 9-7. The national dropout rate of 17 percent is overshadowed by the 22 percent rate for blacks and the 40 percent rate for Hispanics. The failure of a significant proportion of the population to earn a high school diploma encourages the development of an undereducated minority class.

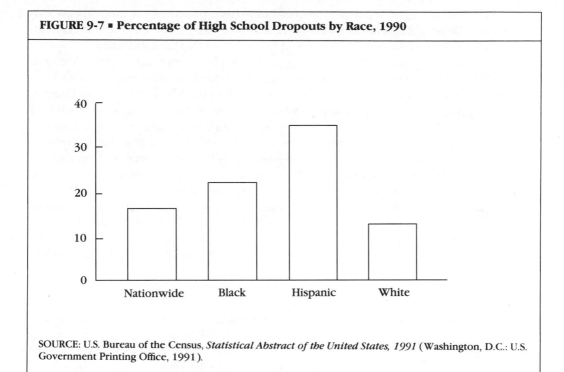

FIGURE 9-7 ▪ **Percentage of High School Dropouts by Race, 1990**

SOURCE: U.S. Bureau of the Census, *Statistical Abstract of the United States, 1991* (Washington, D.C.: U.S. Government Printing Office, 1991).

Changing Priorities in Federal Education Policy

The changing priorities of education policy are reflected in the changes of policy preferences at the federal level. The domestic policies of President Johnson, as embodied in his Great Society programs, emphasized the elimination of poverty and the removal of limitations on individual opportunity in order to promote greater equality. The federal government took the lead in encouraging new and innovative programs aimed at the educational needs of disadvantaged groups. Although the level of federal education spending did not increase dramatically, there was a general expectation that the proportion of federal aid would continue to increase.

President Nixon sought to shift the direction of federal education policy. Because the programs initiated under the umbrella of the Great Society had not yet offered positive proof of major achievements, the federal role in financing education was not expanded. An orientation toward limiting the role of the federal government in education policy dominated the agenda during the Nixon and Ford presidencies.

The Carter administration shifted slightly toward federal leadership in education policy. The Department of Education was created and renewed emphasis was placed on governmental involvement in fostering equal educational opportunity. Federal financial support for educational programs remained largely unchanged, although it did reach a high point during this administration.

The election of President Reagan in 1980 led to another shift in education policy, with attempts to transfer responsibility for education policy back to the state level. President Reagan was unsuccessful in his advocacy of major shifts in education policy, including a constitutional amendment to prohibit busing to achieve integration, the allowance of prayer and Bible reading in schools, approval of tax credits to allow greater access to private schools, the teaching of creation science in public schools, and the elimination of the Department of Education.

The 1980s also involved debate over curriculum content and reform. Two model curricula were developed by the Education Department. *James Madison High School* (1987) and *James Madison Elementary School* (1988), published by the Department of Education, embodied an emphasis on "classical" education with a college-preparatory focus. For example, the English requirement consisted of a four-year literature sequence: introduction to literature, American literature, British literature, and world literature. Three full years of mathematics included an emphasis on algebra, geometry, trigonometry, statistics, and calculus. Little discretion existed within the curriculum.

Although the approach pleased some, especially conservatives because of its emphasis on traditional values, others were critical. Liberals, although commending the model's rigor, felt that it was overly narrow. While students were to read Homer, Shakespeare, the Bible, and other great literature, they would not be exposed to the works of contemporary women and minority and ethnic authors. Notably absent from the curriculum reform proposals were federal funds to finance implementation, in the absence of which the recommendations remain only as points for policy debate.

President Reagan was also temporarily successful in changing sexual discrimination policies in education. Title IX of the 1974 Educational Amendment prohibits sexual discrimination in any program that receives federal aid. This has been traditionally interpreted to mean that if discrimination exists in one component receiving federal aid, then federal aid can be eliminated from all programs at the institution. The Justice Department was successful before the Supreme Court in *Grove City College* v. *Bell* (1984)[26] in effecting change. Grove City College, a private school in Pennsylvania, received no direct federal aid, but some students did receive federal aid in the form of grants or loans. The college argued that it should be exempt from filing nondiscrimination forms with the federal government because it did not receive federal aid directly. The Supreme Court agreed with the Grove City College position. There were never any charges that Grove City engaged in sexual discrimination, but the case did establish an important precedent. If an institution discriminates in one program (for example, athletics or admission to medical school), only the specific program involved will be cut off from federal funds. The *Grove City* decision was overturned by congressional action in 1988.

Priorities in the 1990s

> The centerpiece of our National Education Strategy is not a program, it's not a test. It's a new challenge: to reinvent American education—to design new American schools for the year 2000 and beyond.
>
> —President Bush in *America 2000,* 1991.

George Bush assumed the presidency in 1989 with a pledge to be the "education president." A major impediment to this pledge is the burden of the annual budget deficit (see Chapter 3), which has impinged on the budget proposals for education. The budget deficit was one factor in the president's requesting less federal spending on education for 1990 than had been spent in 1988.

In mid-1991, President Bush and Secretary of Education Lamar Alexander released *America 2000: An Education Strategy.* The education policy goals presented in *America 2000* are summarized in Box 9-2. While *America 2000* presents very broad goals for the United States, some very specific policy preferences are clearly involved.

An American achievement test. A nationwide test to assess achievement of students in core academic disciplines will be developed. Use of the test by local districts will be on a voluntary basis; however, universities will be encouraged to use the test in the admissions process.

BOX 9-2
America 2000: National Education Goals

By the year 2000:

1. All children in America will start school ready to learn.

2. The high school graduation rate will increase to at least 90 percent.

3. American students will leave grades four, eight, and twelve having demonstrated competency in challenging subject matter including English, mathematics, science, history, and geography; and every school in America will ensure that all students learn to think clearly so they will be prepared for responsible citizenship, further learning, and productive employment in a modern economy.

4. U.S. students will be first in the world in science and mathematics achievement.

5. Every adult American will be literate and will possess the knowledge and skills necessary to compete in a global economy and exercise the rights and responsibilities of citizenship.

6. Every school in America will be free of drugs and violence and will offer a disciplined environment conducive to learning.

Annual national and state report cards.   The Department of Education will prepare an annual report indicating how local schools, districts, states, and the nation as a whole are performing in terms of student achievement.

Differential teacher pay.   Increased compensation will be provided to teachers in "dangerous and challenging" environments. Teachers of core subjects will receive additional salary and outstanding teachers will receive merit pay.

Private-sector skills and standards.   The private sector will be encouraged to take an active role in defining the skills necessary for the United States to compete successfully in a global economy.

Expansion of school choice options.   Through vouchers and other mechanisms parents will be able to choose which school (public or private) their child will attend.

Limited federal financial role.   The federal government will provide assessment and informational services and will limit its financial contributions to "seed" money and research and development activities. In the words of the report: "State and local governments provide more than 90 percent of education funding. They should continue to bear that lion's share of the load."

In the absence of federal funds to implement *America 2000,* doubt remains concerning the policy impact of these goals and specific proposals. Successful implementation would most probably produce an educational system of federal mandates and standards funded by states and local districts. The absence of federal money probably will mean the evaporation of this policy initiative.

An unwillingness to increase federal spending means that education spending will not increase dramatically during the 1990s. Figure 9-8 illustrates that total spending on education, when measured as a percentage of GNP, rose in the 1960s and then declined from 1975 to 1980 and has remained relatively constant during the past decade. There is no indication that the trend will change.

Unresolved Education Issues

A number of unresolved issues remain on the education policy agenda.

Drugs in the schools.   Drug abuse remains a serious problem for schools today. Figure 9-9 reflects the fact that almost 45 percent of the American public is now concerned about drug abuse by the young. Drug usage contributes to educational problems by interfering with learning, leading students to drop out, and creating a climate of fear, violence, and lack of respect for educational values. Such concerns can overwhelm the ability of students, parents, and educational professionals to concentrate on the curricular matters at the heart of education.

National teacher certification.   The qualifications of teachers are an increasingly important issue. The nongovernmental National Board for Professional Teaching Standards was created by professional educators in 1987 in response to the publication of a report by the Carnegie Forum on Education and the Economy titled *A Nation Prepared* (1986). The primary focus of this report was the establishment of *national* standards to assess and certify teachers, as opposed to the uncoordinated process used by the fifty states today. If the quality of education is a

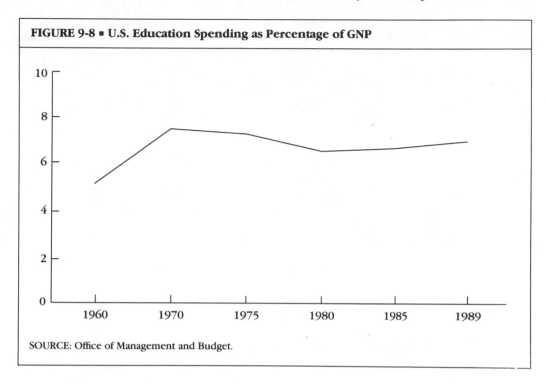

FIGURE 9-8 ▪ U.S. Education Spending as Percentage of GNP

SOURCE: Office of Management and Budget.

national priority, proponents argue, teacher certification is too important to leave to the states to develop fragmented and uncoordinated standards.[27] Educational groups remain divided on this point, but individual professional groups are moving in that direction. For example, the National Association of School Psychologists is in the process of developing a voluntary national certification system.

Workforce preparation.   Historically, the American public education system was charged with producing two types of graduates. One group was students on a college track who would later become managers, decision makers, and scientific or technical experts. The second group consisted of students who, after high school graduation, would assume nontechnical positions in the nation's factories. Today, the nation requires workers who are capable of rapid and continuous learning to improve productivity and enhance the global competitiveness of the nation.[28] American business will increasingly require trained, well-motivated, and creative employees. American industrial and economic security is linked to the caliber of students produced by the nation's schools.

National student assessment standards.   The National Assessment of Educational Progress (NAEP), mentioned earlier, gathers information on students in grades four, eight, and eleven. The program has been in place for almost twenty years. Given the emphasis on standardized tests to measure student achievement and the increasing demand by parents and other groups for comparative data on school performance, national assessment will continue to be discussed.[29]

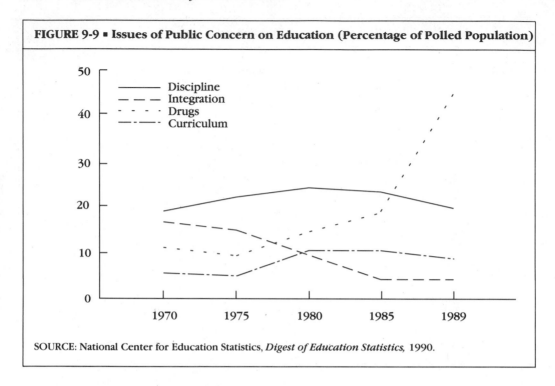

FIGURE 9-9 ▪ Issues of Public Concern on Education (Percentage of Polled Population)

SOURCE: National Center for Education Statistics, *Digest of Education Statistics,* 1990.

Moral education.   Conservatives have argued that the schools have an obligation to provide a moral foundation for the nation's children through an emphasis on traditional values. The Northwest Ordinance in 1787 clearly linked "religion, morality, and knowledge" to good government. The federal legislation of the twentieth century did not emphasize moral foundations but stressed rather values such as national security, equality, and separation of church and state. Both liberals and conservatives are increasingly concerned that moral foundations be linked to the education process.[30] However, differences over substance are divisive. Conservatives emphasize individual values, whereas liberals place greater emphasis on social values. The issue will remain on the agenda.

Alternative certification.   Alternative certification is the practice of providing teaching certification to individuals without traditional educational training. Alternative certification is one method of meeting the coming teacher shortage by using other career professionals rather than recruiting students into undergraduate education programs.[31] Questions concerning quality of instruction, accountability, and professional standards remain unanswered by proponents of this policy, but discussion will continue.

Minority teachers.   Currently, minority teachers comprise slightly over 10 percent of the teaching profession. Some projections indicate that the low salary structure for teachers causes many minority college students to reject teaching as a profession. It is predicted that by the year 2000, only 5 percent of the teaching profession will be minority Americans. This reduction in the proportion of minority teachers will occur at a time when minority children attending public schools will increase from the currently 25 percent to about 33 percent of the school-age population.

Back to the basics.   This movement implies an increased emphasis on basic skills such as reading, writing, and arithmetic but also may incorporate the traditional values of respect, obedience, and moral content.[32] The movement first emerged in the late 1950s after the Soviet Union launched Sputnik. During this early period, the emphasis was on basic education as a foundation for national security through excellence. Basic skills of the 1950s were not centered on individual and personal goal attainment, but rather on the individual's responsibility to use attained basic skills to contribute to the national good.

The current movement emerged during a period of inflation and economic instability. Concern over low student performance was linked to individual, not national, economic survival. Critics charge that the current movement emphasizes employment skill levels rather than educational excellence and national advancement. The debate over curriculum is linked directly to the "back-to-the-basics" movement.

SUMMARY

The United States has a long tradition of free public education, which can be traced to the earliest periods of the American experience, when education was first utilized as part of the political socialization process to build a sense of national identity.

For nearly all its existence, the federal government exercised only a limited role in education. In fact, prior to 1965, that role was insignificant and indirect, with limited programs targeted for specific problems. But with the enactment of the Elementary and Secondary Education Act (1965), the federal government began to expand its role. Federal aid became a more important source of revenue for both local school districts and the nation's universities.

Education has been used to further the struggle for equality in the United States. One concern has been equality of opportunity. The Coleman Report, although controversial in the eyes of many minority activists, did advance the move toward integration and racially balanced schools.

One unresolved problem that adversely affects educational equality is inequity in school finances. Because school districts rely heavily on the property tax as a source of revenue, the unequal distribution of resources results in a wide disparity in the level of per-pupil expenditures within the states and across the nation. Attempts to reform the school finance system have failed in the federal courts and have met with only limited success at the state level. The outlook for the future indicates the continued existence of financial inequities.

National standardized tests, such as the SAT and ACT, have indicated a progressive decline in student performance since the early 1960s, a phenomenon that some link to liberal curricular policies. A reaction to this has been the "back-to-basics" education movement. Here the major emphasis is on reading, writing, and arithmetic.

Concern with the quality of education has led to the development of minimum competency tests for both students and teachers. MCTs attempt to measure student achievement, and passing such an exam is required to receive a high school diploma in many states.

Competency tests for teachers have been devised and are being used by an increasing number of school districts in screening new applicants. Although the NEA and AFT oppose these tests as failing to measure performance accurately, their use seems likely to grow. Proposals for merit pay for teachers and for master teacher programs reflect the same concern for instructional competence.

Community control of education has always been a fundamental American principle. The federal government's reversal of this trend over the past two decades has brought many changes in how and by whom schools are run. This federal intrusion continues to be resisted by local communities who fear centralized control over education for a variety of reasons. Often these reasons pit conservatives against minorities. The issue of control remains unresolved. The consolidation of schools into ever larger districts has further reduced the influence of parents and the general public over education policy, and the power and influence of professional educators continues to grow.

General dissatisfaction with the public school system has caused increasing numbers of parents to send their children to private schools. A relatively recent phenomenon is the rapid increase in the size and number of fundamentalist Christian schools. Parents have sought out these schools as educational institutions committed to traditional values and moral absolutes.

The issue of vouchers and tax credits for private school tuition as a method of assisting the growth of private schools is hotly debated, raising serious ideological and constitutional questions.

Although presidential preferences in education policy have changed priorities in the last two decades, a general trend toward moderate federal intervention has prevailed. The Reagan administration pursued policy options designed to reduce the role of the federal government in education, but this loss of federal revenue placed additional financial burdens on the state governments and school districts.

The Reagan administration advocated reforms in the education system as presented by the commission on excellence. The reform proposals focused on curriculum reform and competency testing and called for expanded responsibility at the state level. The report was consistent with the Reagan administration's view that the federal government should curtail its role in education policy matters.

President Reagan largely kept his 1980 campaign promises. He did persistently seek congressional approval of tuition tax credit legislation as well as tax-free education savings accounts. He continued to urge less federal aid to schools, more state involvement, and more self-help programs for college students. He sought to restrict the involvement of the federal government in the operation and financing of public schools. Reagan's voucher proposals and unstinting approval of more competition from private schools were indicative of his commitment to lessening federal involvement.

President Bush announced his desire to be known as the "education president." As of 1991, his education policy agenda reflected only relatively minor shifts from Reagan-era policies. Funding levels for education programs remained unaltered, and the role of the federal government in education policy was not projected to expand.

NOTES

1. Quoted in S. E. Frost, Jr. and Kenneth P. Bailey, *Historical and Philosophical Foundations of Western Education,* 2d ed. (Columbus, Ohio: Chas. E. Merrill, 1973), p. 340.

2. William M. French, *America's Educational Tradition* (Lexington, Mass.: Heath, 1964), pp. 54–60.

3. Norman C. Thomas, *Education in National Politics* (New York: D. McKay, 1975), p. 21.

4. Robert L. Church, *Education in the United States* (New York: Free Press, 1976), p. 420.

5. U.S. Bureau of the Census, *Statistical Abstract of the United States, 1990* (Washington, D.C.: U.S. Government Printing Office, 1990).

6. Michael Timpane, *The Federal Interest in Financing Schooling* (Cambridge, Mass: Ballinger, 1978), p. 121.

7. *Serrano* v. *Priest,* 5 Cal. 3d 584.

8. *San Antonio Independent School District* v. *Rodriguez,* 411 U.S. 1 (1973).

9. The National Commission on Excellence in Education, *A Nation at Risk: The Imperative for Educational Reform* (Washington, D.C.: U.S. Government Printing Office, 1983), p. 4.

10. Michael Harrington, *The Other America* (New York: Macmillan, 1962).

11. N. F. Ashline, T. R. Pezzullo, and C. I. Norris, eds., *Education, Inequality and National Policy* (Lexington, Mass: Heath, 1976), p. 49.

12. Christopher Jencks et al., *Inequality: A Reassessment of the Effect of Family and Schooling in America* (New York: Basic Books, 1972), p. 7.

13. James S. Coleman, *Equality of Educational Opportunity* (Washington, D.C.: U.S. Government Printing Office, 1966).

14. U.S. Commission on Civil Rights, *Racial Isolation in the Public Schools,* 2 vols. (Washington, D.C.: U.S. Government Printing Office, 1967).

15. See, for example, Donald Rock et al., *Factors Associated With Decline of Test Scores of High School Seniors, 1972–1980* (Washington, D.C.: Center for Statistics, Department of Education, 1985).

16. See Education Commission of the States, *Student Minimum Competency Testing* (Denver: Education Commission of the States, 1983) for a discussion of the specific requirements in each state.

17. Donald M. Lewis, "Testing and Its Legal Limits—The Florida Decision," *Today's Education,* 68 (November–December 1979), 25–28.

18. Diana Pullin, "Minimum Competency Testing, the Denied Diploma and the Pursuit of Educational Opportunity and Educational Adequacy" (ERIC Document Reproduction Service No. ED 228–279, 1982).

19. Gerald W. Bracey, "On the Compelling Need to Go Beyond Minimum Competency" (ERIC Document Reproduction Service No. ED 223–645, 1982).

20. George H. Gallup, "The 15th Annual Gallup Poll of the Public's Attitude Toward the Public Schools," *Phi Delta Kappan,* 65 (1983).

21. Speech delivered at Seton Hall University, South Orange, N.J., May 1983.

22. See Susan M. Johnson, "Merit Pay for Teachers: A Poor Prescription for Reform," *Harvard Educational Review,* 54 (May 1984), 175–188.

23. James Yates, "Baker De Kanter Review: Inappropriate Conclusions on the Efficacy of Bilingual Education" (ERIC Document Reproduction Service No. ED 226–611, 1982).

24. James S. Coleman, *Public and Private Schools* (Chicago: National Opinion Research Center, March 1981). Also see James S. Coleman, "Social Capital and the Development of Youth," *Momentum,* 18 (November, 1987).

25. *A Nation at Risk,* p. 5.

26. *Grove City College* v. *Bell,* 79 L Ed 2d 516 (1984).

27. Lee Shulman and Gary Sykes, *A National Board for Teaching? In Search of a Bold Standard* (Palo Alto, Calif.: Stanford University School of Education, March 1986).

28. Benjamin Duke, *Japanese Schools: Lessons for Industrial America* (New York: Praeger, 1986).

29. U.S. Department of Education, *The Nation's Report Card: Improving the Assessment of Student Achievement* (Washington, D.C.: U.S. Government Printing Office, 1987).

30. Carl Kaestle, "Moral Education and Common Schools in America: A Historian's View," *Journal of Moral Education,* (May 1984).

31. L. Darling-Hammond, B. Mittman, and N. Carey, *Recruiting Mathematics and Science Teachers Through Nontraditional Programs: A Survey* (New York: Rand Corp., 1988).

32. Ellen V. Leininger, "Back to the Basics: Underlying Concepts and Controversy," *Elementary School Journal* 79. (No. 3, 1979), 167–173.

SUGGESTED READINGS

Austin, Gilbert, ed. *The Rise and Fall of National Test Scores.* New York: Academic Press, 1982.

Bennett, William J. *James Madison Elementary School: A Curriculum for American Students.* Washington, D.C.: U.S. Department of Education, August 1988.

Bennett, William J. *James Madison High School: A Curriculum for American Students.* Washington, D.C.: U.S. Department of Education, December 1987.

Carey, Lori. *Measuring and Evaluating School Learning.* Boston: Allyn and Bacon, 1988.

Chubb, John, and Moe, Terry. *Politics, Markets, and America's Schools.* Washington, D.C.: Brookings, 1990.

Coleman, James S. *Public and Private High School: The Impact of Communities.* New York: Basic Books, 1987.

Dorr-Bremme, Donald W. *Assessing Student Achievement: A Profile for Classroom Practices.* Los Angeles: Center for the Study of Evaluation, UCLA Graduate School of Education, 1986.

Everhart, Robert, ed. *The Public School Monopoly: Critical Analysis of Education and the State in American Society.* Cambridge, Mass.: Ballinger, 1982.

Jencks, Christopher et al. *Inequality.* New York: Basic Books, 1972.

Kozol, Jonathan. *Savage Inequalities.* New York: Crown, 1991.

National Commission on Excellence in Education. *Meeting the Challenge: Recent Efforts to Improve Education across the Nation.* Washington, D.C.: U.S. Government Printing Office, 1983.

National Commission on Excellence in Education. *A Nation at Risk: The Imperative for Educational Reform.* Washington, D.C.: U.S. Government Printing Office, 1983.

Reese, William J. *Power and the Promise of School Reform: Grassroots Movements during the Progressive Era.* Boston: Routledge and Kegan Paul, 1986.

Schlesinger, Arthur M., Jr. *The Disuniting of America: Reflections on a Multicultural Society.* New York: Norton, 1992.

Spring, Joel H. *American Education: An Introduction to Social and Political Aspects.* New York: Longman, 1982.

Timpane, Michael, ed. *The Federal Interest in Financing Schooling.* Cambridge, Mass.: Ballinger, 1978.

Wirt, Frederick, and Kirst, Michael. *Schools in Conflict: The Politics of Education.* Berkeley, Calif.: McCutchan, 1982.

Worthen, Blaine R. *Educational Evaluation: Alternative Approaches and Practical Guidelines.* New York: Longman, 1987.

CHAPTER 10

Legal and Social Equality

Few concepts in the context of either domestic or international politics are capable of generating as much symbolic and emotional appeal as that of equality. Traceable in some form as far back as the concept of justice, its roots precede Plato. The term *equality* is certainly a familiar and recurring one in the history of Western thought.

Yet despite its strong symbolism and cultural familiarity, the substantive content of the term has remained imprecise, inconsistent, or both. A central theme of this chapter is that three distinguishable conceptualizations of equality have existed: equality under law, equality of opportunity, and equality of material well-being. Each conceptualization implies different goals for public policy, and the dominant reading of the term has changed over time.

This chapter will demonstrate that an expanding sense of equality of material well-being has come to dominate the policy process. Meanwhile, the roster of groups identified by the policy process and the media as official victims of discrimination has been expanding, although the number of categories that are constitutionally "suspect" (see below) has remained the same. To the evils of racism (referring to discrimination against blacks, Hispanics, and Native Americans) and sexism (referring to discrimination against women) have been added ageism (discrimination against the elderly), ableism (discrimination against the handicapped), homophobia (discrimination against homosexuals), and nativism (discrimination against foreign-born or immigrants).

ISSUE BACKGROUND: THE IDEA OF EQUALITY

Equality under Law

The first conceptualization, equality under law, may be thought of as the minimum position, in that if the term means anything, it means at least this much. The concept of *equality under law* implies that government should treat people as individuals rather than as members of social groups, and that when those categorizations are made, they impose a heavy burden of proof on government to show that there is a valid and widely accepted public purpose behind them. Clearly, the law does make many categorizations of people. It distinguishes criminals from noncriminals, the psychotic from the sane, children from adults, and so forth. The reason why law permits these categories is that there is widespread consensus that these categories are based on behavioral distinctions. Thus we assume that criminals behave differently from noncriminals, psychotics from those defined as sane, and children from adults. However, insofar as the law has now completely rejected the belief that there are behavior patterns or dispositions that are intrinsic to members of a given race, at the very least, classification by race is inconsistent with the concept of equality under law.

Suspect categories.   The courts have said that some categorizations are inherently "suspect"; that is, they are presumed unconstitutional unless government can satisfy a "heavy burden of proof" that they satisfy a "compelling public need." The specific suspect categorizations identified by the Court to date are race, alienage (being foreign born), and, according to four of the nine Supreme Court justices, sex.[1] However, the list is capable of being expanded. It should be noted that such categorizations are not always unconstitutional. Government conceivably could satisfy the required burden of proof.

Accordingly, some categorizations, such as sex, may be constitutional for some purposes but not for others. The law has come to reject the assumption that men are intrinsically more intelligent than women; therefore laws banning women from occupations in which intelligence is the main qualifying criterion would violate the concept of equality under law. However, the law may protect some residual assumptions that women are intrinsically less aggressive than men by excluding them from combat roles in the military. It will become apparent from our discussion of sex discrimination that society's assumptions about the intrinsic properties of women are undergoing a process of evolution and that this process is affecting law and policy. Legal principles distinguishing the sexes that went unchallenged a generation ago are now being found to be in violation of the right to equal protection of the law or are now banned by statute, and women are increasingly appearing in roles previously assumed to be beyond the competence of the typical woman. A similar flexibility of roles is beginning to emerge for men. Thus one can now find women working as doctors, lawyers, or judges, and men working as nurses, flight attendants, or grade-school teachers. Despite the breakdown of the exclusive domination of certain roles by one sex or the other, many roles remain dominated by the sex conventionally associated with that role. Most lawyers, doctors, and professors are men despite the inroads of the feminist movement, and most housekeepers, raisers of children, secretaries, receptionists, and grade-school teachers are women. (See Figure 10-1.)

Equality under law in U.S. history.   The concept of equality under law historically has had a liberal implication. For many years in Western history, it was directed against legally mandated privileges of the various aristocracies or other dominant groups. These privileges included weighted voting and laws stipulating who could or could not own land, enter prestigious occupations, and so forth. Even in the United States, dominant groups were legally able to have laws—or rules supported by laws—that restricted the accessibility of social values to subordinate groups. It is well known that before the historic Supreme Court decision in *Brown* v. *Board of Education of Topeka, Kansas,* which struck down legally required racial segregation in public schools (as noted in Chapter 9), laws

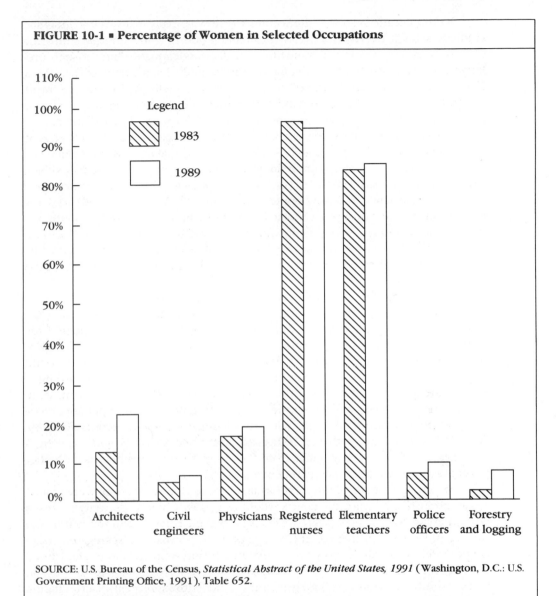

FIGURE 10-1 ▪ Percentage of Women in Selected Occupations

SOURCE: U.S. Bureau of the Census, *Statistical Abstract of the United States, 1991* (Washington, D.C.: U.S. Government Printing Office, 1991), Table 652.

existed to reserve the best public schools and facilities for whites. Furthermore, laws sanctioned discrimination in facilities licensed by the state to serve the public.[2] Inns and restaurants across the country freely and openly, with the blessing of the Supreme Court, restricted their clientele to the dominant groups. Although blacks, women, Hispanics, and Jews were the most commonly excluded groups, Asians and Native Americans also have suffered severe discrimination, especially in the western states.

Until a decade or so after the Second World War, many major law schools and graduate schools overtly or covertly maintained quotas restricting the admission of Jews—who, it was feared, constituted a disproportionate share of such professions—regardless of the credentials of the individual applicants. In the 1920s, Harvard University, under the direction of the president, A. Lawrence Lowell, attempted to reduce the number of Jewish students by various means: by limiting the amount of scholarship aid available to them; by devising disguised quotas (the committee on admissions consistently rejected the use of quotas per se); by requiring photographs on admissions applications; by making "character" a qualification for admission and then defining the term in such a way as to exclude negative attributes that Jews were considered to possess. Also tried was a system of geographical balance whereby applicants from New York City, with its large Jewish population, were passed over in favor of candidates from the South and West, regions with sparse Jewish populations. No method worked satisfactorily. In 1926, admissions officers began to reject candidates known or presumed to be Jewish without any stated reason. The number of Jewish students did in fact drop from 25 percent to 15 percent.[3]

It was alleged in 1988 that the University of California was using such an unofficial quota to restrict the proportion of high-achieving Asians among the students accepted to its several campuses. Although the university denied the charge, it is a fact that the percentage of Asians admitted was substantially lower than that of successful applicants whose objective qualifications (grade point averages and SAT scores) were inferior to those of the Asian students. According to Ernest Koenigsburg, a Berkeley professor who served on several admissions committees, black and Hispanic applicants are twenty times, or 2,000 percent, more likely to be admitted than Asians with the identical academic records. In 1989, Berkeley rejected more than 2,500 Asian and white students with straight A averages. Asians as a group suffer from this more than whites because a higher percentage of them attain such credentials.[4]

In mid-nineteenth century California, Chinese victims of crime were unable to obtain justice because the courts would not allow Chinese to testify against a white person. Special taxes were levied against their laundries. In the first half of this century, laws prohibited intermarriage with Asians and segregated Asian schoolchildren. Asians were virtually excluded from immigration to the United States in the 1920s, and those who were already here were denied citizenship and were prohibited from owning agricultural land. Although legal discrimination against Asians is not as widely known to this generation of Americans as is discrimination against blacks and Hispanics, "the intensity of discrimination against Japanese-Americans in the first half of the twentieth century greatly exceeded that encountered by Mexican Americans."[5]

One of the most blatant examples of inequality under American law in this century was the compulsory internment during World War II of Americans of Japanese ancestry in what critics called concentration camps. The government euphemistically called them "relocation centers." This internment took place regardless of the behavior or status of the individuals involved. These Japanese

Americans were clearly deprived of their liberty and much of their property (homes and businesses had to be disposed of on short notice at great loss) solely on the basis of race. This was accomplished by an executive order in the name of national security and subsequently upheld by the Supreme Court.[6] It is worth noting that the Caucasian German Americans were not similarly perceived as a threat. Thus the German Americans, who possessed the physical attributes of the majority of Americans of European background, escaped the harassment suffered by the Japanese Americans. As one scholar pointed out, "The actions of Germans was [sic] attributed to sick and evil individuals, but the actions of the Japanese were attributed to an evil race."[7]

In 1988, the U.S. Congress did belatedly pay reparations to survivors of the Japanese internment, a move that generated pockets of vociferous opposition. This payment reflected a consensus among opinion leaders in the United States that the internment was a gross, racially motivated denial of basic due process of law.

For much of American history there was an explicit legal denial to Native Americans of equal access to the values of our society, a fact manifested in their being herded en masse off their land and confined to residual pieces of unwanted territory called reservations.

Of course, the denial of equality under law to blacks has been a well-known and widespread phenomenon. The Black Codes were one of the more blatant examples of this. These were a series of laws passed in many parts of the Old South after Reconstruction to attempt to nullify the reality of the Thirteenth Amendment's prohibition of overt slavery. The effect of these laws was to restore the almost complete black dependence on and subservience to the former slaveholders. Blacks were forbidden to hold jobs, receive an education, or even to wander the streets of cities and towns without permission from whites.[8] Until the impact of the *Brown* school desegregation case was finally established in the late 1960s, blacks continued to be singled out by law for specified disadvantages. They were routinely excluded from public facilities in the Old South.

Women have also been denied equality under law. Until the passage of the Nineteenth Amendment, they were not allowed to vote in national elections. Political wisdom was apparently held to correlate with gender. Many vestiges of the notion of female inferiority continued until recently. In seven of the eight states with community property laws, whereby husband and wife could hold property in common, the community property was under the control of the husband. Five states limited a woman's freedom to venture into business. Most states denied a woman the same rights as her husband to establish a separate domicile.[9]

It is argued that although the United States has never had a formal aristocracy to unseat and despite the commitment in American ideology to the idea of equality under law, there has been a more or less identifiable dominant group in this country, a group definable by gender and race or ethnicity, which directly or indirectly has used the law in addition to social discrimination to maintain other groups in a subordinate status. This dominant group has been white, male, and largely Protestant, especially the older, nonevangelical sects such as Episcopal,

Congregational, or Methodist—as opposed to Baptist, Church of Christ, and Pentecostal.

Inequality in the Western world. Dominant groups throughout the Western world create institutional arrangements to perpetuate their status and to minimize social mobility.

The educational system has often functioned as this kind of selective institution in Western nations. In Great Britain and France, for example, rigorous competitive examinations determine who goes on to a university. England had its "eleven plus" exams and France still uses the *baccalaureat,* but what the exams really test are those skills and attributes passed from parent to child in middle- and upper-class families. In England there is a select system of private and expensive secondary education that is the major avenue to Oxford and Cambridge, which educate most of Britain's elite. There is a similar system of preparatory schools in the United States that improves the chance of admission to prestigious higher education for the children of the affluent.

The dominant groups may be defined along ethnic, racial, or religious lines where there is diversity of such attributes. In nations where there is more ethnic or racial homogeneity, stratification is mainly along the lines of social class.

Nations with distinct subcultures, such as Belgium, the Netherlands, Canada, and Austria, usually contain one such subculture that is perceived as dominant and others as subordinate. Frequently these divisions are along religious or linguistic lines. It is fair to generalize that whenever cultural, religious, racial, ethnic, or linguistic attributes are congruent with socioeconomic divisions, the political conflict between dominant and subordinate groups is intensified.

Equality of Opportunity

Laws that treat each individual equally do not necessarily have an equal impact on each individual. The impact of a law on an individual is a function not only of the substance of the law itself but also of the circumstances and attributes of the individual. Equality under law does not necessarily create genuine equality of opportunity.

Equality of opportunity refers to the right of all individuals to realize their human potential to become whatever their wishes and personal abilities allow them to become, free from barriers imposed by society and its institutions. When government reserves certain roles or rewards in society for particular groups or classes of individuals, irrespective of performance or behavior, this in effect impedes the goal achievement of others. This would constitute a violation of equality of opportunity as well as of equality under law.

It is clear, however, that social and economic barriers exist, even though neither law nor public policy assigns privileges or disabilities to specified groups or individuals. The unequal distribution of resources such as wealth, abilities, and health will bestow advantages or disadvantages on individuals in competition for social or material values even when law and policies are neutral. People acquire things they value through the successful investment of resources they already possess. Those who lack such resources cannot use them for self-improvement even when permitted to do so by law. This is especially true in a capitalist system in which capital is used to beget capital. One may need to be clever to succeed in the stock market, but one first needs capital to invest. Even such things as leisure time, transportation, and good health are resources that can be invested for self-improvement, but they are not evenly distributed throughout the population. Furthermore, people and institutions may make goal achievement more difficult for some than for others through mechanisms such as prejudice.

Thus it may be argued that governmental or legal neutrality perpetuates the existing inequalities of opportunity by permitting those who have superior resources to use them to maintain or increase their status relative to the have-nots. Without governmental regulation of the market, the gap between those who have more and those who have less tends to increase.

It is clearly unrealistic to assert that a child born to and raised by a poor, semiliterate black family in one of America's urban ghettos has the same chance of achieving high socioeconomic status as does the child of upper-middle-class, well-educated parents in an affluent suburb, even assuming that all legally imposed distinctions between these groups have been eliminated. The latter set of parents will impart skills, values, and resources to their offspring that the former parents cannot offer. Although it is true that some individuals with superior talents and motivations may rise in Horatio Alger fashion from rags to riches, when genetically acquired properties are about equal, the child of affluence has a much higher probability of reaching his or her potential.

Consequently, the discrimination that makes a group of people socially and economically unequal will tend to cause the offspring of that group to continue to be socially and economically unequal after the original discrimination is discontinued and the current rules of the game apply equally to all. President Johnson, in defending his "affirmative action" policy, suggested the following analogy to explain the logic of this persisting impact of previous discrimination. If two runners begin a race and the legs of one are shackled together, the other runner will gain a substantial advantage. If the shackles are then removed and the race allowed to proceed from that point with no further advantage or disadvantage to either runner, would the race then be fair? Should not the shackled runner be given a special advantage to catch up before the race resumes?[10]

The example describes an unequal opportunity that is generated from previous, legally imposed inequalities. A somewhat different unequal opportunity stems from differences in the talents and values that one is either born with or acquires early in life, that do not stem from any socially or legally imposed discrimination. Here it is a question of whether the government has an obligation to remedy the lower probabilities that one will realize one's potential that stem from such personal qualities as lack of talent and ambition.

The idea of *meritocracy,* essentially a conception of what is meant by social justice, holds that the allocation of social values and status should be on the basis of performance standards in part derived from perceived contributions to the public good. Meritocracy entails the following assumptions: (1) some social roles contribute more to the good of the community than others do, and so rewards should be proportionate to such contributions; (2) the fulfillment of such roles frequently requires long and difficult training or rare talents; (3) special inducements are required to persuade people to fill these important and difficult roles; and (4) both justice and public need require that the occupants of some roles be rewarded a disproportionate share of social values. It is important to note that the concept of meritocracy entails the principle that people are rewarded on the basis of what they do rather than who they are.

It is also important to keep in mind that the assumption that performance is a function of material reward is one that has not been conclusively or even, to some, convincingly demonstrated. People contribute to the social order for many reasons, and it is unclear how large a role in such behavior is based on the prospect of material reward.

It might be said that a consensus exists in America that people ought to be differently rewarded on the basis of performance standards, based in turn on talent, effort, and contribution to the social good; there is, however, a lack of consensus on how performance or social contribution should be measured. There is the question, for instance, as to whether the standards for admission to higher socioeconomic status in the United States, such as success in the educational system, reflect talent and potential social contribution or merely the cultural experiences of the dominant middle-class group. Does a higher grade point average, a standard on which certain groups consistently fall short, indicate a probability of being a superior physician, lawyer, or scientist? To answer such a question, one would have to be able to measure precisely performance in such roles. Because such measurement cannot now be made to the satisfaction of everyone regardless of their values, it remains impossible either to demonstrate or justify the social relevance of the performance standards on which a meritocracy is based.

Equality of Material Well-being

Because of the aforementioned difficulties in using the principle of meritocracy to legitimate the material inequalities that exist in all societies, spokespersons for relatively disadvantaged groups and individuals have been arguing that government has a moral obligation to engineer a more equal distribution of material values, irrespective of traditional performance standards. Furthermore, because one's actual opportunities for upward social mobility depend on the resources with which one starts life, it is argued that equality of opportunity requires equality of material well-being. In short, equality of opportunity is held to be inseparable from equality of result.

Proportional equality.   The concept of equality of material well-being (sometimes called equality of result) would have to be precisely defined in order to be applied to actual social policy. The most extreme form of the concept, the idea that all individuals should possess the same income or wealth, has never been widely advocated as a public policy goal in this country. Rather, the policy goal has been formulated in terms of the proportionate equality of designated social groups. *Proportionate equality* refers to the idea that a social group's percentage in the overall population should be equaled by its share of certain benefits, such as income and wealth, or the holding of desired social roles, such as membership in the professions, high socioeconomic status, and admission to professional schools. According to this notion, for example, if blacks make up 12 percent of the population, they should make up approximately 12 percent of doctors, lawyers, and executives. It is further inferred that if a group has less than its share of social values—for example, the 12 percent of blacks contains less than 1 percent of the nation's physicians—this is evidence that institutional factors, such as systematic discrimination or its pervasive effects, are operating to bring about "underrepresentation." It is therefore implicitly assumed that if discrimination were not present, each group would acquire its proportionate share of society's goods. The distance between proportional equality and the actual inequality of the races is illustrated in Figures 10-2 and 10-3.

The concept of proportional equality is important because it ultimately became the key tool of the social reforms championed by the American civil rights movement. That movement, however, came to this consensus only after a lengthy period of trial and error with other political tactics.

Civil Rights and Affirmative Action

The civil rights movement appears to have gone through three distinct stages in its political evolution. The first stage, dating from the first great school desegregation case to the middle 1960s, concentrated on legal equality. Goals were formulated for the elimination of Jim Crow laws that segregated blacks and imposed legal disabilities on them. Although this first stage was mostly successful, expectations for a more profound change in the life-style of the typical lower-class black individual were not realized, leading to disappointment and dissatisfaction among civil rights leaders. With the goals of legal equality largely realized, the second stage of the movement, in about the mid-1960s, concentrated on other goals: (1) legislation to secure access to jobs and to public facilities such as restaurants and places of accommodation (the 1964 Civil Rights Act); (2) legislation to secure the right to vote (the 1965 Civil Rights Act); and (3) legislation to end discrimination in the sale and rental of housing (the 1968 Civil Rights Act). In the late 1960s, the movement began to press for proportional equality, an effort that focused to a large extent on bureaucratic agencies such as the Department of Health and Human Services (HHS).

Affirmative action.   Beginning in the late 1960s, government began to institute a number of specific policies to effect the redistribution of social benefits to those groups who had less than their share—the goal of proportional equality. These various policies have come to be lumped together under the collective term of affirmative action.

Affirmative action refers to a series of policies or active government efforts to bring into valued roles a number of members of designated disadvantaged groups in rough proportion to their percentage of the population at large. It is

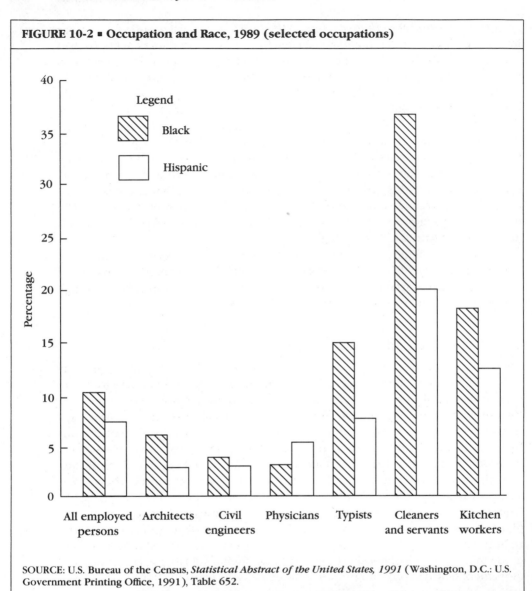

FIGURE 10-2 ▪ Occupation and Race, 1989 (selected occupations)

SOURCE: U.S. Bureau of the Census, *Statistical Abstract of the United States, 1991* (Washington, D.C.: U.S. Government Printing Office, 1991), Table 652.

defended primarily in terms of compensatory justice. That is, justice requires that these groups be given compensation for the harm done to them by previous social policies. The term was coined by President Johnson. It announced the intention of the national government to be no longer neutral toward disproportionate distribution of society's values, whether among racial or ethnic groups, between the sexes, or in the sense of underrepresentation of these groups in valued social roles. Sometimes affirmative action has taken the form of direct government action, as in

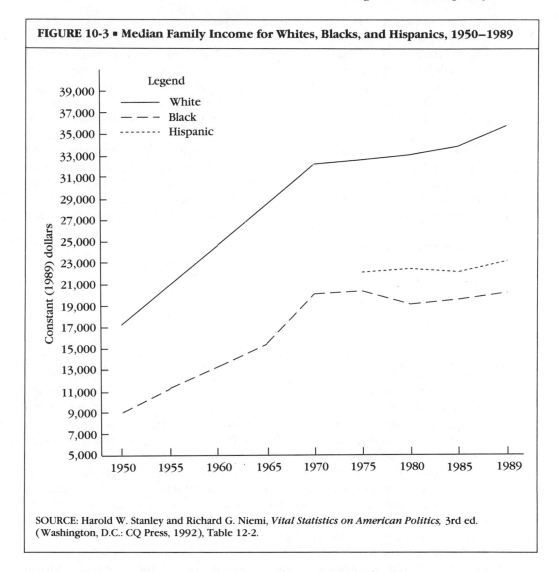

FIGURE 10-3 ▪ Median Family Income for Whites, Blacks, and Hispanics, 1950–1989

SOURCE: Harold W. Stanley and Richard G. Niemi, *Vital Statistics on American Politics,* 3rd ed. (Washington, D.C.: CQ Press, 1992), Table 12-2.

the preferential hiring or promotion of government employees from among the groups designated for such benefits. More often it has been the encouragement of others to take such steps, by the promise or threat of granting or withholding federal funds or by direct government order.

The concept of affirmative action can be narrowly or broadly defined. It could include a number of government regulations and judicial decisions, as illustrated by the following examples. The requirement that a given percentage of those hired, promoted, or admitted to desired roles must be from designated groups (a policy known by the term *quotas*) fits into affirmative action's definition, as does the pressure to grant some form of preferential consideration to members of target groups. Court-ordered busing of schoolchildren seeks to place a proportionate share of designated groups in more desirable schools or classrooms. The meaning of the term can even be extended to include a readjustment of standards by which society is run to accommodate the inability of a proportionate number of targeted groups to meet those standards. The decision by a Michigan federal judge to require courses in "black English" as an alternative to conventional English in the Detroit public schools is an example of this. Another illustration is the court challenge to the tests of reading skills, passage of which is required for a high school diploma irrespective of high school grades. Most states now require competency tests for teachers (discussed in Chapter 9). Blacks and Hispanics fail such tests at a disproportionate rate. For instance, in Florida in 1983, 90 percent of the whites taking the teacher competency tests passed, whereas only 35 percent of blacks passed. Two-thirds of all candidates have passed the Basic Education Skills Test since 1983, but only 21 percent of the blacks and 38 percent of the Hispanics have passed it.

The tactic of attacking selection criteria that are racially and gender neutral on their face but that have a discriminatory impact came to a head in early 1989 when the National Collegiate Athletic Association adopted a new rule, Proposition 42, regarding the eligibility of incoming freshmen for athletic scholarships. The new rule is that a student must have at least a 2.0 grade-point average in addition to a 700 on the SAT or 15 on the ACT to be eligible for such a scholarship. This tightens up the old rule, Proposition 48, which granted eligibility if the scholarship recipient met either one of these requirements. The change took place in the context of a series of scandals about rule breaking and surreptitious professionalization of intercollegiate athletics. A number of black leaders, led by Georgetown University basketball coach John Thompson, charged that the new policy was discriminatory because it is estimated that 90 percent of those who would lose scholarships by failing to meet these standards would be black. Thompson walked off the court prior to a scheduled game for his team to protest the new policy. Defenders of the policy argue that under the existing standards many young men were brought into colleges for athletics without a reasonable chance of actually graduating, and the lower standards lead colleges to manipulate records to keep academically marginal athletes eligible to play. This controversy raised the old issue of whether such standardized tests that are disproportionally failed by members of target groups are racially biased or are valid predictors of the probability of academic success.

Support for affirmative action.   Those who challenge such traditional performance standards claim that they do not really measure what they purport to measure. It is frequently charged that such standards are attributes of the dominant groups in society and therefore these standards perpetuate the existing stratification system. For instance, critics express skepticism that college grade point averages really show one's potential for becoming a good doctor, lawyer, businessperson, or scientist or that the general abilities test given as part of the civil service examination measures one's potential for becoming a good bureaucrat. In other areas such performance standards have been challenged in court, including whether a score on an IQ test is relevant to selecting a good police officer,[11] whether a high school diploma is relevant to selecting power company employees,[12] or whether publications and prestigious degrees are relevant to selecting college teachers. These requirements are being questioned in the first place because the targeted disadvantaged groups fail in disproportionate numbers to meet these performance standards, and the gap between those who have more and those who have less widens still further.

The basic defense of affirmative action rests on the continuing impact of previous discrimination. Because it is now recognized that poverty is self-perpetuating both for individuals and across generations, policies that place a group in a disadvantaged position can be blamed for that group's continuing disadvantaged position even after the discriminatory policies themselves have ended.

Another justification for affirmative action policies designed to place a number of members of targeted minorities in valued roles is that they become role models for the youth of their group. Young blacks, for instance, may be motivated to aim higher if they can see black doctors, attorneys, teachers, and executives. Such role models may provide hope of redemption within the confines of the system and thereby head off pervasive alienation.

The zero-sum aspect of affirmative action programs, the fact that resources assigned to targeted groups must be taken from nontargeted groups (for instance, white men), is defended by claiming that the dominant position of the nontargeted groups was attained at the expense of the subordinate target groups. In other words, whites have become dominant by exploiting blacks and Hispanics, and so whites should pay the cost of correcting the consequences of that exploitation.

Opposition to affirmative action.   Despite the compelling logic of the case for affirmative action, such policies remain among the most controversial of our time and generate persisting and often bitter opposition, which sometimes comes from the very people who supported the civil rights movement when its goal was primarily legal equality. The case against affirmative action has been based on both logical arguments and the self-interest of groups not favored by the policy.

Perhaps the main logical or philosophical objection to affirmative action is that it seems to deny the principle of equality under law. In the final analysis, affirmative action policies reward or penalize individuals on the basis of who they are—their racial, ethnic, or sexual attributes—rather than on the basis of what they do. Furthermore, this aspect of affirmative action reintroduces the relevance of racial and ethnic categories as permissible in American legislation. Yet, as was noted in the discussion of equality under law, the struggle to label certain categories as suspect has been viewed as a liberal and progressive struggle, and the triumph of meritocracy over privilege based on the accidents of birth has been traditionally seen as one of the attributes of both a liberal and a more developed society. Some opponents of affirmative action warn that if race can be used for benign purposes, it will henceforth be more difficult to prevent race from being used in other ways. After all, suppose that defining what constitutes a "benign" policy becomes a judgment by those in power?

Thus, critics claim, affirmative action works against the principles of individualism and meritocracy. Moreover, in technologically advanced societies with the high skill levels required to fill more complex social and economic roles, modification of the principles of meritocracy seems to threaten overall productivity.

Some opponents of affirmative action question the selection of its beneficiaries. They argue that many groups have suffered serious discrimination. It was described earlier how Asian immigrants once suffered worse discrimination and more disadvantages than Mexican immigrants did; yet the latter are designated as affirmative action beneficiaries, whereas the former are frequently classed with the white majority. Poles, Irish, Jews, and Italians all in their turn suffered social and/or legal discrimination; yet none of these groups is targeted for affirmative action benefits. By what criterion, affirmative action opponents ask, are some groups selected for benefits? They argue that because most groups are numerical minorities, the criterion cannot be numerical.

The attribute that distinguishes the target groups seems to be that statistically they have lower success levels than other groups do; they have lower mean incomes, lower mean indices of socioeconomic status, and higher levels of poverty. In other words, the recipients of affirmative action benefits are members of groups that, in the aggregate, have been unable to overcome the impact of discrimination.

The above generally agreed-upon definition of affirmative action recipients raises two key observations from critics. First, individual members of groups not targeted by affirmative action often suffer real penalties as compensations are awarded to the disadvantaged group. The resources of society are finite; when a resource is assigned to one who would not have earned it by meeting society's performance standards, it must be denied to another who would have met them. For each black, Hispanic, or other designated beneficiary who is put in law school, medical school, a management-training program, or some other upward-mobility program to which that person would not otherwise have been admitted, a member of a nontargeted group who may otherwise have "earned" admission must be kept out. To members of nontargeted groups who also see themselves as victims of systematic persecution, such as Jews and Asians, such policies generate particular hostility. These people see their group as being in effect penalized for its success in overcoming the effects of past discrimination. This would seem to be inconsistent with the approval of competitive success that has been widely identified as a basic attribute of American culture.

Members of such groups deny that their success is simply a result of exploiting blacks and Hispanics. As we pointed out, many of the more successful groups have themselves suffered discrimination. Moreover, the cultural dispositions of some groups are more conducive to success in this system than others. For example, David McClelland notes that the child-rearing patterns of some groups foster an "achieving personality."[13]

Second, many critics ask whether affirmative action policies actually help those members of targeted groups who are most disadvantaged. Affirmative action policies stipulate that members of certain groups be selected for desired roles without specifically stipulating which individuals may be chosen or what attributes they may or may not possess; that is, these policies tend only to say that they must be members of the designated group. Because those who design and administer affirmative action programs are reluctant to abandon performance standards entirely, those members of the designated groups who are the best qualified by traditional performance standards tend to be the ones selected for desired roles. This means that middle-class blacks and Hispanics, not hard-core unemployed school dropouts (who are mainly responsible for their group's statistically disadvantaged status), are often the ones who benefit most from affirmative action. This fact illustrates the often observed weakness of the assumption that what is true for relationships among groups (the white race is better off than the black race as a whole) holds true for individuals within those groups (therefore a given white individual must be assumed to be better off than any given black individual). It is, in fact, quite likely that the best nonwhites selected for affirmative action positions may come from less disadvantaged backgrounds than do those whites they displace, whites who would have only marginally succeeded in being selected by conventional performance standards.

It should be noted that some of the opposition to affirmative action programs is based in part on grounds of self-interest rather than principle. Those who are not members of the designated beneficiary groups, such as white men, find that with selected social rewards being set aside for members of designated minority groups, there are fewer rewards for white men to allocate among themselves. Thus, for instance, when corporate personnel departments in a given field succumb to governmental pressure to hire more nonwhites, it becomes harder for white men to find jobs in that field.

Blacks and Jews: A broken alliance.   American Jews epitomize this phenomenon. They populate high-status roles well in excess of their proportion of the population. For example, although comprising only 2.9 percent of the total population, Jewish teachers constitute nearly half of all Ivy League faculties. Thus, when white men in general are restricted (by quotas favoring minorities) from competing for a stipulated number of academic positions, Jewish men are disproportionately excluded, as they are being partially barred from an area of traditional high employment. Therefore, although Jews helped lead the struggle for legal equality of blacks—as many legally supported restrictions applied to them as well—Jewish writers and publications have often taken strong editorial stands against the affirmative action direction of the black civil rights movement. This opposition has generated tension between these formerly allied ethnic groups, as was manifested in the 1984 and 1988 presidential nomination bids of the Reverend Jesse Jackson. The 1984 campaign was marked by anti-Jewish remarks by both Jackson himself and more blatantly by a friend and supporter, Louis Farakhan. This provoked Jewish opposition to the Jackson candidacy. Blacks currently manifest more anti-Jewish attitudes than do any other American ethnic or racial group, and these attitudes are more common among the younger and better-educated blacks.[14] Anti-Semitism in other groups generally is found in older and less well educated people; among blacks, such attitudes are strengthening over time, whereas they are fading among other groups. Meanwhile, hostility to the major aims of black civil rights leaders is growing among major Jewish leaders. It appears that the differences in interests between these two former allies is growing into an emotional, deeply felt antipathy between them.

The mutual hostility was highly visible in 1990 and 1991. Jesse Jackson contributed an anti-Zionist statement to a book sponsored by the League of Arab States. At the City University of New York, paired incidents occurred: The former chairman of the Black Studies Department, Leonard Jeffries, Jr., in the course of several anti-Semitic speeches, claimed that Jews had financed the slave trade and that Jews controlled the American media and film industry and conspired to exclude blacks from both. And a philosophy professor, Michael Levin, was telling his classes that blacks are for genetic reasons less intelligent than whites and that blacks should be segregated in the New York subways for reasons of public safety. In this same period, anti-Semitic lyrics, often violent, were turning up in the songs of two popular rap groups. And neighborhood tensions were high in several cities, most notably in the Crown Heights section of Brooklyn, where large black and Hasidic Jewish neighborhoods intersect. Violent demonstrations took place after a black child was struck and killed by a van driven by a Hasidic Jew (ironically, a black driver had struck and killed a Jewish child in the same neighborhood two years before). A young Hasidic scholar from Australia was killed by one of the roving mobs.[15]

The Erosion of the Fourteenth Amendment

After the Thirteenth Amendment (1865) ended outright slavery in the United States, laws continued to exist that singled out blacks and other racial and ethnic groups for discriminatory treatment. The Fourteenth Amendment (1868) was intended to end such discriminatory legislation by state governments, but two important decisions by the Supreme Court, *The Civil Rights Cases of 1883* and *Plessy* v. *Ferguson* (1896), greatly weakened the amendment's role and in fact legitimized existing forms of discrimination, specifically in education and access to public facilities. It is important to understand this weak interpretation of the intent of the Fourteenth Amendment because, in varying ways, each of the policy areas to be discussed in the next section—school desegregation and integration, equal opportunity in employment and higher education, and equal rights for women— was an attempt to circumvent this eroded interpretation.

Restrictions on the concept of state action.   A key portion of the Fourteenth Amendment has been the subject of much litigation concerning the struggle for equality over the years. It reads, ". . . nor shall any state deprive any person of life, liberty or property without due process of law; nor deny to any person within its jurisdiction the equal protection of the laws." Among the important points to note about this passage are (1) that the language does not prohibit purely individual discrimination and (2) that the language is passive—it tells what the state cannot do, but it does not explicitly command the state to do something actively.

After the Civil War and the enactment of the Fourteenth Amendment, it was assumed by many that the scope of the amendment was intended to encourage state governments to take action per se and also to extend such actions to businesses licensed by the state to serve the public. Because it is assumed by established common law principles that such businesses perform a public function under state aegis, they have customarily been considered state agents. In other words, because they derive their income from the public, they have an obligation to the public. Such an interpretation would have brought this form of discrimination, the most pervasive in our society, within the purview of the Fourteenth Amendment. For instance, under this conception of the Fourteenth Amendment restaurants, hotels, and stores would have been prevented from excluding blacks and other nonwhites as they had done in the United States over the years.

The Supreme Court rejected this traditional interpretation of the amendment in *The Civil Rights Cases of 1883* when it ruled that businesses licensed by the state to serve the public did not come under the concept of state action for the purposes of the amendment,[16] an interpretation that still is in effect. This ruling emasculated the amendment's effectiveness in dealing with this form of discrimination. Congress therefore turned to the Constitution's "commerce clause" for a remedy.

Expanding the Constitution's "commerce clause."   After the Second World War, a changing political climate and new values required that this problem of business discrimination be readdressed, and another constitutional provision had to be expanded by Congress for this purpose. In the 1964 Civil Rights Act, the power to regulate interstate commerce was used to forbid discrimination by businesses directly or indirectly involved in such commerce. This was upheld in the *Heart of Atlanta Motel* case in 1964. Another case that year, *Katzenbach* v. *McClung,* permitted the extension of the law's application to businesses whose only connections to interstate commerce were purchases from a national market.[17] Thus a restaurant well removed from any interstate route was held to be included in the act's antidiscrimination provisions because if that restaurant could discriminate, so could all other such establishments. Cumulatively, that could have an impact on the interstate market that the single restaurant lacked. The need to expand the commerce clause to deal with a problem for which it was clearly not intended by its framers was created by the Court's much earlier emasculation of that part of the Constitution intended to deal with the problem, the Fourteenth Amendment.

CONTEMPORARY POLICY: STRENGTHENING CONSTITUTIONAL GUARANTEES OF EQUALITY

Ending Segregation

The emasculation of the Fourteenth Amendment as an effective instrument against segregation soon went even further than it had under *The Civil Rights Cases of 1883.* The Court ruled in 1896 to legalize active state intervention to segregate public facilities, including public schools. In *Plessy* v. *Ferguson,* the Court held that the equal protection clause of the amendment did not forbid laws requiring separation of the races.[18] Separation, the Court held, did not necessarily mean inequality. The opinion of the Court argued that any implication of black inferiority to be derived from such Jim Crow laws was solely a function of the perceptions of blacks themselves. Hence, in enunciating the so-called separate-but-equal doctrine, the Court officially legitimated such segregation laws. Moreover, in asserting that separation was legal, neither the Court nor society paid much heed to the equality portion of that doctrine. It was an accepted fact that the public facilities available to blacks in localities where segregation was officially practiced, the states of the Old South, were not at all equal to facilities for whites.

It is interesting that the memorable dissenting opinion by Justice John Marshall Harlan argued that "the Constitution is color blind," meaning that race is not a constitutionally permissible criterion for classifying people. That principle, uttered and later quoted in the name of black equality, was in this century to become ammunition for the opponents of black-supported affirmative action plans.

The *Plessy* separate-but-equal principle remained in effect until 1954. After a series of cases that made inroads on its logic, *Plessy* was formally overruled in the 1954 landmark case of *Brown* v. *Board of Education of Topeka, Kansas,* which held that any state-mandated segregation in the field of education inherently violates the equal protection clause of the Fourteenth Amendment.[19] That 1954 decision is now known as *Brown I.* Chief Justice Warren, speaking for a unanimous court, held that the fact of segregation was widely understood as a badge of nonwhite inferiority and that this perception was likely to have a permanent destructive impact on the psychological development of black children, irrespective of the physical equality of the facilities in question. In fact, Topeka, Kansas, was deliberately selected because the physical inequality of black schools was not a serious issue there and therefore the issue of the inherent inequality of segregated schools was brought to the fore. The unconstitutionality of Jim Crow laws was eventually applied to all other public facilities, such as parks, cemeteries, and hospitals.

It was one thing to hand down a principle of law; it is quite another to see that it is carried out. The step of policy implementation, as pointed out in the introductory chapter, is separate from policy adoption and is usually a difficult process in its own right. The response of the southern state governments was by and large to resist the integration of their school systems as forcefully and as long as possible. Recognizing that the immediate dismantling of the dual school system would be disruptive and expensive, the Court had, in a separate opinion (known as *Brown II*), ordered the implementation of its *Brown I* decision "with all deliberate speed."[20] There was sufficient ambiguity in that standard to permit those southern politicians who wished to do so to interpret the phrase as referring to the indefinite future, which in practical terms meant never. Accordingly, with the exception of the border states, the Old South moved slowly toward the termination of its dual school systems. Mississippi did not make its first token integration of its public schools until 1964, ten years after *Brown I.* By 1964, only about 2 percent of the black schoolchildren in eleven Old South states were attending integrated schools. As late as 1969, the Court was forced in *Alexander* v. *Holmes County* to inform a Mississippi school board that the time for "all deliberate speed" had run out and that further delays could not be granted.[21] The request for a new postponement by the Holmes County Board of Education had had the support of President Nixon. Previously, President Eisenhower had withheld his prestigious support from the implementation of the *Brown* decision, remaining silent on the issue until Arkansas's Governor Orval E. Faubus forced a confrontation. Faubus ordered the state's national guard to block the implementation of the desegregation order. The resulting national publicity forced Eisenhower to react, and he nationalized the guard to carry out the desegregation order. Such failures of national administration to pressure local districts on desegregation made it easier for such districts to delay the implementation of *Brown.*

However, the *Holmes County* case ended the last legal justification for the operation of dual school systems. Meanwhile, under the Civil Rights Act of 1964, pressure was placed on local school districts to comply with the intent of *Brown I* by the threat of withholding federal funds from districts that did not satisfactorily respond. Under such pressures, desegregation in the Old South finally proceeded rapidly in the late 1960s. By 1970, a greater percentage of blacks were attending schools with whites in that region than in the North. Thus the first major goal of the civil rights movement, the elimination of Jim Crow laws, had succeeded. The movement had already turned its attention to the reality that the demise of such state-mandated segregation had failed to provide integration.

Enforcing Integration

Persisting discrimination against blacks and Hispanics in the sale and rental of housing has exacerbated a widespread tendency in urban America toward racial and ethnic homogeneity in housing and residential patterns. Although each group of immigrants, Italian, Irish, Greek, Polish, and so forth, had displayed some tendency to seek out and live in neighborhoods peopled by those of its own derivation, housing discrimination against blacks and Hispanics has added to the racial homogeneity of the neighborhoods of these latter two groups. Because nondiscriminatory assignment to public schools has traditionally been on the basis of sending children to their neighborhood schools, the traditional policy perpetuated the reality of racially homogeneous public schools. This racial separation of students due to the effects of discriminatory housing patterns is a form of *de facto* segregation. (De facto segregation is that not caused by law or public policy. *De jure* segregation is that so caused.)

Dissatisfaction with the mere end of de jure (state-mandated) school segregation was given impetus by the Coleman Report of 1966, a study of the causes of educational achievement involving over a half-million students. This report, described in Chapter 9, found that among educational attributes, the one factor that had a significant effect on scholastic achievement was an intermingling of higher achievers and lower achievers. Peer group influence tended to upgrade the performance of the lower achievers without harming that of higher achievers. Moreover, the U.S. Civil Rights Commission found specifically that blacks attending predominantly white schools had significantly higher levels of scholastic achievement than did blacks attending predominantly black schools when family background was held constant.[22] Again, as noted in Chapter 9, these results were interpreted to mean that actual intermingling of and interaction among black and white students would be the most effective technique for upgrading the educational performance of black students.

This interpretation, of course, assumes a correlation between race and educational performance, a correlation that is statistically significant but far from perfect. To a large extent, the apparent correlation between race and educational performance and other behaviors or attributes, such as crime rates and unemployment, actually reflects a correlation between race and social class. Blacks and Hispanics are more likely to be among the lower socioeconomic class than whites are, and lower-class individuals are more likely to be academic underachievers than are those from the middle and upper classes. Therefore it is an oversimplification to assume that white students are always high achievers, whereas blacks and Hispanics are always scholastic lower achievers. Coleman's study was concerned with school achievement levels, and the racial implications were largely read into it by others. It may be that simply mixing high- and low-achieving students, regardless of race, is what Coleman's data suggest, a policy contradicted by the widespread practice of "tracking," or grouping students by ability.

It has also been widely assumed that white schools have been superior to black schools in terms of identifiable concrete attributes, such as the physical plant, school equipment, teacher salaries, and student-teacher ratios. Further, it has been assumed that segregation, even de facto segregation, perpetuates this, as white-controlled school boards are likely to allocate scarce resources to schools attended by white children. Although these assumptions were doubtless fairly descriptive of the Old South prior to desegregation and possibly of the North at one time, Coleman's data from the 1960s draw these assumptions into question. He found little difference between black and white schools in terms of measurable criteria and "most of the variation lies within the same school, very little of it between schools."[23]

In any event, the goals of the civil rights movement with respect to education came to be redefined in terms of the racial balance of the student body and faculty of each school, a goal first stipulated by the Supreme Court in *Green* v. *School Board of New Kent County* (1969).[24] Once this standard is accepted as the imperative of the Fourteenth Amendment, an active governmental role in assigning students to schools on a racial basis is inescapable. The *Green* case required the school board to abandon a "freedom of choice" plan in which, due to tradition and social pressure, whites went to one school and blacks to another. That plan was to be replaced by a kind of school zoning designed to take advantage of that county's rare lack of residential segregation by racially mixing the population of each school. Most communities, however, do not have such integrated residential patterns; therefore the only way to meet the racial balance criterion laid down in

Green would be to require the compulsory transportation of students from one neighborhood school zone to another zone, that is, busing.

The explicit judicial mandate for compulsory busing came in *Swann* v. *Charlotte-Mecklenburg Board of Education* (1971).[25] The Court specifically stated that the lower courts may require busing as one means of achieving the racial balance goal, a goal that was expressed in terms of specific percentages (71 percent white to 29 percent nonwhite), but it held this up as a norm to be striven for rather than a rigid quota. The courts could not require busing to remedy racial imbalance that was purely de facto, that is, had occurred wholly independently of government action; however, any governmental activity, such as the opening or closing of schools, that contributed to such imbalance would justify a court-ordered busing remedy. Yet, although the Court preserved a legal distinction between de facto and de jure segregation, in practice the broad range of governmental actions that have been held to justify busing orders, irrespective of any showing of governmental intent, rendered the distinction unimportant.[26] In other words, the fact of racial imbalance itself has constituted grounds for inferring correctable segregation if any past government action can be shown to have somehow contributed to that imbalance.

Based on *Swann* v. *Charlotte-Mecklenburg,* many court-ordered busing programs have been instituted in cities and smaller communities around the country. More than any other means, busing for racial balance has become the essential tool for solving segregation and promoting true integration. Progress in school integration is shown in Figure 10-4.

The Struggle for Racial Balance in Employment and Higher Education

The Civil Rights Act of 1964.   Busing dealt with the integration of the public schools. This left the underrepresentation of the designated disadvantaged groups—usually blacks and Hispanics, but occasionally including all nonwhites and women—untouched in various sectors of the American economy and in higher education. The Civil Rights Act of 1964, in its Title VII provisions, set up the Equal Employment Opportunity Commission (EEOC) to implement policy toward ending discrimination by any employer or labor union with twenty-five or more persons. Title VI of the same act requires that it shall be the responsibility of each federal agency to require an end to discrimination in any program or institution to which it allocates federal funds. The Office of Federal Contract Compliance is responsible for implementing this policy. As discussed earlier, the goal of ending discrimination has been interpreted as the achievement of proportional representation for designated groups in various valued social roles. Although the EEOC cannot require either quotas or preferential treatment from the mere fact of racial imbalance, it can use such imbalance as evidence of discrimination. The assumption again is that if discrimination were not at work, these groups would be present in various sectors in rough proportion to their numbers in society as a whole.

The adoption of proportionality as a criterion of discrimination came into

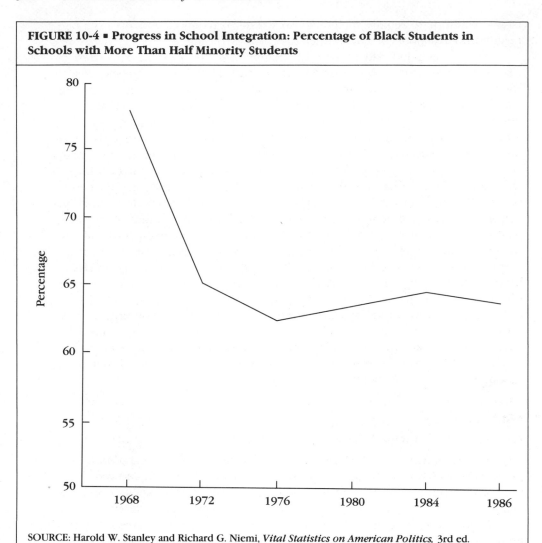

FIGURE 10-4 ▪ Progress in School Integration: Percentage of Black Students in Schools with More Than Half Minority Students

SOURCE: Harold W. Stanley and Richard G. Niemi, *Vital Statistics on American Politics,* 3rd ed. (Washington, D.C.: CQ Press, 1992), Table 12-13.

being largely because much discrimination is covert rather than overt and is thus hard to prove. For example, a school wishing to keep blacks out may deliberately adopt entrance requirements that it knows blacks will disproportionately fail; similarly, it is frequently difficult to establish why a particular job applicant was not hired for a job.

The remedies to imbalance in employment, in the composition of professions, or in admissions to higher education consist of some form of preferential treatment for members of the underrepresented groups or of an attack on the standards by which people are selected. Accordingly, the Office of Federal Contract Compliance and the EEOC have laid down guidelines to the effect that any test for employment, promotion, or membership that is disproportionately failed by members of the designated groups constitutes evidence of illegal discrimination unless the job relevance of that test can be shown. In other words, it must be shown that those who score higher on the test or selection criteria actually perform better in the roles for which they are being selected.

These guidelines were upheld by the Court in *Griggs* v. *Duke Power* (1971).[27] By holding that Congress had in Title VII outlawed criteria for employment disproportionately failed by a protected group, the Court in effect threatened the legality of any performance criteria. The job relevance of such criteria is nearly impossible to prove because it is rarely possible precisely to measure job performance. For example, how can one say that requiring particular academic credentials for a job serves to select better teachers unless one can precisely measure how good one is as a teacher, a judgment on which reasonable people usually disagree?

A seemingly contradictory decision was delivered in the case of *Washington* v. *Davis* (1976).[28] This case involved the disproportionate failure of blacks to pass the written test for becoming a police officer in Washington, D.C. Four times as many blacks as whites failed the test. The Court held that this failure rate in and of itself was insufficient to invalidate the test unless it could be shown that the tests were adopted with discriminatory intent. Unlike *Griggs,* this case was not decided under Title VII, which did not apply at this time to governmental units. Rather, it was decided under the Fifth Amendment's due process clause, the city of Washington, D.C., being an agent of the federal government. Thus two different rulings had been handed down for what are essentially undifferentiated situations: Under Title VII of the Civil Rights Act, a test that designated groups disproportionately fail is presumed invalid unless the job relevance of the test can be demonstrated; under the Constitution, such a test is presumed valid unless intent to discriminate can be shown. Subsequent decisions in the appellate courts applied the latter standard of placing the burden of proof on the plaintiff alleging discrimination. It is this new rule of law that the controversial 1991 Civil Rights Act sought to overturn (this is also discussed below).

Preferential treatment plans vary from using membership in one of the designated groups as one positive factor to be taken into consideration to rigid quotas that require a set proportion of those selected to be members of such groups. But strict quotas generate considerable emotional hostility among some groups, for example, among Jews, because quotas were once used against them to exclude them from prestigious schools and professions.

The challenge to racial preference.   The opposition to racial preference plans, although frequently emanating from perceived self-interest, has been argued in terms of an interpretation of the equal protection clause of the Fourteenth Amendment. It is contended that preferential treatment for nonwhites unconstitutionally discriminates against whites.

In the Alan Bakke case in 1978, the constitutional issue was addressed with great expectation that the Court would resolve it. This case involved the admissions procedure for the University of California Medical School at Davis, which had rejected Bakke's application for admission. This school had set aside a fixed number, sixteen places out of one hundred, for nonwhites. Because scores were compiled for each applicant on grade point averages (GPA), the Medical College Aptitude Test (MCAT), and a personal interview, the procedure created two separate applicant pools. It is important to note that the interview clearly brought subjective criteria into the process, somewhat weakening Bakke's claim that those who were selected over him were "objectively" less qualified.

Although the applicants for the sixteen minority seats had to meet minimum standards on the above criteria and in that sense were qualified, the records of those selected from the minority pool on the two objective scores (GPA and MCAT) were significantly inferior to those selected from the regular pool and, perhaps more significantly, well below the record of some of those, like Bakke, who were rejected under the regular admission process. In fact, the average percentile ranking on MCAT scores of those admitted under the special program were from thirty-six to fifty-two percentile points below those selected from the general applicant pool in the years studied.[29] The GPA of regular admittees averaged 3.5 and 3.4 for those years, whereas the special admittees averaged 2.6 and 2.4.

There was widespread expectation that the Court might resolve the question of the constitutionality of programs involving the preferential treatment of certain racial groups under the equal protection clause. This would, of course, be the judicial resolution of an issue that was still very much in controversy, a resolution based on an ambiguous legal mandate. The Court found itself as divided on the legality of such a program as society is divided over the issue.

Four justices (Burger, Rehnquist, Stevens, and Stewart) held that the use of racial criteria violated Title VII of the Civil Rights Act of 1964. Therefore Bakke should be ordered admitted without considering whether such admissions policies violated the equal protection clause. By deciding the case on statutory rather than constitutional grounds, these justices gave Congress the opportunity of overriding the decision by ordinary legislation rather than constitutional amendment.

Four other justices (Blackmun, Brennan, Marshall, and White) argued that neither the Constitution's equal protection clause nor Title VII prevented the use of racial categories to remedy the effects of past discrimination. Whether race is a permissible category is here held to depend on whether the purposes of the categorization are "benign," a clearly subjective judgment. This group of justices would have placed the judicial stamp of approval on all uses of race to benefit designated racial groups.

Four-to-four stalemates do not make for constitutional decisions on a nine-person Court. It was left to Justice Powell as the swing vote to dispose of the case. His opinion constituted the official Opinion of the Court, although none concurred with it, thereby reducing its force as legal precedent. Agreeing that racial categorizations are suspect categories that place a severe burden of proof on the state to show a compelling public purpose, Powell held that this burden was satisfied by the need to secure "a diverse student body." However, Powell saw fit to distinguish a fixed quota of student slots assigned on the basis of race—a policy he found incompatible with the equal protection clause—from the use of race as one among several factors in selecting from an open applicant pool—a policy he approvingly endorsed on the basis of the description of such a system at Harvard. Powell found the Davis program invalid on equal protection grounds, whereas the Burger group invalidated it on Title VII grounds; nevertheless, Powell and the other group made a motley majority of five to order Bakke admitted.[30]

Conclusion.   Today, it is government policy, based on the Civil Rights Act of 1964, and confirmed in the 1991 Civil Rights Act, to ameliorate the underrepresentation of targeted groups in the economy and in higher education.

Equality and the Women's Movement

As noted earlier, three "suspect categories" have been identified by the Court: race, sex, and alienage. Although only four justices have explicitly held sex to be a suspect category, in *Craig* v. *Boren* (1976) the Court did set standards for when sex may be used to classify people: The government must convince the Court that its purpose is an important one and that the sex classification is "substantially related" to achieving that purpose.[31] This case invalidated a law that set a higher legal drinking age for boys than for girls. The Court was called upon to apply this standard in *Rostker* v. *Goldberg* (1981) when it upheld the right of Congress to exempt women from selective service.[32] However, some have said that the standard was poorly applied, if not completely abandoned, here; the defenders of selective service law make no real effort to show that the exclusion of women is substantially related to the goal of raising an army. This case appears to leave the legality of classification by sex with an uncertain status. Many affirmative action programs and laws, such as Titles VI and VII of the Civil Rights Act of 1964, identify women as one of the beneficiary groups. Other such programs focus on only specified racial minorities, such as those that were under contention in the *Bakke* case, while classifying white women with white males.

In the sense of proportional equality, women have been and remain underrepresented in higher-status positions (for example, doctors, lawyers, business executives, and professors) and overrepresented in lower-status positions (for example, elementary school teachers, secretaries, and nurses). (See Figure 10-1 above.) Even the minimal goal of equal pay for equal work has been difficult to obtain. The median income for women was only 60 percent that of men only a decade ago. By 1988, this gap had narrowed to the point where the median income for women was 66 percent that of men (see Figure 10-5), progress that was attributed more to the increased entry of women into occupations formerly dominated by men than to any increase in the pay for those occupational roles traditionally held by women. Although this progress was hailed by supporters of the feminist movement, they took pains to point out that the gap remains unjustifiably large. Part of this large differential still reflects the tendency for women to be channeled into lower-status and thus lower-paying roles. Nevertheless, part of so large a difference

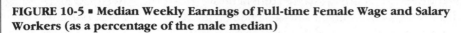

FIGURE 10-5 ▪ **Median Weekly Earnings of Full-time Female Wage and Salary Workers (as a percentage of the male median)**

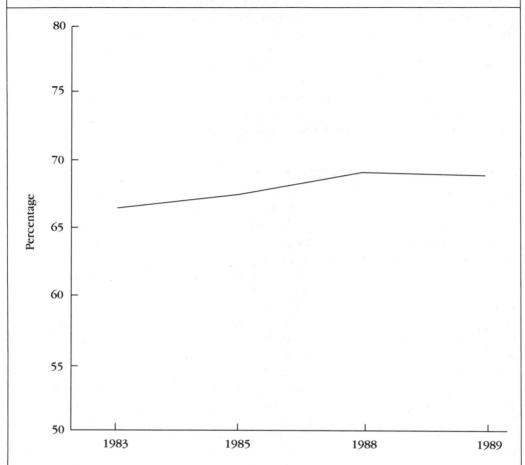

SOURCE: U.S. Bureau of the Census, *Statistical Abstract of the United States, 1991* (Washington, D.C.: U.S. Government Printing Office, 1991), Table 678.

probably also reflects the tendency to pay women less for some of the same jobs that men have. "Pink collar" jobs, those traditionally held by women, often pay less than do those jobs traditionally held by men when the levels of skill or training demanded by the respective sets of jobs are comparable. Although men are increasingly occupying such pink collar jobs and women are increasingly moving into traditionally male jobs, most people still occupy roles conforming to gender-based expectations. Therefore the movement for sexual equality concentrates on requiring equal pay for jobs of "comparable worth" (equal pay for different jobs requiring equal levels of skill, training, or respectability). There is no reason, it is argued, why secretaries should be paid less than plumbers are, when comparable levels of training and responsibility are involved. But President Reagan's chairman of the Council of Economic Advisors referred to the comparable-worth concept as "a ridiculous idea," and the Reagan administration fought it strenuously. The Bush administration is also opposed.

Unemployment rates are higher for women than for men. This further reflects the overall economic discrimination against women that remains an ongoing reality in American society. But the inferior status of women, as with other disadvantaged groups, is not entirely a function of public policy. Widely held stereotypes regarding the appropriate roles of each gender see prestigious tasks demanding intelligence, creativity, courage, or other admirable traits as being by definition "man's work," whereas a woman's natural role is seen as housekeeper and mother.

Overcoming these sex-role stereotypes is one of the most difficult tasks for the women's movement because they appear to retain a greater persistence in the public mind even than racial stereotypes. The creation of a more favorable public perception of efforts to alter the status of women is perhaps impeded by the fact that the National Organization of Women (NOW) is regarded by many as being outside the American mainstream and dominated by misanthropic extremists. In general, the major women's organizations do not take a negative stance against men but rather concern themselves with the maximization of social and economic choices available to women and focus intently on marketplace equity and reproductive freedom.

Part of the subtle denial of marketplace equity to women may be traced to the fact that access to business opportunities was long restricted to male-dominated bastions. The effort of feminists to penetrate traditional male domains received a boost when the Supreme Court upheld a New York City ordinance that banned discrimination by private clubs on the basis of race, gender, creed, or national origin in *New York State Club Association* v. *City of New York* (1988).[33] The clubs in question were those membership associations in which business deals were actually concluded, employment decisions made, and professional contacts established, thereby preserving an "old boys network" in the upper echelons of American business. The exclusion of women and minorities from membership in such associations served, therefore, effectively to exclude them from equal opportunities for success. Such clubs have not only been restricted to whites but have also generally excluded women. The law defined the clubs covered in terms of the size of membership and the fact that they offered regular meal service and regularly received dues or fees from nonmembers for the use of space and services. Such clubs were considered not "distinctly private." Given the state's compelling interest in ensuring equality of opportunity in business and professional life, the First and Fourteenth Amendment values that might conflict with that interest were overridden.

Although sex-role stereotypes have had much to do with the formation of discriminatory laws against women, it is helpful to distinguish between their subtler effects and the blatant use of law to define the female role. The legal disabilities that women have faced should not be minimized. They did not obtain the right to vote, for example, until 1920, fifty years after black men were accorded the right. Women also were once denied the right to serve on juries, work in bars, and pursue various other callings. Some laws with the ostensible purpose of protecting women—such as limiting the amount of weight they could be required to lift on the job or the maximum hours they could be required to work—had the negative effect of keeping women out of many jobs. Some critics have argued that this was deliberate. Such laws assume inexorable connections between men and physical strength and between women and less strength, relationships that exist but are far from certain. Nevertheless, most of the discrimination against women has been the product of social attitudes and sex-role stereotypes rather than the law per se.

It is not unusual, for instance, for men in hiring positions to avoid considering women for jobs in the belief that they will only quit to get married or have babies. Prospective employers can continue to apply such sexist standards surreptitiously as long as they do not have to justify not hiring any particular applicant. Furthermore, for years colleges and universities have spent many times as much on men's athletics as on women's, principally for two discriminatory reasons. First, society in general regards athletic prowess as a male prerogative; that is, male athletes are admired, whereas their female counterparts are chided for being unfeminine. Second, given such attitudes toward women athletes, their sports have not been good collegiate revenue producers because, until recently, they did not attract large paying audiences. However, Title VII of the Civil Rights Act of 1964 bans discrimination on the basis of sex as well as race, and Title IX of the Educational Amendment Acts of 1972 forbids any institution from receiving federal funds to engage in sex discrimination. Accordingly, the government now requires colleges and universities to equalize the amount spent on interscholastic athletics. This has caused vociferous opposition from supporters of expensive but profitable football programs, and so the cost of these programs has been exempted from the cost equation. But the *Grove City* decision, discussed in the previous chapter, limited the impact of Title IX, until it was nullified by an act of Congress in 1988 (passed over President Reagan's veto).

Issues central to the concerns of the leaders of the women's movement include the freedom to receive legal abortions and the achievement of equity in job status and indices of material well-being. These are issues of symbolic and emotional as well as of substantive content.

Abortion, birth control, and the law.   Prior to 1973, most states criminalized most abortions. The common exceptions were abortions permitted when necessary to save the life of the mother. *Roe* v. *Wade* (1973) overturned these laws as a violation of the right of privacy, a right not specifically mentioned in the Constitution but inferred from the Fourth, Fifth, and Ninth Amendments and applied to the states through the Fourteenth Amendment.[34] Specifically, the opinion said that states are forbidden to ban abortions in the first trimester (three months) of pregnancy; states may regulate abortions in the interest of the health of the mother in the second trimester; and the state may choose to ban abortions in the final trimester unless the health of the mother is in danger. The Court found that states had no "compelling interest" to intervene during the first trimester in the private decision of a pregnant woman to abort. Abortions are statistically safer than childbirth for the mother during the first trimester, when performed by competent medical personnel in sanitary surroundings. However, abortions become progressively more dangerous during the second trimester; this gives states a compelling interest in protecting the health of the mother. At around the beginning of the third trimester, the fetus becomes viable outside the womb, and the now potentially independent new life becomes another compelling interest. These three legal distinctions in time are, of course, approximations. Fetuses born in the second trimester have survived, and fetuses born after the second trimester sometimes do not live. Moreover, the trimester division comes increasingly under question as medical advances place the viability of fetuses earlier in pregnancy. A Missouri law upheld in 1989 requires fetal viability tests on any fetus over twenty weeks old.[35] Critics argue that no fetus could survive at that early age and that the tests are dangerous and inconclusive. Anti-abortion, or pro-life, forces have alleged that the *Roe* v. *Wade* decision has resulted in a "holocaust" of killing the unborn (appropriating the imagery of the Nazi slaughter of the Jews and thereby drawing an inference of equivalence between a sixty-cell blastocyst shortly after conception and the slaughter of conscious, active human beings. This inference is resented by pro-choice forces and by Jews who feel that the Holocaust was a unique event). The recorded rate of abortion has almost doubled since *Roe* v. *Wade* from around 15 per 100,000 live births to around 28. However, it should be noted that the pre-*Roe* figure may be low because illegal abortions have not been accurately recorded.

Despite charges that *Roe* grants the right to "abortion on demand," that case affords no absolute constitutional right to a third-stage abortion. And despite the imagery employed by pro-life forces, as in Bernard Nathanson's film, *The Silent Scream,* well over ninety-five percent of all abortions are performed in the first trimester. Second-trimester abortions occur principally because of the availability of amniocentesis, a procedure that shows whether a fetus is seriously flawed, as with spina bifida. Amniocentesis is possible only in the fourth month of the gestation period. No physician has to perform, nor does any health care professional have to participate in, any abortion unwillingly. Although hundreds of third-trimester abortions do take place, it is difficult to find physicians willing to perform them. The *New York Times* reported that as of January 5, 1992, only three physicians in the United States were performing late-stage abortions on a regular basis.

The ease by which a pregnancy may be terminated was enhanced by the development of a pill (RU-486) in France in 1988 that induces a spontaneous expulsion of a newly implanted embryo without the necessity of any further medical procedure. The Roman Catholic Church in France forced the pharmaceutical firm that produced the pill to withdraw it from the market, but President Mitterand ordered the pill placed back on the market. The Food and Drug Administration in the United States must give its usually time-consuming approval before the pill can be released to the American market. Not surprisingly, both pro-choice and pro-life camps are mobilizing to apply the appropriate pressure for their respective causes.

The Supreme Court's *Roe* decision does not require any physician to give an abortion. Rather, it says in effect that when physicians decide to give abortions to patients who freely seek them at a time when the procedure is safer than childbirth itself, it is none of the state's business. Many hospitals, especially religiously sponsored ones, refuse to permit abortions to be performed in their facilities. In some areas, this makes legal abortions unavailable to persons who want them and who are willing and able to pay.

Recent developments in the matter of abortion.   The year 1991 saw the Bush administration supporting two controversial attempts to circumscribe the right to legal abortion in the "abortion gag rule" and in the Pennsylvania abortion law. The former case involved a 1988 administrative ruling by the Department of Health and Human Services that prohibits doctors, or other health care professionals working in medical clinics receiving Title X federal funds, from providing any information regarding the availability of abortion to their patients, regardless of the circumstances of the pregnancy, on the penalty of losing the nearly indispensable funding. Thus, under this ruling, a minor patient who had been impregnated by being raped by her father could not be informed that she had the option of terminating that pregnancy. Since the clinics funded under Title X predominantly serve the poor who cannot pay for private medical care, the gag rule operates to render knowledge of medical options a function of one's economic well-being. The administration, operating to satisfy the strong pro-life component of its political constituency, contended that the right under *Roe* does not entail the right to have federal money used to facilitate the exercise of that right. The opponents of the rule, including many health care professionals speaking through the American Medical Association and the American College of Obstetricians and Gynecologists, contended that the issue was one of free speech and that denying such professionals the right to give "competent medical advice" raised serious questions of malpractice.

The Supreme Court in 1991, in the case of *Rust* v. *Sullivan,* upheld the gag rule in a narrow five-to-four decision.[36] Congress immediately passed the Chafee Bill, in effect reversing the 1988 regulation by barring its implementation. The president, again representing the pro-life forces, vetoed the Chafee Bill and Congress narrowly failed to override the veto following a strong lobbying effort by then presidential chief of staff, John Sununu.

Meanwhile, Pennsylvania enacted a law erecting a number of barriers to the exercise of abortion rights: a mandatory 24-hour waiting period for women seeking abortions, a requirement that a doctor inform the patient of the development of the fetus and of alternatives to abortions, and that minors seeking an abortion obtain the consent of one parent or a judge. The federal appeals court upheld that law in *Planned Parenthood of Southeastern Pennsylvania* v. *Casey,* citing the standard enunciated earlier by Justice Sandra Day O'Connor, but not adopted by the Court majority, that restrictions on abortions were constitutional if they did not place "an undue burden" on women seeking abortions. Both pro-choice and pro-life forces saw the case as providing an instrument for the Supreme Court to issue a definitive reevaluation of the constitutionality of *Roe,* in which, it was widely believed, *Roe* would be overturned by a Court with a pro-life majority.[37] This expectation had been reinforced by the Court's decision in 1990 in *Hodgson* v. *Minnesota,* which upheld a state requirement that minors seeking an abortion had to obtain either the formal approval of both parents or formal judicial approval.[38]

Pro-choice groups also requested that the Court hear the Pennsylvania case. Their strategy, apparently, was either to procure a definitive reaffirmation of *Roe* or, in the more likely case, to compel a reversal of *Roe* right before the presidential election, an event that they hoped would energize what they saw as the pro-choice majority against the reelection of the president and for involvement in state-level politics, where access to legal abortions in many states is likely to remain protected for the foreseeable future. In June, 1992, the Supreme Court upheld the Pennsylvania law's abortion restrictions, with several justices citing the "undue burden" standard. The Court also, however, explicitly upheld *Roe*'s right to abortion.

Of course, abortions are not cheap, and economic considerations limit their availability to the poor. Congress has perpetuated this situation by forbidding the use of Medicaid funds for abortions (which during much of the 1970s were provided under the program) except to save the life of the mother, even in cases of rape or incest. However, it is important to note that one study showed that the cutoff in Medicaid funds has not substantially reduced the incidence of legal abortions. Apparently, women who want legal abortions will undergo other sacrifices or find other means to pay for them. Abortion is of central concern to the women's movement because the ability to control one's fecundity maximizes one's life choices.

Contraception. The same logic that impels concern over the availability of safe, legal abortion applies to the availability of effective contraception. The argument of pro-life forces that abortion should not be used for birth control is plausible if effective contraception is realistically available. Yet some conservative forces have opposed the promotion of effective contraception. One example of this is the opposition of such groups to sex education in the schools on the grounds that it would encourage promiscuity. Another is the example of the so-called squeal rule established by the Reagan administration and avidly supported by forces of the religious right. This was an executive order denying federal funds to any clinic that provided contraception aid to minors unless the parents of such minors were notified. Supporters of this pointed to the value of parental responsibility and control of minors. Opponents argued that such a rule would only discourage minors from seeking such aid, not from engaging in sexual activity. This would result in exacerbating the already critical level of unwanted teenage pregnancy. The conservative assumption appears to be that the ability to have illicit sex without the risks of pregnancy encourages promiscuity. The liberal position is that sexual activity is inevitable and therefore denying access to abortion and birth control merely will produce the spillover effect of unwanted pregnancy. In any event, the squeal rule was defeated after a two-year struggle.

Another objection of some to abortion is based not only on a concern for the unborn but also on the belief that sex ought to be reserved for procreation. This group therefore regards as immoral anything that enables people to engage in sexual activity for mere pleasure while avoiding its natural consequences. The same logic underlies the dispute over the distribution of free condoms in the New York City schools and other school districts as a means to slow the spread of AIDS. Opponents on the social and political right argue that the step would implicitly condone and thereby increase teenage sexual activity. As with their argument against abortion as a remedy to the epidemic of teenage pregnancy, the counsel of these conservatives is abstention from sex outside marriage. Supporters of the condom policy, many of whom also are concerned with the availability of safe, legal abortions, argue that abstention from sexual activity may be desirable but that it is not realistic to expect it. They point to survey data indicating that most teenagers are in fact sexually active.

Women's liberation.   The equal rights amendment (ERA) that was rejected in 1982, an issue of great emotional significance to the supporters of the women's movement, was viewed as an instrument to eradicate most gender-based classifications in law and public policy as well as a symbolic public stand against such gender-based discrimination. But some of the strongest opposition to the amendment came from women, partly because they realized that women would lose not only burdens but also privileges. Laws and social policies in many situations favor women over men. For instance, courts and judges are overwhelmingly disposed to award child custody to women whenever such custody is contested in divorce proceedings. Some states have laws stating that the woman automatically wins custody unless the father can prove that she is an unfit mother. Some states permit alimony payments to women but not to men, irrespective of the relative financial status of the divorcing spouses. An Illinois law allows unwed mothers to acquire custody of illegitimate children but does not even allow unwed fathers a hearing, automatically presuming them to be unfit.

Such policies are under increasing attack by men. In fact, women's liberation is also "men's liberation," and some women fear that the financial and other responsibilities that men assume toward the women they marry would be open to challenge if gender-based distinctions in the law were abolished. Although the gender-based distinctions heretofore found in law and public policy may hinder those women who aspire to fill what were traditionally male roles, such distinctions do in some ways protect women in traditionally female roles (for example, housewife and mother).

Bias against Homosexuals, the Handicapped, and Native Americans

Homosexuals ("gays" and lesbians) are another group claiming to have suffered discrimination in American society and increasingly asserting its legal and constitutional rights to combat such discrimination. Homosexuals differ from the other targeted groups in that they are traditionally defined not on the basis of attributes but on the basis of behavior.

One of the primary concerns of opponents of homosexual rights is the fear that homosexuals will somehow influence or recruit heterosexual but impressionable children to join their ranks. This fear conflicts with the prevailing psychological opinion that homosexuality is more an involuntary than a conscious choice, by either school-age children or adults. A study done in 1991, moreover, concluded that there are measurable genetic differences between the brains of homosexual men and those of heterosexual men. The implication of this study is that one is born with one's sexual orientation and that orientation will be unaffected by any system of rewards and punishments. Therefore it does not make sense to regard homosexuality as something that can be deterred through criminal law. The study also suggests that the danger of heterosexual minors' being "recruited" into the homosexual community is overstated and virtually nonexistent.

An Oklahoma law typified the widespread efforts to bar or remove homosexuals from teaching positions. The law criminalized "advocating, soliciting or promoting public or private homosexual activity in such a manner that creates a substantial risk that such conduct will come to the attention of school children. . . ." Note that the law criminalized the advocacy of homosexuality, not the attributes of being a homosexual. However, a U.S. court of appeals struck down the law on the grounds that advocacy cannot be criminalized (especially when it is not carried out in a context of incitement; see Chapter 11). The Supreme Court upheld this ruling in 1985.

The Court has refused, in a series of cases, to protect homosexuals from dismissal from the armed forces. Therefore, although homosexuality and its practice may be protected in some ways by lower or general appellate court decisions, the Court appears prepared to accept spaciotemporal limits to the right to practice homosexuality.

In the 1986 case of *Bower* v. *Hardwick,* the Court upheld the Georgia sodomy statute with reference to its ban on homosexual behavior, a statute that criminalizes sex "against the laws of nature." A year later, the Court refused to review a case out of Texas upholding that state's more narrowly drawn ban on homosexuality.[39]

The movement toward greater social tolerance of homosexuals and toward reducing the discrimination they suffer in law and social policy has received a setback in the past few years because of the spread of the contagious and nearly uniformly fatal disease, acquired immunodeficiency syndrome, or AIDS. Homosexual men have constituted one of the high-risk groups in the United States and have widely been perceived as one of the major sources of contagion, which has generated widespread fear in the population in general. While there is a lack of certainty in this regard, the consensus among medical experts is that the disease is spread primarily through a kind of sexual activity especially prevalent among male homosexuals and through sharing of contaminated needles among intravenous drug users. Medical experts reassure us that casual contact (drinking fountains, toilet seats, etc.) would not transmit the disease. However, because of perceived uncertainty about how it can be transmitted and the fatal nature of the disease (resulting in about 133,000 American deaths by 1991), the public is in many cases not reassured. This has led to public pressure to identify and isolate homosexuals, costing them their jobs and the right to function in the broader society. It has even led to the denial of the right to attend school to hemophiliac children who have contracted the infection through the transfusion of contaminated blood products.

The spread of AIDS through the male homosexual population, resulting in the tragic death of many of their number, was exacerbated by the sexually promiscuous life-style that was common among many homosexual men, a life-style that was to some extent encouraged by the lack of social legitimacy for a homosexual orientation. In fact, it is now believed that the disease was brought to the United States and established an immediate foothold by the extremely promiscuous activity of the first known carrier in this country, a French Canadian flight steward, Gaetan Dugas, whose professional mobility allowed him quickly to infect dozens of others all over the country. It is widely believed that the transmission of AIDS through transfusions of blood and blood products (a phenomenon that has made hemophiliacs a higher-risk group and put at risk anyone who has surgery), and through contaminated needles among drug users, is still attributable largely to homosexual and bisexual males who have irresponsibly donated blood or shared needles. This has led members of the general public, fearful of the disease and seeking a scapegoat, to blame and want to punish this group, although the shared use of needles by intravenous drug users has actually become the most important factor in the spread of AIDS. Although the incidence of AIDS among the general heterosexual population is still small, it is rising and many people predict a geometric increase in the next decade or so.

The specific policy issues related to AIDS and homosexuality involve the delicate balance of the right of homosexuals and of AIDS victims to live out their lives free from harassment, with the public right to be given all possible protection against a usually fatal affliction. Proposals to bar homosexuals from donating blood have been rejected as overly broad. Instead, blood is regularly screened for AIDS antibodies. Yet some people lack confidence in the thoroughness and reliability of such screening. Public identification of carriers of the virus and identification of their sexual partners would help people who are sexually active to protect themselves from contracting the infection, but it would subject such carriers to public harassment and social ostracism. Proposals for mandatory testing of some sectors of the population carry the same potential benefits and risks. Such proposals also raise the questions of who shall be tested and at what cost. Another problem with proposals for mandatory testing is the fact that the tests are imperfect. Not only would the test fail to detect some people carrying the virus, but it would incorrectly turn out positive for some noninfected people. These noninfected "positives" would be subject to the same mental anguish and social ostracism as those who actually carry the virus. These issues involve the balancing of the right of AIDS victims and of homosexuals to confidentiality regarding their sexual activity and the right of the public to be protected as much as possible.

The handicapped.   Handicapped people have also recently become a visible minority with an agenda of demands. The nature of their demands, however, differs considerably from those of the aforementioned groups. The demands of the handicapped concentrate on access to public places and various public benefits—for example, demands for ramps where only stairs had been present, the availability of material in Braille for the blind, closed-captioned television for the hearing impaired, and the like—with much less concern for proportional equality, the placement of set or targeted proportions of handicapped people in valued roles. The concern of the leaders of the handicapped appears to fit the idea of equalizing competition rather than the idea of equality of results. The goals are the amelioration of the present effects of their disabilities rather than any compensation for the effects of past discrimination, and so their claims have generated less controversy than have those of the other groups previously discussed.

The most important legislation protecting the rights of persons with disabilities is the Americans with Disabilities Act of 1990. Its primary provisions extend the kinds of protections granted to minorities and women in the 1964 Civil Rights Act to handicapped persons. This legislation prohibits discrimination on the basis of disability in employment, public services, and public accommodations. In employment, a qualified disabled person is one who, with or without reasonable accommodations, can perform the essential functions of a particular job. The law also requires new buses and trains, as well as public buildings, to be accessible to the disabled, and it mandates communications companies to operate relay systems that will allow speech- and hearing-impaired persons access to telephone services.

Native Americans.   Native Americans constitute another group that has historically been subject to oppression by the dominant culture. From Plymouth, Massachusetts, to Wounded Knee, South Dakota, their numbers were systematically reduced, and they were forced onto desolate and often infertile reservations. They were caricatured as malevolent and ignorant savages in countless western films. Their standard of living is substantially below the national norm, and they are beset today by structural unemployment, alcoholism, and other symptoms of alienation.

In 1991, Native Americans took up as a target of protest the names of certain athletic teams. When the Atlanta Braves went to the World Series and in early 1992 when the Washington Redskins went to the Super Bowl, demonstrations were organized around both events. Defenders argued that the team names were traditional and had never been meant to disparage, and that, in any case, the protests begged the issue of the undeniably deep social and economic problems of the Native Americans. The five hundredth anniversary of Christopher Columbus's voyage of discovery, as noted in Chapter 9, also became an opportunity to debate the effect of American society on the original population.

POLICY EVALUATION: QUESTIONING A DECADE OF AFFIRMATIVE ACTION TACTICS

The impact of public policy on the issues of inequality examined in the preceding section is complex, but focusing on three important areas—busing for racial balance, the effect of the Supreme Court's decisions on EEOC-mandated employment and college-admissions quotas, and the polarized abortion issue—will tell us much about present general trends.

Busing for Racial Balance

It has been argued by some that because students have always been bused to school, no particular hardship or social cost is imposed by court-ordered busing. The opposition to such busing to achieve racial balance must therefore reveal an opposition to the goal of school desegregation itself. Opponents of busing, regardless of their high-flown rhetoric, are widely regarded by proponents of busing as thinly veiled bigots. Although this is doubtless an accurate description of many opponents of busing, it is not an accurate description of all of them.

First, there is a cost to busing for racial balance. In the case of *Charlotte-Mecklenburg,* the district court's order necessitated doubling the existing bus fleet at an additional cost of $1.5 million. Although before the order 27 percent of the pupils were bused to school, after the order 61 percent were bused. To the monetary cost must be added the expenditure of time as a resource, an expenditure that can vary from around a half-hour each way in smaller communities to several hours per day for some of those bused in Los Angeles. Either the student loses school time or must leave home earlier and return later, time that may be used more productively elsewhere. Thus, at best, busing is a brief inconvenience, and frequently it can make significant inroads into the pupil's day, curtailing time available for other extracurricular activities.

Obviously, an important policy question is whether or not such busing produces social benefits that can justify the social cost. The answer may depend on what busing is supposed to achieve. Is it supposed to balance schools racially to bring about actual social interaction among racial groups? Or is its purpose restricted to upgrading the school performance of designated groups? Busing can bring about racially balanced schools without creating actual integration. Frequently, students are grouped in classes according to previous test scores or grades (tracking) so that the higher-achieving middle-class students will be taking college preparatory academic subjects, and lower-achieving minority students will be taking vocational education or remedial courses. This practice, of course, defeats the purpose envisioned by believers in the Coleman Report, the intermingling of high and low achievers. The categorization of low achievers becomes a self-sustaining one as those students continue in school unexposed to the material they would need to master to be reclassified on subsequent tests.

As to whether busing has had any impact on academic performance, the evidence is at best mixed and inconclusive. Sociologist David Armor published an empirical study that concluded that after several years of busing the academic performance of desegregated black students showed no significant improvement.[40] Others have criticized Armor's findings, claiming that his conclusions do not necessarily follow from the evidence and that his work does not recognize busing's importance for the goal of an integrated society.[41] It is certainly true that Armor's work is not conclusive on this topic, but to attack his work because the conclusions are inconvenient for one's goals is not a rejection of those conclusions on scientific grounds.

It seems fair to say that busing has not yet provided the educational panacea for underachieving minorities that its supporters may have hoped for. Beyond the problem of tracking within the schools, the hostility and other negative emotions generated on this issue by those concerned could impede the kind of social interaction among the races that busing was supposed to bring about and that the Coleman Report suggested as a tool for upgrading the school performance of underachievers. Moreover, as Coleman himself warned a few years later, busing may exacerbate white movement out of the city school districts to the suburbs, a trend that has the effect of increasing segregation.

The impact of such de facto segregation is even greater today than it was in the 1960s, at least legally speaking, as the effectiveness of busing as a tool to achieve racial balance in the schools of many northern urban areas was severely curtailed by the more conservative Burger Court in the mid-1970s. In *Milliken* v. *Bradley* (1974), the Court held that busing could not be required across school district lines.[42] In many metropolitan areas, whites have moved to the suburbs with their own independent school districts, and so blacks now dominate the population of the city proper. A number of major American cities have black majorities or a very large black minority citizenry. Thus Chicago, with a population slightly less than 50 percent black in 1989, has a public school population that is over two-thirds black.

Trends and projections show that the inner cities are becoming populated overwhelmingly by blacks, and the suburbs are remaining overwhelmingly white. Thus, because city boundaries frequently constitute the school district boundaries, moving students about within mostly black cities or nearly all-white suburbs will not contribute much to the racial balance of the schools.

Despite the foregoing doubts, busing is defended as the only available remedy to the widespread reality of racial isolation in America's public schools. That busing is ineffectively implemented by allowing its purpose to be defeated by tracking or suburban de facto segregation does not necessarily condemn the potential of busing itself.

Whether or not it is actually a cost-efficient means of achieving widely agreed-upon goals of public policy, busing for racial balance appears to be here to stay. It is an issue of great symbolic and emotional content: a commitment to busing has been widely perceived by black leaders and their supporters as inseparable from a commitment to the broader goal of racial equality, making it difficult to question the efficacy of one without seeming to oppose the other. Moreover, the courts have officially declared busing to be an imperative of the Constitution and have expended some of their capital of legitimacy for it. Busing is now the law of the land, and it would be difficult for the courts to back down and reverse themselves on this point without damaging their own legitimacy. Nevertheless, the Court does not have to turn around completely in order to make changes in the status of busing. For example, in a 1991 case, *Oklahoma City Board of Education* v. *Dowell,* the Supreme Court ruled that school districts can be freed from court desegregation orders if they have complied in "good faith" with such orders and have eliminated the vestiges of segregation "to the extent practicable." The key issue will be the ability of school districts to convince federal judges that they have met this test.

Limited Retreat on Racial Preference Programs

Despite the outcry of rage and concern from many black leaders and their followers, the *Bakke* decision, which ended the exclusive reliance on racial quotas to enhance racial balance in some institutions, posed little threat to affirmative action in general. The outcome of the case—Bakke "won" and was ordered admitted— must be distinguished from the principles of law that emerged from it. In fact, the Supreme Court's Justice Powell, in conjunction with the four dissenters, actually provided a majority of five in implicit support of most affirmative action programs, which are in fact mostly similar to Harvard's (the affirmative action model approved by *Bakke*), in the sense that they use race as one factor but do not require strict quotas. The *Bakke* case therefore did not conclusively settle the question of the legality of affirmative action.

The *Bakke* case did appear to cast doubt on the validity of direct quotas in educational admissions. In *Kaiser Aluminum* v. *Weber* and *United Steelworkers of America* v. *Weber* (1979), the Court confronted the legality of a "voluntary" quota to balance racially a training program leading to promotion at Kaiser Aluminum.[43] Weber's allegation was that Title VII of the 1964 Civil Rights Act forbade the company, with the union's concurrence, from voluntarily adopting such a racially preferential program that involuntarily excluded Weber from an opportunity to which he otherwise would have been entitled. That law forbade a covered employer from discriminating

> against any individual with respect to his compensation, terms, condition or privileges of employment because of such individual's race, color, religion, sex, or national origin; or to limit, segregate or classify his employees . . . in any way which would . . . adversely affect his status as an employee because of such individual's race, color, religion, sex, or national origin.

The Kaiser program, which led to promotions, selected individuals on the basis of seniority with the exception that it also provided for every white selected, one black must be selected. Thus, though Weber was excluded, some blacks with less seniority than Weber were selected. There was no evidence or allegation of previous discrimination by either Kaiser or the union.

In holding that Title VII did not prohibit Kaiser's racial preference program, Justice Brennan, speaking for the Court, distinguished between the literal meaning of the law and the purposes that he inferred Congress had in mind in adopting that law. Brennan saw the purpose of Congress as correcting the problems of black unemployment and black underrepresentation in management or higher-status jobs. He reasoned that because the program is aimed at this purpose, Congress could not have intended Title VII to preclude the program, even though that is what the words of the law say.

However, a careful examination of the legislative debate over the adoption of the law may also lead to the conclusion that Congress intended Title VII to prevent race from being used as a basis for hiring, firing, or employment status, and at least one scholar, quoting the leaders of the House and Senate in this debate, made a powerful case for that interpretation.[44] The author cites extensive references from the Congressional Record showing that congressional leaders were given repeated assurances by the bill's authors that it was intended to outlaw *all* discrimination by race, for or against any given racial group.

The apparent support at this time for affirmative action in general and even for the quotas that one might detect in *Weber* was reinforced by the subsequent *Fullilove* decision (1980), which upheld a policy of setting aside 10 percent of all city contracts for businesses owned by minorities, regardless of who was the lowest bidder.[45]

However, this apparent trend was reversed in the *Stotts* (1984) case, when the Court rejected a claim that relying on a seniority principle to decide who should be laid off from an Ohio fire department violated the equal protection rights of blacks who, being the most recently hired in a recent affirmative action drive and thus the least senior, were disproportionately among those laid off.[46] This apparent new trend of undermining judicial support for affirmative action policies was reinforced in three 1989 decisions (*Richmond* v. *Croson, Wards Cove Packing Co.* v. *Atonio,* and *Martin* v. *Wilks*),[47] in which the Rehnquist Court moved to limit the force and effectiveness of affirmative action. For example, in *Martin* v. *Wilks* the Court gave firefighters in Birmingham, Alabama, the right to challenge in court a consensual hiring and promotion plan negotiated between blacks and the city personnel board and approved by a court. The ability of members of nontargeted groups to challenge voluntary affirmative action plans in court could discourage negotiating such plans. The Court does appear to be headed in a more conservative direction, and the Reagan administration reinforced it by substantially weakening federal affirmative action requirements. Moreover, the administration's appointees to the U.S. Civil Rights Commission were people known for their opposition to various affirmative action policies. The absence of administration support for affirmative action surfaced again in the summer of 1985 when the Justice Department filed a brief in U.S. District Court asking that court to revise consent decrees that the City of Indianapolis, Indiana, had entered into with the Carter administration. These decrees set hiring quotas of 25 percent for blacks and 20 percent for women.

The 1991 Civil Rights Act. Through 1987, the Court had remained basically tolerant of affirmative action plans that mandated preference for members of targeted groups even in the absence of specific patterns of discrimination against those groups. In a noteworthy case, *Johnson* v. *Transportation Agency of Santa Clara County,* the Court upheld the hiring of a woman as a truck dispatcher in Gilroy, California, over *admittedly better qualified* men to correct a general pattern of societal discrimination against women, even though there was no allegation of a pattern of past discrimination by the particular agency.[48]

The issue of reverse discrimination remains far from settled. The policy of minority set-asides that was apparently nullified in the 1978 *Fullilove* case with regard to a federal statute was resurrected by Richmond, Virginia, when that city enacted a statute requiring that 30 percent of all of the city contracts go to firms in which a targeted minority controlled at least 51 percent. These targeted groups, according to the statute, include "citizens of the United States who are Black, Spanish-speaking, Orientals, Indians, Eskimos, or Aleuts." Apparently, Richmond modeled its statute after the *Fullilove* statute in choosing favored groups, although the groups other than blacks amount to just 1.82 percent of Richmond's population. The statute was clearly aimed at blacks, who account for about half of that city's population. A federal district court upheld the statute in the face of a challenge by the J. A. Croson Company on the basis of the *Fullilove* precedent, but that decision was overturned on appeal.

The basis of the appellate court ruling was a decision in the 1986 case of *Wygant* v. *Board of Education.*[49] The Court held in *Wygant* that a rule requiring nonminority teachers to be laid off before minority teachers regardless of other factors violated the equal protection clause of the Fourteenth Amendment, a ruling that seemed to put the Court at that time clearly in opposition to racial preference plans. The Supreme Court, however, rejected the Richmond statute in *Richmond* v. *Croson.*

The key issue that emerged from the *Johnson* case and from the *Croson* case is whether racial preference plans may be implemented in the absence of evidence of specific discrimination by the firm or institution instituting the plan and, if past discrimination must be shown, what kinds of evidence must be used as the basis of that conclusion. The policy instituted by the city of Richmond was based on a statistical discrepancy between the percentage of contracts awarded to MBEs (minority business enterprises) and the percentage of the targeted groups in that community. Some argue that a more realistic policy might be based on any discrepancy between the percentage of contracts awarded to MBEs and the percentage of MBEs among the firms seeking such contracts. The issue is whether the first kind of statistical discrepancy justifies the inference that discrimination is the necessary cause. The *Croson* and *Wards Cove* cases showed that the Court, as of 1989, was unprepared to accept simple statistical evidence to justify racial preference policies.

The Congress, controlled by the Democratic Party, sought legislative reversal of these decisions in the Civil Rights Act of 1991. The essential provision of the act is to reverse the burden of proof in charges of employment discrimination and thereby to render it easier for minorities to initiate and win litigation in such disputes. The law requires employers charged with discrimination on the basis of a statistical underrepresentation of targeted groups in their work force to justify their hiring criteria in terms of job relevance or "business necessity" as in the *Griggs* ruling discussed above, a requirement that effectively negates the *Wards Cove* decision.

President Bush opposed the act and vetoed earlier versions with the claim that it was a "quota bill," although, as its proponents pointed out, the bill specifically denied that it requires quotas. Quotas, as was pointed out earlier, probably constitute the aspect of affirmative action with the least public support. The administration and congressional Democrats both acted as if they recognized that branding the bill a "quota bill" was a serious attack on it.

It is true that the bill specifically outlaws quotas. However, it made statistical disparities in the work force *prima facie* evidence of employment discrimination and placed the burden of proof on employers to show business necessity for such disparities. The effect of this provision, opponents of the bill argued, is to invite a deluge of litigation against employers in whose work-force target group members are statistically underrepresented, lawsuits that are expensive, time-consuming, and stressful even if one wins. Therefore it would be rational for employers to try to avert the increasing prospect of being sued by avoiding statistical disparities in their workplaces, in other words, to institute "voluntary" quotas. In this manner, the law that specifically stated that employers are not legally obliged to hire on the basis of quotas in effect places great pressure on employers voluntarily to impose such quotas.

Although the Bush veto of the bill was upheld in Congress, the bill was passed again in Fall, 1991, with some minor modifications and, under great pressure from those sympathetic to the leadership of the Civil Rights establishment, Bush signed the amended version. Bush was immediately under attack from the right wing of his Republican Party for allegedly capitulating on the quota issue. Indeed, this was one of the major issues cited by Pat Buchanan in announcing his decision to contest the Republican primaries. Despite some heroic efforts of several administration spokespersons to argue that the later version of the act is significantly different from the older version, a significant substantive difference between the two bills is hard to discern. In effect, the *Wards Cove* and *Croson* decisions have been overturned, and the burden of proof is upon employers to justify any statistical discrepancies in their work force.

The Ideological Conflict over Abortion Rights

Opposition to abortion moved outside the legal and orderly channels of the political process in the early months of 1985 with a series of bombings and arson incidents against clinics that performed abortions. In addition, there have been allegations of physical harassment of potential clients of abortion clinics. Although there was some evidence that only a small fraction of the antiabortion activists was actually involved in perpetrating such acts, most activists condemned the bombing and arson but understood the frustrations of those who see abortion as a form of genocide and are unable to change the situation by other means.

Opponents of such acts stress that people will be injured or killed if the violence continues. But those who defend such acts point to the much larger number of "unborn children" killed by the continuing availability of abortion and imply that the cost is an acceptable one for the goal of saving so many of the unborn. The extent to which these violent and illegal actions have received some sympathy and understanding, if not actual support, indicates the greater importance of the goals of the pro-life movement to some of its members than that of the democratic rules of the game. The passion on both sides of the issue undermines the legitimacy of the political process itself when the policy outcome becomes more important than the democratic process.

The opponents of abortion base their opposition mainly on the premise that the fetus is in fact a human being; therefore legal abortions are tantamount to the legalization of murder. The point of disagreement is whether life begins at the point of conception. Many aver that human life commences at birth or when the fetus becomes viable outside the womb. Opponents of abortion—led by many New Right conservatives and religious groups—argue that legalized abortions encourage greater use of this procedure, to the point that the procedure becomes a form of birth control and that moral considerations require the state to take a stand against what these opponents see as legalized killing. The data seem to support the claim that the number of abortions has increased considerably since abortion was made legal, and it is undeniable that many fetuses are aborted by pregnant women simply because they do not want the child, rather than for reasons of health.

However, supporters of legal abortion—who tend to be liberal, better educated, and religiously secularized—object to the contentions of pro-life groups on two grounds. First, whether legal or not, women who need abortions will seek them out. Second, the availability of legal abortions is fundamentally an issue of protecting the *civil right* of women (like men) to make their own decisions about themselves—in this case, that is, the right not to allow the state to dictate what choices they may make about their own bodies.

First, the pro-choice activists point out that abortion has long been a widespread reality, legal or otherwise. By criminalizing the procedure, the state may reduce the number of abortions, but it cannot prevent many abortions from occurring. The criminalizing of abortion may have the impact of driving many pregnant women to incompetent and untrained abortionists, with disastrous effects on the lives and health of the women involved, although pro-life forces dispute these claims. When abortion was against the law, many women died each year, from crudely performed, unsanitary, illegal abortions—women who in many cases would have lived had legal abortions been available. Therefore supporters of legal abortion emphasize that the number of unborn children saved by criminalizing abortion must be balanced against the number of pregnant women killed or seriously maimed.

To pro-life groups, these considerations pale in the face of their strongly held beliefs that readily available, affordable, and safe abortion (1) constitutes a form of murder and (2) encourages sexual promiscuity. The arguments on this issue are antithetical moral assumptions that cannot be resolved by discussion. What pro-choice groups call choice or freedom, pro-life groups call promiscuity or irresponsibility. Yet both groups are referring to the ability to engage in sexual activity without suffering undesired consequences. In the same way, what pro-life forces call the inconvenience of an unwanted child, pro-choice forces see as something that irrevocably changes the entire course of a woman's life. The essential facts are not in dispute; rather, the moral interpretation of such facts is the essence of the issue.

Second, the issue of legalized abortion is perceived as a matter of equality for women, as the legal availability of abortions gives women greater decision-making power over their lives. They have greater freedom to pursue sexual activity—as men do—without suffering the consequences of child bearing, and they need not retire from economic pursuits to raise children from unwanted pregnancies. Abortion and birth control offer greater alternative possibilities to women than do their traditional roles of homemaker and raiser of children. On the other hand, many opponents of abortion see such greater sexual freedom as leading to sexual irresponsibility and increased rates of adolescent pregnancy. It should also be noted that the issue of legalized abortion is not seen by everyone as a woman's equality issue. The opponents of legalized abortion see it as a fundamental moral issue, a question of human life and dignity. The 1992 presidential campaign offered voters a clear choice, with the Democratic platform and nominee strongly pro-choice and the Republican platform and nominee strongly pro-life.

FUTURE ALTERNATIVES: THE CHANGING CONCEPTION OF EQUALITY

Race and Equality

The most clearly discernible trend in the struggle for equality is the evolution of the generally understood meaning of the term, which has changed its goals and issues. The meaning of the term once referred to the struggle for eradication of discrimination based on racial, religious, sexual, or ethnic attributes and of laws or social policy that burden or penalize people on the basis of such attributes. It has, in recent decades, come to imply that each identifiable racial or ethnic group and each sex has a right to a proportionate share of the benefits of society. The legitimacy of an uneven distribution of material well-being and of the dominance of certain groups over others has increasingly come under attack.

When a goal of social policy is the redistribution of material well-being, the redistribution of finite values is involved. The benefits accorded to some must be taken from others. What some gain, others must lose. Clearly, there are arguments to be made for some form of compensatory justice in view of the history of discrimination against certain groups. However, because of the confusion between the bigotry or discrimination of groups and those of individuals within those groups, the justice of the matter becomes muddled. The white race may, in the aggregate, be guilty of discrimination, but individuals, Brian Weber or Alan Bakke, pay the debt, even though they may not personally have so discriminated. Nor do the benefits of affirmative action necessarily flow to the most disadvantaged individuals in society. The hard-core unemployed seldom reach professional school under such programs; rather, these programs often benefit middle-class members of designated groups. To change the rules of the game and to deny benefits to the Bakkes of society, benefits to which they were entitled under the old rules, is perceived by some as a denial of their rights. Yet minorities do have a right to combat the persisting impact of the history of social discrimination.

The point is that rights conflict. The intractable difficulty of the equality issue is that it is not a clear case of right and wrong, but one of conflicting rights. Plausible ethical arguments can and have been constructed to support conflicting claims based on powerful interests. In addition, in a stagnating economy in which hopes of perpetual economic growth are being dashed on the reality of scarcity and the finite supply of resources, society is increasingly in a zero-sum situation. This means that to the extent that the total supply of benefits cannot be expanded, those benefits that are reallocated to some must be taken from others. Members of nontargeted groups increasingly perceive that they cannot help target groups without giving up something themselves. Thus the strongest opposition to affirmative action frequently comes from those segments of white society most likely to be displaced by members of target groups, the middle or lower-middle classes. Members of the upper class are less likely to be so displaced, and therefore the support for affirmative action by so-called limousine liberals is without cost. Because of this conflict among plausible rights, issues concerning equality promise to continue to be among the most intractable and divisive of issues facing the country for the indefinite future. The issue of racial equality in higher education was given new life in a 1992 case in which the Supreme Court ruled that Mississippi's system of predominantly black and white universities is discriminatory. Similar systems in nineteen other states will be strongly affected by this ruling.

The struggle for equality by blacks has resulted in an inevitable rise in tensions between blacks and the rest of society, many of whom perceive the progress of the targeted groups toward greater material well-being as coming at their expense. In particular, racial, ethnic, or gender preference plans are deeply resented. A new phase of the struggle of the less well off groups has been entered, in which it is perceived that the goal of such groups has shifted from seeking integration or assimilation in the liberal democratic system, as symbolized by the renowned "I have a dream" speech of the Rev. Dr. Martin Luther King, Jr., to challenging the legitimacy of the system itself. Thus the sympathy of such current black leaders as the Rev. Jesse Jackson for third-world antidemocratic leaders such as Fidel Castro or Hafez Assad is perceived as a threat to the dominant system in a way that King's goals of assimilation were not. Thus, despite all of the progress toward equality documented throughout this chapter, tensions between the targeted less well off groups and the rest of society remain higher than ever. These racial tensions are exacerbated by highly publicized incidents such as the conflict between blacks and Hasidic Jews discussed above. The question of whether black Americans can receive equal justice in the American judicial system is likely to remain salient for the foreseeable future.

Just how difficult it is for blacks and other racial minorities to achieve just treatment was dramatically revealed by two housing studies in 1991. One, conducted by the Federal Reserve Board, found that minority-group home buyers experience much higher rejection rates than whites on mortgage applications in America's major cities (see Figure 10-6). The other study, conducted for the Department of Housing and Urban Development by Syracuse University, employed three thousand paired black, white, and Hispanic prospective home buyers

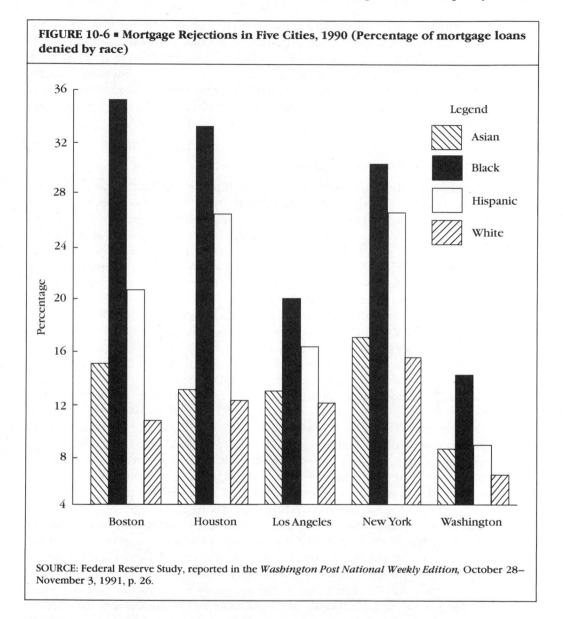

FIGURE 10-6 ▪ Mortgage Rejections in Five Cities, 1990 (Percentage of mortgage loans denied by race)

SOURCE: Federal Reserve Study, reported in the *Washington Post National Weekly Edition,* October 28– November 3, 1991, p. 26.

and renters. It found that blacks experienced some form of discrimination 56 percent of the time they sought to buy and 59 percent of the time they sought to rent a house. Comparable figures for Hispanics were 50 percent and 56 percent.[50]

The levels of racial antagonism and black frustration with continued discrimination and inequality of material well-being were revealed in the 1992 Los Angeles riots that followed the acquittals of the four police officers involved in the beating of black motorist Rodney King. Not only was there generalized outrage at the criminal justice system and at the living conditions of many blacks in urban America, there was specific hatred directed at whites, Hispanics, and Asians. In particular, Korean-owned businesses in black neighborhoods were attacked. Here, the dilemmas of equality discussed in the present chapter intersect with the economic problems of unemployment, the inadequacies of the public assistance system, and the pathologies of the urban underclass discussed in previous chapters.

The Struggle over Abortion

The determination of pro-life forces to criminalize abortion remains unabated despite opinion polls indicating that a majority of Americans support access to legal abortion in certain circumstances. The incidence of direct physical impediment to the operation of clinics or medical facilities performing abortions has intensified. The mobilization for this direct action strategy was coordinated by Operation Rescue, which employed tactics of sit-ins and mass arrests at abortion facilities. The Republican platform of 1988 reflected the most extreme pro-life position of favoring a constitutional amendment to criminalize all abortions in any circumstances including those resulting from rape or incest. Vice-President Quayle explicitly took this position in a nationally televised interview with a teenage interviewer during the campaign—saying she should be required to bear a pregnancy to term even if it resulted from being raped by her father—putting the Bush administration unequivocally in the pro-life camp.

During recent years, each judicial nominee's position on the abortion question was alleged to be a factor in selection for judicial appointments, including those for the Supreme Court, and, with the addition of Clarence Thomas, it appears that a majority of the Court now thinks that *Roe* v. *Wade* was badly decided. It is one thing, however, to say that one would not have written that decision in the first place; it is something else to reverse a decision that has been part of the social fabric and pattern of expectations for two and a half decades.

The pro-life forces perceive that they may have the opportunity for which they have striven so long, a reconsideration by the Court of the *Roe* decision. An opportunity was afforded in 1989 by the case of *Webster* v. *Reproductive Health Services,* coming out of Missouri.[51] The case involved a Missouri law that placed numerous restrictions on the access to legal abortions (e.g., a ban on any public money spent for abortion, a ban on the use of any public facilities or any public employees in the performance of an abortion, and a requirement that doctors determine the viability of any fetus over nineteen weeks into the gestation period) and a declaration that life begins at the point of conception. The appellate court struck these provisions down as incompatible with *Roe.* Missouri appealed that ruling.

In the *Webster* arguments, Justice Sandra Day O'Connor, the swing vote in this case, expressed some concern about the "penumbra" right of privacy which is the cornerstone not only of *Roe* but of the right to contraception and other rights as well. When Missouri Attorney General Webster responded that he was only concerned with a "thread" of the broader right of privacy, the attorney for the Reproductive Health Services defending *Roe* observed that when he pulls a thread, his sleeve falls off. The decision upheld the Missouri law five to four without specifically overturning *Roe.* This decision has the effect of granting the states considerably more leeway in regulating access to legal abortions. For example, the states may now require fetal viability tests, insist that abortions be performed in a hospital, or ban the use of public hospitals for the purpose of abortions. This will in turn have the effect of transferring the passionate debate over abortion rights to the politics of the state legislatures. It is believed that the pro-choice forces are mobilizing for this fight with an intensity formerly limited to the pro-life forces. The *Webster* decision will probably mean that abortion will become less readily available in some states than in others, meaning that legal abortion will be even less readily available to poor women without the means to travel than to more affluent women. The *Casey* case, out of Pennsylvania, was the latest challenge to federal court protection of the right to abortion. The narrow 5–4 majority upholding *Roe* means future challenges are likely and makes future Court appointments crucial for both sides.

Although pro-choice advocates argue with alarm that overruling the *Roe* principle would signal a wholesale return to the days of back-alley coat-hanger abortions, this would not necessarily be the case. Many state court systems have adopted the privacy principle into their state constitutions, and popularly elected state judiciaries are far less accountable to the pressures of the vocal and militant pro-life minority. Hence, even without the protection of access to legal abortions under the federal Constitution, the right may be protected by a number of state constitutions. This would, however, mean that access to legal and medically safe abortion would depend on where one happened to live or on the economic means to move to where abortion is legal, a situation that would produce a perception of inequity. Moreover, the pro-choice forces have been less militant than their opponents because they have taken their right to abortion for granted. However, as leaders of the women's movement warn, overruling *Roe* would mobilize a formerly passive but now intensely angry pro-choice movement.

If *Roe* is reconsidered, the decision would be vulnerable on the inferential nature of the right of privacy that underlies it and on the justification of when the fetus acquires life. The Court's justification for allowing states to ban abortion in the third trimester is based on the presumed point at which the fetus becomes independent of the mother in the sense of survival outside the womb. However, since the decision was handed down in 1973, medical technology has enabled fetuses to survive miscarriage in the second trimester, in rare cases as early as 23 weeks.

Although the right of privacy is an inferred or "penumbra" right, it is a principle that many regard as the essence of the distinction between an open society and one that leans in the direction of totalitarian dictatorship, the staking out of a category of concerns that is none of the state's business. Moreover, this principle is also the basis of the constitutional right of married persons to practice contraception, upheld a little over two decades ago. Overruling *Roe* may encourage some of the pro-life forces that oppose the practice of contraception with equal vehemence once again to place that question on the political agenda. (Joseph Scheidler of the Pro-Life Action Committee, an antiabortion group, has characterized contraception as "obscene . . . a form of mutual masturbation. . . . Sex is not for fun and games.") The Catholic Church, one of the leading institutions in the pro-life coalition, has a well-known position against contraception. Thus the prospects are for intense political conflict to continue on the questions surrounding reproductive rights in the near future.

Meanwhile, the ability of the government at any level to proscribe abortions that are clearly sought by many women, whether legal or otherwise, is further brought into question by the development in France of the abortion-inducing pill, RU-486, which makes it possible to terminate an early pregnancy in the privacy of one's own home. Naturally, pro-life forces would prefer to prevent the introduction of RU-486 in the United States, and a battle over the right to access to this pill is anticipated.

SUMMARY

There are three ways in which the term *equality* has been conceptualized: equality under the law, equality of opportunity, and equality of material well-being. Each conceptualization has its own implications for the imperatives of public policy.

Equality of material well-being, the main thread of this chapter, has been defined as the goal of proportional equality for targeted disadvantaged groups. The various policies designed to realize this goal are collectively designated as affirmative action.

Affirmative action can be defined as compensatory justice for the persisting effects of past discrimination, a definition with which most of its supporters would agree. Its critics attack affirmative action because of its denial of meritocracy, its inconsistency with equality under law, its focus on groups rather than individuals, and its penalizing of competitive success and denial of performance standards. Because plausible cases can be made for either side, the issue comes down to differences in the interests of the groups concerned.

The emasculation of the Fourteenth Amendment by the Supreme Court in dealing with state-mandated segregation or with segregation in businesses serving the public was eventually corrected by the *Brown* desegregation case and by the 1964 Civil Rights Act.

The original intent of the *Brown* decision has been redefined as mandating racially balanced schools. This has led to court-ordered busing as the only way to achieve that goal. After all the controversy in implementing this policy, its impact on either social interaction of the races or on the school performance of racial minorities remains to be demonstrated. Yet busing does impose social costs in money, time, and other resources.

When performance standards have been failed disproportionately by target groups, they have been challenged as discriminatory, that is, in violation of Title VII of the Civil Rights Act and the due process clause of the Constitution. The passage of the 1991 Civil Rights Act suggests that in the event of such a challenge, the burden of proof will be on the employer to show a rational basis for hiring decisions.

The drive for racial balance in employment and higher education led to racial preference plans in these areas. Such plans were challenged in the *Bakke, Fullilove,* and *Weber* cases. Cumulative rulings in these cases have left a modified affirmative action structure in place: Strict quotas in academic admissions may violate either the Civil Rights Act or the Constitution, but other uses of race for the purpose of racial balance appear to be acceptable. However, recent decisions suggest a Court much less sympathetic to affirmative action claims in the future.

Women remain disadvantaged by proportional standards and have been identified in some respects as a targeted group. Although some discrimination against women has been legal, much of it can be traced to sex-role stereotypes. The Civil Rights Act of 1964 also bans discrimination on the basis of sex. Two issues of great emotional and symbolic significance to the women's movement, abortion and comparable worth, have generated much passionate controversy. Proponents of the right to abortion argue that it occupies an area outside the state's jurisdiction; opponents argue that the state does have the right to interfere in a woman's decision about her body when that decision affects another life. The definition of when life begins—a central controversy in this movement—was avoided in the *Roe* v. *Wade* decision.

NOTES

1. *Frontiero* v. *Richardson,* 411 U.S. 677 (1973).
2. *The Civil Rights Cases,* 109 U.S. 3 (1883).
3. For a detailed account of admissions policies at Harvard University, see Alan Dershowitz, *Chutzpah* (Boston: Little, Brown, 1991), pp. 66–74.
4. For full treatment of Berkeley's policies to restrict the admission of Asians, see Dinesh D'Souza, *Illiberal Education* (New York: Free Press, 1991), chap. 2.
5. Peter Uhlenberg, "Demographic Correlates of Group Achievement: Contrasting Patterns of Mexican Americans and Japanese Americans," in Robert K. Yin, ed., *Race, Creed, Color or National Origin* (Itasca, Ill.: Peacock, 1973), p. 86.
6. *Korematsu* v. *United States,* 323 U.S. 214 (1944).
7. Harry L. Katano, *Race Relations* (Englewood Cliffs, N.J.: Prentice-Hall, 1974), p. 218.
8. W. E. B. Dubois, *Black Reconstruction* (New York: Harcourt Brace Jovanovich, 1935), pp. 176ff.
9. Elizabeth Koontz, "Women As a Minority Group," in Yin, ed., *Race,* pp. 288–289.
10. Paraphrased from Daniel Bell, "Meritocracy and Equality," *Public Interest,* 29 (Fall 1972), 44.
11. *Washington* v. *Davis,* 426 U.S. 229 (1976).
12. *Griggs* v. *Duke Power,* 401 U.S. 424 (1971).
13. David McClelland, *The Achieving Society* (New York: Free Press, 1967).
14. See the ADL surveys cited in Nathan Perlmutter and Ruth Ann Perlmutter, *The Real Anti-Semitism in America* (New York: Arbor House, 1982), chap. 8. See also Arthur Liebman, *Jews and the Left* (New York: John Wiley, 1979), pp. 564–568. The 1978 Harris survey also found anti-Semitism to be higher among blacks than other groups.
15. A detailed account of these events may be found in *The New Republic,* October 14, 1991, pp. 21–31.

16. *The Civil Rights Cases,* 109 U.S. 3 (1883).

17. *Heart of Atlanta Motel* v. *United States,* 379 U.S. 241 (1964); *Katzenbach* v. *McClung,* 379 U.S. 294 (1964).

18. *Plessy* v. *Ferguson,* 163 U.S. 537 (1896).

19. *Brown* v. *Board of Education of Topeka, Kansas,* 347 U.S. 483 (1954), known as *Brown I.* The opinion also struck down the segregated school systems of three other states—Delaware, South Carolina, and Virginia—in which companion suits had been filed. And the Court also struck down the constitutionality of government-required segregation in federal-controlled territory, in this case Washington, D.C., in *Bolling* v. *Sharpe,* 347 U.S. 497 (1954). Recall that the Fourteenth Amendment only restricts state government, but the *Bolling* case was decided under the due process clause of the Fifth Amendment.

20. *Brown* v. *Board of Education of Topeka, Kansas,* 349 U.S. 294 (1955), known as *Brown II.*

21. *Alexander* v. *Holmes County Board of Education,* 396 U.S. 19 (1969).

22. James Coleman, *Equality of Educational Opportunity* (Washington, D.C.: U.S. Government Printing Office, 1966); and U.S. Commission on Civil Rights, *Racial Isolation in Public Schools* (Washington, D.C.: U.S. Government Printing Office, 1967).

23. Bell, "Meritocracy," p. 44.

24. *Green* v. *School Board of New Kent County,* 391 U.S. 430 (1969).

25. *Swann* v. *Charlotte-Mecklenburg Board of Education,* 402 U.S. 1 (1971).

26. See the discussion of specific cases in Nathan Glazer, *Affirmative Discrimination* (New York: Basic Books, 1975), pp. 100ff.

27. *Griggs* v. *Duke Power.*

28. *Washington* v. *Davis.*

29. In 1973, the regular admittees averaged in the eighty-third percentile nationally on the science part of the test, and the special admittees averaged in the thirty-fifth. On the verbal test the regular students averaged in the eighty-first percentile, and the special admittees averaged in the forty-sixth. The difference on the quantitative test was from the seventy-sixth percentile to the twenty-fourth, and on the general information test, from the sixty-ninth percentile to the thirty-third. The differences for 1974 were correspondingly from the eighty-second to the thirty-seventh percentiles on science, sixty-ninth to thirty-fourth on verbal, sixty-seventh to thirtieth for quantitative, and seventy-second to eighteenth on general information. Cited in Alan Sindler, *Bakke, DeFunis and Minority Admissions* (New York: Longman, 1978), p. 59.

30. *Bakke* v. *Regents of the University of California,* 438 U.S. 265 (1978).

31. *Craig* v. *Boren,* 429 U.S. 190 (1976).

32. *Rostker* v. *Goldberg,* 453 U.S. 57 (1981).

33. *New York State Club Association* v. *City of New York,* 108 S. Ct. 2225 (1988).

34. *Roe* v. *Wade,* 410 U.S. 113 (1973).

35. *Webster* v. *Reproductive Health Services,* 109 S. Ct. 3040 (1989).

36. *Rust* v. *Sullivan,* 111 S.Ct. 1759 (1991).

37. See the discussion of the Pennsylvania case in the *Washington Post,* Tuesday, October 22, 1991, pp. 1 & 12.

38. *Hodgson* v. *Minnesota,* 58 LW 4957 (1990).

39. *Bowers* v. *Hardwick,* 106 S.Ct. 2841 (1986).

40. David Armor, "The Evidence of Busing," *Public Interest,* 28 (Summer 1972), 90–126.

41. For example, see Thomas Pettigrew, "Busing: A Review of the Evidence," *Public Interest,* 33 (Winter 1973), 88–113.

42. *Milliken* v. *Bradley,* 418 U.S. 717 (1974).

43. *Kaiser Aluminum* v. *Weber* and *United States Steelworkers of America* v. *Weber,* 443 U.S. 193 (1979).

44. Carl Cohen, "Justice Debased: The Weber Decision," *Commentary,* 68 (September 1979), 43–53.

45. *Fullilove* v. *Klutznick,* 448 U.S. 448 (1980).

46. *Firefighters Local Union 1784* v. *Stotts,* 104 S. Ct. 2576 (1984).

47. *Richmond* v. *J. A. Croson Company,* 488 U.S. 469 (1989); *Wards Cove Packing Company* v. *Atonio,* 493 U.S. 802 (1989); and *Martin* v. *Wilks,* 492 U.S. 932 (1989).

48. *Johnson* v. *Transportation Agency of Santa Clara County,* 480 U.S. 616 (1987).

49. *Wygant* v. *Jackson Board of Education,* 476 U.S. 267 (1986).

50. *Baltimore Sun,* August 31, 1991.

51. *Webster* v. *Reproductive Health Services,* 109 S.Ct. 3040 (1989).

SUGGESTED READINGS

Armor, David. "The Evidence of Busing." *Public Interest* 28 (Summer 1972): 119–131.

Bell, Daniel. "Meritocracy and Equality." *Public Interest* 29 (Fall 1972): 29–68.

Berger, Morris. *Equality by Statute: The Revolution in Civil Rights.* rev. ed. New York: Doubleday, 1967.

D'Souza, Dinesh. *Illiberal Education: The Politics of Race and Sex on Campus.* New York: The Free Press, 1991.

Dworkin, Robert. *Taking Rights Seriously.* Cambridge, Mass: Harvard University Press, 1977.

———. *A Matter of Principle.* Cambridge, Mass.: Harvard University Press, 1985.

Edsall, Thomas B. *The New Politics of Inequality.* New York: W. W. Norton, 1984.

Glazer, Nathan. *Affirmative Discrimination.* New York: Basic Books, 1975.

Greer, Germaine. *Sex and Destiny.* New York: Harper & Row, 1984.

Hacker, Andrew. "Asians, Blacks, and Whites Struggle for College." *New York Review of Books,* October 12, 1989, p. 63.

Kristol, Irving. "About Equality." *Commentary* 54 (November 1972): 41–47.

Millet, Kate. *Sexual Politics.* New York: Doubleday, 1969.

Parkin, Frank. *Class, Inequality and Political Order.* New York: Praeger, 1971.

Rawls, John. *A Theory of Justice.* Cambridge, Mass.: Harvard University Press, 1971.

Sindler, Alan. *Bakke, DeFunis and Minority Admissions.* New York: Longman, 1978.

Yin, Robert K., ed. *Race, Color, Creed or National Origin.* Itasca, Ill.: Peacock, 1973.

CHAPTER 11

First Amendment Freedoms in an Open Society

The individual freedoms guaranteed by the First Amendment are widely regarded as essential to the maintenance of a democratic system. Specifically, the First Amendment states that "Congress shall make no law respecting an establishment of religion, or prohibiting the free exercise thereof; or abridging the freedom of speech, or of the press; or the right of the people peaceably to assemble, and to petition the government for a redress of grievances." These freedoms constitute the basis of what is normally understood by the concept of an open society, the type of society that is a necessary foundation for democratic political institutions.

ISSUE BACKGROUND: SAFEGUARDING DEMOCRACY THROUGH CIVIL LIBERTIES

Pluralism and the Tolerance of Diverse Public Ideas

The First Amendment freedoms protect the legitimacy of philosophical, political, and ethical pluralism. The concept of *pluralism* entails tolerance of diversity in social, political, and religious points of view, that is, acknowledgment that different judgments on these subjects all have a right to be held and advocated. Democratic political institutions in the modern world are characterized, at a minimum, by genuine, regular competition among alternative political elites for the occupancy of decision-making roles.[1] This open—and orderly—competition should render governing elites accountable to the governed by compelling them to justify the results of their acts in terms of the public interest.

It is therefore presumed that the different conceptions of the public good, emanating from different interests, will be resolved by a process of bargaining and compromise in which no one group or interest will completely get its way. Each will be restrained by competing interests. The concept of an *open society* thus means that in matters of social, political, or ethical judgments, no one has a monopoly on truth or wisdom; therefore it makes sense to leave the channels of communication open. As Justice Oliver Wendell Holmes said in perhaps one of the most eloquent of all expositions of the concept of freedom of thought:

. . . when men have realized that time has upset many fighting faiths, they may come to believe more than they believe in the very foundations of their own conduct that the ultimate good desired is better reached by free trade in ideas—that the best test of truth is the power of thought to get itself accepted in the competition of the market. . . .[2]

The notion here is that if opinions or philosophies are untrue or pernicious, they will be rejected in an open society aware of competing ideas. It should not be necessary to use the enforcement machinery of the state to repress any set of ideas. Rather, differences in opinion should be dealt with by discussion—the inter-change of ideas.

The various parts of the First Amendment all may be seen as protecting the same democratic value, the legitimacy of a pluralism of ideas and opinions. The amendment should also be seen as protecting the beliefs of minorities, or unpopu-lar ideas—that is, as a constraint on the ability of majorities acting through the democratic political process to impose their ideas and judgments on minorities. Popular ideas or dominant religions do not need First Amendment protection. It is the unpopular ideas that are more likely to be suppressed; it is the adherents of less widely held religions that may be pressured into accepting or bowing to the dominant theological perspective. To believe in freedom of speech, press, assem-bly, or religion only for popular positions is not to believe in it at all! The whole point of the concept of civil liberties is that there are some things that majorities may not do, no matter how politically dominant they may be.

The foregoing suggests a political function for First Amendment freedoms: to protect the process of discussion that underlies our type of political system. A theme of this chapter will be the subtle evolution of the interpretation of these freedoms whereby they have become ends in and of themselves, rather than only means of protecting that system. This evolution is mainly characterized by the shift in the meaning of the First Amendment's freedom of speech clause from protecting discussion (the exchange of ideas) to protecting expression (utterances releasing feelings rather than persuading). Such new conceptions of the amendment's free-doms generate spillover effects into other policy-making areas and raise the issue of trade-offs among competing legitimate values. The issue of trade-offs involves political conflict among legitimate competing interests, conflict that is not easily resolved by a legal pronouncement. Another underlying theme in this chapter is the difficulty of resolving such political conflicts with legal principles.

The Preferred Position Doctrine

There is a philosophy concerning the role that the law and courts ought to play in the democratic political process. This philosophy holds that when there is doubt about the legality or constitutionality of the actions of the political process, judges ought to accept the values implied by that political action rather than impose their own values on society. In other words, when there is doubt as to whether the actions of the political or administrative sectors of society are constitutional, such doubt should be resolved in favor of these actions. This is called the *presumption of constitutionality.*

In the area of First Amendment civil liberties, however, this philosophy of presumed constitutionality underwent considerable modification in the early part of the modern era—roughly from 1895 to the later New Deal (1937). During this time, when America's modern corporate economy was developing, conservative judges tended to read a strict right of property into the Constitution that declared much regulation of business and of the economy unconstitutional. On the other hand, reformists and, later, New Deal liberals, who were actively creating many of the country's first extensive regulatory programs, were arguing for the presumption of constitutionality—that is, that courts ought to accept the legislative regulation of the economy and of corporations. Thus, for a period of about forty-two years (1895–1937), the judiciary actively tried to impose the economic values of laissez-faire, clearly a conservative economic perspective. Liberals, wishing to protect their values of government intervention in the economy, argued that the courts should give the benefit of the doubt to the government when the constitutionality of its actions was challenged.

Ironically, when the issue was the legality of politically imposed constraints on civil liberties (for example, the constraint of freedom of speech to promote greater national security, largely a conservative cause), liberals desired the courts to intervene against much of the then current political practice, that is, to question the presumption of constitutionality in such cases because it did not serve liberal values to uphold it.

Development of the doctrine.   Thus liberals found themselves faced with an uncomfortable paradox. Many who wanted the Supreme Court consistently to uphold liberal social and political values advocated a presumption of constitutionality when the issue was the government's right to regulate the economy. However, when the issue was the government's right to restrict individual rights, liberals did not wish to assume the legality of such actions. Accordingly, liberals are disposed to find censorship laws to be unconstitutional.

The reconciliation of this inconsistency by political liberals with respect to the role of the courts was achieved through the "preferred position doctrine," a modification that emanated from a footnote in the *United States* v. *Carolene Products* case (1938), in which Justice Stone suggested that " . . . there may be a narrower scope for the presumption of constitutionality" in cases involving civil liberties than with regard to other types of legislation.[3] The *preferred position doctrine* holds that civil liberties have a higher priority than do other types of values. In cases involving an alleged infringement of such rights, the burden of proof shifts to the government to prove that what it did was not unconstitutional.

Proponents of the preferred position doctrine argue that civil liberties constitute vested rights of a higher order than economic or social values because civil liberties constitute the essence of the democratic political process itself. Because the very nature of the political process is thus defined by its protection of civil liberties, it makes less sense to defer to the political process (as in presumption of constitutionality) when questions of its infringement on civil liberties are at stake. When such liberties are not protected, the process itself becomes distorted and cannot be relied on to correct itself. In the face of constitutional uncertainty, one may claim to be promoting democracy by accepting majority rule on economic questions. But one cannot claim to be promoting democracy by allowing the suppression of unpopular points of view because that would constitute a suppression of the right of those out of power to supplant those in power by persuasion and political competition. Therefore liberals tend to conclude that the arguments in favor of the presumption of constitutionality that involve deferring to the wishes of a democratic political process do not apply when the political process suppresses the very mechanisms—the First Amendment rights—that create the viability of the democratic process.

Criticism of preferred position. It should be kept in mind that the preferred position doctrine is not self-evident to all constitutional authorities. Some scholars deny that any set of rights or values should be so vigorously protected that they undercut the protection of other values and rights. Although they acknowledge that democracy cannot survive without some protection of First Amendment freedoms, they claim that democracy does not require the absolute protection of such freedoms. Some kinds of public expression clearly contribute more to the free market of ideas than others. It has been questioned, for instance, whether the right to display obscene epithets in public contributes to the exchange of ideas. They also remind us that democracy cannot survive without a measure of public order and security. A more conservative position is that an expressive and incendiary public utterance that contributes nothing to the market of ideas does not promote the maintenance of successful democracy and, further, that the suppression of such utterances may promote democratic values. To hold that utterance in itself must always be held superior to competing values would, in this view, substitute "a self-wielding sword—a talismanic test" (in the words of a leading proponent of this viewpoint) for the judgments that policymakers and judges are supposed to exercise.[4] The public outrage that ensued when the Court declared in the summer of 1989 that burning the flag was a protected form of speech constitutes an illustration of the conservative position that some forms of expression are so offensive to the majority of citizens as to be beyond the pale of constitutional protection. Clearly, the Court did not reinforce that position in this case.

Therefore, although liberals may rely on the preferred position doctrine to defend civil liberties, two other groups, conservatives and those who uphold the presumption of constitutionality, emphatically reject that doctrine, each for different reasons: conservatives, because they frequently dispute the liberal priority of protecting First Amendment values over social order, security, or public morality; the latter, because they object to the judicial reordering of whatever value priorities are set by political or administrative authorities.

The absolute interpretation of the preferred position doctrine. The most extreme version of the preferred position doctrine argues that First Amendment freedoms are absolute. This means that these rights can never be impeded in any way, regardless of their impact on other values in a particular context. One Supreme Court justice, the renowned activist Hugo Black, explicitly argued this position. Pointing out that the amendment says, "Congress shall make *no* law . . . ."

[emphasis added], he argued that "no law" means just that and does not logically allow for exceptions. Black even contended that laws against libel (the publication of malicious untruths about someone) are an unconstitutional invasion of free speech.[5]

In practical terms, this is an untenable position. Examples of the free exercise of speech that any viable government must be able to suppress are not hard to think up. The communication of military secrets to an enemy agent would be one. Deliberate incitement of a riot would be another.

For Black, the meaning of the First Amendment was explicit and unambiguous: "Congress shall make no law . . ."—words, Black argued, that allow no exceptions. However, although that phrase may be unambiguous, its other clauses, such as those on "the establishment of religion" or "freedom of speech," are not. With respect to the last, it is far from self-evident that it includes all human utterance. Freedom of speech does not necessarily include anything that anyone may say, write, film, or paint in any context.

The balancing interpretation of the preferred position doctrine. At the opposite pole from the notion that First Amendment freedoms constitute superior values that must always override competing ones exists another significant idea: that these freedoms must interact with competing values and that the superiority of one set of values over another depends on the context or the situation. In this perspective, each questionable case involves a competition between serious and important values, all of which must be protected to a degree, but no one of which can be protected absolutely. Such cases do not contain a clear right versus a clear wrong so much as they contain conflicting rights. A balance must be struck in each case, in the first instance by the political or administrative authorities making policy and, in the second, by the appellate courts who are merely to review the action's legitimacy. Under the absolute position, such courts may reverse the balance struck by the political or administrative structures in the light of a value priority that they feel must be presumed dominant, but under the balancing position the courts may simply ask whether the balance struck was a reasonable one.

The latter perspective maximizes leeway and discretion for political and administrative officials. Those who wish to minimize the impact of the judiciary applaud the flexibility thus afforded; it allows the government much greater discretion to make policy choices dictated by the circumstances of time and place.

Liberals, however, fear this flexibility. They fear government will infringe on the rights of minorities and those espousing unpopular causes to whatever extent constitutional interpretation allows. In its refusal to set unambiguous rules on the limits of governmental conduct, the balancing position places the burden on the individual to initiate litigation to determine the limits of government infringement in every specific instance. This is, in most cases, an impractical recourse. Government, unfettered by the supremacy of First Amendment guarantees, would be for the most part free to interpret the Constitution to pursue its own objectives or other public purposes at the expense of individual rights. Governments would be inclined to balance in favor of those other values because by definition civil rights entail the protection of minorities and less popular ideas against the will of a politically potent majority. Were these ideas, religious perspectives, or philosophies popular ones, it would not be necessary to invoke constitutionally guaranteed rights to protect them; they would be protected by political means. The idea of balance—the idea that no rights are absolute—has in principle been accepted. But the questions of how to strike the balance in any particular instance and the extent to which the courts should overturn balances struck in the political sector remain at issue.

CONTEMPORARY POLICY: TESTING THE LIMITS OF FIRST AMENDMENT FREEDOMS

Freedom of Speech

Once the absolute position, which holds that the freedom of speech clause encompasses all utterances, is rejected, it follows that the clause refers to some utterances and not to others. Courts then must address the task of making the distinction. Courts operate most legitimately when deriving their decisions from some generic principle, a standard or criterion that applies to a whole category of cases. Courts have been engaged in devising such principles or criteria to distinguish those utterances that are encompassed by the phrase "freedom of speech" from those that are not.

Prior restraint.   The idea that freedom of speech limits a government's ability to punish a speaker or writer for the consequences of what is written or spoken is a modern interpretation of that concept. Traditionally, in the English common law, the concept of freedom of speech merely entailed a restriction on the right of government to suppress what was being said or written in advance of the utterance; in other words, it prohibited censorship.[6] This doctrine, that freedom of speech merely meant the absence of previous or prior restraints, gave government full authority to punish speakers or writers for what was called seditious libel, that is, false criticism of the government.

This concept of freedom of speech would protect only against the suppression of utterance before it is spoken; seditious libel would be punishable without any constitutional question. It was in the context of this earlier limited conception of the meaning of freedom of speech that the now repudiated Alien and Sedition Acts of 1798 could be passed. Far from constricting the existing conception of freedom, however, these laws actually expanded it by making truth a defense when one was accused of sedition. In this step, the laws went beyond the famous British reform in this area embodied in the Fox Libel Act of 1792.

Freedom of speech now means more than the absence of prior restraint, but the concept has always meant at least that much. In that sense, the absence of prior restraint is a minimal conception of freedom of speech. An exercise of prior restraint, or censorship, places a particularly heavy burden of justification on a government taking such action. Denial of licenses to speak, injunctions not to publish, and the like are strongly presumed to be unconstitutional unless it is clearly demonstrated otherwise. But even prior restraint is not an absolute doctrine. The burden of proof, however heavy, may be satisfied. One may conceive of some utterances the effects of which are regarded as so pernicious that the government is under no obligation to allow their dissemination in the first place. Which utterances fit this category depends on one's values. Some may regard explicitly obscene material as irredeemably harmful, whereas others may not. And some may deem certain utterances to be irremediably destructive of national security, whereas others may regard the same utterances as a tolerable risk.

Although exercises in prior restraint require a particularly heavy burden of justification, to say that a governmental action is prior restraint is not automatically to say that it is unconstitutional. It is, however, especially difficult to reconcile censorship with the concept of a democratic system presented in these pages. Censorship, after all, pertains to a small elite, often self-designated, telling the general population of presumably rational adults what they are to be permitted to read, hear, or view. But the concept of an open society entails the assumption that rational adults are the best judges of their own interests, that they are able to choose among the many ideas and values to which they are exposed.

Evolution of the danger test.   Because the concept of freedom of speech means more than the absence of prior restraint but falls somewhere short of Black's absolute position, it follows that some speech may be punished and other speech is protected. A clear, consistent standard is needed to determine what speech the amendment defends. Justice Oliver Wendell Holmes tried to fill this need with the clear and present danger test, a test that has perhaps been cited in speech cases more than any other single test and has almost come to symbolize the liberal interpretation of vigorous freedom of speech protection.

As originally conceived in the *Schenck* v. *United States* case in 1919, this test focuses on the intent of the speaker or writer to bring about an illegal act "that Congress has a right to prevent."[7] Here Schenck intended to prevent the implementation of conscription by urging conscripts not to report for induction. Schenck was not trying to persuade others that the war was wrong; he was trying to incite action that would stop the war. However, as Holmes later complained, "Every idea is an incitement. It offers itself for belief and, if believed, is acted upon unless some other belief outweighs it."[8] Therefore, the clear and present danger test is meant to determine whether the intended consequence of an utterance is persuasion or is an action of such severity and of such an immediate potential threat as to foreclose the consideration of countervailing belief. In other words, the test is whether the intent is to bring about the desired result by persuasion with the force of one's ideas or by physical compulsion. As elaborated in his *Abrams* and *Gitlow* dissents, Holmes made clear that the purpose of the test and of the free speech clause of the First Amendment is to protect discussion, "the market of ideas," rather than expression or "words that may have all the effects of force." If the intent of the speaker or writer was to incite immediate, illegal action, it did not matter that it was improbable that the preventable evil would actually occur.

Surely Schenck, an obscure radical grinding out pamphlets urging draft avoidance, was not likely to impede the American war effort. Therefore the decision unanimously upholding his conviction turned on Schenck's intent to incite illegal action of such proximity and degree that it would foreclose rather than promote discussion.

Thus Holmes's danger test implied that freedom of speech had an instrumental value; its value depended on its role in protecting an open, democratic system. More recently, the freedom has come to be a value in itself, and expressive speech that may even be intent on offense or coercion only (not part of discussion) has been protected, often using the same phrase, "clear and present danger," as a judicial rationale. Cited to protect virtually any utterance, the danger test has become devoid of any concrete meaning. Today, any utterance is protected, regardless of purpose, unless one can show that an intolerable occurrence was a likely result of that utterance. Thus, when a defrocked priest, one Termeniello, was convicted of disturbing the peace following an incendiary speech replete with racial and religious slurs, the conviction was overturned in a 1949 decision, citing an interpretation of the danger test.[9] Here Justice Douglas argued that an unpopular position (that we should have aided the Nazis in exterminating the Jews) is precisely what the First Amendment was designed to protect. The prospect of some disorder due to a hostile audience is not a clear or great enough danger to justify the inhibition of free speech. This position is directly opposite to that taken by the Supreme Court in the *Feiner* case (1951), in which a much less incendiary speech was halted and the speaker arrested in the face of potential hostility from the audience.[10] Here the Court judged that the balance struck by the police between freedom and order was a reasonable one and allowed the conviction to stand. The point of the *Termeniello* case in this discussion is that despite the use of the danger test in the opinion of the Court, discussion or persuasion was never at issue; yet the freedom of speech protection sheltered the defendant nonetheless. The clause's interpretation has changed greatly over time.

From discussion to expression: The decline of the fighting words test.   Perhaps the best illustration of how much the freedom of speech clause has been expanded by judicial interpretation to protect expressive utterance is the demise of the "fighting words" doctrine. As laid down in the *Chaplinsky* case (1942), this doctrine held that

> There are certain well defined and limited classes of speech, the prevention and punishment of which has never been thought to raise any Constitutional problem. These include the lewd and obscene, the profane, the libelous and the insulting or "fighting" words—those that by their very utterance inflict injury or tend to incite a breach of the peace. It has been well observed that such utterances are no essential part of any exposition of ideas and are of such slight value as a step to the truth that any benefit that may be derived from them is clearly outweighed by the social interest in order and morality.[11]

The erosion of the fighting words principle became apparent in the *Cohen* v. *California* case (1971), in which the Court overturned Cohen's conviction for inciting a disturbance of the peace (Cohen had worn a jacket in the halls of the Los Angeles County Courthouse bearing the epithet, "Fuck the draft").[12] The Court held that times change and that words that offend at one time and place may not offend elsewhere; in other words, no phrase is inherently and necessarily beyond First Amendment protection. In this case, there was no evidence that Cohen intended to offend anyone or that anyone was actually offended.

The coup de grace to the fighting words doctrine came in the 1978 controversy surrounding the attempt by the Chicago branch of the American Nazi party to conduct a parade and rally, complete with swastikas, SS uniforms, and jackboots, in Skokie, Illinois, a community with a preponderantly Jewish population and numerous survivors of Nazi extermination camps. Clearly, no persuasion was likely to take place in this context. What was being protected was the symbolic and explicit expression of racial and anti-Semitic slurs. The city of Skokie had attempted to prevent the march by several means, including the requirement of a confiscatory bond against potential damage and, perhaps more significantly, an injunction against utterances that castigated any racial or religious group. The U.S. district court held that racial slurs are a protected form of speech, and the Illinois Supreme Court held that

> . . . the display of the swastika in Skokie cannot be enjoined under the fighting words exception to free speech, nor can the anticipation of a hostile reaction justify prior restraint.[13]

This overrules the fighting words doctrine, for if anti-Semitic slurs by avowed Nazis to concentration camp survivors are not fighting words in the *Chaplinsky* sense of the term, it is hard to imagine any other utterance that would so qualify. In striking down the injunction against racial slurs, the district court reasoned as follows:

> The question is not whether there are some ideas that are unacceptable in a civilized society. Rather the question is which danger is greater: the danger that allowing the government to punish "unacceptable" ideas will lead to the suppression of ideas that are merely uncomfortable to those in power; or the danger that permitting free debate on such unacceptable ideas will encourage their acceptance rather than discouraging them by revealing their pernicious quality.

The district court found the former danger the greater, a decision affirmed by the U.S. Supreme Court.[14] The *Cohen* and *Skokie* cases have very nearly transformed the political interpretation of the freedom of speech clause to embrace any form of expressive utterance, regardless of its relevance to the democratic process.

Protection against Insensitive Speech

The *Skokie* case has apparently not laid the issue of the constitutional protection of inflammatory speech to rest, especially with regard to the protection of "racial slurs." Although the courts have not negated the Skokie decisions, growing public pressure from practicing lawyers and constitutional scholars has suggested reconsidering the constitutional status of such slurs. There has even been some discussion of resurrecting the old (1952) *Beauharnais* v. *Illinois* principle of "group libel," which states that the concept of libel can apply to the defamation of whole categories of people without naming or even implicitly referring to particular individuals. While it was not specifically overruled, the pattern of precedents over the years has implicitly negated that principle, a principle that is close to what is understood by the term *racial slurs.* The heightened sensitivity of the racial or religious groups that are frequently the target of racial slurs renders such speech increasingly illegitimate or unacceptable in public discourse.

A more recent example of the Supreme Court's protection of a form of expression designed by its very nature to incite disruptive behavior was the decision of the putatively conservative Rehnquist Court in July, 1989, to declare that burning the American flag was a form of protected speech. By a 5 to 4 vote, the Court struck down state and federal laws preventing desecration of the flag, thus voiding the conviction of radical Marxist Gregory Lee Johnson for burning the flag outside the Republican convention in Dallas. The *Johnson* flag burning case appears to indicate that symbolic speech, even when it constitutes an affront to deeply and widely held values, is now given First Amendment protection. Public outcry was highlighted by President Bush's call for a constitutional amendment to criminalize such desecration, and Senator Joseph Biden's amendment to a child care bill to establish a federal legislative ban on flag desecration passed the Senate by a vote of 97 to 3. Ironically, the conservative Court has been more protective of freedom of speech than leaders of academe.

The "political correctness" controversy.   Academe has taken the lead in the attempt to suppress speech that is regarded as insensitive to targeted racial and ethnic groups. In some cases, conservative critics of such suppression charge that the leaders in academic communities and the media have imposed a criterion of "political correctness" on permissible expression. The vagueness of the definition of racial or ethnic insensitivity is seen by some as allowing its use as a tool to limit the expression of positions that contradict a liberal perspective.

For example, Harvard University has now defined "racial harassment" as any actions or words "which cause another individual or group to feel demeaned or abused because of their racial or ethnic background." The offense, in this reading, consists not in what the speech in question actually says, but how some people feel about it. In February, 1988, Stephan Thernstrom, Winthrop Professor of History at Harvard, was charged with racial insensitivity because he had quoted southern plantation owners on the subject of black character during his lectures. Although his tenure was not threatened, Thernstrom was chastised by university officials and warned to avoid "possible insensitivity in lecturing." He claimed that he was quoting for analytical purposes, not expressing his own views, and that he was unaware of having given offense. A similar event occurred at the University of Maryland when a professor of Latin American History read to his class a description of Native Americans written by Spanish conquistadors. The professor was required to read a formal apology to his class for "racist speech." Such examples of insensitivity are based upon subjective perceptions of those most easily offended and appear to be impermissibly vague by any interpretation of the First Amendment.

The campaign to suppress speech offensive to some oppressed groups arose from a spate of racial insults on American college campuses. At the University of Michigan, for example, in 1987, a radio talk show host at the university-run station called for listeners to contribute their favorite racial jokes. In 1988, a black student walked into his French class and found scrawled on the board, "A mind is a terrible thing to waste—especially on a nigger." In 1988, at Yale University, someone painted a swastika and the phrase "white power" on the Afro-American Center.

The University of Michigan took the lead in late 1988 in adopting a rule restricting speech that members of targeted groups found offensive. The policy adopted defined as punishable "any behavior, verbal or physical, that stigmatizes or victimizes an individual on the basis of ethnicity, religion, sex, sexual orientation, creed, national origin, ancestry, age, marital status, handicap, or Vietnam-era veteran status." University officials averred that freedom of speech does not include the right to harass or injure others. Harassment or injury is further described as a situation in which a person perceives that he or she is in "a hostile learning environment." Sanctions may vary from reprimand to expulsion. Several other schools have adopted policies of speech censorship patterned after the Michigan model. They include Middlebury College, Brown University, Pennsylvania State University, Tufts University, Stanford University, and the Universities of California, Connecticut, North Carolina, Pennsylvania, and Wisconsin. Other schools are considering such policies.[15] Clearly, the protection of minorities against being offended by hate speech is taking priority over more rigorous interpretations of freedom of speech.

The campaign to restrain expression is not limited to insensitivity to racial and ethnic groups but has at times required conformity to the values of the intellectual left in general. During the 1991 war in the Persian Gulf, for instance, administrators at the University of Maryland ruled that students might not fly the American flag in support of the war effort because such displays might offend those (including many administrators) who opposed the resort to arms. Expressed antipathy to homosexuals is similarly forbidden. A University of Connecticut student was banned from her dormitory and dining hall for displaying a poster on the door of her room referring to "homos," a pejorative epithet.

Many charge that the nation's universities, heretofore counted on to defend the unfettered exchange of ideas, have now taken the lead in suppressing the expression of ideas that are regarded as "politically incorrect."

One of the ironies of the political correctness debate is that conservatives, who have resisted the extension of freedom of discussion to freedom of expression, now protest against "politically correct" restrictions on expression. Liberals, on the other hand, face a similar irony. Many doubt that the dominant groups on most college campuses are in fact minorities and women, who, they argue, still face significant barriers to full participation in higher education. Liberals often see "political correctness" as highly exaggerated. Yet, in view of their judgment about the barriers facing certain groups, many liberals who argued for the extension of freedom to expressive speech, now favor some restrictions on the types of expressive speech discussed above. It is, moreover, unlikely that university bans on insensitive speech are likely to achieve their purpose. For example, University of Wisconsin Chancellor Donna Shalala instituted a revised "code of conduct" (U.W.S. 17) that stipulates that students may be disciplined for

> racist or discriminatory comments, epithets, or other expressive behavior directed at an individual or on separate occasions at different individuals [that] intentionally demean the race, sex, religion, color, creed, disability, sexual orientation, national origin, ancestry, or age of the individual or individuals; and create an intimidating, hostile, or demeaning environment for education, university-related work, or other university-authorized activity.

It is widely felt, in light of the Skokie incidents, that the First Amendment protects the right to express pejorative claims about a group; therefore these codes are carefully drawn to proscribe only insults directed at individuals. Yet the incidents that gave rise to these codes frequently involved insults to groups as a whole. In the Wisconsin instance, a fraternity had held a mock slave auction with white students performing in black face and Afro wigs, an example of bad taste that nevertheless did not single out an individual.[16]

Limitations on the protection of coercive expression, or speech plus. Although any ideas are protected, no matter how heinous, and various forms of expression not part of discussion are also protected with regard to their content, it does not follow that any means to disseminate an utterance or idea is similarly protected. Although a person may try to persuade another to adopt his or her point of view, no matter how stupid or venal that point of view may be, the Constitution does not protect anyone's right physically to force another to act according to his or her wishes. Such compulsion involves more than mere speech; it involves what is sometimes called "speech plus." For example, wearing black armbands as a form of protest in high school has been protected, but the burning of draft cards has not. The question appears to be whether the courts find the symbolic actions undertaken with the speech to be a serious enough threat to public order or public purpose to overcome the protection due to the expression of ideas.[17] The *Johnson* flag burning case indicates that some symbolic speech, even when it constitutes an affront to deeply held values, can receive First Amendment protection.

The Legal Concept of Obscenity

The concept of obscenity in Anglo-American law has been limited to materials that deal with sex in unacceptable ways. Although such material as the graphic depiction of gore or violence may offend the values of some people, traditionally it has not been subsumed under the heading of obscenity.

The moral principles of the dominant groups in America have always been more concerned with what is considered to be the sin of human sexuality than with violence and other human misery. From the time of Puritan New England, sexual indulgence in marriage not intended to lead to procreation has been associated with sin. Dominant rule-making groups have also sought to proscribe activities that support sexual indulgence, such as widely available abortion and effective education regarding contraception. Because it has been widely assumed that sexually explicit material encourages sexual indulgence, it is not surprising that dominant groups imbued with the Puritan tradition have pressed for the suppression of such material.

It should be noted that the material in question in obscenity legislation rarely contributes to the free exchange of ideas. Much of it does not even qualify as worthwhile artistic expression by the standards of most critics. But a great deal of material that is regarded as artistically valuable has in some places been suppressed on obscenity grounds; most good literature, attempting to deal with life in a realistic way, does not ignore the reality of human sexuality. The origin of obscenity legislation, however, never rested on critical measures of aesthetic worth; instead, it sought to protect communities from the perceived social evils of sexually explicit material in any context. Essentially, such legislation had two goals: the reduction of sexual stimulation and the perpetuation of the deeply rooted Christian principle that sex for pleasure is an avoidable and undesirable aspect of human personality and interaction. The origins of this principle can be traced, if not to St. Paul, then clearly to the second- and third-century church fathers who felt that physical indulgence was inconsistent with spiritual well-being. The Puritan tradition in America, once characterized by H. L. Mencken as the nagging fear that somewhere someone may be enjoying himself, was the heir of this view. The suppression of information about sex, however, has been a spillover effect of obscenity legislation.

One source of controversy in this arena is that different individuals have differing levels of tolerance for sexually related material. Some are greatly offended by any four-letter expletive or a reference to a bed or bathroom; others are untroubled by graphic depictions of sex acts. Those who are most easily offended tend to be the most active in trying to obtain legislation and ensure its enforcement of their more restrictive moral standards on others. People who are less easily offended are generally less concerned about pornography, and they have left the field to the wishes of the moralists. Moreover, there is an additional pressure that tends to prevent those with a more tolerant attitude from defending pornography too vigorously, for there is a certain stigma attached to taking such a position; one risks being identified as a consumer of pornography and an oversexed deviant. Thus the censor's position seems more legitimate than that of the defenders of freedom of speech and expression.

The courts have never taken the position that obscenity, defined here as materials the primary purpose of which is to arouse erotic impulses, should itself be granted First Amendment protection. The difficulty is that much material that might otherwise be deserving of such protection contains sexually explicit elements. The constitutional problem has been to devise principles that will allow society to shield its citizens from being unduly sexually stimulated or offended without closing off their access to art, literature, and ideas that are protected by the freedom of speech clause.

From Hicklin to Miller.   The common-law interpretation of the freedom of speech clause gave wide latitude to the discretion of the censors in the suppression of sexually relevant material. The nineteenth-century *Hicklin* test (1868) judged matter to be obscene if any isolated passage in the material has a "tendency to corrupt and deprave those who are open to such immoral influence. . . ."[18] In other words, material that contains any passage that is likely to arouse someone who is particularly susceptible to being so aroused may, by this test, be censored. Because it is possible to find some individuals who are offended and aroused by the most innocuous material and because many pieces of serious writing contain some isolated passage that may offend such people, the *Hicklin* test puts freedom of speech on very tenuous grounds. Consequently there was pressure to liberalize this standard to afford greater protection to art and literature against suppression by the censors.

Accordingly, a more liberal standard was finally handed down in the *Roth* case in 1957. The so-called *Roth* rule has become the standard that subsequent obscenity decisions either assume or modify. It modified the *Hicklin* test in three important ways: First, the test no longer focused on any isolated passage or words but rather on whether "the dominant theme of the material, taken as a whole, appeals to prurient (sexual) interests"; second, its standard of measure became whether the material appeals to the prurient interests of the "average" person, not a particularly susceptible segment of society; third, the treatment of sex in the material under question was not to justify censorship unless it was "utterly without redeeming social importance."[19]

Now material can no longer be censored because of some isolated passage or because some individual can find a sexual innuendo where the thought would not occur to most people. On the other hand, the stipulation that only works "utterly without redeeming social importance" can be censored leaves very little material without First Amendment protection. Material that most people would find to be predominantly trash may have some small measure of social value. Although *Roth* suggests that a small, peripheral part of sexually relevant material would not condemn a work, it also appears to say that a small, peripheral amount of worthwhile material might save an otherwise worthless piece of sexual exploitation. This part of the *Roth* rule appears inconsistent with its dominant theme.

The *Roth* rule was later modified in two important ways in the *Miller* v. *California* case (1973).[20] The Supreme Court dropped the key problematic phrase quoted above in favor of saying that, in order to be legally censored, material must lack *serious* literary, artistic, political, or scientific values (LAPS values). This seems more in line with judging the work as a whole rather than on the basis of some isolated passages. Presumably, under the *Miller* criterion of serious LAPS values, an isolated article in an otherwise provocative "girlie" magazine or a discussion of the healthful benefits of sunshine in an illustrated nudist publication would not, in and of itself, save such material from censorship.

The second way in which the *Miller* case modifies the *Roth* rule has especially serious implications. *Miller* defines the concept of community as local rather than national. The Court explicitly rejected the idea that there can or should be a national standard for what can or cannot be censored. Yet the very purpose of the First Amendment is to provide some national standards for freedom of speech. The Constitution is national law, and law by definition must apply uniformly throughout its realm. The Constitution cannot mean one thing in one state and something else in another state or it would not be law.

Publishing, film, and broadcasting are examples of national commerce, and the legal status of their enormous investments must be predictable throughout the country. One cannot profitably produce the output of such media only for liberal East and West Coast cities; one must also be certain, to borrow a phrase from former presidential advisor John Erlichman, that "it will play in Peoria." Without national standards, the standards for the nation as a whole become the standards of what the most prudish local prosecutors or juries are wont to censor, the lowest common denominator, in effect completely negating the average-person criterion of *Roth.* By the *Miller* standard, any community should be able to censor whatever sexually explicit material dominant groups choose to censor without violating the Constitution. To the question of what the standards are for the material the Constitution protects, the answer is that there are no standards. *Miller* is not merely bad law; it is no law!

The Court backed off from the implications of the local community standard in *Jenkins* v. *Georgia* (1974) when it ruled that Georgia could not ban the critically acclaimed film *Carnal Knowledge* on obscenity grounds. The Court rejected a reading of *Miller* "that juries have unbridled discretion to determine what is 'patently offensive.' "[21] Thus a community is not free to censor the mere depiction of sex; the material had to be "patently offensive." The Court even offered a list of the kinds of things that may be censored. But this implies national standards that constrain community discretion. In 1987, the Court backed further away from community standards, substituting a "reasonable man" test, a criterion that would allow the repression of speech that is obscene to ordinary, sane individuals.

There may be a useful distinction between obscenity and pornography. One may accept the concept that the avoidance of sexual stimulation is not a value of sufficient weight to justify the discretion given to censors; yet one may still argue that there remains a category of material that is beyond mere salaciousness; it is "patently offensive." This is material that is less likely to titillate the average person and more likely to offend. In July, 1989, the Court further elaborated on the distinction between what may be censored in obscenity cases and what is protected from such challenges by the First Amendment in the "dial-a-porn" case, *Sable Communications* v. *Federal Communications Commission.* The Court struck down an amendment to the communications act that banned "indecent" interstate calls. The Court said that while obscene calls may be banned, the denial to adults of access to calls that are merely indecent violates the First Amendment.

There is, of course, a problem in drawing the line, but most know intuitively where it is. Justice Steward put it best in the *Jacobellis* v. *Ohio* case (1964):

> I have reached the conclusion that . . . under the First and Fourteenth Amendments, criminal laws in this area are limited to hard-core pornography. I shall not today attempt to further define the kinds of material I understand to be embraced within that short hand description; and perhaps I shall never succeed in doing so. But I know it when I see it. . . .[22]

Regardless of which test one prefers, the use of either still constitutes censorship. It was noted earlier that the origins of obscenity legislation were aimed at controlling sexuality, not somehow ensuring that only "artistic" products intelligently and maturely reflected that area of human behavior. To this day, society's goals in regulating sexually explicit material are very mixed.

Censorship, sex, and the arts.   The expansion of the concept of protected expression generated controversy over government funding of artistic work with sexual content that was offensive to the moral sensibilities of significant segments of the population. Here the issue was one of government funding, not government suppression. In the one instance, the government funded a photographic exhibition produced by a well-known photographer, Robert Mapplethorpe, including some explicit homoerotica and some photographs involving the genitalia of children. Other funded projects that were offensive to many Americans included a photograph of a crucifix in a glass of urine and a nude dancer smearing herself with chocolate and moving her hands on her body in a highly suggestive fashion.

The debate over funding such projects demonstrated the absence of any objective criteria over what constitutes artistic merit that would override the public interest in the preservation of public morality. Those who opposed funding these projects argued that they went beyond the bounds of common perceptions of artistic value and that, in any event, whatever rights may exist to freedom of expression do not extend to a right to public funding, especially when the material in question is deeply offensive to a majority. Those who support funding of these projects argue that representatives of the artistic community should determine what is art and what deserves to be funded. Since market forces are not presumed to identify and reward genuine artistic merit, the issue of public funding is an important one. An atonal rap group will sell many more recordings than a classical violinist. Without public subsidies, many widely respected creators of classical music, dance, drama, and the like could not survive. Some conservative politicians, such as North Carolina Senator Jesse Helms, used this controversy as political capital in an election campaign to mobilize the constituency that fears the erosion of conventional moral standards. Congress threatened to cut off funding to the arts in general. It becomes apparent that as the frontiers of what is perceived as having artistic value is expanded further, public tolerance of extending protection to such expression may continue to weaken.

Freedom of the Press

Balancing libel against freedom of the press. *Libel* means the publication or dissemination of false and defamatory remarks, impressions, or images of another. The need for libel laws arises out of the reality that when such false, defamatory remarks are disseminated in the mass media, they do find a large and believing audience. The average person does not have comparable access to the ear of the mass public, and so the recourse of the marketplace of ideas does not apply. Truth cannot fairly compete with falsehood when the latter has the advantage of the mass media. Therefore the idea that libel is outside the concept of freedom of speech has a long common-law tradition. The potential threat of court action against the irresponsible use of mass media to damage a person's reputation can help render the media more accountable for their vast influence. Presumably, the availability of such legal recourse will have a dampening effect on public dissemination of falsehood.

The availability of libel suits has discouraged the publication of pejorative untruths about individuals. In general, this is an eminently desirable result. However, discouraging publication of vigorous criticism of one class of individuals, public officials in their official roles, is not so desirable. One of the principal tasks of a free and independent press in a democracy is to mobilize opinion and provide information against the government. This function of the media is crucial in making the government truly accountable.

Accordingly, the Court has held that insofar as libel law is concerned, published criticism of public officials is in a different category from published criticism of private individuals. The principle from *New York Times* v. *Sullivan* (1964) is that in order to render a judgment of libel against a public official in pursuit of his or her duties, the courts must find that malicious intent was present as well as pejorative errors of fact.[23] It is not enough to show that the published material about a public official is technically untrue because when criticizing public officials, one cannot be certain that every alleged fact is entirely accurate. The case in question involved an advertisement in the *New York Times* criticizing the actions of an Alabama sheriff during a civil rights demonstration. Certain minor errors of fact were present in the advertisement. Clearly, the *Times,* publishing hundreds of pages of news from around the world each day, cannot absolutely guarantee the literal accuracy of every statement it prints; it takes some reports on trust. But the Alabama court system, anxious to punish such hated symbols of outside liberal opinion as the *Times,* awarded the plaintiff the prohibitive sum of a half-million dollars, even though the inaccuracies did not change the essence of the story. Such a sum would certainly serve to discourage the media from taking the risk of publishing much criticism of public officials. Subsequently the Court formulated the malicious intent principle, a principle that frees innocent inaccuracies from libel judgments.

The *Sullivan* doctrine has been extended to public figures other than officials as well.[24] The reasoning is that public figures outside government not only have a significant influence on public policy but also possess an access to public opinion that enables them to answer criticism in the print or broadcast media without recourse to civil suit. Additionally, it is held that when one makes a voluntary decision to enter public life, one accepts a disproportionate risk of being subject to a broad range of published criticism. The several Hollywood entertainment figures suing a widely read gossip sheet, the *National Enquirer,* for libel in 1981 faced the task of proving not only untruth but also malicious intent. The publicity surrounding their litigation afforded these plaintiffs substantial opportunity to counteract the *Enquirer*'s allegations; yet, despite the widely held position that a public figure does not need the same protection against libel as does an ordinary citizen, the court in this case did find that the defendant had libeled. It found that the *Enquirer* had engaged in "reckless disregard of the truth," thus satisfying the "malicious intent" standard. However, it remains to be seen whether the precedent will weaken the *Sullivan* standard. It also remains to be seen whether the victory of the plaintiffs and the award to actress Carol Burnett of substantial damages ($800,000, reduced from $1.6 million) will have a dampening effect on vigorous criticism of public figures. The Court has refused to extend the *Sullivan* principle of malicious intent to nonpublic figures who find themselves newsworthy in public events.

The *Sullivan* rule appears to apply to the $120 million lawsuit by William C. Westmoreland tried in late 1984 and early 1985, a suit alleging that CBS had libeled the former general in a "60 Minutes" broadcast. The broadcast claimed that the general had falsified casualty reports in order to create a misleading optimism about the progress of the Vietnam War.

This case illustrates the rationale of the *Sullivan* rule. If Westmoreland could have won that staggering sum without meeting the more demanding malicious intent standard, the major media would have been discouraged from vigorous criticism of major public officials. Meanwhile, Westmoreland, a well-known public figure, articulated his version of the facts in question in various media outlets on numerous occasions. His access to public opinion was comparable to that of one CBS program, and so the marketplace of ideas rather than law courts gave him an appropriate vehicle to defend his honor without the chilling effect on the press's role as a watchdog of government that emanated from such a libel suit.

Former Israeli Minister of Defense Ariel Sharon also instituted in 1985 a celebrated libel suit with *Sullivan* rule implications. Sharon sued *Time* magazine for its claim that Sharon had discussed the strategy of revenge against the Palestinians for the murder of the newly elected Lebanese president, Bashir Gemayel, thereby knowingly encouraging and becoming an accessory to the subsequent massacres of Palestinians in their refugee camps by elements of the Lebanese Christian militia. Here again, Sharon, clearly a public person with independent access to public opinion with which to counterbalance *Time*'s allegation, operated under the need to show malicious intent.

The jury found that Sharon had been harmed and that *Time*'s charges were factually unsubstantiated; however, on the malicious intent finding, the jury found that *Time* had not acted with reckless disregard of the truth. Although Sharon did not collect any money, he claimed that he had been vindicated by the finding that *Time*'s charges were unsubstantiated.

Scholars generally remain concerned that the prevalence and ease of such libel suits, even when unsuccessful, may discourage investigative journalism. Even though Westmoreland finally withdrew his suit, its effects may discourage further investigative reporting by CBS and others because of the huge amounts of money, time, and effort expended by CBS and *Time* in their defense. Unsuccessful suits still have a stifling effect on media criticism of public persons. Even frivolous suits could discourage the media from taking the risk of exposing themselves to such actions.

In early 1988, the Supreme Court made it even more difficult for public persons to win libel judgments when it reversed a substantial judgment won in a lower court by evangelist Jerry Falwell against *Hustler Magazine* for a pornographic parody of him. The Court ruled that no reasonable person would take the satire seriously, a judgment based upon public knowledge of Falwell's character. This strengthens the *Sullivan* rule premise that public persons are less in need of the protection of libel laws than are nonpublic persons.[25] The question of how far the press may go in probing the lives of public figures was dramatically illustrated by the *Miami Herald* surveillance of presidential candidate Gary Hart's home in 1987. The reports generated allegations of a liaison with model Donna Rice, a charge that devastated his 1988 presidential campaign.

A similar incident occurred in the opening stage of the 1992 presidential election campaign. During the New Hampshire primary, a national tabloid newspaper reported the claim of a young woman that she had had a twelve-year affair with Governor Bill Clinton of Arkansas, the main contender for the Democratic nomination. Clinton admitted to former marital difficulties but insisted that the allegations were false. Nevertheless, all the media gave the story intensive coverage, with an almost assuredly damaging effect on Clinton's reputation and campaign. Even if the option of a libel suit had been open to Clinton, it could not have lessened the damage. The undeniable harm done by the incident was to the campaign itself: The serious issues on which the campaign should have centered— the current recession, the American response to the collapse of Soviet communism, health care, the Middle East situation—were entirely buried by the scandal.

Reporting trials fairly.   Because trials are supposed to be conducted on the basis of law and fact under specified rules of evidence, there is some justification for seeking to insulate the conduct of trials from the pressures of public opinion. Yet this goal can and has come into conflict with the value of freedom of the press, a value often framed in terms of "the public's right to know." Extensive reporting about the details of an impending trial sometimes so inflames public opinion that it becomes difficult to find unbiased jurors. Judges who are elected rather than appointed may also find the pressures of public opinion hard to resist. Opinion on how open courts should be to journalists tends to divide along liberal/conservative lines. Liberals are more concerned with protecting freedom of the press, whereas conservatives focus on fair trial considerations. Although the liberals' stand is consistent with their attitude toward First Amendment values, defendants' rights—another traditional liberal concern—frequently benefit from limiting freedom of the press based on fair trial considerations.

Convictions have been reversed on the basis of the effects of the media on trials. Flagrant pretrial publicity, especially involving speculation or allegations about the guilt of the accused, has been a cause, as has extensive media coverage of the trials themselves.[26] But in a potentially notorious trial, the judge does not have the option of avoiding prejudicial publicity by imposing a total ban on news coverage of the proceedings in advance. This is known as a gag rule and has been held to violate the test of prior restraint.[27] However, judges may forbid parties to a case from speaking to the press under certain circumstances—another form of gag rule.

Americans have been more solicitous of the value of freedom of the press in this regard than have the British, who permit only a factual reporting of who was arrested and charged with what crime, and who ban any reporting of the details of the crime or the trial itself. Yet the British press does not appear to be noticeably hampered in exercising its political function of vigorous criticism of public officials and policy. The issue may be the question of what the public has a right to know. Perhaps banning the American press from all courtrooms might only restrict it from reporting all the gory details of murder cases without affecting the nature of the system or political accountability. Other trials, however, do carry a political significance. The criminal processing of the original Watergate burglers comes to mind. The subsequent investigative reporting was instrumental in bringing down a president.

In such politically sensitive trials, the interest of the public is more substantial. Moreover, it is not always clear in advance which trials will have political significance and which will not. In this regard, the Supreme Court has recently ruled that a judge may bar reporters from the pretrial stages of judicial proceedings. Had such a ban been in effect, Woodward and Bernstein might never have begun their unraveling of the Watergate story. Naturally, liberals consider this a dangerous infringement on freedom of the press.

Students and the press.   The prediction that the Rehnquist Court would be less sympathetic to First Amendment claims than other Courts of recent decades was initially borne out in the 1988 case of *Hazlewood School District* v. *Kuhlmeier,* [28] a decision that had far-reaching impact on the concept of freedom of the press and on the question of how far First Amendment rights extend to students in school. The case involved a story printed in a high school newspaper about teenage pregnancy and the effects of divorce on children, a story that appeared also in a metropolitan newspaper, the *St. Louis Globe-Democrat.* Arguing that the stories were "too sensitive" for high school students, the school administrators censored them. The Court rejected the claim of freedom of the press and speech and upheld the administrators on the ground that the school paper is a teaching tool and as such is the property of the school administration to use as it sees fit. The Court rejected the premise that a school newspaper is a vehicle for the dissemination of ideas protected by the First Amendment. In doing so, the Court implicitly undercut much of the force of *Tinker* v. *Des Moines School District,* which, in protecting the right of high school students to wear black armbands to protest the Vietnam War, declared the principle that First Amendment rights do not stop at the schoolhouse door.[29] Clearly, the distinction in

Kuhlmeier between what can legitimately be carried in the metropolitan news-paper and what the school newspaper has a right to print is implicitly resurrecting the distinction between the rights of students in the school and the rights of the public at large. However, the subsequent decisions of the Rehnquist Court in the flag burning and "dial-a-porn" cases reveal a surprising sympathy by this putatively conservative Court to First Amendment claims. The flag burning case further reinforces *Tinker* with respect to the protection of symbolic speech.

Conflicting Priorities: Freedom of Association versus National Security

Implicit in the concept of an open society is not only the right to speak or publish freely but also the freedom to associate and interact with others on the basis of some shared outlook or interest. This freedom, inferred from the First Amendment guarantees of speech and assembly, has in particular come into conflict with the perceived requirements of national security.

Freedom of association was most seriously threatened during the decade of the 1950s by the effort of legislative investigating committees at both the state and national levels to combat a perceived threat of communist subversion. The most notorious of these were the U.S. House Un-American Activities Committee (HUAC) and Senator Joseph McCarthy's Internal Security Subcommittee of the Justice Committee. The senator so epitomized a disregard for due process in the goal of a zealous quest for security that the period became known as the McCarthy era, and government infringement on individual rights is still frequently called McCarthyism.

The difficulty with the use of legislative committees for this purpose is that though they have a de facto power to pronounce guilt and to cause punishment to be assessed, they, unlike courts of law, are not constrained by the rules of evidence and due process of law. They therefore have performed a judicial function while frequently denying the accused constitutionally guaranteed protections. Essen-tially, the HUAC and McCarthy committees attempted to identify and make public people who had either belonged to organizations that were identified as sub-versive by the national or state attorneys general or had associated with people identified in some way as subversives.

The McCarthy period had a highly dampening effect on political discourse and activity. To explore unpopular positions, one had to take a very real risk of social ostracism and professional ruin. Hundreds of careers and lives were de-stroyed on the basis of innuendo, baseless accusation, or innocent interaction with the wrong people. Yet it is difficult to identify any genuine enemy agents un-covered or any increment of security gained by the entire enterprise of congres-sional inquisition. McCarthyism has thus come to symbolize a willingness to suspend due process and First Amendment freedoms in the face of perceived dangers. Constitutional guarantees carried little weight during this period of collective fear. Given the probability that this nation will be facing threats to security in the future, this is a sobering realization.

Freedom of and from Religion

Previous sections have shown how the First Amendment protects pluralism, the legitimate coexistence of various points of view and belief systems. The religion clauses of the First Amendment protect the legitimacy of divergent religious orientations, including agnosticism and atheism. If the right to choose one's own views and to evaluate ideas for oneself is a hallmark of the concept of the open society, surely this principle also applies to religion, which touches fundamental and intensely held sets of values and beliefs. It is therefore fitting that the two religion clauses of the Bill of Rights are included in the First Amendment, which is devoted to the protection and legitimacy of pluralism and the open society.

There are two distinct religion clauses in the First Amendment: the establishment clause and the free exercise clause:

> Congress shall make no law respecting an establishment of religion, or prohibiting the free exercise thereof; . . .

The *establishment clause* is concerned with preventing the government from promoting or aiding religion; the *free exercise clause* is concerned with preventing the government from interfering with the practice of religion. To the extent that government implements either of these clauses to its logical extreme, it may be held to violate a conception of the other clause. For example, when government does nothing that may indirectly aid religion, such as not permitting religious practices in public schools even when a decisive majority desires such activity, government may be seen as preventing the dominant forces in the community from practicing their religion as they see fit. In short, these clauses may come into conflict with each other; therefore to uphold one clause absolutely would endanger the other.

The establishment clause and public schools. There is, of course, considerable ambiguity in the phrase "Congress shall make no law respecting an establishment of religion." Reasonable people can and do disagree about precisely what government is prohibited from doing. At a minimum, it is understood that government may not sanction a particular religious sect as the official state religion, a practice common in most European nations. In England, the Anglican church is the state church; in Scotland, it is the Presbyterian church; in France, Italy, and Spain, the Catholic church has official status; and in Scandinavia, the Lutheran church is the official state religion. A state church or religion means that the head of state normally must be a member of that church, that he or she officially appoints the leading clerics in that church (usually on the advice of political and religious leaders), and that the church and its schools receive overt financial support from the state. In some places it may mean that the religion's moral views are enacted into law, as exemplified by the bans on divorce, contraception, and abortion in some Catholic countries. Although it has meant in the past that members of minority or nonofficial religions lost their religious freedoms and even their property and lives, members of the nonofficial religions are no longer so threatened in Western democracies. The Western world, on the official level at least, is now generally a model of toleration of religious pluralism, despite the continued existence of established churches.

Beyond this prohibition of an official national church, it is generally agreed that government in the United States may not legislatively bestow advantages on one or more sects over other religions. That is, any government activities that aid one religious sect must similarly aid all religions. This is known as the "accommodationist" interpretation of the establishment clause. If the clause meant no more than this, this interpretation would allow government to promote religion in general as long as one sect was not favored over others.

The Supreme Court has taken the position, however, that the establishment clause does mean more than this, that it is more restrictive of government activities having the effect of aiding or promoting religion. The Court has come to the position that government may not directly aid or promote religion in general over nonreligion. This position is sometimes called the "wall of separation" position, using the words of Thomas Jefferson. Not only does this position itself generate controversy, as it is not self-evident that the establishment clause forbids government aid to all religions equally; the wall of separation doctrine also generates controversy even among its ostensible adherents concerning precisely what the government may do without breaching the wall. For example, in the 1947 *Everson* case, the Court ruled that it is constitutional to use public money to reimburse parents for bus transportation to both public and parochial schools.[30] Justice Black's opinion explicitly used the wall metaphor in upholding the legislation, although the four dissenters thought the wall was breached in this instance. The case implicitly established the precedent that the wall of separation doctrine does not prevent some government activities that provide some secondary or spillover benefits to religion if the primary purposes of the policy are secular ones and, in the case of parochial education, if the primary beneficiary is the schoolchild. Thus the question of where to draw the line went unanswered by the wall of separation position.

Prayer in school.   The solution seems on the surface to be simple: no devotional activity, no matter how voluntary or nondenominational it may be, may be sponsored by the public schools. Of course, the concepts of devotional activity and school sponsorship are not unambiguous. In two separate decisions—the Bible-reading cases, *Schempp* and *Murray* (1963), and the New York regents prayer case *Engle* v. *Vitale* (1962)—the Court seemed to take an unequivocal position. In the first case, the Court ruled that devotional reading, without comment, from the New Testament is inconsistent with the establishment clause, even when objecting students are excused from class.[31] In the second it ruled that prayer sponsored by school authorities, regardless of who actually reads it and regardless of how nonsectarian or voluntary the prayer may be, is in violation of the establishment clause.[32] In fact, the prayer in question may be the most innocuous, nonsectarian, and inoffensive prayer conceivable. In striking down such a prayer, the Court made clear that any prayer sponsored by public school officials is on its face unconstitutional. There is no way that any amount of tinkering with the nature of a school prayer or the mode of its presentation can render that prayer logically consistent with the constraints imposed by the school prayer decision. In the summer of 1985, the Court struck down an Alabama law requiring silent meditation or prayer as an organized activity in its public schools. The Court's opinion did hint, however, that some form of silent meditation might pass constitutional muster. The Court has also ruled that it is unconstitutional to distribute Gideon Bibles in public schools, even though students have the right to refuse to accept one, and that the Ten Commandments may not be posted in the classroom.

Both President Reagan and the 1984 Republican party platform explicitly supported both a constitutional amendment to overturn the *Vitale* decision and the right to "voluntary prayer" in the public schools. In a sense, students still have the right of voluntary prayer. It is important to realize that the courts have in no way limited the right of individuals in school to pray in any private manner they choose. Rather, only organized devotional activity, sponsored by the school, has been banned. Some religious leaders have held that such private prayer is actually more meaningful, as it comes from within an individual by choice rather than being recited by compulsion as part of a group exercise. The advantage of the school-sponsored group prayer that the proposed constitutional amendment would ostensibly protect is that it gives the dominant group leverage to compel others to pray and to do so in a manner determined by the dominant group. As Justice Frankfurter observed, "The law of imitation operates, and non-conformity is not an outstanding characteristic of children."[33] Peer pressure to participate will be strong and accordingly, in the case of organized, school-sponsored religious activities, participation is never really voluntary. Some fundamentalist religious leaders still argue that such organized prayer in the schools is essential to restoring the nation's moral foundations, whereas other religious leaders contend that prayer must be private and voluntary in order to be meaningful. The Senate in 1984 rejected a proposed constitutional amendment to permit such prayer.

The prayer and Bible-reading decisions reinforced a tendency for the Court to compel the complete secularization of America's public schools that had previously been apparent in the *McCollum* v. *Board of Education* case (1948), which had struck down "voluntary" religious training by leaders of the major religions during the school day and on school time.[34] Both the hostile public reaction and noncompliance to this decision were extensive in many public school districts throughout the nation. It has been estimated that almost half of such programs continued after *McCollum,* although they were clearly inconsistent with the decision. In the face of such public resistance, the Court backed off somewhat from the implications of *McCollum* and held in a New York case that students could be released for religious instruction during the school day if the instruction took place off the school campus.[35] In doing so, they implicitly rejected much of the logic in the *McCollum* decision.

The *McCollum* rationale held that the voluntary aspect of such religious practices was more formal than real. As the concurring opinion in the case pointed out, because schoolchildren are not noted for their tolerance of nonconformity, there is a definite peer group pressure on the school-aged members of minority religious persuasions to go along with the practices. Given this pressure, the promotion of religious practices during the school day provides the religious leaders with a captive audience gathered by the enforcement machinery of the state (like truant officers). The school audience will be larger than the audience they could gather for religious instruction after school, especially as the students' choice will be between religious training and algebra or study hall.

Furthermore, the released-time program directly impinges on the educational process for the students who do not wish to attend religious services. The same logic might be applied to any other religious activities that have gone on in the public schools. Although students may, with some effort and courage, avoid such activities, it is unlikely that they will be receiving much secular education during that period, which is, after all, the major function of public schools.

Those who seek to ban religion in public schools argue that a related function of mass public education is socialization into a common culture and promotion of a sense of unity among all citizens. Religion, however, can be a divisive phenomenon, appealing as it does at the level of people's most fundamental values and beliefs. Thus the introduction of religious practices in the public schools can detract from the integrative function of those schools.

But all do not agree with the socialization argument. The trend toward noncompliance with bans on public school religious observances has been a continuous obstacle to the Court-mandated secularization of those schools. Not only were there periods of strife following each of the major policy decisions, but pressures for noncompliance continue today. The theoretically simple solution to the degree of religious activity constitutionally allowable (none) has proved more complex than anticipated.

Other establishment clause issues.   The forces that have promoted the secularization of the public schools have broadened their efforts to promote the secularization of other aspects of public life. These efforts came to a head in the lawsuit challenging the right of Pawtucket, Rhode Island, to display a life-sized nativity scene at city expense. The Supreme Court continued its tradition of permitting Christmas pageants, Easter celebrations, and the like in public schools (and therefore presumably in public life) on the grounds that these holidays have become so much a part of the American culture that they have significance beyond their sectarian religious meaning. In *Lynch* v. *Donnelly* (1984), the Court ruled that the Pawtucket display merely "engenders a friendly community spirit of good will in keeping with the season."[36] Yet the new conservative majority (Scalia, Kennedy, Rehnquist, White, and O'Connor) in 1989 struck down the public display of a nativity scene with overt Christian messages ("Jesus is Lord," etc.) while in a separate decision it upheld the public display of a Jewish menorah (the candle holder commemorating the Chanukah season). The menorah was accompanied by symbols of the secular aspects of Christmas in "the spirit of religious pluralism." Thus this ostensibly conservative Court has handed down several First Amendment decisions that reflect the liberal perspective on these matters.

The issue of prayer in the schools arose again in 1991 in *Lee* v. *Weisman.* Ironically this case involved a challenge by a Jewish parent to a prayer offered at 1991 graduation ceremonies by a Jewish rabbi. Despite this unusual circumstance, in the overwhelming preponderance of cases such prayers are offered in the dominant religion of the community. The suit raised the distinction between private prayers and prayers or other devotional activities sponsored by the government. The Bush administration filed a brief for the school district, arguing that government promotion of religion should be considered valid unless

> the practice at issue provides direct benefits to *a* religion in a manner that threatens the establishment of *an* official church [or] it compels persons to participate in a religion or religious exercise contrary to their consciences.

This interpretation would reverse *Engle, Schempp, McCollum,* and other cases, undoing three decades of precedent. It would abandon the wall of separation position in favor of the no preference or accommodation position and would legitimize an increase in officially mandated sectarian religious activity in public schools. In 1992 the Supreme Court ruled such graduation prayers unconstitutional, thereby maintaining exclusion of officially sponsored prayer in public schools.

The free exercise clause. The tension between the establishment clause and the free exercise clause ("Congress shall make no law . . . prohibiting the free exercise" of religion) was discussed at the beginning of this section. In light of this tension, the latter clause is most frequently mentioned in conjunction with values threatened by the vigorous enforcement of the former. Thus the effort to secularize the public schools, an effort justified by the establishment clause, is frequently opposed in the name of the free exercise clause.

The free exercise clause has been invoked to protect numerous socially questionable practices performed in the name of religion, practices that would be otherwise illegal or would violate dominant moral imperatives. The courts have tended to reject the free exercise argument in such cases and to allow the states to ban such practices. Among the otherwise illegal or objectionable practices for which free exercise protection has been denied are polygamy, the use of mind-altering drugs, sexual license, and exposure to poisonous snakes as a test of faith.[37] Furthermore, the free exercise clause does not give parents the right to withhold vaccinations, essential medical care, or education in the name of religion.[38] For instance, a couple was convicted of involuntary manslaughter after they refused medical treatment on religious grounds for their daughter, critically ill with pneumonia, who died. Only the absence of evidence that the parents were aware of the seriousness of the illness prevented the convictions from standing.[39] In 1984, a faith-healing couple from Albion, Indiana, was sentenced to ten years in prison for withholding medical care from their nine-year-old daughter who had died a "preventable death" from meningitis. The superior court rejected their free exercise claim in finding them guilty of reckless homicide.

A difficult issue is presented by faith healers or cult leaders using the free exercise clause to counter charges of fraud. Clearly, the courts cannot inquire into the truth or falsity of beliefs, or all religions would be in trouble. However, the Supreme Court did hold in the case of a preacher who claimed that he could cure all ailments and take the spots off clothing that it is permissible to inquire into the *sincerity* of one's beliefs.[40] With the growing popularity of religious and political cults—highlighted by the mass suicide of the followers of James Jones—the efforts of unorthodox movements to use the free exercise clause as a shield will increase. The pattern of decisions thus far raises considerable doubt on the extent to which the free exercise clause can be used to block the regulation in the public interest of harmful behavior or movements. However, the clause has been used to protect the right of believers to proselytize door-to-door, to refuse to pledge allegiance to the flag, and to refuse to work on Saturdays for religious reasons—while still receiving unemployment benefits.[41] Of course, such daily religious practices as worship, preaching, and religious education are protected by the free exercise clause.

   Conscientious objection.   The free exercise clause has also been used to justify an expansion of the grounds for conscientious objection to compulsory military service in a war. Once it was a settled rule that to claim religious grounds for excusal from military service one had to be a member of a sect that explicitly disavowed military service, such as the Quakers. Pressures to expand this definition became intense during the Vietnam War, when some of the strongest opposition to the war came from leftists who tended to be nonreligious in the conventional sense. The Court allowed an expansion of the grounds for conscientious objection in the case of war protester Daniel Seeger.[42] The law states that such an exemption may be granted on the basis of "religious training and belief" based on "an individual's belief in relation to a Supreme Being involving duties superior to those arising from any human relations." Seeger admitted that he did not believe in God "except in the remotest sense" but based his objections to military service on a "purely ethical creed." In this and other cases, the Court allowed such ethical justifications for refusal to submit to induction, the only serious qualification being that the objection must be to war in general rather than to a particular war. Selective objectors to particular wars may have been penalized for being more honest than other conscientious objectors; a wave of conscientious objection accompanied the widely hated Vietnam conflict, and it is likely that the desire to avoid its particular horrors generated some of the conscientious objection to war in general.

   Beyond that, it is arguable that this significant expansion of the grounds for conscientious objection will make it difficult to disallow such claims from virtually anyone who does not wish to serve. Conservatives fear that the government's ability to coerce military service and thus protect the nation's security will be severely compromised. Liberals tend to applaud the government's inability to conduct an unpopular war. There is, however, little disagreement that the conscientious objector decisions detract from the effectiveness of the selective service system. Thus the conscientious objector question has implications well beyond the free exercise clause.

POLICY EVALUATION: IMPACTS OF CURRENT FIRST AMENDMENT INTERPRETATIONS

The preceding section examined a variety of social policies that have emanated from First Amendment protections in the modern era. Some of these policies

represent fairly stable societal views at present on what the amendment's pertinent language aims to protect or to prohibit. For example, freedom of
association—although always a right to be guarded—is not today under the threat
it was in the McCarthy era of the 1950s, nor is it undergoing significant reinterpre-
tation or expansion. Other First Amendment policy areas, on the other hand, are in
a continuing state of flux. The goals and implementation of the critical judicial
rulings in these evolving areas are especially important, as we turn to evaluating
the impact of policies on civil liberties.

From the Protection of Discussion to the Protection of Expression

With the erosion of the fighting words principle by the *Cohen* and especially the
Skokie cases, the meaning of freedom of speech was expanded. In the first case, as
noted earlier, the Supreme Court recognized that the climate of society changes,
and it held that no language (including "the lewd and obscene" repudiated by the
original decision) was automatically outside First Amendment protection. In the
second case, the Court ruled that the need for safeguarding the expression of
unpopular ideas outweighed the need to punish or prohibit the expression of
morally "unacceptable" ones (recall that the *Skokie* case dealt with the American
Nazi party's desire to stage a parade through a mostly Jewish area near Chicago).

The second case, together with the 1989 flag burning case, represents the
culmination of a liberalizing trend in the interpretation of the freedom of speech
clause, a trend that sought to safeguard free political expression from majority
whims, even if this meant defending that right in the kind of expression outlined
above. In the Skokie case, the fundamental issue was not whether it was desirable
to have this particular demonstration occur or even whether it was desirable to
have Nazism promoted in some fashion. Instead, liberals fear that if we allow
dominant groups to prohibit certain ideas from the democratic political arena,
outlawing their expression, the line beyond which most ideas may not be so
excluded may become difficult to draw. One cannot say that a particular point of
view is suppressible without establishing the precedent that other ideas may be so
suppressed by the dominant group. The *Skokie* case sought to enjoin the demonstration, not because of the manner in which the Nazi ideas would be presented,
but because the town found the content of the ideas too obscene and heinous to
tolerate. Conservatives argue that some ideas are clearly outside the democratic
arena and are so heinous and obscene as to be beyond the pale of public discussion. If any ideas by their nature could be called obscene, Nazism would be among
the first to qualify. But once the principle is established that certain ideas may not
be legally advocated, the category tends to become expanded by those in power to
include much of what they do not like. President Nixon and his followers believed
that active support for his Democratic presidential opponent or opposition to
Nixon's policies should be covertly suppressed in the "national interest." Accordingly, the administration evaded the democratic rules of the game and used the
supposedly neutral but awesome powers of the national government to do so.
Because of this danger of an ever-widening definition of what may be censored, the

concept of obscenity, that which is so hostile to our fundamental values as to be suppressible, has been limited in Anglo-American law to sexually explicit material.

American public policy has now come close to the principle that certain ideas cannot be suppressed because of their nature or content, no matter how worthless or heinous they may seem to most citizens. Even utterances that cannot be reasonably held to be part of discussion, part of the market of ideas, appear to be protected. Expression has come to be a constitutional value for its own sake, irrespective of its role in the democratic process. Freedom of speech is no longer limited to its political role, and most forms of utterance are now protected.

This area illustrates the core of the difference between liberals and conservatives on the speech issues. On the one hand, liberals tend to elevate all forms of utterance to a paramount value through the preferred position doctrine and a presumption of *unconstitutionality* for restrictions on utterance. On the other hand, conservatives are rather more inclined to the concept of balancing the protection of utterance against such other social interests as order, security, public morality, and fair trials.

The Debate over Censorship and Obscenity

A lingering question in the ongoing controversy over obscenity legislation is what social value is preserved by allowing the censorship of patently offensive, hard-core pornography, even assuming that such material can be adequately distinguished. Is the goal of obscenity legislation to protect people from being offended, or is it assumed that certain preventable, harmful behavior and events would be the consequence of the unrestricted dissemination of hard-core pornography? If the former is the value being guarded, government is in the business of controlling thought rather than restricting itself to the control of behavior. Of course, so-called kiddie porn, the use of children to produce pornographic books and films, goes beyond thought control, raising issues of the exploitation of those unable to exercise independent judgment. The law has always distinguished the protection needed by children from the needs of adults.

Justices Black and Douglas took the position that such control of thought is not compatible with an open society. In their dissent from the *Roth* decision, they attacked the central premise of obscenity legislation, that it is permissible to "punish mere speech or publication that the judge or jury thinks has an undesirable impact on thought but is not shown to be part of any unlawful action. . . . " They disagreed with the *Roth* rule because it permits the state to censor material that arouses sexual impulses, whether or not it results in particular forms of behavior. They were suggesting that utterances or ideas that have not been shown to have a likely impact on some unlawful behavior or to cause the physical impeding of some lawful activity are protected by the First Amendment, no matter how much they may offend the moral standards of any particular part of the community. The distinction between the impact of material on thought and its impact on action is easier to make in practice than that between hard-core pornography that is patently offensive and soft-core pornography that is mildly offensive. Because these two liberal justices did not believe that material can be censored on the basis of its content, they were the only justices who did not read or review the material at issue in obscenity cases. To them, the material was constitutionally protected, regardless of what it contained.

Some data are available on pornography's impact on behavior. A commission established under President Johnson and reporting years later during the Nixon administration systematically searched for a causal connection between exposure to sexually explicit material and the disposition to engage in antisocial behavior.[43] The commission used both experimental techniques and aggregate data analysis with a large, representative sample of the population. It failed to find any systematic evidence of such a connection. Accordingly, the commission recommended the abolition of all laws that proscribe the dissemination of sexually explicit material among consenting adults.

Arguments for censorship.   Opponents challenged these findings on several grounds. They were carried out on volunteers who are to that extent unrepresentative of the population at large. The effects on children were not considered. Nor were long-term effects taken into account. Sociological and anthropological research on the long-range effects of sexual permissiveness leans toward the conclusion that such permissiveness is dysfunctional for creative energy and cultural development.[44]

Late in the Reagan administration, Attorney General Edwin Meese released a Justice Department–sponsored study purporting to show the harmful effects of pornography. Critics charged that it lumped together a wide range of sex-related material and did not prove the connection it alleged between pornography and criminal actions. It seems fair to say that there is some systematic evidence that pornography does not in fact produce undesirable behavior but that the evidence is not without flaws and there is a fair amount of thought to the contrary. The issue has not been resolved.

Despite such data, a majority of the population clings to the belief that pornography leads people to commit sex crimes. A 1978 survey by the Roper organization found that 57 percent of a national sample agreed with the statement, "Sexual materials lead people to commit rape." Only 36 percent disagreed, and 7 percent did not know.[45] These findings are consistent with the popularity of the solicitor general for the county encompassing Atlanta, Georgia, who defended his concentrating the resources at his disposal on driving pornography out of the city with the bald assertion, "I'm convinced that the use of obscene materials results in many antisocial acts . . . rape, sodomy, and the molesting of young children."[46] Such persistent beliefs in the face of all contrary evidence are a political reality that can both affect and undermine whatever legal principles may protect sexually relevant material.

Arguments against censorship.   Given the lack of evidence to support an alleged causal effect of pornography on antisocial behavior, liberals argue that what consenting adults read or view is none of the state's business. This concept of the "consenting adult" implies that people do not have such material involuntarily foisted on them and that the probability is very remote that they could naively or unwittingly place themselves in contact with such material. For example, a theater showing X-rated films should be clearly so identified, and no one should be pressured or even implored to enter. The notion of consenting adults also implies a distinction between what is available to adults and what is available to minors, a distinction the Court clearly upheld when it struck down a law banning the sale "to the general reading public" of any book "tending to incite minors to depraved or immoral acts" or "tending to the corruption of the morals of youth." The Court held that this law reduced the adult population of Michigan to reading only what is fit for children.[47] The argument that individuals must be presumed able to decide for themselves what material is fit for them to read or view does not apply with equal force to minors. Assuming that the availability of sexually explicit materials is effectively limited to consenting adults and that there is no demonstrated causal connection between adult exposure to pornography and socially disruptive behavior, why not allow rational adults to choose for themselves what materials they can view without becoming morally offended or depraved? The Supreme Court came close to this position in the *Stanley* v. *Georgia* case (1969), which involved the seizure of sexually explicit films in a private home. The Court held that "if the First Amendment means anything, it means that a state has no business telling a man, sitting alone in his own house, what books he may read or what films he may see."[48] One may read into this decision the principle that consenting adults have the right to read or view whatever they choose as long as they do not force such material on unwilling adults or allow its availability to minors. The Court, however, refused to adopt this logical entailment of *Stanley* when in the *Reidel* case (1971) it upheld a state ban on the buying and selling of pornography by consenting adults.[49] The Court explicitly rejected the position that if someone has a right to read what he or she wants in private, he or she also has a right to buy it from someone willing to sell it. Because it was also held in the *Twelve 200 Foot Reels* case (1973) that one may be prosecuted for importing salacious materials for one's own personal use, one has no right legally to acquire the materials that *Stanley* gives that person a right to read or see.[50]

The consenting adults argument was more explicitly rejected in *Paris Adult Theater* v. *Slaton* (1973), in which the Court upheld the right of the state to close down a theater specializing in X-rated films.[51] It was admitted that the theater was so clearly marked that it was impossible to enter it unaware of the sexual nature of the films being shown. It was further admitted that minors were effectively excluded. Nevertheless, the Court still perceived some legitimate state interests in permitting censorship to override any First Amendment values involved. These state interests include "the interest of the public in the quality of life and total community environment, the tone of commerce in the great city centers and, possibly, the public safety itself." The Court further held that even though it had not been shown that there is a causal relationship between exposure to pornography and deviant or objectionable behavior, a state may nevertheless reasonably assume that such a relationship exists in asserting a legitimate interest in regulating what consenting adults may view or read. Why a state may "reasonably assume" something to be true contrary to available evidence was not discussed.

Supporters of censorship correctly point out that much of the material in obscenity cases is obviously trash and hardly worth protecting. Such material contributes very little if anything to the political purpose of the First Amendment, the free trade in socially relevant ideas. Moreover, although censorship in effect imposes the moral standards of dominant groups on other members of society, such principles may be part of the essence of that society. Even if unwilling adults do not actually see pornography, its very presence is held to lend an unsavory moral climate to the environment. In neighborhoods characterized by widely available pornography, crime rates tend to be significantly higher than average. Furthermore, the suppression of pornography would, many believe, bring about the diminishment if not the disappearance of some notorious abuses associated with the production of pornography. Child pornography is one of the more egregious examples of such abuses.

New attacks on pornography.　A new attack on pornography has been mounted by a group of feminists, led by law professor Catherine MacKinnon and writer Andrea Dworkin, involving the strategy of obtaining legislation to the effect that such material demeans women and thereby violates their civil rights. The remedy invited by such legislation is civil action against either the producers or the distributors of such material, including the bookseller. Because the criminal process is not involved, the burden of proof is altered from previous strategies of criminalizing the production and distribution of sexually explicit material.

The first example of this was a 1984 law passed by the Minneapolis city council but vetoed by the mayor. Other such ordinances were introduced in Indianapolis and Los Angeles. These ordinances have come under severe criticism on freedom of speech grounds. The critics charge that the standards for determining what may be considered demeaning to the dignity of women are left very imprecise and therefore any bookseller, publisher, or other disseminator of sexually relevant material may find himself or herself the defendant in a lawsuit initiated by any woman who was so offended. Even if the defendant wins, the costs of being party to such litigation would be great, and so such litigation could cause a severe dampening effect on the willingness of people to handle any sexually relevant material that may offend those most easily offended. The public would then almost be limited to having access only to material inoffensive to the most sensitive women. Laws granting women the right to sue booksellers who distribute salacious material that the plaintiff believes demeans women were tested in *The American Association of Booksellers* v. *Hudnut* (1984), a case challenging the Indianapolis law. The judge, a woman, found that the law presented an unconstitutional deterrent to free speech.

It is argued, on the other hand, that pornography does promote and legitimate the image of women merely as sex objects rather than as complete and equal persons. Moreover, some sadomasochistic, hard-core pornography fosters the idea of the physical abuse of women as a manly thing to do. Such material characterized by simulated rape and violence toward women is increasingly typical of hard-core pornography today, whereas material formerly considered hard-core (explicit but normal sexual activity) is now relegated to soft-core status, such as that found in such mainstream outlets as *Playboy.* The dissemination of such material thus may actually pose a physical danger to women. Pornography in general depicts sex as a conquest, something that men do *to* women rather than as a mutual expression of affection that men and women do *with* each other. Studies after the 1970 President's Commission Report discussed above do indicate that exposure to the new violent, hard-core pornography does soften attitudes toward rape and the sexual exploitation of women. Indeed, men exposed to such material become more tolerant of sexual violence, according to psychologist Edward Donnerstein. Of course, to the extent that it can be shown that the violent forms of pornography make men more tolerant of such violence, the argument is no longer simply one of competing moral perspectives but rather a question of the right of the state to protect the well-being of its female citizens. But whatever the case for censorship on moral grounds, censorship of the kinds of material that can be shown to pose a physical danger to women is another matter.

Producers of pornography. The concept of blaming the source— producers or sellers of reading or viewing material—for the acts performed by consumers of such material, which was struck down in the *Hudnut* case, was resurrected in 1992 by Senate sponsors of the Pornography Victim's Compensation Bill, which would allow civil litigation against the purveyors of pornography by the victims of sexual violence. The bill makes three assumptions. First, as in the MacKinnon-Dworkin laws struck down in *Hudnut,* it assumes that sellers of books, magazines, or video cassettes should be acquainted with the content of everything they sell. If the basis of the litigation intended by the bill is that the material in question may incite lust, that charge could be made of much serious adult material. The second assumption, given some recent support by the claims of confessed serial killer Theodore Bundy, is that viewing or reading sexually relevant material causes people to commit sexually violent acts, a proposition rejected by the 1970 President's Commission Report. Third, the bill assumes that violent sex crimes are an expression of uncontrollable lust. Current research indicates, however, that such crimes are expressions of hatred of women and a desire for power over them. The bill, being so fundamentally flawed, would be useless in curbing this tragic social malady whose incidence is growing. It has not been passed by Congress as of this writing.

Censorship and the open society. The problem with censorship on the grounds that material is immoral or offensive is that one cannot appoint a censor selectively to stamp out this particular worthless piece of trash or that particular despicable point of view. Censorship is, by definition, delegating the power to one or more persons to decide for everyone else in the jurisdiction which of all future utterances they may see, hear, or read. The adult members of society lose the right to decide for themselves what material is trash and what materials have value, what ideas are legitimate and worthy of consideration, and what ideas are so heinous as to be outside the democratic political arena.

To give a censor power is to give that person discretion to choose what material to suppress. The record does not support optimism that such discretion will be used judiciously. Although most Americans can agree that some materials are offensive and worthless, the record is replete with examples of overzealous censors suppressing material that most Americans would find harmless and often of considerable artistic value. The critically acclaimed films *Midnight Cowboy* and *Carnal Knowledge* were censored in some places, even though the Supreme Court found that the latter film did not "depict sexual conduct in a patently offensive way." Another critically acclaimed film, *Paper Moon,* a comedy involving very little that was even implicitly sexual, was challenged because of the use of profane language. The 1960s saw numerous attempts to ban the well-respected novel *Catcher in the Rye* from school libraries. John Steinbeck's *East of Eden, The Grapes of Wrath, The Red Pony,* and *Of Mice and Men* have all been banned in various places in the United States on obscenity grounds, as were several Hemingway novels.

Boycotts. One recent tactic used to protect society from putatively salacious material is not direct censorship by a public official but rather a boycott of the products of firms that sponsor shows on television allegedly containing such material, a boycott organized and promoted by a nongovernmental source. The chilling effect of the threat of such a boycott has caused sponsorships to be withdrawn in more than one instance. The extent to which the selection and content of shows have been altered because of the boycott threat is unclear. These boycotts are not formally censorship in the traditional sense of a public official banning the dissemination of certain material by law or edict; instead, they constitute a less formal kind of censorship, whereby materials are eliminated from dissemination through the mechanism of socioeconomic pressure.

Another version of these less formal tactics is the pressure to eliminate certain kinds of material from public school textbooks. The testimony at textbook adoption hearings seems to be dominated by those who want material expurgated from the books; live-and-let-live people who welcome new ideas tend to vacate this field. Some people have become almost fixtures at such hearings in the attempt to make textbooks reflect their view of the world. It is the familiar case of a vocal and passionate minority controlling policy over the more passive majority.

Norma and Martin Gabler of Texas have gained considerable notoriety by devoting their lives and fortunes to the cause of having what they consider to be a liberal view of the world expurgated from schoolbooks. They tend to attack books that contain references to sex, evolution, feminist values, or suggestions that the United States may not always have been right in its foreign affairs. In anticipation of such attacks, many publishers self-censor their textbooks in advance. For example, Scott Foresman expurgated four hundred potentially offensive lines from its high school version of Shakespeare's *Romeo and Juliet,* in an effort to eliminate any suggestion of carnal lust between those star-crossed lovers.

The right wing does not have a monopoly on such attempts to control the content of textbooks. Feminists, for example, show up to complain about demeaning depictions of women. Blacks have caused the censorship of such works as *The Adventures of Huckleberry Finn* and *Gone with the Wind* because they used the word *nigger,* and Jews have caused the removal of Shakespeare's *The Merchant of Venice* from school districts because of the portrayal of Shylock as a wicked Jew.

Liberal groups, though less concerned with sexual morality, have tried to pressure the networks to reduce the violence content of television shows. Network executives claim to have reduced such content, although much violence apparently remains in the current programming. There is some circumstantial evidence, mostly of an illustrative variety, that exposure to television violence can result in violent behavior. (A case in point is the man who set fire to his wife in October, 1984, after watching "The Burning Bed.") However, the evidence is inconclusive and the debate continues.

If a major premise of an open society is that reasonable adults are capable of assessing the value of competing ideas, should they also be presumed capable of making moral choices for themselves, provided that such choices do not harm others? When a censor presumes to tell such reasonable, consenting adults what material is too immoral for them to see or read, is that censor not presuming to make moral choices for others? If so, by what criteria can a censor be presumed to be more fit to make moral choices for other people than the people themselves? Thus the central premise of censorship, that reasonable adults cannot be trusted to make social, political, and moral choices for themselves, is a denial of the essence of an open society.

Continuing Conflict over the Role of Religion in U.S. Education

Ban on public school prayer.   The secularization of public schools by judicial fiat was received with widespread hostility and noncompliance. Recall the general observation that the constitutional principles in Supreme Court decisions are not self-implementing. This means, for instance, that although any school-sponsored or school-sanctioned prayer in any school district is logically irreconcilable with the original Supreme Court school prayer case, the legal force of the initial Court order banning prayer applies only to the parties in that particular lawsuit. Persons concerned about the religious practices in other school districts would have to file separate lawsuits citing the original school prayer case as a precedent. Given this reality, widespread misinformation about the imperatives of the decisions, and the social and political pressure of extensive popular opposition to secularizing the public schools, the existence of many pockets of noncompliance is not surprising.

For instance, one national random sample of public school teachers found 28 percent still reciting daily classroom prayers two years after the prayer decision. This does not mean, however, that the decision had no effect in secularizing schools around the country, as the same survey showed 64 percent of the teachers leading prayers before the decision.[52] Moreover, there was extensive regional variation in the rates of noncompliance, with the greatest rates in the South, where more than half of all classrooms were not in compliance.

The Bible-reading decisions evoked the same pattern of noncompliance. Noncompliance was widespread and heaviest in the "Bible Belt" South. For instance, a survey of 121 of Tennessee's 152 school districts found that only one had eliminated such practices altogether. Reading the Bible in school was not required by state law, and the state commissioner of education erroneously opined that the case permitted "voluntary" Bible reading. There was a widespread feeling among administrative personnel that as long as state law did not require Bible reading, teachers were free to do as they pleased in their own classrooms.[53] Inasmuch as teachers act as official agents of the school and the district, this is clearly an erroneous reading of the prayer decision; however, this perception undoubtedly led to widespread noncompliance.

The dual meaning of the religion clauses.   This resistance to the Bible-reading and prayer decisions was further justified by the argument that in forcibly taking "religion out of the schools," the courts were violating the free exercise clause. Yet these decisions did not prohibit people from reading the Bible or praying. Children are in school for about seven hours per day. Presumably, this leaves nine waking hours in which to practice religion to whatever extent they or their parents wish. There are many things the children are presumably free to do but cannot do during school time because such things would interfere with the functions schools are supposed to perform. Although a person is free to practice religion, one may not necessarily do so whenever and wherever one pleases. Moreover, others have a right not to exercise a given religion. Accordingly, the adherent of any religion may not use the powerful enforcement machinery of the state to pressure others to exercise that religion or religion in general. One of the entailments of the religion clauses is that we have both freedom *of* and freedom *from* religion.

Opposition to the removal of religion from the public schools has come from conservatives and religious people, but not all conservatives share this perspective. For example, libertarians and the new religious right support similar policies in some policy areas, but the former oppose government-sponsored religiosity, whereas the latter strongly supports it. Supporters of religion in the public schools argue that religion is a necessary part of our heritage and that schools should reflect the dominant culture. They further contend that the secularization of the school is tantamount to teaching a "religion of humanism," a vague concept implying the elevation of humanity to the place of God.

Aid to parochial schools.   It will be recalled that the *Everson* case (1947), in upholding the reimbursement of public funds to parents for the costs of busing their children to sectarian schools, laid down the child benefit standards. This means that if the primary effect of the aid is to benefit the pupil in the attainment of a secular education, a spillover effect of some benefit to a religious institution does not in itself rule that legislation unconstitutional.

The Court applied this principle in the *Allen* case (1968) in holding that it is legal for the state to lend textbooks on secular subjects approved by public school officials to pupils in sectarian schools.[54] It was argued in dissent that books are a major instrument in propagating a creed and that religious school officials would choose books suitable to their purposes and place powerful pressures on secular school officials to approve them. Such textbooks might reflect the dominant religious creed in that community, thus infringing on both secular rights and rights of minority religious persuasions. Although the Court was willing to approve the loan of textbooks, it drew the line in another case on state reimbursement for the purchase of books and payment of teachers' salaries by sectarian schools.[55] The Court was willing to accept the claim that secular authorities would exercise control in ensuring the religious neutrality of lent textbooks, but it faced the reality that the state could not ensure the religious neutrality of sectarian school teachers, whose salaries they would be paying, when they worked under independent religious school administrations in the protected environment of their classrooms. However, the Court appeared to reverse direction when it voted five to four to uphold a Minnesota law allowing parents a state income tax deduction for certain expenses of a private parochial education as well as for public education.[56]

The uncertainty in devising a precise legal principle for dealing with state aid to sectarian schools reflects the practical political and social dilemma presented by this issue. Like most of the social and political issues discussed in this book, persuasive arguments can be framed both for and against public aid to sectarian schools.

Arguments for aid.   First, arguments for such aid begin with the fact that sectarian schools do a respectable job in providing a secular education, that is, training pupils in subjects like mathematics, English, science, and geography. In fact, many people feel that in general sectarian schools do a better job in that regard than do most public schools. Thus, because sectarian schools perform an important public function, they are said to deserve public support. Moreover, if sectarian schools were to cease to function tomorrow, the existing public school systems would be unable to handle the large population of religious school pupils they would discharge into the public schools. The money not spent on sectarian schools would then have to be spent on a substantial expansion of the public schools.

Second, parents of parochial school pupils carry a double burden: They must pay the property taxes that support public schools and must finance the parochial education of their own children. In effect, they are financially penalized for choosing a religious school education for their children. Therefore it is argued that the lack of public support for parochial education goes beyond neutrality toward religion. Although it is true that parochial school pupils are free to take advantage of the public school system, if any great number of them did so, that system would collapse if not supported by greatly increased taxation. Presidents Reagan and Bush supported a plan for tax credits or vouchers for parochial school tuition, a plan that would alleviate the double taxation burden.

Arguments against aid.   The argument against public aid to parochial schools is framed more in terms of emotion and symbolism. For example, some of the most vigorous opposition to such aid comes from portions of the Jewish community. This opposition is based on a perception, however right or wrong, that the theology taught in many Christian schools contributes to anti-Jewish feelings among their pupils. They question why they should have to finance the teaching of anti-Semitism. In some nations, however, Jews support public financing of sectarian education, as it also supports a network of Jewish day schools, or

Yeshivas. This is part of the reason for the large Jewish population in Montreal; predominantly Catholic Quebec generously supports all religious schools.

Other opponents of aid to parochial education see such aid as the first potential break in the symbolic wall that separates church and state, a breach that will make subsequent breaches more likely. Their objection is based more on the principle of a secular political system for its own sake than on any adverse effect such aid would have on their interests and well-being.

Although these objections may be principled and reasonable they are intensely felt, making the issue difficult to resolve, especially in light of the ambiguity of the constitutional mandate. Although the arguments are generally framed in legal logic, they sometimes emanate from underlying emotions of need for or hostility to the institutions of organized religion. Thus the people who argue that aid of some kind to parochial schools is unconstitutional are often those who feel hostility to organized religion or to the particular religion whose schools dominate their area, more frequently the Catholic church than any other. Those who contend that aid is constitutional frequently feel sympathy toward or belong to the church whose institutions benefit from such aid. And on the point of benefit there is little real challenge: One may argue whether the benefit is direct or indirect, substantial in insubstantial, but it is undeniable that aid to parochial schools benefits those organized religions that maintain a substantial network of religious schools.

In the light of the intense emotion surrounding religion, the danger of parochial school aid is that the benefits will not be allocated equally among all religions, not to mention between organized religion and nonreligion. Any aid policy will benefit the members and institutions of some religions to the exclusion of those who do not belong to those religions, as different religions have different levels of commitment to parochial education. Perhaps this is one justification for a secularized school system in a society with a variety of religious orientations.

FUTURE ALTERNATIVES: CREATIONISM, SECULAR HUMANISM, AND THE CONTINUED PROTECTION OF EXPRESSION

Creationism

The removal of prayer and Bible reading from public schools does not complete their secularization. Public schools still engage in Christmas pageants and related exercises that can readily be viewed as religious. Christmas is clearly a Christian holiday, and other celebrations observed in public schools, such as Halloween and Saint Valentine's Day, have their genesis in Christian traditions. The Court backed off from barring such exercises by ruling that they are more a fixture in the American cultural tradition than strictly religious exercises. Therefore the law now says that although atheists, Moslems, and Jews are protected from being exposed to an innocuous, nonsectarian prayer, they may be compelled either to isolate themselves or to participate in an extensive Christmas pageant under the Court declaration that Christmas is not a religious holiday. Moreover, federal law gives students the right to organize religious clubs and activities on school property outside school hours. Clearly, the establishment clause is imperfectly successful in resisting the inevitable social pressures placed on others to adhere to the imperatives of a dominant religious orientation.

The extent of noncompliance with the Court dictates in the religion cases described earlier illustrates the difficulty in attempting by judicial fiat to secularize the institutions of a nonsecularized culture. Communities have come to expect that the schools that teach their children should reflect the values of that community, and a mere pronouncement by a distant tribunal, a pronouncement that they may well not have heard of and that they almost certainly have not read or studied, is not going to change that expectation. Thus the famous *Scopes* "monkey trial" involved the question of whether a community can bar the teaching of the theory of evolution—a theory almost universally accepted by the scientific establishment—because it conflicts with the dominant religious doctrine of that community. Yet as late as 1968 the Court was forced to rule such efforts unconstitutional, as Arkansas had brazenly passed a law nearly identical with the one challenged in the *Scopes* trial.[57] Despite this, Arkansas and Louisiana passed laws in the early 1980s requiring that "scientific creationism" be taught. The Supreme Court declared such laws unconstitutional in 1987.

Such establishment clause cases are a classic example of the Court's preventing a clear majority from exercising its strongly felt will. At the very least, such religious majorities feel that the biblical account of creation should be taught in addition to evolution, and they continue to exert pressures to have this done. Yet it must be remembered that the point of the concept of civil liberties is that there are some things that a majority cannot do to a minority, no matter how strong that majority may be and no matter how intensely it may want to do so. The efforts to reverse the Court on the prayer issue and to circumvent rulings on pornography suggest that no resolution of issues involving morality and religion can be deemed permanent. Such issues will continue to occupy the public in the decades ahead.

Secular Humanism

A major issue that has been raised in recent years is the right of religious fundamentalist parents to shield their children from the influence of what they call "secular humanism." This vaguely defined term has almost become symbolic of everything many fundamentalists disdain about the modern world. Its general connotation, however, is that humans can, to some extent, control their fate and are not totally subject to the will of the deity. Moreover, it is a legitimate and worthwhile enterprise to strive to improve the quality of life on earth independent of the assistance of God and independent of considerations of salvation. The declining importance of religion in the modern world has created a perceived threat of the encroachment of secular humanism on traditional religious values. The issue is whether secular humanism is merely the declining salience of traditional religious observance and belief or is an alternative religious perspective.

The issue was manifested in the refusal of a group of fundamentalist parents to allow their children to participate in the assigned reading in their public schools because, the parents argued, the books promoted the philosophy of secular humanism and thereby interfered with the right of these parents to raise their children in the religious orientation of their own choosing. The school officials, on the other hand, argued that the educational goals of the school would be undermined if parents refused to allow their children to share a common set of readings and educational experiences. The federal district court upheld the rights of the parents, but a federal appellate court overruled that decision.

The case of the parents was weakened in the eyes of many nonfundamentalist Americans by the innocuousness of some of the passages to which the fundamentalists objected. For example, one of the offending passages merely declared that people ought to strive for self-improvement and to gain increasing control over their own destiny. This decision reinforces the principle that one of the values of the educational system is to socialize children into shared or common sets of values or a common identity. But the decision does not end the dispute over the extent to which religious values may be recognized in the public schools.

Free Expression and Free Exercise

Two recent episodes test the limits of free exercise and free expression in different contexts.

In attempts to deal with offensive behavior and speech, municipal ordinances and state statutes have been passed in many localities. The issues raised by these ordinances parallel those discussed above regarding "political correctness" on college campuses and antipornography statutes. The compatibility of these laws with First Amendment provisions was central in a case brought to the Supreme Court in 1992, *Viktora* v. *St. Paul.* Raymond Viktora had burned a cross in the front yard of a black family. He could have been prosecuted for trespass or under a local ordinance against terrorist threats that carries a prison term of up to five years. Instead, the prosecution chose to charge Viktora under a St. Paul ordinance criminalizing any expression that the defendant should reasonably know will "arouse anger, alarm, or resentment in others on the basis of race, color, creed, religion, or gender," which carries a maximum penalty of only ninety days in jail. The intent of the prosecution thus appeared to be to obtain Supreme Court approval of the legitimacy of such "hate-speech" statutes and the political advantage of a stand against racially offensive behavior, rather than the most likely conviction or the severest punishment for the defendant. In June, 1992, the Supreme Court unanimously struck down the St. Paul ordinance as a content-based restriction on First Amendment–protected expression. This ruling places most campus speech codes in jeopardy.

The point at issue, that the hostile or potential hostile reactions of listeners cannot be used as a justification for limiting freedom, was described as the "heckler's veto" in the 1969 case *Street* v. *New York.*[58] The utter confounding of supposedly liberal and conservative sentiments that occurs in such cases is apparent in *Viktora.* William Kunstler, the civil rights advocate, who almost invariably supports minority rights, spoke against the ordinance. On the other hand, feminist attorney Catherine MacKinnon, whose work underlay *Hudnut,* supported the prosecution. At the same time, People for the American Way, normally among the leading defenders of First Amendment questions, expressed support for the statute.

The complexities of proscribing speech perceived as insensitive are further illustrated by a paid advertisement, written by an outsider, that appeared in the November 5, 1991, edition of Duke University's student newspaper, *The Chronicle.* The piece was presented as historical revisionism, although the writer lacked any training as a historian. The article claimed that the Holocaust was a lie invented by an international Jewish conspiracy to support Zionist objectives. The myth of an international Jewish conspiracy is a traditional staple of anti-Semitism and in any guise is highly offensive, but the editor of the newspaper chose to publish it, without criticism or rebuttal, on free speech grounds. Similar incidents have occurred on other campuses, although usually with editorial critique or rebuttal. Such events make it apparent that vigilance against insensitivity at the expense of free speech is essentially selective; the sensibilities of some groups are protected while those of others are not.

Free exercise controversy.   A major issue in the interpretation of the free exercise clause was opened in 1990, when the Supreme Court reinterpreted the meaning of that clause of the First Amendment. In the case of *Employment Division* v. *Smith* the Court upheld the dismissal from their jobs of two members of the Native American Church for the use of peyote as part of their religious ritual.[59] The case is not significant so much for that particular result, as it is for the reasoning used by the Court.

In this decision, the Court majority overturned the long-standing interpretation of the free exercise clause that placed the burden on the government to justify impingement on the religious practices of citizens. Formerly, state authorities had had to show a "compelling state interest" in the regulations that restrict religious exercise. This gives a significant degree of protection to religious practices that may diverge from mainstream American religion. In the *Smith* case, however, the Court majority established a test that permits far more government intrusion. It allows such intrusion when it is merely the incidental effect of a generally applicable state law. In other words, as long as a regulation does not explicitly single out religion, it can restrict religious practice.

Religious groups from all parts of the theological and political spectrum have reacted in alarm to this new interpretation of the meaning of the First Amendment's protection of freedom of religion. They fear that, if it stands, religion will in fact not have any special protection. These religious leaders and many members of Congress have joined in support of a proposed piece of legislation, the Religious Freedom Restoration Act, that would mandate that the Court return to the earlier interpretation of free exercise overturned in *Smith.*

SUMMARY

First Amendment freedoms protect the legitimacy and tolerance of different social, political, and religious perspectives. The environment in which such different perspectives can legitimately coexist is called pluralism, or an open society. In protecting this pluralism, First Amendment freedoms are essential to the maintenance of a democratic system.

Because of their role in protecting the democratic political process itself, some argue that First Amendment values must be presumed to outweigh such competing values as protection of property, civil order, and national security. This elevation of civil liberties to the highest priority is the preferred position doctrine. Others deny that some values are more important to democracy than others are.

Some advocates carry the preferred position doctrine a step further and argue that First Amendment rights must be protected without exception; this is the absolute position. Given the reality that rights conflict, this would amount to a denial of other rights. Others argue that the amendment's guarantees must be balanced against competing rights in any political or administrative decision; this is the balancing position.

The minimal or common-law definition of freedom of speech is the absence of prior restraint (prior censorship), a doctrine that allows the state complete leeway to punish the consequences of utterances. The right to punish the effects of what has already been said or shown has, however, been restricted by the clear and present danger test, a test designed by Justice Holmes to protect the exchange of ideas.

Because the danger test originally limited the protection of the freedom of speech clause to discussion, the fighting words doctrine held that insults, ethnic and racial slurs, and profanity not contributing to discussion were beyond First Amendment protection. This doctrine was eroded and finally discarded to allow the American Nazi party to taunt Jews in Skokie, Illinois. Free expression has come to replace free discussion as the goal of the First Amendment. But action to force one's point of view on others by physical compulsion, "speech plus," is not as firmly protected as is "pure speech."

Issues of hate-speech and political correctness test the limits of freedom of expression. Obscenity refers in American law to sexually explicit material. The *Roth* rule, as modified by the *Miller* case, is the major standard for what may be censored as obscene. Although most pornography as such is not worth defending, censors have banned much worthwhile material. Yet studies have failed to find any systematic evidence that pornography leads to harmful behavior. Feminists have been active in their attempt to make the distribution of pornography an offense subject to civil lawsuit. Censors, in presuming to tell reasonable, consenting adults what materials they may read or view, appear to deny a basic assumption of an open society, that such adults are presumed competent to make such judgments for themselves.

Libel laws protect individuals against the disproportionate power of the mass media in the market of truth claims. Public officials or public figures must, however, show malicious intent in order to win libel suits, because criticism of such public figures is an important political function of the media, and public persons have recourse to the ear of public opinion that private persons lack.

The McCarthy era constituted the principal threat to freedom of association, another basic attribute of open societies.

Religious pluralism and toleration are also attributes of an open society. There are two religion clauses in the First Amendment—the establishment clause and the free exercise clause—and these often conflict with each other. The Court has leaned toward the establishment clause in trying, with limited success, to secularize the public schools. Prayer and devotional Bible reading, even when nonsectarian and voluntary, have been explicitly banned by the Court, but there remains much noncompliance with the decisions.

Certain kinds of public aid to parochial schools and the loan of textbooks to such schools have been upheld by the Court because such schools perform a public function and the primary beneficiary is judged to be the child. However, public payment of teachers' salaries in such schools and general aid have been ruled unconstitutional.

The free exercise clause may conflict with the rigid enforcement of the establishment clause. The free exercise clause does not give the right to engage in activities that the state can otherwise ban or to allow parents to withhold education or medical care from children in the name of religion. The clause has allowed the courts to interpret the Selective Service Act to expand the grounds for conscientious objection to military service. Finally, prayer in the public schools and the teaching of evolution are areas of continuing controversy.

NOTES

1. This minimal definition may be found expostulated most notably in Joseph Schumpeter's classic, *Capitalism, Socialism and Democracy* (New York: Harper Torchbooks, 1942 and 1962), chap. 22.
2. Dissenting opinion in *Abrams* v. *United States*, 250 U.S. 616 (1919), at p. 630.
3. Justice Stone's now famous footnote 4 in *United States* v. *Carolene Products*, 304 U.S. 144(1938), at p. 152.
4. Justice Frankfurter in *Kingsley Books* v. *Brown*, 354 U.S. 436 (1957), at p. 441.
5. Edmund Cahn, "Justice Black and First Amendment Absolutes: A Public Interview," 37 *New York University Law Review* 549, (1962).
6. For a scholarly inquiry into the meaning of the freedom of speech clause for its authors, which concludes that they understood it merely to encompass this common-law definition, see Leonard Levy, *The Legacy of Suppression* (Cambridge, Mass.: Harvard University Press, 1960).
7. *Schenck* v. *United States*, 249 U.S. 47 (1919).
8. *Gitlow* v. *New York*, 268 U.S. 652 (1925).
9. *Termeniello* v. *Chicago*, 337 U.S. 1 (1949).
10. *Feiner* v. *New York*, 340 U.S. 315 (1951).
11. *Chaplinsky* v. *New Hampshire*, 315 U.S. 568 (1942).
12. *Cohen* v. *California*, 403 U.S. 15 (1971).
13. *Village of Skokie* v. *National Socialist Party of America*, 46 L.W. 2396 (1978).
14. *Smith* v. *Collin*, 99 S.Ct. 291 (1978).

15. The discussion of the Michigan policy is drawn from Dinesh D'Souza, *Illiberal Education* (New York: Free Press, 1991), pp. 140–144.

16. The discussion of the Wisconsin policy relies on Ken Emerson, "Only Correct," *New Republic,* Feb. 18, 1991, pp. 18–19.

17. See, for example, *Adderly* v. *Florida,* 385 U.S. 39 (1966).

18. *Regina* v. *Hicklin,* L.R. 3 Q.B. (1868).

19. *Roth* v. *United States,* 354 U.S. 476 (1957).

20. *Miller* v. *California,* 413 U.S. 15 (1973).

21. *Jenkins* v. *Georgia,* 418 U.S. 153 (1974).

22. *Jacobellis* v. *Ohio,* 378 U.S. 84 (1964), concurring opinion at p. 197.

23. *New York Times* v. *Sullivan,* 376 U.S. 254 (1964).

24. *Curtis Publishing Company* v. *Butts,* 388 U.S. 130 (1967).

25. *Hustler Magazine* v. *Falwell,* 108 S. Ct. 876 (1988).

26. *Sheppard* v. *Maxwell,* 384 U.S. 333 (1966), involved a celebrated case in which a wealthy osteopath was accused of murdering his wife. The press and television cameras so dominated the courtroom that the Court referred to "the carnival atmosphere at the trial."

27. *Nebraska Press Association* v. *Stewart,* 44 L.W. 5149 (1976).

28. *Hazlewood School District* v. *Kuhlmeier,* 168 S. Ct. 562 (1988).

29. *Tinker* v. *Des Moines School District,* 393 U.S. 503 (1969).

30. *Everson* v. *Board of Education,* 330 U.S. 1 (1947).

31. *School District of Abington Township* v. *Schempp* and *Murray* v. *Curlett,* 374 U.S. 203 (1963).

32. *Engle* v. *Vitale,* 370 U.S. 421 (1962).

33. *Illinois ex. rel. McCollum* v. *Board of Education,* 333 U.S. 203 (1948), at p. 227.

34. *McCollum.*

35. *Zorach* v. *Clauson,* 343 U.S. 306 (1952).

36. *Lynch* v. *Donnelly,* 104 S.Ct. 1355 (1984).

37. See, among such cases, *Reynolds* v. *United States,* 98 U.S. 145 (1879), and *Hardin* v. *Tennessee,* 188 Tenn 17 (1949).

38. For example, *Jacobson* v. *Massachusetts,* 197 U.S. 11 (1955).

39. *Craig* v. *Maryland,* 220 Md 590 (1959).

40. *United States* v. *Ballard,* 322 U.S. 78 (1944).

41. *Cantwell* v. *Connecticut,* 310 U.S. 296 (1940); *West Virginia State Board of Education* v. *Barnette,* 319 U.S. 624 (1943); and *Sherbert* v. *Verner,* 374 U.S. 398 (1963).

42. *United States* v. *Seeger,* 380 U.S. 163 (1965).

43. The *Report of the Commission on Obscenity and Pornography* (Washington, D.C.: U.S. Government Printing Office, 1970).

44. James Q. Wilson, "Violence, Pornography, and Social Science," *Public Interest,* 22 (Winter 1971), 45–61; J. D. Unwin, *Sex and Culture* (London: Oxford University Press, 1934). These arguments are well summarized in Harry M. Clor, "Commentary on the Report of the Commission on Obscenity and Pornography," in Clor, ed., *Censorship and Freedom of Expression* (Skokie, Ill.: Rand McNally, 1971), pp. 119–129.

45. U.S. Department of Justice, *Sourcebook of Criminal Justice Statistics, 1980* (Washington, D.C.: U.S. Government Printing Office, 1980), p. 223.

46. Quoted in *Newsweek,* May 25, 1981, p. 46.

47. *Butler* v. *Michigan,* 352 U.S. 380 (1957), at pp. 383–384.

48. *Stanley* v. *Georgia,* 394 U.S. 557 (1969).

49. *United States* v. *Reidel,* 402 U.S. 351 (1971).

50. *United States* v. *Twelve 200 Foot Reels of Super 8mm Film,* 413 U.S. 123 (1973).

51. *Paris Adult Theater* v. *Slaton,* 413 U.S. 49 (1973).

52. Frank Way, "Survey Research on Judicial Decisions: The Prayer and Bible Reading Cases," *Western Political Quarterly,* 21 (June 1968), 189–205.

53. Cited in Stephen Wasby, *The Impact of the United States Supreme Court: Some Perspectives* (Homewood, Ill.: Dorsey Press, 1970), pp. 134–135.

54. *Board of Education* v. *Allen,* 392 U.S. 236 (1968).

55. *Lemon* v. *Kurtzman,* 403 U.S. 602 (1971).

56. *Mueller* v. *Allen,* 77 L Ed 2d 721 (1983).

57. *Epperson* v. *Arkansas,* 393 U.S. 97 (1968).

58. *Street* v. *New York,* 394 U.S. 576 (1969).

59. *Employment Division* v. *Smith,* 110 S.Ct. 1595 (1990).

SUGGESTED READINGS

Abraham, Henry J. *Freedom and the Court,* 5th ed. New York: Oxford University Press, 1988. See especially chaps. 1, 5, 6.

Alley, Robert S., ed. *The Supreme Court on Church and State.* New York: Oxford University Press, 1988.

Bickel, Alexander. *The Least Dangerous Branch.* Indianapolis: Bobbs-Merrill, 1962.

Chaffee, Zachariah. *Free Speech in the United States.* Cambridge, Mass.: Harvard University Press, 1954.

Chopper, Jesse. *Judicial Review and the National Political Process.* Chicago: University of Chicago Press, 1980.

Clor, Harry M., ed. *Censorship and Freedom of Expression.* Skokie, Ill.: Rand McNally, 1971.

Ducat, Craig R. *Modes of Constitutional Interpretation.* St. Paul: West Publishing, 1978.

Emerson, Thomas I. *The System of Freedom of Expression.* New York: Vintage Books, 1970.

———. *Toward a General Theory of the First Amendment.* New York: Vintage, 1967.

Fortas, Abe. *Concerning Dissent and Civil Disobedience.* New York: NAL, 1977.

Meikeljohn, Alexander. *Free Speech in Relation to Self-Government.* New York: Harper & Row, 1948.

———. *Political Freedom.* New York: Oxford University Press, 1965.

Morgan, Richard. *The Supreme Court and Religion.* New York: Free Press, 1972.

Reddish, Martin. *Freedom of Expression: A Critical Analysis.* Charlottesville, Va.: Mitchie, 1984.

Rice, Charles. *Freedom of Association.* New York: New York University Press, 1962.

Shapiro, Martin. *Freedom of Speech: The Supreme Court and Judicial Review.* Englewood Cliffs, N.J.: Prentice-Hall, 1966.

CHAPTER 12

Dangerous Games: Issues in Foreign and Defense Policy

In the contemporary world, people and nations have become highly interdependent. A drought in Russia has economic, political, and social consequences for the people of the United States. Similarly, an election in the United States affects the people and governments of every nation in the world. Because of the interdependence of nations, virtually any major action by one country has consequences for others. Often their effects, although not necessarily intended, may nevertheless cause problems in relations among nations. Other actions, such as the Iraqi invasion of Kuwait or a United States embargo on Haiti are intentional, meant to bring pressure on another government to behave in a manner desired by the nation taking the action. *Foreign policy* refers to the intentional actions and decisions by one government in dealing with other nations. *Defense policy* is one instrument by which foreign policy is implemented.

ISSUE BACKGROUND: KEY CONCEPTS AND HISTORIC VIEWPOINTS

Purposes of Foreign and Defense Policies

The goals of foreign and defense policies vary from nation to nation but usually focus on three factors. Nations typically develop foreign and defense policies to (1) preserve their national security, (2) promote their own economic interests, and (3) advance their own influence over world affairs so as to make them predictable for their own interests. In addition to these objectives, the foreign and defense policies of the United States and some other nations also have been couched in terms of promoting international peace and stability. For some nations, however, "controlled" instability might be preferable in the short run if it led to an expansion of their international influence. The Soviet Union often was accused of fomenting instability so that it could manipulate a chaotic situation after internal conflict had torn apart a political system. Some evidence suggests that the United States may not be totally innocent of such tactics either, especially in Latin America. However, at least in public justifications, the purposes of the United States' foreign and defense policies have included altruistic goals of peace, stability, and democracy. Of course, the stated policy and what actually takes place are not always the same.

There are many ways by which nations conduct their foreign policies. *Diplomacy,* the major instrument of foreign policy, is a process whereby nations negotiate and compromise their differences so as to reduce conflict. Through diplomatic relations, nations communicate with one another and develop various types of interchange, and through cultural, social, and economic exchanges, national leaders develop an understanding of one another. Such understanding makes it possible for each to comprehend better the positions of others. When conflicts develop among nations, they normally try to resolve them through communicating with one another and often through negotiating over differences. As John Spanier suggested, however, Americans have never been very comfortable with this "classical" approach to diplomacy.[1] Convinced that theirs is the morally right position, Americans tend to find compromise offensive. After all, one cannot compromise with those who are immoral, and foreign enemies are usually characterized as such.

There are many times, of course, when differences are not settled through communication and negotiation. In such instances, nations may resort to political actions in seeking desired results. Diplomatic relations may be broken, or complaints may be lodged with the United Nations or other international agencies to bring pressure on the offending nation. Economic sanctions are commonly invoked to influence another country's position as well. Trade embargoes may be used to punish a nation that is acting contrary to the wishes of another. All of these approaches were used by the United States against Iraq during the course of the 1990–91 Persian Gulf crisis.

The ultimate method by which one nation may try to implement its foreign policy is military force. A country with superior military power often can impose its will on others when force is used to settle disputes, although great damage may be sustained by the dominant power itself. The use of force is associated with another factor, the implicit or explicit threat of force. Threatening to use force often is seen as a deterrent to actual hostile action by another. Much of post–World War II foreign policy between the United States and the Soviet Union was based on deterrence by both sides' building up their military capacity. Although superior military capacity may seem to be an effective means of ensuring one's influence over others, sometimes that power can also be a constraining force. When one nation has the power to destroy others, it may feel obliged to react carefully when provoked. Power brings with it some obligations to use it with discretion. Thus the United States was virtually paralyzed by Iran's holding of American hostages in 1980, even though it had the power to inflict immense damage on or to totally destroy Iran. There are, of course, factors other than power that affect the ability of a nation to take such action. For example, considerations of world reaction to the Iran confrontation, America's own moral or ideological orientations, the safety of the hostages, and the potential involvement of other nations in the matter were just a few constraints the United States faced in trying to decide on a course of action during that crisis, which lasted for more than a year.

Isolationism versus Interventionism

There always has been a division in the United States between those who believe foreign affairs to be a distraction to America's more important internal concerns and those who see the United States as a leader in an interdependent world. President Washington's farewell address often has been invoked to support the position that the country should remain free from involvement in the affairs of other nations. The inward focus of early foreign policy was, in part, a pragmatic approach, as the newly independent nation had little power to influence affairs in other parts of the world. Instead, it concentrated on its own internal development.

The isolationist stance of the United States taken by early administrations persisted well into the twentieth century, although there were occasional instances of active intervention in world affairs. The Spanish-American War (1898), in which the United States took Spain's colonies of Puerto Rico, Cuba, Guam, and the Philippines, was one break from isolationism. Following the war, however, the nation withdrew again into noninvolvement. Another return to the world arena took place with the United States' participation in World War I and President Woodrow Wilson's attempt to bring the country into the League of Nations, which he played a major role in creating. Unsuccessful in his attempts to get the United States to join, he saw the country revert to its isolationist role in world affairs.

Wilson's approach epitomizes the ideals on which one American foreign policy tradition has been based. It was Wilson's belief that America was somehow different from the rest of the world and should set an example to be followed by others. As a democracy convinced of its superior moral virtue, America had the mission of leading and assisting other countries by becoming involved in world affairs. Thus World War I was a struggle fought to end all wars. The idealism of Wilson and others suggested that if America could demonstrate the virtue of its way of life, peace and prosperity would ensue for all. A corollary to this approach is that power is evil and those who exercise it only cause problems in international relations. Thus American foreign policy was based on an erroneous dismissal of power politics as a basis for international relations.

World War II produced a fundamental change in the American approach to the world at large. Determined that the country would help shape global affairs in such a way that future wars would be prevented, the United States assumed an active international role. Part of its activism resulted from a concern in the postwar period that the Soviet Union would try to dominate the structure of world affairs. Two camps had formed—the Soviet Union and other communist nations, on the one hand, and the United States and its allies, on the other—and the conflicts between them evolved into the Cold War. The Cold War witnessed efforts by each side, especially the United States and the Soviet Union, to establish spheres of influence. In the immediate postwar period, international politics developed into a bipolar system, with each bloc competing for the allegiance of other nations.

Even in the efforts to gain allegiance of other nations, however, there have been many variations in the United States' role in world affairs. Though generally playing a leadership role after World War II, there have been pressures for less involvement as well. Especially after the United States' disengagement from Vietnam, the Nixon, Ford, and Carter administrations emphasized to its allies that they should assume greater responsibility for their own security. With the election of 1980, change came once again as the Reagan administration attempted to reassert the United States' influence around the world. The 1988 election campaign rhetoric of President George Bush suggested an aggressive stance. The swift military action in the Persian Gulf despite apparent urgings of caution by many of his advisors, including the chair of the Joint Chiefs of Staff, reflects that stance.

CONTEMPORARY POLICY: FROM COLD WAR TO COOPERATION

The Politics of a Bipolar World

The containment of communism has been, until recently, a cornerstone of American foreign policy since World War II.[2] Although each administration has had its own approach to implementing it, postwar policy was based on three objectives, listed here as outlined by Charles Kegley, Jr., and Eugene Wittkopf:

1. The United States must permanently reject isolationism and substitute for it an active responsibility in international affairs.
2. Communism constitutes the principal danger in the world, and American conduct must be directed against this threat.
3. Because the Soviet Union is the spearhead of the communist challenge, American foreign policy must be dedicated to the containment of Soviet expansionist tendencies and influence.[3]

The policy of containment attempted to keep the Soviet Union from expanding its influence any further than it already had. In the early postwar period the emphasis was in Europe, where the Soviet Union had brought Eastern Europe under its influence, and Western efforts were directed at preventing further expansion. Although the rhetoric of some administrations, such as that of Eisenhower, went further, suggesting that they would actively encourage "liberation" of nations already under Soviet domination, actual policy implementation fostered containment. The concept of containment emanated from the Truman Doctrine, which pledged support to those nations being pressured by the Soviet Union and communism. Although the Truman Doctrine was based primarily on granting economic and financial aid, it also left the door open for the military assistance that became a conventional practice in later years.

To stem the expansion of Soviet influence, the United States sponsored and joined numerous alliances around the world. This approach is referred to as collective security. The first and most important was the North Atlantic Treaty Organization (NATO), which is an alliance of the United States and many of the nations of Western Europe. Security agreements were also signed with nations in Southeast Asia, the Middle East, and Latin America. These treaties pledged the member nations to come to the defense of any other member threatened by a third nation. Although the agreements did provide security for smaller nations, they also were a means for the United States to exert influence in various parts of the world. The one-sidedness of the security arrangements in most of these alliances—the likelihood of other members' coming to the assistance of the United States was slight—underscores the fact that the United States had other reasons for joining them. One of the major benefits to the United States was having access to foreign territory for locating military installations and to foreign markets for economic activity. While the United States was developing these alliances, the Soviet Union was doing the same, particularly in Eastern Europe.

To implement the alliances, the two blocs found it necessary to develop military arsenals. In this way emerged the Cold War and an unprecedented arms race. Some critics of American foreign policy believe that American policymakers never really understood power politics until after World War II, that it was the Soviets' intransigence and expansionist policies beginning then that led them to an appreciation of the role of force in international affairs.[4] Even with the development of military and security alliances, the United States was not wholly able to stem the tide of communist bloc activities. The American public, accustomed to foreign involvement in the form of all-out war with relatively quick results, became frustrated with the seemingly stalemated containment policies. Instead of taking decisive action and then retreating to domestic affairs, the Cold War meant prolonged foreign involvement without easily discernible effects. An impatient public reacted with frustration directed at President Truman in the early postwar period.

The Korean War.   The Korean War epitomized this frustration. The United States, as an agent of the United Nations, seemed to be mired in a prolonged, costly conflict for no reason. People could not understand why the powerful United States could not unleash its awesome military power, defeat North Korean aggression, and then leave. The Truman administration recognized other potential implications of all-out force, however, such as bringing Soviet troops directly into the conflict and possibly starting World War III. General Douglas MacArthur, the field commander, advocated striking at China, which was supplying "volunteers" to the North Korean effort. When MacArthur decided to challenge Truman by stirring up public opinion in support of his own position, Truman exercised his powers as commander in chief and relieved MacArthur of his command.

The Republican party exploited the frustration with containment by promising to get rid of the "communist menace" if it were in office, rather than live with it indefinitely. They nominated a war hero to run for president, General Dwight D. Eisenhower, who promised to go to Korea, implying he could bring a quick end to the conflict by bringing the full diplomatic prestige of the office of president to bear on the situation. With the election of Eisenhower, John Foster Dulles became secretary of state. He began a moral crusade in United States foreign policy; goals were formulated in ethical terms focusing on "good" and "evil" rather than on conflicts of interest in international politics. Dulles began promising to liberate those nations dominated by the Soviet Union and thus roll back Soviet influence.

The massive retaliation strategy. Domestic anticommunist rhetoric did not translate into comparable action. Instead, the administration did little when in 1956 Hungarian patriots attempted to revolt against their communist government. The administration let the Soviet Union know that it would not intervene in the situation, thereby continuing the policy of containing rather than attempting to overthrow communist rule. However, the administration was faced with strong anticommunist sentiment at home, which it had helped foster and could not ignore. Partially to appease that sentiment, the policy of massive retaliation was developed. Massive retaliation, a variation of containment policy, threatened to use nuclear force to strike at Soviet expansionism or aggression. Thus the Soviet Union and China would risk total destruction for aggression. The American public could relate to such a policy because it once again presented the traditional American view that war, once entered into, should be "won." Deterrence through the threat of military force now became the key to containment.

Threats of massive retaliation, however, are deterrents only as long as they are credible. Such threats actually gave the Soviet Union and China the opportunity of testing the risk of aggressive activities. They calculated their moves carefully to discover whether the United States would really engage in all-out war to defend any particular nation. Indochina (Vietnam in particular) became the scene of the test of this doctrine in 1954 when the Eisenhower administration demonstrated that it was not willing to follow through on its warnings to China and the Soviet Union. Because the new foreign policy of the administration depended on air power and bombing capabilities rather than ground forces, much of the ground forces had been demobilized. The United States therefore began to provide economic and military aid to France, which had colonized Vietnam and was fighting Vietnamese nationalists in an effort to retain control over it. Thus began the efforts to resist "communist aggression" from the North. That the United States would enter all-out nuclear war to save Vietnam was, however, not very credible (just as it would avoid a head-to-head collision two years later in refusing to save Soviet-occupied Hungary). Because the administration was unwilling to follow through on its own warnings, the policy proved to be a rhetorical one. Perhaps it was expected that warnings would be enough. But such warnings can succeed only if the parties involved really believe the threats will be carried out.[5] The lack of intent to implement a policy tends to immobilize its advocate's options to react and, in effect, nullifies that policy.

The limited war strategy and Vietnam. As massive retaliation became an implausible policy, the United States began to develop a limited war capability once again and to utilize conventional warfare techniques in Vietnam. Involvement in Vietnam deepened. By the middle of the 1960s the United States had committed more than a half-million troops to the war. Debate on its strategy raged, with some wishing to use all-out force to wipe out the "aggressors" and others arguing, successfully, for a war of attrition to weaken the North Vietnamese and Viet Cong to the point of surrender. Many times, the American public was told that it would soon be over, but the war was a prolonged one, and frustration once again built. Along with those who were impatient for swift, effective action to end the war militarily, there were added many voices challenging the war on other grounds.

A great deal of debate over the war in Vietnam centered on moral issues. Many citizens questioned the propriety of the United States' participating in what they viewed as a civil war. Others viewed the war as a necessary stand against communist aggression. Protestors took to the streets, and a new constituency of draft resisters and political activists demonstrated their outrage at the war. The realities of war—Americans saw actual battle scenes displayed on their home television screens—the questions being raised on moral grounds, and disenchantment with how the war was proceeding all resulted in a gradual decline after 1966 in public support for and an increase in opposition to the United States' involvement. The Johnson administration lost much support as a result of that involvement. And once again the Republicans, led this time by Richard Nixon, used disenchantment with foreign involvement as a major issue in winning election to the presidency. Nixon promised an end to the conflict, but his secret plan for ending it did not materialize, and it was not until after his second term began that a ceasefire was arranged and the United States withdrew in 1973. By April, 1975, the United States' Vietnamese allies had totally collapsed, and the communists took over South Vietnam, Cambodia, and Laos. Ironically, all the efforts expended in protecting the world from communist domination ended with the United States' once again withdrawing from international involvement.

The failure of containment in Vietnam contributed much to the movement toward détente (relaxation of strained relations between the United States and the Soviet Union) in the Nixon, Ford, and Carter administrations. The Reagan administration seemed to be more committed to containment than détente at the start. The highly publicized United States invasion of the tiny island nation of Grenada in October, 1983, to restore democracy and oust the allies of the Soviet Union and Cuba was a symbol of the president's affection for bold strikes to contain communism.

In its second term, however, the administration emphasized cooperation and held four summit meetings with Soviet leaders to lessen tensions between the two nations. With the collapse of Communism in Eastern Europe in 1989 and 1990, the stage was set for vastly improved relations. President Bush and Soviet leaders declared an end to the Cold War and pledged to work together. The cooperative effort in reacting to Saddam Hussein's Iraqi invasion of Kuwait represented a historic occasion symbolizing the new era in United States–Soviet relations. In 1991, the Soviet Union collapsed and the United States now is providing humanitarian aid to parts of the former Soviet Union, including Russia.

Efforts in El Salvador, Nicaragua, and other Central American nations also represented the Reagan administration's intent to control Soviet communism. In the face of inconsistent congressional support for its efforts, the Reagan administration in 1985 seemed to modify its boldness in opposing the pro-Soviet Sandinista regime in Nicaragua. Originally calling for the regime's overthrow, the president seemed to back off from those statements. Although originally asking for direct U.S. military aid for the "Contras," the revolutionaries seeking to overthrow the Sandinista government, the president finally settled for an ambiguous package of so-called humanitarian aid. These efforts and the domestic reactions to them began to resemble the foreign policy and domestic resistance prominent during the Vietnam War years, and the administration's Central American policy became a highly volatile issue. The president and Congress could never agree on Central American policy; therefore the issue was left to the Bush administration in early 1989, which fashioned a compromise with Congress to provide humanitarian aid for a limited time.

The Bush administration attempted to be assertive with Panama in the wake of its election fiasco of May, 1989. After holding elections (observed by several United States luminaries, including former President Carter), President Manuel Noriega abruptly declared the election void when charges of corruption and stealing the election were made. President Bush then called on the people of Panama to get rid of Noriega and began moving U.S. military dependents from Panama. In December, 1989, the U.S. engineered the downfall of the Noriega regime and captured Noriega, who was later convicted on drug trafficking and other charges in Miami. A new government in Nicaragua provides hope to U.S. policymakers that stability will develop there and negotiations among conflicting groups in El Salvador also give hope for some resolution to problems in establishing stable government there.

An interesting assumption underlying most post–World War II policy is that the United States always will react to the actions of the aggressor communist bloc but never initiate its own. Such an approach is consistent with the moral values traditionally used as symbols in the United States' foreign policy. Because war is "evil," the United States will not start one but would react if an "evil" power did so. But because of this orientation, the United States always is at the disadvantage, letting the place and timing of initial action be controlled by the other side. The action in Grenada perhaps represented a different approach by the Reagan administration. Similarly, the quick action in the Persian Gulf reflected the Bush administration's resolve.

New Approaches for a Multipolar World

The Cold War developed in a bipolar world in which two major powers competed, each supported by a group of allies. As the Cold War continued, however, India, for example, wished to remain neutral in the conflict. As neutrality began to develop in the 1950s and early 1960s, there was some negative reaction by both the Soviet Union and the United States. Neutral nations were considered by both sides to be in the enemy camp if they did not clearly ally with the Americans or the Soviets. The desertion of China from the Soviet camp was the most important of several divisions in alliances that began to develop at this time. The United States exploited that division, just as the Soviet Union exploited disagreements between the United States and some of its allies, as in the Middle East during the 1950s when conflicts erupted between the United States and many Arab countries, notably Egypt.

The result of neutrality, divisions in alliances, and new alignments of developing nations led to what has come to be known as multipolarity or polycentrism. A *multipolar* world is one in which numerous centers of power exist, making it impossible for one or two nations and their allies alone to dominate international affairs. The nuclear capability of nations such as France, China, Israel, and India, among others, creates a situation that is much less predictable than when only one or two have nuclear arms. The actions and reactions of new members of the nuclear club have to be taken into account when planning foreign policy.

Added to the military and nuclear power of many nations are new concerns for the world. The economic power of Japan, for example, affects the world economy and thus international affairs. The impact of Japan's auto, steel, shipbuilding, optical, machinery, and electronics industries on the rest of the world has been phenomenal during the postwar years, and its effects on other economies have led to tensions between governments. Similarly, the power of the Organization of Petroleum Exporting Countries (OPEC) to jolt the international economic system, as described in Chapter 4, was much in evidence during the 1970s. Oil became a weapon in international conflict, for whenever critical commodities can be held back or increased in price, they can be used for political gain in the power struggles of foreign policy. Moreover, with the dissolution of the Soviet bloc, severe economic disruption is occurring and affecting the whole world economy. Economic disruption has the potential for political instability.

Proliferation of nuclear weapons has created a situation in which world affairs are more unpredictable (see Table 12-1). Now foreign policy leaders have to be concerned about what many nations with nuclear power might do. If Saddam Hussein, for example, had nuclear bombs at his disposal, the world would have to be concerned about how he might use that power. Additionally, concerns now focus on who controls the nuclear arsenal of the former Soviet Union.

TABLE 12-1 ▪ Nations in the Nuclear Club

Nuclear Powers	*Now produce nuclear weapons with ability to deploy*	*Working on them*	*Believed capable of building nuclear bomb*
United States	Argentina	Libya	Canada
Soviet Union (former)	Brazil	Iraq	Germany
China	India	North Korea	Italy
France	South Africa	Iran	Japan
Great Britain	Pakistan		Romania
	Israel		Sweden
			Switzerland

SOURCE: Based on *NATO Defense and the INF Treaty,* Senate Hearings, Committee on Armed Services, 100th Congress, 2nd Session, January 25, 26, and 27, 1988.

Conflicts with allies such as Greece, Turkey, Spain, Portugal, and the Philippines developed in the 1980s. Most of these conflicts revolve around the existence of United States military bases in those nations. Fierce internal opposition to United States presence from strong nationalist groups causes problems for the leaders of those nations. As a result, negotiations to retain military bases have become difficult, and many bases are being closed. Similarly, disputes arose between the United States and New Zealand (and eventually Australia) about the presence of U.S. nuclear-equipped vessels in their ports. Emotional reactions to these concerns cause leaders of other nations to act carefully in their alliances with the United States.

American-Soviet Arms Negotiations

Even though the United States was mired in Vietnam trying to stem the spread of communism, the 1960s also signaled the beginnings of accommodation with the Soviet bloc. Even with the strident rhetoric of the Eisenhower administration, summit meetings with Soviet leaders were arranged, and the Kennedy and Johnson administrations expanded efforts to resolve conflicts over the bargaining table. During the 1960s the Partial Test Ban Treaty (1963), Outer Space Treaty (1967), and Nuclear Nonproliferation Treaty (1968) were negotiated and signed. Just as the later approach of détente did not totally abandon the concept of containment, so steps initiated by Kennedy and Johnson opened some new doors while still fostering containment objectives. It was a period of transition, during which the emphasis was changing from confrontation to limitation of the buildup of military power, as both sides began to fear the proliferation of advanced military technology in an unstable political environment.

The presidential and congressional elections of 1980, 1984, and 1988 indicate public support for a stronger national defense. President Reagan, as a candidate, promised an increase in defense spending, and as president he led the nation in the largest peacetime arms buildup in history. But conflict over the deficit slowed the buildup considerably by the end of the 1980s, with President Bush agreeing to a $4 billion cut in defense spending for fiscal year 1990. President Bush promised to continue a strong defense program, although details were not forthcoming during the election campaign. The end of the Cold War eroded support for military spending, although the success of the Persian Gulf war created a new sense of pride in the military and debates over new weaponry and appropriate arsenals were rekindled. As the nation approached the 1992 presidential elections, debates emerged between President Bush and Democratic presidential candidate Bill Clinton on just how large cuts in defense spending should be. People who expected a large "peace dividend" with the end of the Cold War have found little transfer of defense spending to domestic problems.

Arms limitation talks had been undertaken to relieve the insecurity the major powers felt about the proliferation of nuclear arms among many nations and to find ways to reduce the costs and dangers of the arms race. In part, by setting an example on arms limitation, the United States and the Soviet Union could influence others to restrain themselves and perhaps to bring some balance to the situation. But arms limitation negotiations are difficult, if only because neither side wants to give up an existing advantage. Thus conventional wisdom has it that a nation bargains only from a position of strength, a philosophy that is repeatedly espoused in any discussion of United States participation in such negotiations. Obviously, it is an advantage to bargain from a position of strength, and the way to do so is to build up one's military power in preparation for negotiations. The difficulty is that both sides view the situation in the same way, and so the preparation itself for the negotiations results in an arms race. Americans were often unwilling to accept the idea that the Soviet Union needs to bargain from a position of strength as much as does the United States. Each cannot be stronger than the other. There must be compromise before talks can start. These perceptions fundamentally affected the Strategic Arms Limitation Treaty (SALT) negotiations, which took place during the Nixon, Ford, and Carter administrations, and the Strategic Arms Reduction Talks (START) of the Reagan administration (see Table 12-2).

SALT I talks started the process of reducing arms buildups and SALT II continued that process. SALT II was initialed in 1979 but never ratified. When the Reagan administration took office in 1981, the president refused to meet with leaders of the Soviet Union until after the 1984 election when meetings between representatives of the two countries resumed. But little substance resulted, and the administration's Strategic Defense Initiative ("Star Wars") proposal, which would attempt to develop a protective shield in space, became a stumbling block. In a surprise move in 1985, President Reagan announced that the United States would dismantle a submarine to bring the nation into compliance with the unra-

---

TABLE 12-2 ▪ Arms Limitations Negotiations

Year of Agreement	Negotiations or Treaty	Results
1972	SALT I	1. Limits on number of strategic weapons, particularly antiballistic missiles (ABMs). 2. Intercontinental Ballistic Missiles (ICBMs) frozen at 1972 levels.
1977	SALT II	1. Limits on the number of strategic launchers, including Multiple Independently Targetable Reentry Vehicles (MIRVs). 2. Dismantling of 270 Soviet strategic weapons. 3. Restrictions on improvement of weapons technology. 4. Equality in number of strategic weapons held by the United States and the Soviet Union.
1981–84	START	No substantive agreement.
1987	Intermediate Range Nuclear Forces (INF)	All INF to be eliminated within three years— withdrawal and destruction of all nuclear missiles with ranges of 300–3,400 miles.

tified SALT II agreement. The action was seen as an invitation to the Soviet Union to engage in serious disarmament negotiations.

In March, 1985, arms reduction talks resumed in Geneva, and the Soviet Union dropped its insistence that the United States halt deployment of medium-range missiles in Europe. The door was open for a new relationship between President Reagan and the Soviet leadership. In November, Reagan held his first summit with a Soviet leader, Mikhail Gorbachev, in Geneva. Those talks were followed by a meeting in Reykjavik, Iceland, in October, 1986, but this session fell apart because of a dispute over Reagan's Star Wars (SDI) proposals, which the Soviets wanted dropped. Relations cooled until December, 1987, when Gorbachev visited Washington. Reagan then visited Moscow in May, 1988, the first time a U.S. president had done so since 1974. These events underscore a dramatic turnaround in U.S.-Soviet relations. The Reagan administration came to office with a very hostile stance toward the Soviet Union and maintained that stance until the half-way point of the president's second term. Then, in the last two years, dramatic developments to lessen hostility and foster cooperative efforts took place.

In December, 1987, an Intermediate Range Nuclear Forces (INF) treaty was negotiated with the Soviet Union to eliminate all INF missiles within three years. The treaty was ratified by the Senate in 1988. The treaty requires withdrawal and destruction of all nuclear missiles with ranges of 300 to 3,400 miles. The Soviet Union had 1,752 such missiles, and the United States had 859. While agreement on reduction has been reached, there are still problems to be worked out on verification of the cuts. Problems in verification are even more significant in continuing negotiations on strategic arms reductions.

Of course, these changes would not have come about without changes in the Soviet perspective as well. Gorbachev made some bold moves in making concessions and proposing ways of reducing the arms race. His most dramatic move was in an address to the United Nations in December, 1988, when he announced a unilateral cut in the size of the Soviet and Warsaw Pact forces. Although cuts left the Warsaw Pact with an advantage over NATO, the move was an important symbol in the search for better relations between the superpowers. Clearly, there were other reasons, especially economic, for Gorbachev's moves. However, at no time since the beginning of the Cold War had prospects been better for reduction of tensions. The Bush administration kept the initiative alive. In July of 1991, Presidents Bush and Gorbachev met in London and agreed to a new START treaty numbering more than 700 pages which was signed later in Moscow. Capping nine years of on-again, off-again negotiations, the treaty actually rolls levels of strategic weapons back to what existed when negotiations first began nine years earlier. There were many facets to the treaty (see Box 12-1). With the dissolution of the Soviet Union, the Russians are ill-prepared to continue development of military weaponry, and President Boris Yeltsin is focusing on cooperation and gaining economic and humanitarian aid. There still are questions about who will control the nuclear stockpile of the former Soviet Union although President Yeltsin indicates that a unified command will report to him. It is not clear, however, that all the other republics in which nuclear weapons are stockpiled agree. Nonetheless, Bush and Yeltsin agreed to further major weapons reductions in June, 1992.

BOX 12-1.
1991 Strategic Arms Reduction Treaty

Overall Goal   A roughly 50 percent cut in Soviet ballistic missile warheads and a roughly 35 percent cut in U.S. ballistic missile warheads within seven years of treaty approval, with two intermediate cuts to equal levels.

Delivery Systems   Ceiling of 1,600 strategic offensive delivery systems, defined as missiles deployed in silos and on submarines, plus "heavy" bombers and mobile missile launchers—roughly 36 percent below current Soviet levels and 11 percent below the U.S. level.

Throw-weight   A 46 percent cut in the warhead-carrying capability of all land- and sea-based ballistic missiles, from Soviet levels on the date the treaty is signed.

Warheads   No more than 6,000 warheads on 1,600 delivery vehicles such as missiles and airplanes. No more than 4,900 warheads on ballistic missiles, including no more than 1,100 land-based, mobile missile warheads.

"Heavy" Missiles   No new "heavy" or large missiles. A limit of 1,540 warheads on 154 deployed Soviet SS-18 missiles, half the current total. No changes in the SS-18 launch weight or throw-weight.

Mobile, Land-Based Missiles   Deployed missiles limited to 1,100 warheads; nondeployed or spare missiles limited to 250 and nondeployed launchers to 110.

Counting Rules   All but three types of existing missiles on each side are counted as carrying the number of warheads agreed to in December, 1987; this will be verified by a specified number of short-notice, on-site inspections. Heavy bombers carrying up to 20 or so short-range attack missiles or gravity bombs are counted as "one" warhead within the 6,000 limit.

Nuclear Force Operations   Mobile land-based missiles must be deployed within designated areas of 9.65 square miles and can be broadly dispersed only for testing and repair or during national crises. Bombers that do not carry cruise missiles must be kept separate from those that carry such weapons and from cruise missile storage depots; conventionally armed bombers must be based separately from those carrying nuclear arms. No testing or deployment of missile launchers that can be rapidly reloaded.

Air-Launched Cruise Missiles   Most bombers counted as carrying 8 to 10 nuclear-armed missiles, half the maximum possible. Only missiles with a range of more than 370 miles are counted. No limits on the numbers of missiles armed with non-nuclear warheads or on those held in storage.

Sea-Launched Cruise Missiles   Long-range nuclear-armed missiles are constrained by a special, unverified, nontreaty limit of 880, more than either side wants to deploy.

Verification   Weapons data exchange and on-site inspections of weapons facilities declared in advance, including continuous monitoring of facilities involved in mobile missile production. Short-notice inspections of suspect, undeclared facilities may be requested; some can be refused if concerns are otherwise resolved.

Space Weapons   The two sides will skirt a dispute about the Strategic Defense Initiative program to develop a U.S. missile defense that would violate the 1972 U.S.-Soviet Anti-Ballistic Missile Treaty. Moscow will reiterate its right to withdraw from the START treaty if SDI tests go beyond the ABM Treaty.

Duration   Treaty will be in effect for fifteen years and can be extended for successive five-year periods, until replaced by another treaty.

SOURCES: The *Washington Post*; Arms Control Association.
Reprinted from *The Washington Post National Weekly Edition*, July 22–28, 1991, p.16.

U.S. Relations with China

During World War II, the United States recognized the importance of friends and stability in Asia. China, having long had friendly relations with the United States and being the largest nation in the area, was the obvious choice for the role.[6]

After the war, efforts were made to stabilize China's internal politics as well as to provide aid for military and economic development. To signify *further* the intent to give China status as a major power, it was granted a permanent seat on the United Nations Security Council as one of the "big five" powers of the world. Stabilization of China's internal situation, however, was doomed to failure because of the intense split between the nationalists and the communists. The nationalists, led by Chiang Kai-shek, were corrupt and inept and seemed to do everything to play into the hands of the communists. Eventually the communists ousted the nationalists, who fled to the island of Taiwan and continued the Republic of China from that province. The mainland Chinese called themselves the People's Republic of China.

Intransigent support for the Nationalist Chinese and opposition to the People's Republic became embedded in foreign policy and popular belief. President Nixon, however, with impeccable conservative credentials, was able to move the nation to recognize the enduring reality of the People's Republic, that it was here to stay and represented the majority of Chinese. In one of the Nixon administration's main accomplishments, the People's Republic of China was officially recognized and assumed the Chinese seat on the United Nations Security Council. President Reagan made a highly publicized visit to China in 1984 and continued to exploit the differences between it and the Soviet Union. Cultural and diplomatic exchanges have continued, but the changes in U.S.-Soviet relations have overshadowed U.S.-China relations.

The Chinese government's bloody suppression of the democracy movement in June 1989 posed a major dilemma for United States foreign policy. The Bush administration did not wish to appear to condone the brutality of the crackdown in Tiananmen Square. At the same time, the administration is concerned about jeopardizing cultural and economic relations, which have been important in building relations with China. Despite much criticism, the Bush administration granted China most favored nation status in trade, with no concessions from the Chinese on the issue of human rights.

The emergence of the People's Republic of China as a major force in Asia has enormous implications for foreign affairs. Because it is a communist nation, it had some natural ideological links to the Soviet Union and some suspicion of the United States. With the demise of the Soviet bloc and the Soviet Union, relations with China no longer are much affected by the old alignments. As the United States and former republics and nations of the Soviet bloc move increasingly to mutual cooperation, China is left as a big imponderable in international affairs. So far, it has demonstrated little interest in accommodation with either the United States or the new Commonwealth of Independent States made up of eleven of the former Soviet republics. Its size and its increasing military capability make it a force to be dealt with, especially as it apparently is supplying military technology to countries hostile to the United States. On May 21, 1992, China detonated one of the most powerful nuclear weapons ever used in an underground test.

Defense Strategies

Closely allied to the foreign policy of any nation is its defense posture. Because the military strength of a nation is normally viewed as the means for enforcing its foreign policies, it is inevitable that foreign and defense policy are linked. Not surprisingly, views on defense capabilities and alternatives vary according to perspectives on foreign policy. Only a few disagree with the idea of a strong defense, but what constitutes a strong defense is subject to debate. This controversy is always intensified during election years, when candidates appeal to the patriotic impulses of the American public.

One tradition argues that America's defense capability should be limited to protecting only our own territory and lives, and a few even contend that pacifism is the most effective method of doing so. Others believe that we need continually to achieve the strongest military position possible. They are willing to provide the defense establishment with virtually whatever it requests, with little question of how it contributes to overall foreign policy or affects domestic policies.

Since World War II, the United States has witnessed dramatic change in worldwide military power. Immediately after the war, the United States was in a clearly dominant position, having both a strong conventional military capability and the world's only arsenal of atomic weapons. As a result, its allies depended on the United States, and its enemies had reason to fear it. Within a decade and a half, however, nuclear capability had spread, and both allies and enemies developed the means to create their own nuclear weapons. Such developments led to a situation in which both allies and antagonists could be more independent in their actions and thus could ignore the desires and pressures of the United States to a much greater extent. Having their own nuclear capability, allies such as France could operate more independently of the United States' influence, and the Soviet Union could compete more effectively.

Cold War impact on defense policies.   Defense policies during the Cold War were based on fear and distrust of the Soviet Union. Fueled by the belief that the Soviets intended to overrun and control the world, the American public and its political leadership decided to build an unrivaled military establishment. During the 1950s and most of the 1960s, defense expenditures were virtually unquestioned, but by the late 1960s, many liberals were beginning to object to many expenditures as wasteful and unnecessary. Instead of competing in an arms race, they argued, the United States should seek accommodation with the Soviet Union. In the early Reagan years, perspectives once again changed to a more hostile view of that nation. After 1984, however, the administration took a more conciliatory approach.

Suspicion of the Soviet Union's intentions developed as a result of the duplicity of its leaders in Eastern Europe immediately after World War II. Its consolidation of control over Eastern Europe and tensions in Berlin (1948–1949) and in Greece and Turkey (1947) convinced the United States that it would have to maintain military superiority to compete with the Soviets. The Soviets responded in kind.

Consequently, the United States and the Soviet Union armed themselves with the most sophisticated military equipment available. In addition to spending on military hardware, the United States built installations throughout the world and provided substantial economic and military aid to other nations so that they could become links in America's defense network. The Soviet Union and its allies responded by attempting to catch up to and surpass the United States in military capability. These actions resulted in the arms race discussed earlier in which each bloc attempted to develop superiority over the other. The arms race had important side effects for the U.S. economy, not the least significant being prosperity in terms of high employment along with good profits for defense industry contractors. At the same time, however, waste and fraud tended to be overlooked in the haste to fund all kinds of projects.

During the 1960s, many people began to worry about the overall implications of the arms race and, in particular, about the real possibility of nuclear disaster. Fears mounted that continued proliferation of nuclear weapons would inevitably lead to their use. Disarmament proposals became common matters of debate during the middle and late 1960s, and the formal arms limitation negotiations described above became regular features of United States–Soviet relations. Although an Arms Control and Disarmament Agency was created in the executive branch, it was and remains controversial because it advocates less dependence on military arsenals and more emphasis on working to reduce arms buildups.

However, with the sweeping political changes in Eastern Europe and the dissolution of the Soviet Union and the ensuing economic problems, most defense analysts believe that the need for large sophisticated arsenals is greatly reduced. Just as many were speculating on what to do with the "peace dividend" resulting from reduced expenditures, Iraq invaded Kuwait and the United States (under United Nations auspices) became involved in a costly war in the Persian Gulf. The fact that the former Soviet Union supported the United Nations initiative attested to a major reduction in tensions between the superpowers and renewed hope for arms reductions. Finally, the START treaty signed in August, 1991, signaled continued movement toward reducing strategic military stockpiles. Nonetheless, many conservatives argue that there is still need for a strong military because it is impossible to tell what is going to happen in the new world order and we must be prepared to deal with any eventuality. President Bush is pushing for continued strength of the military arsenal, in part to assuage the conservative challenges to his administration, at the same time that he and Russian President Boris Yeltsin attempt to agree on further arms reductions.

Instruments of defense.   Defense policy outputs consist of military weaponry and military personnel. Each is necessary to an effective defense posture, but there is disagreement about the ratio one should have to the other and how each should be provided. In this era of high technology it is often assumed that conventional warfare with hand-to-hand combat and limited air warfare is obsolete. Such an assumption leads to the conclusion that sophisticated weapons should be developed and used as a means of defense and that large conventional forces should be downplayed. If wars were to be conducted on the basis of the most advanced technology available, it would make sense to adopt such a strategy. However, because of the serious consequences of nuclear warfare, it becomes difficult to justify the virtual elimination of conventional forces. Instead, armed forces personnel are needed to defend against minor irritations or limited incursions by an enemy. Otherwise, every act of the enemy would have to be met with the ultimate weapon and, as discussed earlier, it is highly unlikely that such weapons would actually be used. Therefore the enemy might be capable of making limited inroads because it calculates that the United States will not react with massive destruction that risks possible destruction to itself. Because of these limits, strategic military hardware is complemented by tactical ground forces and weapons. The Persian Gulf war, with high dependence on conventional forces, underscored the need for balance.

Military weaponry.   Military weaponry consists of defensive, tactical, and strategic arms. It is often difficult to separate these, but an obviously defensive instrument is an antiballistic missile that intercepts and destroys an enemy missile on the attack. Tactical weapons are used to conduct theater or limited war. Strategic weapons are those used to make a strike against the enemy's heartland. The strike may be preemptive (designed to stop the enemy from action) or retaliative for some first action by the enemy. Part of the efforts of both the United States and the Soviet Union was to try to develop the most advanced weaponry in order to stay constantly ahead of the other.

Deterrence.   The strategy of deterrence and the assumptions behind it are critical to its success. Deterrence assumes that one nation will have sufficient military hardware to inflict unacceptably severe damage on the nation making the first strike and that a potential foe not only believes we can and would launch the second strike but also regards the damage as unacceptable. Thus, if the nation striking first were able to neutralize counterattack capabilities, it would have a distinct advantage. Because the assumption in American policy is that the enemy would strike first and American action would be a reaction to the first strike, it is important that the second strike capability be survivable. The emphasis in SALT I and II was on prohibiting one nation from developing the capacity to eliminate the other's counterattack forces. This second strike capability by both sides is often referred to as Mutual Assured Destruction Deterrence (MADD).

A nuclear freeze became a popular rallying cry for disarmament-prone liberals in the mid-1980s. The idea was that both the major superpowers would not add any new nuclear weapons systems. Proponents of the freeze idea argued that it does not call for disarmament of existing nuclear weapons and therefore does not harm the strategy of deterrence. Opponents pointed out, however, that such a freeze would prevent the United States from deploying those weapons systems most likely to be survivable and to give us a retaliatory capacity into the 1990s: the Trident submarine, the Cruise Missile, and the B-1 and Stealth Bombers. The current generation of nuclear submarines is probably detectable and thus vulnerable, but the Trident can travel farther and stay submerged longer, making it survivable under foreseeable technology.

A similar rallying cry among liberals in the 1980s was the concept of no first use of nuclear weapons. The idea here was that we would retain our willingness and ability to respond to a nuclear attack but that we would pledge in advance that we would not introduce nuclear weapons in any conflict. This idea is based upon the belief that once nuclear weapons are introduced into a conventional conflict, the last restraint on the scope of the conflict has been removed, and the conflict will then inevitably escalate into an all-out thermonuclear conflagration. Opponents of this position point out that, since the potential aggressor knows where it will strike and can concentrate its forces there while the defenders must spread their forces, the defender is at a great disadvantage. Therefore the no first use pledge would be virtually an open invitation to aggressors, that if they were to attack with conventional forces, the United States would not respond in the only manner that could repel such an attack, with tactical nuclear weapons.

Preemptive strikes are based on a different set of assumptions. A preemptive strike is a first strike strategy to cause the other side to decide against striking. Thus, if enough damage can be done to make the other side calculate that it can only lose disastrously by deploying the remains of its counterattack capability, it may decide against reacting in kind. Preemptive strikes are contrary to United States policy.

Strategies. There are dangers in attempting to calculate the action or reaction of another nation. There is no way of knowing how much damage the enemy will consider too much and thus what risks it will take. Neither can the enemy be sure of our calculations. Yet another issue is how believable the whole policy is. Military strength can only deter if a potential foe knows we have it and believes we would use it. Presumably, war will not occur if the other party does as we wish it to do. But if war breaks out anyway, there is no deterrent value in our actions.[7] The whole idea of using military arsenals as a deterrent assumes rational behavior by both parties, but what is rational to one may not be so to the other.

Sometimes conflicts between the major parties manifest themselves in other ways. Thus proxy wars may be waged in which each of the superpowers participates in a conflict in a third nation. Such activity is particularly common in Third World nations. The Soviets' support of Syrian aggression and the United States' and the Soviets' support of factions in Lebanon are examples of ways in which the two nations engaged in war without direct confrontation. Of course, the Soviet Union was usually accused of fostering instability by supporting terrorist or insurrectionist activities in nations around the world. But the United States was not innocent of such activity. The support of anti-Allende forces in Chile, aid to the Contras, and not-so-secret CIA involvement in mining Nicaraguan ports illustrate American engagement in those types of efforts.

Debate surrounds two new weapons systems: the MX missile (nicknamed "Peacekeeper" by President Reagan) and the Strategic Defense Initiative (SDI) (nicknamed "Star Wars" by its opponents). These are being discussed at home and were strongly opposed by the Soviet Union, because they have the potential to change the whole defensive strategy from MADD to either a first strike strategy or a strategy of defending against nuclear attacks. The MX is the newest MIRVed land-based missile in the American arsenal. It is highly accurate but also, under current basing modes, highly vulnerable to attack. Thus the fear is that it would have to be used as a first strike weapon or at least "launched on warning" of an attack, either of which would be deviations from the current strategic deterrence doctrine. SDI, which is currently only under research, is a combination of new high technologies, such as advanced radars, lasers, particle beams, pulsed power, and missile guidance, based partly on satellites. SDI weapons would be used to shoot down attacking missiles. It thus could change our strategy from that of deterring any nuclear exchange to one of accepting the possibility of such warfare and defending against it, a concept rejected in the ABM treaty. Scientists vigorously disagree on whether the SDI system could work. President Reagan met significant opposition in Congress, and even among NATO allies, with respect to research, development, and procurement of the two systems. The Bush administration has continued to support them although it scaled back the scope. Overall, the administration is proposing a $50 billion cut in defense spending while the Democratic leadership of Congress suggests that the cut should be larger. Some members of Congress suggest scrapping SDI entirely and are supporting a ground-based missile defense system. Debate continues while the new environment created by the dramatic changes in the former Soviet Union and Eastern Europe continue to complicate the world situation. The uncertainty in emerging international relationships makes defense planning difficult.

Military personnel. The deployment of troops is another instrument of defense policy. The draft was established in 1940 as a means by which young men could be obtained for military service. Under a draft system, the government always had personnel to staff its military needs. Because of numerous factors, including reactions to the Vietnam War and a general desire to lessen military involvement in world affairs, the draft was ended in 1973, and an all-volunteer force was established. Advocates of the all-volunteer force argued that good pay and benefits would attract capable personnel and keep them in the armed services, thus meeting the needs of military policy. The experience with the all-volunteer force has been disappointing to its supporters. Turnover rates have remained high, keeping costs up, and there are many criticisms of the quality of personnel recruited. As a reaction partly to the problems with the all-volunteer force and partly to international tensions, the registration of eighteen-year-olds for a possible draft was reinstituted in 1980. Although the Carter administration said it was not anticipating reinstitution of the draft, there was opposition to registration on the basis that the draft was likely to be resurrected. With the current downsizing of the military, recruitment is not a problem. Instead, many service personnel are being discharged early to reach the goals for a smaller armed forces.

The latest controversies surround whether women should be permitted to perform combat roles (they are now prohibited from doing so) and whether homosexuals should continue to be banned from the military services. The administration opposes changes in both policies but many members of Congress are pressuring the Defense Department to alter both. Both issues are emotionally charged. Opponents of both changes raise issues of morale and potential for sexual activity and abuse resulting from changes. Supporters of change argue that performance should be the sole basis for decisions on serving in the military and in all activities of it. The changing demographics of the military generally engender debate. During the Persian Gulf war, for example, many critics raised issues of an increasingly minority military force fighting a war which was decided upon by a largely white administration and Congress. The Persian Gulf war resulted in a large number of pregnancies, further fueling the debate.

Military intelligence.   Intelligence activities are also part of the instruments of defense. In order to counter the efforts of opponents it is necessary to understand their motives, activities, and capabilities. Military plans, force levels, and strategies are normally secret information; therefore it becomes necessary to conduct intelligence activities to obtain desired information. The Central Intelligence Agency (CIA) and other intelligence-gathering agencies in the Departments of State, Defense, and Justice came in for much criticism starting in the late 1970s with the disclosure of numerous instances of American participation in deposing and installing governments in foreign nations and of violations of the rights of American citizens. Controversy arose anew in 1991 during confirmation hearings on the nominee to head the CIA, Robert Gates. Questions were raised about his role in the Iran-Contra affair and whether he had been truthful with Congress in its investigation of the affair. The incident involved sale of weapons to Iran through intermediaries during the Reagan administration and diversion of money from the sales to the Contra rebels in Nicaragua. The role of the CIA has been hotly debated with much conflicting information about its involvement and how much the administration knew about what was happening.

The record of intelligence agencies during the Iranian hostage crisis, the Soviet invasion of Afghanistan, and Iraq's invasion of Kuwait also occasioned significant criticism. That the administration seemed surprised by these events raised many questions about the effectiveness of the intelligence establishment. As a result, many critics are proposing a lifting of restrictions on the agencies, thus giving them more freedom to do the jobs for which they were created. The Reagan and Bush administrations supported this position but also faced strong opposition from those who fear a renewal of the abuses that have come to light in recent years. The debate over defense policy is tinged with emotion, and it is difficult to strike a compromise between the views of those who believe that we must be prepared for any military eventuality and those who believe that the change in the world order has made military defense less of an issue.

POLICY EVALUATION: A NEW ROLE FOR THE UNITED STATES?

In recent administrations, foreign policy has been a major factor in judging administration performance. The Johnson and Carter administrations were objects of particularly harsh criticism. The Nixon administration, on the other hand, has its foreign policy to thank for any positive evaluation it receives, as it became mired in one of the worst domestic scandals in presidential history. The Reagan administration received high praise for restoring the honor and pride of America around the world, although there were many critics as well. Even the Democrats in Congress, in their reply to Reagan's final radio address, praised and thanked him for his efforts, especially in foreign affairs.

President Bush initially had such high popularity in the aftermath of the Persian Gulf war that the Democrats seemed to have little enthusiasm for a 1992 race against him. By early 1992, however, his popularity took a dramatic downward spiral as domestic issues began to dominate the attention of voters, dramatically improving the chances of challenger Bill Clinton. A recession (long denied by the administration) and intransigent social problems overtook foreign policy in importance to citizens.

Why is it that foreign policy has such an impact? Part of the answer probably lies in the expectations that Americans have of their ability to control the destiny of the world. American citizens in the postwar era became used to winning, and war heroes have been glorified through movies and television. The public's expectations usually do not include much awareness of the factors that constrain action in the world arena. Because America has the technology to act, many feel it should act. Inaction is seen as a sign of weakness of will. The constraints imposed by the realities of nuclear proliferation and the powers of others to act if provoked are not always part of the typical citizen's evaluation of how to behave in the world. Political leaders, however, must consider the repercussions of their actions, and they tend to be more cautious than many of their critics. However, that same caution often is cited as an example of an administration's lack of will.

A Return to Diplomacy

The experience in Vietnam sometimes is viewed as the end of American innocence in foreign affairs.[8] Since that time, the use of power has become politically risky for

U.S. leaders. Too many people cannot forget the Vietnam debacle—some because it seemed a violation of American ideals, a disillusioning glimpse of American arrogance; others because of its military futility. Given the Vietnam experience, people are now especially wary of military intervention. For instance, considerable criticism was generated when the Reagan administration sent military advisers to El Salvador. Similarly, the mining of Nicaraguan harbors under CIA direction created an angry outburst even from those who usually support the administration. Many people are concerned that such actions in Central America could lead us into another Vietnam, as the United States' involvement there began in much the same way. Because the existence of power often tempts its possessors to use it, there is always danger that the military community will be overeager to test its capacities in such theoretically limited warfare. The military establishment and political leadership are often at odds over the extent to which force should be used. Because United States tradition holds that force is basically evil and that it must be employed only as a last resort, leaders usually have difficulty convincing the rest of society of their position.

The recent desire to disentangle the United States from foreign military involvements was first enunciated by the Nixon administration and was continued by the Ford and Carter administrations. Although the Reagan administration's actions in Grenada and Central America suggested a return to policing the world with military power, such policing has generally been deemphasized. Instead, current efforts tend to focus on providing support to other nations while requiring them to bear the primary burden of their own security. Japan and Western Europe are being asked to assume increasing shares of their defense costs, and they do not always respond favorably. Japan and Germany were demilitarized by treaties signed at the end of World War II. Japan was prohibited from developing its own military force, and limitations were imposed on Germany's rearmament. Those prohibitions have been cited by Japan as reasons for not bearing more of the cost of its own military security. However, constant pressure from the United States has resulted in some relenting on Japan's part, and agreements are being reached to share costs.

The Gulf War

Reluctance to use military force was significantly overcome in 1991. The persisting American faith in the attainability of a worldwide cooperative order, a manifestation of Wilsonian idealism intensified by the sudden relaxation of Cold War tensions in 1989, was shattered in August, 1990, by the Iraqi invasion of Kuwait. Iraq had just emerged from its eight-year war with Iran; it possessed the fourth largest military establishment in the world and the capability to produce and use poison gas. Iraq also was working toward the production of nuclear power that most observers believe was for military purposes.

The United States quickly condemned what appeared to be one of the clearest cases of unprovoked aggression since World War II. President Bush put together a remarkably diverse coalition of nations to cooperate in the assembly of a large armed force in the Persian Gulf to deter further aggression and to institute rigid sanctions against Iraq. (See Map 12-1.) These moves were legitimated by resolutions of the United Nations Security Council. Between August and the end of the year, the grip of sanctions imposed an increasing burden on the Iraqi people. Some people argued that if kept in place long enough, these sanctions would force President Saddam Hussein to withdraw his forces from Kuwait and restore the *status quo ante bellum.* Others argued that Hussein would not be moved by the hardship of the Iraqi people, given his previous record of mass torture and killing of that population. President Bush concluded that sanctions would not produce the desired effect within the time that the coalition could maintain its forces in the Gulf.

Bush's decision to resort to the military to force Iraq out of Kuwait was opposed by most of the Democratic party leadership. The opposition was attacked by Republicans as indicative of unwillingness of a potential Democratic administration to use force as necessary to assert America's vital interests. The president initially used the popularity of the military action with the general public to

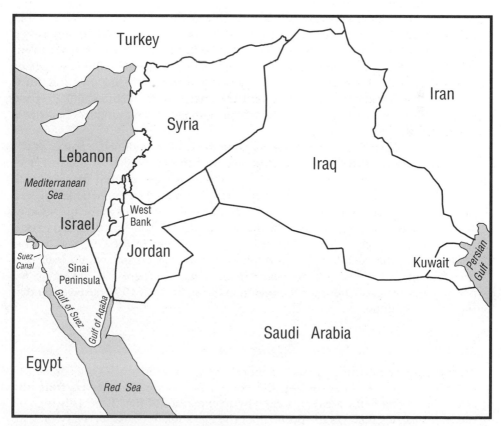

MAP 12-1 Area of the Persian Gulf War

solidify his electoral position and frighten off many potential Democratic candidates for the presidency.

There was much confusion about the objectives of United States policy, although the administration indicated that the objective was to reestablish the status quo in Kuwait as sanctioned by the United Nations resolutions. However, others argued that an unstable and aggressive leader like Hussein could not be permitted to threaten his neighbors with the widely believed capability to use weapons of mass destruction. Hussein had clearly demonstrated a hostility toward the West and its values, and many worried that an expansive Iraq could control the Middle East oil reserves to the serious detriment of the United States and its Western allies. These people wanted Hussein driven from power.

Despite this confusion, the allied coalition launched saturation air strikes against Iraqi forces, followed by a ground attack that routed the Iraqis with surprising ease. Rather than demolish the country's military capacity, however, the coalition suddenly broke off the attack once the Iraqis were out of Kuwait. The administration reportedly was concerned that the destruction of Iraqi power would create a vacuum which would prove tempting to other radical Arab forces in the region, particularly Iran.

President Bush expressed hope that internal forces would drive Hussein from power. However, the Iraqi army used its air power brutally to suppress a rebellion by Iraq's chief dissident minorities, the Kurds and Shiite Moslems. Eventually, the U.S. and coalition forces did provide some protection while assurances were worked out for safe return of many Kurds who fled the suppression. Bush realized that impatience with long military engagements could quickly erode support for the effort and brought the troops home to several months of patriotic celebrations.

The essential status quo was restored in the Gulf, including the power of the defeated Saddam Hussein. It is unclear whether the credibility of the threat of American use of force to protect its vital interests was restored by the quick reaction of the coalition to Hussein's seizure of Kuwait. Analysts who supported the military option argued that that was one of the major issues in the question of whether to use force, especially once the liberation of Kuwait was declared to be a vital American interest. Thus, despite a popular victory in the Gulf war, it was unclear what the coalition had won. Many hoped that victory would lead to a breakthrough in the search for peace in the region. Progress in arranging for possible peace negotiations for the region in the summer of 1991 raised hope that such a breakthrough was possible.

Israel and the Palestinian Question

The perennial American hope for a comprehensive solution to all of the conflicts in the Middle East was boosted by the good will Americans received from the numerous forces in the area threatened by an expansionist Iraq. Especially high on the American agenda was the problem of the Palestinian Arabs. Secretary of State James Baker was dispatched on several trips to the area to revitalize the peace process. These attempts were based on the land-for-peace formula that has been discussed since the Six-Day War of 1967, when Israel acquired territory formerly occupied by Arabs. The plan requires that Israel relinquish control of these acquired territories, specifically the West Bank (the area between the original 1947 eastern border of Israel and the Jordan River), the Gaza Strip, and the Golan Heights. The formula has already been applied to the Sinai Peninsula, which was returned to Egypt as part of the Camp David accords, a peace agreement between Israel and Egypt. Under some proposals, the West Bank and Gaza Strip would become a state for Palestinian Arabs displaced by the founding of the state of Israel. (See Map 12-2.)

American policymakers have become rather impatient with Israel's reluctance to cooperate with the administration's plan to solve all of the area's problems

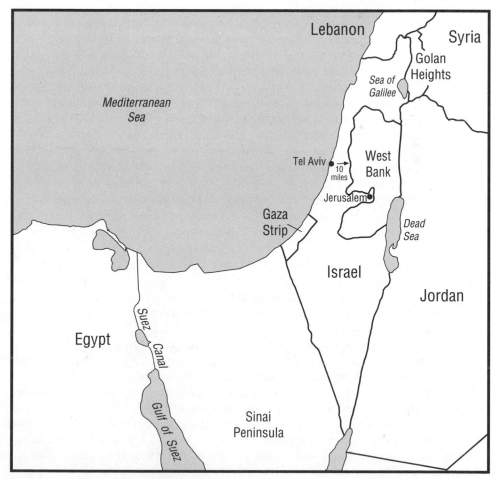

MAP 12-2 Israel and Neighboring States

of instability by turning what they call "the occupied territories" into a Palestinian state, thereby resolving the essential grievance against the West, the plight of the Palestinians. Israelis have, in fact, been building settlements on the West Bank in increasing numbers, thereby rendering their surrender of this territory more unlikely. Those Israelis who have sympathized with the land-for-peace formula have become less numerous and largely discredited in their own country since the Gulf war, and the adoption of the relatively hard line of the right-wing Likud party. Several factors and developments account for the growing skepticism of Israelis about trading land for peace. In late 1991 and 1992, more pressure was put on Israel to engage in peace talks, and the process of direct negotiations began. Although the United States pressured the parties to negotiate, it was not a direct participant in the talks.

First, the perceived importance of the West Bank as an Israeli security buffer was reinforced by the SCUD missile attacks on Israel by Iraq in the Gulf war. Iraq had to use long-range missiles that could not carry the chemical warheads Hussein was thought to possess. However, if the Iraqis could have fired them from a West Bank state, more accurate missiles with deadlier warheads could have been used. Since Israel is only eight to twelve miles wide in its middle part, Israel's major population centers would have been within mortar range from the border of a West Bank state. The cheering reactions of Palestinians as the missiles hit Israeli residential centers caused Israelis to doubt the sincerity of the moderation of the Palestinians. Additionally, the support of the Palestine Liberation Organization (PLO) leadership for Saddam Hussein and Iraqi policy caused concern among many Israelis.

Second, the immigration of hundreds of thousands of Soviet Jews to Israel is placing strains on that country for living space and housing. As the country becomes more crowded, the pressure to keep the territories will strengthen.

Third, in light of the foregoing factors, Israelis are reassessing the theory that a Palestinian rump state on the West Bank living peacefully alongside a Jewish state will assuage Arab grievances and end the hostility between these two peoples. Attempts have been made to negotiate peace treaties in the past with return of territories for guarantees of nonaggression against the Jewish state. Since much of the rhetoric of the Palestinian leadership has suggested destruction of Israel as a state, Israelis are not convinced that establishing a Palestinian state would result in acceptance of the right of Israel to exist.

Fourth, the various Arab leaders demand that negotiations proceed through a comprehensive peace conference sponsored by the United Nations. Israelis do not perceive the United Nations as being sympathetic to their cause. They prefer face-to-face negotiations with the Arab states. The Arab states, in turn, resist such negotiations since they would imply recognition of the Jewish state. There have indeed been numerous secret meetings over the years between Israel and Arab states such as Syria, and now the initiatives by Secretary of State Baker have led to direct negotiations. The Labor Party victory in the 1992 Israeli elections has slowed down West Bank settlement and created a more conciliatory Israeli government.

Even if agreement with the Palestinians were reached or if Israel were eliminated from the area, peace and stability would remain elusive. Arab struggles against other Arabs have gone on since long before the establishment of Israel. It may well be that, as Chapter 13 suggests is often true of social and political problems, no real solution exists and the only prospect for a kind of stability for the near future may be the existing stalemate. It goes against the dominant American liberal optimism and Wilsonian idealism in foreign policy to concede that a solution may not exist for all problems; hence the persisting search for a comprehensive solution to the problems of the area.

Sanctions as Instruments of Policy

Other efforts to influence international developments include economic sanctions, such as the wheat embargo against the Soviet Union and boycott of the 1980 Moscow Summer Olympics in response to the Soviet invasion of Afghanistan, and the freezing of Iran's monetary assets in reaction to that country's seizing of American hostages. These nonmilitary efforts to influence behavior of other nations are not without criticism. For example, many Americans became impatient with the waiting game regarding sanctions against Iraq and pressed for military action as the only recourse. Despite the military success in the Gulf war, there is a general reluctance to use force, given the many possible negative or destabilizing consequences suggested elsewhere in this chapter. American reliance on other methods of accomplishing foreign policy objectives is likely to continue.

Human rights.   Concerned about atrocities against the political victims of many governments, the Carter administration emphasized human rights as a cornerstone of its foreign policy. Pressures were brought to bear—mostly in the form of denunciations—on many nations that violated human rights, in the hopes that policies would change. Nations as varied as South Africa, Israel, Iran, and the Soviet Union were condemned by the administration for violation of basic human rights, as were numerous Latin American nations. Though agreeing that the cause of human rights is a noble one, conservative critics of the Carter administration urged a more pragmatic approach. They suggested, along with the vilified nations themselves, that condemnation on those grounds is interference in the internal affairs of other nations and only alienates political friends. America's international enemies, the critics pointed out, remained unaffected by mere denunciations, because the Carter policy called for no direct intervention—the only way truly to effect change among these totalitarian states. Supporters of the administration's position argued that public censure brought world pressure to bear on the offending governments, thus encouraging them to change their behavior. The debates over the appropriate role of the United States in Nicaragua and El Salvador exemplify the human rights controversy, and the Reagan administration's action there clearly demonstrated a preference for supporting friends, regardless of their human rights record. This perspective of the Reagan administration was reflected in its policy of "constructive engagement" toward South Africa, which refused direct sanctions against the nation to pressure it to alter its policy of apartheid. The summer of

1985 saw increasing demonstrations in the United States and elsewhere for the government to pressure the South African regime to alter its racial policies. Increasing riots and civil disorder that same summer in South Africa itself kept the apartheid issue in the public consciousness. However, the Reagan administration contended that sanctions of an economic nature would hurt blacks more than the government by generating unemployment. Supporters of the administration also contended that it is unfair to single out South Africa in the face of many other outrages against human rights, many by some of the regimes most critical of South Africa. The Reagan administration, however, was vocal in its denunciation of human rights violations in the Soviet Union and its allies. Strong economic sanctions against South Africa ultimately were approved by Congress. The Bush administration lifted the sanctions in 1991, declaring that South Africa had done what had been asked. Bush was criticized soundly, because he was at the same time urging most favored nation status for China.

The arguments over human rights represent fundamental differences in perspective. Although conservatives argue that they are interested in human rights, they also note that the United States must be practical in dealing with other governments. With their former concern for maintaining stability and preventing the communist bloc from any further expansion, conservatives feel that it is better to remain friends with noncommunist nations not predisposed toward American views on human rights rather than alienate them by denouncing them or applying other kinds of pressures. Additionally, conservatives tend to feel that raising the human rights issue encourages instability within those nations and risks the possibility that some adversary will move in and exploit the situation. In the long run, conservatives feel that world stability and peace, along with increasing prosperity, will contribute most to the cause of human rights.

Liberals, on the other hand, feel that it is immoral for the United States to support dictatorships and other governments insensitive to their citizens. They believe America should help people everywhere strive for basic rights and should use whatever peaceful means are available to do so. Liberals also tend to believe that by setting an example for the rest of the world, the United States can also serve the cause of human rights. Thus they tend to be critical of many internal American practices, such as the unfair treatment of minorities, women, and the poor. Liberals tend to argue especially that human life should not be traded for political support and that the only way to protect the rights of people is to maintain pressure on violators of human rights. They advocate withdrawing foreign aid, particularly military aid, from any government that does violate basic human rights.

The Destabilizing Impact of Independent Nongovernmental Actors

The ready availability of weapons technology has created a new problem for foreign policymakers. Terrorism has become a common phenomenon in the modern world. Groups with little stake in the stability of the system may be inclined to use destructive weapons such as nuclear bombs to gain their demands.

The potential for nuclear blackmail exists, and national leaders now have few mechanisms for dealing with such an eventuality. Terrorist groups exist all over the world and can stir up problems anywhere. Groups such as the Irish Republican Army (IRA) and the Palestinian Liberation Organization (PLO) are among well-known terrorist organizations that have used violence to attempt to intimidate governments and gain their objectives. Their tactics include bombings, hostage-taking, assassination, and kidnapping for ransom. Because such organizations are not official parts of governments, they are not subject to the same kinds of pressures and actions as a governmental unit. Furthermore, because existing governments seem unable to coordinate a policy for dealing with such groups, they operate almost free of control and follow none of the accepted modes of dealing with nations. Some organizations have attempted to shed the terrorist image and gain respectability in the international arena. The PLO, for example, has improved its image in some quarters and is viewed by some as increasingly responsible in pursuing its goals. The PLO has been somewhat successful in presenting itself as an army of liberation with legitimate concern about Palestinian rights, although its avowed goal of the total destruction of the state of Israel continued to be a problem until its implicit recognition of Israel in December 1988.

Terrorism has emerged in recent years as a major threat to the foreign policy integrity as well as to the citizens and property of Western powers in general. The United States in particular, as a symbol of the capitalist West and as a supporter of Israel, has become one of the primary targets of terrorist attacks.

Terrorism consists of random attacks against innocent civilians and property of value to the country whose policies the terrorists wish to change or whose existence they wish to challenge. It is a means by which movements, organizations, or small states can successfully hurt or coerce nations much stronger than themselves. Since determined terrorists can almost always attack or seize some individuals of value to a greater power, perfect security against terrorism is impossible to achieve.

The frustration of dealing with terrorists was made painstakingly clear when Shiite extremists highjacked a TWA jet and held 39 Americans hostage for eighteen days in June, 1985. The Reagan administration found itself unable to act to rescue the hostages and was forced to work behind the scenes to arrange release of 735 Lebanese Shiite prisoners held by Israel. Declaring that there would be no negotiation with terrorists, the administration, in fact, brought pressure on Syria and Israel to work out an agreement that was acceptable to the highjackers. Although the crisis was resolved, one United States military service hostage was murdered, and there is no assurance that similar terrorist acts will not occur.

A factor that makes terrorism against powerful nations such as the United States an attractive technique is that, given our values, terrorism is almost certainly risk- and cost-free to those who plan and direct it. It is sometimes possible to catch and punish those responsible—for example, Palestinian terrorists who slip into Israel to plant bombs or shoot civilians. Those who plan and direct such acts, however, frequently are difficult to identify with precision. When powerful and aggressive nations, such as Syria or Libya, are thought to have had a major role in planning or encouraging terrorism, retaliation carries the risk of generating much wider conflict or of wreaking death and mayhem among innocent civilians. Retaliation against suspected terrorists without a due process determination of guilt and at the cost of innocent lives or property offends basic American values. However, not to retaliate renders such terrorism effective. The data on the question of whether retaliation actually discourages future terrorism are mixed and inconclusive.

The United States acted on the retaliation theory in 1987 when President Reagan ordered an air raid against Libya after a group headed by Abu Nidal, a well-known Palestinian extremist given sanctuary by Libya, seized a cruise ship, the *Achille Lauro,* and brutally murdered a wheelchair-bound elderly American Jew, Leon Klinghoffer. Nidal was the same individual who had been identified as the mastermind of a massacre of passengers at Rome's airport in 1986. Terrorist acts sponsored by the Libyans ceased for about a year after the raid, giving rise to the assertion that serious retaliation against the sponsoring nation will deter state-sponsored terrorism. However, Syria continued to sponsor terrorism and presents a more difficult case for retaliation. Syria is stronger and more heavily armed than Libya, thereby posing more of a threat to potential attackers.

The continued threat of terrorism was brought to the attention of all the world on December 21, 1988, when a Pan American jet en route from Germany to the United States via London exploded in the sky over Lockerbie, Scotland, killing all 258 persons aboard. A bomb, probably plastic explosives with a barometric fuse, caused the airliner to explode, but the identity of the persons or organizations responsible proved difficult to determine. Groups linked to Iran and to Abu Nidal claimed responsibility for the act. The United States charged Libyan agents with the bombing. The difficulty of detecting such explosives in luggage and the problems in identifying and retaliating against the perpetrators contribute to the continuing threats of terrorism. With the release of the hostages held by terrorists in Lebanon in 1992, the situation has been defused to some extent. It appears that terrorists do not see much to gain by holding hostages at present, but there is no assurance that some new strategy will not be used.

In recent years, other kinds of nongovernmental groups have also organized and acted with significant impact on foreign affairs. OPEC, as we saw in Chapter 4, is an example of one such group. Its decisions on levels of oil production and pricing created tensions in and among importing nations. The economic and social consequences of OPEC's actions were immense and stimulated efforts by other nations to work together to adjust to the consequences of OPEC policies. The inflationary effects, in particular, strained relations among nations. Other types of producer nations, for example, coffee producers, have also discussed developing cartels similar to OPEC, but they so far have not been successful.

Large corporations such as IBM and Exxon are examples of multinational corporations that also affect international affairs. With their massive economic resources, they can influence the policies of nations. Their influence in decision making became public as tales of international bribery and the like surfaced during and after the Watergate scandals. In the past, the multinational corporations were criticized for exploiting developing nations by draining their natural resources and returning little or nothing to them. In recent years, it has become apparent that multinational corporations have also engaged in efforts to influence the policy of the United States and other nations through various methods, including bribery.

FUTURE ALTERNATIVES IN AN UNSTABLE WORLD

Up until the many changes in the world order beginning in 1989, the major focus of United States foreign and defense policy was on maintaining military superiority over the Soviet Union. With the dissolution of the Soviet bloc and then of the Soviet Union, attention has shifted. Although there is still strong support for maintaining a viable defense system, there are many other concerns. In 1981, 72 percent of the public supported increased defense spending, whereas 18 percent supported it in 1991.[9] With the collapse of the communist bloc, concern has shifted toward stabilizing Eastern Europe and the newly formed Commonwealth of Independent States (former Soviet republics). Because economic problems contribute to political unrest, the United States is trying to find a way to provide assistance to these countries as they convert from centrally planned to free-market economies. The economic chaos has been severe in Eastern Europe and in most of the former Soviet republics. As a result, support for economic aid is widespread although there is considerable opposition as well, given the poor state of the United States economy.

Economic issues will be major factors in foreign policy in the 1990s. The European Economic Community (EEC) has many Americans worried that it will develop into a major international power. A unified Europe could pose serious problems to enterprise in the United States and dictate economic policies. Similarly, the impact of the Japanese on the world economy is growing. By 1992, criticism of Japan had become common in the United States as people look for a scapegoat for the economic problems at home. Scandals in Japan's financial system were causing international ripples. Another series of scandals involved the Bank of Credit and Commerce International (BCCI), which had engaged in massive speculative loans and lost almost $900 million while engaging in shady arms deals, money laundering, and diversion of money to foreign leaders, all of which sent shudders through the world banking community and created instability in stock markets.

Political instability in many of the former Soviet republics and Eastern European nations also raises alarm. As authoritarian control crumbled, nationalism and ethnic conflict reappeared in many regions. Yugoslavia has been faced with severe ethnic conflicts as have Armenia and Uzbekistan among others. These conflicts have long-standing historic roots and divert energies from economic development, which could solve the nations' structural problems. With fear about control over military and nuclear resources, the rest of the world is understandably apprehensive.

SUMMARY

Foreign and defense policies are designed to protect the nation's security, pro-mote economic interests, and enable the nation to influence world affairs to the nation's benefit.

Diplomacy is the main channel whereby foreign affairs are conducted, but when the give-and-take of diplomatic relations fails to achieve the desired objec-tives, nations often resort to other means. Other methods include the use of political and economic sanctions, which may be the severing of diplomatic rela-tions, economic boycotts, and embargoes against trade. If none of these methods works, military force also can be used.

The United States began its existence with a very limited interest and role in international affairs. It became impossible to maintain an isolationist stance, however, as events such as the Spanish-American War, World War I, and World War II kept drawing the country into world events. Finally, after World War II, the United States became an active shaper of world affairs and through its efforts attempted to create a stable and peaceful world order.

In response to Soviet attempts to spread its influence, the United States made alliances with other nations and brought pressure through threats of all-out war to contain Soviet communism. The policy of containment appeared to work in Western Europe, but there were difficulties in applying it in areas with different cultures and needs. A major test came in the Far East as China fell to the Commu-nists. The Korean War and the frustration of the American people with the seeming inability to win it signaled a new phase of relations with the communist bloc.

When the United States was the only nation possessing an atomic bomb, it was able to use its force to threaten other nations. However, as other nations, especially the Soviet Union, developed nuclear capability, strategy had to shift once again. A nuclear arms race began in which each side attempted to build more highly sophisticated arms. Especially during the Eisenhower administration, threats to use that weaponry were employed as a deterrent to communist aggres-sion. The policies proved ineffective, however, because threats that can never be carried out—such as massive nuclear retaliation—soon lose their credibility.

The world is now one in which many nations exert influence. With the independence of Eastern Europe from the Soviet Union and the break-up of the Soviet Union itself, the world order has changed dramatically. No longer are two superpowers the major players. Even before the changes in the Soviet sphere, Japan and other nations such as the oil-producing countries exerted much influ-ence through their economic power. The development of the European Economic Community and its tremendous economic potential present another challenge. Similarly, the presence of nuclear capacity in several smaller nations make pre-dictability difficult.

Defense policy is one aspect of foreign policy in that defense capabilities are used as instruments of foreign policy. Defense policy is based on an arsenal of arms and personnel. The United States and the Soviet Union engaged in an arms race after the end of World War II, and that race led to a proliferation of nuclear arms among many nations. This proliferation in turn resulted in pressures for limitations on development of arms. The Strategic Arms Limitation Talks (SALT) and Intermediate Range Nuclear Forces (INF) negotiations attempted to establish agreements between the United States and the Soviet Union concerning limitations on weapons capacity.

The end of the Cold War has reduced the debate over military preparedness to some extent as tensions have diminished. However, as the Persian Gulf war demonstrated, there still are potential threats and the United States maintains the capacity to deal with them. Debate has now shifted to how much of a reduction in capacity is appropriate.

A complicating factor in foreign and defense policy is the rise of terrorism in the past twenty years. Groups take innocent civilians as hostages and bomb civilian airplanes. There seems to be no effective way of dealing with them. However, there also appears to be a reduction in terrorist activities and thus hope for a period of calm.

NOTES

1. John Spanier, *American Foreign Policy Since World War II,* 12th ed. (New York: Praeger, 1991).
2. Charles W. Kegley, Jr., and Eugene R. Wittkopf, *American Foreign Policy: Pattern and Process,* 4th ed. (New York: St. Martin's Press, 1991), pp. 1–3.
3. Ibid., p. 30.
4. This perspective is apparent throughout E. H. Carr, *The Twenty Years Crisis, 1919–1939,* 2nd ed. (New York: St. Martin's Press, 1964); and Kenneth W. Thompson, *Political Realism and the Crisis of World Politics* (Princeton, N.J.: Princeton University Press, 1960).
5. Reo M. Christenson raised some provocative questions on this issue in *Heresies Right and Left: Some Political Assumptions Reexamined* (New York: Harper & Row, 1973).
6. This discussion is based on Spanier, *American Foreign Policy,* chap. 4.
7. See Robert Jarvis, *The Illogic of American Nuclear Strategy* (Ithaca, N.Y.: Cornell University Press, 1984), pp. 165–167.
8. This discussion is based on Spanier, *American Foreign Policy,* ch. 8.
9. "Opinion Roundup—Defense Spending: Keep It Where It Is," *Public Opinion,* 10 (March/April, 1988), p. 24, and *The Gallup Poll,* No. 308 (May, 1991), p. 39.

SUGGESTED READINGS

Ackley, Richard T. "Strategic Arms Limitation: The Problem of Mutual Deterrence." In *Foreign Policy and U.S. National Security,* edited by William W. Whitson, pp. 221–245. New York: Praeger, 1976.

Allison, Graham T. *Essence of Decision: Explaining the Cuban Missile Crisis.* Boston: Little, Brown, 1971.

Blechman, Barry M. *U.S. Security in the Twenty-First Century.* Boulder, Colo.: Westview, 1987.

Chace, James, and Carr, Caleb. *America Invulnerable: The Quest for Absolute Security from 1812 to Star Wars.* New York: Summit Books, 1988.

Cimbala, Stephen J., ed. *National Security Strategy: Choices and Limits.* New York: Praeger, 1984.

Hilsman, Roger. *The Politics of Policy Making in Defense and Foreign Affairs.* Englewood Cliffs, N.J.: Prentice-Hall, 1990.

Hosmer, Stephen T. *Constraints on U.S. Strategy in Third World Conflicts.* New York: Crane Russak, 1987.

Kaufman, William W. *A Reasonable Defense.* Washington, D.C.: Brookings Institution, 1986.

Kegley, Charles W., Jr., and Wittkopf, Eugene R. *American Foreign Policy: Pattern and Process.* 4th ed. New York: St. Martin's Press, 1991.

McGowan, Pat, and Kegley, Charles W., Jr., eds. *Threats, Weapons and Foreign Policy.* Beverly Hills, Calif.: Sage, 1980.

Peters, Joan. *From Time Immemorial: The Origins of the Arab-Jewish Conflict over Palestine.* New York: Harper & Row, 1984.

Smoke, Richard. *National Security and the Nuclear Dilemma.* Reading, Mass.: Addison-Wesley, 1984.

Scowcroft, Brent; Woolsey, A. James; and Etzold, Thomas H. *Defending Freedom: Toward Strategic Stability in the Year 2000.* Lanham, Md.: University Press of America, 1988.

Spanier, John. *American Foreign Policy Since World War II.* 12th ed. New York: Praeger, 1991.

Sylvan, Donald A., and Chan, Steve, eds. *Foreign Policy Decision Making: Perception, Cognition, and Artificial Intelligence.* New York: Praeger, 1984.

CHAPTER 13

The Continuing Policy Debates

The first edition of this text was written during the early months of the first Reagan administration. This edition was written during the 1992 presidential campaign.

Political actors.   The first point is to remember that although the president is the most visible actor on the American political stage, he is not the dominant actor. From time to time it may seem that way, but Congress, especially, and others frequently take the leading role. Thus, although the Reagan and Bush administrations had a substantial impact on public policy, the direction of that impact was shaped by other agents as well, often in directions that the president did not particularly foresee.

Presidents are most influential in foreign and defense policy, and President Reagan's agenda for challenging communism throughout the world and for strengthening American military forces illustrates this truth. Much that he planned, he accomplished. Yet his early harsh criticism of the Soviet Union and of the Carter administration's attempts at warm relations with the Soviet Union turned into even warmer relations with the Soviets by the end of the Reagan years. The INF and START treaties and progress on other arms reduction agreements in those years were at variance with his earlier demeanor and with some of the policy choices of conservatives, many of whom opposed the agreements struck in 1987 and 1988.

Events in the Soviet Union and Eastern Europe rapidly overtook the plans and policies of President Bush, who largely reacted to the rapid pace of change there and to the end of the Cold War. Moreover, the limits of a president's reliance on foreign and defense policy for his reputation were illustrated by the rapid disappearance of Bush's foreign-policy-based popularity during 1992.

On the domestic front, President Reagan's 1980 promise to balance the budget within three years turned into eight years of the largest budget deficits in American history. Promises to cut taxes produced some early cuts, but the mid-1980s produced tax increases and finally a tax reform bill that contained only part of what the president had wanted. Spending-cut proposals in health, education, public assistance, housing, environment, revenue sharing, transportation, and other domestic programs were partially successful, particularly in the first years of the Reagan presidency. But later years brought increasing resistance to such cuts and budget stalemates that colored the Bush years. Although the president was successful in scaling back the institutions and policies of much of the active state that he so strongly opposed, the fundamental programs were preserved by congressional opposition to his initiatives. The "Reagan revolution" was successful only at the margins. And President Bush increased spending in some areas targeted for deep cuts by his political mentor.

The larger issues.   One legacy of the policy changes of the 1980s that may very well last far into the 1990s is renewed vitality in federalism through state policy initiatives. (See Chapter 5.) Significant policy experiments have been undertaken by both liberal and conservative governors and legislatures in the states in areas of environmental regulation, health care provision and cost control, work programs for public assistance recipients, elementary and secondary education, and economic development. Recent federal legislation, such as the 1988 welfare reform bill, has assumed and built upon such state and local policy experimentation. Because these emphases run in cycles, it is difficult to predict just how long this renewed emphasis on federalism will last, but it is a significant development of the last decade. This uncertainty was heightened by the effects of the poor economy of the late 1980s and the recession of the early 1990s. These put heavy pressure on state governments, whose tax revenues were declining just as they were being asked to do more. Sharp state spending increases for crime control, prison construction, unemployment compensation, and health care meant sharp reductions in many states for education, transportation, public assistance, parks, and other state programs. The general national mood of fiscal conservatism affected all levels of government, but the states did not have the federal government's borrowing capacity to cushion the shocks of budgetary shortfalls.

The demographic shifts described in Chapter 1 and their policy consequences have been significant themes in many of the substantive policy chapters. The economy must contend with a work force that contains more women and single parents than ever before, and with an aging "baby boom" generation as well. The aging of the population places intense pressure on the social insurance and health care systems. And the frequency of divorce places many children and their mothers in poverty. Crime policy, too, has to respond to the economic and social pressures that changes in the family structure place upon adolescents. The educational system must respond to a generation with a substantial portion of its numbers growing up in broken homes, poverty, and ill health.

The increasing numbers of racial minorities, especially Hispanics, and the failure of public policy to address the problems of the underclass and of the effects of racial discrimination will also demand response from the policy system in the last decade of this century. There is a danger that the United States is becoming a two-tiered society, with many citizens achieving unprecedented levels of affluence and a significant minority moving deeper into poverty. These trends are exacerbated by competitive pressures on our economic system generated by newly emerging economic powers overseas. The end of the Cold War heightens concern for domestic conditions and world economic competition.

During the 1990s, American public policy will have to reassess the commitments of one generation to the others. What are the obligations of the generation of workers to the aged, to children, to generations to come? This question pervades the pressing issues in health care, Social Security, and education. But it also runs through policy debates over day care, job training, economic revitalization, and the size of the national debt.

Another set of pressing issues has to do with limits on individual freedom in a nation that prides itself on its commitment to such freedom. With the emergence of the new religious right and with public policy impinging upon the traditional institutions of church and family, new questions of religious liberty have emerged in the last fifteen years. Abortion policy poses questions of an unborn child's right to life and of a woman's freedom; medical technology produces dramatic questions of the right to die. The epidemic of drug addiction and drug-related crimes and accidents generates pressure for drug-testing programs that raise substantial questions of individual freedom, as do testing proposals for the AIDS virus.

These last issues recall the cultural conflicts that run through many of the policy areas discussed in this book. Questions of the best approach to poverty, urban unrest, drug addiction, AIDS, women's equality, and multicultural education arc not simply questions of the best means to achieve agreed-upon goals. Instead, they touch on the deep divisions in beliefs, principles, and behavior that characterize America in the 1990s.

On one thing, however, most Americans are unified—deep distrust of politicians and political institutions. This frustration with government has produced a backlash against President Bush, demands for tax reduction and term limitations, and reduced interest in politics and elections. The abortive presidential candidacy of Ross Perot is one symptom of this distrust.

This cultural trend has had significant impact on many policy areas. It has produced an economic policy stalemate in which taxes needed to pay for desired government programs or deficit reduction cannot be advocated, but neither can reduced spending, which is perceived as political unconcern for the plight of the middle class. Voters are worried about the state of the economy, doubt that government can or will do anything about it, but nevertheless hold elected officials, especially the president, responsible. An electorate that fundamentally distrusts its leaders is unlikely to look to them for creative approaches to health care, poverty reduction, improved education, or environmental protection.

In foreign and defense policy, a new multipolar world presents America with new questions and challenges concerning its diplomatic, military, and economic role in the world. Are we and should we attempt to be the dominant political, military, and economic actor of the free world? How should we respond to the changes in the communist world and to changes in our own allies? The greatest foreign and defense policy issues facing the president will turn on these questions.

In neither foreign nor domestic policy are the issues entirely clear or the answers easy. Whatever one's political perspective, it is necessary to recognize limits on achieving all of one's desired goals. The preceding chapters have described a large number of such limitations and constraints on policy-making, but these can be summarized and described more systematically as well.

It should be clear after reading this book that public policy in the United States is affected by many factors in the political environment. Although some people perceive policy and pursue policy goals from a conservative, liberal, or radical perspective, it is highly unlikely that any individual or group will always be satisfied with the policy results. Rather, it is likely that each participant in public policy-making will realize only some of his or her desired outcomes. Partial fulfillment of the desired goal leads participants to continue to attempt to influence policy.

Pluralism. Because ours is a pluralistic political system, political reality dictates compromise in the policy-making arena. In order to move toward their ultimate policy goals, participants must be able to build support with other participants, or they will fall short of getting the votes of legislative bodies or other decision-making units. The building of support normally requires modifying positions so that resulting policy is a compromise of alternative proposals. For example, the advocates of a flat-tax system found much support for their position, but they also realized that there were strong interest groups that have access to the political decision makers who must be accommodated if the flat tax was to be achieved. They were willing to accept continuation of such deductions as mortgage interest payments and state and local property taxes, for they realized that without those accommodations the 1986 tax reform would have been impossible. The Family Support Act also illustrates such compromise. Even though they may compromise in the short run, most policy advocates see the compromises as a temporary step as they work toward the ideal goal they have set for themselves. Of course, goals also change as people change their values and become aware of different issues and alternatives.

Values are at the base of different perspectives on how problems should be resolved. An important difference in values is that people differ on whether government ought to intervene in many problems at all. That debate has been heightened in recent years with the election of many political leaders, including President Reagan, who believe that government ought to reduce its presence. The debate over the role of the federal government has been intense in many policy areas. The Reagan administration and congressional conservatives were successful in reducing federal activity in environmental and energy regulation; they relied more on state government in public assistance and health policy; and they weakened federal intervention in business for reasons of affirmative action. On the other hand, continued liberal strength prevented abolition of the Departments of Energy and Education and blunted the severest attacks on health and welfare policies. The continuing debates during the 1990s over taxes and government spending, returning programs to the states, assistance to agriculture, and abortion rights all are, at least partly, issues of the extent of government intervention into economic, personal, and social life.

Even if there is agreement on the need for intervention, differing values will then dictate how people view what should be done and how it should be accomplished. For example, it is agreed that there is a governmental obligation to provide education. Beyond that agreement, however, there is a wide diversity in opinion about what should be provided. Should it be for elementary and secondary levels only, or should public universities be supported as well? Should education be only the three Rs, or should it also include vocational education and education in the arts and entertainment? People also differ on whether public education should refer only to the actual operation of public schools or whether it should also include the concept of vouchers and tuition tax credits, which can be used to pay for tuition at private schools. Every policy area is subject to differing perspectives on the appropriateness and forms of intervention.

The question of government intervention also asks whether free-market forces or government regulation should be used to accomplish public goals. The debate over economic regulation, federal deficits, fiscal policy, and taxes, for example, includes issues of which kinds of government policy can best work with and stimulate market forces for economic prosperity. The debate over cost control in health care policy means deciding whether to rely on market forces or public regulation.

In addition to the political realities of public policy-making and issues of government intervention, the forces of policy demand are also important. If a policy is developed and no one is aware of or interested in it, the policy will not be very effective. Most policies are established as a result of a demand to do something about a particular problem; thus there is already a market for the policy. But the size of the market may be critical. That an environmental policy advocated by an environmental group may, in fact, be beneficial to a large portion of the population does not ensure that it will be enacted into policy. It is just as likely that it will be opposed strongly by interests that would be negatively affected by the proposed policy. Frequently, interest groups help develop the demand, but sometimes this is done after the fact by agencies set to administer the policy.

The limits of public policy.   Yet another aspect of public policy is its cost. Any government program has costs, and in this day of cutback management, there are conflicts over the ability of government to underwrite new activities or to maintain old programs. The debate over the deficit, which has dominated economic policy for over a decade, has brought the cost question and cost trade-offs to the forefront. There are conflicts over which programs are to survive and at what level of activity. As long as governmental funds are limited and public officials are under pressure to cut expenditures, such conflicts are likely to escalate. Thus the policies discussed in this book should not be examined in isolation from one another. Time, attention, and money devoted to defense mean less of these available for health, crime, or education, for example. Devoting large sums of money to Social Security for the aged means less available for the education of the young. Increased attention to health needs can result in less attention to highways.

It should also be clear that there are interdependencies among policies and that policies do not have only the effects they are created to have. Instead, many unintended consequences occur that may affect other policies or require modifying their approaches in order to accommodate some new difficulty. Many of the interdependent features of policy become apparent in the debates over a given policy. For example, the environmentalists are usually confronted by those who worry about the effects of environmental controls on economic development. The conflicts between industrialists and environmentalists are well known, but accommodations have been made by both sides. Less commonly understood, however, are some of the unintended consequences. For example, the energy conservation policies of the 1970s led to the increased use of wood as a fuel for heating homes. Such a development was encouraged and applauded as a way of conserving fossil fuels. In recent years, however, many states in the western United States have recognized a need for regulating the use of wood fuel, as it has exacerbated the smog problem. Furthermore, some health experts claim that wood smoke in the home resulting from open fires is as dangerous to health as is smoking cigarettes. Other examples of unintended consequences are the stiff enforcement of drug laws leading to increased crime, public assistance programs discouraging work, and tax deductions for health insurance driving up health care costs.

The interrelatedness of policies does not stop at the borders of a country. Foreign and defense policies are closely intertwined with economic and other domestic policies. As indicated in the consideration of these policies, the fortunes of U.S. business interests are often tied to foreign policies. Similarly, economic policies that affect the strength of the American dollar affect our relations with other nations on many other fronts. A strong American dollar and high American interest rates encourage foreign investments and imports into the United States and discourage American exports.

"Problem" and "solution."   When something is a "problem," Americans believe it must have a "solution." After all, in school every math problem has a correct solution, even if we cannot discover it on our own! Citizens often approach public policy with a characteristically American problem-solving mentality, and they can become very disillusioned when, for example, new anticrime programs do not solve the problem of crime or when cities continue to decay after billions of dollars are spent on urban renewal. If these same observers knew more about the incredible complexity of many such problems, they would be far less likely to have such high expectations and be better equipped to appreciate partial victories when they occur.

A public policy may fail to achieve improved conditions in an issue area for a variety of reasons. First, often there is no general agreement on what the issues are. For example, some believe that the primary economic difficulty is inflation, others unemployment. Second, when the perceptions of issues differ so much, it is likely that any policies formulated will have conflicting goals or will have goals that are too limited to deal adequately with the conditions demanding a response. Third, the costs of a complete solution may be too high or public resources too few, even if such a total solution is theoretically possible. Fourth, the dilemma being faced may change before a policy has had time to have its intended impact, or other dilemmas may intervene, drawing attention and resources away from the first. (Economic policy is particularly subject to this difficulty. Given the time lag between adoption and impact, the original problem may have diminished by the time the effect is felt, and thus the program may create a new problem of its own.) Fifth, some problems are inherently unsolvable. Crime will never be totally prevented; there will always be threats to national security. The difficulty is keeping crime and threats at manageable levels. Sixth, government is limited in its rationality, efficiency, and authority. Bureaucracy, departmental jealousies, petty politicking, and the simple limits of time, attention, and information all prevent government from formulating fully rational policy, even when the conflict over goals is minimal. Moreover, even when policy is well formulated, the difficulties of implementation may still be formidable. Thus the cards are often stacked against the effectiveness of public policy, almost from the start.

Additionally, government is constitutionally prevented from adopting certain kinds of policies to attack issues. The U.S. Constitution reflects what is culturally and politically unacceptable in America—for example, it forbids torture as a means of deterring crime. Not all such limits are constitutional, however. Letting the poor starve to death to "solve" the problem of poverty would be politically and socially unacceptable. Finally, although issues that become matters of public concern often have more than one cause, government response is limited to acting on only those causes within its scope of authority. For example, one cause of the financial problems of Social Security is the aging of the population, a factor not under government control. And both policy evaluation and issue understanding are tempered by many of these same limitations. The study of public policy rapidly teaches the lesson that not all problems have solutions. Public policy has so many inherent limitations that it may be best not to speak of solving problems at all but, rather, of facing dilemmas, addressing issues, improving conditions, or responding to challenges. To expect too much of public policy is to face certain disappointment and disillusionment, conditions that may obscure the real, though limited, accomplishments of public programs.

Policy-making is not the only aspect of policy that should be considered. Often it is assumed that if a policy is developed, it will automatically solve the problem to which it is addressed. Unfortunately, such is not the case. Instead, implementation is necessary, and there can be as many disagreements about the method of implementation as over the content of the policy. Furthermore, implementation depends on the administrator charged with carrying out the policy. Different administrators and agencies have different interpretations of what a policy means, and these will affect its development.

Similarly, the evaluation of policies produces different results. Because people have different perspectives on policies, they also view the results differently. Personal values affect the way citizens view the effects of any policy or program. Understanding of the intent of the policy also varies and thus leads to different evaluations of the effectiveness of that policy.

Ultimately the question is whether American public policy is in the best interests of its citizens. In order to make that assessment, it is necessary to know what is in the public interest. That is a concept on which there is little agreement; nonetheless, most people have some sense of what seems to be in the public interest. Because of the variation in what is in the interests of the citizens, evaluations also vary widely. For these reasons and because of the sharp ideological disagreements over the role of government, the necessary trade-offs between policy areas, and the compromises necessary within an issue area, public policy always diverges from the ideal, both in procedure and substance. Those who expect a policy to solve completely a public concern will always be disappointed. And they should not be surprised when, as has happened frequently in the last decade, stalemate characterizes numerous policy arenas. The task of policymakers and citizens alike is not to expect perfection or immediate action but to develop a way of keeping policymakers and implementers accountable for their actions. In this way policy can be adjusted when failures occur. Adjustment in response to citizen demand is a central feature of a democratic political system.

Index